Fish and Shell-fish

TX
747

Simms, A.E.

Fish and shell-fish.

Fish and Shell-fish

EDITOR: **A. E. Simms** F.H.C.I.M.A., F.R.S.H.
ASSISTANT EDITOR: **Mabel Quin**
PREFACE BY: **Professor John Fuller** F.H.C.I.M.A., F.R.S.H.

VIRTUE & COMPANY LIMITED
London, Dublin and Coulsdon

British Library Cataloguing in Publication Data

Fish and shell-fish.
1. Cookery (Fish)
2. Cookery (Seafood)
I. Simms, A E
641.6'9'2 TX747

ISBN 0-900778-03-2

First published in Great Britain, 1973
Reprinted 1979, 1981

Printed in Great Britain by Ebenezer Baylis & Son Limited
The Trinity Press, Worcester, and London.

Contents

Colour Plates

COLD HORS D'OEUVRE

HOT ENTRÉES

BUFFETS

SALT WATER FISH

Four formal table settings pages ix to xii ▶

FRESH WATER FISH

SHELL-FISH

Acknowledgements

The original edition of this book was conceived, designed and produced by René Kramer of Castagnola, Switzerland, gastronome and publisher.

A large number of personalities from the culinary world, including numerous chefs de cuisine, have contributed from their knowledge and wealth of experience. We thank the following contributors:

Austria	KARL DUCH
Belgium	ANDRÉ BÉGHIN
Denmark	ERIK CEDERHOLM
Finland	ERICK HAACK
France	PIERRE MENGELATTE, WILLEM E. L. TE MEIJ, LUCIEN LEHEU, WALTER BICKEL
Germany	WALTER BICKEL, WERNER FISCHER
Great Britain	PROFESSOR JOHN FULLER, JOHN MCKEE, A. E. SIMMS
Holland	WILLEM E. L. TE MEIJ
Hungary	EMIL TUROS
Israel	HERMANN WOHL
Italy	PAOLO CASCINO, CESARE GOSI, LUIGI MORANDI, FRANCO CORPORA
Spain	KARL HECKH
Sweden	ERIK CARLSTRÖM
Switzerland	WILLI BARTENBACH, EMERICO BIANCHI, ARTHUR BOLLI, WALTER HUG, RENÉ KRAMER, EMIL WAELTI
United States	GEORGE K. WALDNER

Translators of the English edition are Steve Combes and John Galleymore

We are pleased to acknowledge and thank the following, who have contributed towards the production of the dishes:

Hotel La Palma au Lac, Locarno
Arthur Bolli, proprietor
Walter Hug, chef de cuisine, assisted by Artino de Marchi, Helmut Rumpf, Mario Viri, and Dario Brizzio, maître d'hôtel

Hotel Gritti-Palace, Venice
Fred Laubi, director
Cesar Gosi, chef de cuisine

Grand Hotel Eden au Lac, Lugano-Paradiso
Giorgio Huhn, proprietor
Emerico Bianchi, chef de cuisine

Hotel Intercontinental, Frankfurt
Wilhelm Jungbluth, chef de cuisine
Rudolf Braun, larder chef

Parkhotel, Frankfurt
Fred Eggert, director
Otto Brust, chef de cuisine

Hotel Pilter, Salzburg
Max Dick, chef de cuisine

The Ritz Restaurant, Berlin
Werner Fischer, proprietor and chef de cuisine

The Poorthuys Restaurant, Zierikzee (Holland)
Willem E. L. Te Mey, proprietor and chef de cuisine

Hotel Olivella au Lac, Morcote (Switzerland)
Lionello Colombo, chef de cuisine

Hotel des Bains, Morat-Montilier (Switzerland)
Kurt Fasnacht, proprietor and chef de cuisine

Scotts Restaurant, London
H. Slack, Sous Chef de Cuisine

Public Schools Club, London
L. Howe, Chef de Cuisine

Normandie Hotel, London
Bartholomew Calderoni, former Chef de Cuisine

Dorchester Hotel, London
Eugen Käufeler, Maître de Cuisine

Queens Hotel, Cheltenham
Henry Duthaler, Junior Chef de Cuisine

La Cigogne, London
Marcel Haentzler, former Chef de Cuisine

Grand Hotel, Birmingham
J. F. Beer, former Chef de Cuisine

Mr. W. E. L. Te Mey, Holland, has suggested the basis of this work and has taken care of the general principles and the classical recipes.

Preface

by Professor John Fuller F.H.C.I.M.A., F.R.S.H.,

Chairman, City and Guilds of London Institute's Advisory Committee for Catering and Food.

Formerly Director, Scottish Hotel School, University of Strathclyde

Reasons abound for my pleasure at being asked to contribute a preface to this English edition of a most handsome and useful book on an important sector of cookery, *Fish and Shell-fish.*

Not least is the fact that I contributed to the original French language edition in 1969. On its first appearance then, I was greatly impressed both by the text from an international team of culinary experts and also by the fine-quality illustrations. The colour and black and white pictures do not merely enhance or decorate the text but perform a most practical function in helping to instruct and in demonstrating how to present. In that the first appeal of food is to the eye, cookery is very much a visual art. This book recognises that in a singularly helpful way.

Another reason for welcoming this book is because I have for some time been a member of the White Fish Advisory Council of the United Kingdom. I have thus a long-standing concern that the merits of fish and shell-fish should not merely be more appreciated in this country but that this appreciation should be stimulated by more and better knowledge of how to use, cook and present fish for all occasions from the most simple to the most festive. This book does just that.

Not only do British people like fish; but in the world of professional catering their liking for it means that fish and chips has long been a "take-away" and a "sit-down" best seller. So dominant has been this dish in terms of ordinary eating that it has, perhaps, been allowed too long to overshadow the superb raw material for other kinds of fine fare for which our fishing grounds and rivers give such ample opportunity. Lobster, salmon, oysters, mussels, herrings and the white fish yield of our trawlers bring an abundance of gastronomically and nutritionally excellent fare for our table. The fish and chip syndrome may, too, have confused many caterers about an increasingly knowledgeable consumer demand for "different" fish food.

If the time is ripe for chefs and cooks to have a thoroughly professional book as their aid to an extended repertoire of exciting fish dishes, it is certainly just as timely for customers. The British customer, eating out in restaurant or café or canteen, whether in traditional, classic or ethnic style is growing ever more cosmopolitan in taste. He has an interest in eating international. Moreover, the appearance of seafood restaurants not only in London but in towns and cities throughout the Western world testify that there is a place for good fish fare at the sophisticated end of the dining out market, as well as in the middle or popular brackets.

With *Fish and Shell-fish* at their elbow, chefs, cordons bleus and domestic cooks now have an encyclopaedic guide to the exploitation for table purposes of all piscatorial riches of the world.

John Fuller,
Headington, Oxford.

How to use this Book

Example:

Barbue amiral

For 6 persons: *1 brill weighing 1 kg. 500; 50 gr. red butter; ½ litre court-bouillon (containing white wine); 200 gr. shelled crayfish; 12 large poached and bearded mussels; 12 poached and bearded oysters; 12 mushroom heads; 12 bouchées mignonnes; ½ litre sauce Villeroi; ½ litre sauce normande; 30 gr. crayfish butter; 2 eggs; breadcrumbs; 12 thin slices of truffle.* Cooking time: approximately 40 minutes.

Brill: See DESCRIPTION OF FISH

Court-bouillon: See BASIC PREPARATIONS, section on court-bouillon

Mushroom heads: See ACCOMPANYING DISHES AND GARNISHES

Bouchées and bouchées mignonnes (very small bouchées): See HOT ENTRÉES

Sauce Villeroi: See FISH SAUCES

Sauce Normande: See FISH SAUCES

Crayfish butter: See SAVOURY BUTTERS

Place the brill on the buttered grid of a turbot-kettle (turbotière), moisten with the court-bouillon, cover with a sheet of buttered paper, and cook covered with a lid in a medium oven. After cooking, drain the fish, and arrange it on a serving dish. Brush the surface of the fish with the red butter. Coat the mussels and oysters with the sauce Villeroi, egg and breadcrumbs, and fry them. Use the shelled crayfish to make a salpicon, bind it with a little of the sauce normande, and use it to fill the bouchées mignonnes. Surround the brill with the mussels, oysters, bouchées mignonnes, mushrooms, and slices of truffle. Serve separately the sauce normande (containing a little reduced braising stock finished with the crayfish butter), and plain boiled potatoes.

To poach: See GLOSSARY

To moisten: See GLOSSARY

To drain: See GLOSSARY

Salpicon: See GLOSSARY

We believe this book to be truly comprehensive. There may, however, be fish which are available in some parts of the world which are not given a mention in these pages. If so, the chef should always bear in mind that the sauces and methods of preparation can, of course, be readily adapted for different types of fish.

Part I

GENERAL

Tables

SOLIDS

A kilogramme (kg) is subdivided into 1000 grammes (g). Measurements of less than 1 oz are usually measured in spoonfuls, e.g. ½ oz flour is equivalent to 1 rounded tablespoonful.

ounces	grammes
1	28
2	56
3	85
4	113
5	141
6	170
7	198
8	226
9	255
10	283
11	311
12	340
13	368
14	396
15	425
16	453

pounds ←	lb → kg	kilogrammes
2·20	**1**	0·45
4	**2**	0·91
6	**3**	1·36
8	**4**	1·81
11	**5**	2·27
13	**6**	2·72
15	**7**	3·18
17	**8**	3·63
19	**9**	4·08
22	**10**	4·54
30	**14**	6·35
44	**20**	9·07
61	**28**	12·70
220	**100**	45·36
246	**112**	50·80

Metric (grammes)	Imperial (ounces)
100	3½
125	4½
500	17½ (1·1 lbs)
1000 (1 kg)	35¼ (2·2 lbs)

Note Since most recipes are based on proportions (e.g. half fat to flour), rather than attempt to convert imperial measures to exact equivalents it is easier to work on the basis that 1 ounce equals about 25 grammes, e.g. 4 oz flour is equivalent to approximately 100 g. Recipes based on 25 g units can be used with existing equipment.

FLUIDS

A litre is subdivided into 1000 millilitres (ml)
100 centilitres (cl)
10 decilitres (dl)

gallons ←	gal → litres	litres
0·22	**1**	4·5
0·44	**2**	9·1
0·66	**3**	13·6
0·88	**4**	18·2
1·10	**5**	22·7
1·32	**6**	27·3
1·54	**7**	31·8
1·76	**8**	36·4
1·98	**9**	40·9
2·20	**10**	45·5
4·40	**20**	90·9
6·60	**30**	136·4
8·80	**40**	181·8
11·00	**50**	227·3
22·00	**100**	454·6

fluid ounces	ml (cc)
1	28
2	56
3	85
4	113
5	142
6	170
7	198
8	227
9	255
10	284
11	312
12	341
13	369
14	397
15	426
16	454
17	483
18	511
19	539
20	568

TEMPERATURE

Oven temperatures

Present electric scale °F	Gas marks	Suggested Celsius scale °C
225	¼	110
250	½	130
275	1	140
300	2	150
325	3	170
350	4	180
375	5	190
400	6	200
425	7	220
450	8	230
475	9	240

Oil temperatures
Ingredients should be added after 190°C or 375°F has been reached.

Descriptions of Fish, Shellfish and Molluscs

FAMILIES OF FISH

Clupeoids

Family to which the following belong:

shad
sprat
herring
sardine

These fish are slender, their scales are large and thin and easily detachable. The fins are small and narrow; there is only one dorsal fin. The back is greenish and the sides are silvery.
The clupeoids live in 'families', near the coast or in the open sea. Herring and sardine fishing is of considerable economic importance.
This family includes about 200 species and sub-species. The largest of the clupeoids is the *tarpon* (*Megalops atlanticus*) found around the Antilles. Some rare species, such as the shad and the American shad, ascend rivers to spawn.

Gadoids

Family to which the following belong:

haddock
cod
hake
dorse
rock salmon
ling, blue ling
whiting
pollack

These fish have a long body, the maximum size of which comes just after the head, which is usually developed. The scales are small. There are one to three dorsal fins. A few gadoids have a barbel under the jaws.
The gadoids live in cold or temperate waters. Their fishing, as, for example, cod (*morue*, *cabillaud*), is of great importance. The flesh is of good quality and very nutritious (100 gr. of fish = 33 calories) with 8% of proteins and vitamins A, B_1, B_2 and C.

Pleuronectoids

Family to which the following belong:

brill
plaice
flounder
dab
sole
turbot

The pleuronectoids are flat fish with a flattened body, oval in shape. In the adult state, these fish, living in the depths and swimming by an undulating movement, have both eyes on the same side of the body.
The pleuronectoids vary considerably in colour (the blind side being almost always whitish) in order to adapt to the bottom on which they lie.
In this family are the most prized fish for cooking, such as the sole and the turbot.

Scombroids

Family to which the following belong:

bonito
bonitol
mackerel
white tunny or albacore
tunny (red tunny)

These fish have a slender or elongated and finely formed body, of a slightly tapering spindle shape.
Their fishing is important. They are often preserved in various ways: marinated mackerel, tunny in oil, etc.
Preparation requires much care. The flesh is rather tasty but not very digestible.
To this family are commonly added the carangoids: *horse mackerel*, *goggler* or *scad*.

SALT WATER FISH

Haddock *(Gadoids)*

Latin: *Melanogrammus aeglefinus*
French: *aiglefin*
German: *Schellfisch*
Italian: *nasella*
Spanish: *merluza*
Dutch: *schelvis*

Description. *General appearance:* see page 2; *colour:* back and head dark, sides grey, stomach white, a characteristic black spot on the side at the level of the first dorsal fin; *size and weight:* 30 to 50 cm., rarely more, 2 to 3 kg.

Characteristics. *Food:* worms, shellfish, echinoderms, sand-eels, herring spawn, herring fry; *where found:* North Atlantic, both American and European, Iceland, and at the South of the Bay of Biscay. The North Sea is the centre of its European habitat.

Culinary applications. Fine white fish, particularly tasty from summer to the end of the year (spawning-season from February to March). Fresh and frozen fillets. Preparation with *court-bouillon* and as for cod. The haddock split in two, lightly smoked and salted, is known as *smoked haddock* or *finnan haddie.*

Anchovy *(Engrauloids)*

Latin: *Engraulis encrasicholus*
French: *anchois*
German: *Sardelle*
Italian: *acciuga*
Spanish: *anchoa*
Dutch: *ansjovis*

Description: *General appearance:* a lengthened body with a pointed head, the caudal fin is hardly rounded at all, no scales, disproportionately large opening for the mouth; *size:* 9 to 15 cm., rarely 20 cm.

Characteristics. Inhabits the depths, only leaving them to spawn; *food:* very small crustaceans; *where found:* coasts of France, Italy, England, Norway, etc. where great quantities are taken at the spawning-season (June to July in the Atlantic and May to September in the Mediterranean).

Culinary applications. Fresh anchovies, like fresh sardines, are eaten only in coastal areas. The greatest part of the catch is salted for a year at least. Anchovies are also smoked. Anchovy fillets are much used in cooking: in oil, salted, rolled, and for making paste and essence.

Conger Eel *(Anguilloids)*

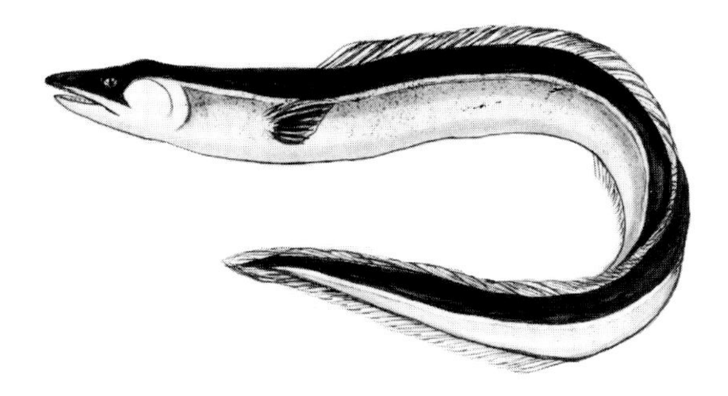

Latin: *Conger vulgaris* Cuvier
French: *anguille de mer*
German: *Meeraal*
Italian: *grongo*
Spanish: *congrio*
Dutch: *zeepaling*

Description. *General appearance:* as the eel (see page 23); *colour:* a little clearer than that of the river eel. The colour of the fish has probably adapted to that of the sea bottom; *size and weight:* the female up to 2 m. or longer, the male smaller. The *muraena* or *murry* belongs to the same species (Latin: *Muraena helena* French: *murène*; German: *Muräne*); this is browner in colour with clear spots; its size varies from 1 m. to 1·50. m. and its weight reaches 6 kg.

Characteristics. The adult fish is coastal, living between 40 and 100 m. deep; *food:* this dangerous carnivore feeds on fish such as herring and dorse, and on small crustaceans, sometimes cuttlefish, and the female can easily devour the small male; *where found:* west and south of the British Isles, Biscay, the Mediterranean, the Atlantic coast of North America, Japan, South Africa, Australia, India.

Culinary applications. The flesh is less tasty than that of the fresh-water eel; it is used more for soups, *bouillabaisse* and *matelotes.* The murry is as tasty as the fresh-water eel.

Bass *(Serranoids)*

Latin: *Labrax lupus*
French: *bar*
German: *Meer-* or *Seebarsch*
Italian: *spigola*
Spanish: *robelo*
Dutch: *zeebars*

Description. *General appearance:* very elongated body with two dorsal fins; *colour:* greyish-blue back, bright silver, very white stomach; *size:* average length 35 to 50 cm., maximum 80 cm.

Characteristics. Hunting near the shores it can escape being caught by nets; *food:* small kinds of fish living close to the land; *where found:* the Mediterranean and the Atlantic, but never North of the Channel; the spawning-season is from May to August.

Culinary applications. Excellent and expensive fish, most frequently grilled (with or without fennel), the largest are poached or prepared with a *court-bouillon*, the smallest fried or in *bouillabaisse*. In France the bass is well known by the name of '*loup*' or '*loubine*'. The striped bass is the nearest variety (Latin: *Roccus saxatilis*; French: *bar rayé*; German: *Streifenbarsch*), living near the North American coast and in the Pacific: considerably larger than the bass it often attains a weight of 9 kg. and sometimes 40 kg.

Brill *(Pleuronectoids)*

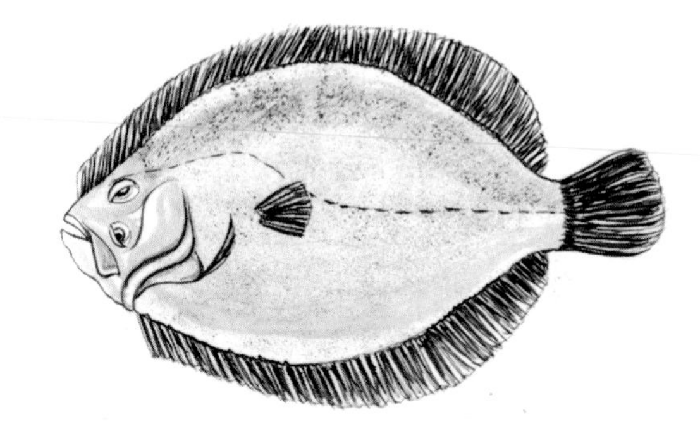

Latin: *Rhombus laevis*
French: *barbue*
German: *Glattbutt*
Italian: *barbutta*
Spanish: *barbadar*
Dutch: *griet*

Description. *General appearance:* very similar to that of the turbot (see page 20), a little more oval and lengthened, the part before the dorsal fin is divided; smooth skin without any protuberance; *colour:* greyish-yellow, a dark spot at the end of the lateral line; *size:* 30 to 75 cm. (rarely 1 m).

Characteristics. A coastal fish preferring rather deep water with a sandy or muddy bottom; *food:* fish, small crustaceans; *where found:* from the Mediterranean to the Baltic, but only as far as Mecklenburg.

Culinary applications. Excellent flesh, a little less fine than turbot or sole. Preparation is as for turbot.

Angler *(Lophioids)*

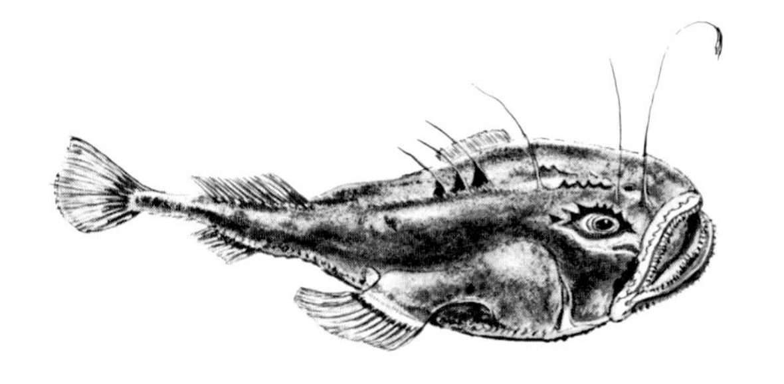

Latin: *Lophius piscatorius*
French: *baudroie* (*lotte* or *diable de mer*)
German: *Seeteufel*
Italian: *rospo di mare*
Spanish: *rape*
Dutch: *zeeduivel*

Description. *General appearance:* the head is very peculiar, disproportionate in size and almost circular with an enormous mouth and a large number of solid pointed teeth. The repulsive appearance of the angler fish is added to by the moveable element on its head; *colour:* the back is a darkish brown striped with black and the stomach is white; *size:* according to the species, from 70 cm. to 2 m.

Characteristics. According to age, it lives near the bottom at a depth of 10 m. to 500 m.; *food:* carnivorous, waiting for and attracting its prey, other fish and even skate and small sharks; *where found:* European coasts from Iceland to the Mediterranean. Similar species are found along the African and American coasts. The spawning season is from March onwards, depending on the latitude.

Culinary applications. The head is so ugly that it is always cut off and the body is sold; the flesh is snowy white, firm and tasty; it is used for *bouillabaisse* and *bourride* but also scalloped, fried or grilled. There is also smoked angler.

Cod *(Gadoids)*

Latin: *Gadus morrhua*
French: *cabillaud* (*morue*)
German: *Kabeljau*
Italian: *merluzzo fresco*
Spanish: *merluza*
Dutch: *Kabeljauw*

Description. *General appearance:* elongated body, at its largest just behind the head, then becoming more spindle-shaped, large head, prominent lower jaw with rather large and strong barbels; *colour:* olive-green turning to marbled-brown; the young adapt to the colour of their surroundings; *size and weight:* at 5 years old the cod is 80 cm. then 1 m. and up to 20 kg. in weight; the cod of the Baltic are a 'dwarf' kind (dorse) and are never more than 1 kg. in weight.

Characteristics. Rapid swimmer in cold waters; *food:* a voracious fish, eating small fish and their fry: herring, smelt etc.; *where found:* north of the Atlantic (Newfoundland, Iceland, etc.), the Arctic and the North Sea; its southern limit is the Channel.

Culinary applications. Delicate and tasty flesh, the fish can be cooked whole (without the head) and in slices; the fillets can be fried; it can be prepared *meunière* or poached; it makes good *quenelles.*

The cod fishery is only next in importance to that of the herring. Opened and dried the cod becomes the *Stookfisch* or dried cod (*morue sèche*); salted and dried it is salted cod (*morue salée—Klippfisch*), salted on board when taken and put into barrels, it is known as *laberdan*. The celebrated oil is made from the liver. Fillets are often frozen.

Plaice *(Pleuronectoids)*

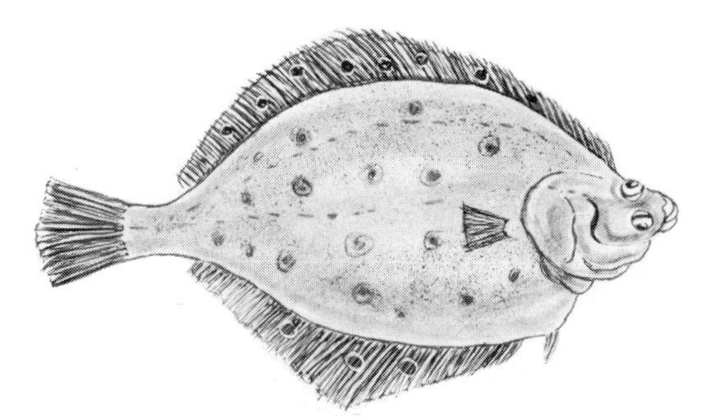

Latin: *Pleuronectes platessae*
French: *carrelet* (*plie franche*)
German: *Scholle*
Italian: *passera*
Spanish: *platija*
Dutch: *schol*

Description. *General appearance:* a flat fish, the line of the right side curved slightly inwards near the pectoral fin; *colour:* the upper part smooth and brownish, the eye side covered with numerous orange spots; the blind side is transparent white; *size and weight:* it can reach a size of 1 m.; in the trade three sizes are recognised: large of about 40 to 50 cm., weighing 1 kg.; medium of 25 to 35 cm., weighing 300 to 350 gr, and small for frying.

Characteristics. In winter the plaice eats very little, seeking calm areas where it can bury itself in the sand. Young plaice go deeper and more firmly in than the adult and thus avoid being caught in nets; *food:* small crustaceans, mussels, worms; *where found:* European coasts of the Atlantic from Portugal to the White Sea, as well as the western and central regions of the Baltic; each sea has its own particular species.

Culinary applications. The flesh of the plaice is white and tasty. It is sold fresh, smoked, marinated or frozen. Small plaice are cooked *meunière*, the largest are cut into *tronçons*, *court-bouillonnés* with different sauces, or fried, or poached.

Hake *(Gadoids)*

Latin: *Merluccius vulgaris*
French: *colin* (*merlus*)
German: *Seehecht, Hechtdorsch*
Italian: *merluzzo*
Spanish: *merluza*
Dutch: *koolvis*

Description. *General appearance:* elongated body, jutting lower jaw, without barbels; *colour:* metallic grey, black skin on the inside of the mouth; *size and weight:* average 50 cm., it can reach 1 m. and 10 kg.

Characteristics. Fish living in depths of 200 to 300 m. or more; *food:* sardines, mackerel, herring, whiting, cuttlefish; *where found:* western and south-western coasts of Europe from the Atlantic to Norway and Iceland and towards the south on the African coasts. Smaller species are found in the Mediterranean; the spawning season is from spring to summer, according to region.

Culinary applications. The hake has white flesh of excellent taste; it is much used in professional cookery, particularly in France and Great Britain. It can be poached whole. The fillets can be fried, grilled or poached or prepared *meunière*. Its flavour is at its best in June. It is the skinned and boned middle part of the body that is specially used. Slices or *darnes* of hake are often served. Also known in the south of France, incorrectly, as *merlan*.

Gilt-Poll *(Sparoids)*

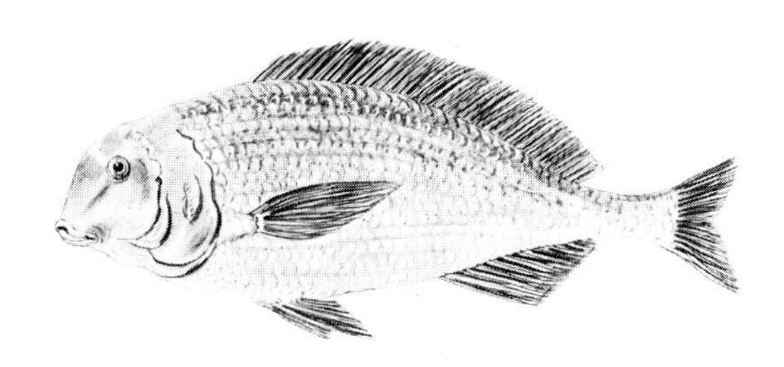

Latin: *Chrysophrys aurata*
French: *daurade*
German: *Goldbrassen*
Italian: *orata*
Spanish: *dorado*
Dutch: *goudbrasem*

Description. *General appearance:* oval, flattened along the sides, one only dorsal fin, large eyes; *colour:* dark blue on the back, silvery yellow sides with gold reflections; *size and weight:* average 30 to 50 cm. and up to 7 kg.

Characteristics. A coastal fish, often entering the oversalt or rather saltless pools or lagoons along the coast; *food:* molluscs, crustaceans, fry; *where found:* especially in the Mediterranean as well as in the Atlantic, particularly in the Gulf of Gascony; very rare in the Channel; spawning, from May to July, is in the open sea. The young measure about 20 cm. at the end of a year and are all male, the change to female comes later.

Culinary applications. The true gilt-poll is a fine and tasty fish, but fish sold as gilt-poll in markets are often far from it (see under *Sea-bream*). Small gilt-poll can be fried or grilled, their fillets prepared as fillets of sole; large fish can be larded or stuffed, roasted in the oven or served in buttered paper.

Common dorados *(Sparoids)*

SEA-BREAM
Latin: *Pagellus centrodontus*
French: *centrodonte, rousseau* or *gros yeux*
German: *gewöhnlicher Meerbrassen*
Dutch: *zeebrasem*

GILTHEAD
Latin: *Pagellus erythrinus*
French: *pageau* or *pagel*
German: *Rotbrassen*

BECKER
Latin: *Pagrus vulgaris*
French: *pagre*
German: *rötlicher Brassen*

and other varieties.

All these fish of the sparoid family are often sold as gilt-poll. They are more or less like it in shape and colour. They are excellent fish, not so fine as the true gilt-poll but prepared in the same way.

Smelt *(Salmonoids)*

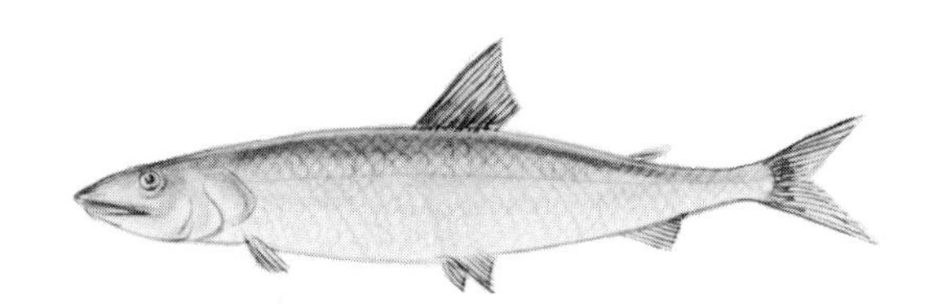

Latin: *Osmerus eperlanus*
French: *éperlan*
German: *Stint*
Italian: *eperlano*
Spanish: *esperinque*
Dutch: *spiering*

Description. *General appearance:* a small fish with elongated body like a flattened torpedo on the sides, mouth opening extends beyond the eyes; *colour:* back greyish-green, sides and stomach silvery; *size and weight:* 20 to 25 cm., 60 to 100 gr.
The *spirlin* of Northern and Eastern France and Central Europe is incorrectly called the fresh water smelt: it is a smaller fish (up to 15 cm.).

Characteristics. *Food:* plankton and animalcules from the sea bottom, fish; *where found:* coasts of the North Sea and the Baltic, Channel, Atlantic, estuaries of rivers; the spawning season is from February to the end of May.

Culinary applications. Smelt is usually in the market from June to September. The smaller fish make an excellent fry. The larger can be fried or prepared in the same way as whiting; they are also marinated.

Flounder *(Pleuronectoids)*

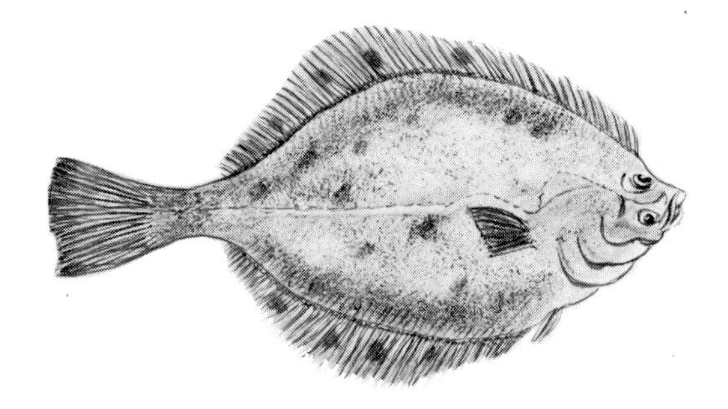

Latin: *Pleuronectes flesus*
French: *flet*
German: *Flunder*
Italian: *passera*
Spanish: *platija*
Dutch: *bot*

Description. *General appearance:* flat fish with a rather straight line on the side, slightly curved inwards from the pectoral fin; *colour:* greyish-brown, yellowish rather orange coloured spots, paler and less visible than those on the plaice, blind side white with, sometimes, various shades; *size:* from 30 to 40 cm., but can attain 80 cm. and live until 40 years old.

Characteristics. A typical fish of rather shallow coastal waters: when young it can often be found in brackish waters to which it returns after spawning; *food:* like that of the plaice with a preference for small crustaceans; *where found:* European coasts from the Black Sea to the White Sea, including the Baltic and the Gulf of Bothnia; it ascends rivers quite far in spite of industrial obstacles.

Culinary applications. For a long time the greater part of these fish were smoked. Nowadays the flounder is prepared fresh. Its flesh is oilier and less fine than that of the plaice. It is prepared *meunière* but fillets can also be fried.

Halibut *(Pleuronectoids)*

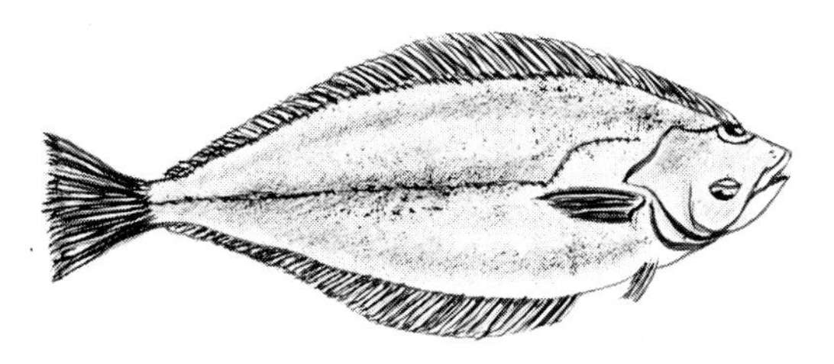

Latin: *Hippoglossus*
French: *flétan*
German: *Heilbutt*
Italian: *fletano*
Spanish: *mero*
Dutch: *heilbot*

Description. *General appearance:* elongated; the largest of the flat fish; the body is covered with round scales of even size and the fish is smooth; *colour:* the side on which the eyes are situated is greyish-brown and the fish becomes darker, almost black, with age; the blind side is white; *size and weight:* it grows relatively quickly and, not counting the caudal fin, it attains 45 to 62 cm. at 4 years old, 1·10 m. at 10, 1·45 to 2 m. at 15; at this size of 1·45 to 2 m. it weighs 45 to 114 kg.; specimens of 2 to 3 m. exist but are rare. The known maximum age of these fish is 20 to 30 years.

Characteristics. A sea-bottom fish, at 100 to 200 m. deep; on rare occasions it can go down to 700 m.; *food:* young cod or other fish of the same family; *where found:* Atlantic and North Pacific coasts. The most important fishing areas are Iceland, Spitzbergen, Greenland and the western coast of America. It has great economic importance due to the large size of the fish; the catch well exceeds that of brill and turbot.

Culinary applications. Its flesh is very tasty and appetising; it is white but less firm than that of brill or turbot. It is prepared in *darnes* in a *court-bouillon,* and it can be cut up into fillets or portions, then fried, poached or served *meunière.*

Rock Salmon *(Gadoids)*

Latin: *Gadus virens*
French: *grelin (lieu noir)*
German, *Seelachs, Köhler*

Italian: *gado*
Spanish: *gado*
Dutch: *Zwarte koolvis*

Description. *General appearance:* see page 1; *colour:* olive green, very dark green, almost black, the mouth is black from which comes its German name meaning charcoal-burner; *size:* up to 1 m. The pollack (Latin: *Gadus pollachius*, French: *lieu jaune*, German: *Pollack*) is rather similar to the rock salmon. It is found along the western coasts of Europe as far as Iceland and even in the Baltic and the Mediterranean; it attains a length of 60 cm., its flesh is finer than that of the rock salmon (*lieu noir*).

Characteristics. A fish living in cold and temperate water; *food:* carnivorous, feeding especially on herring, the young live on plankton; *where found:* from Biscay to Greenland, the principal fishing grounds being the coasts of Scotland, Iceland and Norway; in North America it is known as the *coalfish.*

Culinary applications. Inferior in quality but with flesh which stays firm. It is eaten fresh, in fillets, frozen and smoked; salted cod (*morue*) is made from it. There is the occasional attempt to use it instead of smoked salmon. Prepared as cod (*cabillaud*) and fried fish balls.

Grey Gurnard *(Trigloids)*

Latin: *Trigla gurnadus*
French: *grondin*
German: *grauer Knurrhahn*
Italian: *grondino*
Spanish: *trigla*
Dutch: *knorhaan, grauwe poon*

Description. *General appearance:* elongated body, strong head covered with bony sections, the lower spines of the pectoral fins are *fingers* used by the gurnard to move along the sea-bottom and probably have a tactile role; the name, as can easily be recognised in French and Italian, comes from the rumblings the fish can make because of the powerful muscles of its gaseous swimming-bladder; *colour:* great variation according to species; *size:* grey gurnard 30 cm., red 40 cm., sea swallow 50 cm. at most.

Characteristics. The species of this fish live at very variable depths (e.g. the *grondin lyre* and the sea swallow at 300 to 400 m.); *food:* crustaceans, molluscs, small fish; *where found:* the grey gurnard lives from the Murmansk and north Norway coast down to the Adriatic; it has white dots on the back and these are sometimes within black circles on a yellowish ground.

Culinary applications. Very white and tasty flesh but there is appreciable waste; the fillets can be fried or poached; grey and red gurnard or gurnet are good for *bouillabaisse.* The red gurnet is often sold as red mullet: this is incorrect and is often a trick.

RED GURNARD
Latin: *Trigla cuculus*
French: *grondin rouge*
German: *roter Knurrhahn*
Dutch: *Engelse poon*

SEA SWALLOW
Latin: *Trigla hirundo*
French: *grondin perlon*
German: *See schwalbe*

Herring *(Clupeoids)*

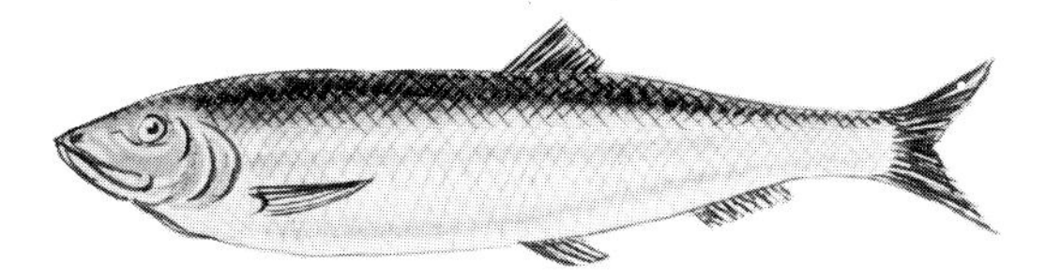

Latin: *Clupea harengus*
French: *hareng*
German: *Hering*
Italian: *aringa*
Spanish: *arenque*
Dutch: *haring*

Description. *General appearance:* see page 1; *colour:* greenish back, silver sides, body covered with soft, easily detached scales; *size:* average 30 cm., rarely 50 cm.

Characteristics. Herrings live in shoals at successive stages in their life; *food:* crustaceans, and small fry, etc.; *where found:* there are numerous kinds in the north Atlantic, Biscay, the Arctic Circle, Spitzbergen and the White Sea; there are also localised kinds; the Baltic herring and the North Sea kind as well as the Iceland and Norwegian types.

Culinary applications. Fish of primordial and vital importance over a long period of time (a basic food in the Middle Ages); fresh herring (*hareng vert*) has a tasty flesh, fried or grilled. Usually the herring, with the head removed, is salted and put into casks and barrels on board, when caught. The red herring is gutted and smoked after refrigeration. The bloater is salted then smoked. The kipper is quickly salted in brine then smoked. According to age there are three classifications: the herring without eggs or soft roe, the herring with soft roe or eggs, and the herring which has spawned.

Dab *(Pleuronectoids)*

Latin: *Pleuronectes limanda*
French: *limande*
German: *Kliesche*
Italian: *limanda*
Spanish: *pescado gallo*
Dutch: *schar*

Description. *General appearance:* see page 2; *colour:* light yellowish brown with a few irregular paler spots; *size:* from 20 to 40 cm.

Characteristics. Typical fish of rather shallow waters of 20 to 30 m. deep; it is rarely found at a depth of more than 100 m.; *food:* crustaceans, echinoderms, worms, small fish of the herring family; *where found:* from Biscay to Iceland; the Baltic and Jutland; the spawning season is from December to June.

Culinary applications. Excellent fish, inferior to the plaice or flounder. Difficult to preserve, it is dried when caught. Preparation is as for plaice and the best method is *meunière.*

Lemon Sole *(Pleuronectoids)*

Latin: *Pleuronectes cynoglossus*
French: *limande-sole*
German: *Rotzunge*
Italian: *limanda*
Spanish: *limanda*
Dutch: *tongschar*

Description. *General appearance:* almost like the sole but with a more pointed head and short caudal fin; *colour:* reddish or greyish brown, black pectoral fin; *size and weight:* 30 to 50 cm. and up to 1 kg. There are two fish which are usually called lemon-sole: the 'true' lemon-sole (*Pleuronectes microcephalus* Don), the head of which is very small and which is more like the plaice, and the 'false' lemon-sole (*Hippoglossoides limandoides* Bloch) also called a halibut-sole (*sole-flétan*), of inferior quality, with a rough and scaly skin; this fish attains a length of 30 to 40 cm.

Characteristics. A coastal fish inhabiting moderately deep water with a muddy bottom; *food:* crustaceans, worms, mussels, etc.; *where found:* European coasts from northern Norway to the Channel and the north-east of the British Isles as far as the Skagerrak and near Iceland; found also in small numbers in the Baltic, on the coasts of North America as far as Cape Cod; the spawning season takes place from April to September.

Culinary applications. Prepared *meunière* and like sole which this fish sometimes replaces because of its lower price; the flesh is white and tasty but not so firm as that of the sole.

Ling *(Gadoids)*

Latin: *Molva molva*
French: *lingue*
German: *Lengfisch*
Italian: *molva allungata*
Dutch: *leng*

Description. *General appearance:* see page 1; rounded caudal fin; *colour:* white edged fins uneven in number with black markings on them; *size:* can attain 1·50 m. The blue ling (Latin: *Molva* *byrkelange* Walb; French: *lingue bleue*; German: *Blauleng*) has a finer tail, large eyes and teeth and short barbels; its back has metallic reflections whence its name; it is fished mostly near Iceland.

Characteristics. Fish living between 150 and 300 m. deep; *food:* crustaceans and fish; the ling is often caught by trawlers because of its habit of following shoals of herring; *where found:* the Channel and North Sea as far as Norway and even in the Kattegat and also, rarely, in the Baltic.

Culinary applications. The quality of the ling is inferior to that of the cod. The fillets can be fried and smoked. In northern countries ling is used to make *stockfisch.*

Mackerel *(Scombroids)*

Latin: *Scomber scombrus*
French: *maquereau*
German: *Makrele*
Italian: *sgombro*
Spanish: *caballa*
Dutch: *makreel*

Description. *General appearance:* see page 2, sharply cut caudal fin, scales diminishing in size from the head to the tail; *colour:* back bright dark brownish green with transversal black stripes, pearly sides, white stomach; *size:* average 30 to 50 cm. rarely attaining 60 cm.

Characteristics. The study of the mackerel, in order to improve its fishing, has made it possible to determine its migrations according to the seasons; *food:* animalcules, then herrings, sardines, sprats and small gadoids; *where found:* the Atlantic, in the north as far as Norway and in the south as far as the Canaries; abundant in the North Sea, less abundant in the Kattegat and the Baltic (in summer only); it is found in the Mediterranean, on the west coast of North America and in the Pacific. It spawns in the Mediterranean in March and April and in the Atlantic from June to August.

Culinary applications. Tasty flesh which must be eaten very fresh before it turns bitter. The mackerel can be fried, grilled or poached or prepared *meunière*; smoked or marinated it is also much appreciated. The *horse mackerel* is much less well considered and has hardly any value except smoked. In Spain and Portugal the small *goggler* are preserved in oil and sold cheaply.

HORSE MACKEREL, GOGGLER
Latin: *Caranx trachurus*
French: *maquereau bâtard, maquereuse, chinchard*
German: *Bastardmakrele*
Portuguese: *chicharros*
Dutch: *horsmakreel*

Very similar to the mackerel, body less rounded and without stripes; in all seas from the Cape of Good Hope to Northern Norway.

Whiting *(Gadoids)*

Latin: *Gadus merlangus*
French: *merlan*
German: *Wittling, Weissling*
Italian: *masello*
Spanish: *pescadilla*
Dutch: *wijting*

Description. *General appearance:* see page 1; *colour:* greyish green or olive back, sides almost white beige with sometimes irregular yellow stripes; *size:* average 30 cm. and a maximum of 50 to 60 cm.

Characteristics. The whiting lives in rather scattered shoals not far from the sea-bottom and usually not deeper than about 60 m.; it sometimes ascends rivers; *food:* herring and herring fry, shrimps and small whiting; *where found:* in the north from Murmansk and Iceland to the south as far as the Black Sea and the Mediterranean; a few small whiting are found in the Baltic.

Culinary applications. One of the best sea fish with very tasty tender flesh. Fragile fish which must be eaten very fresh. It can be fried in deep fat or used for *farces* but it can also be prepared *meunière*.

Wolf-fish *(Anarrhichadides)*

Latin: *Anarrhichas lupus*
French: *poisson-loup*
German: *Seewolf*
Dutch: *zeewolf*

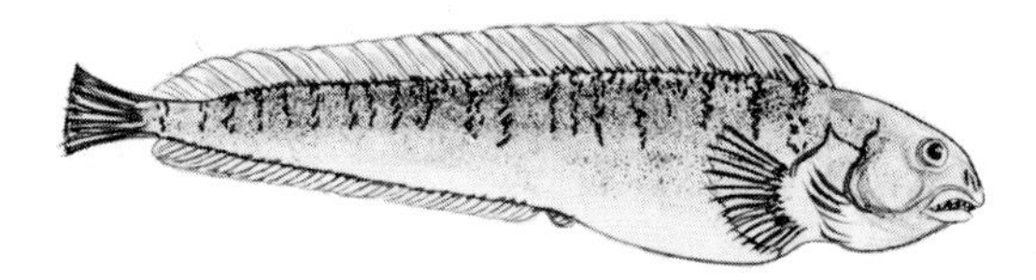

Description. *General appearance:* almost cylindrical body slightly diminishing in diameter towards the tail; medium sized head, mouth with flesh-eating teeth; *colour:* grey to greyish brown, marked with blackish brown vertical bands, stomach lighter; *size:* maximum 1·20 m.
The mottled sea-wolf (*loup marin tacheté*) is close to the sea-wolf (*Anarrhichas minor* Olafsen); it is more elongated with numerous round markings, stomach lighter and without markings; it attains 2 m. in length.

Characteristics. Coastal fish; *food:* mussels, sea-urchins, crustaceans, starfish; *where found:* North Sea, the Atlantic and rarely the French coasts, Greenland, Iceland, the American coast as far as Cape Hatteras.

Culinary applications. Tasty flesh which is cut into fillets allowing preparation *meunière* and also used in soups. Occasionally sold smoked.

Thornback Ray *(Rajoids)*

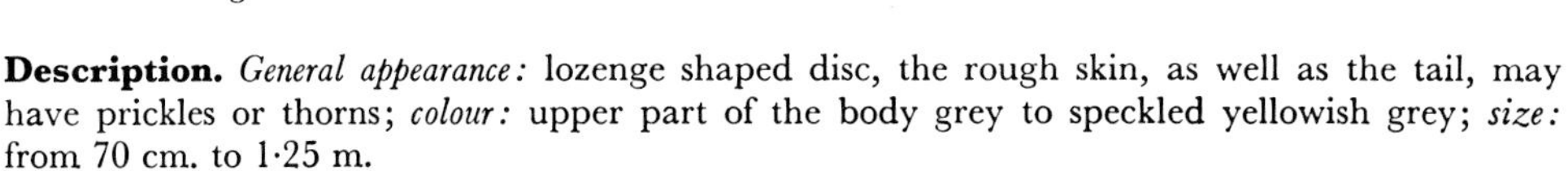

Latin: *Raia clavata*
French: *raie bouclée*
German: *Nagelrochen*
Italian: *razza*
Spanish: *raja*
Dutch: *stekelrog*

Description. *General appearance:* lozenge shaped disc, the rough skin, as well as the tail, may have prickles or thorns; *colour:* upper part of the body grey to speckled yellowish grey; *size:* from 70 cm. to 1·25 m.
The *raie cendrés* or ashgrey-ray resembles the thornback-ray but its skin is smooth and it has no caudal fin; this fish can attain 2·50 m. and 75 kg.; it is found from the North Sea to Iceland. In certain northern countries it is salted and also smoked. It is said to be more tasty than the thornback-ray.

Characteristics. A coastal fish; *food:* fish, crustaceans, sea-urchins, mussels; *where found:* coasts of Madeira and the Mediterranean; they can be found as far as Iceland and a few specimens are taken in the western North Sea.

Culinary applications. The ray is mostly eaten poached and then prepared in different ways. It must be absolutely fresh otherwise it develops an insupportable smell of ammonia.

Norway Haddock *(Scorpenoids)*
(Red-Fish)

Latin: *Sebastus marinus*
French: *rascasse du nord*
(*chèvre, sébaste*)
German: *Rotbarsch*
Italian: *scarpena rossa, scorfano rosso*

Description. *General appearance:* not a very long body, head strong and partly plated, solid and irregular scales, lower jaw thrust forward, large eyes; *colour:* back a brilliant red becoming lighter towards the stomach; *size and weight:* average 30 to 50 cm., from 1 to 2 kg.; rare specimens of 80 cm. to 1 m. are found.

Characteristics. Lives in shoals on rocky bottoms, always more than 100 m. deep, sometimes reaching 1000 m.; *food:* crustaceans, molluscs and fish; *where found:* north Atlantic coasts; European limit is the Kattegat and the American limit Cape Cod; found very rarely in the North Sea or the Baltic, and only if the fish has got lost there.

Culinary applications. Fish only known in European markets since 1890. Its flesh is oily. Its fillets can be fried, *sauté*, or poached.

Red Mullet *(Mulloids)*

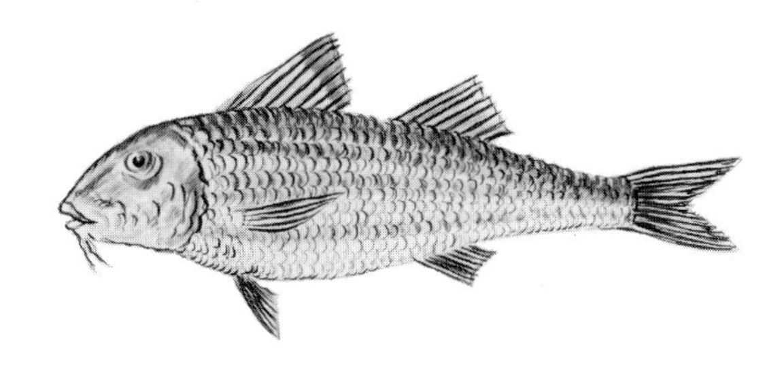

Latin: *Mullus barbatus* and
Mullus surmuletus
French: *rouget barbet*
German: *Rotbarbe*
Italian: *triglia*
Spanish: *sargo*
Dutch: *zeebarbeel*

Description. *General appearance:* elongated body, moderately flattened, large scales; under the chin two 'barbels' which can move in any direction; *colour:* the red mullet only becomes reddish pink after death; alive it is a greenish brown along the back and silver on the sides and stomach; *size and weight:* a maximum of 25 cm. for the red mullet inhabiting areas of a muddy bottom and of 35 to 40 cm. for the surmullet or red mullet of rocky areas.

Characteristics. Living in small families in coastal areas; *food:* worms and small crustaceans; *where found:* very abundant in the Mediterranean, rather more rare in the Atlantic; spawns in spring. The flesh is tastier from May to September.

Culinary applications. The flesh is particularly tasty: it is therefore desirable to give it a simple preparation. The mullet having no gall it is not necessary to gut it; hence also its name 'sea woodcock'. It may be prepared grilled or *sauté*, or *en papillote* (for this it is preferable to let it marinate beforehand). The mullet from rocky areas has the better reputation.

Sardine *(Clupeoids)*

Latin: *Clupea pilchardus* Walb
French: *sardine*
German: *Sardine*
Italian: *sardina*
Spanish: *sardina*
Dutch: *sardien*

Description. *General appearance:* see page 1; jutting lower jaw, rather large scales, caudal fin widely forked and flattened; *colour:* silvery; *size:* 10 to 15 cm. and up to 25 cm.
The pilchard (Latin: *Sardina pilchardus*; French: *royan*; German: *Pilchard*) is probably a particular species.

Characteristics. Sometimes forms enormous shoals; *food:* worms, molluscs, fry; *where found:* from the south of the Canaries to Norwegian waters; found in great quantities in the Mediterranean as well as on the south and south-west coasts of England; spawning takes place all the year round in the Mediterranean and, elsewhere, in spring and summer.

Culinary applications. The fresh sardine is a very delicate fish and is only eaten near the coastal fishing areas: France, Spain, Portugal (from July to September) and the south of England (until December). Sardines preserved in arachis oil, or preferably olive oil, are justly famous and come into many other preparations.

Sole *(Soloids)*

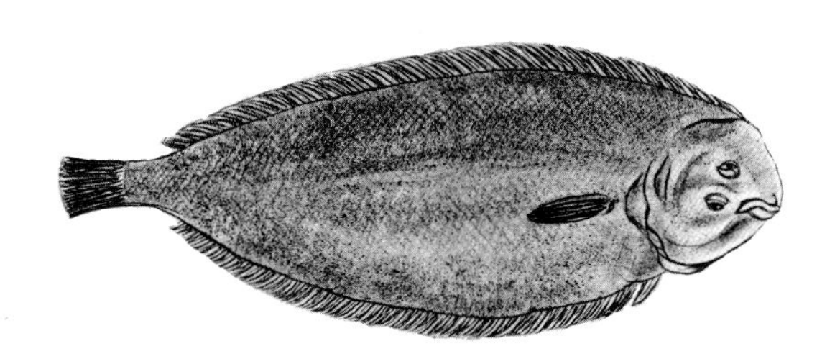

Latin: *Solea vulgaris* and *Solea solea*
French: *sole*
German: *Seezunge*
Italian: *sogliola*
Spanish: *lenguado*
Dutch: *tong*

Description. *General appearance:* see page 2; mouth in the shape of a parrot's beak, dorsal fin continuing the caudal fin almost as far as the eyes; *colour:* grey or greyish brown with variable spots which allow the sole to adapt to the colour of the sandy or muddy bottom it prefers; *size:* the sole can attain a size of 66 cm. and there are three main categories for purposes of sale: large, of about 250 gr. or more; medium, of 170 to 250 gr., and small, of 170 gr. or less.

Characteristics. The sole lives at a depth of 20 to 30 m., with its body buried in the mud except for its head; *food:* worms, crustaceans, sand-eels, small fish; *where found:* the Mediterranean, Biscay as far as the Channel and up to Trondheim, the Kattegat and the west of the Baltic. The commercial interest in the fish continues throughout the year.

Culinary applications. White, firm and very tasty flesh. The true sole is among the most sought after fish. It can be fried, cooked *meunière*, poached, cut into fillets, rolled into *paupiettes,* and it can be served hot or cold. There are a great number of recipes.

Sprat *(Clupeoids)*

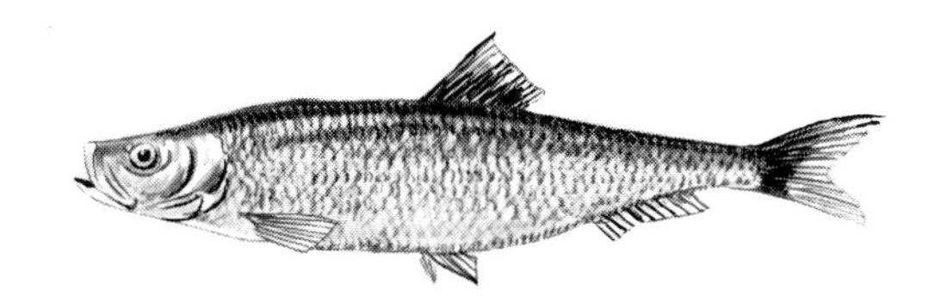

Latin: *Lupea sprottus*
French: *sprat* (*esprot*)
German: *Sprotte*
Italian: *spratto*
Spanish: *sprat*
Dutch: *sprot*

Description. *General appearance:* see page 1; very similar to the young herring but with larger eyes; *colour:* see *herring*; *size:* 9 to 12 cm., rarely 15 cm.

Characteristics. *Food:* preference for small crustaceans and worms; *where found:* northern coasts of Europe down to the Mediterranean and the Black Sea; abundant in the western Baltic.

Culinary applications. Like sardines, grilled or fried; but best known preserved, marinated or smoked.

Tunny *(Scombroids)*

Latin: *Thunnus thynnus*
French: *thon*
German: *Thunfisch*
Italian: *tonno*
Spanish: *atun*
Dutch: *tonijn*

Description. *General appearance:* a large and almost spindle-shaped fish with narrow fins; *colour:* dark blue on the back with grey sides and white stomach; the yellow tunny (*thon jaune, Neothunnus macropterus*) is very rare; *size and weight:* average 2m. and 100 kg. but, exceptionally, it can attain up to 5 m. and up to 500 kg.

Characteristics. A powerful and rapid swimmer the tunny travels considerable distances; *food:* it lives entirely on other fish, attacking shoals of sardines, herrings and mackerel and even larger and better armed fish; *where found:* the Mediterranean and the Atlantic, the North Sea. Spawning takes place in June.

Culinary applications. The flesh is very well thought of. Fresh tunny can be grilled, braised or fried and it is, of course, chilled and smoked. It can be preserved, especially in oil. Tunny in oil is very usefully and agreeably used in the preparation of *hors d'œuvre.*

BONITO
Latin: *Pelamys thynnus*
French: *bonite*
German: *Bonito*

The same type of fish with long horizontal brown bands; the bonito is found in many areas including the Black Sea and Japan.

BONITOL
Latin: *Thunnus mediterraneus*
French: *boniton*
German: *Bonitol*

A small and exclusively Mediterranean bonito; firmer and better flesh than that of the bonito.

ALBACORE (White tunny)
Latin: *Thunnus germo*
French: *germon (thon blanc)*
German: *Germon*

This fish is easily recognised by its very lengthened pectoral fins which have the appearance of wings; it is found in the Mediterranean and in the West Indies.
The bonito, bonitol and the albacore are prepared in the same way as tunny. Tinned albacore gives a white and firm flesh.

Turbot *(Pleuronectoids)*

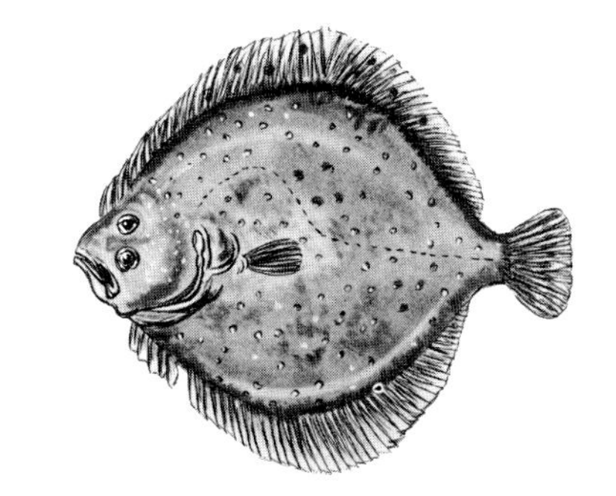

Latin: *Rhombus maximus*
French: *turbot*
German: *Steinbutt*
Italian: *rombo*
Spanish: *rodaballo*
Dutch: *tarbot*

Description. *General appearance:* almost circular, skin without scales and with numerous protuberances, powerful teeth; *colour:* basically yellowish-grey with markings; *size and weight:* it can attain 1 m. and even 2 m. and 40 kg.

Characteristics. The turbot likes rather shallow water with a sandy or muddy bottom; *food:* it eats all kinds of other fish; *where found:* from the Mediterranean to the coasts of Norway.

Culinary applications. White firm flesh, very well thought of. The turbot can be served whole, braised or moistened with a cooking-liquor; it is cut into fillets or thick slices which can be poached. Cold turbot is a very decorative dish.

Weever *(Trachinoids)*

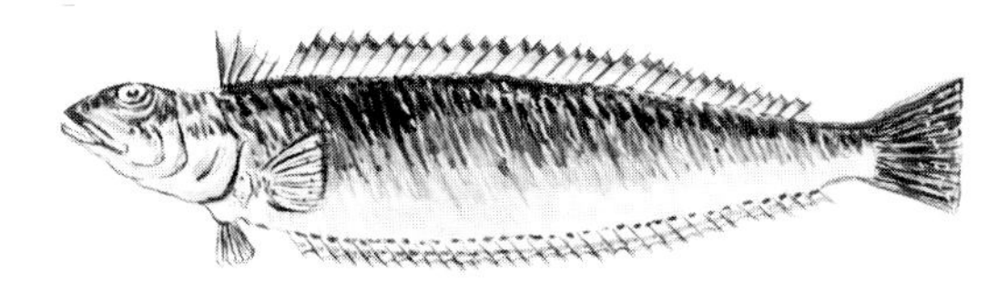

Latin: *Trachinus draco*
French: *dragon de mer (le grande vive)*
German: *Peterännchen*
Italian: *dragone, vipera di mare*
Spanish: *traquino*
Dutch: *pieterman*

Description. *General appearance:* elongated and compressed body with a rather large oblique mouth and a small head. The spines of the first dorsal fin are poisonous as well as the backward pointing spine of the gill-cover; *colour:* body varying from yellow to brown with bluish tints and stripes; *size:* 20 to 30 cm., sometimes 40 cm.

Characteristics. A fish which buries itself in the sand to wait for its prey; *food:* small fish; *where found:* from the African coasts of the Atlantic to the coasts of Norway, the Mediterranean; rare in the North Sea and the Baltic; spawning takes place in July and August; the poisonous spines of the weever can be dangerous.

Culinary applications. White and savoury flesh used especially in *bouillabaisse.* The weever can have the same preparation as the whiting, or can be smoked.

FRESH WATER AND MIGRATORY FISH

Shad *(Clupeoids)*

Latin: *Alosa vulgaris*
French: *alose*
German: *Alse, Maifisch*
Italian: *alosa*
Spanish: *sabalo*
Dutch: *elft*

Description. *General appearance:* see page 1; large thin scales, distinctive eyelids; *colour:* a bright greenish blue on the back, sides a golden colour with dark markings behind the gills; *size and weight:* 50 cm. (up to 75 cm.), and up to 3 kg. There is a smaller species.

Characteristics. The only clupeoid ascending rivers to spawn; *where found:* the western coasts of Europe, North America and the Mediterranean. Ascends as far as the lakes of Tessino and even the Rhine where it is fished.

Culinary applications. Tender and delicate fish, very tasty but not very digestible. It is prepared poached whole or cut up. It can be grilled and fried. The roe is much esteemed in North America, where the shad, prepared in the oven, is something of a speciality.

Eel *(Anguilloids)*

Latin: *Anguilla anguilla*
French: *anguille*
German: *Aal*
Italian: *anguilla*
Spanish: *anguila*
Dutch: *aal, paling*

Description. *General appearance:* elongated and cylindrical body, two pectoral fins, the dorsal and anal fin join together, simulated scales in a thick squamous skin; *colour:* grey, brown or olive-green back, stomach yellowish or greenish becoming a silvery white at the time of migration; *size:* the males attain 50 cm. and the females up to 1·50 m.

Characteristics. Migratory fish originating in the ocean depths (the Sargasso Sea), arriving at the estuaries of rivers to find their way into salty and fresh waters; at sexual maturity (8 to 10 years old for the male, and 12 to 15 for the female), the eel will travel thousands of miles to its spawning grounds; the eel has a preference for a muddy or slimy bottom, streams, ponds and pools; *where found:* eastern coasts of the Atlantic, North Sea and the Baltic, and even the Mediterranean; *food:* according to species the eel is a voracious feeder on crustaceans, molluscs, fish, spawn and fry.

Culinary applications. Remarkable table fish with firm and oily flesh. It can be fried, grilled or prepared *en matelote, au bleu,* and *au vert,* etc. It can also be marinated and is particularly appreciated when smoked.

Barbel *(Cyprinoids)*

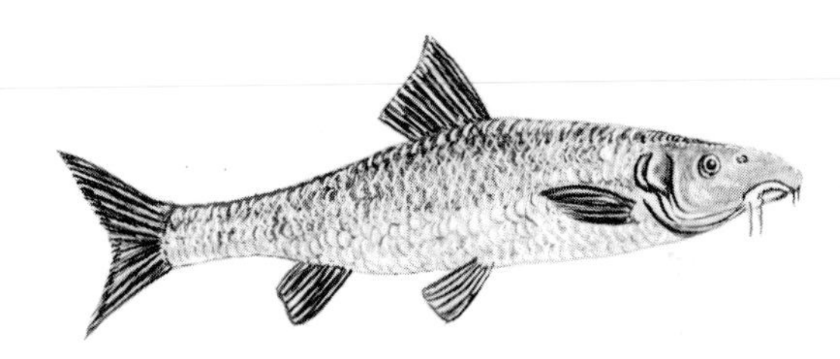

Latin: *Barbus barbus*
French: *barbeau*
German: *Barbe, Flussbarbe*
Italian: *barbio*
Spanish: *barbo*
Dutch: *barbeel*

Description. *General appearance:* oval with a short dorsal fin and a long head; its upper jaw has four short barbels; *colour:* back greenish grey, sides a lighter colour; there are yellow or golden coloured specimens; *size and weight:* from 30 cm. to 90 cm. and up to 8 kg.

Characteristics. Preference for swiftly flowing water with a sandy or pebbly bottom; *food:* worms, larvae, slugs, spawn; *where found:* central Europe, western Balkans, England and France; spawning takes place from May to July, season of the great migrations upstream and to fishing areas.

Culinary applications. White and tasty flesh, very digestible but full of bones. The larger pieces are poached in a *court-bouillon* and served with a sharp sauce; the smaller are grilled, fried, or prepared *meunière* or *en matelote.* The spawn are poisonous.

Bream *(Cyprinoids)*

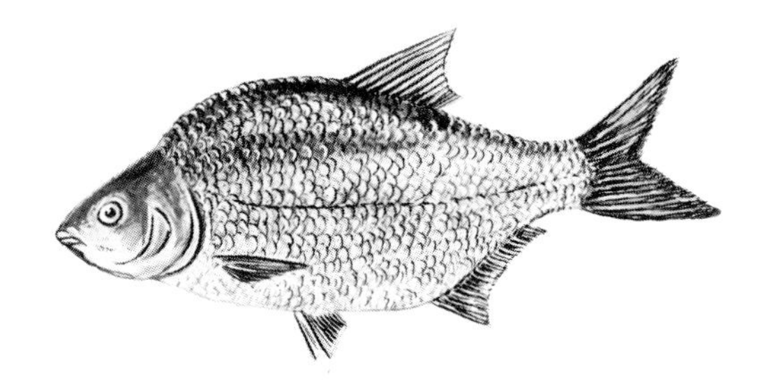

Latin: *Abramis brama*
French: *brème*
German: *Brachsen, Blei*
Italian: *sarago*
Spanish: *sargo*
Dutch: *brasem*

Description. *General appearance:* a laterally compressed body swelling up on the back; the adult fish attains a length three times as much as its height; the upper jaw juts over the lower; *colour:* the back and the top of the head a leaden grey, almost black, with a greenish tint, sides a lighter colour, stomach a rather iridescent white or whitish; *size and weight:* 30 to 50 cm. and up to 70 cm., up to 6 or 7 kg.

Characteristics. Living in rivers and lakes, in warm and sluggish waters; *food:* omnivorous, the bream eats larvae, molluscs and worms; in winter it searches along the bottom with its prominent jaw; *where found:* Central Europe, Northern and Western Europe, scarcely going beyond the centre of France; spawning takes place from May to July in waters with abundant vegetation.

Culinary applications. The flesh of the bream is much like that of the barbel with just as many bones. Large specimens are prepared in the same way as carp; small ones are fried or used in soup.

Pike *(Esocoids)*

Latin: *Esox lucius*
French: *brochet*
German: *Hecht*
Italian: *luccio*
Spanish: *lucio*
Dutch: *snoek*

Description. *General appearance:* long, slim body, slightly flattened on the sides, the front part of the head flattens into the shape of a duck's bill over a large mouth well provided with strong teeth; *colour:* the back varies, according to the area or location, and can be olive-green or olive-brown or greenish grey, the sides being lighter with dark markings, the stomach is white; small pike are usually a light green; *size and weight:* from 40 cm. to 1 m. the best weight is from 2 to 3 kg.; pike are found weighing up to 10 kg. and even up to 20 and 30 kg.

Characteristics. The fish is a sedentary type lurking along the banks of a river or lake or under overhangs; *food:* most voracious, the pike will eat all fish, toads, frogs, birds, and even small mammals; it is sometimes put into hatcheries in order to eat the useless species; *where found:* the whole of Europe except the south, and the zones of similar climate in Asia and North America; spawning takes place from February to May.

Culinary applications. The flesh of the young pike is firm and white without many bones, but it is not very digestible. Older fish have a rather fibrous flesh with very many small bones. The best pike come from running water; the liver is excellent; the eggs can be toxic. Preparation can be *au bleu* and *au vert*, braised and *en matelote*; the flesh is used for *farces* and for *quenelles*, a speciality much in demand.

Carp *(Cyprinoids)*

Latin: *Cyprinus carpio*
French: *carpe*
German: *Karpfen*
Italian: *carpa*
Spanish: *carpa*
Dutch: *karper*

Description. *General appearance:* elongated body, slightly flattened on the sides, two barbels on each side of the jaw; there are three main varieties: the common carp (French: *carpe commune*; German: *Schuppenkarpfen*) entirely covered with regular scales; the mirror carp or king carp (French: *carpe-miroir*; German: *Spiegelkarpfen*) covered irregularly with large scaly plates in two or three longitudinal bands; the leather carp (French: *carpe-cuir*; German: *Lederkarpfen*) almost entirely without scales; the mirror carp and the leather carp have been produced by a process of continual selection; *colour:* carp are of very differing colours, the back going from bluish green to brownish green, the sides from bluish green to a golden yellow, lighter towards the stomach; the fins, except the dorsal one, are bluish green with reddish tints; *size and weight:* on average from 25 to 50 cm. and from 1 to 3 kg.; it can attain 1 m. and 20 kg.

Characteristics. The carp prefers shallow warm waters, lakes and pools rich in vegetation and food of all kinds; it hibernates in shallow waters; *food:* fauna found on the bottom or from the banks, and vegetation; *where found:* originating from the Far East, it is found throughout Europe except in the extreme north; spawning takes place from May to June.

Culinary applications. A fish very rightly well thought of, with a tasty and oily flesh; it is prepared *au bleu*, served with melted butter or sauce *hollandaise*, braised with red wine, stuffed or roasted in the oven. The soft roe of the carp, a great delicacy, has a variety of uses.

Chub *(Cyprinoids)*

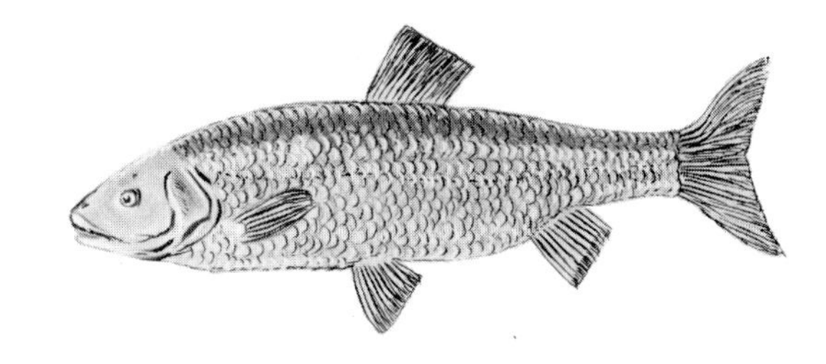

Latin: *Squalius cephalus*
French: *chevaine* (*chevesne, cabot*)
German: *Döbel, Aitel, Rohrkarpfen*
Italian: *cavedine*
Dutch: *kopvoorn, meun*

Description. *General appearance:* a rather wide elongated body with a wide head rounded in shape in front, the upper jaw juts over the lower, the scales are large and strong; *colour:* the back and the top of the head are dark grey with greenish brown tints, the sides have yellowish or silvery tints, the stomach is white with metal coloured tints, the stomach and anal fins are red; *size and weight:* from 30 to 50 cm. and up to 60 cm. and 3 kg.

Characteristics. It likes lakes of low or medium altitude, swiftly flowing rivers and has a preference for waterfalls and eddies such as downstream from mills and factories, etc.; *food:* first of all plants, insects and very small fresh water animal life, then small fish, frogs and spawn; *where found:* Central, Southern and Western Europe, Asia Minor; not found in Denmark, Ireland or Sicily; spawning takes place from April to June; the young live together and the adult fish are solitary.

Culinary applications. The flesh is of good quality but full of bones. Small chub are prepared as trout and large fish as carp. Used also *en matelote.*

Sturgeon *(Acipenseroids)*

Latin: *Acipenser sturio*
French: *esturgeon*
German: *Stör*
Italian: *storione*
Spanish: *esturion*
Dutch: *steur*

Description. *General appearance:* a torpedo shaped body, almost completely cartilaginous, toothless protrusile mouth, the skin without scales furnished with five rows of large, carinated, bony plates; *colour:* the back is greenish brown or greyish brown and the sides are lighter, the stomach yellowish or white; *size and weight:* up to 2 m. for the male and 4 to 6 m. for the female, from 40 to 200 kg.

Characteristics. Its growth is achieved in the sea and then it ascends rivers; *food:* the young eat infusoria, minute crustaceans, etc.; the adult fish feed on worms, molluscs, crustaceans and small fish which they seek in the mud; *where found:* the Atlantic, the North Sea, the Baltic and in rivers; in France it is now only rarely found in certain parts of the Rhone and the Garonne; spawning takes place from April to June.

Culinary applications. Very tasty flesh which is cut up for braising; slices are grilled or fried; also sold smoked. The sturgeon's eggs, prepared and salted, provide the very highly esteemed caviar.

Whitefish *(Salmonoids)*

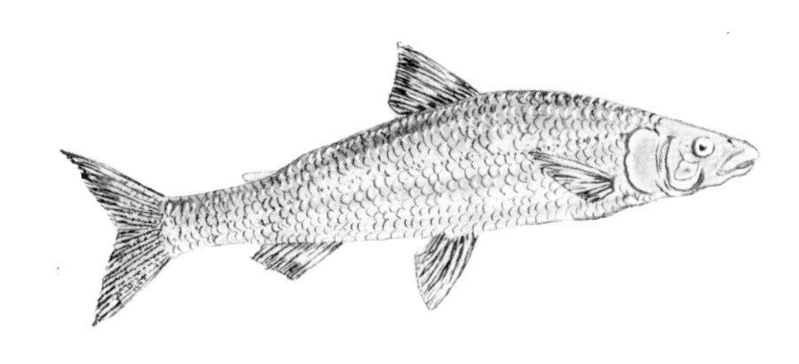

Latin: *Coregonus wartmanni* Bloch
French: *féra*
German: *Blaufelchen, Reinanke*
Italian: *lavareto*
Spanish: *salmonete*
Dutch: *grote marene*

Description. *General appearance:* body in the shape of a flattened torpedo, strong raised head; *colour:* back bluish green, or dark green, head and gill covers with golden and pink tints, the sides and stomach silvery white; *size:* 30 to 40 cm.

Characteristics. The whitefish lives chiefly in the deep cold and pure waters of great lakes, rich in oxygen; *food:* worms, insects, molluscs, plankton; *where found:* Alpine and pre-Alpine areas of northern Europe and northern Germany; spawning takes place as soon as the temperature of the water drops below 8 degrees Centigrade (November–December); it is fished a great deal in Lake Geneva and is bred and reared in Lake Constance.

Culinary applications. Fish of excellent and tasty flesh, often prepared as trout.

Gudgeon *(Cyprinoids)*

Latin: *Gobio gobio*
French: *goujon*
German: *Gründling*
Italian: *ghiozzo d'acqua dolce*
Spanish: *gobio*
Dutch: *grondel*

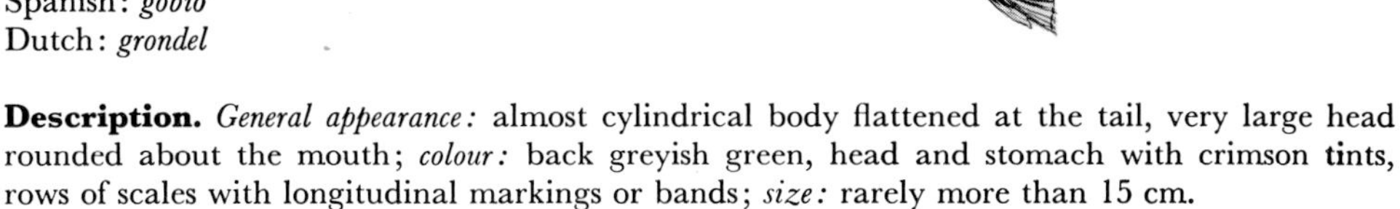

Description. *General appearance:* almost cylindrical body flattened at the tail, very large head rounded about the mouth; *colour:* back greyish green, head and stomach with crimson tints, rows of scales with longitudinal markings or bands; *size:* rarely more than 15 cm.

Characteristics. A fish of rapid and clear rivers, living with others of the same species on sand or gravel bottoms; *food:* worms, molluscs, larvae, spawn and vegetation; *where found:* the whole of Europe, except southern Italy, Norway and Scotland, and even as far as China; spawning takes place from May to June.

Culinary applications. A delicate fish although full of bones and is prepared fried as a dish, or as a garnish.

Hucho *(Salmonoids)*

Latin: *Salmo huco*
French: *huch*
German: *Huchen, Donaulachs*
Italian: *huco*
Dutch: *Donauzalm*

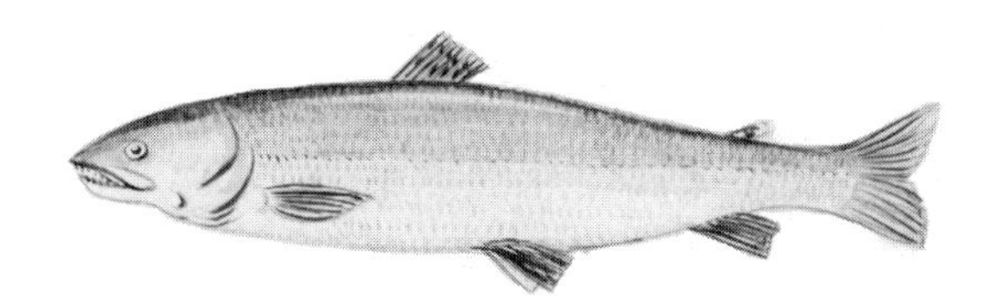

Description. *General appearance:* elongated, almost cylindrical body, a little flattened; long head with a large mouth; *colour:* back dark brown almost violet or greyish green, sides lighter with red shades, stomach silvery white; *size and weight:* average 60 cm. to 1·20 m., can attain 2 m. and 50 kg.

Characteristics. *Food:* plankton and fry, then all fish within its range it can attack; *where found:* only in the Danube basin and especially the tributaries of its right bank; the hucho is gradually disappearing; spawning takes place from March to May.

Culinary applications. White, rather firm, tasty flesh; all preparations for salmon are applicable.

Lamprey *(Petromyzonoids)*

RIVER LAMPREY
Latin: *Lampetra fluviatilis*
French: *lamproie de rivière*
German: *Fluzzneunauge*
Italian: *lampreda*
Spanish: *lamprea*
Dutch: *rivierprik*

Description. *General appearance:* cylindrical body, eel-like, with a round sucking mouth in the shape of a funnel, without maxillary bone or movable jaws; *colour:* slate-coloured back, greyish-brown, olive green or bluish green, the sides are lighter, the stomach is white with silvery tints; *size:* 30 to 50 cm.

Characteristics. Migratory fish ascending rivers; *food:* plankton, animalcules, then eggs of fish, small crustaceans and even small fish; *where found:* coastal waters of Europe as far as Siberia and Greenland where they go at the age of about 4 to 5; when fully grown they return to the sea and then ascend rivers to spawn and often to die; spawning takes place in April and May.

SEA LAMPREY
Latin: *Petromyzon marinus*
French: *lamproie marine*
German: *Meerneunauge* or *Lamprete*
Dutch: *zeeprik*

Description. *General appearance:* see *river lamprey*; *colour:* dark brown or dark olive green mottling on a light coloured back with a silvery white stomach; *size:* 50 cm. to 90 cm.

Characteristics. Also migratory; *food:* similar to that of the river lamprey; *where found:* Atlantic coasts of Europe, from the White Sea and Iceland down to Gibraltar, the coasts of North America, sometimes the Baltic and even the Gulf of Bothnia, the western Mediterranean and the Adriatic; spawning takes place from March to May.

Culinary applications. The sea lamprey is more appreciated than the river lamprey; the flesh is tasty but more difficult to digest. It is used in *pâtés, en matelote,* in fried or grilled *darnes*; it can also be prepared in the same way as eel.

Lavaret *(Salmonoids)*

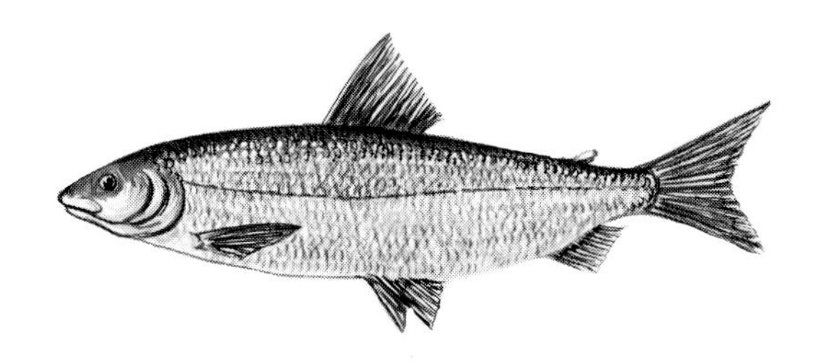

Latin: *Coregonus oxyrhynchus*
French: *lavaret*
German: *Schnäpel*
Italian: *pevarello corègono*
Spanish: *coregono*
Dutch: *houting*

Description. *General appearance:* like the whitefish except for the pointed snout and jutting mouth; *colour:* greyish blue or olive blue, with a blue snout; *size:* 25 to 40 cm. and up to 50 cm.

Characteristics. Coastal fish ascending rivers in autumn where it spawns on sandy and pebbly bottoms; *food:* plankton, animalcules of the bottom; *where found:* the south-east coasts of the North Sea and western coasts of the Baltic; spawning takes place in November and December.

Culinary applications. As *whitefish*, *salmon* and *trout.*

Burbot, Eel Pout *(Gadoids)*

Latin: *Lota lota*
French: *lotte de riviere*
German: *Aalquappe, Trüsche, Aalrutte*
Italian: *lasca*
Spanish: *lota*
Dutch: *kwabaal*

Description. *General appearance:* elongated cylindrical body with the hind part slightly flattened, thick and sticky skin, small scales; *colour:* the back between brown and olive yellow, the sides lighter, the stomach yellowish white; mottlings over the head and the top of the body; the young are darker; *size:* 30 to 60 cm., often 80 cm. and exceptionally 1 m.

Characteristics. The burbot lives in stagnant or very slow moving water; it likes fresh and clear water at up to 2000 m. altitude; *food:* the young eat the larvae of insects, worms, animalcules; the adult fish are voracious and carnivorous eating other fish, even in captivity; *where found:* Europe and northern and central Asia, the limit being the east of France; it lives also in river estuaries in the Baltic; spawning takes place from November to March.

Culinary applications. Tender and firm flesh, almost without bones, rather oily and tasty; the liver (white) is much esteemed: it must be roasted or fried, taking an appreciable time. The burbot must always be skinned before cooking. It can be poached with red wine, roasted in the oven after being larded; the flesh is used for *farces* and *quenelles*, and cut slantwise to breadcrumb for frying.

Sea Char *(Salmonoids)*

Latin: *Salvelinus alpinus*
French: *omble chevalier*
German: *Seesaibling, Rotforelle, Ritter*
Spanish: *ombla chevalier*
Dutch: *ridder*

Description. *General appearance:* slender when young, elongated and torpedo shaped and, like the trout, the sea char later becomes thicker; *colour:* bluish green or greyish green back becoming

a pink or yellowish colour on the sides with yellow markings, the stomach is a pale pink or yellow; *size and weight:* average 25 to 40 cm. with specimens up to 80 cm. and 10 kg.; the *common char* only attains 100 to 300 gr. and the *black char* 100 gr.
The brook-char (Latin: *Salvelinus fontinalis*; French: *omble de fontaine*; German: *Bachsaibling*) resembles the sea char; its mouth is larger and its sides lighter in colour; the fins are edged with black and white; imported from North America in 1884, this fish now lives in Europe as trout do; spawning takes place from October to March.

Characteristics. The char lives in cold water lakes, well oxygenated, at an altitude of 2000 m. or more; particular local forms exist; *food:* the young eat animalcules and plankton; the adults are carnivorous; *where found:* lakes in the Alps, Great Britain, Finland, Scandinavia, Russia, Iceland, etc., and the lakes of western North America; spawning takes place sometimes the whole year round but more often from September to January.

Culinary applications. The flesh is much esteemed; the larger fish are prepared as salmon, the smaller as trout. The black char, smoked, is of excellent taste.

Grayling *(Salmonoids)*

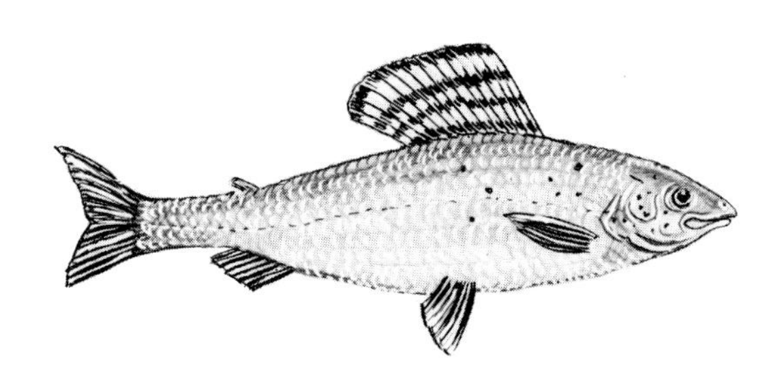

Latin: *Thymallus thymallus*
French: *ombre écailles*
German: *Aesche*
Italian: *témolo*
Spanish: *umbra*
Dutch: *vlagzalm*

Description. General appearance: elongated body with a small head and small mouth, very developed dorsal fin, average and solid scales; *colour:* the back and upper part of the head is greenish grey or bluish grey, the sides and stomach a silvery white, almost yellow, the first dorsal fin has dark markings forming a kind of chess-board pattern; *size and weight:* it does not exceed 25 to 50 cm. and 400 to 600 gr.

Characteristics. It lives in swiftly flowing and fresh waters; *food:* insects, larvae, slugs, worms, spawn of other fish; *where found:* almost through the whole of Europe in lakes; spawning takes place from March to May.

Culinary applications. Much esteemed for its delicacy, the grayling is as highly thought of as the trout in some regions. It is very difficult to keep alive once taken from the water. The small fish are prepared as trout, the larger as salmon trout.

Perch *(Percoids)*

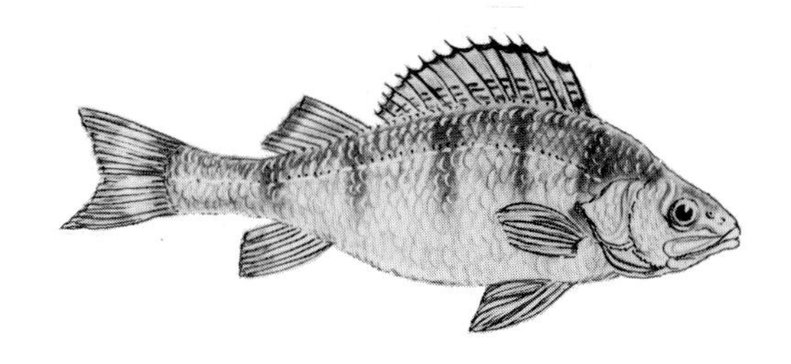

Latin: *Perca fluviatilis*
French: *perche*
German: *Barsch, Flussbarsch*
Italian: *pesce persico*
Spanish: *perca*
Dutch: *baars*

Description. *General appearance:* a regular shaped body covered with scales, the dorsal fin has prickly spines, the mouth is large with numerous teeth; *colour:* the back goes from dark grey to bluish green sometimes approaching brown or yellow, the stomach is almost white; *size and weight:* 15 to 50 cm.; it remains small in rivers but in lakes can attain 4 kg.

Characteristics. Lives in streams, rivers and lakes of different temperatures, up to an altitude of 1000 m., as well as in some salty waters; *food:* young eat animalcules, and adults become carnivorous, stealing spawn and eating fish; *where found:* Europe, North America and northern Asia; spawning takes place from May to June.

Culinary applications. Small perch are prepared as trout, large fish are better as fried fillets or cooked *meunière.*

Pike-Perch *(Percoids)*

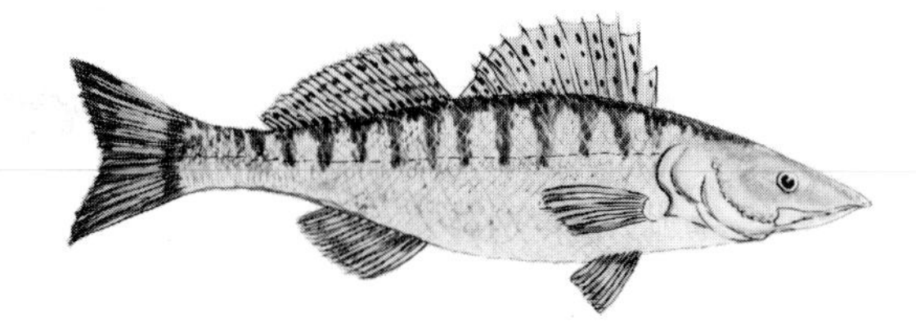

Latin: *Sander lucioperca*
French: *sandre*
German: *Zander, Schill, Fogasch*
Italian: *luccioperca*
Spanish: *luciperca*
Dutch: *snoekbaars*

Description. *General appearance:* body of a regular or normal shape covered with scales and like that of the pike, with a large mouth well provided with teeth, including canines; *colour:* greenish grey to bluish grey on the back and sides, with a dull greyish white stomach and the sides of the head mottled; *size:* average 40 to 50 cm. and up to 1 m.

Characteristics. A lake fish, living in fresh and even brackish flowing water; *food:* animalcules, then spawn, fry and other fish; *where found:* Central Europe, as far as Russia to the east and northern Italy to the south, as well as in the slightly salt waters of the Baltic; the pike-perch is reared in pools and ponds, and in this manner an excellent variety, known as *fogasch,* is found in Lake Balaton; spawning takes place from April to June.

Culinary applications. White and tasty flesh which does not keep long. Small fish are poached or fried whole, larger ones are cut into slices or fillets; pike-perch fillets are prepared in the same way as fillets of sole.

Salmon *(Salmonoids)*

Latin: *Salmo salar*
French: *saumon*
German: *Lachs, Salm*
Italian: *salmone*
Spanish: *salmon*
Dutch: *zalm*

Description. *General appearance:* a splendid fish with a well-shaped body and a wide tail, the snout is slender and elongated; *colour:* the adult has a greyish brown back, silvery sides and a brilliant white stomach; ascending towards the spawning areas the fish takes on brighter colouring; *size and weight:* average, for the European salmon, 60 cm., and 6 to 8 kg., but it can attain 1·50 m. and 50 kg.

Besides the European salmon, three kinds are imported:

royal salmon (Latin: *Oncorhynchus tschawytscha*) (Alaska and north Japan down to California), attaining a weight of 16 kg.,

red salmon (Latin: *Oncorhynchus nerka*) (north Japan down to the Bay of San Francisco), 1 m. and 6 kg.,

pink salmon or *rump-backed salmon* (Latin: *Oncorhynchus gorbusha*), the smallest of the Alaska salmon, 1·5 kg. to 2·5 kg., and, rarely, up to 5 kg.

Characteristics. A migratory fish spending its period of growth in rivers, departing to the sea and then returning to spawn and often to die exhausted; its extraordinary journeys, even against the strongest currents, sometimes take it over distances of more than 2000 miles; *food:* the salmon is carnivorous and a voracious feeder; the adult fish eats herrings, sprats and other fish; *where found:* a fish found over very wide areas, on European coasts of the north Atlantic as far as Greenland and on American coasts as far as Cape Cod; in the Gulf of Bothnia, the Bay of Finland, the White Sea and the North Sea. It is also found in Alaska, in British Columbia, in Canada and Asia as far as Japan. A migratory fish, it is even found in France, England and Scotland, and especially in Norway, where there is considerable fishing. The rivers of Siberia flowing into the Chukotsk Sea have salmon and so do some of those flowing into the Pacific. Spawning takes place mostly in December and January.

Culinary applications. The flesh of the salmon on its way to spawn is oily and clear red in colour; the higher it ascends a river the darker the flesh becomes and it loses its oily nature. It is one of the finest fish and the most delicate and tasty. The salmon of the Rhine, the Loire and the rivers of Scotland, Ireland and Norway become rare because of the obstacles to the ascent produced by industries and because of pollution: but they are the best fish. The salmon comes to market fresh, frozen, canned and, of course, in the form of that remarkable speciality, smoked salmon. Fresh salmon is chiefly prepared with a *court-bouillon*, accompanied with a fine sauce, but can be served grilled or poached. It is used in cold *hors d'œuvre* and fish cocktails. Cold salmon *en bellevue* is a great luxury calling for every technique and artistry.

Sheat-fish, *Silure (Siluroids)*

Latin: *Silurus glanis*
French: *silure*
German: *Wels, Waller*
Italian: *siluro*
Spanish: *siluro*
Dutch: *sterlet*

Description. *General appearance:* a cylindrical body near the head, diminishing and flattening towards the tail, a large mouth with two barbels on the upper jaw and four on the lower one; *colour:* bluish black, greenish olive or dark violet on the back, with greyish white sides sometimes having golden tints, the stomach is often reddish; *size and weight:* average of 1 to 2 m. and can attain 3 m. and 300 kg.

The *dwarf catfish* (Latin: *Ameiurus nebulosus*; French: *poisson-chat*; German: *Katzenwels, Zwergwels*) lives chiefly in the United States, to the east of the Rocky Mountains; a voracious fish which can also eat its own young.

Characteristics. The sheat-fish is an inhabitant of lakes and waters offering little movement and muddy bottoms; *food:* animalcules, then fish, frogs, and even birds and small mammals; *where found:* central Europe and eastern Europe up to 60 degrees latitude North and even in certain gulfs of the Baltic; it is also found in the Caspian and a few regions of western Asia; spawning takes place from May to June.

Culinary applications. Tasty and oily flesh but not very digestible. It can be larded in large pieces for braising with wine, sliced on the bias to breadcrumb and fry; it also has its place in a *matelote.* The flesh of the dwarf catfish is slightly orange coloured, sweetish and tasty. It is treated like burbot.

Sterlet *(Acipenseroids)*

Latin: *Acipenser ruthenus*
French: *sterlet*
German: *Sterlet*
Italian: *sterleto*
Spanish: *sterleto*
Dutch: *sterlet*

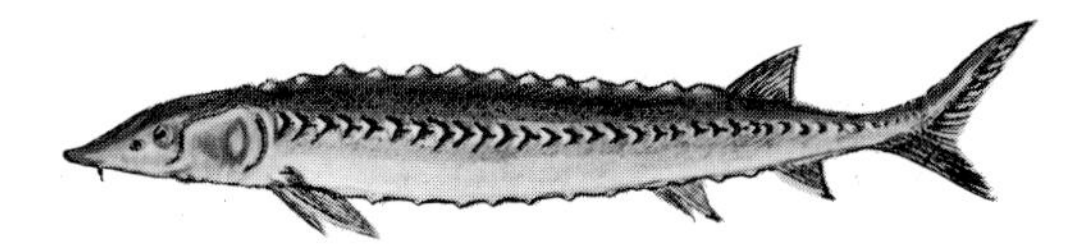

Description. *General appearance:* rather spindle-shaped, with a long and pointed head, the skin has no scales but is furnished with five rows of bony plates; *colour:* brownish grey or blackish on the back with a whitish stomach; *size and weight:* average 40 to 60 cm., and can attain 1 m., and 10 to 15 kg.

Characteristics. A river fish; *food:* snails, worms, insects, larvae and spawn; *where found:* the Black Sea and the Sea of Azov and their rivers. Northern Russia and Siberia, the Danube sometimes as far as Ulm; spawning takes place in May and June. The main fishing is in Russia, and rearing along the Volga and in Hungary. It is rare in western European markets.

Culinary applications. Flesh of excellent quality, tender and tasty; the small fish are poached, slices of the large fish are larded and braised. It is smoked and it is salted. The caviar of the sterlet is a great delicacy.

Tench *(Cyprinoids)*

Latin: *Tinca tinca*
French: *tanche*
German: *Schleie*
Italian: *tinca*
Spanish: *tenca*
Dutch: *zeelt*

Description. *General appearance:* squat body and a mouth with a small opening; scales under a skin which is superficial, thick and viscous; *colour:* from green with golden tints to darkish brown on the back and sides, the stomach is lighter and the fins are dark; *size and weight:* average 20 to 30 cm., up to 50 cm., and even 70 cm. in eastern Europe, and up to 2 kg.

Characteristics. A fish living at the bottom of still or very slightly moving waters, hibernating in deep mud; *food:* plants and small aquatic animals; *where found:* the whole of Europe except central and northern Scandinavia, Iceland and the Baltic region; spawning takes place from May to July.

Culinary applications. The flesh is tender, tasty and oily but not very digestible; fish of 350 gr. to 500 gr. are best. The tench is sometimes reared. Used in *matelote, au bleu, meunière, à la Bercy,* fried or gratinated.

Trout *(Brook or River Trout) (Salmonoids)*

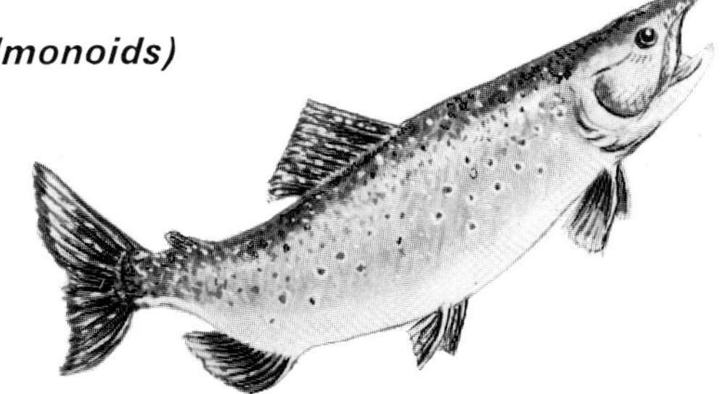

Latin: *Salmo trutta forma fario*
French: *truite*
German: *Flussforelle*
Italian: *trota*
Spanish: *trucha*
Dutch: *beekforel*

Description. *General appearance:* the brook or river trout has the appearance of a flattened torpedo; *colour:* variable even among fish of the same habitat; generally brownish green back with lighter sides and very light stomach; the head and sides have golden tints, the sides are spotted with red and black; the so-called white trout has a very light coloured back and the so-called black trout has a very dark back; *size:* average 25 to 40 cm.

Characteristics. The trout likes flowing water or the cold oxygenated waters of lakes (20 degrees Centigrade), and ascends rivers; *food:* tadpoles, fish and even aquatic plants; *where found:* the whole of Europe as far as the Urals, Ireland, Iceland and even Asia Minor; introduced into parts of North America, Africa, India and New Zealand; spawning takes place from October to January.

Culinary applications. The trout is a very well thought of fish and the demand for it is such that there is a great increase in the number of hatcheries and in the artificial rearing of the fish, although such trout are not so good as those from natural conditions. The sale and the purchase of the natural 'wild' trout is sometimes forbidden, as in France, where this was done to stop commercial poaching and other large-scale fishing. Trout is prepared *au bleu* or *meunière*, but it is also poached in white wine, etc.

Rainbow Trout

Latin: *Salmo iridens*
French: *truite arc-en-ciel*
German: *Regenbogenforelle*
Dutch: *regenboogforel*

The mouth is more elongated and it has bright colouring on the sides; variable with metallic tints. The rainbow trout comes from North America and was introduced into Europe in 1880. It is essentially a fish for artificial rearing and is of very rapid growth. It is prepared like river trout.

Lake Trout

Latin: *Salmo trutta forma lacustris*
French: *truite lacustre*
German: *Seeforelle*
Dutch: *meerforel, schotje*

The sides are speckled with colours which can be very different: orange, red, brown, with contrasting rings; this fish can attain 1·40 m. and 40 kg., but its average size is 40 to 80 cm.; it lives in the deep lakes of the Alps, in Germany and in the lakes of Scotland and Scandinavia.

Salmon Trout, Sea-Trout

Latin: *Salmo trutta*
French: *truite saumonee*
German: *Meerforelle*
Italian: *trota salmonata*
Spanish: *trucha salmonada*
Dutch: *zeeforel*

This fish is often confused with the salmon but its body is more thick-set, the mouth is rounder and smaller and the eyes are situated more forward; the back is silvery white and the sides are black. It lives in the North Sea, the Baltic and the north Atlantic; it ascends rivers to spawn in November and December; it attains 80 cm. and from 1 to 5 kg. It is a fish with very tasty flesh which is particularly good for the preparation of cold dishes.

SHELL-FISH (CRUSTACES)

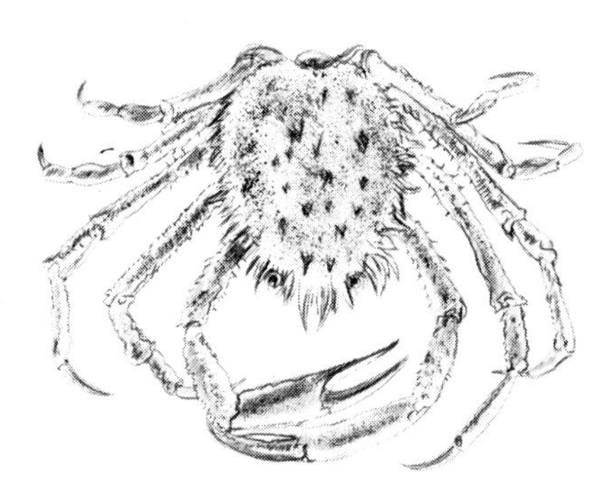

Spider Crab *(Decapoda brachyura)*

Latin: *Maia squinado*
French: *araignée de mer*
German: *Seespinne, Spinnekrebs*
Italian: *granchio*
Spanish: *centolla*
Dutch: *spinkrab*

Description and characteristics. A rounded body, almost heart-shaped; two points, separated from each other, between the eyes; numerous protuberances; sharp elongated claws; long legs arranged like those of the spider from which it gets its name; upper part of the body reddish yellow, lower part whitish yellow; maximum length 20 cm. Lazy and heavy, it lives on the sea bottom, covered with sand or debris. Found in the Adriatic, the Mediterranean, and sometimes, though more rarely, on Atlantic coasts.

Culinary applications. The same preparation as for crab.

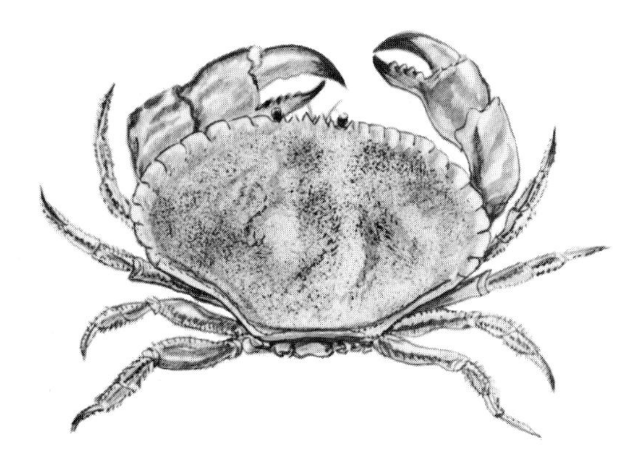

Crab *(Decapoda brachyura)*

Latin: *Cancer pagurus*
French: *crabe*
German: *Taschenkrebs*
Italian: *granceola*
Spanish: *cangrechio de marcambaro*
Dutch: *krab*

Description and characteristics. Numerous species: blue crab, etc.; ten legs, of which the two front ones are claws; very strong shell; pedunculated eyes; the common crab has a reddish brown back and is lighter, rather yellowish, underneath; at 5 years old it is adult and its shell attains 20 cm.; it can attain 30 to 40 cm. and weighs 6 kg.; it lives in the coastal waters of the Atlantic from the Bay of Biscay to Norway, in the Adriatic and the Mediterranean, in the Pacific and on the American coasts as far as the Bahamas and Cuba; it prefers rocky crevices in which it can lodge and lie flat so that it can easily defend itself against enemies with its powerful claws and catch its prey; small crustaceans, molluscs and mussels, etc.

Culinary applications. It contains little flesh in comparison with its size; the liver and creamy substance of its body are very tasty; the essential part of the flesh is in the claws. Crabs cooked in salt water (like all crustaceans) can be prepared hot or cold; hot—in soups, croquettes, gratinated *en coquille*, or in their shell; cold—in cocktails, salds, on *canapés*, etc.

KING CRAB (Decapoda brachyura)
Latin: *Cancer magister*
French: *crabe géant*
German: *Königskrebs*
Italian: *paguro*
Spanish: *pagurido*
Dutch: *reuzenkrab*

Description and characteristics. It belongs to the group of spider crabs; the upper part of its body is brownish and the lower part lighter; average size 50 cm. in diameter; its legs can attain 2 m. in length. All the crabs in this group live in deep waters; the cold waters of the North Pacific, the Behring Sea, near Kamtchatka, Canada, Newfoundland and the southern point of the Argentine.

Culinary applications. Rarely sold alive, it is usually available under the name of crabmeat, frozen or tinned. It is particularly used for cocktails, salads, with mayonnaise, or for *croquettes* or *bouchées*.

Shrimp *(Decapoda caroids)*

Latin: *Crangon vulgaris*
French: *crevette grise*
German: *Sandgarnele*
Italian: *gamberetto grigio*
Spanish: *camarone*
Dutch: *garnaal*

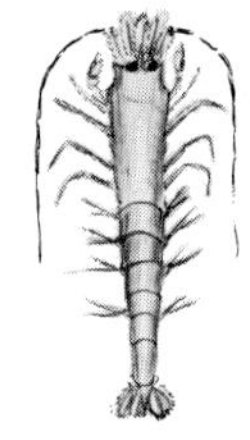

Description and characteristics. An almost smooth body, pale greyish brown which becomes a brownish red during cooking; length 6 to 7 cm., the female is 9 cm. in length; fished in enormous quantities in the North Sea and near all European coasts.

PRAWN
Latin: *Palaemon squilla*
French: *crevette rose* (*bouquet*)
German: *Steingarnele*
Dutch: *steurkrab*

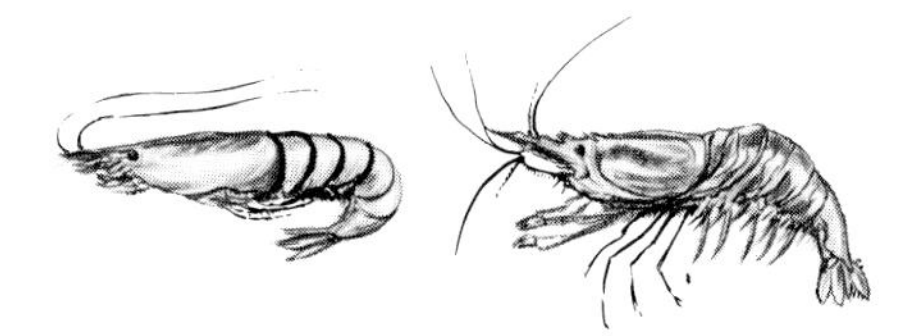

Description and characteristics. A very curving body, the head is provided with a toothed point which is hard and long; the eyes are large; the colour is a light bronze with brown bands, becoming a pinkish red during cooking while the flesh remains white; it attains 8 to 10 cm. in length. Found in the Mediterranean and near the French coasts of the Atlantic.

BALTIC SHRIMP
Latin: *Leander adspersus*
French: *crevette baltique*
German: *Ostseegarnele*
Dutch: *Oostzeegarnaal*

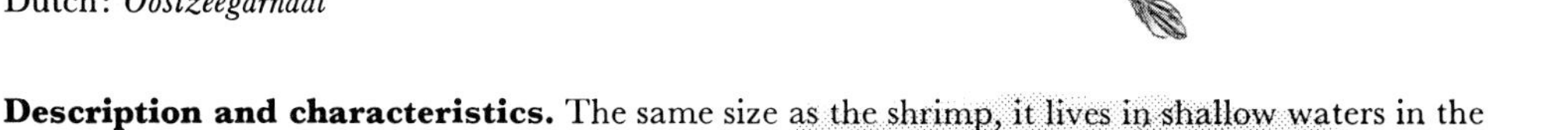

Description and characteristics. The same size as the shrimp, it lives in shallow waters in the west Baltic.

SAW-SHRIMP
Latin: *Palaemon serratus*
French: *crevette scie*
German: *Sägegarnele*
Dutch: *garnaal*

Description and characteristics. Similar in appearance to the prawn, attaining 7 cm. in length. It is found near the French Atlantic and North Sea coasts, and in the Mediterranean.

Culinary applications. Very delicate, they are usually cooked on board fishing boats and must be eaten promptly. Used for soups, sauces, cold *hors d'œuvre*, hot *entrées* and as a garnish.

Crayfish *(Decapoda astacoids)*

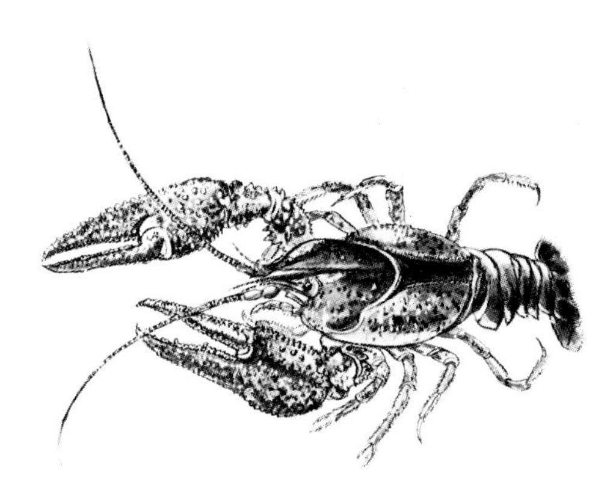

French: *écrevisse*
German: *Krebs*
Italian: *gambero*
Spanish: *cangrejo*
Dutch: *kreeft* (*rivierkreeft*)

RIVER CRAYFISH
Latin: *Astacus fluviatilis*

Characteristics. Found throughout Europe with the exception of the British Isles, central and northern Scandinavia, Greece, Italy and Spain.

BROOK CRAYFISH
Latin: *Astacus torrentium*

Characteristics. Found especially in mountainous countries; south Germany, Switzerland, Austria, certain regions of Czechoslovakia and of Hungary and Yugoslavia.

COMMON CRAYFISH
Latin: *Astacus pallipes*

Characteristics. Found in France, Great Britain and a few islands of the Mediterranean.

MARSH CRAYFISH
Latin: *Astacus leptodactylus*

Characteristics. Found in European Russia, Poland, Hungary, and as far as the Istrian peninsula. The claws are particularly long and thin; flesh of poor quality.
There are other species of little importance.
Of all the crayfish the best is *Astacus fluviatilis*; the name is not particularly correct because the crayfish lives not only in rivers but also in inland lakes, streams and ponds, if the water is clean, oxygenated and offers enough hiding places. It is omnivorous and eats small fish, snails, aquatic insects and the larvae of insects, as well as calcareous plants. It is erroneously believed that it lives on putrefying meat. It casts its shell several times a year to assure its growth: eight times in the first year, five in the second, and once from the fourth year onwards, that being the year when it attains sexual maturity. Its colour varies according to the water in which it lives. It prefers living in a wet state rather than in the water, and its hiding places are in the banks. *Size:* 15 mm. in the first year, 10 cm. at sexual maturity, and then 15 cm. and from 100 to 120 gr. at 12 years old.

Culinary applications. The taste of the crayfish depends on the water in which it lives and also on its food: the best are those from fresh flowing water. It is claimed that the meat of the crayfish eaten in the months 'without an "r"' is the best, but it is particularly good sometimes in September and October. The essential condition is to eat them very fresh, in which case the tail curls up while cooking; a tail which remains stretched out is an indication that the crayfish is not fresh. They are used for soups, *hors d'œuvre*, *entrées* and as a garnish.

Lobster *(Decapoda asticoids)*

Latin: *Homarus vulgaris*
French: *homard*
German: *Hummer*
Italian: *astaco*
Spanish: *bogavante*
Dutch: *zeekreeft*

Description and characteristics. Elongated body with a well-developed tail, part having a wide caudal fan; the first pair of antennae are long, the second are not developed. Of the claws, one, either the right or the left, is really a prehensile leg, the other is thicker and tougher; the former seizes its prey and the other one breaks it. The shell is very hard and rigid and is cast regularly; average length is 25 to 45 cm., and can attain 60 cm. and several kilos; *colour:* bluish black with brown or purple tints. It lives on the rocky sea-bottom near coasts. Found along all the coasts of Europe, especially the French, Danish, Swedish, Norwegian, Belgian, German and eastern coasts of Scotland. It lives on mussels, snails and various sea animals.

Culinary applications. The most esteemed meat is that of lobsters weighing 400 to 800 g. The average length of lobsters permitted for sale in Europe is fixed at 20 cm. It is cooked with a *court-bouillon,* and cooled. It is prepared simply for salads or in cocktails with mayonnaise; for hot dishes it is grilled *américaine, Thermidor,* and in many other ways.

Crawfish, Spiny Lobster *(Decapoda loricata)*

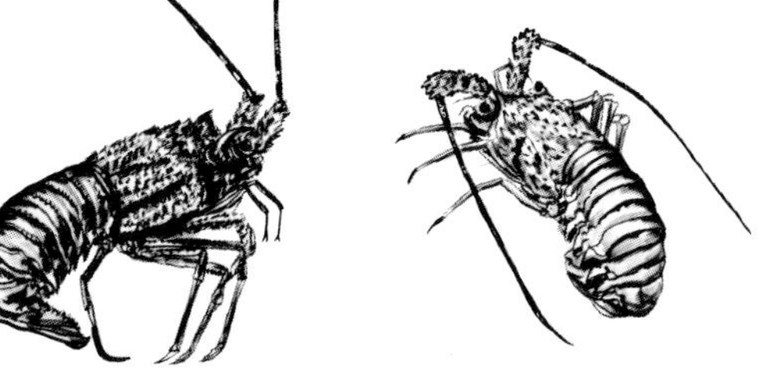

Latin: *Palinarus vulgaris*
French: *langouste*
German: *Languste, Panzerkrebs*
Italian: *aragosta*
Spanish: *langosta*
Dutch: *pantserkreeft, doornkreeft, langoest*

Description and characteristics. It is distinguished from the lobster by the absence of claws and by a tail which is longer and wider in proportion to its body; very long antennae; length with tail stretched out—20 to 50 cm., weight varies from less than 1 to 7 kg.; the colouring is brownish purple with small yellowish spots for the European crawfish; the North African crawfish (*Palinarus mauritanicus* or *langouste royale*) goes from pale green to olive green with a more squat body, while the crawfish taken on the east and west coasts of Africa has tints going from pale green to dark green or from blackish green to purple. The crawfish lives in winding passages or hidden amongst the seaweed on rocky bottoms near coasts, and it prefers mussels for food. It is found very widely, passing through the Adriatic and the Mediterranean as far as the western and southern coasts of England and Ireland; the English Channel is its north-eastern limit; it is also fished in the Gulf of Aden, on the coast of Chile, in Australia, the Far East and at the Cape of Good Hope.

Culinary applications. Crawfish must be alive until preparation; commercially considerable quantities of crawfish tails are obtainable frozen. The rock lobster tails of South Africa are excellent both for hot dishes and for a garnish. For important dishes needing a fine presentation, only fresh crawfish, alive until prepared, may be used.

Dublin Bay Prawn, Norway Lobster

(Decapoda astacoids)

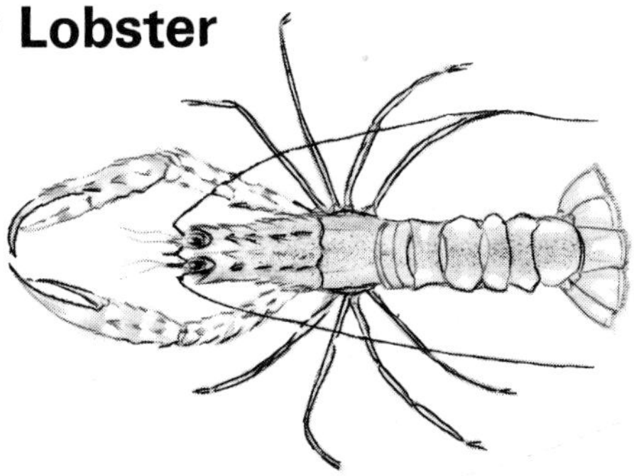

Latin: *Nephrops norvegicus*
French: *langoustine* (*homard de Norvège*)
German: *Kaisergranat, schlanker Hummer*
Italian: *scampo*
Spanish: *langosta*
Dutch: *Noorse kreeft, langoestine*

Description and characteristics. A near relative of the lobster, with a long tail, large protuberant eyes and elongated claws with sharp teeth; its colour goes from brick red to salmon red, with, sometimes, brownish markings. The colour does not change with cooking. Smaller than the lobster, it can however attain 30 cm. It feeds on small molluscs which it crushes with its toothed claws. It is mainly found near the Atlantic coasts of France, Spain, Portugal, the North Adriatic and also to the west of the British Isles. In the Irish Sea and near the eastern coast of Scotland it is known as the *Dublin Bay prawn*, near the French coasts it is the *langoustine*, and in the Adriatic it is the *scampo*.

Culinary applications. Very delicate and tasty meat (the claws contain very little); it is fresh or frozen on the market; it is prepared in numerous ways—in cold *entrées* or cocktails, with egg and breadcrumbs, grilled on skewers and in crowns of rice with an appropriate sauce.

SHELL-FISH (COQUILLAGES)

French Mussel

Latin: *Venerupis decussatus*
French: *clovisse*
German: *Teppichmuschel*
Italian: *vongola*
Spanish: *almeja*
Dutch: *Middellandse-Zee-tapijtschelp*

Description. Fawn colouring, fluted, with three lines of dark brown markings. Length 3 to 6 cm.

Culinary applications. All these shellfish are eaten raw; a few can be prepared in the same way as scollops and others as mussels.

Cockle *(Lamellibranch molluscs)*

Latin: *Cardium edule*
French: *coque*
German: *gewöhnliche Herzmuschel*
Italian: *cuore*
Spanish: *berberecho*
Dutch: *kokkel*

The best known has a length of 4·5 cm.

Latin: *Cardium echinatum*
French: *bucarde*
German: *dornige Herzmuschel*
Italian: *tellina*

Length 4 to 5 cm.; the shell has 25 to 30 ridges, rough or prickly.

Latin: *Cardium aculeatum*
German: *grosse Herzmuschel*

Diameter 3·5 to 8 cm.; the prickles or rough part are in the shape of hooks.

Description and characteristics. A white shell striped with brown; found in the Mediterranean, on the French and English coasts of the Atlantic, especially in low water, estuaries, and lagoons; lives on plankton, water being constantly brought into the shell by vibrating lashes.

Scollop *(Lamellibranch or pelecoid molluscs)*

Latin: *Pecten maximus, Pecten jacobaeus*
French: *coquille Saint-Jacques*
German: *Pilgermuschel, Jakobsmuschel*
Italian: *conchiglia di San Iacopo*
Spanish: *conchas peregrinas*
Dutch: *sint-jakobsschelp*

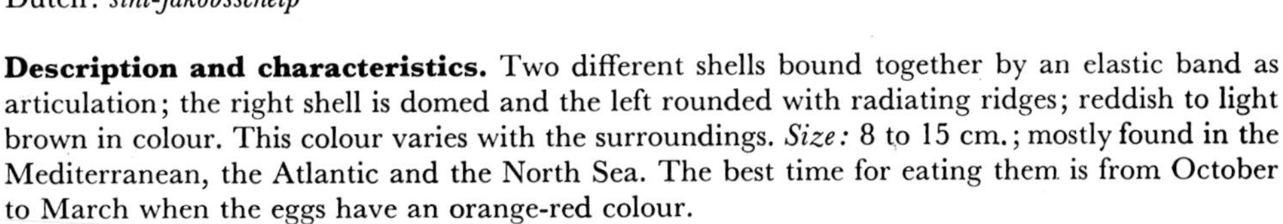

Description and characteristics. Two different shells bound together by an elastic band as articulation; the right shell is domed and the left rounded with radiating ridges; reddish to light brown in colour. This colour varies with the surroundings. *Size:* 8 to 15 cm.; mostly found in the Mediterranean, the Atlantic and the North Sea. The best time for eating them is from October to March when the eggs have an orange-red colour.

Culinary applications. Bearded and with the dark parts removed it is prepared stewed in white wine and served with white wine sauce and mushrooms; it can be gratinated on the shell, grilled and used as a garnish for other dishes.

Oyster *(Lamellibranch molluscs)*

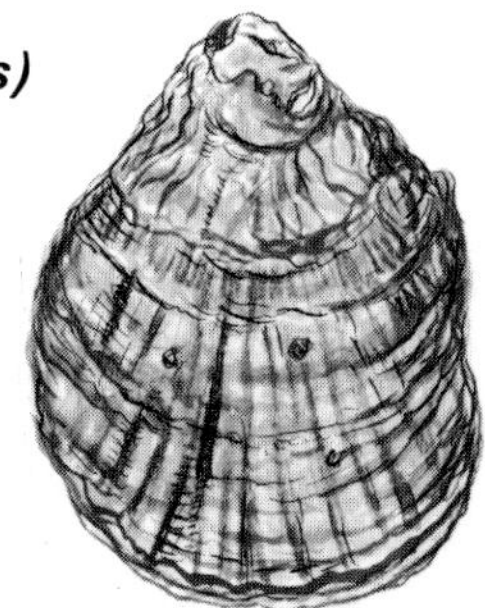

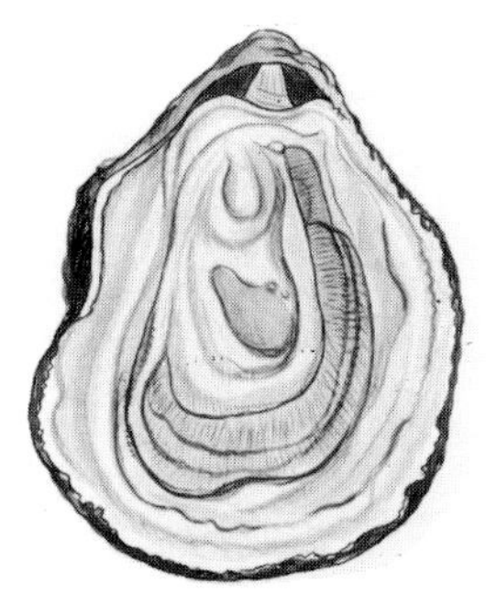

Latin: *Ostrea edulis*
French: *huître*
German: *Auster*
Italian: *ostrica*
Spanish: *ostra*
Dutch: *oester*

Description and characteristics. The upper shell is flattened and the lower one, with which the oyster clings to the rock, is domed; they live in colonies on rocks or fixed hard objects at a depth varying from 10 to 40 m.; they feed on plankton which is taken in with the water filtered by the branchiae and then rejected. The oyster is hermaphrodite but its power of reproduction is very great (one oyster alone can produce a million eggs), although most oysters die, a prey to other marine species. The greatest number of oysters come from artificial culture beds. They need water containing from 2 to 3% of salt, and their development takes from 3 to 6 years.

Amongst the best known kinds are:

Whitstable, Colchester (Great Britain)
Galway Bay (Ireland)
Marennes, Belons, Portugaises (France)
Imperial (Holland)
Ostend (Belgium)
large Limfjords (Denmark)

Culinary applications. A food rich in phosphorus, calcium and vitamin A; the siliceous seaweed on which it feeds determines its development, the growth of the liver, and the colour, which is greenish for the Marennes and Portugaises (*Gryphaea angulata*), reddish for the Belons. Oysters are usually served raw; they can also be poached, fried, gratinated or used as a garnish.

Mussel *(Lamellibranch molluscs)*

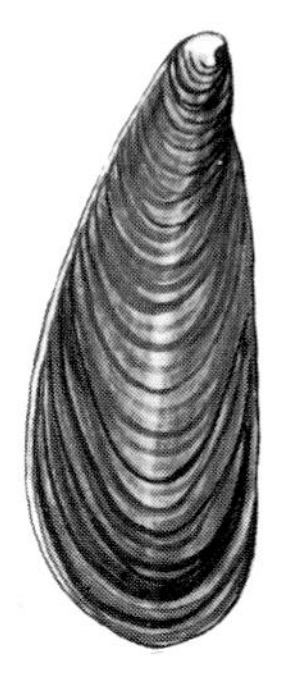

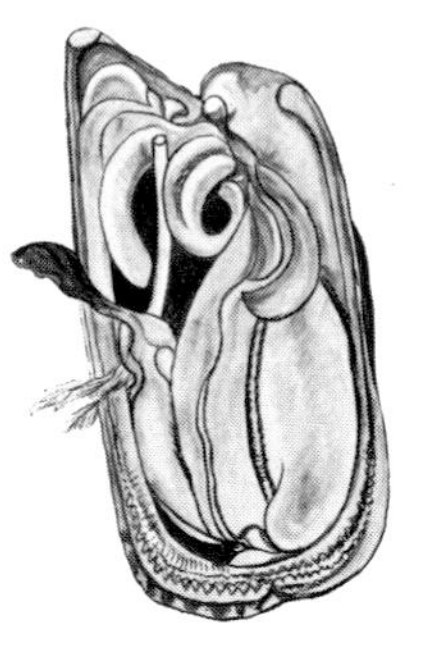

Latin: *Mytilus edulis*
French: *moule*
German: *Miesmuschel, Pfahlmuschel*
Italian: *mitilo*
Spanish: *concha*
Dutch: *mossel*

Description and characteristics. Two identical shells, elongated and oblique in shape, held together by an elastic band which closes them very tightly; the colour is bluish black, purple blue, sometimes lighter with violet or purple markings. They live clinging to sandbanks, rocks, posts, or suspended in clusters by fine threads produced by the secretion of a gland. The mussel can attain 6 to 8 cm. in length. The majority arriving for sale are artificially produced: found on the western coasts of France, Belgium, Holland and Schleswig-Holstein; they are gathered from October to May and their development takes from 3½ years.

Culinary Applications. Only tightly shut mussels are still alive and fit to eat. They are prepared *marinière*, in a white sauce, grilled on skewers, *Villeroi*, in stews, salads, and as a garnish, and in many other ways.

Venus' Shell

Latin: *Macrocallista chione*
French: *palourde*
German: *braune Herzmuschel*
Italian: *isolone*
Spanish: *concha*
Dutch: *tapijtschelp*

Description. An oblong and smooth shell; fawn colouring with striped bands; found on the Atlantic coasts.

Fan-shell

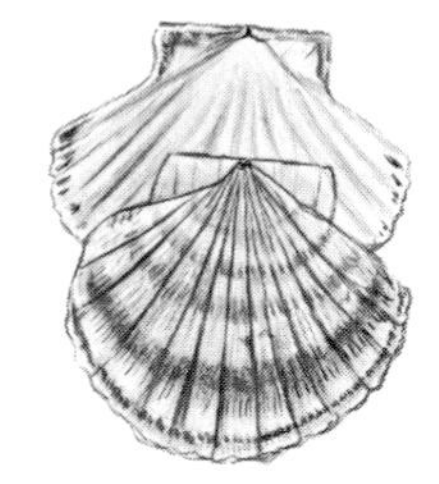

Latin: *Clamys varia*
French: *pétoncle*
German: *Kammuschel*
Italian: *canestrello*
Dutch: *bonte mantel*

Description. Very similar to the scollop, but its two shells are domed and the radiating ridges are more numerous with very many colour tones from white to red; *size:* from 6 to 8 cm.

Culinary applications. The same preparation as for scollops.

Clam

Latin: *Venus verrucosa*
French: *praire*
German: *warzige Venusmuschel*
Italian: *caparozolo*
Spanish: *escupina gravada*
Dutch: *ruwe venusschelp*

Description. A shell covered with irregular small plates in a concentric pattern with verrucous pimples; the colouring is rust to reddish yellow; *length:* 3 to 5 cm.

MOLLUSCS

Squid *(Cephalopod molluscs)*

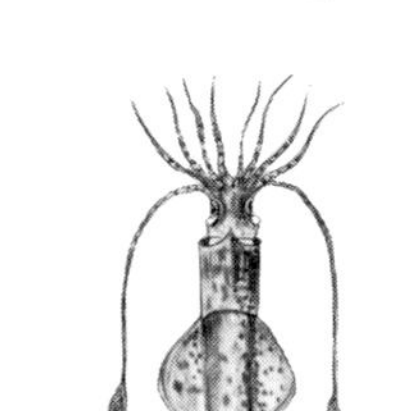

Latin: *Loligo vulgaris*
French: *calmar*
German: *Kalmar*
Italian: *calamaro*
Spanish: *calamar*
Dutch: *pijlinktvis*

Description and characteristics. Like all cephalopods, the head is distinctly separated from the body, large eyes, a mouth provided with a tongue and two jaws, surrounded with several very mobile arms provided with suckers which serve to crawl, to feel and seize a prey; propulsion is assured by the forceful ejection to the rear of water taken in through a crack in front. Most cephalopods possess a gland which enables them, if attacked, to squirt a brownish black liquid (sepia). The squid has ten arms and a body like a bag having a pair of wide and triangular fins adjacent to the pointed rear end; a violet colour, average size 30 to 40 cm. It lives on the western coasts of the Atlantic and especially, in large numbers, in the Mediterranean.

Culinary applications. Squid of the length of a hand have a particularly tasty white flesh. All cephalopods are prepared with a *farce* made from their arms, with eggs and mixed herbs, then grilled or braised with wine. They can also be marinated and prepared for cold *hors d'œuvre.*

Octopus *(Cephalopod molluscs)*

Latin: *Octopus vulgaris*
French: *poulpe*

German: *gemeine Krake, Meerpolyp*
Italian: *polpo*
Spanish: *polipo*
Dutch: *achtarmige poliep, kraak*

Description and characteristics. Like all cephalopods (see *squid*), but only eight arms; colouring is reddish brown; found especially in the Mediterranean in the nooks and crannies of rocks where it waits for its prey; it feeds particularly on crustaceans which it catches with the help of its arms provided with suckers and which it kills with the poison from its salivary glands.

Culinary applications. The flesh is tasty if the octopus is young, weighing from 500 gr. to 1 kg. maximum. It is prepared like other cephalopods (see *squid*).

Cuttlefish *(Cephalopod molluscs)*

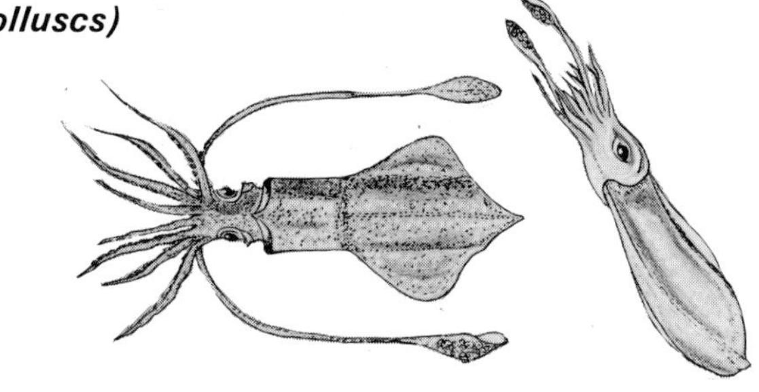

Latin: *Sepia officinalis*
French: *seiche*
German: *Tintenfish*
Italian: *mitilo*
Spanish: *sepia*
Dutch: *zeekat*

Description and characteristics. Like the other cephalopods (see *polyp, squid*) but with an oval, flattened body, the back is streaked with blackish brown giving a zebra-like appearance, the stomach is silvery, the body is contained in a muscular sac which expands along the whole margin into a narrow fin; and it has a bone under the skin of the back. It has ten arms, eight shorter than those of the octopus and often folded back; the other two arms are longer and serve to seize its prey; it lives mostly in the Mediterranean, on dark and rocky bottoms; it feeds on crustaceans and fish. Average weight: 500 gr. to 1 kg.

Culinary applications. Like other cephalopods (see *squid*) but a necessary precaution is to open the upper part most carefully to withdraw the sac containing the colouring liquid.

The Choice and Preparation of Fish

Fish as Food

The flesh of the fish is very different from that of animals, the meat of which is coloured by the greater contribution of blood. Blood vessels are much less numerous in fish, thus the whiteness of flesh. When it is coloured or tinted it is due to the particular feeding habits of the fish.
The flesh of the fish is seldom tough as is often the case with animal flesh containing muscle and sinew. The connective tissues of the fish are protected by delicate membranes which surround the flesh.
The presence of fatty matter in fish is less than in animals. Fat which is present in fish does not present itself as a subcutaneous layer, except in the eel, but is distributed in the muscular tissue.
A distinction is made, of course, between oily fish and lean fish but in fact there is not much difference. There is more oil in mackerel, salmon, grey gurnard and herring. More frequently, however, the culinary preparations of fish require fatty foodstuffs to be added such as butter, oil, etc. Let us note at the same time that fish oils and albumin have the same nutritive value as those of butcher's meat.
Connective tissue and sinews do not exist in fish; cooking-time is therefore very appreciably reduced in comparison with that of butcher's meat.
Essences and aromatic juices of fish are much less dense than those of meat; thus a fish 'juice' would be poor. Meat stocks, juices, glazes and essences are composed of numerous elements of strong flavour scarcely to be found in fish fumets. The number of combinations with a fish base is also limited.
The nutritive value of 500 gr. of fish is generally reckoned to be equivalent to that of 300 gr. of meat. Moreover fish, being very easily digested, rarely gives those eating it any feeling of having eaten too much.
On the other hand fish contains a great quantity of vitamins, notably A and D, very useful for growth. This is not so with butcher's meat. The presence of iodine, particularly helpful for the human organism, should also not be forgotten.
The spawning season varies according to the species. It extends from January to June. Fish is of distinctly better quality out of the spawning season.
The predominant smell of fish can be diminished by adding a little vinegar or white wine to the poaching stock or the court-bouillons.
The water content of fish varies from 60 to 80%. It is considerably reduced by drying or smoking.

Lean fish are more easily digested than oily fish: poached, they are especially recommendable for sick people, and often prescribed.

Purchase and Preparation

The price of fish varies appreciably according to season, inclement weather and arrival. The law of supply and demand considerably affects the market. Of course the quality of the fish can produce serious fluctuation.
All the same, throughout the whole year, fish can be found at modest prices, such as herring, flounder, dab, plaice, etc., as well as freshwater fish.
For every recipe only fish of perfect freshness is to be used—for the firmness of its flesh and its good taste. It is necessary to avoid the muddy taste of some fish from stagnant water. We have already alluded to the spawning season during which the fish is less agreeable in texture.
Unlike butcher's meat, fish has no need to be tenderised by hanging. The sooner it is prepared after being taken from the sea the better it is.
Before preparing fish of large size such as turbot, halibut or brill, they should be allowed to drain of blood completely. To do this the fish is cut near the tail.
The skin of the fish protects the flesh. For this reason it must not be damaged.
Refrigerated or deep-frozen fish has to be brought slowly and naturally to a normal temperature to avoid loss of natural juices.
Dried or salted fish must be white fleshed. Dried fish must not soak too long as this would give it a disagreeable odour.
Fish cooked by steam or smoked fish can develop mould on the skin. This is removed by rubbing with oil.

Trimmings

It is worth noting that whole fresh fish leave a large proportion of trimmings:

turbot and brill	up to about: 55%
carp, fresh cod, sole, flounder	,, ,, ,, 50%
bass	,, ,, ,, 47%
trout, sea char, lavaret, perch	,, ,, ,, 45%
whiting	,, ,, ,, 45%
small fish for frying (smelt, gudgeon)	,, ,, ,, 40%
sardine	,, ,, ,, 25%

Advice of a General Kind

A fish which is very fresh can be recognised by the smell which must be agreeable. The eye should be clear and the skin shining. Its flesh is both firm and elastic, and skin under the gills a true red. A very fresh fish is difficult to skin, the skin adheres to the flesh.
As soon as the fish arrives in the kitchen, remove the gills and gut it. Certain fish must be skinned and others scaled, this being done with a special scaling knife.
The fish once gutted is washed in plenty of fresh water and then wiped. After this it is kept in a closed receptacle in the lower part of the refrigerator or ice box. It used to be kept on ice.

The preparation of fish always requires much care and attention. A great number of elements come into play. The products used whether for the main dish or for the garnishes and sauces, play a determining role, not only for taste but also for consistency and even their colour. Recipes are very varied and the sauces are of capital importance. Almost always they contain the specific taste of the fish used. The bones and trimmings are therefore of much importance: they serve for the preparation of stocks, fumets, sauces etc.

One method much used is the court-bouillon, a poaching or cooking liquor.

But there are others:

cooking in a court-bouillon with vegetables;
braising;
poaching;
frying;
grilling;
shallow frying or meunière;
cooking au bleu.

For deep frying or for shallow frying, the oil or butter must be very hot. To egg and breadcrumb a fish, a little oil or butter must always be added. Shallots are usually better than onion for the preparation of fish recipes.

Quantities to serve per person are about 500 gr. of unboned fish or 200 gr. of trimmed fillets for a main dish. For an entrée or hors d'oeuvre, 100 gr. is sufficient. It must also be noted that the quantities to serve will vary according to the country and its own custom: differences can be considerable.

Hot fish must always be served on a hot serving dish. Fish cooked au bleu will be sprinkled with a little hot fish stock so that the skin does not stick to the dish. If, by chance, fish knives and forks are not available, two forks should be placed on the table.

The Cooking of Fish: Principles and Bases

Basic Preparations

COURT-BOUILLONS

In most cases the court-bouillons must be prepared in advance to develop flavour and aroma, particularly if the fish must be cooked in less than half an hour.
When the fish requires more than half an hour to be cooked, they are put in a cold court-bouillon and this is slowly brought to the boil. For cold preparations, fish and shellfish prepared in court-bouillon must cool completely in the liquid; this must be allowed for in the cooking-time.
When using a court-bouillon prepared with white wine or red wine, the fish should be immersed only up to two-thirds in the cold liquid. During the cooking they must be basted regularly with their court-bouillon.
If fish or shellfish are served with their court-bouillon, the vegetable garnishes will be cut up into a julienne or into fine fluted small thin slices. This julienne of vegetables is then served at the same time as the dish.
(See Culinary Technique, page 86.)

Some Examples of Court-Bouillons

(for 3 litres)

Court-bouillon A

For salmon, salmon and trout darnes

2½ litres of water; 1 dl. vinegar; 20 gr. salt; 300 gr. minced carrots; 200 gr. chopped onion; 50 gr. parsley stalks; 1 bayleaf; a few crushed peppercorns.

Allow the court-bouillon to cook for about 1 hour, then pass through the conical strainer or muslin.

Court-bouillon B

For eel, pike, etc.

2½ litres of water; 1½ litres of dry white wine; a little thyme; 1 bayleaf; a few crushed peppercorns; 30 parsley stalks; 30 gr. salt; 300 gr. sliced onion.

Cook for 30 minutes and pass through a muslin or the conical strainer.

Court-bouillon C

For fish stew with red or white wine
For matelote of carp, trout, salmon

Proceed as for the court-bouillon B. Replace the white wine with red and add 300 gr. of sliced carrots.

Court-bouillon D

For large pieces of turbot, brill and halibut

Put the fish in enough cold water for it to be covered. Add 15 gr. of salt, 1 dl. of milk per litre of water and 1 peeled and pipped lemon.

Court-bouillon E

For shrimps, crab, crawfish, lobster, crayfish, Dublin Bay prawns, etc.

Proceed as for court-bouillon A, with 15 gr. of salt per litre of court-bouillon.

Court-bouillon F

For haddock, cod and perch

Prepared with water and simply 15 gr. of salt per litre of water.

FARCES AND QUENELLES

Farces to Garnish Fish

Farce A

250 gr. chopped raw soft roe; 180 gr. fresh white breadcrumbs soaked in milk and squeezed dry; 50 gr. butter; 1 whole egg; 3 yolks of egg; 10 gr. chopped chives; 10 gr. chopped parsley; 5 gr. salt; 2 gr. pepper.

Mix the skinned and chopped soft roes together with soaked and pressed white crumbs, melted butter, whole egg and yolks. Pass through a hair sieve, season and work well with a spatula, finish with the chopped chives and parsley.

Farce B

200 gr. fresh white breadcrumbs soaked in milk and squeezed dry; 75 gr. finely chopped mushrooms; 25 gr. finely chopped onion and 25 gr. finely chopped shallot; ½ crushed clove of garlic; 3 yolks of egg; 30 gr. butter.

Cook together in butter without coloration the onion, shallot and mushrooms and allow to cool. Add the squeezed breadcrumbs, yolks of egg and chopped garlic, season with salt, pepper and a pinch of powdered nutmeg. Work together thoroughly with a wooden spatula.

Farce mousseline

500 gr. of raw fish flesh (pike, whiting, salmon, trout, etc.); 2 whites of egg; ¾ litre fresh cream; 8 to 10 gr. salt; 2 gr. white pepper.

Pound the flesh of the fish in a mortar with the seasoning or pass through the finest plate of a mincer and then through a hair sieve. Place into a saucepan and add the egg whites working well with the spatula. Place on ice for 2 hours or into the refrigerator. Add the chilled cream a little at a time working over ice until well incorporated. Test a little of the mixture in boiling water for texture and if too soft add a little more white of egg or if too firm a little more cream. This farce is used mainly for mousses, mousseline, soufflés, quenelles or for stuffing larger fish which is to be braised whole.

Farce zephyr

Adopt the same procedure as for farce mousseline, but soften the farce with the addition of a further ½ litre of fresh cream and finally incorporate ¼ litre of whipped chilled cream. This mixture is normally employed for very light mousses and mousselines.

Other Fish Farces

Farce A with pike

500 gr. net pike flesh; 250 gr. flour panada; 1 egg; 3 yolks of egg; 200 gr. butter.

Dice the pike flesh and pound with salt and pepper in a mortar or pass through the finest plate of the mincer, place into a bowl, add melted butter and the panada mixing well, add the yolks of egg one at a time and continue beating, finishing finally with the whole egg. Pass through a hair sieve and work the mixture thoroughly with a spatula. Test the mixture for texture and correct seasoning.

Farce B with pike

500 gr. net pike flesh; 4 dl. thick cold sauce béchamel; 2 whole eggs; 4 yolks of egg.

Prepare a fine farce with the pike flesh as for Farce A. Add the cold béchamel, working well with a wooden spoon, add the eggs one at a time beating well and finally the egg yolks. Pass through a hair sieve, work the farce well with a spatula and test the mixture for texture. Correct seasoning. The pike may be replaced with carp, salmon, turbot or trout.

Farce for fish pâtés

500 gr. raw flesh of pike, salmon, carp, etc.; 250 gr. choux paste.

Prepare a fine farce with the flesh of the chosen fish, incorporating very cold basic unsweetened choux paste in place of béchamel. Heighten the flavour with a point of Cayenne pepper.

Shellfish farce

500 gr. raw shellfish meat (lobster, crawfish, crayfish, etc.); 2 whites of egg; ¾ litre fresh cream; 9 gr. salt; 1 gr. white pepper.

Using the above ingredients prepare a farce by the method given for farce mousseline.

Farces for Fish Quenelles

Farce de brochet lyonnaise

500 gr. net raw pike flesh; 500 gr. kidney suet; 500 gr. frangipane panada; 4 whites of egg; 15 gr. salt; 1 gr. grated nutmeg.

Pass the pike flesh and kidney suet twice through the finest plate of a mincer. Add the panada, season, add egg whites one by one mixing well with a spatula, then pass the mixture through a hair sieve. Test the mixture for texture as in farce mousseline adding more egg white if necessary. Reserve the mixture in a terrine, levelled off and keep in a cool place until required.

Basic farce for quenelles

250 gr. net of pike; 125 gr. ordinary choux paste; 100 gr. butter; 4 eggs; about 5 cl. fresh cream; 1 soup-spoonful mixed herbs.

Prepare a fine farce with the raw pike flesh, season and work in the very cold unsweetened choux paste, mixed herbs and melted butter. Pass through a hair sieve, add the eggs one at a time mixing well and add sufficient fresh chilled cream to obtain the required texture. Test as for farce mousseline.

Quenelles are moulded in different shapes and sizes:
moulded cylindrically with the aid of floured hands
oval shaped using coffee spoons
spoon-shaped ovals using two tablespoons
soup quenelles, squiggle shaped, using paper cornet.

Quenelles classified as lyonnaise are usually moulded with tablespoons, average weight 70 gr. Quenelles used for garnishes average not more than 30–40 gr., smaller ones using basic quenelles mixture vary between 10–12 gr. Basically they are cooked in boiling salted water or poached in a fish or white wine stock. Quenelles are also made from farce mousseline.

Essences

Essences are strongly reduced stocks giving a concentrated form. If the sauce has a sufficiently pronounced flavour it does not need an essence. Essences only serve to heighten the flavour of a weak taste. Rather than use an essence it is better to make direct use of an excellent stock for the preparation of sauces. Amongst aromatic essences are the essences of celery, truffle, mushroom. In many sauce preparations the essence can be added to the stock at the moment it is being cooked. It is always useful to have glazes and essences handy.

Fish essence

2 kg. fish trimmings and bones; 125 gr. chopped onion; 50 gr. parsley stalks; 200 gr. mushroom trimmings; 3 dl. white wine; 1½ litres of fish stock; 100 gr. butter; juices of 1 lemon. Cooking time: 15 minutes.

Sweat in butter without coloration the mushroom parings and the parsley stalks, add the fish bones and trimmings and sweat together for 15 minutes with a lid on. Moisten with white wine fish stock and lemon juice. Simmer very slowly for a further 15 minutes. Pass through a fine chinois or muslin, season sparingly with salt.

Fish Glaze

Fish glaze, like fish essence, is obtained by the reduction of fish stock to obtain a highly concentrated flavour and a consistency of syrup. Glaze is used to thicken sauces and improve them. Fish glaze is superior to essence and is an excellent ingredient. It does wonders. Whipped cream or butter are often incorporated giving it richness. It is obvious that glazes, like essences, are only used in the case of insufficiency of stock or sauce. Ready prepared fish glaze, kept in reserve, allows economy and saves time. Its preparation with a base of trimmings and bones is not expensive. It only takes time and care.

Roux

Roux is a combination of butter (or other fats) and flour, cooked for varying degrees of time. It is one of the elements for thickening sauces. Its preparation requires care and attention. There are three types of roux: white, blond and brown.

Brown roux

Made by slowly cooking together 200 gr. clarified fat and 300 gr. of flour, stirring frequently over a low heat until a light brown colour is obtained.

Blond roux

Prepared from 200 gr. of butter and 300 gr. flour, blended together over a low heat until a sandy texture and a pale straw colour are obtained.

White roux

Prepared with 250 gr. of butter and 300 gr. of flour, cooked together over a low heat until a sandy texture is obtained, but stirring constantly to prevent coloration.

The brown roux is the thickening base for sauce espagnole and its derivative half-glaze. The pale roux forms the base of the veloutés, and the white roux for sauce béchamel and cream soups.

Panadas

Flour panada

300 gr. flour; 100 gr. butter; 6 dl. water; 4 to 5 gr. salt.

Bring the water to the boil together with the salt and butter. Add, away from the fire, the sifted flour; mix well and dry out over a good heat until the mixture leaves the bottom and sides of the pan. Place in a terrine and allow to cool. This panada forms a base for choux paste as well as other uses indicated.

Panada frangipane

250 gr. flour; 175 gr. melted butter; 8 egg yolks; ½ litre of milk; 4 gr. salt; 2 gr. white pepper; a pinch of powdered nutmeg.

Mix together in a pan the flour and the egg yolks, add the melted butter and the seasoning. Dilute gradually over the heat with the boiling milk, whisking well for 5–6 minutes until the mixture is thick and smooth. Put into a buttered earthenware dish and allow to cool.

Bread panada

500 gr. of white breadcrumbs; 6 dl. boiling milk; 12 gr. salt.

Soak the breadcrumbs in the boiling milk until the milk is completely absorbed. Place on the stove and stir with a wooden spatula until the mixture leaves the sides and bottom of the pan. Spread on a buttered dish and allow to cool.

Stocks

At the end of the last century, the preparation of stocks took a great deal of time. The work was very complicated. Today the time needed is appreciably shorter. Simplified methods get comparable results, on condition that the basic elements are of perfect quality and the greatest care is given to the preparation.
It must not be forgotten that stocks enter into the composition of soups, sauces, glazes and essences.

Fish stock

For 4 litres: *3–4 kg. of fish bones and trimmings; 200 gr. sliced onions; 60 gr. parsley stalks; ½ litre of white wine; juice of 1 lemon; 4 litres of water; 5 gr. white peppercorns added 10 minutes before straining the stock.* Cooking time: 30 minutes.

Layer the bottom of the pan with onions and aromatics. Add the bones and trimmings; moisten with white wine, water and lemon juice. Bring to the boil and skim, simmer slowly for 20 minutes. Add the peppercorns and cook for a further 10 minutes. Pass through a tammy cloth or muslin.

Fish stock with red wine

For 4 litres: *100 gr. mushroom parings; 2 kg. fish trimmings and bones; 2 litres of red wine; 2 litres of water; 300 gr. sliced onions; 100 gr. parsley stalks; 2 bayleaves; 5 cloves of garlic.*

Prepare as for fish stock. For fish stews, poach the fish in red wine. The majority of fish dishes being served without bones, there is need for fish stock with red wine. The trimmings of the fish from which the sauce is made are used.

Lenten stock

For 5 litres: *7½ litres of water; 400 gr. carrots; 400 gr. onions; 200 gr. leeks; 100 gr. butter; 8 parsley stalks; 300 gr. celery; 30 gr. salt; 20 gr. sugar; 400 gr. of mushroom parings.*

Sweat in butter the vegetables cut in a julienne, with salt and sugar. Add the mushroom trimmings, and a sprig of thyme. Moisten with the water, simmer and reduce to 5 litres. Pass through a muslin cloth. This stock is used as a base for lenten soups and sauces.

Other Preparations

Cooked tomato fondue or fondue portugaise

To produce ½ litre: *50 gr. chopped onion; 500 gr. skinned, pipped and diced tomatoes; 1 crushed clove of garlic; 40 gr. butter or 4 cl. of oil.* Cooking time: 12 to 15 minutes.

Stew in butter or oil the chopped onion; add the tomatoes, crushed garlic, salt and pepper. Cook slowly until all the liquid has evaporated. According to the degree of ripeness of the tomatoes, the acidity can be adjusted by adding a pinch of sugar.

Fish jelly

For 3 litres: *1 kg. 500 of heads, bones and trimmings of turbot, sole, pike or whiting; 50 gr. parsley stalks; 200 gr. sliced onions; 100 gr. mushroom pairings; 10 white peppercorns; ½ litre of dry white wine; 4 litres of water; 15 gr. salt.* Cooking time: 30 minutes.

Layer the pan with the aromatics and place the fish heads and trimmings on top. Moisten and place on the open fire; bring to the boil and skim; simmer slowly for 20 minutes. Add the peppercorns, continue simmering for a further 10 minutes and pass through a muslin cloth.

Clarification of jelly

3 egg whites; 200 gr. minced or finely chopped whiting flesh; 6 leaves of soaked gelatine; 50 gr. mushroom parings.

Place the whiting flesh in a saucepan together with the whites of egg, trimmings of mushroom and soaked gelatine; pour on the tepid or cold fish stock and whisk well together. Bring to the boil very slowly to ensure clarification by the whites of egg and flesh. Simmer gently for 15 minutes. Pass through a wet muslin. If the fish stock used is very strong, then it need only be clarified with egg white. It may require more or less gelatine according to the time of year.

Matignon or bed of roots

125 gr. red of carrot; 125 gr. of onions; 50 gr. celery; 100 gr. raw ham; 1 small bayleaf; sprig of thyme; 50 gr. butter; 5 cl. madeira.

Slice the onion and carrot into small rings and the celery and ham into dice. Stew in butter with the bayleaf and thyme; deglaze with madeira and reserve in an earthenware dish.

Mirepoix

125 gr. carrots; 125 gr. onion; 50 gr. celery; 100 gr. lean bacon; 1 small bayleaf and a sprig of thyme.

Cut the vegetables into medium-sized dice, according to the nature of the intended usage. Add the blanched diced bacon, thyme and bayleaf, and stew together in butter.

Mirepoix bordelaise

125 gr. red of carrot; 125 gr. onion; 30 gr. parsley stalks; 1 pinch of powdered thyme and bayleaf.

Cut the carrot, onion and parsley stalks into a very fine dice. Sprinkle with thyme and bayleaf; stew in butter until completely cooked. Place in a small earthenware dish covered with a buttered paper until required. Mirepoix bordelaise is used particularly for the cooking of lobsters and crayfish. It must be prepared in advance.

Short pastry for pastry-cases (tartelettes, barquettes)

500 gr. flour; 250 gr. butter; 2 eggs; 5 cl. water; about 10 gr. of salt.

Sift the flour on to the table and make a bay. In the centre place the softened butter, eggs, water and salt. Mix these ingredients together incorporating the flour a little at a time until all is absorbed. Without overworking, form the paste into a ball, cover with a damp cloth and keep in the cool for several hours before use.

Choux pastry

100 gr. butter; 300 gr. sifted flour; 6–7 eggs; 5 gr. salt; ½ litre of water.

Place together in a saucepan, the water, salt and butter. Bring to the boil; draw to the side and add the flour, stirring briskly. Reheat until the mixture leaves the sides and bottom of the pan; allow to cool, then add the eggs one by one according to size, mixing well. The mixture should not be too firm, but should drop from the spatula.

Frying batter

125 gr. sifted flour; 2 spoonfuls of olive oil; 2 dl. water; 2 whites of egg.

Mix together in an earthenware bowl the flour, a pinch of salt, oil and the tepid water. Mix in the flour, carefully folding in to prevent elasticity. Rest for 1 hour and when required for use fold in the stiffly beaten egg whites.

Pizza paste

For 12 persons: *700 gr. flour; 200 gr. butter; 2 eggs; 3 dl. milk; 20 gr. yeast; salt.*

Divide the butter into small pieces and work it until creamy in an earthenware bowl; add the eggs one by one. Dilute the yeast in a little milk at blood heat. Sieve the flour and make a bay, add the liquid and the softened butter and a pinch of salt and work the mixture to a medium consistency, or until it does not stick to the fingers. Cover and leave to rest for 30 minutes before use. (Italy.)

Spices and Aromatic Plants

Aniseed

For preparing fish, and for pastry. Grown in Spain, the East and most sub-tropical countries. Italian and Spanish seeds are larger than those from Germany, Soviet Russia and Syria. Aniseed oil is produced by distillation, and the characteristic flavour of aniseed comes from the active constituent called anethol.

Basil

For preparing soups, sauces, salads, and fish galantines (q.v.). Grown in Western Europe.

Bayleaves

Used in soups and sauces, and also for wrapping liquorice, dates and figs. Bayleaves are an essential ingredient among those aromatics which are also good preservatives. They come from Mediterranean countries, and dried leaves of top quality must be leathery, sinuous, highly aromatic, and pale green in colour.

Black peppercorns

The vine which produces black peppercorns is cultivated in tropical forests of the monsoon regions of Asia, and also in most other tropical countries with a warm, wet climate. These include Brazil, Malagasy, India, Ceylon and Indonesia. It favours conditions of partial shade, and is often encouraged to climb posts or shaded trees in coffee plantations.
Black peppercorns have many culinary uses, as they contain the gastric stimulant piperine. The berries of the vine are picked when green and unripe. Drying in the sun shrivels the flesh and gives the peppercorns their characteristic black colour.

Burnet

Used principally in salads, and grown in Western Europe.

Capers

Often used as a garnish for fish dishes, and consisting of the small flower-buds of the Capparis spinosa, a plant which grows about one metre high. A caper is of about the same size as a small garden pea. The buds are picked before flowering, salted, and then pickled in vinegar.

Caraway

Used in liqueurs, and in making cheese, cakes and generally in bakery. Grown in Holland, Soviet Russia, England and Germany. The seeds are rich in volatile oils.

Cardamom

For preparing curry, liqueurs, exotic dishes and pastry.

Cayenne pepper

Used in seasoning and in the making of curry powder. The main areas of supply are Africa, Japan and tropical America. This pepper is related to the pimento, and the flavouring content is found in the red epicarp (outermost layer). The flavour is strong, and easily predominates.

Celery

Used in preparing soups and sauces. Celery is a plant whose brightly-coloured leaves are rich in volatile oils and aromatic content. In spring, the young plants bring forth shoots. Celeriac is obtained by covering the plants with soil, as is the case with asparagus, to prevent the forming of leaves. In cookery, celery is esteemed for its aroma and colour.

Chervil

Used in the preparation of soups and sauces, and as an ingredient for garnishes containing mixed herbs.

Chives

Used in preparing soups, sauces and salads, occasionally replacing onions. Very tasty in garnishes, but without having a dominant flavour. Grown in Western Europe, chives have a more distinctive flavour than onions.

Cinnamon

Used almost exclusively in pastry. In Ceylon, new plantations are frequently being established. In ancient times, the Greeks obtained their cinnamon from the Syrians, and cinnamon bark was one of the most important products of the East India Company. This is, therefore, one of the most ancient spices, and the flavour of the bark depends on the soil in which the tree is grown.

Cloves

Cloves are grown in Madagascar. The cloves themselves are the dried flower-buds of the clove tree. The residue of clove oil provides a chemical vanilla which is a substitute for the natural vanilla product.

Coriander

Used in pickles and marinades. Coriander is an ingredient of curry powder.

Curry

Often used in the preparation of soups and fish sauces. Curry powder is a mixture of spices such as turmeric (giving the yellow colour), coriander, black pepper, pimentoes, ginger, cardamom, caraway, cinnamon, mace and cloves, in fixed proportions. These powdered spices must be thoroughly mixed together.

Dill

For preparing soups, sauces and salads, and for pickling gherkins. This spice is highly appreciated in the cookery of all Scandinavian countries, and is grown in Western Europe.

Fennel

Indispensable in pickling gherkins and onions. Fennel is grown in Mediterranean areas, and is related to aniseed.

Garlic

A bulbous plant frequently used in preparing soups, sauces and salads. If well dried, garlic will keep for a long time.

Ginger

Chinese cookery uses ginger as a main ingredient, but ginger is also found in pastry cookery. The Jamaican variety is the best, followed by ginger from China, India and Japan. The best ginger comes from one-year-old rhizomes, which are gathered and then peeled like potatoes. Particularly in China, the rhizomes are fermented, and then cooked in a highly sweetened syrup.

Horse-radish

A root used in preparing mustard, and in preserving gherkins, onions and fish. Grown throughout Europe, horse-radish is used raw, both whole and grated. The aroma of mustard oil given off during the grating process is caused by the disassimilation of glucoside.

Lovage

Used in soups and sauces. The flavour of this Western European plant makes it smell rather like beef broth.

Mace

Used in ragoûts, soups and sauces. Mace is the outer bark of the nutmeg, and, when fresh, is red in colour.

Mint

Used in cookery and pastries, and grown for its aromatic oil.

Mustard

The use of mustard in cookery is well known. To make it, the seeds are dried, milled and pressed, then mixed with spices, sugar, wine, must, vinegar, water and salt.

Nutmeg

Used in preparing ragoûts, soups, sauces and vegetables. Whereas Molucca was once the sole supplier of nutmeg, it is now grown throughout the Indonesian archipelago, which also produces the best nutmeg. Second-quality nutmeg is sold ready grated.

Onion

The onion is used as a vegetable as much as a spice. Together with the shallot and the chive, it is one of the most frequently used aromatic plants. The majority of sauces, ragoûts and many other dishes could not be made without onions.

Paprika

Mild paprika is used in preparing soups and sauces. It looks rather like the tomato, and is grown in Hungary, Portugal and Spain. It is sold fresh, or powdered, or preserved whole, or even, in recent times, diced and canned. There is another variety of paprika which has a stronger flavour.

Parsley

The freshly-chopped leaves of this aromatic plant are widely used in cookery. Parsley roots are indispensable in preparing fish sauces. 'Curly' parsley is useful and pleasant as a garnish, whether raw or fried.

Pepper

The pepper plant, a climbing shrub, is grown in all tropical regions. A distinction can be made between white and black pepper even though they come from the same shrub. The inside of the fruit of the pepper plant is the white peppercorn, from which white pepper is milled. The red skin, when dried and milled, becomes black pepper. The names of the various kinds of pepper come from the names of the growing areas.

Pimento

The pimento, belonging to the plant family Solanaceae, produces a fruit of highly piquant flavour used as a spice. The best pimentoes come from Mozambique.

Rosemary

The fresh or dried leaves of this aromatic plant are used in the flavouring of soups and sauces. Oil of rosemary is used in medicine and perfumery.

Saffron

European saffron comes, in general, from Spain, Italy and the south of France. It is the head of the pistil of Crocus sativus, and 15,000 pistils are required to produce 100 gr. of saffron. Saffron contains a high concentration of volatile oil and colouring matter.

Savory

Used fresh or dried, and especially in the preparation of broad beans. It is strongly flavoured.

Sorrel

Used in preparing soups and with vegetables. Sorrel, both wild and cultivated, grows in Western Europe. Its leaves are crisp and covered with light down, and its general appearance is that of coarse spinach.

Sweet marjoram

Used in sausages, soups and sauces, and grown in Morocco. The parts used are pieces of the root and the oval leaves covered with small 'hairs'. When the leaves are held up to the light, oily cells are visible.

Tarragon

Used for flavouring vinegar, in marinades, for garnishes containing mixed herbs, and in the preparation of salads.

Thyme

Thyme is absolutely necessary in certain sauces, especially brown sauces. The fresh leaves have more flavour than the dried ones.

Turmeric

Used as colouring matter and for the preparation of mustards and pickles. It comes from the curcuma plant grown in India, and the roots contain a volatile oil, yellow in colour and with a resinous taste. Turmeric is the principal ingredient of curry powder.

Wild marjoram

Although this herb can be cultivated in temperate zones, its growth and use are particularly associated with Mediterranean countries. It consists of the dried leaves of a plant of the same family as mint, with a more pungent flavour than that of sweet marjoram.

Cooking Methods

Braising

This method of cooking is applicable to whole fish such as: salmon, salmon-trout, carp, pike, brill, turbot and chicken-turbot as well as the larger cuts of these fish. To braise, a fish-kettle or other suitable pan which can be tightly covered should be used.
Well butter and line the base of the pan with sliced onion, carrot and shallots, previously tossed in butter. Add a few parsley stalks. Arrange the fish on top. Sometimes the fish is studded on one side with truffles, carrots or gherkins suitably cut to size. Cover the fish with a buttered paper, or, if preferred, slices of fat bacon. According to the sauce which is to accompany the fish, moisten to three-quarters of its height and braise, loosely covered in the oven, so that the stock is reduced as the fish is cooked. When almost done, remove the cover and continue cooking, basting frequently to glaze the fish. Drain well and dress on a suitable dish. Cover to keep warm. Pass the cooking liquor, skim off surplus fat, reduce if necessary and add to the fish sauce. Braised fish is usually accompanied by an appropriate garnish.

Poaching

This method of cooking can be applied to sole, turbot, brill, halibut and fillets of other fish.
Butter a suitable fireproof dish, fish tray or shallow pan, and place on it the fish, salt lightly and sprinkle with fish stock and mushroom cooking liquor or dry white wine, cover with a buttered paper and cook in a medium oven. The fish is usually accompanied by a suitable garnish according to designation. The cooking liquor is reduced and added to the appropriate sauce.

Deep Frying

Frequently the method of frying in deep oil or fat is carried out at a frying temperature of 300° F. plus when frying small fish. Large pieces of fish are incised to allow for the penetration of the frying fat and to prevent drying out of the fish. To fry a fish on both sides, pass through salted milk, then through flour. White fish is often breadcrumbed.

It is essential to regulate the frying temperature according to the thickness and weight of the fish. Fried fish is dressed on a napkin accompanied by fried parsley and lemon quarters.

Grilling

For this method of cooking one uses in general medium sized or cut fish. The whole fish are incised in order to allow the heat to penetrate. Fish which dry out quickly are previously floured, oiled or brushed with butter. In this way a crust is formed which prevents the fish drying out. Oily fish such as salmon, mackerel, herring, trout, have no need of this treatment and can be grilled, simply passed through oil.
Grilled fish are accompanied by a savoury butter, for example pistachio butter, or a sauce, for example sauce béarnaise, Choron, Vincent. (See Culinary Technique, mackerel, page 84.)

Shallow or Pan Frying (Meunière)

Smaller fish, such as sole, mackerel and trout are fried entirely in clarified butter in the pan. Large fish are cut into slices or darnes. This method of cooking also applies to whole fish not above 1 kg. 500. For this method of cooking, use half oil and half clarified butter.
Season the fish with salt and pepper, pass through flour. Lay it in a frying pan containing hot butter. Colour it golden on both sides, then arrange it on a dish and sprinkle with lemon-juice, chopped parsley and noisette butter. (See Culinary Technique, page 72.)

Au Bleu Cooking

To cook fish au bleu, it is indispensable to have live fish. Only small fish are treated in this way such as young pike, small carp, trout and other small fish of the salmonides family such as white fish, lake trout, sea char, etc.
Ten minutes before preparing the fish, take it from the water and kill it with a blow on the head, quickly gut it and wash it. The fish must not be touched too much in order not to remove the external mucosity which gives the fish its bluish colour in cooking. The mucosity clings to the scales and thus the fish is not scaled.
The classical method requires the fish to be poached in the court-bouillon A, and, before putting into the court-bouillon, the fish is passed through tepid vinegar. We do not recommend this method, vinegar not being necessary to cook a fish au bleu. Indeed vinegar affects the delicacy of the taste, especially of trout and similar fish. It is enough to put the fish into boiling salt water or in a court-bouillon without vingear. If the fish has not lost its mucosity it will always cook au bleu. A freshly killed fish is recognised by the way its flesh is easily flaked. Fish cooked au bleu are used for hot or cold dishes. For cold dishes the fish must be killed at least an hour in advance so that the flesh remains firm.

Illustrated Culinary Techniques

COD

Place the fish on a chopping board.

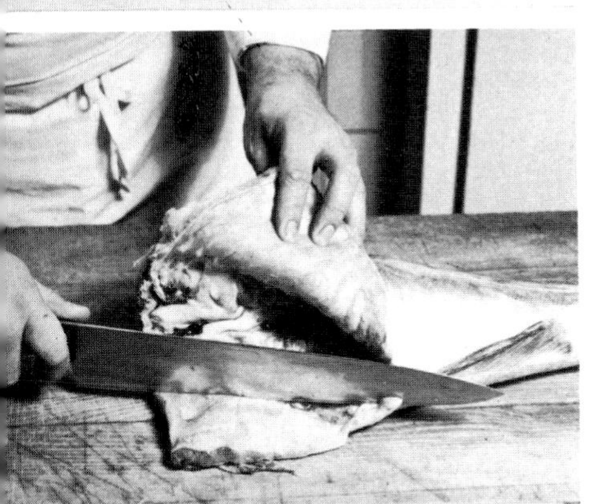

Lay on its side and cut away the stomach flaps.

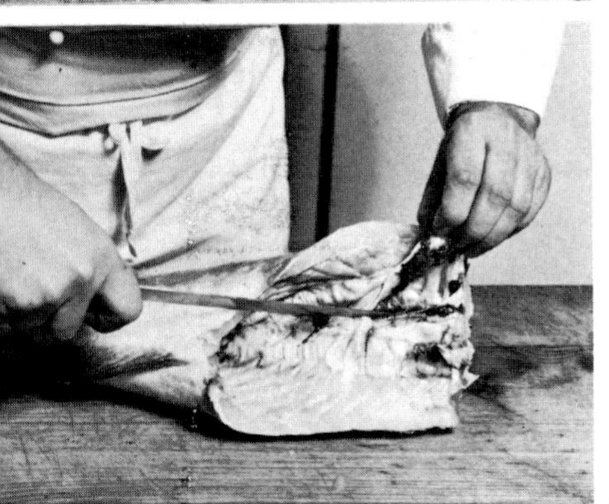

Remove the fine black membranes and all traces of blood.

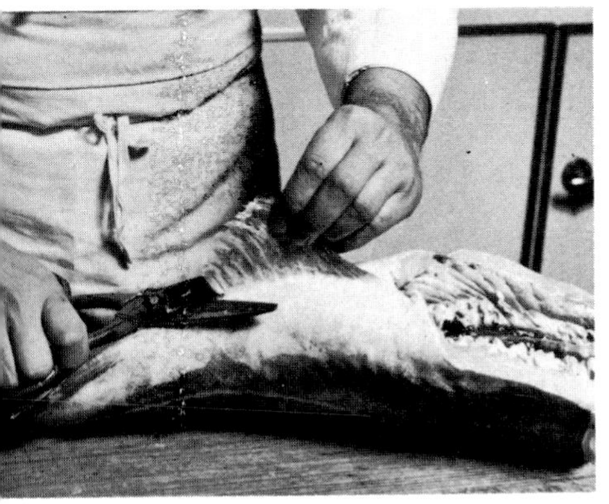

Remove the fins with scissors.

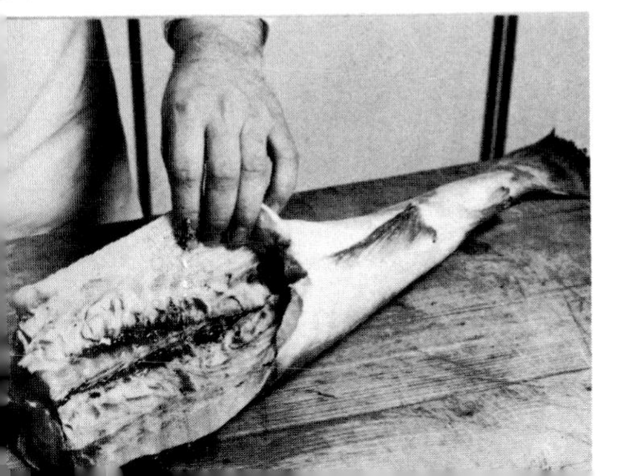

To fillet:

COD (cont)

Incise on each side of the backbone.

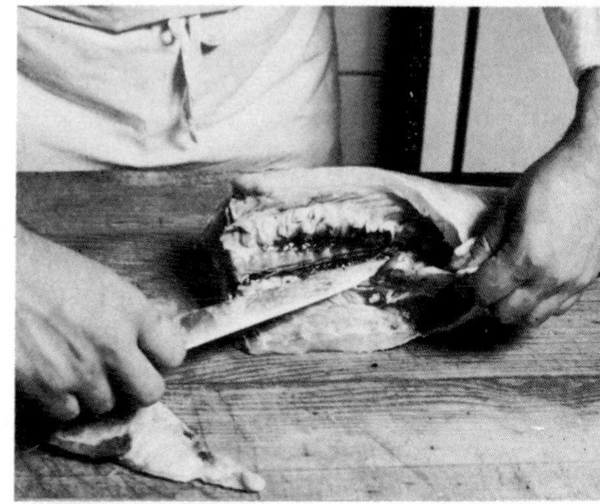

Follow the bone very carefully, lifting at the same time.

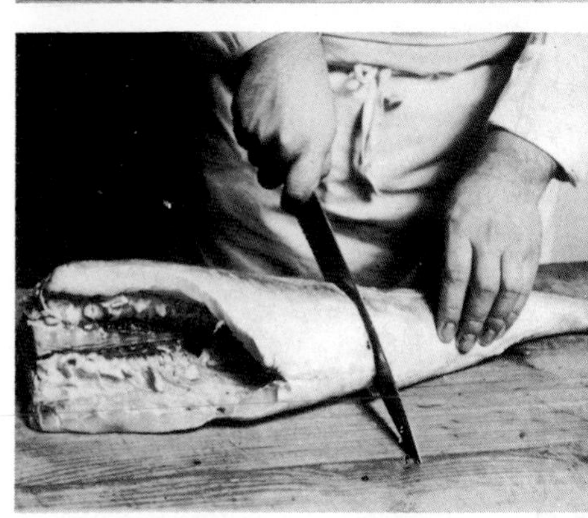

Cut in two.

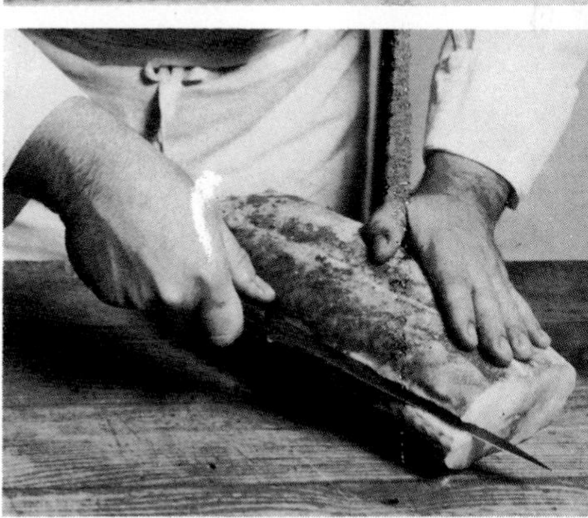

Fillet by making an incision on either side of the backbone.

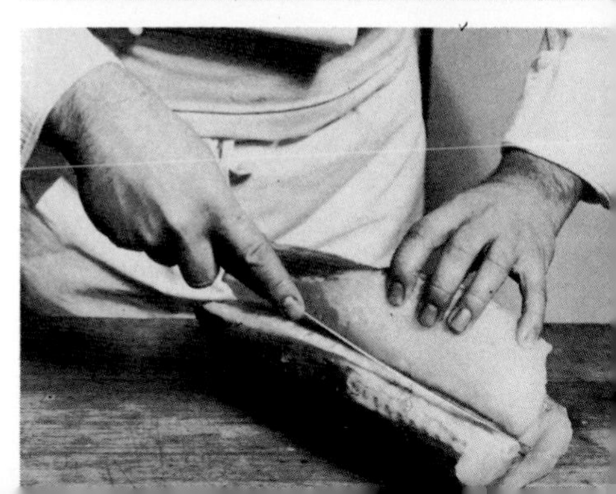

Lifting and using long sweeping strokes of a sharp flexible knife

COD (cont)

Remove the small bones.

Cut the fillet into even slices.

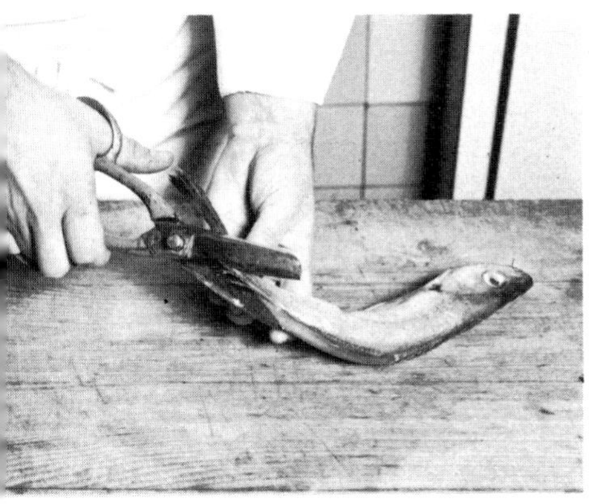

WHITING

Remove the fins with a pair of scissors.

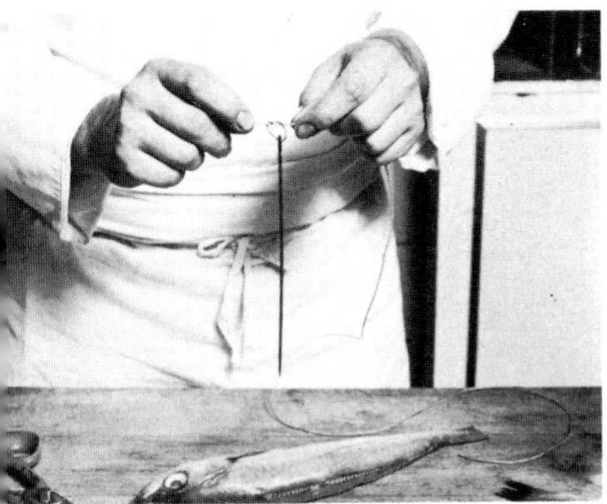

En colère:

Prepare a trussing needle with thin string.

Insert the point of the needle under the tail bone.

Next thread the needle through a gill into the mouth; pull out the needle.

With the help of the string pull the head and tail tightly together to make a knot. Pass through milk, then flour and cook in hot deep fat.

En lorgnette:

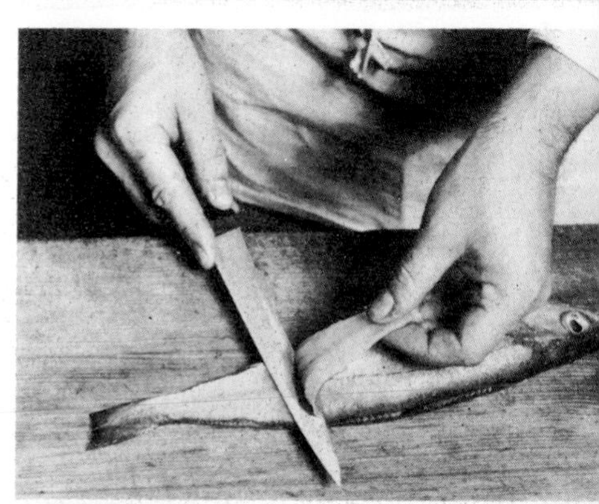

Split the whiting on each side of the backbone . . .

carefully keeping the knife against the bone up to just short of the head.

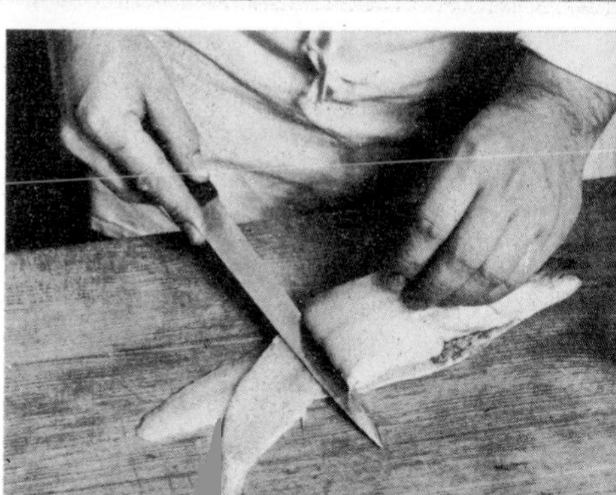

Turn the fish over and release the second fillet similarly.

WHITING (cont)

Remove the backbone with a pair of scissors.

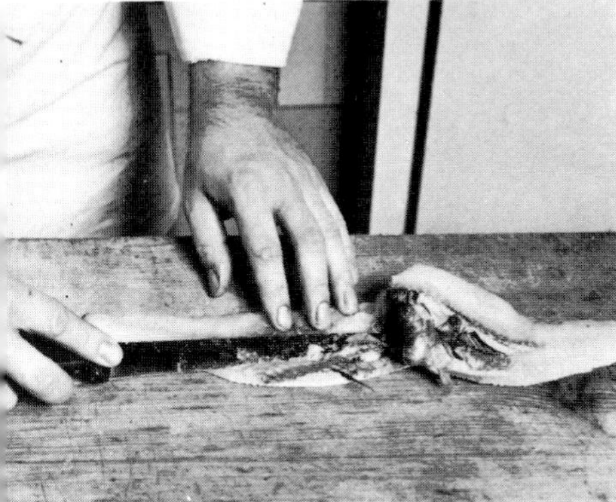

Take out the small bones and inedible superfluities.

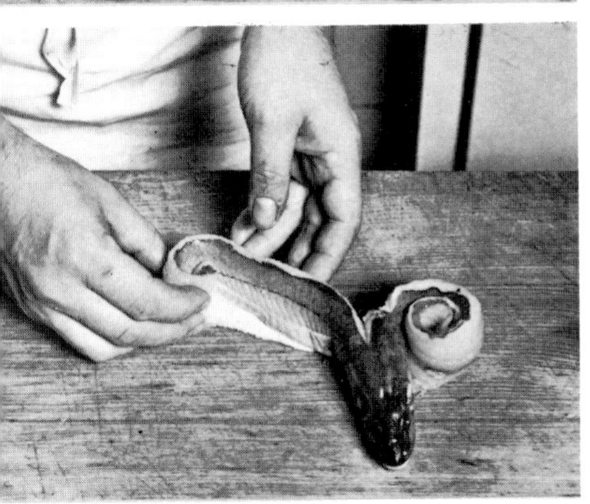

Roll the fillets in the opposite direction to each other towards the head to produce the effect of a lorgnette.

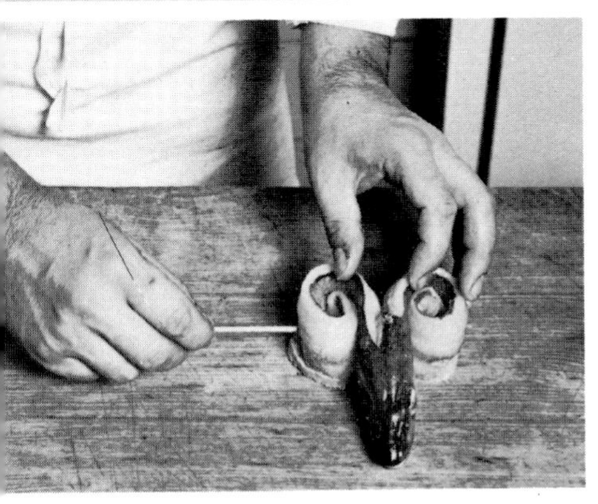

Skewer to keep in position while deep frying.

SOLE

Removing the skin:

Place the fish with the white skin down on the table. Snip off the tail fin. Make a small incision in the skin as near to this as possible.

SOLE (cont)

Lift carefully the skin with the thumb-nail, seize the skin . . .

and rip off with a sharp tearing movement . . .

holding the sole flat.

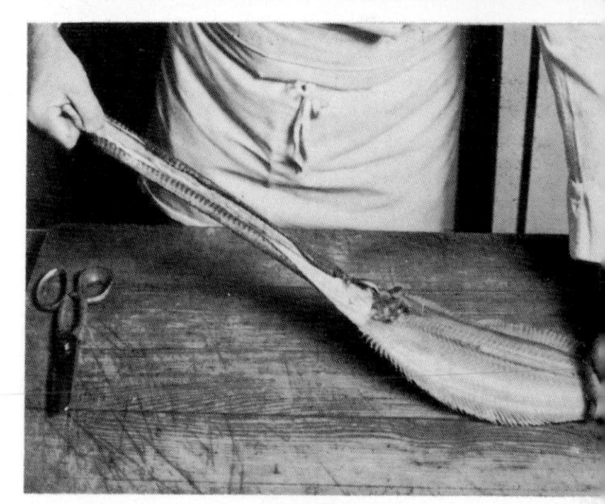

To fillet:

Cut off the fins with a pair of scissors.

Incise against the backbone.

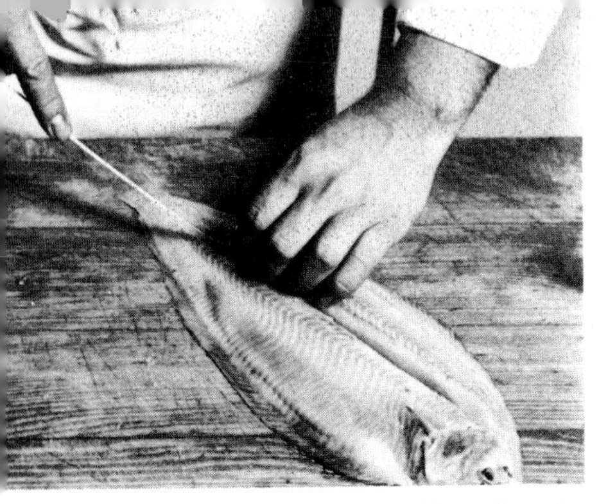

SOLE (cont)

from head to tail.

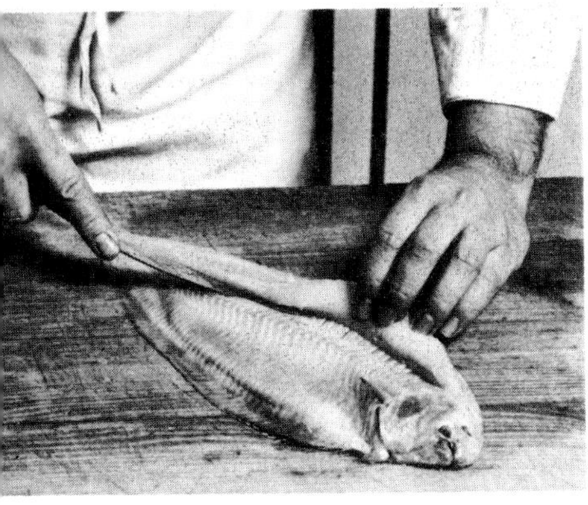

Slide the blade of a flexible knife between the backbone and the fillet . . .

to lift it off. Turn the fish round and remove the second fillet in the same way.
Turn the sole over and remove carefully the fillets on the other side.

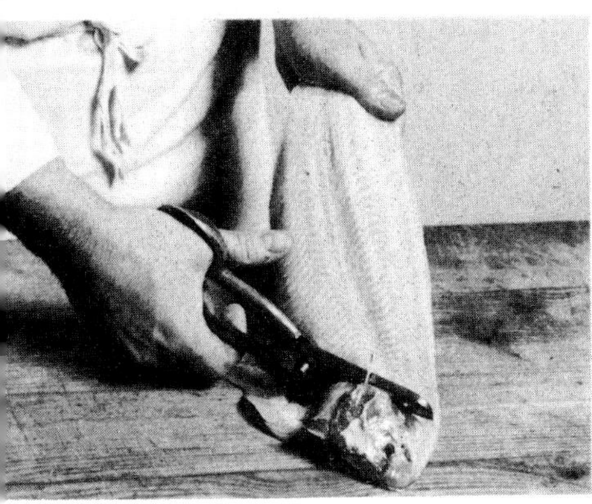

Sole meunière:

Remove the skin and cut off the head with a pair of scissors . . .

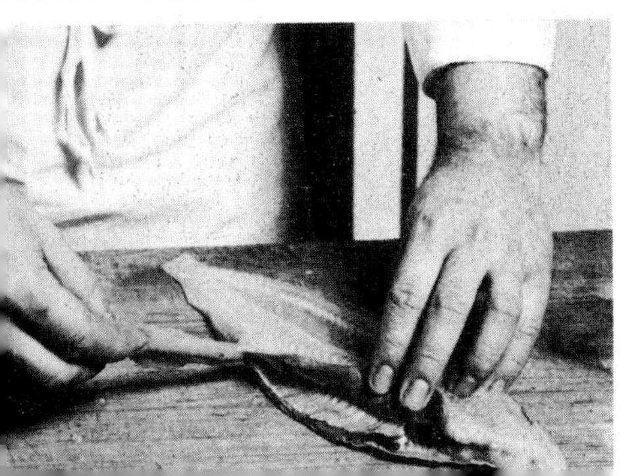

make an incision in the stomach and gut and clean the fish. Season, pass through flour and cook in the frying pan in hot butter, skinned side down.

SOLE (cont)

Goujons:

Cut the fillets of sole slantwise to represent the appearance of a gudgeon.

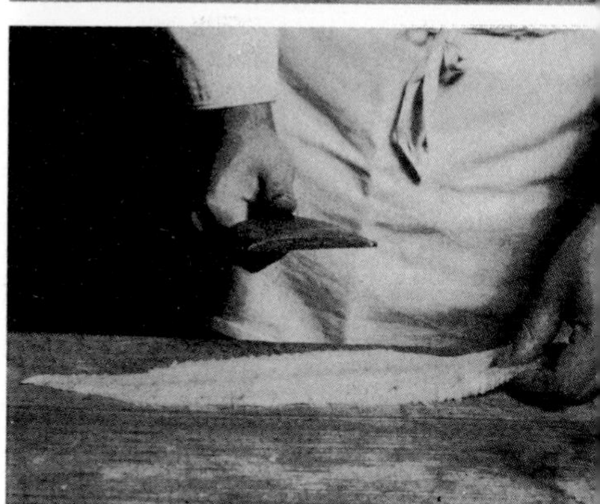

Paupiettes simples:

Lightly beat the fillets to prevent curling up.

Season and roll up.

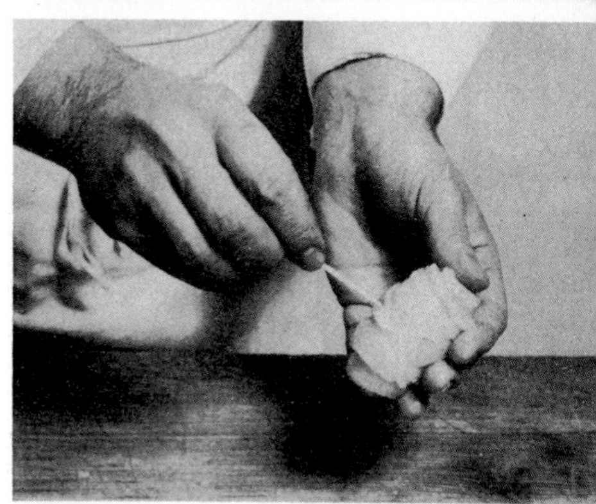

Fasten the fillets with a skewer.

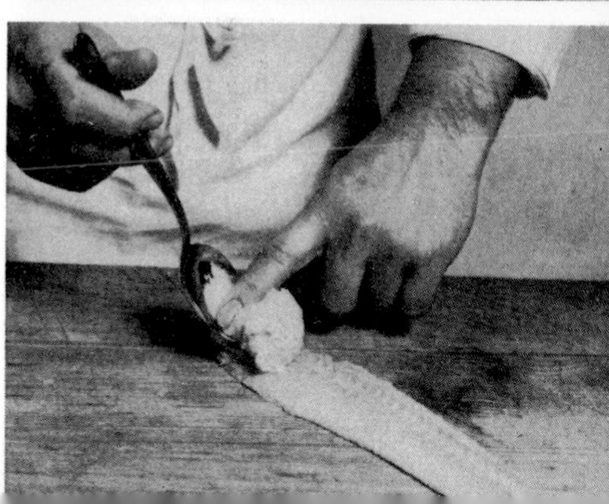

Stuffed paupiettes:

Lightly beat the fillets to prevent curling up. Arrange the farce with the aid of a spoon or a piping-bag with a plain tube.

SOLE (cont)

Roll the fillet to make a paupiette.

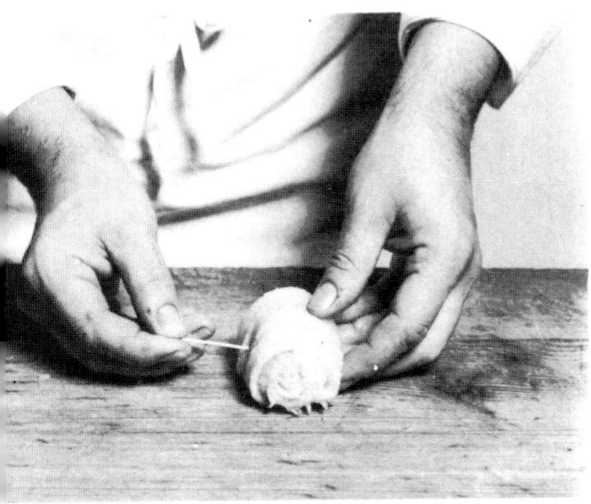

Secure with a skewer.

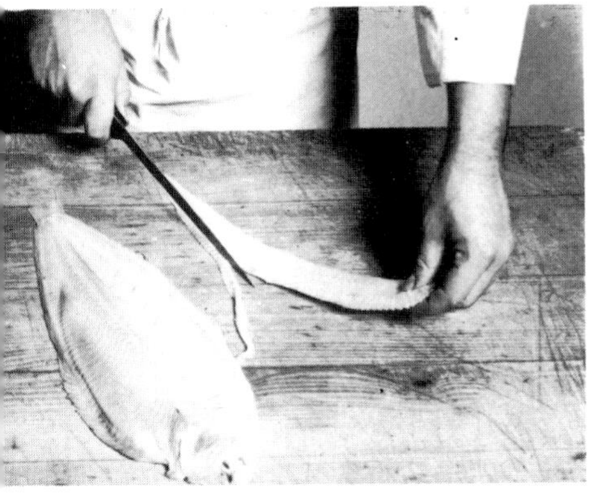

Preparation of fillets for poaching:

Trim the fillets.

Beat to prevent curling and fold.

The folded fillet ready for poaching.

Sole Colbert:

Remove the black skin and scale the white skin. On the skinned side make an incision right along the bone, partially lift the fillets . . .

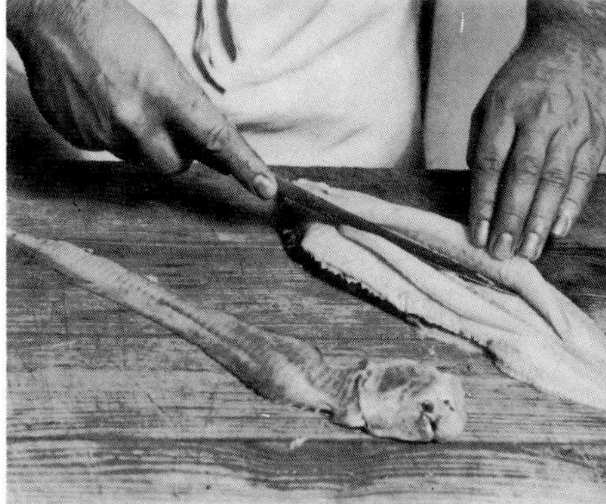

without removing them. Repeat the operation on the other side.

Break the bone at the head and tail to facilitate removal of backbone after cooking.

Turban de filets de sole:

Butter a ring mould with a brush. Arrange the lightly beaten fillets in the mould.

Fill the mould with a prepared farce. Turn back the ends of the fillets over the farce. Cook au bain-marie in the oven.

SOLE (cont)

Filets de sole en chaud-froid

Recipe: *Filets de sole Domino* (see page 231 and page 249).

Allow the poached fillets, folded before cooking, to cool and pass the white sauce chaud-froid through a tammy cloth . . .

with pressure.

According to the desired presentation give the fillets an even shape, trimming with a knife. Mask the fillets with sauce and allow to set.

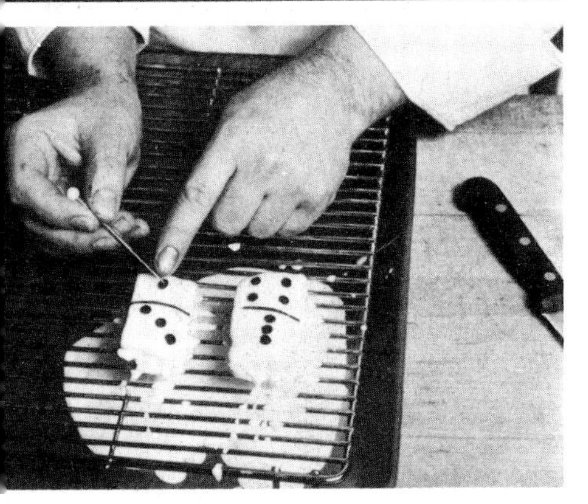

Place the decorations on top according to the recipe or desired presentation.

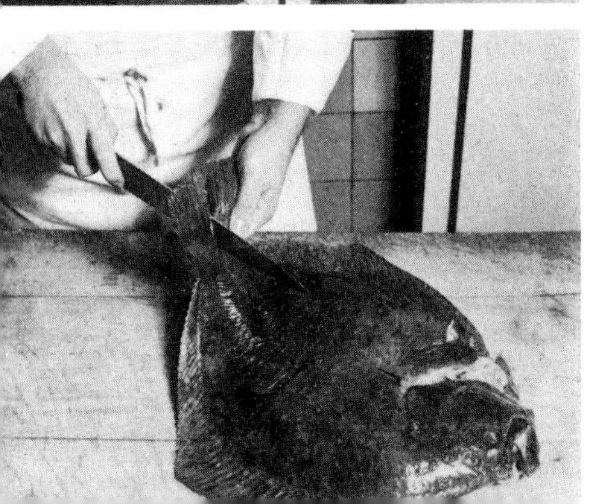

TURBOT

Place the fish on the chopping board, the tail fin towards you. Incise from the tail . . .

TURBOT (cont)

and split the turbot in two with a large knife,

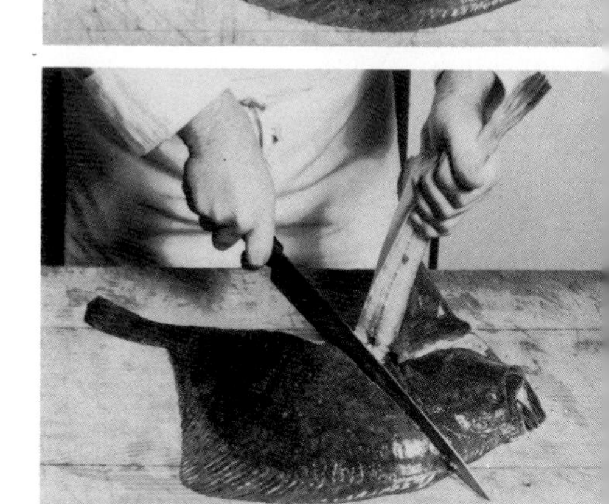

holding the edge of the stomach side and
gradually turning the fish

continuing the separation to obtain two pieces:
(a) the dorsal side
(b) the head with the stomach side.

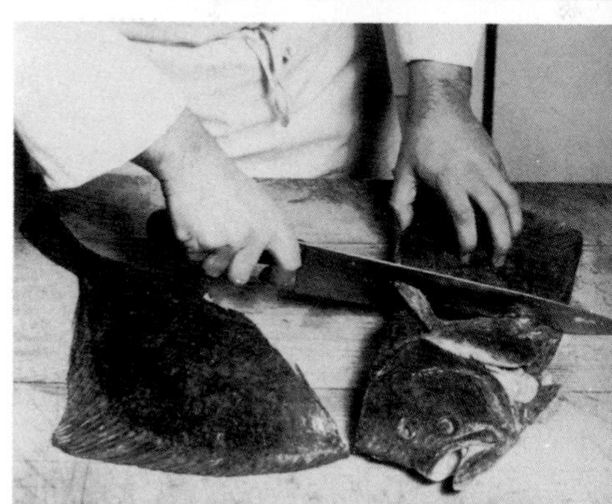

Cut off the head

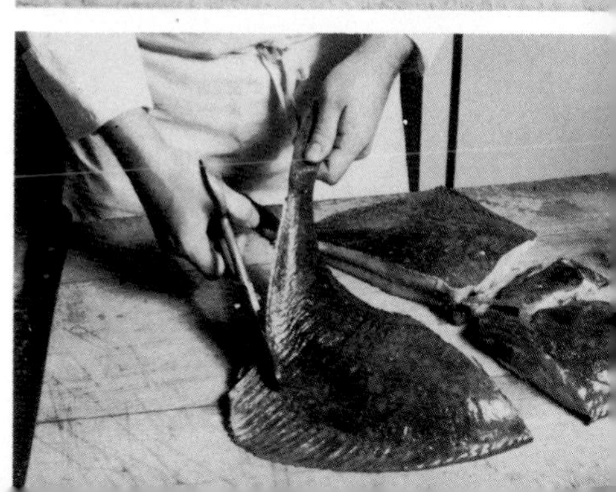

Remove the fins with scissors.

TURBOT (cont)

Cut off the stomach side.

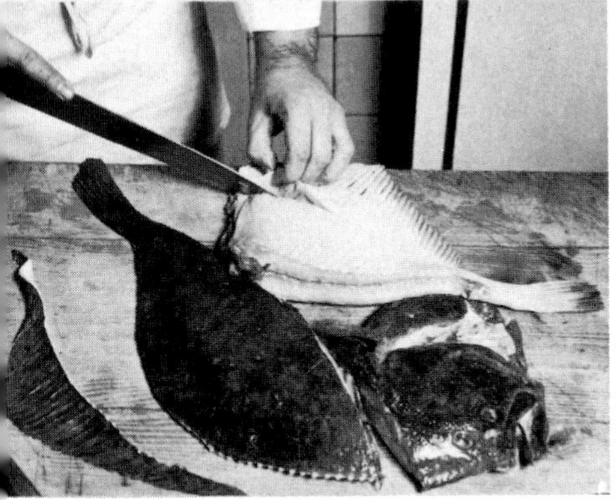

Make first an incision with a knife . . .

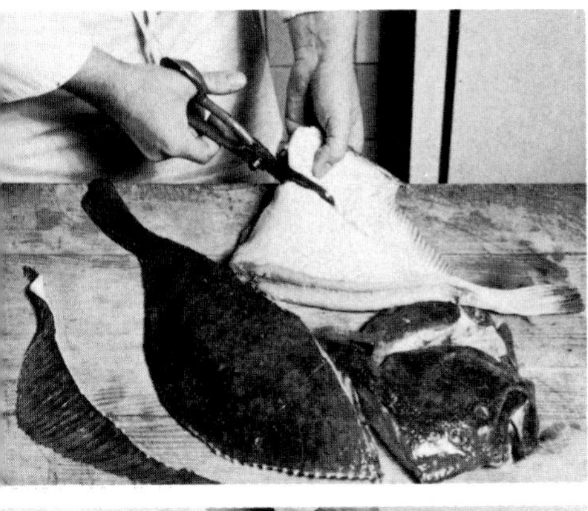

and trim with scissors

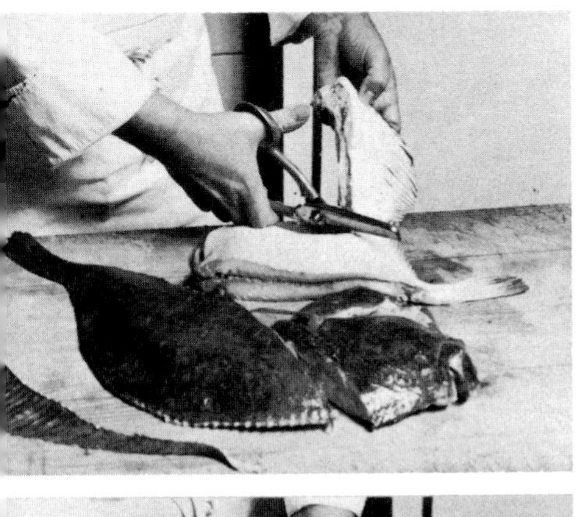

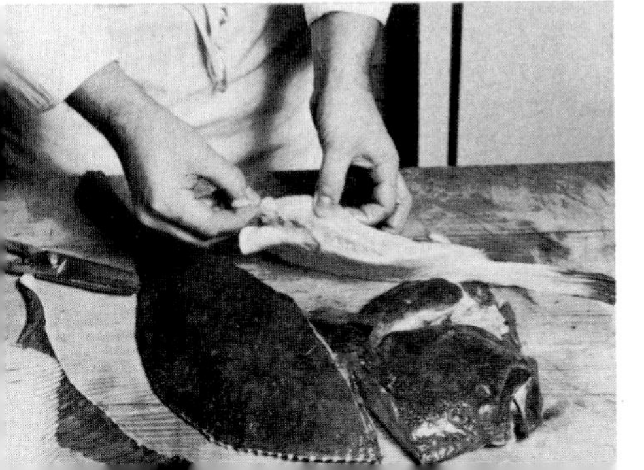

Cut the stomach open on the black side to loosen and remove the stomach.

TURBOT (cont)

Cut the turbot into slices.

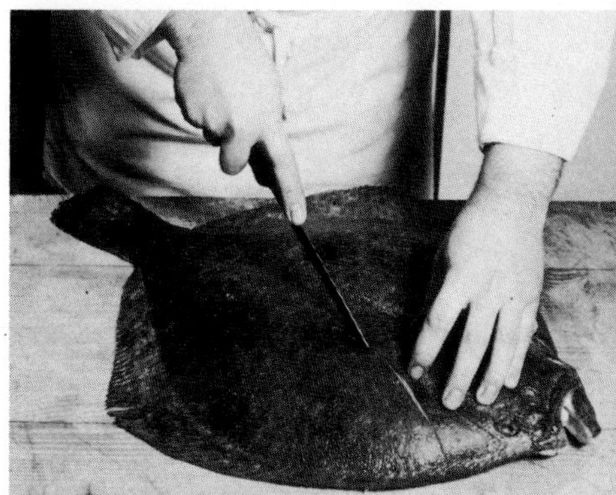

To fillet:

Place the fish flat on the board with the tail towards you. Make an incision in the flesh of the outside towards the centre, along the backbone . . .

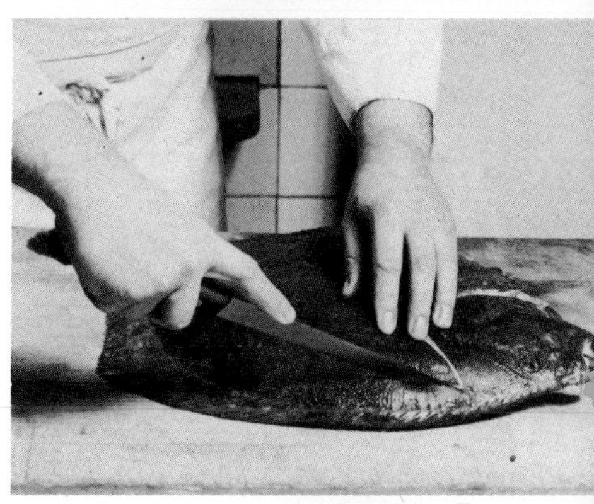

sliding the knife along towards the tail bone.

Incise, sliding the flexible knife between the bone and the flesh . . .

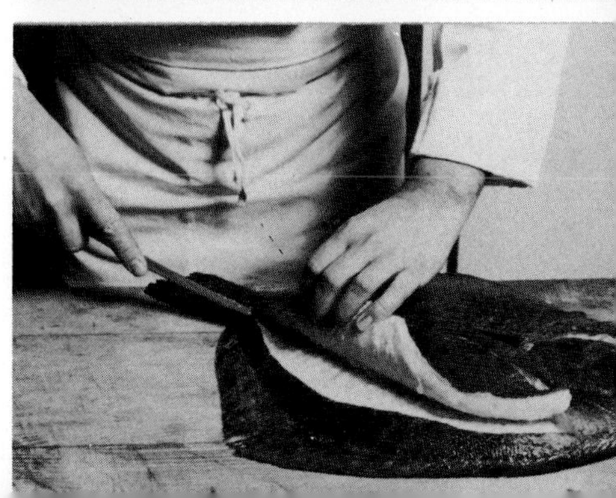

to detach the fillet.

TURBOT (cont)

Remove the fillet.

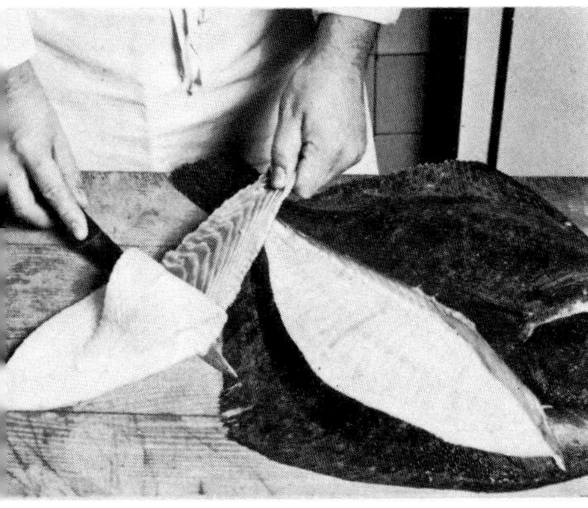

Lift the skin sliding the knife between the skin and the fillet.

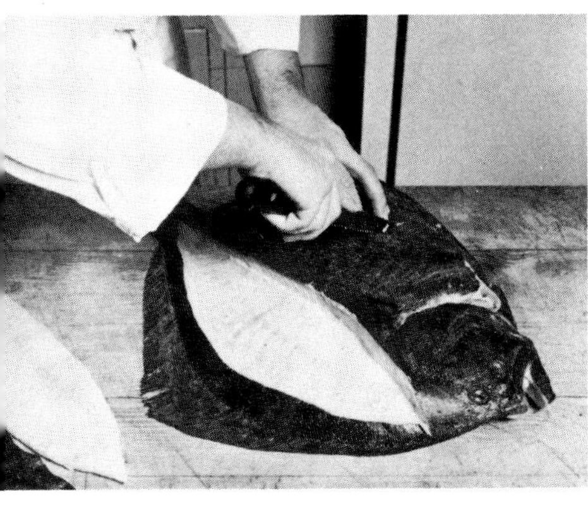

Remove the second fillet . . .

with the same procedure as for the first.

See the first fillet.

TURBOT (cont)

See the first fillet.

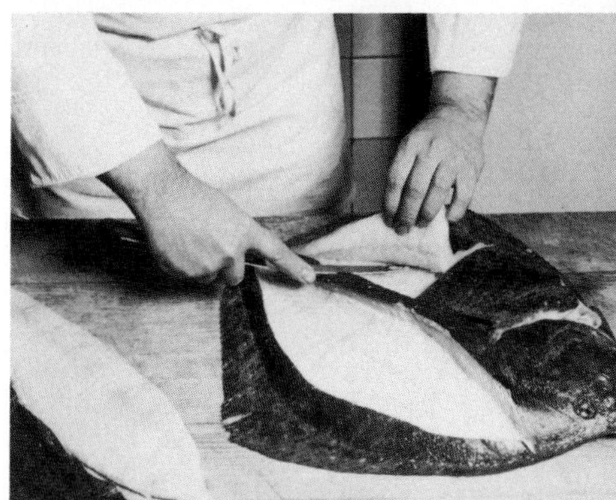

See the first fillet.

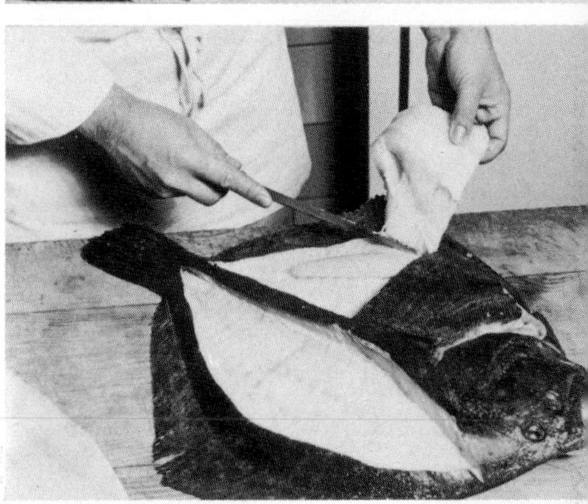

Detach the fillet with the help of a knife.

Remove the skin.

Turbot Taj Mahal (see page 225 and page 235).

Incise the fillet, sliding the blade of the knife . . .

TURBOT (cont)

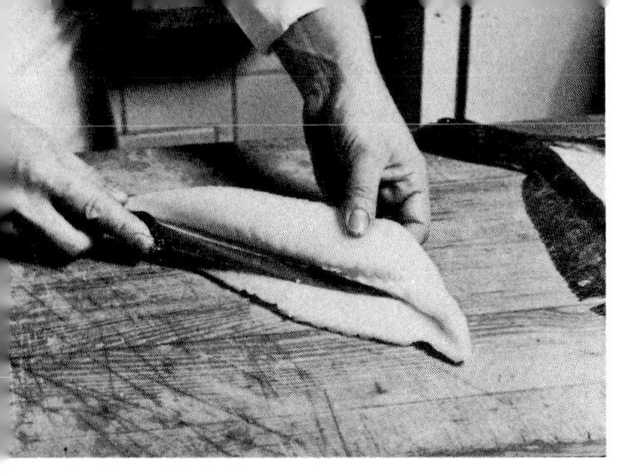

to divide it, taking care not to cut it in two.

Open the pocket obtained in this way and lightly beat to prevent curling.

Arrange the farce.

Roll the fillet.

Equalise the two ends of the roll thus obtained.

TURBOT (cont)

Place the roll on a damp cloth, roll over and over as if for making a galantine.

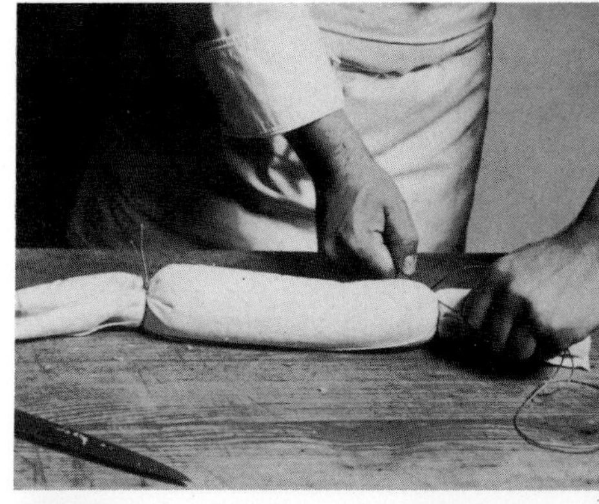

First tie each end.

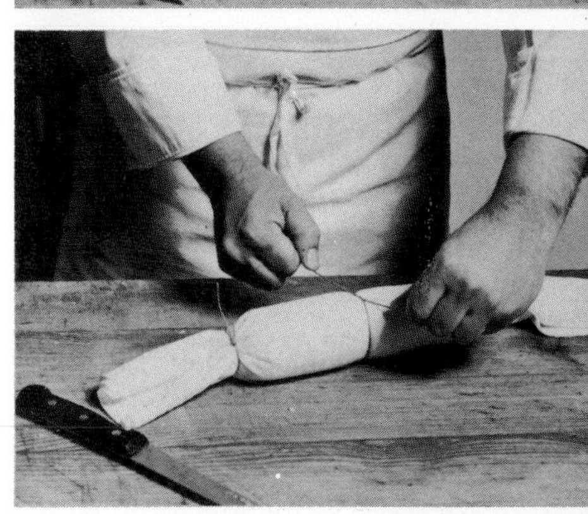

And then the middle . . .

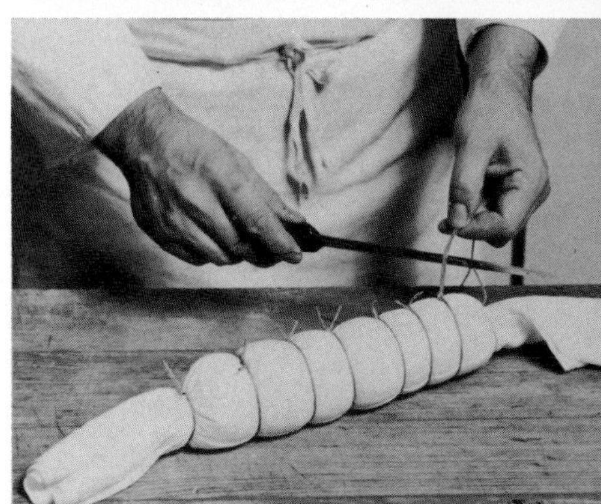

continue to tie the galantine alternating from either end. Poach.

MACKEREL

To fillet:

Cut off the head.

MACKEREL (cont)

Place the fish on the board, incise . . .

and cut along the stomach side to open the fish.

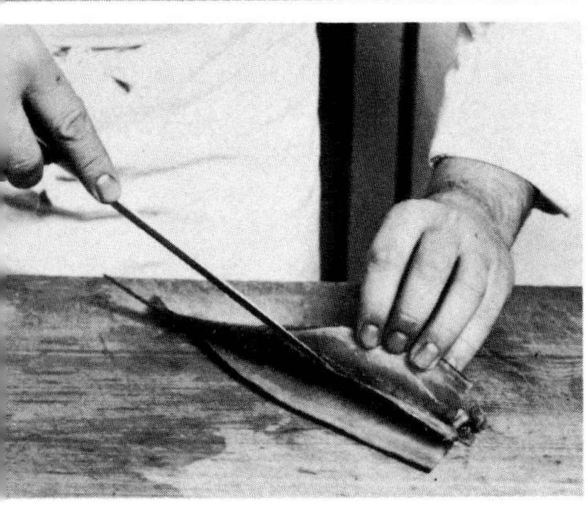

To remove the backbone, slit carefully and follow delicately the stomach bones.

Tear out the backbone.

Make an incision with the scissors to flatten the fish.

MACKEREL (cont)

The flattened fillets ready to be grilled.

SARDINES

Scale with a strong knife, holding very flat to avoid penetrating the flesh.

Incise the small fish to facilitate the cooking.

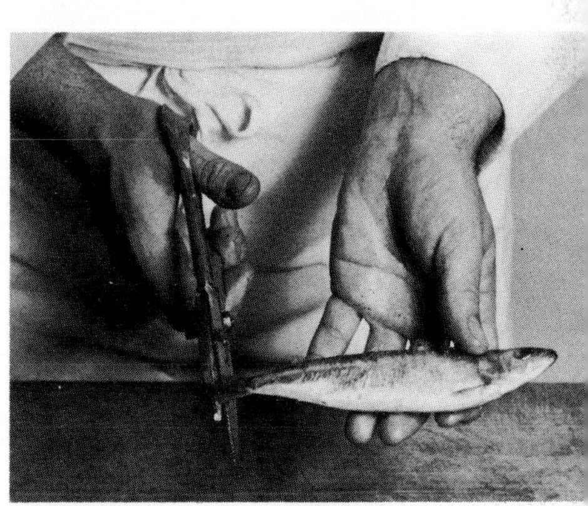

Cut off the tail fin.

To gut the sardines, carefully cut a strip in the stomach part . . .

SARDINES (cont)

and cut the head on the slant.

Introduce the index finger into the opening and remove with care the inedible superfluities.

Remove the intestine. The fish is ready for cooking. Sardines are preferably grilled.

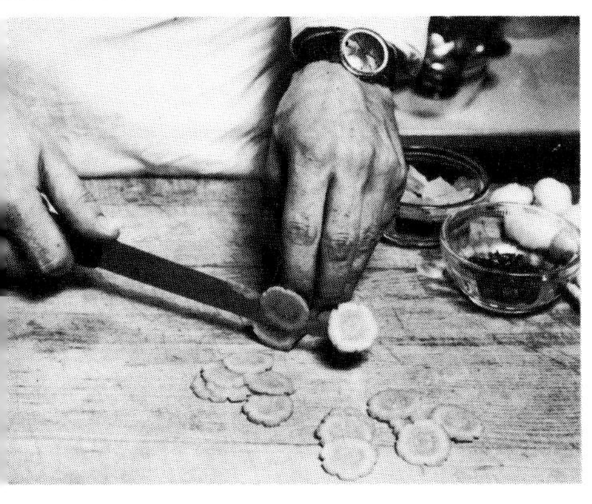

THE COURT-BOUILLON

(Recipes pages 53–54.)

Flute the vegetables (carrot, celeriac), and cut into roundels. Cut the onions into rings.

Fill the fish-kettle with water, add wine and vinegar, add the vegetables, bay leaf, clove and peppercorn.

DECORATION OF HARD-BOILED EGGS FOR COLD BUFFET

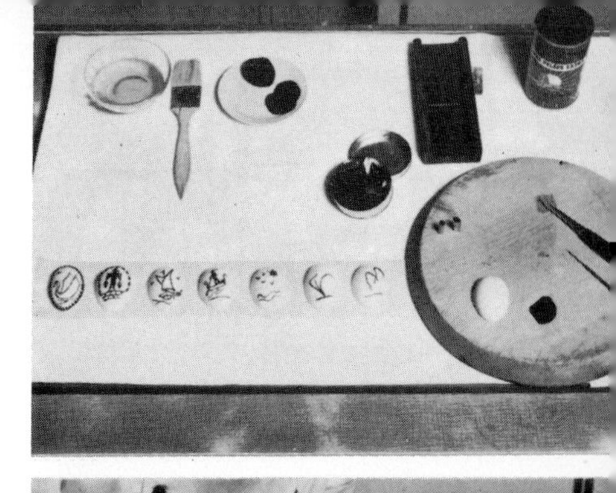

Divide the hard-boiled eggs lengthwise and put them on grease-proof paper. Cut the truffle into very fine slices and into strips or other decoration desired.

With a needle put these strips on the egg and decorate according to taste. Glaze with jelly. It is recommended to prepare a sketch of the decoration before cutting the truffle to avoid waste.

SALMON (large fish)

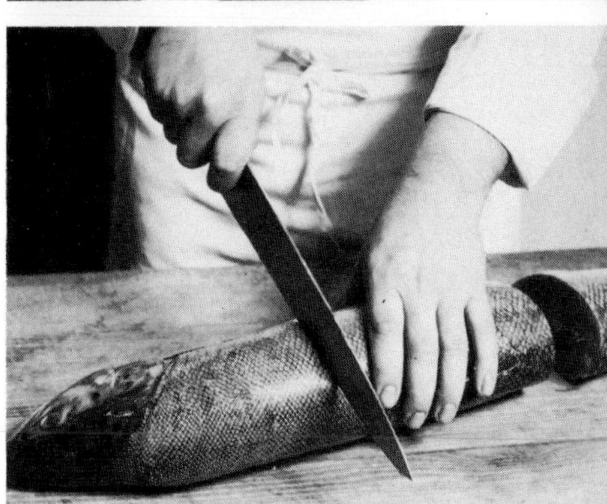

Cut the fins with scissors, scale with the back of a knife and cut up into thick darnes.

Cut off the stomach flap.

Cut the tail up into individual portions (darnes).

TROUT (large fish)

Remove the fins with the scissors, scale with the back of a knife to prevent cutting into the flesh.

For cold buffets:

Prepare and empty the trout through the gills. Secure to the grill of the fish kettle with the help of a strip of gauze or cotton. Never use string which would cut into the flesh.

To fillet:

Cut off the head.

Incise along the backbone.

Carefully follow the backbone sliding the knife towards the stomach and lifting the top fillet as you go . . .

TROUT (cont)

until the two fillets are freed.

Remove the bones and the inedible superfluities.

Cut off the ventral fin.

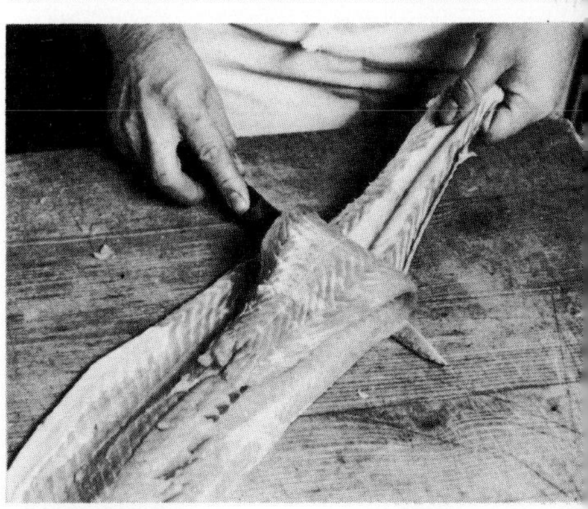

Lift the fillet and slide the knife between the flesh and the skin.

Cut up into suitable portions.

TROUT (cont)

For braising: butter a sauteuse, sprinkle with finely chopped shallots, arrange the fillet on top . . .

and sprinkle with white wine.

RIVER TROUT

To fillet:

Make an incision on the side of the head and . . .

follow carefully the backbone from the head to the tail to remove the first fillet. Cut along the stomach to separate the fillet completely. Turn the fish over and repeat the operation.

Remove the small bones and trim.

RIVER TROUT (cont)

Remove the skin

Paupiettes:

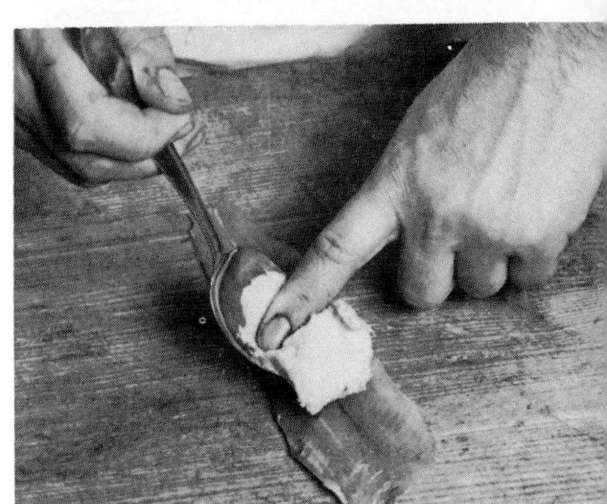

Spread with farce.

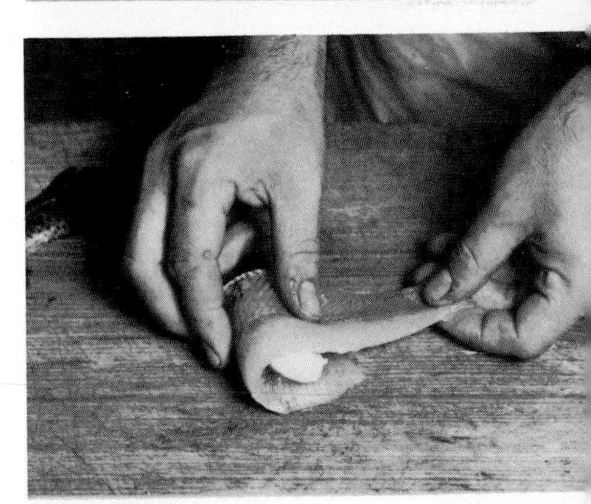

Roll the stuffed fillet to form a paupiette.

EEL

To skin an eel make a circular incision at the base of the head.

Turn the skin back . . .

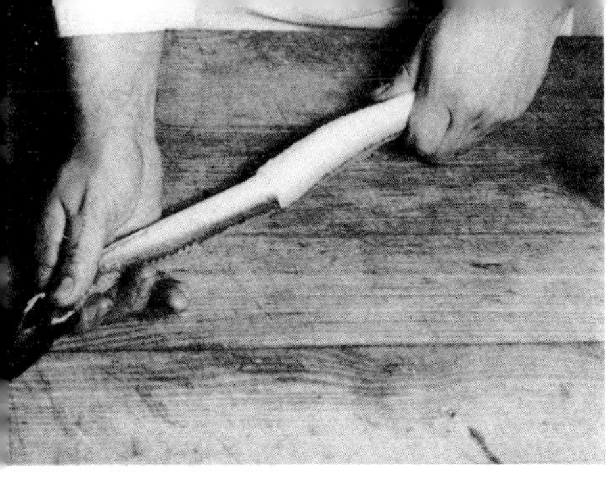

EEL (cont)

and rip it off briskly, holding the upper part of the fish firmly with one hand.

To fillet:

Cut the flesh along the backbone.

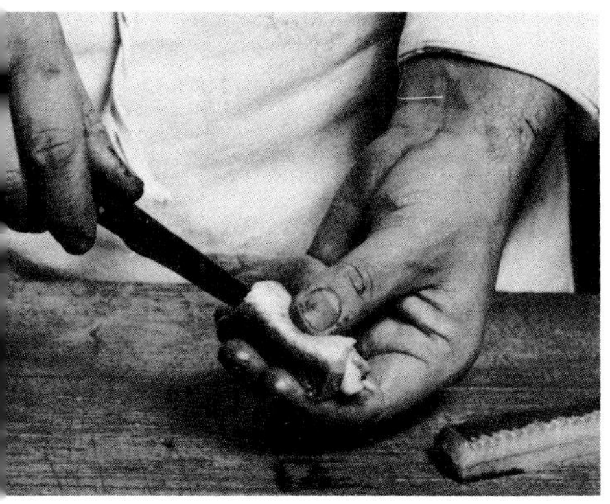

Cut the eel into troncons. Gut them by introducing a very pointed knife firmly into the stomach part . . .

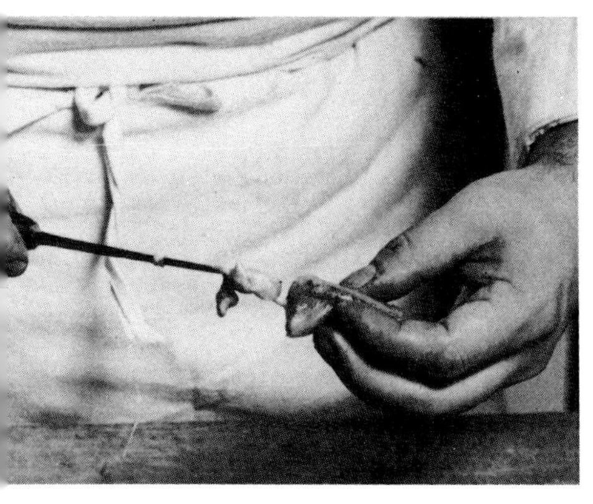

and push the intestines towards the outside. Remove the intestines by introducing the knife and withdrawing with a spiral movement.

CARP

Scale the carp.

CARP (cont)

To fillet:

Cut off the fins with scissors.

Cut off the head.

Remove the fillets by incising along the backbone according to the normal method used for large fish (see trout).

Trim the fillets.

Skin.

CARP (cont)

Cut the fillet into equal slices for braising.

WHITEFISH (small fish)

Au bleu:

Scale with a knife.

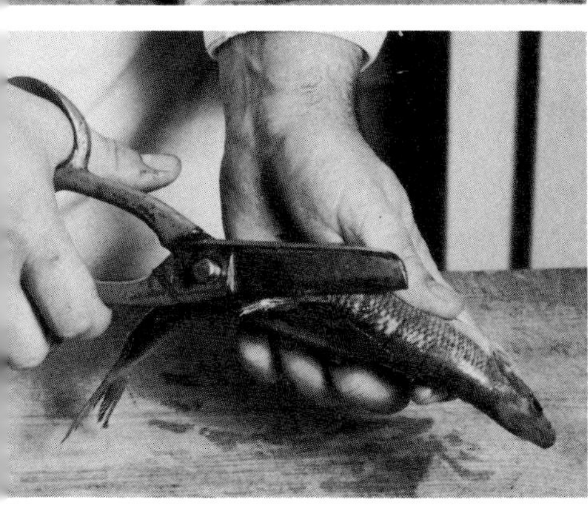

Cut off the fins with scissors.

Open the stomach and gut the fish.

Marinated fillets of whitefish:

(same method as for herrings etc.)

Incise . . .

WHITEFISH (cont)

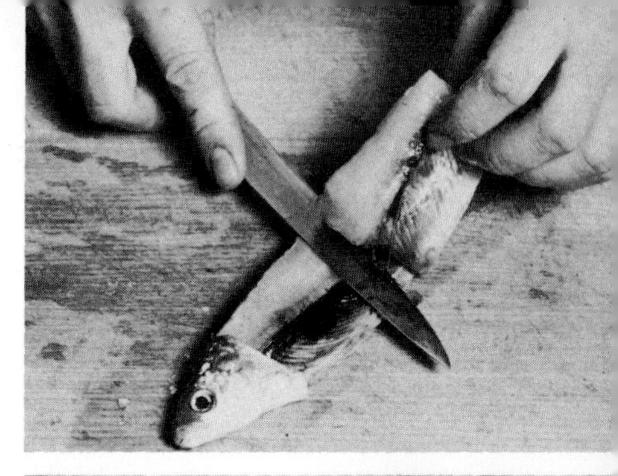

and slide the knife along the backbone, holding with the left hand the fillet being detached.

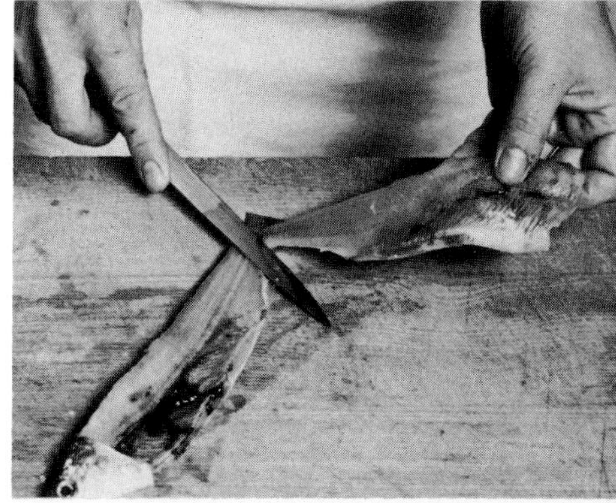

With the knife separate the end of the fillet from the backbone.

Detach the second fillet.

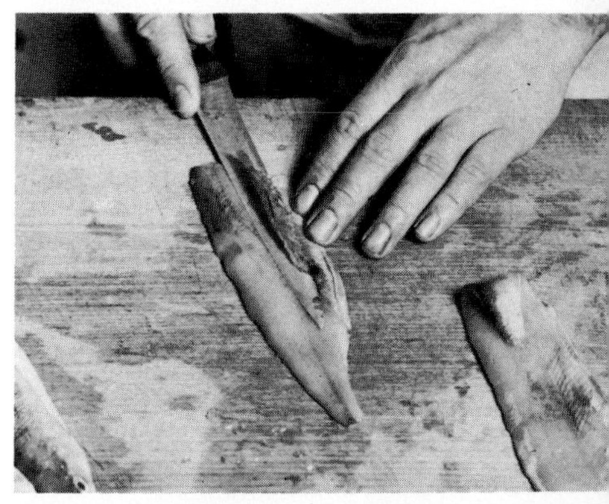

Trim and clean.

Season.

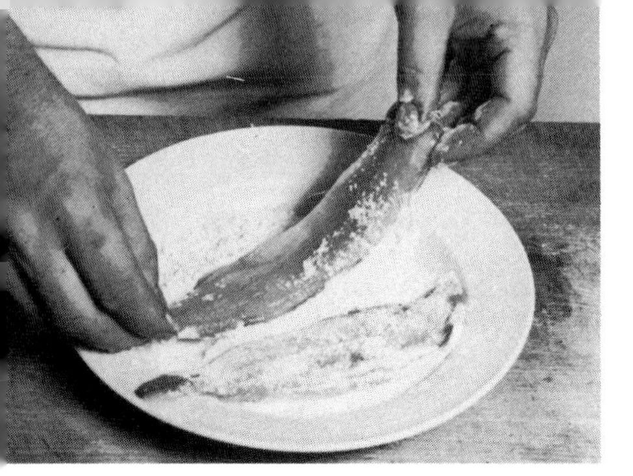

WHITEFISH (cont)

Flour and fry.

Put in a deep fire-proof dish, place roundels of lemon, bay leaves and peppercorns on the fish, sprinkle with a few drops of vinegar and stock or consommé.

LOBSTER AMERICAINE

Take a live lobster and remove the claws.

First method:

Split the lobster in two lengthwise.

Cut the joints to facilitate the removal of the meat of the claws and arms.

Crack the shells . . .

to remove the meat.

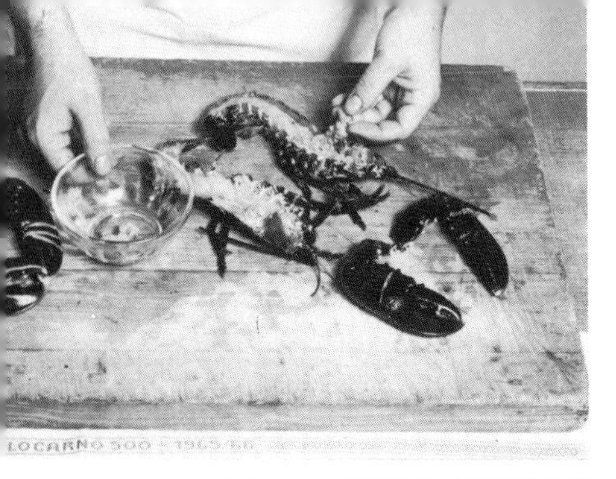

LOBSTER (cont)

Carefully retain the creamy part and the coral and put on one side.

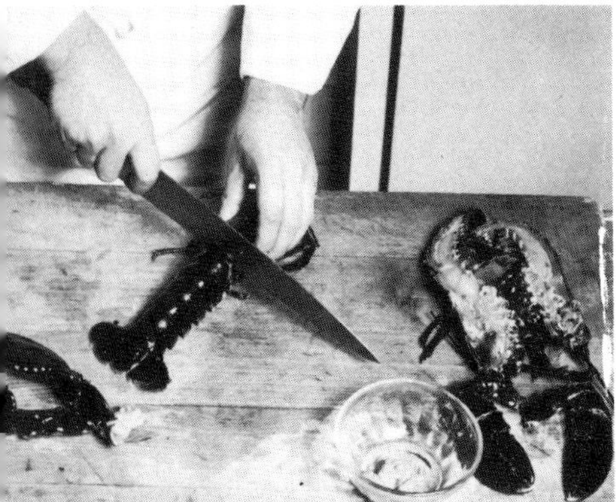

Second method:

Quickly chop the live lobster in troncons.

Split the head . . .

with a single stroke.

Remove the creamy parts and the coral and place on one side. These will be used for the preparation of the sauce.

COLD CRAWFISH

Fix the live crawfish on a small board . . .

with the help of string to keep it straight during cooking.

Tie round several times.

Secure the antennae.

COLD LOBSTER

Proceed as for the preparation of crawfish.

Crawfish and lobster ready for cooking.

COLD LOBSTER (cont)

How to split a cooked lobster.

Presentation for buffets:

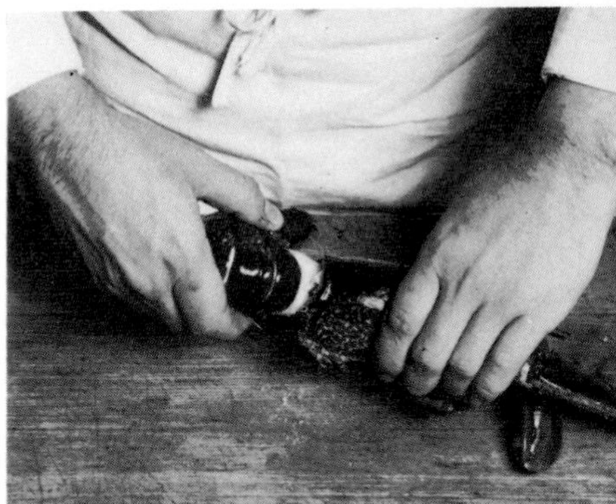

Carefully detach the tail by twisting it.

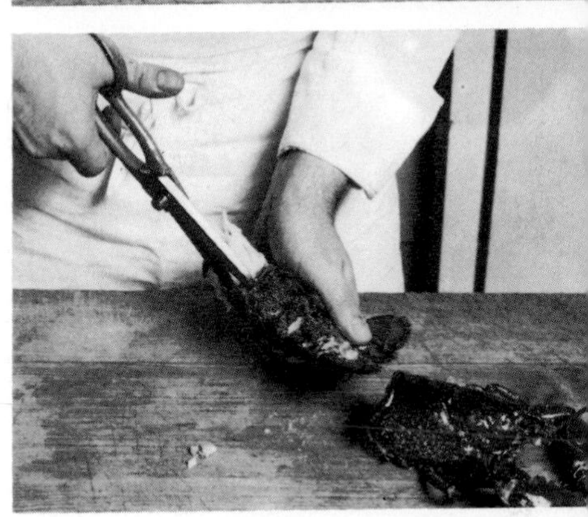

Make two incisions in the lower part.

Remove the meat carefully.

Continue removing the meat and cut into even medallions.

Continuation: see crawfish, page 99.

CRAWFISH PARISIENNE

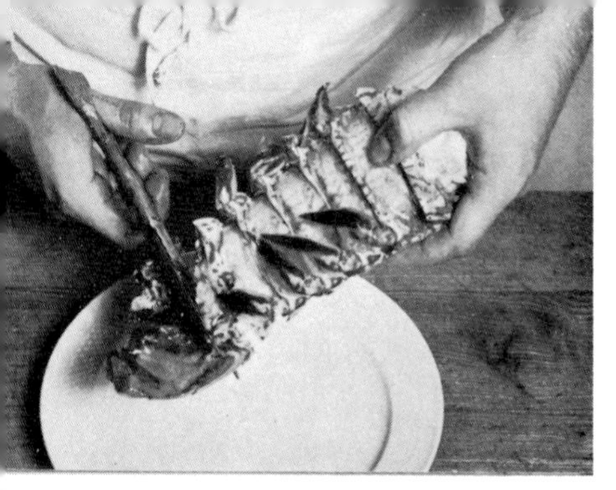

Detach the tail from the body and cut the ends.

Cut both sides of the lower part.

Remove the meat . . .

in one piece.

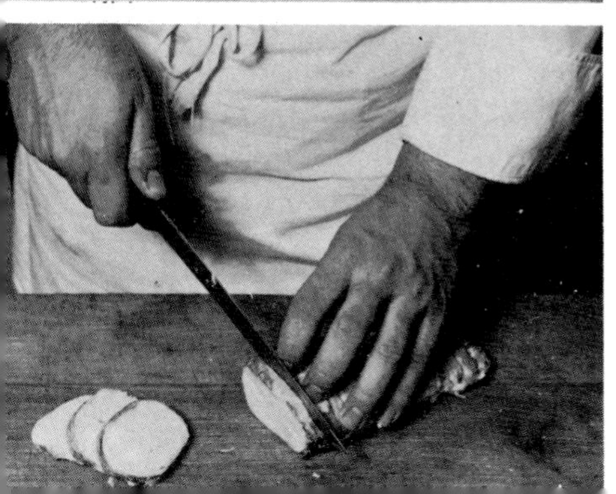

Cut into medallions.

CRAWFISH (cont)

With the help of a column cutter make suitable decorations in truffle blades, and, using a needle, place them on the medallions.

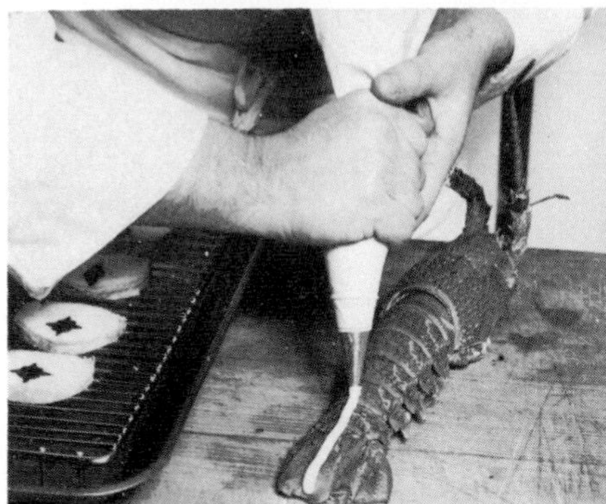

Glaze the medallions decorated in this way with jelly. Using a piping-bag and tube arrange a cordon of jellied mayonnaise on the empty shell . . .

and put the medallions on top, one slightly overlapping the other, the largest near the head.

CRAYFISH ASPIC

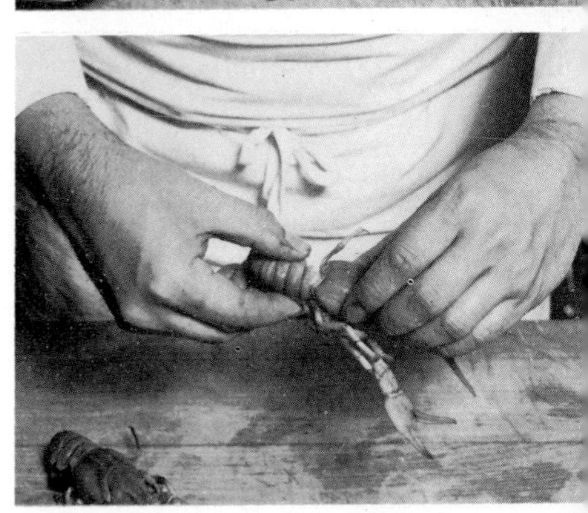

Detach the tail from the head.

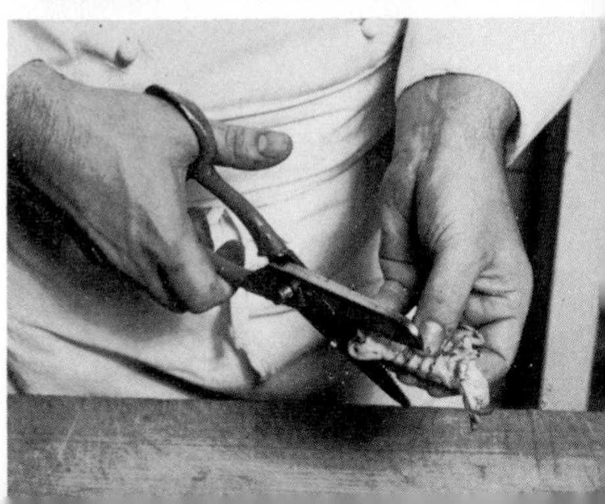

Remove the meat, by making two incisions with scissors in the lower part of the shell.

CRAYFISH ASPIC (cont)

Carefully remove the meat from the shell . . .

in one piece . . .

detach the arms and claws . .

and remove the meat: crack the shell with scissors.

And extract the meat with the hands.

CRAYFISH ASPIC (cont)

Preparation of aspic.

Embed the mould in crushed ice:
Pour in the liquid jelly.

Allow to stand until the jelly is set.

Pour off any liquid jelly, to leave a uniform layer of jelly on the bottom and sides.

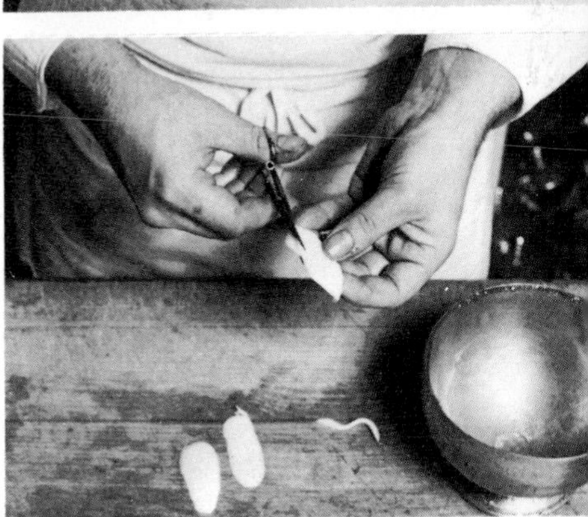

Cut decorations from cooked white of hard-boiled egg, for example flower petals.

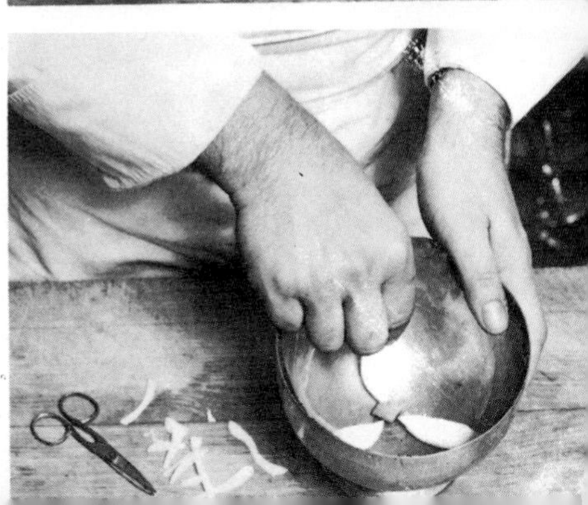

Place a roundel of gherkin in the centre with petals around.

CRAYFISH ASPIC (cont)

Carefully run a little jelly over the decorations with the help of a brush.

Re-embed the mould in the ice to set the jelly.

Line the mould with crayfish tails superimposed above each other. Fill the centre left empty either with a farce or jelly.

CRAB

Presentation of cooked crab.

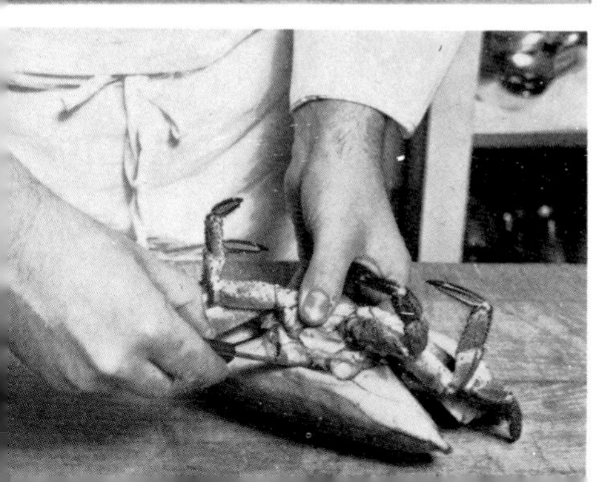

Make an incision . . .

CRAB (cont)

and introduce the knife into the shell.

Detach the legs, claws, tail, as well as the ventral part of the shell.

Remove the contents of the shell, scraping to remove completely. Flake the meat as well as that of the legs and claws.

SCAMPI

How to shell raw scampi (the same as for lobster, crawfish and crayfish).

OYSTERS

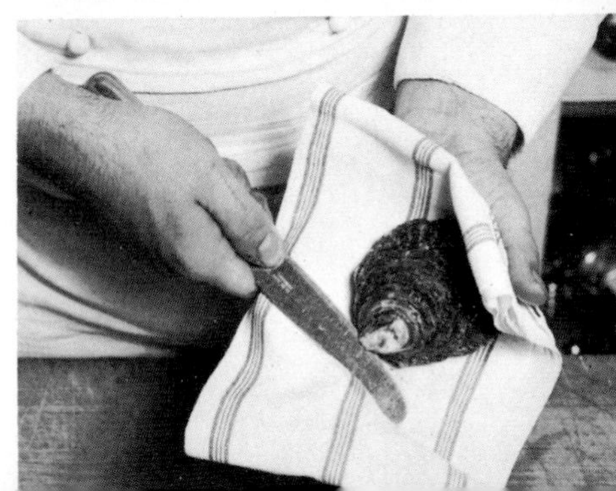

Open them at the moment of serving by forcing in the blade of a knife, using if possible a special oyster knife, starting from the hinge of the oyster.

OYSTERS (cont)

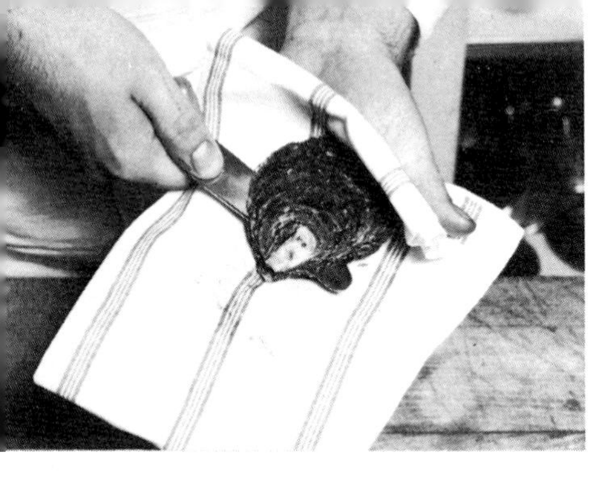

Break the ligament.

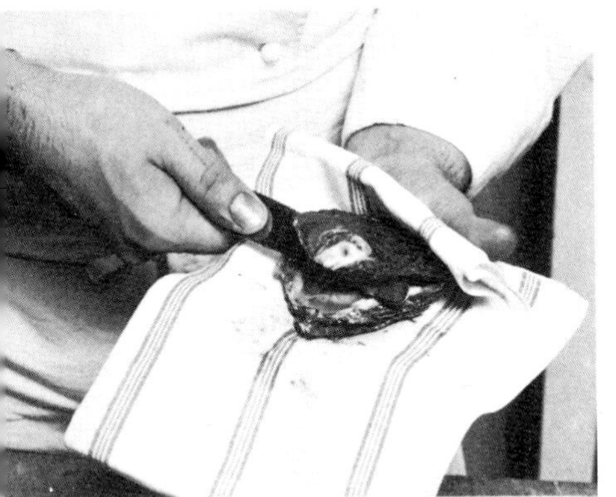

Cut the muscle.

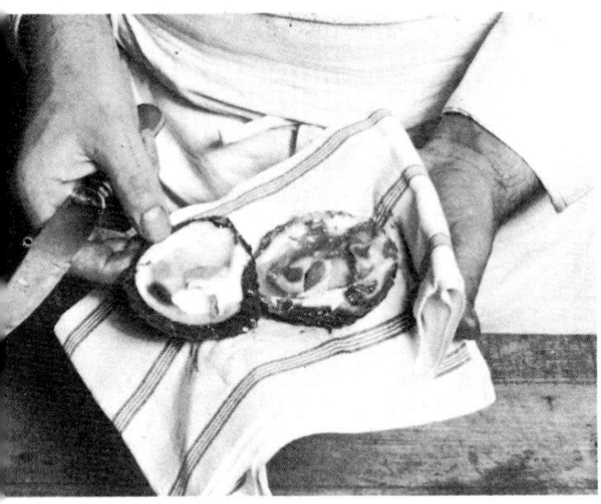

Lift the flat shell.

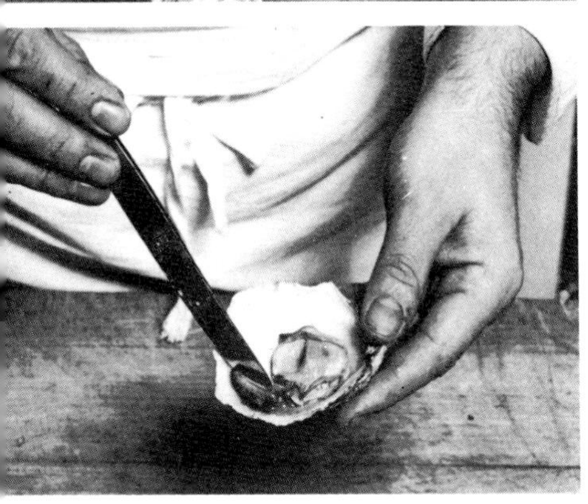

The oyster detached.

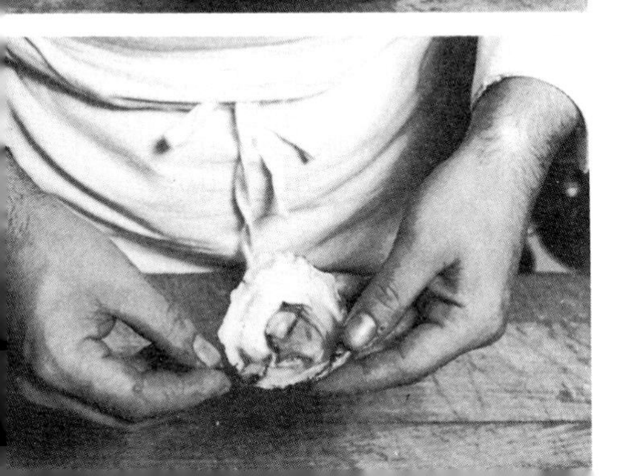

Eliminate the small flakes produced while opening.
Beard the oyster.

OYSTERS (cont)

Arrange the oysters in their deep shells on a bed of crushed ice, and, separately, lemons, and slices of brown bread and butter.

PRESENTATION OF CAVIAR

Caviar being very perishable it must be kept refrigerated. Served in its original tin on a socle of ice (for buffets) or, in an appropriate crystal bowl, on crushed ice, accompanied by lemon, toast and butter. In certain countries caviar is served accompanied by finely chopped onions and sour cream, always served separately as shown in the illustration

SCOLLOPS

Carefully introduce the blade of a knife between the two shells.

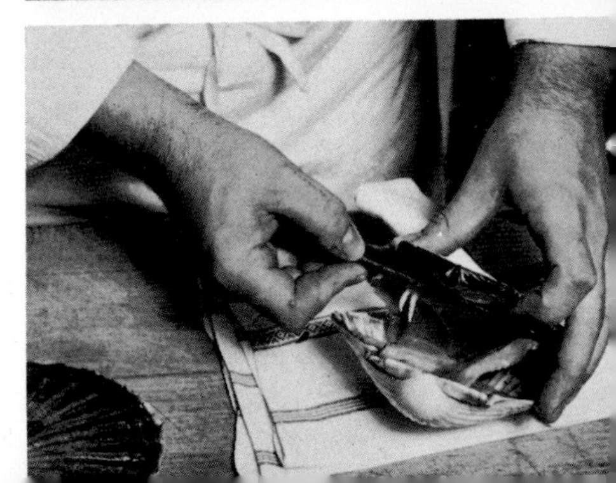

Lift the flat shell by fully twisting the knife just away from the membrane which is noticeable by its resistance.

SCOLLOPS (cont)

Loosen the scollop clinging to the flat or concave shell.

With the help of a knife with a flexible blade remove the scollop.

Detach from the shell.

Carefully separate the membrane and the beards surrounding the scollop . . .

as well as the reddish part, the coral. Clean the scollop and the coral in water to remove all trace of sand.

SCOLLOPS (cont)

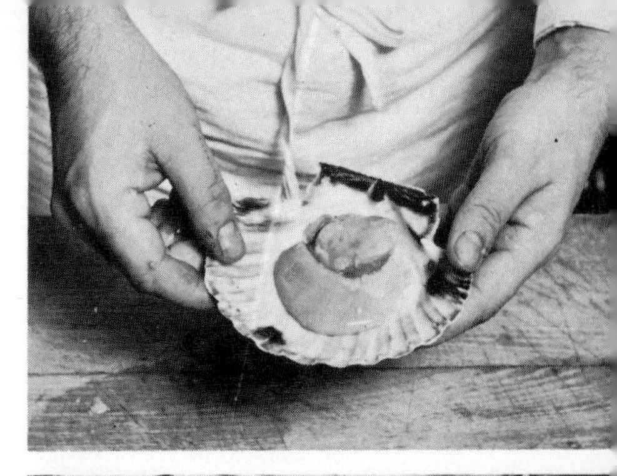

Wash the deep shell with care. It is used for the arrangement of the scollop according to the chosen recipe.

For poaching, butter a sauteuse and sprinkle with finely chopped shallot, place the meat and the coral in it, sprinkle with white wine and poach.

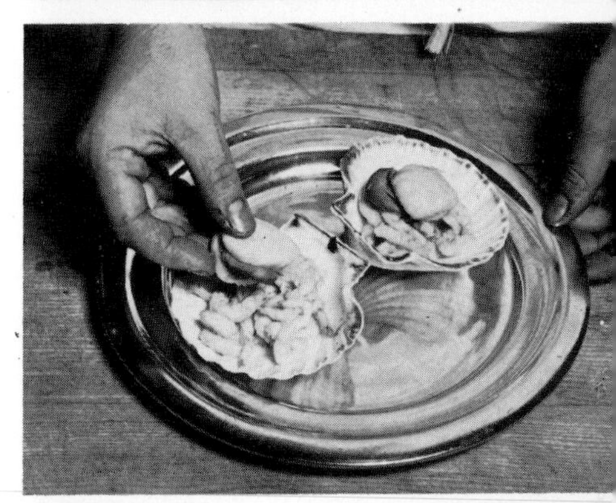

Example of preparation and presentation: Arrange picked shrimps in the shell and place the scollop and the coral on top.

Prepare a thick smooth sauce with fish velouté, sauce béarnaise and whipped cream. Work up this sauce . . .

and mask the sea-food with it. Gratinate under the salamander.

SCOLLOPS (cont)

Decorate the gratinated shells with a slice of truffle and a puff pastry crescent (fleuron).

Skewered scollops

Cut slices of smoked salmon into small rectangles of the same size as the scollop and the coral.

Skewer alternately scollops, coral and smoked salmon. Grill. Smoked salmon serves especially as an oily agent during the grilling.

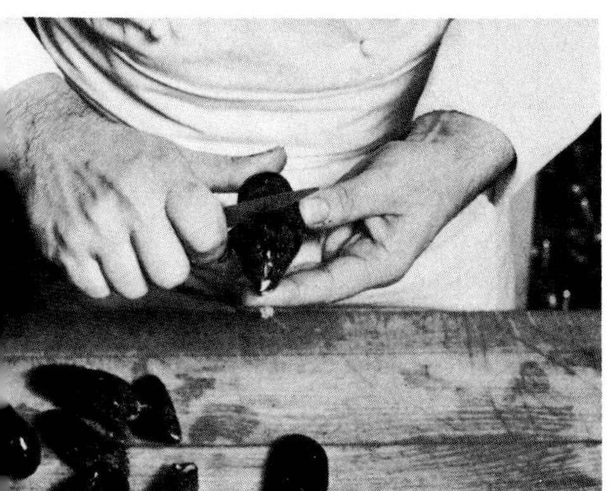

MUSSELS

Scrape and carefully remove the barnacles on the shells. Wash in plenty of water to rid them of sand.

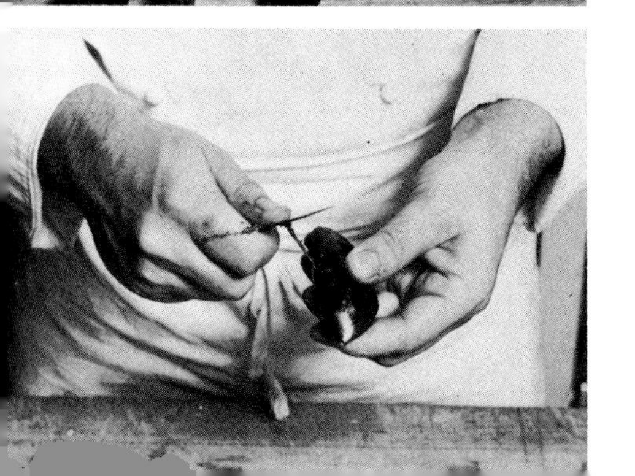

Beard them.

MUSSELS (cont)

Cooking marinière

Cook the mussels with white wine, chopped shallot and pepper—no salt.

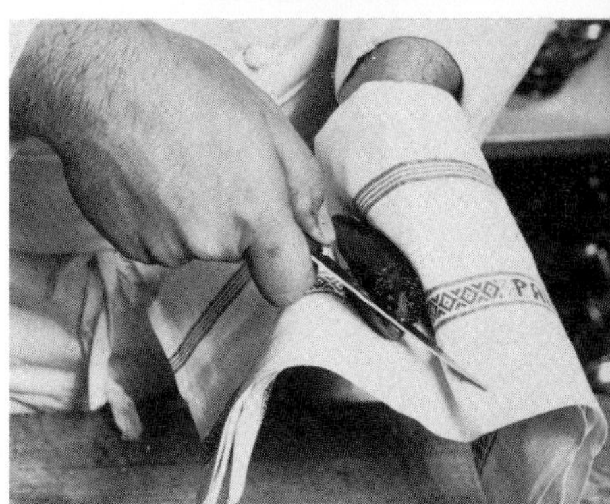

Raw mussels

The same procedure as for oysters. (See page 107.)

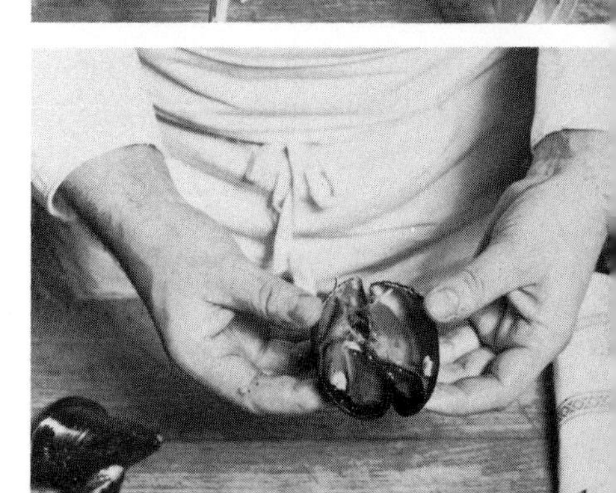

Presentation on crushed ice.

BROWN BREAD AND BUTTER (OR RYE BREAD)

Indispensable accompaniment with the serving of oysters or mussels for eating raw. Cut the brown bread (or rye bread) into thin slices.

BROWN BREAD AND BUTTER (cont)

Butter the slices . . .

and place on top of each other in regular layers. Divide up this cube . . .

and cut finger slices through it to be arranged on a serviette or paper napkin overlapping each other.

This arrangement is more attractive than the presentation of brown bread and butter in the form of triangles cut from sliced buttered brown bread.

POMMES DUCHESSE

It is important to utilise the appareil while still hot. With the help of a piping bag and suitable tube, pipe on to a buttered tray. Various shapes may be fashioned.

Restaurant Service

LOBSTER COCKTAIL

An ideal arrangement showing correct mise en place. (From the grillroom of the Coq d'Or, Hotel La Palma au Lac, Locarno.)

Place the lobster on the board with tail fully extended. Split the cold lobster lengthwise with a heavy knife, first the tail, then turn the lobster round and split the head.

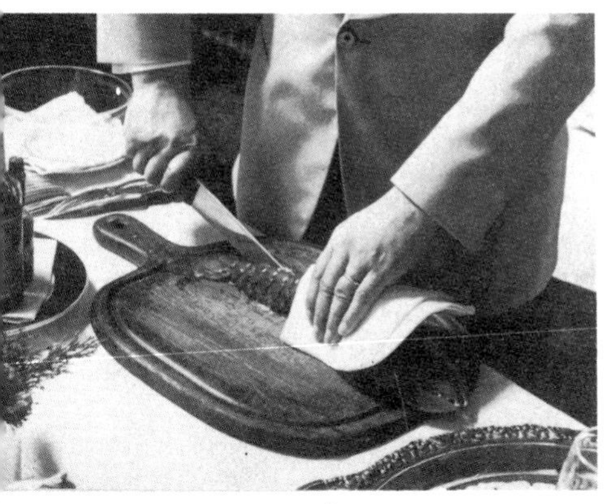

Insert the knife in between head and tail, holding the head with a napkin.

Remove the intestinal cord. Using a spoon and fork loosen the meat from the shell.

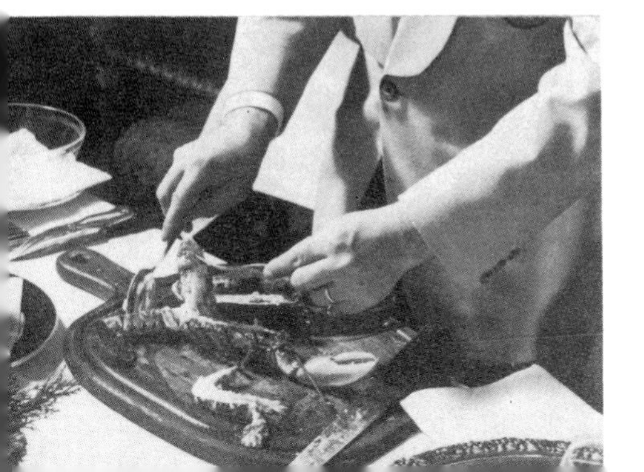

And lift out the meat with the fork.

LOBSTER COCKTAIL (cont)

With a knife remove the pincers and the arms to crack them.

Split the pincer in two, holding it from one side with a serviette.

Repeat the same operation if the arms are thick enough.

Detach . . .

and remove the claw-meat with the lobster-fork. and similarly any remaining meat from the arms,

LOBSTER COCKTAIL (cont)

Cut the tail-meat slantwise into scollops
of medium thickness.

Preparation of the cocktail sauce.

Put in the bottom of the cocktail goblet finely
shredded lettuce or other green salad.

Place the lobster meat on top.
Sprinkle with cognac or sherry according to the

taste and wishes of the customer.

LOBSTER COCKTAIL (cont)

Mask with cocktail sauce.

Garnish with a roundel of hard-boiled egg decorated with half a stoned black olive.

Garnish each cocktail with a lobster claw

PRAWN COCKTAIL

Using prawns proceed as for the preparation of lobster cocktail.

SOLE MEUNIERE

Presentation of the dish.

Lift the sole out of the serving-dish on to a hot plate.

Carefully remove the fin bones with a fish knife.

Make an incision from the head to the tail sliding the fish-knife along the backbone, as far as the tail.

Remove the fillet . . .

SOLE MEUNIERE (cont)

and put it back into the serving-dish.

Repeat the same operation with the second fillet.

Lift off the backbone and separate the fillets.

Re-form the fillets in the serving-dish, garnish with slices of lemon and serve.

CARPE AU BLEU

Presentation in a silver fish-kettle.

CARPE AU BLEU (cont)

Carefully lift the grill and suspend slantwise across the kettle, the tail of the fish towards the head-waiter.

Separate the vegetable garnish of the court-bouillon and set it aside.

Make an incision just behind the head, a second at the base of the tail and continue the length of the back following the backbone.

Make a second incision halfway down the fish above the backbone.

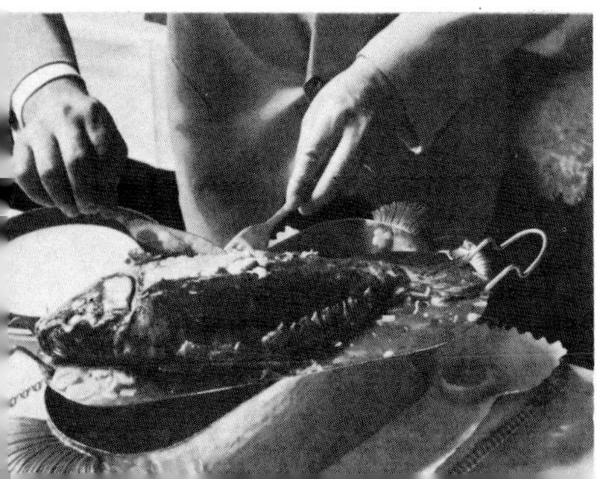

The skin is turned back and lifted off from the bottom.

CARPE AU BLEU (cont)

Skin the tail part.

Detach the fillet which lifts off easily.

Cut the fillet into portions on the slant.

The fillets lift off very easily. Re-assemble the fish on a serving-dish or serve individual portions on hot plates.

TRUITE DE RIVIERE AU BLEU

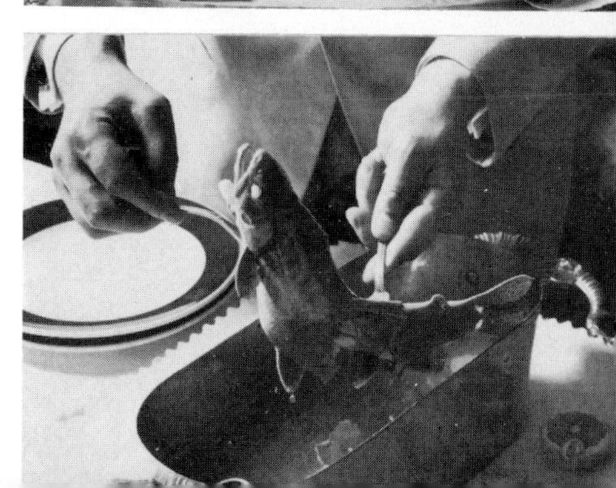

Take the trout out of the court-bouillon and lift it from the fish-kettle.

TRUITE DE RIVIERE AU BLEU (cont)

Place it on a hot plate and skin it with the help of a fish knife.

Remove the fins.

Slide the trout on to the customer's plate. (If he prefers present the trout in fillets: Remove the head, separate the fish into two fillets, sliding a knife between flesh and bone. Remove the fins. Arrange the two fillets on his hot plate.)

SCAMPI OR DUBLIN BAY PRAWNS FLAMBES

Recipe and method of M. Dario Brizzio, head-waiter, Hotel La Palma au Lac, Locarno. Ideal presentation and mise en place.

SCAMPI FLAMBES (cont)

Salt the scampi, presented raw on their shell.

Pepper: give a turn of the mill.

Melt table butter in the two pans a flamber one for the cooking of the scampi, the other for the preparation of the sauce.

Take care that the butter does not colour,

Stiffen the scampi in butter, sprinkle with Pernod.

SCAMPI FLAMBES (cont)

Flame the scampi with cognac.

Continue the cooking.

Preparation of the sauce in the other pan:

add some fish stock to melted butter.

Add dry white wine for the sauce.

Turn the scampi during their cooking.
Leave the sauce to cook gently in the other pan.

SCAMPI FLAMBES (cont)

Add the chopped parsley to the sauce.

Incorporate the cream with the sauce, stirring with the fork.

Baste the scampi with their own cooking-liquor and repeat continually.

Pour Pernod in the sauce.

Pour cognac over the scampi and flame.

SCAMPI FLAMBES (cont)

Remove the scampi from their cooking pan and put them into the sauce.

Baste the scampi copiously with sauce.

Repeat the operation several times.

Incorporate butter working it up to bind the sauce.

Add the yolk of egg, away from the fire, stir, and mask the scampi.

Preservation Procedures

Smoking

This very ancient method of preserving fish is used for herring, salmon, shad and several other fish. A different method is employed for the mackerel family and the scombrides. Smoked fish such as salmon and eel are expensive because of the difficulties in the operation for which there is a lack of highly skilled personnel.
Some firms smoke salted or frozen Canadian salmon. Obviously frozen salmon is not so good as fresh for this purpose. The best salmon for smoking come from Scotland, Norway and Ireland. The production of smoked trout is making progress in Germany and Holland and smoked and salted red herring is becoming popular in these countries.

Freezing

The most modern method of preservation of fish is freezing. This is done today on board fishing boats having large refrigerating rooms. The fresher the fish when frozen, the better it is; the more so since most fish are sold in portions.
There are several methods for freezing fish. According to the Ottensen method the temperature of the fish is reduced to 0° Centigrade and the fish is then plunged into a brine solution at —15° Centigrade. This rapid cooling prevents the cell tissues from any notable change. To prevent the fish from deteriorating the salt property of the solution must not be too strong. In other methods the fish is packeted and frozen at a speed of 1 cm. per hour at a temperature of —30° to —40° Centigrade. The temperature at the middle of the packeted portion must be —15° Centigrade or less. The fish is then stocked at —18° Centigrade.
The freezing of fish and shellfish is more or less universal. The gadoids, pleuronectes, salmonoids, shrimps, scampi, crawfish tails, etc. are also equally well frozen. Fatty fish when frozen develop an oily taste if they are stocked too long.
For restaurants with a large trade, fish portions, packeted and frozen, are a useful and practical solution.

Refrigeration

The cold prevents the development of micro-organisms and neutralises their action but does not destroy them. Refrigeration only prolongs the freshness for a short time. Refrigeration is not freezing. Fish used to be transported or kept in ice which caused appreciable damage.

Marinating

A marinade is an aromatised liquid used for impregnating fish. Marinades with white wine or vinegar are the best. To aromatise, tarragon or other plants are often added. The time for marinating is 3 to 4 days in summer and 6 to 7 days in the cold season. The herring is particularly good for marinating.

Salting and Brining

Salting is an excellent procedure for preserving, but foodstuff treated in this way changes its appearance, taste and smell. Salting without adding other elements is used for herring, cod, haddock, fresh cod, dried cod, and caviar.
Salting is rather like brining which is a composition of salt, sugar and saltpetre. Foodstuffs for brining can be kept in the solution for a long time.

Dehydration

The object of drying is to reduce the water-content in foodstuffs. It is done by exposure to the sun, hanging in fresh air or warm air. Freezing is sometimes done before drying. Cod and other fish of the same gadoids family are dried by hanging in the air. Thus the Stockfisch is a cod dried in the air and the Klippfisch is a salted cod dried in the air.

Sterilisation and Pasteurisation

Micro-organisms (bacteria, moulds, etc.) which are not resistant to a high temperature can be destroyed by sterilisation and pasteurisation.
Pasteurisation takes place at a temperature of 60° to 80° Centigrade. This method is particularly useful in dairy work.
Sterilisation is only achieved at a temperature above 100° Centigrade. Sterilisation is used for domestic and especially industrial preservation. Sterilisation is used to preserve in tins: shrimps, lobster, king crabmeat, crawfish, and fish, particularly salmon.

Canned Salmon

Canada, Japan, Siberia and Columbia are the main producers of tinned salmon.
Tinned salmon contains vitamins A and D; its average composition is 61% water, 20% albumin; 16% fatty matter, 3% salts. The category of the salmon is nearly always stated on the tin. Some varieties have artificial colouring.

The following distinctions are made:

Sockeye salmon: excellent quality, dull red colour, firm consistency and very small vertebrae.
Chinook salmon, spring salmon: of great value, lighter in colour, less firm in consistency, very large vertebrae.
Coho or silver salmon: less value, reddish-orange in colour, thick large vertebrae.
Pink salmon: mediocre value, pale pink colour, tender in consistency.
Chum salmon: mediocre value, grey and not very attractive colour, very large vertebrae.

Fish Sauces

Fish-Base Sauces

Sauce béchamel

Basic white sauce

For 2 litres: *325 gr. white roux; 2½ litres milk; 40 gr. minced onion; 1 sprig of thyme; 12 gr. salt; ½ bayleaf; 2 gr. crushed peppercorns; a pinch of nutmeg.*

Prepare a white roux. Moisten the roux with the boiling milk, add the onion and aromatics, salt, peppercorn and nutmeg, allow to cook gently for 1 hour, strain and cover with nuts of butter.

Sauce espagnole maigre

Lenten Spanish sauce for fish
Basic brown sauce with fish stock

For 5 litres: *500 gr. roux made with butter; 10 litres fish fumet; 100 gr. butter; 250 gr. carrots; 150 gr. onions; 250 gr. mushroom peelings; a sprig of thyme; 1 bayleaf; 1 dl. white wine; 2 kg. fresh tomatoes or the equivalent in tomato purée.* Cooking time: 5 hours.

Bring the fumet to the boil, bind with the prepared roux. Bring to the boil again, add the mirepoix of vegetables well coloured in hot shallow butter and deglazed with white wine. Allow the whole to cook for 2 hours over a low fire. Strain, allow to reduce for a further 2 hours, adding the tomato purée, or the fresh tomatoes. Strain and cover with buttered paper.

Sauce velouté de poisson

Basic fish sauce

For 5 litres: *6 litres fish fumet; 625 gr. blond roux.*

Moisten the roux with the fish fumet. Bring to the boil while stirring, allow to simmer for 1½ hours. Pass through a tammy cloth, cover with buttered paper.

Sauce allemande

Basic fish sauce with butter

For 2½ litres: *2 litres fish velouté; 1 litre fish fumet; ½ litre mushroom cooking liquor; 10 yolks of egg; nutmeg; white pepper; 1 lemon.* Cooking time: 12 to 15 minutes.

Put together in a sauteuse the cold velouté, the fish fumet, the mushroom cooking liquor and the yolks of egg. Mix well. Reduce by a good third at full heat while stirring constantly with a spatula. Season with a pinch of pepper and a pinch of grated nutmeg, add the lemon juice, pass through the tammy cloth.

Sauce chaud-froid de poisson

For 2 litres: *1½ litres fish velouté; 1 litre fish jelly; ½ litre fresh cream.* Cooking time: 15 minutes.

Put together in a sauteuse the velouté, the jelly and the fresh cream. Reduce by a third at full heat while stirring constantly with a spatula. Adjust for seasoning and consistency, pass through the tammy cloth.

HOT FISH SAUCES

Sauce américaine

For 6 persons: *1 lobster of 400 gr.; 3 dl. fish velouté; 1 dl. white wine; 1 dl. fish fumet; 2 chopped shallots; 2 peeled, pipped and chopped tomatoes or a soup-spoonful of tomato purée; 2 cl. cognac; 2 soup-spoonfuls of olive oil; 75 gr. butter; ½ a clove of garlic; 1 coffee-spoonful of chopped parsley and tarragon.* Cooking time: 25 to 30 minutes.

Cut the tail of the live lobster into tronçons or thick slices, break the claws to facilitate the extraction of the meat, split the trunk in two lengthwise, throw away the food sac, take out the creamy parts, mix them with 50 gr. of butter. Heat in a sauteuse the oil and the rest of the butter. Sauté the pieces of lobster in this until the shell has taken a fine red colour. Flambé with cognac, deglaze with white wine, add the fish fumet, a point of crushed garlic and the chopped tomatoes. Cover and cook in the oven for 15 minutes. Take out the pieces of lobster and extract the meat. Reduce the cooking liquor to 1 dl. and pass through the strainer (chinois). Heat this coulis, add it to the fish velouté, adjust for seasoning and consistency. Complete, away from the fire, with the butter and the creamy parts of the lobster, add the chopped parsley and tarragon, a pinch of Cayenne pepper, and the lobster meat cut into dice.

Sauce anchois

Anchovy sauce

For 6 persons: *4 dl. sauce normande; 50 gr. anchovy butter; 25 gr. anchovy fillets cut up into small dice.*

Incorporate the anchovy butter into the sauce normande away from the fire, and add the diced anchovies.

Sauce aurore

For 6 persons: *3 dl. fish velouté; 1 dl. tomato purée; 50 gr. butter.* Cooking time: 15 minutes.

Incorporate the tomato purée with the velouté

and work up with the butter at the moment of serving.

Sauce bâtarde

For 6 persons: *175 gr. butter; 30 gr. flour; 2 egg yolks; 1 soup-spoonful of fresh cream; ½ lemon.* Cooking time: 5 to 8 minutes.

Blend 30 gr. of butter with 30 gr. of flour, add quickly to 4 dl. of boiling salt water (5 gr. salt). Mix briskly with the whisk, add a liaison of egg yolks and cream. Pass the sauce through a tammy cloth, work up with the rest of the butter, add a squeeze of lemon, adjust for seasoning and consistency.

Sauce béarnaise

For 6 persons: *2 coffee-spoonfuls of chopped shallot; 1 dl. white wine; 5 cl. tarragon vinegar; 25 gr. chopped tarragon; 2 gr. mignonette pepper; 3 egg yolks; 250 gr. melted butter; 1 small coffee-spoonful of chopped tarragon; ½ soup-spoonful of chopped chervil.* Cooking time: 15 minutes.

Reduce until almost dry the white wine and the tarragon vinegar with the chopped tarragon and chervil and the mignonette pepper. Allow to cool slightly, add the egg yolks, and a pinch of salt. Work au bain-marie until the yolks begin to thicken. Work up little by little with the melted butter. Take care the sauce does not over-heat. Before passing through a tammy cloth, adjust for seasoning and consistency, and season with a pinch of Cayenne pepper. Complete with the chopped tarragon and chervil.

Sauce Bercy

For 6 persons: *4 dl. fish velouté; 1 dl. white wine; 1 dl. fish fumet; 1 coffee-spoonful of chopped shallot; 70 gr. butter; 1 coffee-spoonful of chopped parsley.* Cooking time: about 15 minutes.

Stew the shallot in the butter. Moisten with the white wine and the fish fumet. Reduce by a third, add the velouté, bring to the boil three or four times. Work up the sauce, away from the fire, with the rest of the butter, adjust for seasoning and consistency and complete with the chopped parsley.

Sauce Bonnefoy

For 6 persons: *2 dl. Bordeaux wine (dry Graves); 2 coffee-spoonfuls of chopped shallot; 4 dl. fish velouté; 1 small sprig of thyme; ½ a bayleaf; 1 pinch of mignonette pepper; ½ coffee-spoonful of chopped tarragon.* Cooking time: 15 minutes.

Reduce the white wine by half with: shallot, thyme, bayleaf, crushed mignonette pepper. Add the velouté, bring to the boil two or three times, pass through a tammy cloth. Adjust for seasoning and consistency and complete with the chopped tarragon.

Sauce bretonne

For 6 persons: *20 gr. white of leek; 20 gr. celery; 20 gr. onion; 20 gr. raw mushrooms; 4 dl. fish velouté; 2 soup-spoonfuls of fresh cream; 50 gr. butter.* Cooking time: 15 minutes.

Stew the julienne of leek, celery, onion and mushrooms for 4 to 5 minutes in butter, without colouring. Add the velouté, allow to cook for 5 to 6 minutes. Adjust for seasoning and finish the sauce with the cream and the butter.

Sauce canotière

For 6 persons: *1 litre of court-bouillon with white wine but very little salt and very aromatised; 40 gr. beurre manié; 75 gr. butter; Cayenne pepper.* Cooking time: 15 minutes.

Reduce the court-bouillon by two-thirds, and bind it with the beurre manié. Bring to the boil two or three times, work up with the butter, away from the fire. Adjust for seasoning and consistency and add a pinch of Cayenne pepper. Mixed with small glazed onions and small mushroom heads, this sauce may be served with the same fish as the sauce matelote blanche.

Sauce câpres

Caper sauce

For 6 persons: *4 dl. sauce bâtarde; 2 soup-spoonfuls of capers.*

At the moment of serving, incorporate the capers in the sauce bâtarde.

Sauce cardinal

For 6 persons: *4 dl. thick sauce béchamel; 1 dl. fish fumet; 5 cl. truffle essence; 1 dl. fresh cream; 50 gr. lobster butter.* Cooking time: about 12 minutes.

Reduce by one-quarter the béchamel to which has been added the truffle essence, the fish fumet and the cream. Work up with the lobster butter (or crayfish butter) away from the fire.

Sauce aux champignons

Mushroom sauce

For 6 persons: *5 dl. sauce allemande; 15 cl. mushroom cooking liquor; 60 gr. small cooked mushrooms.* Cooking time: 12 minutes.

Reduce by a good quarter the sauce allemande to which has been added the mushroom cooking liquor. Add the heads of very small mushrooms and bring to the boil again.

Sauce Chivry

For 6 persons: *1 dl. white wine; 5 gr. burnet leaves; 5 gr. tarragon; 5 gr. parsley leaves; 5 gr. chervil leaves; 5 gr. chive; 4 dl. fish velouté; 50 gr. Chivry butter.* Cooking time: 12 to 15 minutes.

With the cover on, infuse the herbs for ten minutes in the hot wine. Pass through a muslin, add the infusion to the velouté. Work up with the Chivry butter, away from the fire.

Sauce Choron

For 6 persons: *4 dl. sauce béarnaise; 3 soup-spoonfuls of very concentrated tomato purée.*

Prepare the sauce béarnaise without the final adding of chopped chervil and tarragon. Add the tomato purée.

Sauce crème

For 6 persons: *3 dl. sauce béchamel; 2 dl. fresh cream; lemon.* Cooking time: 10 minutes.

Reduce by a quarter the béchamel with 1 dl. of cream. Pass through a cloth strainer, heat, incorporate little by little the rest of the cream and the juice of ¼ lemon.

Sauce crevette

Shrimp sauce

For 6 persons: *4 dl. fish velouté; 1 dl. fish fumet; 1 dl. fresh cream; 50 gr. shrimp butter; 50 gr. shelled shrimp tails.* Cooking time: 12 minutes.

Reduce by a quarter the velouté to which the fumet and the cream have been added. Pass through a tammy cloth, and add, away from the fire the butter and shrimp tails. Adjust for seasoning and consistency and season with a pinch of Cayenne pepper.

Sauce curry

For 6 persons: *75 gr. chopped onion; 1 bunch of herbs; 1 pinch of cinnamon; 1 pinch of mace; 40 gr. butter; 1 small coffee-spoonful of curry powder; 3 dl. fish velouté; 2 dl. coconut milk; 1 dl. fresh cream; ½ a lemon.* Cooking time: 20 minutes.

Stew the chopped onion in the butter without colouring. Sprinkle with curry, cinnamon and mace. Moisten with the velouté and the coconut milk. Add the bunch of herbs, allow to cook gently for 15 minutes. Pass through a tammy cloth, add the cream, bring to the boil once or twice, complete with a little lemon juice.

Sauce diplomate

For 6 persons: *35 cl. sauce normande; 50 gr. lobster butter; 1 soup-spoonful of lobster meat in small dice; 1 coffee-spoonful of truffle in small dice.* Cooking time: 5 minutes.

Work up the sauce normande with the lobster butter and truffle and the diced lobster. Adjust seasoning and consistency.

Sauce estragon

Tarragon sauce

For 6 persons: *10 gr. chopped fresh tarragon; 4 dl. fish velouté; ½ a coffee-spoonful of finely-chopped tarragon.* Cooking time: 10 minutes.

Blanch the roughly-chopped tarragon, pound it in a mortar with 3 or 4 spoonfuls of velouté, and pass through a hair sieve. Add this purée to the hot sauce velouté; complete with the finely-chopped tarragon.

Sauce fines herbes

For 6 persons: *4 dl. white wine sauce (sauce vin blanc III); 25 gr. shallot butter; 1 soup-spoonful of parsley, tarragon and chervil in equal parts and chopped together.*

Work up the white wine sauce with the shallot butter. Add the chopped parsley, tarragon and chervil.

Sauce genevoise

For 6 to 8 persons: *6 dl. red wine; ¼ litre meatless half-glaze sauce; 250 gr. salmon head or salmon trout head, or heads of river trout; 1 dl. fish fumet; 70 gr. butter; 50 gr. carrots; 40 gr. onion; 6 parsley stalks; anchovy essence.* Cooking time: about 1½ hours.

Prepare a fine mirepoix with carrot, onion, parsley stalks, sprig of thyme, half a bayleaf. Toss in the butter, add the fish-head, stew for 15 minutes. Moisten with ½ litre of red wine and the half-glaze, allow to cook gently for 45 minutes. Pass through a tammy cloth, allow to stand for a few minutes, skim free from surface fat. Add the fish fumet and 1 dl. red wine, reduce to the desired consistency. Pass through a tammy cloth, complete with 50 gr. butter and a few drops of anchovy essence.

Sauce hachée

For 6 persons: *75 gr. chopped onion; 2 chopped shallots; 1 dl. vinegar; 3 dl. half-glaze; 1 dl. tomato purée; 2 soup-spoonfuls chopped ham; 1 soup-spoonful duxelles; 1 soup-spoonful chopped gherkins and capers; 1 coffee-spoonful chopped parsley; 40 gr. butter.* Cooking time: 15 minutes.

Brown gently in the butter the chopped onions and shallots. Moisten with the vinegar, and reduce by half. Add the half-glaze and the tomato purée, allow to cook slowly for 5 to 6 minutes. Incorporate the ham, duxelles, gherkins, capers and chopped parsley.

Sauce hollandaise

For 6 persons: *3 egg yolks; 300 gr. butter; 1 soup-spoonful of vinegar; 1 pinch of mignonette pepper; ½ a lemon.*

Reduce almost completely the vinegar to which 2 spoonfuls of water have been added. Add the crushed mignonette pepper and a pinch of salt. Allow to cool slightly. Add the egg yolks and a spoonful of cold water. Work au bain-marie with the whisk until thickening starts. Work up with the melted or softened butter, adding one or two coffee-spoonfuls of water. Adjust seasoning with salt and a few drops of lemon juice, and pass through a muslin or tammy cloth. Keep tepid in order not to 'turn' the sauce.

Sauce homard

Lobster sauce

For 6 persons: *35 cl. fish velouté; 7 cl. fresh cream; 30 gr. lobster butter; 20 gr. red butter.* Cooking time: 5 minutes.

Add the cream to the velouté and allow to cook gently for 2 to 3 minutes. Pass. Work up, away from the fire, with the lobster butter and the red butter. Adjust for seasoning and consistency. If the sauce accompanies a boiled whole fish, add a soup-spoonful of cooked lobster meat in small dice.

Sauce aux huîtres

Oyster sauce

For 6 persons: *4 dl. sauce normande; 2 soup-spoonfuls of oyster cooking liquor; 12 very small oysters.* Cooking time: 5 minutes.

Add the oyster cooking liquor to the sauce normande, allow to cook for a moment. Garnish the sauce-boat with the poached and bearded oysters.

Sauce italienne

For 6 persons: *100 gr. chopped raw mushrooms; 15 cl. white wine; 3 dl. meatless half-glaze; 1 dl. tomato sauce; 1 soup-spoonful chopped chervil; parsley and tarragon; 40 gr. butter.* Cooking time: 15 minutes.

Stew the chopped mushrooms in the butter. Moisten with white wine, and reduce by half. Add the half-glaze and the tomato sauce, and allow to cook gently for 6 to 7 minutes. Incorporate the herbs.

Sauce Joinville

For 6 persons: *4 dl. sauce normande; 25 gr. lobster butter; 25 gr. shrimp butter.* Cooking time: 5 minutes.

Work up the sauce normande with the lobster and the shrimp butter. If the sauce is served with a boiled fish without garnishing, add to it 1 coffee-spoonful of julienne of very black truffle.

Sauce Laguipière

For 6 persons: *4 dl. sauce bâtarde; 1 coffee-spoonful of fish glaze; ½ a lemon.*

Mix the sauce bâtarde with the fish glaze. Add the lemon juice.

Sauce livonienne

For 6 persons: *100 gr. julienne of carrot, celery, onion and mushrooms; 4 dl. fish velouté; 50 gr. butter; 20 gr. julienne of truffle.* Cooking time: 10 to 15 minutes.

Stew in the butter the julienne of carrot, onion, celery and mushrooms. Work up the fish velouté with the butter and incorporate the garnishing. Finish with the julienne of truffle.

Sauce marinière

For 6 persons: *4 dl. sauce Bercy; 2 egg yolks; 2 soup-spoonfuls of mussel cooking liquor.* Cooking time: 10 minutes.

Bind the sauce Bercy with the egg yolks and add to it a little mussel cooking liquor, according to the desired consistency.

Sauce matelote

For 6 persons: *4 dl. fish velouté; 25 gr. mushroom peelings; 2 dl. court-bouillon with white wine; 50 gr. butter; 6 small onions; 6 very small mushroom heads.* Cooking time: 15 minutes.

Reduce to a quarter the court-bouillon to which has been added the mushroom peelings. Pass and add to the fish velouté, bring to the boil two or three times. Garnish with the small onions cooked glacés à blanc and the cooked mushroom heads.

Sauce Mornay

For 6 persons: *4 dl. sauce béchamel; 1 dl. fish fumet; 30 gr. butter; 40 gr. grated cheese.* Cooking time: 10 minutes.

Reduce by a quarter the béchamel to which the fish fumet has been added. Add, away from the fire, the grated cheese and complete with the butter.

Sauce mousseline

For 6 persons: *4 dl. sauce hollandaise; 2 soup-spoonfuls of whipped cream.*

Incorporate the stiffly-whipped cream with the sauce hollandaise at the moment of serving.

Sauce mousseuse

For 6 persons: *250 gr. butter; salt; juice of ¼ of a lemon; 2 soup-spoonfuls of whipped cream; about 2 dl. cold water.* Cooking time, 15 minutes.

Heat slightly a shallow stew pan and place in it the butter previously well softened. Season and work constantly with the whisk while adding, little by little, the cold water and a squeeze of lemon. Complete with the very stiffly-whipped cream.

Sauce moutarde

For 6 persons: *4 dl. sauce bâtarde; 1 large soup-spoonful of mustard.* Cooking time: 15 minutes.

Mix the mustard, away from the fire, with the sauce bâtarde. Carefully avoid boiling the sauce after adding the mustard.

Sauce moutarde dijonnaise

For 6 persons: *1 coffee-spoonful of chopped shallot; 1 dl. white wine; 4 dl. white wine sauce; 2 soup-spoonfuls of Dijon mustard; 25 gr. butter.* Cooking time: 10 minutes.

Brown the shallot in the butter, moisten with the white wine, and reduce by three-quarters. Add the white wine sauce, bring to the boil once or twice, and add the mustard, away from the fire.

Sauce Nantua

For 6 persons: *4 dl. béchamel; 15 cl. fresh cream; 50 gr. crayfish butter; 9 small shelled crayfish tails.* Cooking time: 10 minutes.

Reduce by a third the béchamel to which has been added 1 cl. fresh cream. Pass and incorporate the rest of the cream with the sauce. Finish, away from the fire, with the crayfish butter and the crayfish tails.

Sauce Newburg

For 6 persons: *1 lobster of 400 gr.; 3 cl. cognac; 15 cl. madeira or marsala; 2 dl. fish fumet; 2 dl. fresh cream; 60 gr. butter; 2 soup-spoonfuls of olive oil.* Cooking time: about 30 minutes.

Cut up the raw lobster into thick slices, remove the creamy parts and pound them with 30 gr. of butter. Sauté the pieces in the hot oil and the butter until the shell has turned a red colour. Season, flambé in the cognac, deglaze with the madeira. Reduce the wine by two-thirds, add the fish fumet and the cream, and allow the lobster to cook gently for 20 minutes. Take out the pieces, remove the meat and cut it into dice. Add the creamy parts to the sauce, bring to the boil once or twice, and pass. Adjust seasoning and consistency and incorporate the lobster dice in the sauce.

Sauce noisette

For 6 persons: *4 dl. sauce hollandaise; 50 gr. beurre noisette.*

Mix the nut-brown butter with the sauce hollandaise.

Sauce normande

For 6 persons: *5 dl. oyster cooking liquor; 1 dl. mushroom cooking liquor; 2 dl. fumet of sole; 4 dl. fish velouté; 15 cl. fresh cream; 4 egg yolks; ¼ of lemon; 40 gr. butter.* Cooking time: 15 minutes.

Bring together in a sauteuse: the oyster cooking liquor, the mushroom cooking liquor, the fumet of sole, the fish velouté, and a liaison of egg yolks with 1 dl. of cream. Add a squeeze of lemon juice, and reduce by two-thirds at full heat. Add the rest of the cream, pass, work up with the butter, adjust for seasoning and consistency.

Sauce orientale

For 6 persons: *4 dl. sauce américaine; 5 gr. curry powder; 7 cl. fresh cream.* Cooking time: 10 minutes.

While adding the curry powder, reduce the sauce américaine by a quarter. Add the cream, heat without allowing to boil. Adjust for seasoning and consistency.

Sauce Poulette

For 6 persons: *1 dl. mushroom cooking liquor; 4 dl. sauce allemande; 30 gr. butter; 1 spoonful chopped parsley; lemon juice.* Cooking time: 8 to 10 minutes.

Reduce by two-thirds the mushroom cooking liquor. Add the sauce allemande, allow to cook for 2 or 3 minutes. Complete, away from the fire, with the butter, a squeeze of lemon juice and the chopped parsley.

Sauce ravigote

For 6 persons: *5 cl. vinegar; 1 dl. white wine; 4 dl. fish velouté; 50 gr. shallot butter; 1 soup-spoonful of chopped chives; tarragon and parsley in equal parts.* Cooking time: 10 minutes.

Reduce the vinegar and the white wine by three-quarters. Add the fish velouté, bring to the boil, and incorporate, away from the fire, the shallot butter and the herbs.

Sauce Récamier

For 6 persons: *15 cl. Rhine wine; 1 dl. champagne; 1 dl. fish fumet; 4 egg yolks; 150 gr. butter; ½ a lemon.* Preparation: 15 minutes.

Reduce the wine, the champagne and the fish fumet by two-thirds, allow to cool slightly. Mix the yolks with the reduction, let them set au bain-marie as for a hollandaise, and work up with butter. Season with salt, white pepper and lemon juice. Keep tepid in order not to 'turn' the sauce.

Sauce Régence

For 6 persons: *1 dl. Rhine wine; 1 dl. fish fumet; 20 gr. mushroom peelings; 10 gr. raw truffle peelings; 4 dl. thick sauce normande; 1 coffee-spoonful of truffle essence.* Cooking time: 5 to 7 minutes.

Reduce by half the wine and the fish fumet with the mushroom and truffle peelings. Pass the reduction, add it to the sauce normande. Complete with the truffle essence.

Sauce riche

For 6 persons: *4 dl. sauce diplomate; 40 gr. truffle; 1 coffee-spoonful of truffle essence.*

Complete the sauce diplomate with the truffle cut in small dice and the essence of truffle.

Sauce Rubens

For 6 persons: *100 gr. of brunoise of carrot, onion, celery; 1 dl. white wine; 3 dl. fish fumet; 1 soup-spoonful of madeira; 2 egg yolks; 100 gr. butter; 30 gr. lobster butter; 1 dash of anchovy essence.* Cooking time: 25 minutes.

Brown the brunoise in butter, add the white wine and the fish fumet, cook gently for 20 minutes. Pass the reduction through a conical strainer, add the madeira and bind with the egg yolks. Work up with the butter and the lobster butter, season with a dash of anchovy essence.

Sauce Saint-Malo

For 6 persons: *4 dl. white wine sauce (sauce vin blanc I); ½ soup-spoonful of mustard; 40 gr. anchovy butter; 1 dash of anchovy essence.*

Add the mustard and the anchovy butter to the white wine sauce, flavour with the anchovy essence.

Sauce Soubise

For 6 persons: *200 gr. chopped onion; 4 dl. béchamel; 7 cl. fresh cream; 75 gr. butter.* Cooking time: about 40 minutes.

Blanch the onion well, drain it, stew in the butter without colouring. Add the béchamel, season with salt, white pepper, and a pinch of sugar. Cook gently for 20 to 25 minutes. Pass through a tammy cloth, heat, and finish with the cream and a nut of butter.

Sauce Souchet

For 6 persons: *50 gr. carrot; 50 gr. parsley root; 50 gr. celery; 1 dl. white wine; 1 dl. fish fumet; 4 dl. white wine sauce (sauce vin blanc I); 50 gr. butter.* Cooking time: about 20 minutes.

Cut the vegetables into a julienne, and stew in butter. Moisten with the white wine and the fish fumet, reduce to a quarter. Add the julienne to the white wine sauce, bring to the boil once or twice, and adjust seasoning and consistency.

Sauce tomate

For 6 persons: *4 dl. fish velouté; 50 gr. tomato purée or 200 gr. fresh tomatoes; 1 small crushed clove of garlic; 25 gr. butter.* Cooking time: 15 minutes.

Add the tomato purée, or the peeled tomatoes cut into quarters, and the garlic to the velouté. Cook gently. Pass through a tammy cloth. Adjust seasoning and consistency. Complete with a nut of butter.

Sauce tyrolienne

For 6 persons: *1 dl. white wine; 5 cl. tarragon vinegar; 25 gr. chopped tarragon; 20 gr. chervil; 2 chopped shallots; 3 egg yolks; 1 dl. olive oil; 2 soup-spoonfuls of tomato purée; Cayenne pepper.* Preparation: 15 minutes.

Reduce by two-thirds the white wine and the vinegar to which has been added the tarragon, the chervil and the shallots. Pass through a tammy cloth, twisting strongly. Add the tomato purée and the egg yolks. Work up at the side of the fire as for a mayonnaise. Adjust seasoning and consistency and season with a pinch of Cayenne pepper.

Sauce Valois au Foyot

For 6 persons: *3 dl. sauce béarnaise; 1 coffee-spoonful of dissolved meat glaze.*

Mix the meat glaze with the sauce béarnaise.

Sauce vénitienne

For 6 persons: *1 dl. tarragon vinegar; 1 coffee-spoonful of chopped shallot; 10 gr. chervil leaves; 4 dl. white wine sauce (sauce vin blanc I); 35 gr. green butter; 1 coffee-spoonful of chopped tarragon and chervil.* Cooking time: 10 minutes.

Reduce by two-thirds the vinegar with shallot and chervil. Pass through a tammy cloth, twisting well. Add the reduction to the white wine sauce, work up with the green butter, and garnish with tarragon and chervil.

Sauce Véron

For 6 persons: *3 dl. sauce normande; 1 dl. sauce tyrolienne; 1 coffee-spoonful of fish glaze and ½ coffee-spoonful of anchovy essence.*

Mix the sauce normande and sauce tyrolienne and add the fish glaze and the anchovy essence. In place of the anchovy essence, the sauce may be completed with 30 gr. of anchovy butter.

Sauce Victoria

For 6 persons: *4 dl. lobster sauce; 30 gr. lobster meat; 30 gr. truffle.*

Add a garnishing of small diced lobster meat and truffle to the lobster sauce.

Sauce Villeroi

For 6 persons: *5 dl. sauce allemande; 1 soup-spoonful of truffle essence; 1 soup-spoonful of ham essence (optional).* Cooking time: about 10 minutes.

Mix the sauce allemande with the truffle essence and the ham essence. Reduce at full heat with the spatula until the sauce is thick enough to coat the back of the spatula.

Sauce vin blanc I

For 6 persons: *4 dl. fish velouté; 1 dl. fish fumet; 5 cl. white wine; 1 egg yolk; 40 gr. butter.* Cooking time: 10 minutes.

Mix the fish velouté with the white wine, the fish fumet and the egg yolk. Reduce by about a third. Adjust seasoning and consistency, and work up with the butter.

Sauce vin blanc II

For 6 persons: *4 dl. fish velouté; 1 dl. fish fumet; 5 cl. white wine; 4 soup-spoonfuls sauce hollandaise.* Cooking time: 10 minutes.

Mix the velouté with the fish fumet and the white wine. Reduce by a quarter. Adjust seasoning and consistency. Add the hollandaise away from the fire.

Sauce vin blanc III

For 6 persons: *5 cl. fish fumet; 5 cl. white wine; 3 egg yolks; 250 gr. butter; lemon; Cayenne pepper.* Cooking time: 15 minutes.

Reduce by half the fish fumet and the white wine. Allow to cool slightly, add the egg yolks, and work up with the butter as for a hollandaise. Season with a squeeze of lemon juice and a pinch of Cayenne pepper.

COLD FISH SAUCES

Sauce aïoli

For 6 persons: *4 cloves of garlic; 1 egg yolk; 3 cl. olive oil; lemon juice; salt; pepper.*

Pound the garlic finely in a mortar, season with salt and pepper, and incorporate the egg yolk with this purée. Add the olive oil drop by drop and a squeeze of lemon juice while working constantly with a whisk. If the sauce becomes too thick, add a few drops of boiling water.

Sauce albigeoise

For 6 persons: *1 soup-spoonful of capers; 1 soup-spoonful of small gherkins; 2 hard-boiled eggs; ½ a soup-spoonful of parsley; 4 anchovy fillets; 2 soup-spoonfuls of peppers cut in a julienne; 1 clove of garlic; 3 dl. oil; 1 dl. vinegar; salt; pepper.*

Pound well the hard-boiled eggs, the capers, the gherkins and the parsley and garlic, and pass all through a hair sieve. Season this purée with a pinch of salt and a pinch of white pepper, and work up with oil and vinegar as for a mayonnaise. Complete the sauce with the anchovy fillets cut in small squares and a fine julienne of peppers.

Sauce andalouse

For 6 persons: *400 gr. mayonnaise; 15 cl. tomato purée; 50 gr. red peppers.*

Mix the tomato purée with the mayonnaise, and incorporate the red peppers cut in a fine julienne.

Sauce antiboise

For 6 persons: *400 gr. mayonnaise; 1 coffee-spoonful of anchovy sauce; 2 soup-spoonfuls of tomato purée; 1 coffee-spoonful of chopped tarragon.*

Add the anchovy sauce to the mayonnaise and incorporate in it the tomato purée and the tarragon.

Sauce audoise

For 6 persons: *4 dl. sauce aïoli; 3 coffee-spoonfuls of capers, gherkins and shallot in equal parts; ½ coffee-spoonful of chervil and ½ coffee-spoonful of chopped parsley.*

Incorporate all the ingredients, finely chopped, with the sauce aïoli.

Sauce biarrote

For 6 persons: *30 gr. pipped red peppers; 1 soup-spoonful of tomato purée; 25 gr. onion; 15 gr. parsley; 350 gr. thick mayonnaise.*

Chop finely the red peppers, the onion and the parsley, mix them with the tomato purée. Incorporate all with the mayonnaise, and adjust seasoning and consistency.

Sauce bohémienne

For 6 persons: *¼ litre cold béchamel; 3 egg yolks; a dash of vinegar; 2 dl. olive oil; 2 soup-spoonfuls of tarragon vinegar; 1 soup-spoonful of mustard.*

Mix the egg yolks with the béchamel. Add a pinch of salt, a pinch of white pepper and a dash of vinegar. Work up the sauce with the oil and the tarragon vinegar as for a mayonnaise and complete with the mustard.

Sauce Chantilly

For 6 persons: *400 gr. mayonnaise; 3 soup-spoonfuls of whipped cream.*

Prepare the mayonnaise with the lemon juice instead of vinegar, while keeping it very thick. At the moment of serving incorporate in it the very stiffly-whipped cream; adjust seasoning and consistency.

Sauce cypriote

For 6 persons: *finely-chopped yolks of 4 hard-boiled eggs; 2 soup-spoonfuls tomato purée; 2 soup-spoonfuls anchovy butter; 1 coffee-spoonful chopped fennel; 400 gr. mayonnaise.*

Mix the egg yolks with the tomato purée and the anchovy butter, and add the chopped fennel. Incorporate all with the mayonnaise.

Sauce génoise

For 6 persons: *20 gr. pistachio; 15 gr. pine kernels or sweet almonds; 1 soup-spoonful béchamel; 2 egg yolks; 4 dl. oil; juice of 1 lemon; 1 soup-spoonful of mixed herbs; parsley; chervil; chive; tarragon.*

Pound finely the pistachio and the pine kernels with the béchamel, and pass through a fine hair sieve. Mix this purée with the egg yolks, a pinch of salt and a pinch of white pepper. Work up the sauce with the oil and the lemon juice as for a mayonnaise. Finish by incorporating the finely chopped herbs.

Sauce Gribiche

For 6 persons: *yolks of 3 hard-boiled eggs; 1 coffee-spoonful of mustard; 4 dl. oil; 1 soup-spoonful of vinegar; 50 gr. gherkins; 50 gr. capers; the white of 1 hard-boiled egg; 1 coffee-spoonful of chopped mixed herbs; parsley; chervil; tarragon.*

Pass the egg yolks through a hair sieve, and work them into a paste with the mustard, salt, white pepper, and a dash of vinegar. Work up the sauce as for a mayonnaise with the oil and vinegar, add the chopped gherkins and capers, the mixed herbs and the white of egg, cut into a short julienne.

Sauce mayonnaise

For 6 persons: *2 egg yolks; 1 soup-spoonful of vinegar or the equivalent of lemon juice; 3½ dl. oil; 6 gr. salt; 1 gr. white pepper.*

Whisk the egg yolks with the salt, white pepper and a dash of vinegar. Add the oil drop by drop at first and, when the sauce begins to thicken, increase the rate of flow. Break the sauce from time to time by adding vinegar. At the end add a soup-spoonful of boiling water to keep the mayonnaise from 'turning'.

Sauce occitane

For 6 persons: *4 dl. sauce verte; 2 soup-spoonfuls of julienne of peppers; 1 soup-spoonful of finely-chopped mushrooms; 3 cl. oil.*

Soften the julienne of peppers in the oil. After cooling, mix the julienne and the mushrooms with the sauce verte.

Sauce rémoulade

For 6 persons: *400 gr. mayonnaise; 1 coffee-spoonful of mustard; 20 gr. capers; 40 gr. gherkins; ½ soup-spoonful of mixed herbs; ½ coffee-spoonful of anchovy essence.*

Add the mustard to the mayonnaise. Add the capers, gherkins and herbs, all well minced. Bring up with the anchovy essence.

Sauce russe

For 6 persons: *50 gr. of creamy parts of lobster; 50 gr. caviar; 400 gr. mayonnaise; 1 coffee-spoonful of Worcestershire sauce.*

Pass through a fine sieve the creamy parts of lobster and the caviar while adding 2 soup-spoonfuls of mayonnaise. Add this purée to the rest of the mayonnaise. Complete the sauce with the mustard and the Worcestershire sauce.

Sauce tartare

For 6 persons: *yolks of 3 hard-boiled eggs passed through a fine sieve; 4 dl. oil; 1 soup-spoonful of vinegar; 1 soup-spoonful of mayonnaise; 15 gr. chives.*

Work into a smooth paste the egg yolks with a pinch of salt and a pinch of white pepper and the vinegar. Work up the sauce with the oil as for a mayonnaise. Blanch the chives, pound in a mortar, mix with the mayonnaise and pass through a hair sieve. Add this purée to the sauce.

Sauce Tolosa

For 6 persons: *250 gr. very thick mayonnaise; ¼ litre of tomato purée; 1 clove of garlic.*

Mix the mayonnaise with the tomato purée and complete the sauce with the finely-chopped garlic.

Sauce verte

For 6 persons: *20 gr. leaf spinach; 20 gr. watercress; 40 gr. parsley, chervil and tarragon in equal parts; 400 gr. mayonnaise.*

Blanch the herbs, drain, cool, and squeeze thoroughly and pass through a hair sieve while adding 2 soup-spoonfuls of mayonnaise. Mix this purée with the mayonnaise, adjust seasoning and consistency.

Sauce vinaigrette ou ravigote

For 6 persons: *3 dl. oil; 1 dl. vinegar; 20 gr. capers; 25 gr. chopped parsley; 20 gr. chopped chervil, tarragon and chive in equal parts; 30 gr. finely-chopped onion.*

Mix the oil well with the vinegar, season with salt and white pepper. Add the chopped capers, parsley, herbs and onion.

Sauce Vincent

50 gr. sorrel, parsley, tarragon, chive and burnet in equal parts; 30 gr. watercress; 30 gr. leaf spinach; yolks of 3 hard-boiled eggs passed through a hair sieve; 2 raw egg yolks; 4 dl. oil; 1½ soup-spoonfuls of vinegar; 1 coffee-spoonful of Worcestershire sauce.

Blanch the herbs, remove liquid by twisting in a cloth. Pass through a hair sieve with the yolks of hard-boiled eggs, incorporate the raw egg yolks and the vinegar. Work up the sauce with the oil, adjust the seasoning with salt, white pepper and Worcestershire sauce.

Savoury Butters

Garlic butter

100 gr. peeled cloves of garlic; 100 gr. butter.

Blanch the garlic and finely pound in a mortar; incorporate the butter and pass through a hair or fine wire sieve.

Anchovy butter

100 gr. de-salted and sponged fillets of anchovy; 100 gr. butter.

Pound the fillets finely in a mortar together with the butter. Pass through a fine sieve.

Bercy butter

½ soup-spoonful of finely-chopped shallots; 1 dl. white wine; 250 gr. diced beef marrow; 100 gr. softened butter; ½ lemon; 1 tea-spoonful of chopped parsley.

Reduce the white wine by half, together with the shallots. Allow to cool. Add the beef marrow, previously poached and cooled, the butter, lemon juice and chopped parsley, and mix well together. Season with salt and pepper.

Caviar butter

100 gr. caviar; 250 gr. butter.

Pound the caviar, add the butter, mix well together and pass through a hair sieve.

Mushroom butter

100 gr. very white raw mushrooms; 120 gr. butter; juice from ½ lemon.

Slice the mushrooms and toss quickly in hot butter, and pound in a mortar adding the lemon juice. Pass through a very fine sieve and work together with the softened butter. Season with salt and pepper.

Chivry or ravigote butter

125 gr. burnet, parsley, chervil and tarragon in equal proportion; 25 gr. chopped shallot; 125 gr. butter.

Blanch, cool, and remove all moisture from the herbs. Pound together with the blanched shallots, add the butter, and pass through a tammy cloth.

Colbert butter

200 gr. maître d'hôtel butter; 2 tea-spoonfuls of meat glaze; 1 soup-spoonful of chopped tarragon.

Combine the chopped tarragon with the meat glaze and mix with the softened maître d'hôtel butter.

Shrimp butter

150 gr. shelled shrimps; 150 gr. butter.

Finely pound the shrimps and add the butter. Pass through a very fine sieve.

Shallot butter

100 gr. peeled shallots; 125 gr. butter.

Blanch the shallots for 5 minutes, strain and remove all moisture. Pound well in a mortar, adding the butter. Pass through a tammy cloth.

Crayfish butter

150 gr. crayfish trimmings; 150 gr. butter.

Pound the crayfish trimmings cooked en mirepoix; add the butter and pass through a very fine sieve.

Epicure butter

Yolks of 6 hard-boiled eggs; 16 de-salted anchovy fillets; 1 coffee-spoonful of chives and tarragon; pinch of powdered mustard; ½ soup-spoonful of chopped gherkins; 150 gr. butter.

Pound together in a mortar the yolks, anchovy, chives and tarragon. Pass through a fine sieve, add the butter, mix well, season with salt, pepper and the mustard, and incorporate the gherkins.

Snail butter

For two dozen snails: *160 gr. butter; 15 gr. chopped shallots; 5 gr. crushed garlic; 1 soup-spoonful of chopped parsley; 6 gr. salt; 1 gr. white pepper.*

Soften the butter and work well together with the other ingredients. Reserve in the refrigerator.

Tarragon butter

250 gr. butter; 125 gr. very fresh tarragon leaves.

Blanch the tarragon leaves for 2 minutes, strain and squeeze out all moisture. Pound in a mortar with 50 gr. of the butter. Combine with 200 gr. butter, and pass through a hair sieve.

Smoked herring butter

6 fillets of smoked herring in oil; 250 gr. butter.

Drain and cut the herrings into dice, pound well in a mortar, add the butter and mix well. Pass through a fine sieve.

Lobster butter

150 gr. lobster eggs and creamy parts; 150 gr. butter.

Pound these ingredients together in a mortar and pass through a hair sieve.

Soft roe butter

150 gr. soft roes; 250 gr. butter; 1 coffee-spoonful of English mustard.

Poach, cool, and drain the soft roes and pass through a hair sieve, mix with the softened butter and finish with the mustard.

Maître d'hôtel butter

250 gr. butter; 1 soup-spoonful of chopped parsley; juice of ¼ lemon; 6 gr. salt; pinch of white pepper.

Soften the butter without melting until pliable, then mix in well the remaining ingredients.

Montpellier butter

100 gr. watercress, picked parsley, chervil, tarragon and chives in equal quantities; 25 gr. picked leaf spinach; 40 gr. chopped shallot; 1 clove of garlic; 8 fillets of anchovy; 3 gherkins; yolks of 3 hard-boiled eggs; 1 soup-spoonful of pressed capers; 2 dl. oil; 700 gr. butter; 3 raw egg yolks.

Blanch and cool the spinach, herbs and shallots. Squeeze out all moisture. Pound well in a mortar together with the garlic, anchovy and capers to obtain a fine paste. Incorporate the raw and cooked egg yolks, and the finely chopped gherkins. Gradually incorporate the oil and softened butter, mixing well with a whisk. Pass through a hair sieve, correct seasoning and heighten flavour with a dash of Cayenne pepper.

Mustard butter

250 gr. butter; 1½ soup-spoonfuls of dry mustard.

Soften the butter until pliable without melting, and add the mustard. Work well together and reserve in the refrigerator.

Paprika butter

250 gr. butter; 25 gr. pink paprika.

Incorporate the softened (unsalted) butter with the paprika.

Pistachio butter

75 gr. pistachio nuts; 125 gr. butter.

Blanch and skin the nuts. Pound in the mortar, adding a few drops of water. Incorporate the butter and pass through a hair sieve.

Horse-radish butter

250 gr. butter; 100 gr. grated horse-radish.

Pound the horse-radish together with the butter, and pass through a fine sieve.

Red butter

250 gr. of lobster or crayfish shells; 250 gr. butter.

Dry the shells, pound them thoroughly in a mortar, incorporating the butter. Melt in a bain-marie and pass through a muslin into iced water. Collect the solidified matter and press well in a muslin to remove all moisture.

Sardine butter

200 gr. sardines, free from skin and bones; 200 gr. butter.

Pound together in a mortar and pass through a fine sieve.

Smoked salmon butter

150 gr. of smoked salmon; 250 gr. butter.

Pound well together and pass through a fine sieve.

Truffle butter

100 gr. very black truffles; 1 soup-spoonful of sauce béchamel; 200 gr. butter.

Pound the truffles well with the cold sauce béchamel, add the butter and incorporate well together. Pass through a fine sieve.

Green butter

See Chivry butter.

Garnishes

The following are the principal garnishes for fish, simply giving the main ingredients of which they are made and from which they often take their name.

Américaine

Scollops of lobster tails cooked in the américaine style; blades of truffle, sauce américaine; and crescents of puff pastry (fleurons).

Cancalaise

Poached and bearded oysters; picked shrimps; sauce vin blanc.

Cardinal

Scollops of lobster tail; truffle blades; sauce Cardinal; fleurons.

Chambord

Decorated quenelles of fish farce; turned mushrooms; olive-shaped truffle pieces, goujons, egg and breadcrumbed; scollops of soft roes cooked meunière; cooked crayfish; sauce Chambord.

Chauchat

Thick roundels of plain boiled potatoes overlapping on the edge of the serving dish; sauce Mornay.

Commodore

Large fish quenelles decorated with truffle; crayfish tails; sauce normande with crayfish butter.

Dieppoise

Shelled prawns or shrimps; poached and bearded mussels; sauce vin blanc containing reduced poaching liquor.

Doria

Olive-shaped cucumber pieces cooked in butter, surrounding the fish cooked meunière.

Florentine

Bed of buttered leaf spinach; sauce Mornay.

Grand Duc

Buttered asparagus tips; shelled crayfish tails; truffle blades; sauce Mornay.

Joinville

Salpicon of mushrooms, truffles and picked shrimps bound with a sauce Joinville; fish topped with truffle blades; picked shrimps; sauce Joinville.

Marinière

Poached and bearded mussels; picked shrimps; sauce marinière.

Montreuil

Spoon-cut balls or olives of plain boiled potato masked with shrimp sauce, surrounding dish; fish masked with sauce vin blanc.

Nantua

Picked crayfish; truffle blades; sauce Nantua.

Niçoise

Skinned, pipped, diced tomato stewed in oil with a little garlic; anchovy fillets, stoned black olives; capers and chopped tarragon.

Normande

Poached, bearded oysters and mussels; picked shrimps; breadcrumbed deep-fried goujons; turned mushrooms; trussed crayfish; sauce normande; N-shaped fried croûtons.

Régence

Small spoon-shaped quenelles of whiting farce with crayfish butter; poached and bearded oysters; small turned mushrooms; scollops of cooked soft roe; truffle blades; sauce normande with truffle essence.

Riche

Medallions of cooked crawfish; truffle blades; sauce Victoria.

Trouvillaise

Picked shrimps; poached bearded mussels; turned mushrooms; shrimp sauce.

Tsarine

Cucumber olives cooked in butter; turned mushrooms; glazed with sauce Mornay.

Valois

Small olive-shaped plain boiled potatoes; scollops of poached soft roe; trussed crayfish and sauce Valois.

Victoria

Medallions of cooked crawfish; truffle blades; sauce Victoria.

Walewska

Scollops of cooked crawfish or lobster; truffle blades; glazed with sauce Mornay.

Wine and Fish

A work on fish would be incomplete if it did not include a few notions about wine, or rather the wines that go with fish.
Usually dry white wines accompany fish and shellfish. There are exceptions—fish prepared with red wine, for example, a matter of taste rather than any rule.
White Burgundy, dry white Bordeaux, and the wines from the Moselle and the Rhine, as well as the white wines of the Loire, are always recognised as acceptable. There are a great number of them and their names are best seen in a comparative table of years and growths of crûs.
The selection of this or that type of wine is influenced by the taste of the particular fish dish or the degree of condiments in the sauce. The same wine will not be drunk with raie au beurre noir as with grilled sardines or fillets of sole in sauce, or still less with trout au bleu or écrevisses à la nage.
As always in good cookery what matters is achieving the perfect marriage of wines and food. A fish in a sauce with wine in it must be accompanied by a wine of the same family.
A fine rare fish dish may well be accompanied by a splendid long-cherished wine.
Red wine can be taken perfectly well with a matelote or a meurette prepared in the same wine. But it is not obligatory, for it is the taste of the fish that determines the wine accompanying it.
A very dry vin rosé is perfectly suitable and this may be convenient at times. However, it must be a real rosé and not a substitute. This will avoid too heavy a meal which can happen if you have a succession of crûs.
Enthusiasts are not opposed to an 'entirely champagne' meal. True champagne, not mousseux, may well be one of the wines which best accompany grilled fish and shellfish.
We should remember, apart from what our table shows, that one of the most established principles for wine at table is that the progression must be constant. If fish is not the main dish and if your red wine is not very much better than your best white wine, a good dry white wine should be served. It must be at the right temperature, and not too heady. Your guests will be grateful for such a choice.
On the other hand, if the fish dish is the centre of the meal, what a pleasure it is to have one of those great white wines which, too often, are replaced on the wine list by the more sumptuous, but often overwhelming, red wines.

Germany

Caviar	Still and sparkling wines of the Saar and Moselle.
Oysters and shellfish (coquillages) Seafood	Full-bodied wines from Franconia, Baden and Württemberg. Dry mousseux wines.
Shellfish (crustacés) and grilled or poached fish	Full-bodied wines from the Saar and Moselle. Balanced wines from the Rheingau and the Palatinate (Rheinpfalz). Dry mousseux wines.
Fried fish or fish meunière	Wines from the best vineyards of Franconia, Nahe and the Palatinate.
Shellfish (crustacés) and fish in sauce	Still wines of the Nahe, Rheingau or Rhenish Hesse.
Fish cooked in red wine	The same wine as for cooking. For example: Ahrweiler, Assmannshäuser, Walporzheimer.
Fish in light sauce	The elegant growths of the Palatinate, the Rheingau and Rhenish Hesse.

France

Caviar Oysters and shellfish (coquillages) Seafood	Dry: Bordeaux: Bordeaux supérieur, Premières-Côtes, Graves. Burgundy: Chablis, Pouilly-Fuissé, Rully. Loire: Pouilly fumé, Sancerre, Quincy, Saumur, Savennières, Muscadet. Alsace: Riesling. Côtes du Rhône and Midi: Hermitage blanc, Condrieu, Cassis, Bandol, Bellet. True Champagne white wines.
Shellfish (crustacés) and grilled or poached fish	Dry: The same wines as for oysters and also equally recommended: Burgundy: Meursault, Montrachet, Corton-Charlemagne. Côtes du Rhône: White Châteauneuf-du-Pape. Champagne. Vins rosés. Dry rosés from the Midi: Bandol, Cassis, Bellet. Côtes de Provence. Côtes-du-Rhône: Tavel, Chusclan.

Shellfish (crustacés) and fish in sauce	Dry: Bordeaux: Graves. Burgundy: Chablis, Montrachet, Meursault, Pouilly-Fuissé. Loire: Pouilly fumé, Sancerre, Saumur, Anjou sec, Savennière. Alsace: Riesling, Pinot gris. Champagne. Red wines: For fish cooked in red wine, the same wine as for cooking. Lamproie bordelaise: Saint-Émilion, Médoc and Graves corsés.
Fish in light sauce (white butter, sauce mousseline)	Dry: see above. Mellowed: Bordeaux: Sauternes, Barsac, etc. Anjou: Côteaux-du-Layon. Alsace: Gewürztraminer.

Italy

Caviar	Coronata di Genova.
Oysters and shellfish (coquillages) Seafood	Vermentino (Savona). Vittoria (Sicily). Traminer (Bolzano). Cortese (Piedmont).
Shellfish (crustacés) and grilled or poached fish	Lugana (Desenzano). Soave (Verona). Pomino (Florence). Arbia (Siena). Orvieto seco. Verdicchio di Jesi (Umbria). Cinqueterre (Liguria).
Fried fish or fish meunière	Arbia (Siena). Lugana (Desenzano). White Chianti. Soave (Verona). Lacrima Cristi.
Shellfish (crustacés) and fish in sauce	Corvo bianco (Sicily). Lacrima S. Magdalenae bianco (Sicily). Falerno bianco (Naples).
Fish cooked in red wine	The same wine as for cooking. Examples: Bardolino, Valpantena, Valpolicella (serve at 12° Centigrade).

Fish in light sauce	Tokai del Friuli (Lison). Lacrima Cristi. Pomino (Florence).

Switzerland

Oysters and shellfish (coquillages) Seafood	Fine still white wines: Valais: Fendant (zones of Loêche and Monthey). Vaud: Dorin de la Côte, de Lavaux (Vevey-Montreux region). Neuchâtel: all crûs. Geneva: all crûs. Zurich: Riesling-Sylvaner, Räuschling. Ticino: Mendrisiotto. Vins mousseux 'brut'.
Shellfish (crustacés) and grilled or poached fish	(a) the same white wines as above, and also: Valais: Fendant from the best regions (Sierre, Sion, Conthey, Vétroz, Martigny). Riesling, Muscat, Ermitage, Johannisberg. Vaud: Dorin de Lavaux, Aigle and Yvorne. Neuchâtel: vins mousseux 'brut'. (b) rosés: Neuchâtel: Oeil de perdrix.
Fried fish or fish meunière	The same wines as above and also: Neuchâtel: white wines from the best zones: St. Blaise, Auvernier, Cressier. Fribourg: Vully. Berne: Schafiser, Twanner and vins mousseux secs 'brut'.
Shellfish (crustacés) and fish in sauce	Valais: Fendant (réserves spéciales), Ermitage, Amigne, Humagne, Arvine. Vaud: Dezaley, Aigle, Yvorne, Pinot gris. Neuchâtel: white Pinot, Pinot gris, mousseux. Eastern Switzerland: Pinot gris. Schaffhausen: Tokay.
Fish cooked in red wine	The same wine as for cooking. Pinot noir. Merlot VITI (Ticino).
Fish in light sauce (white butter, sauce mousseline)	The same white wines as in the above categories and full-bodied wines such as: Valais: Malmsey (Pinot gris). Pinot blanc and all the crûs bearing the denomination flétris. All the other specialities of French Switzerland, and those of eastern Switzerland, known under the denomination Spätlese.

Part II

RECIPES

Cold Hors-d'oeuvre

Anchovies

To free anchovies after being kept in salt, wash them and steep them in milk for 10 to 12 hours. Fillet and skin, and sponge the fillets. Each fillet may be cut lengthwise into two or three strips. Moisten the fillets with oil before use.

Anchois Côte d'Azur

For 6 persons: *24 anchovy fillets; 300 gr. potato salad; 24 rolled anchovy fillets; 24 stuffed olives; chopped yolk and white of 1 hard-boiled egg; 1 soup-spoonful of chopped parsley.*

Dress half the anchovy fillets on a bed of potato salad. Garnish around the dish with yolk and white of hard-boiled egg, chopped separately, and garnish with the stuffed olives rolled up in the rest of the anchovy fillets. Sprinkle all with chopped parsley. *(See illustration, page 170.)*

Anchois marinés

Marinated anchovies

For 6 persons: *1 kg. fresh anchovies; 2 dl. olive oil; ½ litre wine vinegar; 2 cloves of garlic; 2 bayleaves; 1 sprig of thyme; 8 or 10 peppercorns; 3 cloves; flour.* Cooking time: 4 to 5 minutes.

Gut the anchovies, clean and wash them, dry and flour them, and fry to a golden colour in very hot oil. Remove them from the pan and arrange in layers in an earthenware dish. During this operation bring to the boil the vinegar to which the garlic will have been added. Add bayleaf, thyme, pepper and cloves. Allow to cook gently for 5 minutes. Pass this marinade and pour it while still hot on the anchovies. Allow to marinate at least two days. Serve very cold, sprinkled with a part of the marinade.

Anchois nîmoise

For 6 persons: *24 anchovy fillets in strips; olive oil; chopped yolks of 3 hard-boiled eggs; 24 beetroot crescents.*

Dress the strips of anchovy in a trellis work pattern in the centre of an hors d'oeuvre dish on a bed of lettuce leaves. Sprinkle them with a few drops of oil and with the chopped egg yolk. Surround the hors d'oeuvre dish with the crescents of beetroot. *(See illustration, page 170.)*

Anchois norvégienne ou kilkis

Kilkis are available in tins. Arrange them on the hors d'oeuvre dish with a little of their liquor. Serve with butter and toast, separately. *(International cookery.)*

Anchois en paupiettes

For 6 persons: *24 anchovy fillets; 24 roundels of hard-boiled egg; 75 gr. butter; 24 stuffed olives; picked parsley.*

Trim and flatten the anchovy fillets, roll them into paupiettes. Stuff each paupiette with a nut of softened butter and place an olive on top. Dress the paupiettes on a roundel of hard-boiled egg. Garnish with picked parsley. *(International cookery.) (See illustration, page 171.)*

Anchois au poivron

Anchovies with red pimento

For 6 persons: *24 anchovy fillets; 24 thin strips of canned red pimento; yolk of 1 hard-boiled egg; white of 1 hard-boiled egg; 1 soup-spoonful of capers; 1 soup-spoonful of chopped parsley; olive oil.*

Dress the anchovy fillets on an hors d'oeuvre dish alternating them with the strips of red peppers. Sprinkle them with a few drops of oil. Border the hors d'oeuvre dish with yolk and white of egg, chopped separately, and with chopped parsley. Sprinkle with capers. Note: Fresh green peppers may also be used. *(International cookery.)* *(See illustration, page 171.)*

Rouleaux d'anchois

Anchovy rolls

For 6 persons: *24 anchovy fillets; 120 gr. fish purée; 100 gr. anchovy butter.*

Trim and flatten the anchovy fillets, roll them into paupiettes. Fill the centre with a fish purée using a piping bag. Decorate with anchovy butter. *(International cookery.)*

Anchois des tamarins

For 6 persons: *24 anchovy fillets; 300 gr. boiled potatoes, slightly cooled; 24 black olives; 1 soup-spoonful of chopped mixed herbs; oil; pepper; vinegar.*

Cut the potatoes into a coarse julienne, marinate them with a trickle of oil and a few drops of vinegar. Season with pepper, dress on an hors d'oeuvre dish and sprinkle with mixed herbs. Surround the salad with paupiettes of anchovy garnished with a black olive in the centre. *(International cookery.)*

Anguille fumée

Smoked eel (i)

For 6 persons: *600 gr. smoked eel; 1 lemon; lettuce leaves or jelly.*

Skin and fillet the eel. Cut up into slices of about 6 cm. in length. Dress them on lettuce leaves or on chopped jelly. Serve quarters of lemon, toast and butter, separately. *(International cookery.)*

Smoked eel (ii)

Cut into slices, skin and remove the bone. Re-form. Store as for smoked salmon. Serve on lettuce leaves with a fan of gherkin. Horse-radish sauce is served separately.

Anguille en gelée

Jellied eel

For 6 persons: *900 gr. eel, skinned and boned; 1¼ litres white wine court-bouillon; 2 egg whites; 2 lemons; 8 leaves of gelatine; 2 or 3 gherkins.* Cooking time: 20 minutes.

Cut up the eel into slices about 6 cm. in length and poach gently in a strong court-bouillon with white wine and the juice of a lemon. Drain the pieces, dress them on an hors d'oeuvre dish. Prepare a jelly with ¾ litre of court-bouillon, and the soaked gelatine. Clarify it with the beaten white of egg and a little water. Decorate the eel with roundels of gherkin and peeled half slices of lemon. Pass the jelly through a cloth and allow to cool. Pour this over the eels when it is half set, covering them completely. *(France.)*

Anguille hongroise

For 6 persons: *900 gr. skinned and boned eel; ½ litre court-bouillon; ¼ litre dry white wine; 1 small red pepper and 1 small green pepper; 6 leaves of soaked gelatine; 1 white of egg; 1 coffee-spoonful of pink paprika.* Cooking time: 15 minutes.

Cut up the red and green peppers into a fine julienne, blanch them for 3 or 4 minutes, cool and drain them. Prepare the eel as for the preparation of anguille au vin blanc et paprika. Arrange the fillets on an hors d'oeuvre dish and cover them with the peppers. Mask with jelly. *(International cookery.)* *(See illustration, page 172.)*

Anguille au vin blanc et paprika

For 6 persons: *900 gr. skinned and boned eel; ½ litre court-bouillon; ¼ litre white wine; 6 leaves of soaked gelatine; 1 white of egg; 5 gr. pink paprika.* Cooking time: 15 minutes.

Fillet the eel and cut each one up into 6 pieces. Poach in the court-bouillon and white wine; season with paprika. Drain the pieces and arrange them on an hors d'oeuvre dish. Prepare a jelly with the court-bouillon, the soaked gelatine and the lemon juice. Clarify with the white of egg. Decorate the eel according to taste, mask with jelly. *(International cookery.)*

Avocat Ashdoth

For 6 persons: *3 avocado pears of medium size; 60 gr. fillets of fish of fine flesh such as pike-perch, daurade, sea-perch; 2 apples; 1 red pepper; 3 dl. fish stock; 2 lemons; 5 cl. olive oil; 3 dl. sauce rémoulade; Worcestershire sauce; 6 black olives; wine vinegar.*

Poach the fillets of fish in the fish stock, allow to cool. Peel the apples, pip them and cut into a julienne, sprinkle them with lemon juice to prevent them from turning brown. Cut the pepper, previously pipped, into a julienne. Drain the fish and flake it. Prepare a salad with fish, red pepper, apples, oil, vinegar, salt, pepper and a drop of Worcestershire sauce and allow to marinate. Cut the avocado pears in two and remove the stones; remove the flesh of the fruit just before serving and sprinkle it with a little lemon juice to prevent it from turning brown; make a purée of it and season with lemon juice, salt and white pepper. Fill the empty skins with the fish salad. With the help of a piping bag with fluted tube, border the pears with a crown of purée. Mask with sauce rémoulade and decorate with an olive. *(Israel.)*

(See illustration, page 173.)

Avocat farci Baltimore

Stuffed Avocado Baltimore

For 6 persons: *3 very ripe avocado pears; 250 gr. shelled shrimps or 250 gr. salpicon of crab meat; 200 gr. mayonnaise; 1 hard-boiled egg; yolks of 2 hard-boiled eggs; 50 gr. butter; 1 coffee-spoonful of grated horse-radish; 1 coffee-spoonful of English mustard; 1 small red pimento; 1 lemon.*

Peel the avocado pears thinly and rub with lemon juice. Cut them in two lengthwise and remove the stones. Bind the shrimps with half of the mayonnaise, mix with the horse-radish and the mustard. Pass the yolks of 2 hard-boiled eggs through a hair sieve, mix them with the softened butter and the rest of the mayonnaise. Season strongly. Fill the halves of the avocado pears with the shrimp salad, garnish with a slice of hard-boiled egg and strips of red pimento. With the help of a piping bag with fluted tube, border the pears with the egg, mayonnaise and butter mixture. Dress on lettuce leaves. Serve very cold. *(United States.)*

Barquettes cancalaise

For 6 persons: *12 boat-shaped pâté brisée cases; 240 gr. mousse of haddock or whiting; 24 poached and bearded oysters; 2 dl. fish jelly.*

Fill the pastry cases with the mousse. Garnish each with 2 oysters, glaze lightly with jelly. *(France.)*

Barquettes hollandaise I

For 6 persons: *12 boat-shaped pastry cases; 4 hard-boiled eggs; 125 gr. mayonnaise; 12 small fillets of sprat, skinned and boned; 1 soup-spoonful of chopped parsley.*

Fill the pastry cases with the chopped hard-boiled egg bound with the well-seasoned mayonnaise. Garnish the pastry cases with the fillets of sprat cut into strips. Sprinkle with chopped parsley. *(Holland.)*

Barquettes hollandaise II

For 6 persons: *12 boat-shaped pastry cases; 150 gr. cooked mushrooms; 150 gr. cooked turbot; 100 gr. mayonnaise; 12 roundels of hard-boiled egg; 2 dl. fish jelly.*

Fill the pastry cases with a salpicon of mushrooms and turbot, bound with the mayonnaise seasoned with a pinch of Cayenne pepper. Decorate each pastry case with a roundel of hard-boiled egg, glaze with jelly. *(Holland.)*

Barquettes Marivaux

For 6 persons: *12 boat-shaped pastry cases; 150 gr. mushrooms; 150 gr. shelled shrimp tails; 100 gr. mayonnaise; 2 dl. jelly; 12 roundels of hard-boiled egg; chervil leaves.*

Fill the pastry cases with a salpicon of mushrooms and shelled shrimp tails bound with the mayonnaise lightly jellied. Place on each pastry case a roundel of hard-boiled egg. Decorate with chervil leaves. Glaze with jelly. *(France.)*

Barquette normande

For 6 persons: *12 boat-shaped pastry cases; 200 gr. poached fillets of sole; 150 gr. bearded mussels; 50 gr. truffle; 12 poached and bearded oysters; 2 dl. white sauce chaud-froid; 15 cl. jelly.*

Fill the pastry cases with a salpicon of fillets of sole, mussels and truffle. Mask with sauce chaud-froid. Place an oyster on each pastry case. Glaze with jelly. *(France.)*

Barquettes diverses

Various pastry cases

Fill boat-shaped pastry cases with a salad, mousse, purée or salpicon of fish or shellfish. Decorate to taste. *(International cookery.)*

Bouchées au thon

Tunny bouchées

For 6 persons: *12 small bouchées in puff pastry; 125 gr. tunny in oil; 40 gr. softened butter; 3 soup-spoonfuls of mayonnaise; 1 hard-boiled egg; 1 soup-spoonful of capers; 1 coffee-spoonful of chopped parsley; 12 roundels of stuffed olives; lemon.*

Prepare a purée with the tunny and the butter. Mix it with the mayonnaise. Season and add a few drops of lemon juice. Fill the bouchées with this purée. Sprinkle with capers, chopped parsley and chopped hard-boiled egg. Place a roundel of stuffed olive on each bouchée. *(France.)*

(See illustration, page 175.)

Brioches fourrées aux crevettes

Brioches filled with shrimps

For 6 persons: *6 very fresh brioches without sugar; 120 gr. small shrimp tails; 24 whole shrimps; 1 dl. mayonnaise; 1 soup-spoonful of chopped parsley or chervil; lettuce leaves or parsley.*

Remove the lids of the brioches and hollow them out carefully. Incorporate the chopped parsley with the mayonnaise and use it to bind the shrimp tails. Adjust for seasoning and consistency. Fill the brioches. Put the lids back. Garnish with the whole shrimps and the lettuce leaves. *(Switzerland.)*

Buckling

Prepared and served as for Smoked Trout.

Canapés

Canapés are slices of fresh white bread of different sizes, usually half a centimetre thick. Canapés are grilled or fried in butter. They are garnished with a fluted piping bag or they are spread with varied mixtures.

Canapés à l'amiral

For 6 persons: *12 oval serrated canapés; 120 gr. shrimp butter; 120 gr. shelled shrimp tails; 50 gr. lobster coral.*

Mask the canapés with shrimp butter, and border them with the shrimp tails. Place in the centre a little lobster coral. *(France.)*

Canapés aux anchois

Anchovy canapés

For 6 persons: *12 square canapés; 150 gr. anchovy butter; 48 strips of anchovy fillets; 2 chopped hard-boiled eggs.*

Spread the canapés with anchovy butter. Garnish the centre with a trellis work of anchovies, and sprinkle them with chopped hard-boiled egg. Edge the canapés with a small ribbon of anchovy butter.

Canapés au caviar

Caviar canapés

For 6 persons: *12 round canapés; 100 gr. caviar butter; 60 gr. softened butter; 60 gr. caviar; 1 lemon.*

Spread the canapés with caviar butter. Surround them, using a piping bag with small round tube, with a ribbon of softened butter. Garnish the centre with fresh caviar and place in the middle a small fan-shaped piece of lemon. *(France.)*

Canapés aux crevettes

Shrimp canapés

For 6 persons: *12 round canapés; 150 gr. shrimp butter; 120 gr. shrimps.*

Mask the canapés with shrimp butter. Garnish them with shrimps or prawns, arranged in a rosette, and edge them with shrimp butter, using the piping bag with fluted tube. *(France.)*

Canapés danoise

For 6 persons: *12 rectangular slices of black bread; 120 gr. horse-radish butter; 12 thin strips of smoked salmon; 12 thin strips of herring fillets marinated in white wine; 30 gr. caviar; 1 soup-spoonful of finely-chopped chive.*

Spread the canapés with horse-radish butter. Garnish them with strips of salmon, alternating with the herring fillets and a little caviar. Edge with chopped chive. *(International cookery.)*

Canapés d'écrevisses

Crayfish canapés

For 6 persons: *12 crescent-shaped canapés; 12 shelled crayfish tails; 40 gr. crayfish butter; 20 gr. fresh butter.*

Spread the canapés with crayfish butter. Edge them with a ribbon of fresh butter. Garnish with a fine crayfish tail cut lengthwise, putting the two halves with the rounded sides near each other to form a crescent shape. *(International cookery.)*

Canapés française

For 6 persons: *12 rectangular canapés of black bread; 120 gr. sardine butter; 12 fillets of sardine; 2 dl. sauce ravigote; 1 soup-spoonful of chopped parsley.*

Spread the canapés with sardine butter. Place a sardine on top. Mask with sauce ravigote, and sprinkle with chopped parsley.

Canapés hollandaise

For 6 persons: *12 oval canapés; 100 gr. poached soft herring roe; 2 fillets of herring in thin strips; 50 gr. butter; yolks of 3 hard-boiled eggs; 1 soup-spoonful of chopped chive.*

Prepare a purée with the roe and the softened butter and sieved yolk of hard-boiled egg. Season. Spread the canapés with this purée, garnish them with thin strips of herring in a trellis pattern. Fill the spaces with chopped yolk of hard-boiled egg, and edge the canapés with finely-chopped chive. *(Holland.)*

Canapés rochelaise

For 6 persons: *12 round canapés; 120 gr. soft roe butter; 12 poached oysters; 60 gr. crayfish butter.*

Spread the canapés with soft roe butter. Place in the middle of each canapé a poached oyster, and decorate the edges with the crayfish butter by using a piping bag with fluted tube. *(France.)*

Cantaloup farci Thousand Islands

Stuffed Cantaloup Melon Thousand Islands

For 6 persons: *3 small cantaloup melons; 150 gr. shelled shrimps; 150 gr. lobster meat; 150 gr. crab meat; 2 hard-boiled eggs; 200 gr. mayonnaise; ½ green pepper; ½ red pepper; 10 gr. grated horse-radish; 50 gr. ketchup; 1 coffee-spoonful of chopped mixed herbs, chive, dill, parsley.*

Cut the melons in two lengthways and empty them of seeds, serrate the edges and cool in the refrigerator. Prepare a coarse salpicon with the lobster meat, the crab meat and the shrimps. Fill the melons with it. Mix with the mayonnaise: the ketchup, the finely-chopped peppers, the horse-radish and a chopped hard-boiled egg. Add the mixed herbs and mask the salpicon with this sauce. A few shrimps can be kept to decorate the edges of the melons. Sprinkle the second chopped egg over all. Dress the melons on crushed ice and serve with quarters of lemon. *(United States.)*

Carolines

These are small éclairs made in choux pastry without sugar, very small in size, stuffed with a mousse or purée of fish or shellfish, masked with a sauce of the same kind as the basic ingredient, and glazed with jelly. *(France.)*

Caviar

Caviar is the roe of the fish of the sturgeon family, which has been removed from the freshly caught fish and then cleared of all skin, veins and fat. This roe is then salted and packed in tins or tubs. The main supply, and indeed the best quality, comes from the Black and Caspian Seas, and the fish are caught when spawning during the winter and spring when they swim up the rivers from these seas. The port of Astrakhan exports the majority of the world's supply. The best-known types are:

Beluga —a large grain and light colour
Ship —a medium size grain and light colour
Sevruga—a small grain and a little darker colour
Oscetra —a small grain and a little darker colour.

Generally the best quality roes are lightly salted and therefore do not keep well and, although it is generally true that the lighter-coloured caviar is the best flavoured, the preparation and storage will ultimately determine the quality. Caviar should be stored at approximately 32°F. and should be handled carefully, using a horn, wood or plastic spoon to transfer it to smaller jars for service. If the eggs are crushed, allowed to come in contact with metal, or left exposed to the air, then the flavour will deteriorate. Caviar should look bright, shiny and whole, rather than dull, crushed and oily. Some caviar is pasteurised and packed in airtight jars. 'Pressed' caviar is that which has been prepared by 'blanching' and pressing between cloths and then packed. This type is of inferior quality. It is also packed in airtight jars.
Caviar is served very cold. The best quality is generally served direct from the tin or jar which has been on a socle of ice or surrounded by crushed ice. A portion is approximately 15 gr. or ½ oz. Hot, thick toast, thinly sliced brown bread and butter or blinis are served with caviar; lemon, hard-boiled egg and finely chopped onions are also served. Caviar is also served in pastry barquettes.

Blinis

Ingredients: *453 gr. strong flour; 226 gr. buck-wheat flour; 225 gr. medium flour; 1 pint milk; 30 gr. cream; 30 gr. yeast; 2 eggs; salt to taste.*

Dissolve the yeast with half of the warmed milk, add 226 gr. flour to make a thin paste. Place aside for one hour in a warm place to ferment. Add the remainder of the warm milk and flour, then add the salt and yolks of eggs. Place aside in a warm place for 30 minutes and then add the stiffly-whisked white of egg. The blinis are cooked in small individual iron pans. Heat the pans, add a little clarified butter and then the mixture. Cook in a hot oven or at the side of a hot stove for 6–8 minutes, turning over when set.
Red caviar is prepared from salmon, carp, pike, grey mullet and other fish. The grain is much larger than that of real caviar and is from pink to red in colour. It has not the flavour of real caviar. Dark caviar, a type made from various fish roes, is sold as a cheap substitute for caviar, but it is very inferior in flavour.

Cocktail d'aiglefin

Haddock cocktail

For 6 persons: *300 gr. cooked haddock fillets, cooked under slight pressure; 100 gr. shelled shrimp tails; 30 gr. sweet red pimentoes; 2 dl. fresh cream; 60 gr. ketchup; 2 cl. ginger syrup; 3 cl. olive oil; 1 lemon; 1 soup-spoonful of chopped chervil and parsley.*

Cut up the fish into dice, mix it with the shrimps and the pimentoes, cut up into very small dice. Marinate all with salt, pepper, oil and lemon juice, for one hour. Arrange the mixture in six chilled cocktail or champagne glasses. Mask with the whipped cream to which has been added the chopped chervil and parsley, the ketchup and syrup of ginger, and a pinch of salt. *(International cookery.)*

Cocktail d'anguille

Eel cocktail

For 6 persons: *200 gr. cooked eel fillets; 100 gr. shelled shrimp tails; 100 gr. peeled and cored apples; 50 gr. celeriac; 200 gr. mayonnaise; 5 cl. fresh cream; 20 gr. grated horse-radish; 6 roundels of hard-boiled egg; 1 coffee-spoonful of chopped parsley.*

Fill 6 champagne glasses up to two-thirds with the fillets of eel cut into pieces. Arrange on top the shrimps, the finely minced, chopped apples, the celeriac cut into small dice and previously blanched, cooled and drained. Mask all with the mayonnaise to which have been added the grated horse-radish, the whipped cream, and which has been highly seasoned. Decorate each glass with a roundel of hard-boiled egg on which a pinch of chopped parsley is placed. *(International cookery.)*

Cocktail d'anguille au curry

For 6 persons: *200 gr. stewed fillets of eel; 4 hard-boiled eggs; 200 gr. mayonnaise; 1 dl. fresh cream; ½ a coffee-spoonful of paprika; ½ a coffee-spoonful of curry powder; 1 coffee-spoonful of chopped parsley.*

Cut up the eel into small pieces. Cut up the hard-boiled eggs into dice. Season the mayonnaise with the curry and add the whipped cream. Fill the glasses half-full with eel and hard-boiled egg. Mask with mayonnaise. Decorate the edges with parsley and chopped hard-boiled egg, sprinkle the centre with paprika. *(International cookery.)*

Cocktail d'anguille au homard

For 6 persons: *200 gr. cooked fillets of eel; 150 gr. lobster meat; 6 small medallions of lobster; 200 gr. mayonnaise; 5 cl. fresh cream; 3 soup-spoonfuls of ketchup; 20 gr. finely minced onion; 1 soup-spoonful of chopped lobster coral; 6 slices of truffle; 2 lemons.*

Cut up the eel and the lobster meat into dice. Bind with a sauce composed of mayonnaise, whipped cream and onion. Put into six glasses, sprinkle lightly with ketchup. Place in the middle a medallion of lobster, sprinkle with chopped coral, and top with a slice of truffle. Serve quarters of lemon separately. *(International cookery.)*

Cocktail d'anguille moderne

For 6 persons: *300 gr. eel fillets; poached with white wine and mixed herbs; 200 gr. mayonnaise; 12 small sections of grapefruit; 6 large shelled prawn tails; 1 chopped hard-boiled egg; 1 soup-spoonful of chopped parsley.*

Cut up the fillets into a fine julienne. Reduce the cooking liquor to 3 or 4 cl. and add the mayonnaise. Put the julienne of eel into six glasses and dress each with 2 sections of grapefruit. Mask with chopped hard-boiled eggs. Arrange a large prawn tail on each glass. *(International cookery.)*
(See illustration, page 169.)

Cocktail d'avocat aux crevettes

Avocado pear and shrimp cocktail

For 6 persons: *3 avocado pears; 120 gr. shelled shrimp tails; 75 gr. ketchup; 2 dl. fresh cream; ½ coffee-spoonful of powdered paprika; 2 chopped hard-boiled eggs; 1 soup-spoonful of chopped parsley.*

Peel the avocado pears which must be very ripe, and cut the flesh into dice. Arrange the dice in six glasses and place the shrimps on top. Chill well. Mask with a sharp sauce composed of the ketchup mixed with cream, the powdered paprika and the Worcestershire sauce. Garnish with the yolk of half a hard-boiled egg and with chopped parsley. *(International cookery.)*

Cocktail d'avocat aux scampi

Avocado pear and scampi cocktail

For 6 persons: *9 small shelled scampi tails; 3 avocado pears; 4 oranges; 1 soup-spoonful of mango chutney; 20 gr. grated horse-radish; 200 gr. mayonnaise; 1 lemon; 3 cl. olive oil.*

Cut the avocado pears into two, remove the stones, and hollow them out. Cut up the flesh

into dice and mix it with 6 diced scampi and the orange cut into sections. Marinate for 30 minutes with the orange juice, lemon juice, salt and olive oil. Incorporate with the mayonnaise the chopped mango chutney, the horse-radish and a little of the marinade. Put this mixture into the avocado skins or into the cocktail glasses, mask with the mayonnaise, and garnish each one with a half-tail of scampi. *(International cookery.)*
(See illustration, page 169.)

Cocktail chinois

For 6 persons: *300 gr. shelled shrimp tails; 200 gr. mayonnaise; 50 gr. ketchup; 1 dl. fresh cream; 30 mandarin quarters; ½ a coffee-spoonful of paprika; 1 coffee-spoonful of chopped parsley; 4 cl. dry sherry.*

Marinate the shrimp tails in the sherry for one hour. Garnish the glasses with the shrimps, mask them with a sauce prepared thus: mix the mayonnaise with the ketchup and the sherry of the marinade, add the whipped cream. Sprinkle lightly with chopped parsley and with paprika. With 5 segments of mandarin form a flower on each cocktail. *(International cookery.)*

Cocktail de crevettes I

Shrimp cocktail I

For 6 persons: *300 gr. shelled shrimp tails; 4 skinned and pipped tomatoes; 200 gr. mayonnaise; 3 soup-spoonfuls of ketchup; 100 gr. sweet green pepper; 10 gr. grated horse-radish; ½ a lemon; white of 1 hard-boiled egg; 1 soup-spoonful of chopped parsley and chervil; Worcestershire sauce; tabasco.*

Mix the mayonnaise with the ketchup, the horse-radish and the lemon juice. Season it with a dash of Worcestershire sauce and a few drops of tabasco. Cut up the tomatoes and the sweet green pepper into small dice; add them to the shrimp tails. Put this composition into six cocktail glasses. Mask with mayonnaise, sprinkle with chopped chervil and parsley, then garnish with a julienne of white of egg. *(International cookery.)*

Cocktail de crevettes II

Shrimp cocktail II

For 6 persons: *200 gr. shelled shrimp tails; 2 bananas; ½ a sweet red pepper; 100 gr. mushrooms; ½ a coffee-spoonful of curry powder; 1 coffee-spoonful of mustard; 1 soup-spoonful of mango chutney; 1 dl. fresh cream; 1 lemon; 2 soup-spoonfuls of olive oil; 200 gr. mayonnaise.*

Marinate the shrimp tails, 1½ bananas and the chopped mushrooms with the lemon juice, the oil and a pinch of salt, for 30 minutes. Mix the mayonnaise with the mustard, the curry, and the chopped mango chutney; add the whipped cream. Put in cocktail glasses the shrimps and the other ingredients. Mask with sauce, decorate with roundels of bananas, sprinkle with a fine julienne of red pepper or with a roundel of hard-boiled egg. *(International cookery.)*
(See illustration, page 169.)

Cocktail de crevettes III

For 6 persons: *1 kg. 500 of uncooked prawns; 200 gr. thick mayonnaise; 2 spoonfuls of ketchup; 1 spoonful of chopped dill; 1 bunch of dill; 3 cl. Oloroso sherry; 1 lemon.* Cooking time: 4 to 5 minutes.

Place the prawns in boiling water, salted and aromatised with a bunch of dill. Bring to the boil, poach the prawns and allow them to cool in the cooking liquor. Shell and marinate them in the lemon juice. Mix the mayonnaise with the ketchup and the sherry. Arrange the prawn tails in cocktail glasses, mask with the sauce and sprinkle with chopped dill. *(Spain.)*

Cocktail d'écrevisses

Crayfish cocktail

For 6 persons: *30 shelled crayfish tails; 200 gr. skinned and pipped tomatoes; 200 gr. mayonnaise; 5 cl. fresh cream; 50 gr. ketchup; 10 gr. grated horse-radish; 1 coffee-spoonful of mustard; 1 coffee-spoonful of chopped chervil and tarragon; 1 lettuce heart; 1 hard-boiled egg; tabasco.*

Mix the mayonnaise with the horse-radish, the ketchup, the mustard, the mixed herbs and a few drops of tabasco. Incorporate in it the whipped cream. Shred the lettuce coarsely, put it into the base of the glasses, add the diced tomatoes. Mask with a spoonful of sauce, arrange 4 crayfish tails in each glass, cover with the rest of the sauce. Sprinkle with chopped hard-boiled egg and place a crayfish tail in the centre. *(International cookery.)*

Cocktail de filets de sole et crevettes

Fillet of sole and shrimp cocktail

For 6 persons: *200 gr. shelled shrimp tails; 200 gr. poached fillets of sole; 200 gr. mayonnaise; 50 gr. ketchup; 50 gr. chopped preserved ginger; 1 soup-spoonful chopped parsley; paprika.*

Cut up the shrimps and fillets of sole into dice, bind them with the mayonnaise to which the chopped ginger and ketchup has been added. Season well. Arrange the mixture in six well-cooled glasses. Sprinkle with chopped parsley and dust lightly with paprika. *(International cookery.)*

Cocktail Florida

For 6 persons: *300 gr. crab meat; 200 gr. mayonnaise; 50 gr. ketchup; 5 cl. fresh cream; ½ a coffee-spoonful of curry powder; 2 cl. cognac; 6 quarters of lemon.*

Use only the white of the crab meat, shred and fill six champagne or cocktail glasses. Prepare a sauce with the mayonnaise, the whipped cream and the ketchup. Season it with cognac. Mask the crab meat with this sauce and fix a quarter of lemon on the edge of each glass. Serve hot toast separately. *(International cookery.)*

Cocktail hawaiienne

For 6 persons: *300 gr. shelled shrimp tails; 150 gr. pineapple; 200 gr. mayonnaise; ½ a coffee-spoonful of curry powder; 50 gr. chopped preserved ginger; ¼ of a red pepper; ¼ of a green pepper; 5 cl. fresh cream.*

Mix the shrimp tails and the pineapple cut up into small dice. Arrange in six glasses. Mask with a sauce prepared with the mayonnaise to which has been added the chopped ginger, curry powder and whipped cream. Sprinkle with a fine and short julienne of red and green peppers. *(International cookery.)*

Cocktail de homard

Lobster cocktail

For 6 persons: *300 gr. cooked lobster meat; 200 gr. mayonnaise; 100 gr. ketchup; 2 cl. cognac; 1 soup-spoonful of parsley and chervil; 6 quarters of lemon.*

Cut up the lobster meat into medium sized pieces, bind with the mayonnaise to which has been added the ketchup and the cognac. Arrange the mixture in six well-cooled glasses and sprinkle with chopped parsley and chervil. Serve with segments of lemon and Melba toast, separately. *(International cookery.)*

Cocktail de homard au melon

Lobster and melon cocktail

For 6 persons: *200 gr. cooked lobster meat; 6 small medallions of lobster; 200 gr. small melon balls; 200 gr. mayonnaise; 50 gr. ketchup; 5 cl. fresh cream; 10 gr. grated horse-radish; 2 cl. cognac.*

Prepare a sauce with mayonnaise, ketchup, horse-radish, cognac and whipped cream. Adjust seasoning and consistency. Pour a spoonful of this sauce into six chilled glasses. Add the diced lobster meat. Mask with the rest of the sauce, place a medallion of lobster in the centre and surround with melon balls. *(International cookery.)*

Cocktail d'huîtres I

Oyster cocktail I

For 6 persons: *1 lettuce heart; 24 oysters; 200 gr. mayonnaise; 50 gr. ketchup; 1 soup-spoonful of chopped parsley, chervil and tarragon; 10 gr. chopped horse-radish; Worcestershire sauce; tabasco; chopped whites of 2 hard-boiled eggs; ½ a lemon.*

Prepare a sauce with the mayonnaise, the ketchup, the grated horse-radish and the lemon juice. Flavour it with a dash of Worcestershire sauce and a few drops of tabasco. Shred the lettuce and put it in the bottom of each of six champagne glasses or cocktail glasses. Arrange 3 bearded oysters in each glass and mask with the sauce. Place an oyster sprinkled with the mixed herbs in the centre of each glass and surround it with a julienne of white of egg. *(International cookery.)*

Cocktail d'huîtres II

Oyster cocktail II

For 6 persons: *24 bearded oysters; 1 lettuce heart; 2 small celery hearts; 100 gr. mayonnaise; 1 dl. double cream; raw yolks of 2 eggs; 1 lemon; 2 soup-spoonfuls of ketchup; paprika; ½ a coffee-spoonful of chopped tarragon.*

Shred the lettuce and cut the celery into a fine julienne. Bind all with the mayonnaise and garnish the bottom of each of six cocktail glasses with it. Place on top 4 oysters and mask with a sauce prepared thus: dilute the egg yolks with the lemon juice and the ketchup and mix with the cream. Season with a pinch of salt and a pinch of paprika. Sprinkle lightly with chopped tarragon. *(International cookery.)*

Cocktail de langouste

Crawfish cocktail

For 6 persons: *250 gr. cooked crawfish meat; 6 thin medallions of crawfish; 200 gr. mayonnaise; 1 dl. fresh cream; 50 gr. ketchup; 12 small white asparagus tips; 3 cl. cognac; the juice of ¼ of a lemon; 1 heart of lettuce; tabasco.*

Cut up the lobster meat into small dice and allow to marinate in the cognac for one hour in a cool place. Mix the mayonnaise with the whipped cream, the ketchup, the lemon juice and a few drops of tabasco. Garnish the bottom of each glass with a small spoonful of shredded lettuce. Add the crawfish meat. Mask with the sauce, garnish with a medallion of crawfish and two asparagus tips. *(International cookery.)*

Cocktail de la Mer du Nord

For 6 persons: *150 gr. shelled shrimp tails; 150 gr. cooked lobster meat; 150 gr. crab meat; 12 large raw mushrooms; 1 lettuce; 6 round slices of lemon; 25 gr. caviar; 1 small clove of garlic; olive oil; vinegar.*

Place in each cocktail glass a small spoonful of julienne of lettuce. Arrange on top a salpicon of lobster, crab, minced mushrooms, shrimp tails. Sprinkle with a marinade of oil, vinegar, salt, pepper and crushed garlic. Garnish with a round slice of lemon and place a little caviar in the middle. Serve separately heart-shaped croûtons browned in butter. *(Denmark.)*

Cocktail de poisson aux olives

For 6 persons: *300 gr. poached fillets of turbot, haddock, cod or other fish; 3 tomatoes, skinned and pipped; 200 gr. mayonnaise; 8 green olives; 3 stuffed olives; 2 cl. cognac; 1 lemon; 3 cl. olive oil; 1 lettuce heart; 1 soup-spoonful of capers; 6 roundels of hard-boiled egg; Worcestershire sauce; tabasco.*

Cut the fish and the tomatoes into dice, let them marinate in olive oil, lemon juice, salt and pepper. Stone the olives and cut them into quarters. Bind all with the mayonnaise, flavour with cognac, Worcestershire sauce and a few drops of tabasco. Shred the lettuce and put into six glasses. Arrange the fish salad on top. Garnish with a roundel of hard-boiled egg, a few capers and half a stuffed olive in the centre. *(International cookery.)*

Cocktail de sandre Hashomron

Pike-perch cocktail

For 6 persons: *600 gr. cooked fillets of pike-perch; 3 avocado pears; 3 slices of pineapple; 200 gr. mayonnaise; 100 gr. ketchup; heart of lettuce; 1 coffee-spoonful of chopped dill; 2 cl. cognac; the juice of ½ a lemon; Worcestershire sauce; 3 black olives.*

Peel and skin the avocado pears, remove the flesh in small balls with a spoon cutter, and sprinkle with lemon juice. Marinate the cooled flaked fish, the pineapple in dice, and the balls of avocado in cognac, Worcestershire sauce, salt, pepper, and a pinch of sugar. Incorporate the ketchup with 50 gr. of mayonnaise and the chopped dill with the rest of the mayonnaise. Garnish cocktail or champagne glasses with the lettuce leaves and fill them with the salad. Mask one half with mayonnaise containing the dill, and the other half with mayonnaised ketchup. Place in the centre half a stoned black olive. Serve chilled. *(Israel.)*

Cocktail de scampi au curry

Curried scampi cocktail

For 6 persons: *18 small shelled scampi tails; 4 cl. olive oil; 1 lemon; 200 gr. mayonnaise; 1 dl. fresh cream; 1 soup-spoonful of chopped mango chutney; ½ a coffee-spoonful of curry powder; 1 lettuce heart; 1 soup-spoonful of chopped parsley; chopped yolks of 2 hard-boiled eggs.*

Prepare a sauce with mayonnaise, curry, chopped mango chutney and whipped cream. Shred the lettuce. Marinate the scampi (cut in two lengthwise) with lemon juice, olive oil and pepper for 30 minutes. Arrange the lettuce in champagne glasses, place the scampi on top. Mask with the sauce. Sprinkle with chopped parsley and yolk of egg. *(International cookery.)*

Cocktail de scampi à l'orange

Orange and scampi cocktail

For 6 persons: *12 small shelled scampi tails; 18 segments of orange; 6 lettuce leaves; 1 soup-spoonful of chopped mango chutney; 1 lemon; 3 cl. olive oil; 10 gr. grated horse-radish; 2 dl. double cream; 1 coffee-spoonful of chopped dill; 3 soup-spoonfuls of ketchup; 3 soup-spoonfuls of orange juice.*

Cut the scampi in two lengthwise, and marinate in the lemon and orange juice, olive oil and pepper for at least 30 minutes. Prepare a sauce with double cream, horse-radish, ketchup and mango chutney, adding the scampi marinade. Place a small lettuce leaf in each glass. Place on top 2 scampi and 2 segments of orange. Mask with the sauce, sprinkle with a little chopped dill in the middle, and garnish with a segment of orange. *(International cookery.)*

Cocktail vigneronne

For 6 persons: *300 gr. crab meat; 200 gr. mayonnaise; 5 cl. fresh cream; 100 gr. ketchup; 3 cl. syrup of ginger; 250 gr. fresh grapes, skinned and pipped; yolks of 2 hard-boiled eggs; paprika.*

Place the flaked crab meat into six cocktail glasses. Mask with the well-seasoned mayonnaise mixed with the whipped cream. Sprinkle with ketchup to which has been added the ginger syrup. Sprinkle with chopped yolk of hard-boiled egg, and decorate each cocktail with grapes. *(International cookery.)*

Smoked Cod's Roe

This is purchased whole or ready in jars, and is shaped by spoons into portions and dressed in lettuce leaves. Serve with thinly sliced brown bread and butter.

Concombre danoise

Cucumber cocktail danoise

For 6 persons: *12 thick roundels of blanched cucumber; 120 gr. purée of smoked salmon; 12 anchovy fillets; 1 herring fillet; 1 hard-boiled egg; grated horse-radish.*

Scoop out the centre of the cucumber roundels keeping a base. Garnish them with the purée of smoked salmon mixed with the diced anchovy and herring fillet and the diced hard-boiled egg. Sprinkle with grated horse-radish. *(International cookery.)*
(See illustration, page 216.)

Cornets de saumon fumé

Smoked salmon fillets

For 6 persons: *12 very thin slices of smoked salmon; 200 gr. horse-radish butter; 50 gr. mayonnaise; 2 dl. jelly; picked parsley.*

Cut into triangles the slices of smoked salmon, roll them into cornets, and fill them (using a fluted piping bag) with the horse-radish butter mixed with the mayonnaise. The cornets may also be stuffed with the softened butter mixed with chopped hard-boiled egg, or filled with horse-radish cream lightly jellied. Arrange the cornets on chopped jelly and garnish with picked parsley. *(International cookery.)*

Duchesses

These are small choux paste buns. Using a piping bag they are filled with a fine purée and glazed with jelly without being masked with sauce chaud-froid. *(France.)*

Duchesses au caviar

For 6 persons: *12 small choux buns; 120 gr. caviar; 1 dl. jelly.*

Fill the choux buns with caviar, glaze lightly with jelly. Serve very cold. *(France.)*

Duchesses Nantua

For 6 persons: *12 small choux buns; 120 gr. crayfish purée; 1 dl. fish jelly; 1 soup-spoonful of chopped pistachio.*

Fill the choux buns with the crayfish purée. Glaze them with jelly, sprinkle them with chopped pistachio. *(France.)*

Duchesses norvégienne

For 6 persons: *12 small choux buns; 200 gr. kilkis; 75 gr. mayonnaise; 50 gr. butter; 1 dl. jelly; ½ a lemon.*

Drain and pass the kilkis through a fine hair sieve, mix them with the softened butter and the mayonnaise. Season with white pepper and a few drops of lemon juice. Fill the buns with this purée, glaze them lightly with jelly. *(France.)*

Duchesses au saumon fumé

For 6 persons: *12 small choux buns; 120 gr. purée, or cream of smoked salmon; 12 very small lozenges of smoked salmon; 1 dl. jelly.*

Fill the choux buns with the salmon purée or cream. Decorate each with a small lozenge of smoked salmon, and glaze with jelly. *(France.)*

Fonds d'artichauts garnis

For 6 persons: *12 small artichoke bases; 300 gr. purée of fish or soft roe, or shellfish; oil; vinegar.*

Marinate the artichoke bases with the oil and vinegar and garnish them either with the purée of fish, soft roe, or shellfish, or else with a finely cut salad of fish, shrimps etc., bound with mayonnaise. *(France.)*

Fonds d'artichauts Mazarin

For 6 persons: *12 artichoke bases; 250 gr. lobster meat, or crawfish meat; 80 gr. mayonnaise; 1 chopped hard-boiled egg; 1 soup-spoonful of chopped parsley; 12 shelled prawns; oil; vinegar.*

Marinate the artichoke bases with oil and vinegar. Cut up the lobster meat into dice and bind it with mayonnaise. Garnish the artichoke bases in a dome shape with this salpicon, sprinkle them on one side with chopped hard-boiled egg, and on the other with chopped parsley (half and half on the surface). Stud a prawn in the centre. *(France.)*
(See illustration, page 174.)

Grémilles à la russe

Pope or ruff fish of the perch family

For 6 persons: *12 ruff; 1 litre court-bouillon with white wine; 250 gr. mayonnaise; 1 dl. jelly; 1 soup-spoonful of chopped parsley.* Cooking time: 15 minutes.

Poach the ruff gently in a strongly aromatised court-bouillon and allow them to cool in it. Drain them and sponge them carefully. Mask them with the jellied mayonnaise and sprinkle them with chopped parsley. *(France.)*

Filets de hareng

Herring fillets

For 6 persons: *12 pickled herring fillets, de-salted and flaked; 1 dl. soft roe purée; 3 dl. mayonnaise; 2 soup-spoonfuls onion, parsley, chervil, celery, chive and tarragon, in equal parts; 1 soup-spoonful of vinegar.*

Mix the mayonnaise with the soft roe purée and the mixed herbs, dilute it with vinegar. Season with a pinch of Cayenne pepper. Dress, arrange, and mask the fillets with the sauce. *(France.)*

Filet de hareng livonienne

For 6 persons: *12 small fillets of pickled herring, skinned and boned; 200 gr. cooked and peeled potatoes; 200 gr. pippin apples; 1 dl. oil; 3 cl. vinegar; 1 soup-spoonful of chopped parsley, tarragon and fennel.*

Cut up the fillets into dice. Add the potatoes and the pippin apples similarly diced, with mixed herbs, and season with oil and vinegar. Form in the shape of a herring with this salad and use herring heads and tails to decorate. *(France.)*

Filets de hareng Lucas

For 6 persons: *12 fillets of pickled herring, skinned and boned; 3 dl. oil; 4 cl. vinegar; 1 coffee-spoonful of mustard; yolks of 2 hard-boiled eggs; 1 soup-spoonful of chopped gherkin, shallot and chervil.*

Prepare a sauce composed of yolks of hard-boiled egg passed through a hair sieve; add the oil, vinegar, salt, pepper and mustard worked up as for a mayonnaise, and complete it with chopped herbs. Cut up the fillets of herring into strips and mix them with the sauce. Arrange on an hors d'oeuvre dish. *(France.)*

Filets de hareng russe

For 6 persons: *12 fillets of pickled herring, skinned and boned; 300 gr. slices of cooked and peeled potatoes; 1 dl. oil; 3 cl. vinegar; 1½ soup-spoonfuls of chopped shallot, fennel, chervil and tarragon in equal parts.*

Scollop the fillets of herring. Arrange them on an hors d'oeuvre dish alternating with the roundels of potato. Sprinkle with oil and vinegar and with the chopped mixed herbs. *(France.)*

Bismark Herrings

Ingredients: *2 kg. 268 salted herrings; 340 gr. sliced onions; 7 gr. mustard seed; 12 bayleaves; 7 gr. peppercorns; 12 cloves; 12 chillies; 226 gr. sliced, salted cucumber (Agouris); 1·136 litres wine vinegar; 1·136 litres water.*

Remove the scales from the herrings, cut off the heads, open and remove the bone. After cleaning, soak in cold water for two hours to remove salt. Place the herring in a china bowl and alternate with layers of the garnish. Cover with the mixture of water and vinegar and pickle for three days.

Harengs dieppoise

For 6 persons: *12 very small fresh herrings; 1 dl. white wine; 5 cl. vinegar; 1 carrot; 2 shallots; 2 onions; parsley; 1 bayleaf; 1 sprig of thyme.* Cooking time: 12 minutes.

Prepare a court-bouillon with the white wine and an equal part of water, vinegar, fine roundels of carrot and onion, and finely-chopped shallots, bayleaf, thyme, parsley stalks and a little salt. Poach the herrings, allow to cool in the court-bouillon. Serve the herrings garnished with roundels of carrot, rings of onion and fine slices of lemon masked with the court-bouillon passed through a conical strainer. *(France.)*

▲ Cocktail of fish and shellfish, pp. 163–167

Cocktail of fish and shellfish, pp. 163–167 ▼

▲ Anchois Côte d'Azur, p. 158

Anchois nimoise, p. 158 ▼

▲ Anchois en paupiettes, p. 158

Anchois au poivron, p. 158 ▼

▲ Anguille hongroise, p. 159

Tomates antiboise, p. 180 ▼

▲ Salade de crevettes quimperlaise, p. 178

Avocat Ashdoth, p. 159 ▼

▲ Tartelettes Neptune, p. 180

Fond d'artichauts Mazarin, p. 167 ▼

▲ Bouchées au thon, p. 160

Tartelettes au thon, p. 180 ▼

▲ Melon Eden, p. 177

Melon et homard, p. 177 ▼

Salted herrings

Pack in layers of dry salt. Keep in a cool place in a non-metal container covered with a weighted lid, for at least 2 days before use. Proportions: *453 gr. salt to 4 kg. 268 herrings.*

Soused herrings

Ingredients: *12 herrings (approximately 4 lbs.); 12 oz. onion; 12 oz. sliced cannelèd carrot; 2 bay-leaves; ½ pint malt vinegar; ½ pint water; salt; few peppercorns; parsley stalks.*

Par cook the sliced ringed onions and carrots in the water with the herbs and spices. Add the vinegar and bring to the boil. Season. Meanwhile, prepare the herrings. Scale, clean and remove the heads. Re-wash and score. Arrange in a fairly shallow earthenware or fireproof dish. Pour over the prepared boiling court-bouillon. Cover with greaseproof paper and gently cook in a moderate oven for approximately 20 minutes. The herrings are usually served cold in their own court-bouillon, but they may be served hot.

Médaillons de homard Rhode Island

Lobster Rhode Island, Medallions of

For 6 persons: *2 lobsters of 700 gr.; 400 gr. fine macédoine of vegetables; 200 gr. mayonnaise; 12 slices of truffle; ½ litre fish jelly; 2 leaves of gelatine; 2 lettuce hearts.* Cooking time for the lobsters: 15 minutes.

Cook the lobsters in a court-bouillon, cool in the liquor. Detach claws and tails, extract the creamy parts from the trunks and retain. Shell the tails, and gut. Divide into 6 to 8 good medallions. Decorate each medallion with a roundel of truffle and glaze with jelly. Cut up the meat from the claws and the points of the tails into dice, and mix them with the macédoine. Bind with mayonnaise, incorporating the gelatine, previously soaked and dissolved au bain-marie in a little water. Adjust seasoning and consistency. Fill a timbale mould and put to set in a cool place. Turn out the mixture in the centre of a large round dish and arrange the medallions around, vertically. Garnish with the trunks cut in two lengthwise, and the lettuce hearts cut into quarters. Serve separately a well-seasoned mayonnaise. *(United States.)*

Maquereau marinés

Marinated mackerel

Proceed as for the preparation of harengs dieppoise. *(France.)*

Melon Eden

For 6 persons: *3 cantaloup melons; 12 thin slices of smoked salmon; 600 gr. prawns; ½ litre cocktail sauce.*

Cut the melons in two lengthwise and remove the pips. With a spoon detach most of the flesh leaving sufficient to hold the rind together. Cut the flesh into small pieces, mix it with the prawns, bind with the cocktail sauce and fill the melons. Decorate with the rolled up slices of salmon. Serve on a bed of lettuce. *(Switzerland.)*
(See illustration, page 176.)

Melon et homard

Melon con bogavante

For 6 persons: *2 lobsters of 500 gr.; 3 small cantaloup melons; 5 cl. port wine; 6 soup-spoonfuls of ketchup.* Cooking time: 15 minutes.

Cook the lobsters in a court-bouillon and allow to cool in the cooking liquor. Shell the tails, break the claws, and extract the meat. Cut up the tails into medallions and the claws into large dice. Cut the melons in two lengthwise and remove the pips. Detach the flesh with a spoon, leaving sufficient to hold the rind together, and mix it with the diced meat of the lobster claws. Fill each half with this salpicon and sprinkle with port wine. Arrange the medallions on top and mask with ketchup. Serve very cold. *(Spain.)*
(See illustration, page 176.)

Oeufs farcis Clémence

Eggs, stuffed

For 6 persons: *6 hard-boiled eggs; 150 gr. tunny; 300 gr. potato salad; 200 gr. mayonnaise; 1 soup-spoonful of mixed herbs; 30 gr. butter.*

Cut the hard-boiled eggs in two lengthwise, remove the yolks, pass them through a hair sieve with the tunny. Mix this with the softened butter, season, and stuff the whites using the piping bag with a fluted tube. Garnish the base of the dish with the salad, masked with a fairly light mayonnaise with mixed herbs. Place the stuffed eggs on top. Decorate with a slice of stuffed olive. *(International cookery.)*
(See illustration, page 216.)

Oeufs farcis Venora

For 6 persons: *6 hard-boiled eggs; 100 gr. anchovy fillets; 50 gr. butter; 2 small tomatoes; 12 very small medallions of fish; 6 stuffed olives; 1 dl. jelly.*

Cut the eggs in two, remove the yolks and pass with anchovy fillets through a hair sieve. Work with the softened butter and use this to stuff the whites. Place on top a thin slice of peeled tomato and a medallion of fish. Decorate with half an olive. Glaze with jelly.

Oeufs farcis vivandière

For 6 persons: *6 hard-boiled eggs; 150 gr. shelled shrimp tails; 1 soup-spoonful of mayonnaise; 1 coffee-spoonful of chopped chervil; 40 gr. softened butter.*

Cut the eggs in two, remove the yolks. Fill the whites with shrimps bound with a little mayonnaise mixed with the chervil. Pass the yolks through a hair sieve, work them with butter, season, and decorate the edges of the whites with a piping bag with fluted tube.

Pamplemousse Césarée

For 6 persons: *5 grapefruit of medium size; 600 gr. fillets of white-fleshed fish; 2 apples; 350 gr. celeriac; 250 gr. carrots; 150 gr. hazel-nuts; 200 gr. mayonnaise; 2 soup-spoonfuls of fresh cream; 2 dl. fish stock; 1 tea-spoonful of fresh chopped mint; lemon; fresh mint leaves; 6 maraschino cherries.*

Cook the fish fillets in the fish stock; cook the carrots and the celeriac in salt water. Allow to cool. Halve 3 grapefruit and remove the flesh and the skin. Peel the other 2 grapefruit, and remove the segments leaving neither skin nor pips. Cut into small dice the fish, the segments of grapefruit, the apples, the carrots and the celeriac, and sprinkle with lemon juice; add the chopped hazel-nuts, bind with the mayonnaise and the cream, and complete with the chopped mint and adjust seasoning and consistency. Fill the grapefruit cups with this mixture, and garnish with a maraschino cherry and small leaves of mint. Serve very cold. *(Israel.)*

Rollmops

As for Bismark Herrings, but prepare each fillet by rolling round a piece of salted cucumber. Pack into a jar with the garnish and cover with the liquor.
Another method using soft-roe herrings: Clean and prepare as before. Spread each fillet with a little mustard and finely-chopped onion and then roll, fixing with a small wooden skewer. Place the prepared fillets in a shallow receptacle together with the roes. Boil the garnish of onion etc. with the vinegar and water, allow to simmer for 10 minutes and then strain over the fillets. When cold, remove the roes. Rub these through a sieve. Mix the purée of roe with the liquor, adding ½ pint of oil. Pour the dressing over the fillets and marinate for a few days before using.

Rollmops finlandais

For 6 persons: *1 kg. 500 of small Swedish herrings; ½ litre vinegar; 1 bayleaf; 12 white peppercorns; 1 black peppercorn; 3 tea-spoonfuls of sugar; 1 tea-spoonful of salt; 1 soup-spoonful of chopped dill.* Cooking time: 5 minutes.

Remove the fillets from the herrings. Rinse and salt them. Heat a marinade of: vinegar, pepper, bayleaf and sugar. Roll up the fillets and place them side by side in a shallow stewpan, add the hot marinade, and allow to cook gently. Let them cool in the stock and sprinkle with chopped dill. Serve the rollmops cold with new potatoes. *(Finland.)*

Rougets au safran

Red mullet, with saffron

For 6 persons: *6 red mullet of 125–150 gr.; 2 dl. white wine; 300 gr. peeled, pipped and chopped tomatoes; 1 crushed clove of garlic; 1 very large pinch of saffron; 6 white peppercorns; 4 coriander seeds; 1 soup-spoonful of chopped parsley.* Cooking time: 10 minutes.

Prepare a court-bouillon with the white wine and an equal part of water, the tomatoes, pepper, coriander, garlic, saffron and salt. Clean the mullet, poach in the court-bouillon, and allow them to cool. Dress. Arrange them on a dish, mask with the cooking liquor passed through a tammy cloth, and sprinkle with chopped parsley. *(France.)*

Salade de crevettes quimperlaise

Shrimp salad

For 6 persons: *600 gr. shelled shrimps; 200 gr. mayonnaise; 50 gr. capers; 1 large very ripe tomato; 2 hard-boiled eggs; 2 artichoke hearts; 1 bunch of parsley; 5 black olives; 2 poonfuls of ketchup; 3 cl. brandy; salt and pepper; a few drops of tabasco.*

Marinate the shrimps in the brandy for an hour. Take them out and add the mayonnaise and the ketchup. Adjust the seasoning with a few drops of tabasco and add the whole capers. Decorate with the tomatoes and the hearts of artichoke cut into quarters. Garnish with the hard-boiled eggs cut into roundels and, in the middle of each one, arrange an olive cut in two. Decorate with parsley. *(France.)*
(See illustration, page 173.)

Salade Helsinki

Helsingin salaatti

For 6 persons: *600 gr. cooked flesh of pike or perch; 12 crayfish; ½ tin of peas; 1 lettuce; 350 gr. mayonnaise; wine vinegar; oil.* Cooking time for the crayfish: 10 to 12 minutes.

Cook the crayfish in a court-bouillon, allow to cool in the liquor, shell the tails and the claws. Flake the fish, and drain the peas. Mix and marinate together the flaked fish, the crayfish and the peas. Decorate copiously a salad bowl with leaves from the heart of lettuce and arrange all in the centre of the dish. Cover well with mayonnaise and serve cold. *(Finland.)*

Salade d'oeufs de carpe

Salata de icre de crap

For 6 persons: *125 gr. carp eggs; 50 gr. fresh white breadcrumbs; 2 lemons; ¼ litre of sunflower seed oil; black olives.*

Pass the carp eggs through a fine hair sieve, work them carefully with the breadcrumbs previously soaked and slightly pressed in a little salt and the juice of a lemon. Work up the mass as for a mayonnaise with the oil and adjust the seasoning and consistency. Arrange in a dome shape in a glass dish, and garnish with roundels of lemon and black olives. Serve very cold accompanied with slices of toasted bread. *(Rumania.)*

Saumon fumé

Salmon, smoked

For 6 persons: *18 to 24 very thin slices of smoked salmon; 6 quarters of lemon; leaf parsley.*

Garnish the salmon with quarters of lemon and leaf parsley. Serve separately toast and butter, freshly-milled pepper and, according to taste, a horse-radish cream. *(International cookery.)*

Smoked salmon

Smoked salmon is produced in Scotland, Denmark, Holland, Norway and other countries. Smoked Scotch salmon is pre-eminently the finest.

The flesh side of the smoked salmon is carefully trimmed of the outer hard surface engendered by the smoking and brining process. All bones are carefully removed, the small ones with a pair of tweezers. The flesh is sliced thinly, starting at the tail and cutting at an angle towards the tail. The first slices tend to be dry and should be put on one side for other uses. The salmon is rubbed with oil and wrapped in an oiled paper after it has been trimmed. It is then hung in a cool, dry place. This is done because the salmon quickly absorbs any other flavours. Serve with lemon and thin slices of brown bread and butter.

Saumon mariné à l'aneth

6 to 8 kg. fresh North Sea salmon; 3 kg. salt; 1 spoonful of sugar; 2 soup-spoonfuls of crushed white pepper; 1 coffee-spoonful of saltpetre; 1 kg. chopped dill. Marinating time: 48 hours.

Scale the salmon, gut them and remove the heads, divide lengthwise, remove the bones and trim away the fat parts of the belly and the points of the tails. Do not wash the fish but wipe it with a damp cloth. Mix the salt with the sugar, pepper, saltpetre, and half of the dill. Place a third of the marinade in a deep tray and lay a fillet of salmon on the top with the skin side down. Sprinkle with dill and add more of the marinade. Add the other fillet of salmon with the skin on top. Sprinkle with dill and cover with the rest of the marinade. Pack tightly, cover with a cloth and leave in the refrigerator or in a cold room for 48 hours. After removal from the marinade the fish must be carefully wiped with a cloth. Salmon marinated in this way has a strong taste of dill. The salt mixture has the sole purpose of firming the flesh without penetrating it. Kept in the cool, wrapped in a damp cloth dipped in a little of the marinade, the salmon keeps for a fairly long time.

For the table the salmon is cut into very thin scollops garnished with lettuce leaves and a small bunch of dill and quarters of lemon. It is accompanied by a sauce, for four portions, prepared thus: mix in a soup-plate 1½ spoonfuls of mustard, 1½ spoonfuls of sugar, 1½ spoonfuls of wine vinegar with 6 spoonfuls of olive oil. Season with very little salt and white pepper. Add a drop of water and a little chopped dill. This sauce is prepared at table by the head waiter, and is called: Hovmästersås. *(Sweden.)*

Sprats

For 6 persons: *24 sprats; 2 chopped shallots; 1 soup-spoonful of chopped parsley; oil; vinegar.*

Choose very fat sprats, remove the heads and tails and fillet them. Arrange them on a dish. Sprinkle with finely-chopped parsley and shallot and oil and vinegar, and allow to marinate for 4 to 5 hours before serving. *(International cookery.)*

Tartelette Neptune

For 6 persons: *12 short-pastry tartlets; 100 gr. mushrooms; 150 gr. shelled shrimp tails; 3 soup-spoonfuls of mayonnaise; 40 gr. softened shrimp butter; 6 bearded oysters; 1 dl. jelly.*

Fill the tartlets with a salpicon of mushrooms and shrimp tails bound with the mayonnaise to which the shrimp butter has been added. Place an oyster in the centre, and glaze lightly with the jelly. *(International cookery.)*
(See illustration, page 174.)

Tartelette Stanley

For 6 persons: *12 small oval tartlets; 250 gr. shelled shrimp tails; 80 gr. mayonnaise; 12 small roundels of tomato; 12 roundels of hard-boiled eggs; 1 dl. jelly; curry powder.*

Fill the tartlets with shrimp tails bound with the curried mayonnaise. Garnish them with a roundel of hard-boiled egg and a roundel of tomato. Mask with the jelly and sprinkle with chopped parsley. *(International cookery.)*

Tartelette au thon

Tunny-fish tartelette

For 6 persons: *12 small tartlets; 250 gr. chopped tunny; 80 gr. mayonnaise; 12 very small tunny roundels; 1 coffee-spoonful of chopped parsley; 2 chopped hard-boiled eggs.*

Fill the bottom of the tartlets with the chopped tunny bound with the mayonnaise. Place on top a roundel of tunny and sprinkle with chopped parsley; border the tartlets with the chopped hard-boiled egg. *(France.)*
(See illustration, page 175.)

Thon Marinette

For 6 persons: *12 small slices of tunny; 12 roundels of potatoes; 12 small roundels of tomato; 12 onion rings; 2 dl. sauce vinaigrette; 1 sieved hard-boiled egg; 1 soup-spoonful of chopped parsley.*

Arrange the slices of tunny on a round hors d'oeuvre dish alternating with the roundels of potato, tomato and rings of onion. Sprinkle all with the vinaigrette and with the hard-boiled egg and chopped parsley. *(France.)*

Thon Mirabeau

For 6 persons: *240 gr. tunny; 80 gr. softened butter; 2 soup-spoonfuls of mayonnaise; 2 tomatoes; 24 stoned olives.*

Pass the tunny through a hair sieve with the butter. Work it well with a spatula, incorporate the mayonnaise and adjust seasoning and consistency. Arrange this cream dome-shape in the centre of the dish, stud with olives, border the dish with thin half-roundels of very firm tomatoes. Serve toast separately. *(France.)*

Thon Mireille

For 6 persons: *240 gr. tunny; 80 gr. softened butter; 2 soup-spoonfuls of mayonnaise; 12 small round flat galettes in puff pastry; 12 roundels of hard-boiled egg; 12 small slices of tomato; 1 coffee-spoonful of chopped chervil.*

Prepare the cream as for the preparation Thon Mirabeau and mask the galettes with it. Garnish them with a small slice of tomato and a roundel of hard-boiled egg. Sprinkle lightly with chopped chervil. *(France.)*

Tomates antiboise

For 6 persons: *12 small tomatoes; 200 gr. tunny; 2 hard-boiled eggs; 30 gr. capers; 100 gr. mayonnaise; 1 coffee-spoonful of anchovy essence; 1 soup-spoonful of chopped parsley, chervil and tarragon; oil; vinegar; 1 lemon; leaf parsley.*

Scoop out the tomatoes through a small opening made on the stalk side, season the inside with salt, pepper, oil and vinegar, one hour in advance. Turn over and drain. Prepare a salpicon with the tunny, the hard-boiled egg and the capers; bind with the mayonnaise flavoured with anchovy essence. Incorporate the herbs. Fill the tomatoes with this salpicon, garnish with a half-slice of lemon and with leaf parsley. *(France.)*
(See illustration, page 172.)

Tomates monégasques

For 6 persons: *12 small tomatoes; 200 gr. tunny; 1 hard-boiled egg; 1 coffee-spoonful of chopped onion; 1 soup-spoonful of chopped parsley, chervil and tarragon; 80 gr. mayonnaise; oil; vinegar; leaf parsley.*

Scoop out the tomatoes, as for the preparation Tomates antiboise and let them marinate in the oil and vinegar. Fill them in a dome-shape with a mixture composed of chopped tunny to which has been added chopped hard-boiled egg, onion and herbs, all bound with the mayonnaise. Arrange with picked parsley around them. *(France.)*

Truites marinées

Trout, marinated

For 6 persons: *6 trout of 130 gr. to 175 gr.; ¾ litre court-bouillon; ¼ litre white wine; 2 soup-spoonfuls of mirepoix; 2 dl. vinegar; 6 slices of fluted lemon.* Cooking time: 12 minutes.

Prepare the court-bouillon with the white wine, vinegar and mirepoix. Poach the trout and let them cool in the court-bouillon. Drain, remove the skin, and arrange on an hors d'oeuvre dish. Pour a little passed court-bouillon over the trout, decorate them with slices of fluted lemon. *(France.)*

Filets de truites marinées

For 6 persons: *6 trout of 150 gr.; 200 gr. thick mayonnaise; 300 gr. vegetable salad; 1 soup-spoonful of chopped lobster coral; roundels of cucumber, radish, hard-boiled egg.*

Poach the trout in the court-bouillon as for the preparation Truites marinées. Allow to cool, drain, remove the fillets with care, and remove the skin. Arrange the fillets on the vegetable salad and mask with mayonnaise diluted with a little court-bouillon. Sprinkle with chopped coral, and border with thin roundels of cucumber, radish and hard-boiled egg. *(International cookery.)*

Truites fumés

Smoked trout

The skin is loosened, the lateral and dorsal bones removed, and the skin re-formed to facilitate service in the room. Store as for smoked salmon. Serve on lettuce leaves accompanied by hard-boiled egg, and a fan of gherkin decorated with small slices of lemon. Horse-radish cream is served separately, and thin slices of brown bread and butter.

Fish Soups and Consommés

Fish soups are divided into three categories: clear soups, thickened soups and the unclassified soups.
Clear soup is composed of a clarified stock of fumet of fish or shellfish, often lightly bound with tapioca or arrowroot. A corresponding garnish according to name is added. Thickened soup is prepared in different ways: cream, purée, velouté, etc. The stock or fish fumet serving as a base for soups is always prepared in advance.

Stock, Clarification for Soups, Royale for Fish Soups

Fish stock or fumet for preparation of soups

For 3 litres: *2 kg. or 2½ kg. of heads, bones and trimmings of sole, turbot, pike, whiting, etc.; 3 litres water; ½ litre dry white wine; 30 gr. butter; 80 gr. minced white of leek; 50 gr. minced onion; 30 gr. minced celery; 50 gr. parsley stalks; 1 bay-leaf; 20 gr. salt.* Cooking time: 40 minutes.

Sweat the aromates in the butter, add the fish, and moisten with white wine and the water, and add the salt. Bring to the boil and allow to simmer for 40 minutes. Pass through a fine conical strainer.

Clarification of fish consommés

For 3 litres: *3 litres fish fumet; ½ litre dry white wine; 500 to 600 gr. raw whiting or pike flesh; 3 whites of egg; 50 gr. white of leek and 50 gr. parsley stalks cut into rough dice.* Cooking time: 25 to 35 minutes.

Place together in a suitable pan the chopped fish flesh, the whites of egg, the diced vegetables and the white wine. Mix well, add the tepid fish fumet, and salt lightly. Bring to the boil and cook gently for 25 to 30 minutes. Pass the consommé through a tammy cloth.

Velouté for fish soups

For 3 litres: *300 gr. white roux; 3½ litres fish fumet.* Cooking time: 20 minutes.

Prepare the roux when required, cool and dilute it in the cold fish fumet. Bring to the boil while stirring and simmer gently for 20 minutes. Pass through a fine conical strainer or tammy cloth.

Fish or shellfish royale for garnishing soup

For 6 persons: *60 gr. firm fish flesh or shellfish meat; 1 soup-spoonful of cold béchamel; 1 dl. fresh cream; 3 egg yolks; 15 gr. butter.* Cooking time: 30 minutes.

Prepare a fine purée with the fish poached in butter, or with the cooked shellfish meat. Add the béchamel and the cream. Season with a pinch of salt and a pinch of grated nutmeg. Mix well, bind with the yolks of egg and pour into a buttered mould. Poach au bain-marie, carefully avoiding boiling. The royale is only cut up in the desired form after completely cooling.

Hot Soups and Unclassified Soups

Aïgo-saou

For 6 persons: *750 gr. pieces of cleaned white fish; 50 gr. chopped onion; 2 tomatoes, skinned, pipped and diced; 150 gr. potatoes cut in quarters; 2 crushed cloves of garlic; 1 small bunch of herbs; 15 gr. salt; 1¾ litres water; household bread; olive oil.* Cooking time: 20 minutes.

Put all the ingredients together in a saucepan, add the water, and boil quickly to cook. Arrange slices of bread in the soup-tureen, sprinkle them with a dash of peppered olive oil. Pour the soup over the slices of bread. Serve the fish separately accompanied with the aïoli (garlic sauce). *(France.)*

Bouillabaisse hollandaise

Dutch fish soup

For 6 persons: *1¼ litres fish fumet; 1 kg. flesh of various fish; whiting, sole, mackerel, pike etc. diced; 7 cl. oil; 1 minced white of leek; 1 chopped onion; 3 chopped shallots; 2 crushed cloves of garlic; 2 gr. saffron; 20 gr. lobster butter; 20 gr. tomato purée; ½ litre fish velouté.* Cooking time: 30 minutes.

Colour the diced fish in the oil together with the vegetable garnish. Moisten with the fish fumet. Simmer until cooked, and incorporate the velouté. Mix together the tomato purée, lobster butter and the garlic, and mix well in the soup. Season and serve with slices of toast. Add a little cognac, according to taste. *(Holland.)*

Bouillabaisse marseillaise

French fish soup

For 6 persons: *2 kg. of assorted fish such as John Dory, angler, conger, red mullet, whiting; 600 gr. crawfish; 125 gr. chopped onion; 100 gr. skinned, pipped and diced tomato; 2 crushed cloves of garlic; 1 branch of fennel; 1 small piece of dried orange peel; 2 sprigs of chopped parsley; 1 sprig of thyme; 1 small bayleaf; 1 dl. olive oil; 1 large pinch of saffron.* Cooking time: 18 minutes maximum.

Put in a saucepan the vegetables and the aromatics. Place on top first the crawfish and the fish of firm flesh, cut up into pieces of equal size. Sprinkle with olive oil, season with salt, milled pepper and saffron, and moisten with enough water for the fish to be well covered. Bring to the boil and boil quickly for 7 to 8 minutes. Add the fish of tender flesh, such as the red mullet and the whiting, also cut into equal pieces; complete the cooking, boiling fast, for another 7 to 8 minutes. Pour the cooking liquor of the bouillabaisse over slices of bread placed in a serving dish, and the fish and the crawfish (cut into tronçons) on another dish and sprinkle with roughly chopped parsley. The bread is never fried or toasted for the bouillabaisse marseillaise. The liquor of the bouillabaisse is normally taken as a soup and the other contents eaten as a second course. *(France.)*

Bourride

For 6 persons: *75 gr. various small fish; 2 chopped onions; 2 tomatoes, skinned, pipped and diced; 2 small crushed cloves of garlic; 1 bunch of mixed herbs; 5 cl. olive oil; 1 pinch of saffron; yolks of 2 eggs; ¼ litre aïoli; bread.* Cooking time: 15 minutes.

Pour 1½ litres of water into a saucepan and add to the fish cut into pieces of equal size; add the onion, tomato, garlic, bunch of herbs, oil, saffron, a pinch of salt and a little of the rind of a bitter orange. Bring to the boil and boil quickly. Pass the bouillon through a tammy cloth, crushing the vegetables, and bind this bouillon with the yolks of egg mixed with the aïoli. Bring to the boil two or three times and pour over slices of bread. Serve the fish separately. *(France.)*

Canebière

For 6 persons: *350 gr. various fish (all kinds of fish may be used); 120 gr. brunoise of carrots, onion, leek, celery and parsley; 30 gr. chopped shallots; 60 gr. tomatoes, skinned, pipped and diced; 1½ litres of fish fumet; 30 picked shrimp tails; 30 small pieces of lobster; 30 bearded mussels; ½ litre white wine; 7 cl. oil; pepper and salt; 1 branch of fennel.* Cooking time: 15 minutes.

Cut the fish into pieces of equal size. Colour slightly in hot oil with the vegetables, moisten with the white wine. Add the fish fumet, and cook on a good fire. Two minutes before serving, add the shrimp tails, the mussels, the chopped lobster and fennel. Adjust seasoning and consistency, and complete with a pinch of Cayenne pepper. *(International cookery.)*

Potage d'anguilles

Eel soup

For 6 persons: *1 kg. 200 of eel; 225 gr. prunes; 200 gr. apples; 60 gr. butter; 30 gr. flour; 60 gr. onion; 2 soup-spoonfuls of vinegar; 1 coffee-spoonful of powdered sugar.* For the quenelles: *125 gr. flour; 125 gr. butter; yolks of 4 eggs; ¼ litre of water.* Cooking time: about 30 minutes.

Cut up the eel, already skinned and cleaned, into tronçons of about 3 cm. Salt, allow to stand for 30 minutes. Wipe and cook until tender in water with very little salt and the minced onions. Cook the prunes, previously soaked, in very little water. Prepare a choux paste with the flour, the butter, the water and the egg yolks. Form quenelles with a coffee-spoon, poach in salt water and cool them. Remove the tronçons of eel and keep them hot with a little stock. Prepare a white roux with 40 gr. of butter and 30 gr. of flour, moisten with 1½ litres of eel stock and cook gently. Peel the apples and core them, cut into dice and stew quickly in butter. Pass the soup through a tammy cloth, and season with salt, pepper, vinegar and sugar. Garnish with the tronçons of eel, the prunes, the apples and the quenelles. *(Denmark.)*

Potage aux huîtres

Oyster soup

For 6 persons: *30 oysters; 15 cl. sherry; 15 cl. dry white wine; 1 kg. 500 knuckle of veal; 2 small carrots; 100 gr. leek; 100 gr. celeriac; 50 gr. breadcrumbs; 2 egg yolks; 250 gr. quenelles of fish.* For the quenelles: *125 gr. boned fish flesh (pike, whiting or pike-perch); 15 cl. fresh cream; 1 white of egg; 20 gr. flour; 25 gr. butter.* Cooking time: 3 hours.

Put the knuckle in cold water, bring to the boil and skim. Add the vegetables, very little salt and allow to cook gently for 2 to 2½ hours. Open the oysters, remove and beard them and allow them to marinate in the sherry. Keep the beards and liquor of the oysters. Pass the fish flesh through the finest plate of a mincer, incorporate the flour and the egg white, pass through a hair sieve and allow to cool. Season, work up with the cream and add the cooled melted butter. Form quenelles with a coffee-spoon, poach in salt water and cool them. Remove the knuckle from its bouillon and pass the latter through a conical strainer. Add the oyster liquor and the beards of the oysters as well as the breadcrumbs. Allow to cook gently for half an hour, pass through a tammy cloth, and reduce the soup to 1½ litres. Add the sherry of the marinade and the white wine; bind with the egg yolks mixed with a little bouillon, garnish with the oysters and the quenelles, and serve very hot. *(Denmark.)*

Potage de palourdes Santa Margherita

For 10 persons: *1 kg. 250 of palourdes (small bivalve molluscs, e.g. cockle, venus, clam); 175 gr. tomatoes, skinned, pipped and diced; purée of 3 anchovies; 6 cl. olive oil; 1 small onion; 1 small carrot and 1 small piece of white of leek, all chopped; 1¼ litres fish fumet; 2 dl. white wine; 1 chopped clove of garlic; 1 sprig of thyme; 1 bayleaf; 10 sage leaves; 1 cl. cognac; 80 gr. butter; 400 gr. rice; 1 soup-spoonful of chopped parsley; ½ soup-spoonful of chopped basil; saffron; Cayenne pepper.* Cooking time: about 35 minutes.

Colour lightly in oil the onion, carrot, leek, garlic, thyme, bayleaf and sage. Add the tomatoes, the anchovy purée, the previously cleaned shellfish, salt and pepper. Moisten with the cognac and the white wine, reduce almost completely. Add the fish fumet, cover, and cook on gentle heat for 15 minutes. Take out the shellfish and remove the cooked flesh and reserve. Pass the cooking liquor, bring to the boil, add the rice and a pinch of saffron per person, and allow to cook for another 16 minutes. When the rice is cooked, place the shellfish, parsley and basil, as well as the butter, into a soup-tureen. Add to it the rice and its bouillon, and correct seasoning with a pinch of Cayenne pepper. Serve very hot. *(Italy.)*

Potée de poisson Sturehof

Swedish fish soup
Sturehofs Fysgryta. Speciality of the former Restaurant Sturehof, Stockholm

For 6 persons: *2 whiting, each about 300 gr.; 1 barbel of 500 gr.; 500 gr. salmon trout; 20 raw mussels; 200 gr. carrots; 50 gr. celery and the white of 1 leek all cut into thin, small slices; 250 gr. tomatoes, skinned, pipped and cut into strips; 1 bunch of mixed herbs; 1 dl. white wine; 75 gr. oil or butter; 6 to 8 raw potatoes cut into round slices; 1 soup-spoonful of chopped parsley, dill and chives; 2 crushed cloves of garlic.* Cooking time: about 40 minutes.

Gut, clean and trim the fish and cut up into pieces. Prepare a good stock with heads and trimmings. Stew the vegetables in the oil or butter, moisten with a little stock. Add the pieces of fish, the mussels, brushed, washed and cleaned, the bunch of mixed herbs, the garlic, and moisten with the white wine and about 1¼ litres of the fish stock. Allow to cook gently for 20 minutes. Remove the mixed bunch of herbs and add the potatoes, blanched and cooled, and simmer them together until cooked. At the moment of serving, add the strips of tomato and sprinkle with the herbs. Serve boiling hot. *(Sweden.)*

Soupe aux clams Manhattan

Manhattan clam chowder

For 6 persons: *6 large chowder clams; 50 gr. butter; 250 gr. tomatoes, skinned, pipped and diced; 100 gr. onions; 200 gr. peeled potatoes; 2 green peppers; 2 celery stalks; 50 gr. smoked bacon; thyme.* Cooking time: 1 hour.

Cook the clams in a litre of water. Cut the onions, celery, peppers and bacon into small dice; colour in butter, sprinkle with flour, and colour again for a few minutes. Moisten with the cooking liquor of the clams, add the clams cut into small pieces, the diced potatoes and the tomatoes. Season with salt, pepper, and a little thyme. Cook gently for 1 hour. If necessary thicken with a little diluted potato starch or maize flour. *(United States.)*

Soupe aux moules et aux palourdes à la mode des îles

For 10 persons: *1 kg. mussels; 1 kg. palourdes (shellfish such as cockle, venus, clam); 200 gr. chopped onion; 100 gr. butter; 75 gr. flour; 1½ litres milk; 300 gr. grated gruyère cheese; 3 egg yolks.* Cooking time: about 25 minutes.

Melt the butter; add the onion and heat without coloration. Sprinkle with flour and make a roux, add the hot milk stirring continually; season, and allow to cook gently on a moderate heat for 15 minutes. During this time heat the mussels (previously brushed and washed) until they open. Remove from the shells. Decant carefully the mussel liquor and pass through a tammy cloth. Retain a few spoonfuls. Add it to the white sauce stirring well. Incorporate the gruyère, and allow to cook another 2 minutes with gentle heat. Mix the egg yolks with the retained liquor stock and add to the soup, stirring all the time. Adjust seasoning and consistency. Serve with small croûtons of toasted white bread. The milk can be replaced by bouillon. In this case mix the egg yolks with 2 dl. of cream. A nut of butter may also be added to complete. *(Italy.)*

Soupe au riz et aux crevettes

Rice and shrimp soup

For 10 persons: *450 gr. picked shrimps; 250 gr. rice; 15 cl. milk; 50 gr. chopped onion; 1 crushed clove of garlic; 425 gr. potatoes in small dice; 1 litre fish fumet or water; 160 gr. fresh peas; 200 gr. tomatoes, skinned, pipped and diced; 5 cl. olive oil; 1 soup-spoonful of chopped parsley; pinch of wild marjoram.* Cooking time: 25 minutes.

Cook lightly in the oil the onion, garlic and parsley. Add the tomatoes, colour lightly, moisten with the fish fumet or water, add the potatoes, rice, peas, and season. Leave on the fire until the potatoes are cooked. Add the shrimps to the soup and continue the cooking until the rice is just cooked. Remove from the fire, add the milk, and adjust seasoning and consistency. Serve very hot. *(Italy.)*

Soupe de poisson Constantine

For 6 persons: *450 gr. fillets of fresh cod or haddock; 1 litre of mussels; 125 gr. picked shrimps; 75 gr. onion; 75 gr. rice; 100 gr. white of leek; 250 gr. tomatoes; 1½ litres fish fumet; 5 cl. olive oil; ½ a coffee-spoonful of curry; 2 pipped green peppers; 1 dl. white wine; 1 soup-spoonful of chopped parsley; 1 lemon.* Cooking time: 20 to 25 minutes.

Clean the mussels, cook them with the white wine. When they are fully open, remove from the shells and retain them. Pass the mussel cooking liquor, allow to cool, and decant. Cut the fillets of fish into large squares of 5 cm. on the slant; salt and marinate for 1 hour minimum in the lemon juice. Divide the onions in two and prepare the peppers and leek in a julienne; toss in the olive oil without colouring. Sprinkle with curry, and continue cooking for 2 minutes; moisten with the fish fumet and the cooking liquor from the mussels, bring to the boil, add the rice and allow to cook for 10 minutes. Add the fish and the tomatoes, skinned, pipped and diced; allow to cook gently for another 10 minutes. Add the mussels, the picked shrimp tails and the chopped parsley. Bring to the boil again, and adjust seasoning and consistency. Serve immediately. *(Germany.)*

Soupe de poisson espagnole

For 6 persons: *250 gr. angler; 250 gr. tunny; 250 gr. cockles; 100 gr. prawns; 2 small chopped onions; 1 small chopped clove of garlic; 2 soup-spoonfuls of tomato purée; 100 gr. cooked peas; 1 hard-boiled egg; 2 soup-spoonfuls of chopped parsley; 1 coffee-spoonful of paprika; 4 cl. Pernod; 2 litres fish fumet; croûtons of toast; oil.* Cooking time: 30 minutes.

Colour the onion and garlic in the oil, add the angler and the tunny cut up into large dice; season with salt and paprika, and sauté all for a few minutes. Flame with the Pernod and moisten with the fish fumet. Cook the cockles for 5 minutes and shell them. Shell the shrimps and cook for 5 minutes. Add to the stock with the tomato purée. Allow to cook gently for 10 to 12 minutes, and adjust seasoning and consistency. Before serving, add the peas and the chopped hard-boiled egg; sprinkle with chopped parsley. Serve croûtons of toast separately. *(Spain.)*

Soupe de poisson finlandaise

For 10 persons: *3 kg. fish flounder, perch or small Swedish herrings; 25 mussels; 2 carrots; 2 leeks; 2 onions; 8 tomatoes, skinned, pipped and diced; 1 soup-spoonful of chopped fennel leaves; ¼ litre olive oil; 2 bayleaves; 2 crushed cloves of garlic; 14 white peppercorns; 1 bunch of parsley; 1 sprig of thyme; 1 lemon; 2 gr. saffron.* Cooking time: about 45 minutes.

Fillet the fish. Chop trimmings and bones; moisten with 5 litres of cold water; bring to the boil and skim. Add the bayleaf, thyme, the parsley stalks, the green of the leeks, pepper, salt, and allow to cook gently for 20 to 25 minutes. Cut up the carrots and whites of leek in a coarse julienne. Simmer in the olive oil for about 15 minutes with onion, garlic and fennel. Pass the fish stock through a conical strainer and pour it over the vegetables. Allow to cook for 5 minutes and add the tomatoes, skinned, pipped and diced, and the saffron. Open the mussels in a little boiling fish stock, remove from the shells and beard them. Decant the poaching liquor of the mussels, pass through a muslin, add it to the soup as well as the fillets of fish cut into pieces. Allow to cook for a few moments. Add the mussels and the lemon juice; season and give another boiling. Place the chopped parsley in a hot soup-tureen and pour the soup into it. *(Finland.)*

Soupe de poisson hongroise

For 10 persons: *1 kg. 200 of fillets of fish (carp, pike, sheath fish); 5 gr. paprika; 40 gr. lard; 60 gr. flour; 150 gr. carrots; 150 gr. turnips; 50 gr. minced onion; 3 dl. sour cream; 30 gr. butter; 1 small bunch of chopped parsley; 1 bayleaf; vinegar; white bread.* Cooking time: 1 hour.

Clean the fish, cut it into large pieces and place them in a saucepan. Add 3 dl. of water, 1 bayleaf, pepper and salt and cook for 30 minutes while skimming. Prepare a julienne with carrots and turnips, add the onion, and colour all in another saucepan with a little lard. Add the parsley, moisten with the fish stock, and allow to cook for 20 minutes. In the meantime, prepare a roux with the lard and the flour, sprinkle with paprika, and moisten with a little water. Bind the soup with this roux. Add the sour cream and allow to cook for 10 minutes. Season with a few drops of vinegar, and adjust seasoning and consistency. Colour the diced bread in the butter. Arrange the fish in a soup-tureen and pour the soup over. Serve the croûtons separately. *(Hungary.)*

Soupe de poisson de la Mer du Nord

For 6 persons: *1 kg. of small fish in season—for example, 1 small whiting, 1 plaice, 1 lemon sole, 1 piece of ling, 1 small tail of brill; 1 litre of mussels; 100 gr. picked shrimp tails; 2 dl. dry white wine; about 30 cl. light beer; 75 gr. butter; 2 egg yolks; 1 dl. fresh cream; 25 gr. flour; 2 onions; 1 clove of garlic; 2 branches of celery; 1 bayleaf; 1 sprig of thyme; 1 coffee-spoonful of chopped chervil; 1 lemon; large pinch of saffron.* Cooking time: fish fumet—30 minutes; fish—5 to 6 minutes.

Fillet the fish, skin and bone them, cut up into dice of 1½ cm. Prepare 1 litre of fish fumet with bones, onion, celery, thyme, bayleaf, garlic, beer, lemon juice and water. Cook the mussels with white wine, celery, onion and milled pepper. As soon as cooked, remove from shells and beard. Pass the stock and allow to stand. Arrange the pieces of fish in a deep dish well buttered and pour the cooking liquor of the mussels over them; poach for 5 minutes. Colour the fish fumet with the saffron, pass through a tammy cloth, bind with the flour worked up with 40 gr. of butter. Add the chervil, a liaison of yolks of egg and fresh cream, the shrimp tails and the fish with the cooking liquor. Adjust seasoning and consistency. Serve very hot. *(Belgium.)*

Soupe de poisson russe

For 10 persons: *1 kg. of large or small sturgeon, without skin or bone; 2½ litres of fish fumet; 1 dl. salted cucumber juice; 100 gr. minced onion; 150 gr. salted cucumber; 150 gr. marinated cèpes; 75 gr. capers; 10 roundels of pipped lemon; 50 gr. crayfish butter; 2 soup-spoonfuls of chopped dill; black olives; 2 soup-spoonfuls of oil; rastegais.* Cooking time: about 30 minutes.

Colour lightly the minced onion in the oil, moisten with the fish stock and the cucumber juice, and cook slowly for 10 to 15 minutes. Cut the fish into pieces about 50 gr., poach them in the stock until the fish is just cooked, and add the cucumber, the cèpes, cut into small slices, and the capers. As soon as the fish is cooked, adjust the seasoning of the soup, pour with all the ingredients into a soup-tureen, sprinkle with crayfish butter and chopped dill, and garnish with roundels of lemon. Serve the black olives and the rastegais separately. (Rastegais: small Russion patties filled with a salpicon of salmon.) *(Russia.)*

Soupe de poisson Szeged

For 10 persons: *2 kg. 500 of various fish (carp, if possible live, small pike-perch, sheath-fish, small sturgeon, with eggs and soft roe); 300 gr. minced onion; 100 gr. minced green peppers; 50 gr. tomatoes, skinned, pipped and diced; 30 gr. paprika.* Cooking time: 1 hour 20 minutes.

Fillet the fish, previously gutted, scaled, cleaned and washed. Cut into large pieces. Prepare a stock with the heads and trimmings, onion and 3 litres of water. Cook gently for one hour. Arrange in a saucepan the fish pieces, the eggs, the soft roe of the fish; add the stock passed through a tammy cloth. Add the peppers, the tomatoes, and bring to the boil. Sprinkle with paprika, and shake to incorporate it. Allow to cook, covered, on a gentle heat for 20 minutes. Do not stir. Real fish soup Szeged should be prepared with different kinds of fish, but it can be made with carp only. *(Hungary.)*

Waterzoï des pêcheurs

For 10 persons: *500 gr. fillets of whiting; 500 gr. fillets of sea bream; 600 gr. of angler fish, cut into large dice; 4 fillets of sole, each of 75 gr.; 6 minced whites of leek; 60 gr. chopped onion; 1 bottle of beer; 4 egg yolks; ¼ litre fresh cream; 50 gr. butter; 1 gr. saffron; 15 to 20 mussels; 1 bunch of mixed herbs; 2 soup-spoonfuls of chopped chervil; 1 onion; 2 sticks of celery; 2 dl. white wine; 1 pinch of coriander.* Cooking time: about 30 minutes.

Prepare a fish stock with the bones and trimmings moistened with 1 litre of water; add a bouquet garni. Pass the stock and reduce by half. Cook without colouring in the butter the leeks, diced celery and chopped onion; add the prepared diced fish, season with salt and milled pepper, and sprinkle with saffron and coriander. Heat the beer with the prepared fish stock, pour over the fish, bring to the boil and simmer for 10 minutes. Meanwhile, poach the fillets of sole with a little of the reserved stock. Cook the mussels in white wine with half a chopped onion and a stick of celery. Decant the cooking liquor from both the sole and the mussels and add to the soup. At the last moment add the shelled and bearded mussels and the cooked fillets of sole cut into three pieces. Finish with a liaison of egg yolks and cream.

Clear Soups

Consommé Albion

For 6 persons: *1½ litres consommé of fish; 60 gr. seed tapioca; 120 gr. quenelles of lobster; 60 gr. julienne of truffle.* Cooking time: 12 minutes.

Bring the consommé to the boil and bind it with the tapioca. Add the cooked quenelles and the truffle, as a garnish. *(France.)*

Consommé cancalaise

For 6 persons: *1½ litres fish consommé; 18 poached oysters; 4 fillets of sole cut into julienne and poached; 120 quenelles of whiting; 60 gr. tapioca.* Cooking time: 12 minutes.

Add the cooking liquor from the oysters to the consommé and bind it lightly with the tapioca. Garnish with the julienne of fillets of sole, the quenelles, and the bearded oysters. *(France.)*

Consommé carmélite

For 6 persons: *1½ litres fish consommé; 50 gr. cooked rice; 50 gr. arrowroot; 120 gr. quenelles of whiting, round in shape.* Cooking time: 12 minutes.

Bind the consommé with the arrowroot diluted with a little water, allow to cook gently. Pass through a muslin and garnish with the rice and the quenelles. *(France.)*

Consommé Marie-Louise

For 6 persons: *1½ litres of very clear fish consommé; 30 gr. arrowroot; 120 gr. very small quenelles in truffled fish farce; 12 crayfish tails.* Cooking time: 10 minutes.

Bind the consommé with the arrowroot and add to it the quenelles and the crayfish tails cut into two. *(France.)*

Consommé muscovite I

For 6 persons: *1½ litres of consommé of sterlet with cucumber essence; 60 gr. julienne of cooked mushrooms; 30 gr. vésiga (dried spinal marrow of sturgeon).*

Soak the vésiga overnight, cook it in bouillon or fish fumet, and cut it into dice. Garnish the consommé with the vésiga and the mushrooms. *(Russia.)*

Consommé muscovite II

For 6 persons: *1½ litres of fish consommé; 60 gr. julienne of cooked mushrooms; 60 gr. cooked small cucumber balls; 120 gr. cooked sturgeon flesh.*

Heat the consommé and add the mushrooms, the cucumber balls and the sturgeon cut into small dice. *(Russia).*

Consommé Nelson

For 6 persons: *1½ litres fish consommé; 30 gr. arrowroot; 50 gr. cooked rice; 12 very small choux buns; 120 gr. chopped lobster à l'américaine.* Cooking time: 10 minutes.

Dilute the arrowroot with a little water, and bind the consommé. Allow to cook gently, pass through a muslin. Garnish with the rice. Fill the small choux buns with the hot lobster and serve them separately. *(International cookery.)*

Consommé Vatel

For 6 persons: *1½ litres fish consommé with essence of sole; 4 very small poached fillets of sole; 100 gr. royale of crayfish purée.*

Cut up the fillets of sole in small lozenges and the royale into dice. Add them to the consommé. *(France.)*

Thickened Soups

Bisque de crevettes Boston

Boston shrimp soup

For 6 persons: *500 gr. tails of Jumbo prawns unshelled; 60 gr. butter; 75 gr. chopped onion; 100 gr. rice; 2 dl. white wine; ¼ litre fresh cream; 3 cl. cognac; 2 spoonfuls of vinegar; 1 coffee-spoonful of pink paprika.* Cooking time: 1 hour.

Put the shrimps into 1 dl. of cold water, add the white wine, vinegar, salt and pepper, bring to the boil, and allow to go tepid. Shell and gut the shrimps. Colour in the butter the onion and the shrimp shells, sprinkle with paprika, add the rice, and stew all for a moment. Moisten with the shrimp cooking liquor and allow to cook gently for 1 hour. Pass through a tammy cloth, bind with the cream previously brought to the boil. Add the cognac and the finely-diced shrimp tails, boil again and adjust seasoning and consistency. *(United States.)*

Bisque ou purée d'écrevisses

Crayfish bisque

For 6 persons: *20 small crayfish; 100 gr. butter; 200 gr. mirepoix bordelaise; 1 dl. white wine; 2 cl. cognac; 80 gr. rice; 1½ litres fish stock; 15 cl. fresh cream; 1 sprig of thyme; ⅛ bayleaf; 2 parsley stalks; Cayenne pepper.* Cooking time: about 35 minutes.

Stew the mirepoix in the butter, add the crayfish, gutted and washed, the parsley stalks, thyme and bayleaf, a pinch of salt and a little pepper. Sauté at full heat until the crayfish turn red. Flambé with the cognac; deglaze with the white wine; reduce the wine by two-thirds. Moisten with 2 dl. of fish stock. Cook for 10 minutes. Shell the tails, retain them for the garnishing (12 trunks may also be retained). Cook the rice separately for 20 minutes in 4 dl. of fish stock. Pound the shells with the rice, adding the crayfish cooking liquor. Put this purée into a saucepan, dilute it with the rest of the fish stock, boil for 1 to 2 minutes, and pass through a fine conical strainer. Heat without boiling; add the rest of the butter in small pieces and the cream. Adjust seasoning and consistency, and complete with a pinch of Cayenne pepper. Garnish with the tails cut into dice. The trunks may be added filled with a fish farce, then poached (optional). *(France.)*

Bisque d'écrevisses princesse

For 6 persons: *1½ litres of crayfish bisque; 12 very small quenelles of whiting and crayfish butter; 6 crayfish tails; 6 cooked tips of green asparagus.*

Add to the bisque the asparagus tips, the crayfish tails cut into dice, and the quenelles. *(International cookery.)*

Crème d'anguille hollandaise

For 6 persons: *500 gr. skinned and boned eel; 1 small white of leek; 1 small carrot; 1 small stick of celery; 30 gr. salsify; 1¼ litres fish stock; 2 dl. fresh cream; 3 egg yolks; 1 soup-spoonful of parsley, chervil and sorrel, chopped; a pinch of powdered thyme.* Cooking time: 18 minutes.

Fillet the eel, cut into tronçons of 1 cm. Cut the vegetables into a brunoise. Cook the eel with the brunoise in the fish stock for about 15 minutes. Remove the eels and bind the cooking liquor with the egg yolks and the cream. Adjust the seasoning with a pinch of powdered mace. Put back the tronçons of eel and add chopped parsley, chervil and sorrel, and the powdered thyme. *(Holland.)*

Crème de crevettes

For 6 persons: *250 gr. raw shrimps; 150 gr. mirepoix bordelaise; 50 gr. butter; 1 litre clear béchamel; ¼ litre white wine; ¼ litre of fish stock; 60 gr. picked shrimp tails; 2 dl. fresh cream; 30 gr. shrimp butter.* Cooking time: 25 minutes.

Stew the raw shrimps in the butter with the mirepoix for 5 minutes. Add the white wine, and reduce by two-thirds. Add the béchamel and the fish stock, and allow to cook gently for 20 minutes; strain the liquid and pound the shrimps in a mortar and add the purée to the soup. Heat and pass through a tammy cloth. Bring almost to the boil, bind with the cream and the shrimp butter, and garnish with the picked tails. *(France.)*

Crème divette

For 6 persons: *¾ litre crayfish bisque; 250 gr. smelt; 40 gr. butter; ½ litre clear béchamel; 2 dl. fresh cream; 50 gr. quenelles of smelt farce, in large pearls; 25 gr. very black pearls of truffle; 6 shelled crayfish tails; 1 dl. fish stock.* Cooking time: 20 minutes.

Stew the smelt in the butter, add the fish stock and the béchamel; allow to cook gently for 15 minutes. Pass through a fine hair sieve; add the crayfish bisque; heat, skim, add cream, and adjust seasoning and consistency. Garnish with quenelles, truffles and the crayfish tails cut into dice. *(France.)*

Crème Perette

For 6 persons: *1¼ litres lobster bisque; 2 dl. cream; 2 dl. white wine; 24 large frogs' legs.* Cooking time: 10 minutes.

Poach the frogs' legs in the white wine; allow to cool. Cut up the flesh into dice. Reduce the white wine by two-thirds, add it to the lobster soup, and bind with the cream. Garnish with the frogs' legs. *(International cookery.)*

Potage américaine

For 6 persons: *12 small shelled crayfish tails; ½ litre crayfish bisque; ½ litre tomato soup; ½ litre consommé with tapioca.*

Mix the bisque with the tomato soup and the tapioca consommé kept rather thick. Add the crayfish tails cut into large dice. *(France).*

Potage au crabe

Crab soup

For 6 persons: *120 gr. crab meat; 1½ litres crayfish bisque.*

Cut up the crab meat into dice and add it to the crayfish bisque.

Potage dieppoise

For 6 persons: *1¼ litres fish velouté; ¼ litre mussel cooking liquor; 1 small minced white of leek; 50 gr. mushroom trimmings; 80 gr. picked shrimp tails; 18 mussels poached in white wine; 40 gr. butter; 1 dl. fresh cream; 2 egg yolks.* Cooking time: 20 minutes.

Add the white of leek and the mushroom trimmings to the velouté. Allow to cook gently for 15 minutes, pass through a tammy cloth. Add the mussel poaching liquor, carefully decanted; heat without boiling. Finish with a liaison of cream and yolks of egg; butter and garnish with the bearded mussels and the shrimp tails. *(France.)*

Potage Josselin

For 6 persons: *1 litre fish consommé; ¼ litre mussel poaching liquor, carefully decanted; 6 egg yolks; 3 dl. cream; 60 gr. butter.* Cooking time: 5 to 6 minutes.

Mix the fish consommé and the mussel poaching liquor. Add the egg yolks, diluted with the cream, and stir continually on a slow fire until the mixture coats the back of a spatula. Do not allow to boil. When the liaison is assured, complete the soup, away from the fire, with the butter. Adjust seasoning and consistency. *(France.)*

Potage aux huîtres australienne

Australian oyster soup

For 6 persons: *12 large oysters; ½ litre consommé; 1 dl. fresh cream; 2 egg yolks; 50 gr. diced celeriac stewed in butter; curry.* Cooking time: about 10 minutes.

Open the oysters and retain the liquor. Beard and stiffen the oysters and the beards, in 2 dl. of hot water. Remove the oysters; pass the cooking liquor; mix it with the hot consommé. Add the diced celeriac and bind with the egg yolks diluted with the cream. Season with a little curry. Adjust seasoning and consistency. Serve the soup in hot cups; add the oysters and their liquor at the last minute. *(International cookery.)*

Potage Thermidor

For 6 persons: *1½ litres of lobster bisque; 60 gr. Chivry butter; 1½ dl. cream; 3 egg yolks; 60 gr. quenelles of pike farce; 30 gr. diced red peppers; ¼ litre fish stock.*

Mix the lobster soup with the fish stock; bind with the cream and the egg yolks. Complete away from the fire with the Chivry butter. Garnish with the quenelles and the diced red peppers stewed in butter. *(France.)*

Potage bisque de crevettes

Shrimp bisque

For 6 persons: *600 gr. raw shrimps; 200 gr. mirepoix bordelaise; 50 gr. butter; 1 dl. white wine; 2 cl. cognac; 80 gr. rice; 1¼ litres fish stock; 15 cl. fresh cream; 1 sprig of thyme; ½ bayleaf; 2 parsley stalks; Cayenne pepper; 30 gr. shrimp butter.* Cooking time: 30 minutes.

Prepare the soup as for the preparation of crayfish bisque. Shell half the tails and retain for garnishing. Work up the bisque with the shrimp butter, and add the shelled tails. *(France.)*

Potage bisque de homard

Lobster bisque

For 6 persons: *600 to 750 gr. live lobster; 100 gr. butter; 200 gr. mirepoix bordelaise; 1 dl. white wine; 2 cl. cognac; 80 gr. rice; 1¼ litres fish stock; 15 cl. fresh cream; 1 small bunch of mixed herbs; Cayenne pepper.* Cooking time: about 30 minutes.

Colour the mirepoix in the butter. Add the lobster cut into thick slices, season with a pinch of salt and a little freshly-milled pepper. Sauté on full heat until the lobster turns red. Flame with the cognac; deglaze with the white wine; add the bunch of mixed herbs and 2 dl. fish stock. Allow to cook for 18 minutes. Cook the rice with 4 dl. of fish stock. Shell the lobster; retain the meat. Pound the shells with the rice, and add the lobster cooking liquor. Pass this purée through a hair sieve. Put the purée into a saucepan; dilute it with the rest of the fish stock and allow to boil for 3 to 4 minutes. Pass through a conical strainer. Add 50 gr. of butter and cream, adjust seasoning and consistency, and complete with a pinch of Cayenne pepper. Garnish with the lobster meat cut into dice. *(France.)*

Potage de poisson Carnaro

For 10 persons: *1 kg. sea-food such as mussels, shrimps, etc.; 250 gr. white-bait; 80 gr. butter; 50 gr. chopped onion; 2 small chopped carrots; 1 minced leek; 1 bayleaf; 1 sprig of thyme; 1 crushed clove of garlic; 1 soup-spoonful of chopped parsley; 100 gr. rice; 1 dl. white wine; 2 cl. cognac; 1¼ litres fish stock; 1 dl. fresh cream; Cayenne pepper; bread croûtons.* Cooking time: 30 minutes.

Sauté lightly in the butter the onion, carrots, and leek. Add the bayleaf, thyme, garlic and, to complete, the sea-food previously brushed, washed and cleaned. As soon as the shrimps turn red, flame with the cognac, moisten with the white wine, and add ¼ litre of fish stock and the parsley. Allow to cook until the shells open; cook the rice in 1 litre of fish stock for 12 minutes. Add the whitebait, and allow to simmer for 10 minutes. Add the shelled sea-food and the cooking liquor. Bring to the boil; pass all through a fine hair sieve. To complete, bind the soup with cream, and season with a pinch of Cayenne pepper. Serve with fried bread croûtons. *(Italy.)*

Potage de poisson Kinereth

For 6 persons: *600 gr. sea fish with firm flesh; 300 gr. tomatoes, skinned, pipped and diced; 300 gr. mushrooms; 150 gr. onion; 2 dl. fresh cream; 2 egg yolks; 60 gr. butter; Worcestershire sauce; curry; fish fumet made from: 1 kg. bones and trimmings of sea fish; 50 gr. minced onion; 10 parsley stalks; 25 gr. mushroom trimmings; 5 peppercorns; lemon; ¼ litre white wine.* Cooking time: about 60 minutes.

Prepare a stock with chopped bones and trimmings, onion, parsley, mushroom trimmings, pepper, the juice of half a lemon, 1½ litres of water and 1 dl. white wine. Allow to cook gently for 30 minutes; pass through a conical strainer. Cut the onions and mushrooms into dice; colour them in the butter; add the tomatoes; moisten with the fish stock. Add the fish cut into small pieces; season with salt and pepper, and bring to the boil. Allow to cook on gentle heat for about 20 minutes. Add the rest of the white wine; bring to the boil again, and complete the seasoning with curry and Worcestershire sauce. Bind with the egg yolks mixed with the cream. *(Israel.)*

Velouté Albufera

For 6 persons: *1¼ litres crayfish bisque; 1½ dl. cream; 3 egg yolks; 2 dl. fish stock; 50 gr. crayfish butter.*

Dilute the bisque with the fish stock. Heat, bind with the cream and the egg yolks. Complete with the crayfish butter. *(France.)*

Velouté Borely

For 6 persons: *1¼ litres fish velouté; ½ litre of mussels; 2 dl. white wine; 250 gr. whiting fillets; 2 dl. fish stock; 100 gr. whiting quenelles; 1½ dl. fresh cream; 2 egg yolks; 50 gr. butter.* Cooking time: 15 minutes.

Stew the whiting in the butter and fish stock. Cook the mussels in the white wine. Pass the whiting fillets through a fine sieve. Add this purée and the decanted cooking liquor from the mussels to the velouté. Pass through a conical strainer. Heat without allowing to boil. Complete at the moment of serving with a liaison of cream and egg yolks. Garnish with the bearded mussels and the whiting quenelles. *(France.)*

Velouté cardinal

For 6 persons: *1¼ litres fish velouté; 1½ dl. fresh cream; 3 egg yolks; 40 gr. lobster butter; 40 gr. red butter; 100 gr. lobster royale or 60 gr. lobster meat.*

Heat the velouté; bind it with the cream and the egg yolks. Rectify with the lobster butter and the red butter. Garnish with the royale or the lobster meat, cut into dice. *(France.)*

Velouté de crevettes normande

For 6 persons: *1¼ litres shrimp bisque; 1½ dl. fresh cream; 3 egg yolks; 12 small oysters; 60 gr. picked cooked shrimp tails; 50 gr. shrimp butter.*

Poach the oysters, retain the liquor. Heat the bisque with the oyster liquor; complete it with a liaison of cream and egg yolks, and the shrimp butter. Garnish with the bearded oysters and the shrimp tails. *(France.)*

Velouté Doris

For 6 persons: *1¼ litres velouté of whiting fish stock; 1½ dl. fresh cream; 3 egg yolks; 24 small poached oysters; 50 gr. butter.*

Heat the velouté and complete it at the moment of serving with a liaison of cream and egg yolks and the butter. Garnish with the bearded oysters. *(Holland.)*

Velouté d'écrevisses Joinville

For 6 persons: *1¼ litres crayfish bisque, not creamed; ¼ litre fish stock; 1 dl. fresh cream; 2 egg yolks; 50 gr. crayfish butter; 6 shelled crayfish tails; 30 gr. truffle; 30 gr. cooked mushrooms.*

Mix the bisque, kept rather thick with the fish stock, and heat without allowing to boil. Finish with a liaison of cream and egg yolks and the crayfish butter. Garnish with the truffles, mushrooms and crayfish tails cut into dice. *(France.)*

Velouté d'eperlans

For 6 persons: *100 gr. smelt fillets; 200 gr. whiting flesh; 50 gr. chopped onion; ½ a lemon; 1 litre fish velouté; ¼ litre fish stock; 1½ dl. fresh cream; 3 egg yolks; 60 gr. quenelles of whiting farce; 100 gr. butter.* Cooking time: 20 minutes.

Stew in butter and lemon juice the smelt fillets, the whiting flesh and the chopped onion. Add the fish stock, allow to cook for 15 minutes; pass through a fine sieve. Mix this purée with the fish velouté, and heat without boiling. Complete with a liaison of cream and egg yolks and 50 gr. of butter. Garnish with the smelt fillets. *(France.)*

Velouté d'éperlans dieppoise

For 6 persons: *1¼ litres smelt velouté; ½ litre of mussels; 2 dl. white wine; 60 gr. picked shrimp tails; 1½ dl. fresh cream; 3 egg yolks; 50 gr. butter.*

Cook the mussels in the white wine. Prepare the velouté; dilute it with the poaching liquor of the mussels, carefully decanted. Heat and complete with a liaison of cream and egg yolks and butter. Garnish with the shrimps and the bearded mussels. *(France.)*

Velouté d'éperlans Joinville

For 6 persons: *1 litre smelt velouté; 1½ dl. fresh cream; 3 egg yolks; 50 gr. shrimp butter; 6 crayfish tails; 30 gr. truffle; 60 gr. cooked mushrooms; ¼ litre fish stock.*

Dilute the velouté with the fish stock. Heat and bind with the cream and the egg yolks, and finish with the shrimp butter. Garnish with the truffles and julienne of mushrooms and the diced crayfish tails. *(France.)*

Velouté d'éperlans princesse

For 6 persons: *1 litre smelt velouté; ¼ litre fish stock; 1½ dl. fresh cream; 3 egg yolks; 60 gr. green asparagus tips; 12 small quenelles of smelt farce with crayfish butter.*

Dilute the velouté with the fish stock. Heat and bind with the cream and the egg yolks. Garnish with the diced asparagus tips and the smelt quenelles. *(France.)*

Velouté d'éperlans Saint-Malo

For 6 persons: *1 litre smelt velouté; ¼ litre fish stock; 1½ dl. fresh cream; 3 egg yolks; 50 gr. shrimp butter; 120 gr. quenelles of sole farce.*

Prepare the velouté in the usual way. Garnish it with the sole quenelles. *(France.)*

Velouté Eugénie

For 6 persons: *1¼ litres shrimp velouté; 1½ dl. fresh cream; 120 gr. picked shrimp tails; 1 soup-spoonful of chervil leaves; 3 egg yolks.*

Bind the velouté with the cream and the egg yolks, and add the shrimp tails. At the moment of serving incorporate the chervil leaves. *(France.)*

Velouté de homard Cleveland

For 6 persons: *¾ litre lobster bisque; ½ litre fish velouté; 1½ dl. fresh cream; 3 egg yolks; 60 gr. lobster meat; 2 skinned and pressed tomatoes.*

Mix the bisque with the velouté, bind with the cream and the egg yolks. Garnish with the tomatoes, cut into dice and softened in butter, and the diced lobster meat. *(France.)*

Velouté de homard indienne

For 6 persons: *1¼ litres of lobster bisque; 1½ dl. fresh cream; 3 egg yolks; 50 gr. butter; 5 gr. curry; 60 gr. cooked rice; 50 gr. cooked lobster meat.*

Season the bisque with the curry, bind with the cream and egg yolks. Butter lightly. Garnish with the cooked rice and the diced lobster meat. *(France.)*

Velouté de homard orientale

For 6 persons: *¾ litre lobster soup prepared à la Newburg; ½ litre of fish velouté; 1½ dl. fresh cream; 3 egg yolks; 60 gr. cooked rice; 60 gr. cooked lobster meat.*

Mix the lobster soup with the velouté, and bind with the cream and egg yolks. Garnish with the rice and the diced lobster meat. *(France.)*

Velouté de homard au paprika

For 6 persons: *1 litre fish velouté; ¼ litre fish stock; 30 gr. chopped onion; 10 gr. pink paprika; 25 gr. red and green peppers; 50 gr. butter; 20 gr. tomato purée; 50 gr. cooked rice; 100 gr. lobster butter.* Cooking time: 20 minutes.

Colour the onion in the butter, and add the paprika. Allow to cook for 2 minutes; add the tomato purée, the velouté and the stock. Allow to cook gently for 15 minutes; and pass through a tammy cloth. Bind with the cream and egg yolks. Complete, away from the fire, with the lobster butter. Garnish with the rice and the diced cooked peppers. *(France.)*

Velouté aux huîtres

For 6 persons: *1¼ litres fish velouté; 24 small oysters; 1½ dl. fresh cream; 3 egg yolks; 50 gr. butter.*

Poach the oysters in their liquor. Prepare a smooth fish velouté and add to it the oyster liquor. Complete with a liaison of cream, egg yolks and butter. Garnish with the bearded oysters. *(International cookery.)*

Velouté Jacqueline

For 6 persons: *1¼ litres fish velouté; 1½ dl. fresh cream; 3 egg yolks; 50 gr. cooked rice; 1 soup-spoonful of rouge de carotte in pea-sized balls; 1 soup-spoonful of very small green peas; 1 soup-spoonful of diced asparagus tips; 50 gr. butter.*

Bind the velouté with the cream and the egg yolks, and butter lightly. Garnish with the rice, the rouge de carotte, the peas and the asparagus tips. *(France.)*

Velouté Philippine

For 6 persons: *½ litre mussels; 120 gr. raw shrimps; 2 dl. white wine; 1 litre fish velouté; 50 gr. shrimp butter; 1½ dl. fresh cream; 3 egg yolks; 50 gr. butter.*

Cook the mussels in the white wine, and drain them. Cook the shrimps in this white wine. Heat the velouté with the decanted white wine; bind with the cream and the egg yolks, and complete with the shrimp butter. Garnish with the bearded mussels and the picked shrimp tails. *(France.)*

Cold Soup

Soupe de poisson froide

For 10 persons: *1 kg. 500 of fish, pike sudak, carassin, etc.; 2 litres kvass; 250 gr. skinned peeled cucumber, fresh or salted; 150 gr. chopped sorrel; 100 gr. very tender chopped leek leaves; 1 soup-spoonful of chopped dill; 1 soup-spoonful of chopped chervil; 5 cl. sour cream.*

Cook the fish in slightly salted water, ensuring it remains whole. Allow to cool in the cooking liquor, drain, remove skin and bones, flake the fish with a fork, and put it into an earthenware dish. Remove the seeds from the cucumbers and cut them into small dice, add them to the fish, as well as the dill, chervil, leek and sorrel. Mix with the sour cream, add the kvass, and adjust seasoning with pepper and salt. Serve very cold. *(Russia.)*

Hot Entrées

Allumettes aux anchois

Anchovy sticks

For 6 persons: *250 gr. puff pastry; 200 gr. fish stuffing; 30 gr. anchovy butter; 12 anchovy fillets.* Cooking time: 12 to 14 minutes.

Roll the pastry into a strip 7 cm. long and 4 to 5 cm. thick. Mask with the fish stuffing containing the anchovy butter and cut up into rectangles 3 cm. wide. Place an anchovy fillet on each rectangle, put on a baking sheet and cook in a moderate oven. *(France.)*

Allumettes aux crevettes

Shrimp sticks

For 6 persons: *250 gr. puff pastry; 200 gr. whiting stuffing; 40 gr. shrimp butter; 60 gr. picked shrimp tails.*

Prepare the strips of pastry as above. Mask with whiting stuffing containing the shrimp butter, to which are added the sliced shrimps. *(International cookery.)*

Anchoyade

For 6 persons: *12 slices of household bread; 200 gr. anchovy fillets; 2 hard-boiled eggs; 50 gr. finely-chopped onion; 3 soup-spoonfuls of olive oil; vinegar.* Cooking time: 10 minutes.

Pound the anchovy fillets and pass through a fine sieve. Incorporate with this purée a spoonful of oil and a few drops of vinegar. Spread the bread with this purée, sprinkle with hard-boiled egg and more thickly with onion. Sprinkle with oil and brown in the oven. *(France.)*

Anguille en baton

Eel sticks

For 6 persons: *12 pieces of filleted eel of about 8 cm. in length; ½ litre fish fumet; 250 gr. puff pastry; 1 egg.* Cooking time: 12 to 15 minutes.

Poach the fillets in the fumet, and allow to cool. Roll out the pastry into rectangles of 6 cm. by 10 cm. Place two fillets, one against the other, on each rectangle, wrap them in the pastry. Moisten to seal the edges and place them, with the join on the underside, on a baking sheet. Glaze with egg yolk and cook in a hot oven. *(Holland.)*

Araignée de mer gradoise

For 6 persons: *1 spider crab of 1 kg.; 450 gr. rice; 50 gr. chopped onion; 2 chopped cloves of garlic; 1 coffee-spoonful chopped parsley; 125 gr. butter; 50 gr. grated Parmesan cheese; 5 cl. white wine; 1 litre fish fumet; 2 kg. various seafood (mussels, cockles, or clams, etc.).* Preparation: 40 minutes.

Cook the crab for 15 minutes in the court-bouillon. Shell, remove the meat from the trunk, claws and legs. Sweat the onion and garlic in butter; add the crab meat; colour lightly; add the parsley; moisten with the white wine, and allow to reduce. Add the rice, season, and sprinkle with a sufficient quantity of fish fumet to obtain a risotto with well-separated grains. After 20 minutes cooking, remove from the heat, incorporate with a fork the Parmesan and a good piece of butter. Press the rice into a previously buttered Savarin mould and turn over on a round serving dish. Fill the centre with the seafood prepared à la pizzaiola (see moules pizzaiola, page 463). *(Italy.)*

Attereaux Pahlen

For 6 persons: *12 thin scollops of lobster tail; 12 scolloped mushrooms; 12 slices of truffle; 12 poached and bearded oysters; ½ litre sauce Villeroi; 12 rice croquettes the size of a nut; 2 eggs; fresh white breadcrumbs; parsley.* Cooking time: 7 to 8 minutes.

Thread alternately on to wooden skewers—the lobster scollops, mushrooms, mussels, oysters and truffle slices. Coat with sauce Villeroi and allow to cool. Cover with egg and breadcrumbs giving the preparation a cylindrical shape. Fry at the last moment, replacing the skewers by silver ones studded with rice croquettes; garnish with fried parsley. *(International cookery.)*

Barquettes américaine

For 6 persons: *12 small cases in short pastry (lightly baked); 300 gr. lobster meat; 15 dl. sauce américaine; fresh white breadcrumbs; butter.* Cooking time: 2 to 3 minutes.

Bind the diced lobster meat with the sauce américaine sufficiently reduced. Garnish the cases with this mixture, sprinkle with bread-crumbs fried in butter, and pass through the oven. *(France.)*

Barquettes de crevettes Joinville

For 6 persons: *12 small pastry cases; 200 gr. picked shrimp tails; ¼ litre fish velouté; 30 gr. cray-fish butter; 24 small prawns, with only the tail shelled.*

Fill the cases with diced shrimp tails bound with 1 dl. of the sauce velouté containing the shrimp butter. Mask each case lightly with the remainder of the sauce, and stud two prawns on top. *(France.)*

Barquettes de crevettes Mornay

For 6 persons: *12 small pastry cases; 250 gr. picked shrimp tails; 3 dl. sauce Mornay; 50 gr. grated cheese.* Cooking time: 4 to 5 minutes.

Fill the cases with a dice of shrimps, and mask them with sauce Mornay. Sprinkle with grated cheese. Glaze in a hot oven or under the salamander. *(France.)*

Barquettes d'écrevisses Nantua

For 6 persons: *12 small pastry cases; 250 gr. shelled crayfish tails; 1 dl. fish velouté; 30 gr. cray-fish butter; 2 dl. sauce Nantua; 12 small shelled crayfish tails; 12 crayfish stuffed with Russian salad.*

Fill the cases with diced crayfish tails bound with fish velouté containing the crayfish butter. Mask lightly with sauce Nantua. Decorate each case with a crayfish tail and a stuffed trunk. *(France.)*

Barquettes de filets de sole

For 6 persons: *12 small pastry cases; 150 gr. poached fillets of sole; 60 gr. mushrooms; 40 gr. truffle; 3 dl. sauce normande; 12 small scollops of poached fillets of sole; 12 half-slices of truffle.*

Fill the cases with diced fillets of sole, mush-rooms and truffle, bound with 1 dl. of sauce normande. Lightly mask with the same sauce; complete with the alternating scollops of sole and half slices of truffle. *(France.)*

Barquettes de homard Victoria

For 6 persons: *12 small pastry cases; 150 gr. lobster meat; 60 gr. mushrooms; 40 gr. truffle; 1 dl. lobster sauce; 12 very small scollops of lobster tail; 12 very small slices of truffle.*

Fill the cases with a salpicon of lobster, mush-rooms and truffles, bound with the lobster sauce. Decorate each case with a scollop of lobster and a slice of truffle. *(France.)*

Barquettes aux huîtres

For 6 persons: *6 small cases made from puff pastry trimmings and lightly baked; 24 oysters, poached and bearded; 3 dl. cream sauce; 30 gr. truffle.* Cooking time for oysters: 1 minute.

Fill each pre-heated case with 4 poached oysters. Mask with cream sauce to which has been added the reduced poaching liquor. Sprinkle with chopped truffle. *(France.)*

Barquettes de laitance florentine

For 6 persons: *12 small boat-shaped pastry cases; 300 gr. leaf spinach stewed in butter; 12 large scollops of soft roe; 1 dl. white wine; 3 dl. sauce Mornay; 50 gr. grated Parmesan cheese.* Cooking time: 3 to 4 minutes.

Poach the soft roe scollops in the white wine; drain them. Garnish the pastry cases with the spinach; place a scollop of roe on the spinach. Mask lightly with sauce Mornay, sprinkle with grated Parmesan, and glaze under the salamander. *(France.)*

Barquettes de laitance au parmesan

For 6 persons: *12 small boat-shaped pastry cases; 2 dl. sauce Mornay; 12 scollops of poached soft roe; 1 dl. white wine; 250 gr. Parmesan appareil à soufflé.* Cooking time: 7 to 8 minutes.

Poach the soft roes in white wine and cut into scollops; drain them. Garnish the bottom of the cases with a thin layer of sauce Mornay and on this place a soft roe scollop. Cover with a Parmesan appareil à soufflé, and cook in a moderate oven. *(International cookery.)*

Barquettes aux moules

For 6 persons: *6 small boat-shaped pastry cases, made from puff pastry trimmings; 36 large mussels, poached and bearded; 3 dl. white wine sauce.* Cooking time for the mussels: 6 to 7 minutes.

Fill each case with 6 mussels. Mask with white wine sauce; glaze, and serve immediately. *(France.)*

Barquettes zélandaise

For 6 persons: *12 small boat-shaped pastry cases; 300 gr. fillets of eel; breadcrumbs; parsley; 60 gr. butter.* Cooking time: 10 to 12 minutes.

Cut up the eel fillets into a fine short julienne; season and sauté in butter. Fill the cases with this julienne; sprinkle with breadcrumbs, and pass through the oven for 2 to 3 minutes. Before serving, sprinkle with fried parsley. *(Holland.)*

Beignets

Fritters

Small articles or preparations either coated with frying batter or bound with choux pastry which swells during frying. The fritters are arranged on a serviette and garnished with fried parsley. Fritots are always accompanied with tomato sauce, while real fritters (beignets) are served without sauce.

Anchovy fritters

For 6 persons: *6 roundels of tunny, 4 cm. in diameter and 1½ cm. thick; 36 anchovy fillets; 4 dl. frying batter; parsley.* Cooking time: 6 to 8 minutes.

Wrap the roundels of tunny completely with thin strips of anchovy fillets. Dip in the batter and fry in very hot fat. Arrange in a bunch, and garnish with fried parsley. *(France.)*

Fritters bénédictine

For 6 persons: *300 gr. brandade of cod; 150 gr. potato purée; 4 dl. frying batter; parsley.* Cooking time: 6 to 8 minutes.

Mix the brandade with the potato purée, divide it into small balls the size of a nut, shape into oval quoits, dip in the batter, and fry in hot fat. Garnish with fried parsley. *(France.)*

Fritters cardinal

For 6 persons: *12 soft roes; 2 dl. thick lobster sauce; 4 dl. batter; parsley; court-bouillon.* Cooking time: 10 to 12 minutes.

Poach the soft roes in a court-bouillon for 3 to 4 minutes, and allow to cool under slight pressure. Coat them with reduced, hot lobster sauce; cool. At the moment of serving dip in the batter and fry in hot fat. Garnish with fried parsley. *(France.)*

Soft roe fritters I

For 6 persons: *12 soft herring roes; 1 lemon; chopped parsley; 4 dl. frying batter; 1 dl. white wine.* Cooking time: 10 to 12 minutes.

Poach the soft roes in white wine for 3 to 4 minutes and allow them to marinate in the lemon, chopped parsley and milled pepper. At the moment of serving dip in the batter and fry in very hot fat. Garnish with fried parsley. *(Holland.)*

Soft roe fritters II

For 6 persons: *12 soft herring roes; 4 dl. frying batter; 3 cl. olive oil; 2 lemons; 1 coffee-spoonful of chopped parsley; parsley.* Cooking time: 15 minutes.

Poach the soft roes in the court-bouillon; allow to marinate (30 minutes) with lemon juice, a thin trickle of oil, and chopped parsley. Dip in the batter, and fry at the last moment. Garnish with fried parsley and quarters of lemon. *(Holland.)*

Beignets Mathurine

For 6 persons: *350 gr. choux paste without sugar; 40 gr. herring fillets; 40 gr. sardine fillets.* Cooking time: 7 to 8 minutes.

Cut up the herring and sardine fillets into small dice; incorporate them in the choux paste. Divide this paste into small balls the size of a nut. Plunge them into the moderately hot fat, and increase the heat gradually. *(France.)*

Mussel fritters

For 6 persons: *36 large mussels (poached and bearded); ½ litre frying batter; 2 or 3 lemons; 3 dl. olive oil; parsley.* Cooking time: 4 to 5 minutes.

Allow the mussels to marinate for 30 minutes in olive oil, lemon juice, and milled pepper. Dip them into a light batter, and fry in hot fat. Drain them. Arrange on a serviette with fried parsley and quarters of lemon. *(France.)*

Blanquette ostendaise

For 6 persons: *2 kg. small round fish (whiting, gurnard, gurnet, haddock, sea eel); 1 litre of mussels; 50 gr. picked shrimp tails; 2 sticks of celery; 2 onions; 1 carrot; 1 crushed clove of garlic; 2 cloves; 8 white peppercorns; 1 bayleaf; 1 sprig of thyme; ½ litre white wine; 2 lemons; 60 gr. butter; 40 gr. flour; 2 egg yolks; 5 dl. fresh cream.* Cooking time for the fish: 10 minutes.

Clean, trim and wash the fish, and cut into slices of about 4 cm. Prepare a court-bouillon with the white wine with equal quantity of water, 1 carrot, 1 onion, 1 finely chopped celery stick, bayleaf, thyme, cloves, peppercorns, and garlic. Allow to reduce for 20 minutes. Cook the mussels with 1 stick of celery, 1 onion, pepper, and juice of 1 lemon. As soon as cooked remove from shells and beard. Sieve the cooking liquor, allow to stand, add it to the strained court-bouillon; bring to the boil and add the fish. Season and poach gently. Prepare a white roux with butter and flour; add ¾ litre of the cooking liquor, mix, and allow to cook for 10 minutes. Strain the sauce; add the fish and the shrimps, and allow to simmer an instant more. Thicken, away from the fire, with egg yolks and cream. Adjust seasoning and consistency; add a few drops of lemon juice. Arrange the fish in a timbale. Mask with sauce. Serve separately a creole rice and the rest of the sauce. *(Belgium.)*

Bordure de laitance Mornay

For 6 persons: *300 gr. poached soft roes; 500 gr. purée duchesse; 3 dl. sauce Mornay; 40 gr. grated cheese; 25 gr. butter.* Cooking time: 12 minutes.

Border an earthenware gratinating dish with the purée duchesse, using a fluted piping bag. Scollop the soft roes; arrange them in the middle of the dish. Mask with sauce Mornay, and sprinkle with grated cheese and with melted butter. Brown in a hot oven. *(France.)*

Bordure de seiches et de moules

For 6 persons: *750 gr. of small cuttle-fish; 450 gr. rice; 50 gr. chopped onion; 1 large crushed clove of garlic; 5 cl. dry white wine; 100 gr. grated Parmesan; 100 gr. butter; 1 litre fish stock; 1 bayleaf; mussels pizzaiola.* Cooking time: about 60 minutes.

Clean the cuttle-fish, remove the brown skin, and the ink bladder, and keep it in reserve. Cut the flesh into dice. Sweat in butter half of the onion and the garlic; add the diced cuttle-fish, salt and pepper; moisten with the white wine, and allow to reduce almost completely. Moisten with the fish stock; add the bayleaf, and allow to cook on a gentle fire for 30 minutes. Sweat the remainder of the onion in a saucepan with butter. Add the rice, heat gently, and add the ink (optional). Add the contents of the first saucepan; allow to cook very gently for about 18 minutes until the rice is cooked. Remove from the fire. Add to the rice the grated Parmesan and a nut of butter. Turn out on to a buttered round dish, filling the centre with mussels pizzaiola (see recipe, page 463). Serve very hot. *(Italy.)*

Bouchées

Bouchées are cut from puff pastry with a round, oval or square cutter. The ordinary bouchées have a fluted round shape of 6 cm. in diameter. Very small bouchées, called bouchées mignon, served as hot hors d'oeuvre, are 4 cm. in diameter. In some cases the lid is kept. In others it is replaced by a slice of truffle, a small mushroom head, or other main garnishing element. Cooking time for bouchées: 18 to 20 minutes; very small bouchées: 15 to 18 minutes.

Bouchées dieppoise

For 6 persons: *6 round bouchées; 125 gr. picked shrimp tails; 125 gr. poached and bearded mussels; 2 dl. reduced white wine sauce.*

Fill the bouchées with a salpicon of shrimps and mussels bound with the white wine sauce. *(France.)*

Bouchées aux huîtres

For 6 persons: *6 very small bouchées; 18 oysters, poached and bearded; 100 gr. cooked mushrooms; 2 dl. white wine sauce; 1 soup-spoonful of sauce hollandaise.* Cooking time for the oysters: 1 minute.

Prepare a salpicon with 12 oysters and the mushrooms. Bind with the reduced white wine sauce to which has been added the reduced poaching liquor and the sauce hollandaise; fill the bouchées with it. Place an oyster on each bouchée; lightly mask with sauce. *(France.)*

Bouchées Joinville

For 6 persons: *6 fluted oval bouchées; 150 gr. picked shrimp tails; 60 gr. mushrooms; 40 gr. truffles; 2 dl. sauce Joinville; 6 slices of truffle.*

Fill the bouchées with a salpicon of shrimps, mushrooms and truffles bound with the sauce Joinville. Place a slice of truffle on top, as a lid. *(France.)*

Bouchées aux laitances

For 6 persons: *12 round and fluted bouchées; 300 gr. poached soft roe; 1½ dl. fish velouté; 5 dl. fresh cream.*

Prepare a salpicon with the soft roe; bind it with the reduced and creamed velouté. Fill the bouchées with the salpicon. *(Holland.)*

Bouchées Marie-Rose

For 6 persons: *6 oval-shaped bouchées; 150 gr. picked shrimp tails; 75 gr. scollops in fine farce of smelt; 25 gr. short julienne of truffle; 2 dl. shrimp sauce; 6 thin roundels of smelt farce.*

Fill the bouchées with a salpicon of very small shrimp tails; scollops of smelt farce and truffle bound with shrimp sauce. Place a roundel of poached smelt farce on top, as a lid. *(France.)*

Bouchées monseigneur

For 6 persons: *6 fluted oval-shaped bouchées; 170 gr. soft roe purée; 30 gr. chopped truffle; 2 dl. thick shrimp sauce; 6 thick scollops of truffle.*

Half fill the bouchées with soft roe purée, combined with truffle. Complete the filling with the shrimp sauce, and place on each bouchée a lozenge of truffle. *(France.)*

Bouchées Nantua

For 6 persons: *6 fluted oval bouchées; 250 gr. shelled crayfish; 50 gr. truffles; 2 dl. sauce Nantua; 6 crayfish trunks.*

Fill the bouchées with the salpicon of crayfish and truffles bound with sauce Nantua. Place on top of each bouchée the stuffed crayfish trunk.

Bouchées Victoria

For 6 persons: *6 fluted round bouchées; 225 gr. cooked lobster meat; 50 gr. truffle; 2 dl. reduced lobster sauce.*

Fill the bouchées with a salpicon of lobster and truffle, bound with the reduced lobster sauce. *(France.)*

Brochettes de Cape Cod scollops grillées

For 6 persons: *900 gr. Cape Cod scollops; 12 large mushroom heads; 100 gr. smoked bacon; 2 small green peppers and 2 small red peppers; 2 lemons; 125 gr. butter; 300 gr. rice; 7 cl. oil; 1 coffee-spoonful of curry powder; breadcrumbs.* Cooking time: about 10 minutes.

Stud the scollops on the skewers, alternating with red and green peppers in pieces of 2½ cm. and the bacon in thin slices. Secure on each end of the skewers a mushroom head. Season the skewers, dip them in the oil, roll them in the breadcrumbs, and grill them over moderate heat brushing frequently with oil. Cook the rice, drain it and dry in the oven. Heat 25 gr. of butter with the curry and incorporate it with the rice. Arrange the skewers on the rice and moisten with melted butter mixed with lemon juice. *(United States.)*

Brochettes d'huîtres aux épinards à la crème

For 6 persons: *36 oysters; 36 mushroom heads of equal size; 1 kg. 200 cooked leaf spinach; 2 dl. fresh cream; 100 gr. butter; 20 gr. flour; 2 lemons; fresh white breadcrumbs; nutmeg.* Cooking time: 5 to 6 minutes.

Open the oysters, remove from the shells, beard and poach them. Skewer the oysters alternating with a mushroom; pass them through the melted butter and breadcrumbs. Moisten with melted butter and grill them in a moderate heat. Chop the spinach coarsely, and sauté in butter; sprinkle with flour, mix well, add the cream, and season with salt, pepper and grated nutmeg. Allow to cook for a few minutes. Arrange the skewers on a serviette, garnish with quarters of lemon; serve the spinach separately, in a fireproof dish. *(Denmark.)*
(See illustration, page 215.)

Canapés garnis

Canapés are made from sliced bread, which is toasted without crust. Various kinds of bread may be used, buttered and garnished to taste.

Bloater canapés

For 6 persons: *12 round canapés of about 5 cm. in diameter; 180 gr. smoked bloater fillets; 1 dl. sauce béchamel; 30 gr. butter; 50 gr. grated cheese.* Cooking time: 2 to 3 minutes.

Prepare a purée from the bloater fillets. Bind with béchamel and the butter. Adjust seasoning and consistency. Arrange in a dome-shape on the canapés, and sprinkle with grated cheese. Glaze. *(France.)*

Canapés au cabillaud

Fresh cod canapés

For 6 persons: *12 round canapés; 200 gr. cooked flaked cod; 1 dl. sauce béchamel; 30 gr. butter; 50 gr. grated cheese.* Cooking time: 2 to 3 minutes.

Prepare a purée with the cod, the béchamel and the butter. Adjust seasoning and consistency. Arrange in a dome-shape on the canapés. Sprinkle with grated cheese. Glaze or brown. *(France.)*

Canapés Ivanhoe

For 6 persons: *12 round canapés; 180 gr. poached flaked smoked haddock; 1 dl. sauce béchamel; 50 gr. butter; 12 very small grilled mushroom heads.*

Prepare a purée with the haddock, bind with the béchamel and a nut of butter. Adjust seasoning and consistency. Butter the canapés and arrange on them the hot purée in the shape of a dome. Place a mushroom head in the centre. Serve very hot. *(France.)*

Canapés aux sardines

For 6 persons: *12 rectangular canapés; 60 gr. butter; 24 sardine fillets in oil; 2 hard-boiled eggs; brown breadcrumbs.* Cooking time: 2 to 3 minutes.

Butter the canapés and arrange two sardine fillets on top. Sprinkle with chopped hard-boiled eggs and breadcrumbs, brush over with melted butter, and heat in the oven. *(International cookery.)*

Cannelons de poisson

For 6 persons: *300 gr. puff pastry trimmings (or half-puff pastry); 300 gr. cooked flaked fish (salmon, haddock, turbot, etc.); 2 dl. fish velouté; 1 egg.* Cooking time: 12 to 14 minutes.

Roll the pastry into six strips of 16 cm. in length and 2 cm. in width. Form a cone with each strip of pastry. Brush with beaten egg and bake in a moderate oven. Prepare a salpicon with the flaked fish and much reduced velouté. Garnish the cones with the salpicon. Serve very hot. *(France.)*

Cassolettes

Cassolettes are small fireproof porcelain containers. They are usually filled with the same salpicons as bouchées.

Coquilles

For this preparation shells are used in fireproof porcelain, in silver, or natural scollop shells. With a fluted piping tube they are bordered with a circle of purée duchesse. They are filled with different preparations. The coquilles are usually browned in the oven.

Coquilles de barbue Mornay

Coquilles of brill Mornay

For 6 persons: *300 gr. purée duchesse; 300 gr. poached and flaked brill; 4 dl. sauce Mornay; 60 gr. grated cheese; 30 gr. butter.* Cooking time: 5 to 6 minutes.

Border the shells with a circle of purée duchesse and cover the base of the shell with a small spoonful of sauce Mornay. Fill the shells with the flaked brill, mask with hot sauce Mornay. Sprinkle with grated cheese and brown in a hot oven. Before serving, lightly sprinkle with melted butter. *(France.)*

Coquilles de clam Casino

Baked clam Casino

For 6 persons: *36 Cherrystone clams; ½ a red pepper; ½ a green pepper; 4 chopped shallots; 1 coffee-spoonful of grated horse-radish; 100 gr. lean bacon; 100 gr. butter; 1 lemon; Worcestershire sauce; tabasco sauce; paprika.* Cooking time: 8 to 10 minutes.

Open the raw clams, take a half-shell away and arrange the half-shells containing the clams on a baking sheet covered with kitchen salt. Put on each clam a little Casino butter. Cover with a thin slice of bacon; cook in a hot oven. Casino butter: empty the raw peppers and chop finely; work into the softened butter the shallots, peppers and horse-radish; season with salt, paprika, Worcestershire sauce and a few drops of tabasco sauce. *(United States.)*

Coquilles de crevettes

Shrimp coquilles

For 6 persons: *6 scollop-shells; 300 gr. purée duchesse; 300 gr. picked shrimp tails; 2 dl. sauce béchamel; 40 gr. shrimp butter; 500 gr. grated cheese; 20 gr. butter.* Cooking time: 7 to 8 minutes.

Edge the scollop-shells with purée duchesse. Bind the shrimp tails with the béchamel worked up with the shrimp butter. Fill the shells with this preparation; sprinkle with grated cheese, and sprinkle lightly with melted butter. Brown. *(France.)*

Coquilles de homard

Lobster coquilles

For 6 persons: *6 scollop-shells; 300 gr. purée duchesse; 300 gr. cooked lobster meat; 2 dl. lobster sauce; 50 gr. grated cheese.* Cooking time: 7 to 8 minutes.

Edge the scollop-shells with purée duchesse. Fill them with a salpicon of lobster bound with lobster sauce. Sprinkle with grated cheese, glaze in a hot oven. *(France.)*

Coquilles de laitance hollandaise

Coquilles of soft roe hollandaise

For 6 persons: *6 scollop-shells; 300 gr. purée duchesse; 6 soup-spoonfuls of sauce hollandaise; 300 gr. soft roes of carp, herring or haddock, poached and scolloped; 30 gr. grated cheese; 30 gr. bread-crumbs; 40 gr. butter.* Cooking time: 4 to 5 minutes.

Edge the scollop-shells with purée duchesse; pour into each of them a spoonful of sauce hollandaise. Fill with the scollops of soft roe; sprinkle with grated cheese and breadcrumbs. Sprinkle with melted butter and brown quickly in a hot oven. *(Holland.)*

Coquilles de laitance parisienne

Coquilles of soft roe parisienne

For 6 persons: *6 scollop-shells; 300 gr. poached soft roes; 100 gr. of scolloped cooked mushrooms; 20 gr. chopped truffle; 4 dl. white wine sauce.* Cooking time: 10 to 15 minutes.

Mask the bottom of the shells with a little white wine sauce, mixed with chopped truffle. Fill them with scollops of the poached soft roe, alternating with slices of mushroom. Mask with the same sauce. Glaze quickly. *(France.)*

Coquilles Lucullus

For 6 persons: *6 scollop-shells; 300 gr. purée duchesse; 2 dl. sauce béchamel; 30 gr. crayfish butter; 150 gr. picked shrimp tails; 100 gr. mush-rooms; 50 gr. truffle; 12 small crayfish tails; 50 gr. breadcrumbs; 30 gr. butter.* Cooking time: 7 to 8 minutes.

Edge the scollop-shells with purée duchesse. Garnish them with a salpicon of shrimp tails, mushrooms and truffles in short julienne, bound with the béchamel worked up with the crayfish butter. Sprinkle with breadcrumbs and then with melted butter, and brown in the oven. At the moment of serving, place two crayfish tails on each shell. *(International cookery.)*

Crabes aux champignons gratinés

For 6 persons: *6 small crabs; 600 gr. fresh mushrooms; 2 dl. fresh cream; 2 egg yolks; 50 gr. butter; 3 cl. cognac; 60 gr. grated cheese.* Cooking time for the crabs: 12 to 15 minutes.

Cook the crabs in salt water and allow them to cool in their cooking liquor. Detach claws and legs; open the trunks, remove the meat only and add it to the creamy parts from the shell. Clean the shells; dry them and retain. Clean the mushrooms; cut them into four, and cook them with the cream and season them. Bind, away from the fire, with the egg yolks. Add the cognac, and work up with the butter. Add the crab meat. Fill the shells with this salpicon and sprinkle with grated cheese. Brown in a hot oven. *(Denmark.)*

Crêpes glacées aux fruits de mer

Seafood pancakes

For 10 persons: *10 large shelled scampi; 10 fillets of sole; 200 gr. raw diced pike meat; 200 gr. cooked lobster meat; 200 gr. poached and bearded mussels; 50 gr. butter; 1 dl. fish velouté; 6 large tomatoes, skinned, pipped and very ripe; 3 dl. fresh cream; 5 cl. cognac; 3 soup-spoonfuls of sauce hollandaise; 3 soup-spoonfuls of whipped cream; tabasco. Pancake batter for 16 to 18 small pancakes: 3 dl. milk; 150 gr. flour; 3 eggs; 30 gr. butter; 1 pinch of salt.* Total cooking time: about 20 minutes.

Prepare a salpicon with fish and shellfish. Heat the butter in a sauteuse and place the fish in it. Season with salt, pepper, and a few drops of tabasco. Flambé with the cognac; deglaze with the cream, add the velouté and the finely-chopped tomatoes. Allow to cook on a gentle heat for about 10 minutes. Remove the pan from the fire and take out the fish. Pass the sauce through a strainer; heat it up again and allow it to cook until very creamy. Complete it with whipped cream and sauce hollandaise. Prepare the pancakes which must be very small and very thin. Fill them with the salpicon, roll up, mask them with the sauce, and glaze them in a hot oven or under the salamander. *(Switzerland.)*
(See illustration, page 212.)

Crêpes aux fruits de mer Newburg

Pancakes with seafood Newburg

For 6 persons: *150 gr. cooked lobster meat; 150 gr. cooked crab meat; 150 gr. picked shrimps; 4 dl. béchamel; 4 soup-spoonfuls of sauce hollandaise; 3 soup-spoonfuls of whipped cream; 3 cl. sherry; 100 gr. butter; 50 gr. grated Parmesan. Pancake batter: 180 gr. flour; 2 eggs; 1 egg yolk; 3 dl. milk; 45 gr. melted butter; 1 pinch of salt.*

Prepare 16 to 18 very thin small pancakes. Cut up the lobster meat, the crab meat and the shrimps into a salpicon, and bind it lightly with a little béchamel to which has been added 2 spoonfuls of sauce hollandaise. Flavour with the sherry and a pinch of paprika. Fill the pancakes with the salpicon; roll them up, and arrange them on a buttered fireproof dish for browning. Prepare a sauce with the rest of the béchamel, the sauce hollandaise and the whipped cream. Mask the pancakes, sprinkle with grated Parmesan and glaze quickly under the salamander. *(United States.)*

Crevettes roses Remiche

For 6 persons: *900 gr. shelled prawns; 3 chopped shallots; 40 gr. butter; 150 gr. mayonnaise; 3 soup-spoonfuls of ketchup; 1 soup-spoonful of grated horse-radish; tabasco sauce; 30 gr. grated breadcrumbs; 25 gr. grated Parmesan.* Cooking time: 3 to 4 minutes.

Cook the shallots golden brown in the butter; add the prawns; sauté rapidly. Mix the ketchup with the mayonnaise, incorporating the horse-radish, and season with the tabasco sauce. Arrange the prawns on a gratinating dish; mask with mayonnaise; sprinkle with bread-crumbs and Parmesan, and brown quickly under the salamander. Serve immediately. *(United States.)*

Croquants du littoral

For 6 persons: *100 gr. picked shrimps; 12 thin slices of cooked Dublin Bay prawn tails; 1 coffee-spoonful of chopped truffle; 75 gr. butter; 75 gr. flour; ½ litre milk; 3 egg yolks; 100 gr. grated cheese; 2 eggs; 2 soup-spoonfuls of oil; flour; fresh white breadcrumbs; parsley.* Cooking time: 5 to 6 minutes.

Make a white roux with the melted butter and the flour; moisten with the milk; bring to the boil, and allow to cook for 2 to 3 minutes, while whisking. Incorporate the egg yolks without ceasing to whisk, and give another boiling. Add, away from the fire, grated cheese, truffle, and shrimp tails. Season with salt, pepper, grated nutmeg; mix carefully. Pour the preparation on to an oiled baking sheet and allow to cool. Before completely cold, arrange the slices of Dublin Bay prawns on the preparation, lightly pressing them in. When the mixture has become cold and firm, cut it into squares, each including a slice of Dublin Bay prawn. Flour the squares; pass them through the whipped egg with a little oil, and breadcrumb them. Fry them in deep fat until crisp and golden. Arrange on a dish, garnished with fried parsley. *(Belgium).*

Croquettes

Croquettes are small preparations of different forms composed of a fine salpicon bound with a reduced sauce, and often including egg yolks. The principal ingredient is fish. After the preparation has cooled, the croquettes are formed, egg and breadcrumbed, and fried in deep fat. The average weight of a croquette is 60 to 70 gr. They are served with a sauce appropriate to the principal ingredient.

Croquettes de barbue

Brill croquettes

For 6 persons: *500 gr. cooked brill; 150 gr. mushrooms; 40 gr. truffle; ¼ litre fish velouté; 2 eggs; breadcrumbs; parsley; 4 dl. tomato sauce or shrimp sauce, or sauce Nantua.* Cooking time: 5 to 6 minutes.

Prepare a salpicon of brill, cooked mushrooms and truffle and bind with the reduced velouté. Form into cork-shaped croquettes, coat with egg and breadcrumbs, and fry in very hot deep fat. Arrange on a serviette, garnish with fried parsley, and serve the sauce separately. *(France.)*

Croquettes de crevettes

Shrimp croquettes

For 6 persons: *300 gr. picked shrimps; 200 gr. mushrooms; 2 dl. sauce béchamel; 30 gr. shrimp butter; eggs; fresh white breadcrumbs; parsley; 3 dl. shrimp sauce.* Cooking time: 5 to 6 minutes.

Prepare a salpicon with the shrimp tails and the cooked mushrooms; bind with the reduced béchamel worked up with the shrimp butter. After cooling divide into 12 parts; form cork-shapes, and coat with egg and breadcrumbs. Fry in very hot deep fat; arrange on a serviette and garnish with fried parsley. Serve the shrimp sauce separately. *(France.)*

Croquettes dominicaine

For 6 persons: *24 large poached and bearded oysters; 150 gr. cooked mushrooms; 15 cl. sauce béchamel; 5 cl. purée Soubise; 30 gr. lobster butter; 3 dl. white wine sauce; 2 eggs; fresh white breadcrumbs; parsley.* Cooking time: 4 to 5 minutes.

Prepare a salpicon of oysters and mushrooms. Bind with the reduced béchamel to which has been added the purée Soubise, and finished with the lobster butter. Allow to cool, form into oval croquettes, coat with egg and breadcrumbs, fry in very hot deep fat. Arrange on a serviette with fried parsley. Serve separately the white wine sauce, to which has been added some reduced poached oyster liquid. *(France.)*

Lobster croquettes

For 6 persons: *300 gr. lobster meat; 150 gr. mushrooms; 50 gr. truffle; 2 dl. reduced béchamel sauce; 30 gr. lobster butter; 3 dl. lobster sauce containing chopped parsley.* Cooking time: 5 to 6 minutes.

Bind the salpicon with: reduced béchamel, the diced lobster meat, cooked mushrooms and truffle. Finish with lobster butter. Allow to cool. Form the croquettes into an oval shape, coat with egg and breadcrumbs, and fry in very hot deep fat. Garnish with fried parsley. Serve the lobster sauce separately. *(France.)*

Croquettes indienne

For 6 persons: *150 gr. of rice; ½ litre fish fumet; 200 gr. lobster meat; 1½ dl. reduced sauce béchamel; 5 gr. curry powder; eggs; fresh white breadcrumbs; 3 dl. curry sauce.* Cooking time: 5 to 6 minutes.

Cook the rice in the fish fumet; mix it with the lobster meat, cut into small dice, and bind with the reduced béchamel seasoned with the curry. Form the croquettes into cork shapes, coat with egg and breadcrumbs, and fry them in very hot deep fat. Arrange the croquettes with fried parsley. Serve the curry sauce separately. *(International cookery.)*

Croquettes de morue américaine

Cod croquettes américaine

For 6 persons: *350 gr. of cooked cod; 300 gr. potato duchesse; 7 dl. sauce béchamel; eggs; fresh white breadcrumbs; parsley; 3 dl. tomato sauce.* Cooking time: 5 to 6 minutes.

Mix the finely-flaked fish with the purée duchesse and the reduced béchamel. Adjust seasoning and consistency. Roll the mixture into balls of 60 gr. with the aid of a little flour. Coat with egg and breadcrumbs and fry in clarified butter. Garnish with fried parsley. Serve the tomato sauce separately. *(International cookery.)*

Croquettes nantaise

For 6 persons: *300 gr. cooked flaked fish; 200 gr. mushrooms; 2 dl. reduced fish velouté; eggs; fresh white breadcrumbs; 3 dl. tomato sauce; parsley.* Cooking time: 5 to 6 minutes.

Flake the fish, mix it with the cooked mushrooms, cut into small dice, and bind with the fish velouté. Form the preparation into rectangular croquettes; coat with egg and breadcrumbs, fry and serve immediately. Garnish with fried parsley. Serve the tomato sauce separately. *(France.)*

Cuisses de grenouille au paprika

Frogs' legs with paprika

For 6 persons: *24 large frogs' legs; 60 gr. lard; 15 cl. fresh cream; 10 gr. paprika; 60 gr. minced onion; 100 gr. diced green peppers; 75 gr. peeled, pipped and chopped tomatoes; 15 gr. flour.* Cooking time: 15 minutes.

Trim the frogs' legs and clean by soaking in cold water. Colour the onion in the lard; sprinkle with paprika; moisten with a little water; add peppers and tomatoes, and bring to the boil. Add the frogs' legs; lightly salt, and allow to cook for 10 minutes. Add the cream, thickened with the flour. Allow to cook for another 3 to 4 minutes. Arrange the frogs' legs masked with sauce. Serve accompanied with a rice pilaf. *(Hungary.)*

Dartois

Preparation composed of two bands of puff pastry, the base of one spread with the mixture and covered with the second piece of pastry, brushed with beaten egg, cooked in a hot oven, and cut up into rectangles 3 cm. wide.

Dartois aux anchois

250 gr. puff pastry; 250 gr. whiting stuffing; 50 gr. anchovy butter; 12 anchovy fillets; 1 egg. Cooking time: 20 to 25 minutes.

Roll out the pastry to a thickness of 4 mm. Divide into two bands 8 cm. wide and as long as required. Cover one piece of pastry with the whiting stuffing, combined with the anchovy butter, up to within 1 cm. of the edge. Lay strips of anchovy on the stuffing. Egg wash the edges and cover with the second band, sealing the previously moistened edges. Incise with the point of a small knife; brush with egg. Lightly mask the divisions. Cook in a hot oven. Cut up into rectangles of 3 cm. *(France.)*

Dartois aux filets de sole

250 gr. puff pastry; 250 gr. creamed farce of sole; 100 gr. raw fillets of sole; 1 egg. Cooking time: 20 to 25 minutes.

Proceed as for the making of dartois aux anchois, replacing the whiting stuffing by the sole stuffing, and the anchovy fillets by fine strips of fillets of sole. *(France.)*

Crayfish viennoise

For 6 persons: *18 large crayfish; 300 gr. rice; 50 gr. onion; 125 gr. beef bone-marrow; 150 gr. sliced mushrooms; 6 slices of truffle; 130 gr. butter; 7 dl. veal stock; 3 dl. sauce hollandaise.* Cooking time for the rice: 18 minutes.

Brush and wash the crayfish; cook them gently in slightly salted water, seasoned with caraway and parsley. Shell the tails and pincers and gut the crayfish. Prepare a crayfish butter with 100 gr. of butter, dried and pounded shells, passed through a fine sieve. Blanch the beef marrow; harden it with cold water; dry it; cut into small pieces together with the mushrooms and truffle. Lightly colour the chopped onions in 30 gr. of butter; add the rice and heat with the onions; moisten with the veal stock, and add the mushrooms, the beef marrow, the crayfish claws and half of the tails. Season, cover, allow to cook. Incorporate 75 gr. of crayfish butter with the sauce hollandaise. Press the prepared rice in a Savarin mould, and turn it out on a round dish. Garnish with the other half of the crayfish tails and the slices of truffle. Sprinkle with the rest of the hot crayfish butter. Serve the sauce hollandaise separately. *(Austria.)*

Feuilleté de crevettes cardinal

For 6 persons: *600 gr. picked shrimps; 2 dl. fresh cream; 1 dl. fish fumet; 50 gr. crayfish butter; 3 soup-spoonfuls of sauce hollandaise; 2 soup-spoonfuls of whipped cream; 2 dl. dry white wine; 5 cl. cognac; 25 gr. beurre manié; 6 small oval vol-au-vent.* Cooking time: 15 minutes.

Brown the shrimps in the crayfish butter; flame with the cognac, and moisten with the white wine. Allow to cook gently for 5 minutes; remove the shrimps and keep them hot. Add to the cooking liquor the fish fumet and the cream, reduce by a quarter, and bind with the beurre manié. Replace the shrimps in the sauce; add whipped cream and sauce hollandaise. Mix carefully, and adjust seasoning and consistency. Fill the vol-au-vent with the mixture. Serve very hot. *(Switzerland.)*

Feuilleté Neptune

For 6 persons: *1 large vol-au-vent case; 150 gr. Carolina rice; 4 dl. white stock; 1 small chopped onion; 250 gr. fresh-minced mushrooms; 600 gr. picked shrimps; 24 mussels; poached, bearded and breadcrumbed; 3 dl. fresh cream; 100 gr. butter; ¼ litre sauce Choron; 1 coffee-spoonful of curry; parsley; frying oil.* Cooking time for the rice: 16 to 18 minutes.

Colour the onion lightly in the butter, add the rice and allow to heat. Moisten with the white stock, season, and cook as for a pilaf. Sauté in butter the mushrooms; season, moisten with the cream, and allow to reduce. Combine the curry powder with 25 gr. butter, heat up and add the shrimp tails. Deep fry in hot oil the prepared mussels and the parsley. Mix the sauce Choron with a spoonful of cream. Place the vol-au-vent on a round dish and fill it with a layer of pilaf. Arrange on this the creamed mushrooms and on top arrange the curried shrimps. Mask all with sauce Choron and glaze quickly under the salamander. Add a crown of fried mussels and fill the centre with the fried parsley. *(Sweden.)*

Feuilleté de truite au jambon des Flandres

For 6 persons: *6 trout each of 300 gr.; 6 thin slices of raw Flanders ham each of 45 to 50 gr.; 300 gr. puff pastry; 12 anchovy fillets; 100 gr. butter; 2 chopped shallots; 1 soup-spoonful of flour; 1 coffee-spoonful of paprika; 2 egg yolks; 1 dl. fresh cream.* Cooking time (Oven): 20 minutes.

Fillet the trout, previously cleaned with the heads removed. Place a fillet of trout, seasoned and garnished with a fillet of anchovy on one of the edges of a slice of ham. Begin to roll the ham over itself. Place a nut of butter, then the second fillet of trout and finishing rolling to form a paupiette. Roll thin the puff pastry and cut it up into six squares of about 18 cm. along the side. Place each paupiette in the centre. Egg wash the edges of the pastry; close the puff pastry. Turn over on to a baking sheet with the join underneath; brush over with beaten egg. Make three or four incisions with the point of a sharp knife. Place the paupietettes on a pastry tray; cook in a moderate oven. Make about 2 dl. of fish fumet with the washed trout heads and bones, without the gills. Toss the chopped shallots in 40 gr. of butter, sprinkle with paprika, and allow to cook for a few moments. Add the flour, mix together, and cook for a further few moments. Make a velouté with the fish fumet. Pass through a fine conical strainer; add a liaison of cream and egg yolk. Adjust seasoning and consistency. (The sauce should be a pale pink colour.) Dress the fish turnovers on a serviette. Serve the sauce separately. *(Belgium).*

Fruits de mer gastronomiques

For 6 persons: *120 gr. fillet of sole cut in goujons; 120 gr. fillet of turbot cut into goujons; 12 shelled prawns; 3 scollops; 12 poached and bearded mussels; juice of ½ lemon; 6 tomatoes, skinned, pipped and diced; chopped parsley; 6 turned and cooked mushroom heads; 23 gr. butter; oil; 10 cl. cognac.* Cooking time: 30 minutes.

Divide each scollop into halves, season, pass through flour and sauté in hot oil until half cooked. Add the goujons of sole and turbot previously seasoned and floured. When cooked, drain off the oil and flame with cognac. Add the prawns, mussels, diced tomatoes and cook together for 3 minutes. Arrange on a serving dish, garnish with the turned mushrooms and sprinkle with chopped parsley, and lemon juice. Mask with nut-brown butter (beurre noisette).

Huîtres en coquille Rockefeller

Oysters on half-shell Rockefeller

For 6 persons: *36 large oysters; 500 gr. cooked leaf spinach, drained and coarsely chopped; 60 gr. butter; 20 gr. flour; 1½ dl. white wine; 1 dl. fresh cream; 30 gr. breadcrumbs; 25 gr. grated Parmesan; garlic powder; nutmeg.* Cooking time: 4 to 5 minutes.

▲ Oeufs farcis Vénora, p. 178

Sélection de hors d'oeuvre de poissons ▼

▲ Crevettes indienne, p. 431

Scampi Emerico Bianchi, p. 447 ▼

▲ Brochette de scampi Eden, p. 447

Scampi grillés, p. 448 ▼

▲ Crêpes glacées aux fruits de mer, p. 205

Pizza Chioggia, p. 218 ▼

▲ Feuilleté de crevettes cardinal, p. 208

Croustade de filets de sole, p. 224 ▼

▲ Spaghetti aux moules napolitaine, p. 221

Omelette de homard, p. 218 ▼

▲ Risotto aux fruits de mer, p. 219

Brochettes d'huîtres aux épinards à la crème, p. 203 ▼

▲ Oeufs farcis Clémence, p. 177

Concombres danoise, p. 167 ▼

Open the oysters and retain juice. Remove them and stiffen them with the white wine and their juice and a nut of butter. Clean the half shells; sponge them, and put them on a baking sheet sprinkled with coarse kitchen salt. Prepare a sauce with white roux (30 gr. butter), the flour, the cooking liquor of the oysters, and the cream. Season highly. Sauté the spinach with very little butter and season with salt, pepper, a pinch of nutmeg and garlic powder. Fill each half shell with a small spoonful of spinach; place an oyster on this and mask lightly with sauce. Sprinkle with breadcrumbs and grated Parmesan. Brown in a very hot oven. *(United States.)*

Kedgeree

Ingredients: *900 gr. flaked cooked turbot or other white fish, free from skin and bone; 100 gr. butter; 350 gr. rice into riz pilaf; ½ litre curry sauce; 7·5 dl. cream; 6 hard-boiled eggs; 2 lemons.*

Re-heat the fish in the oven in a well-buttered dish covered with paper. Meanwhile re-boil the curried sauce and add the cream. Lightly mix the fish with half the sauce. Prepare a ring of riz pilaf. Place the fish in the centre and cover with the remainder of the sauce and alternate quarters of hard-boiled egg and quarters of lemon.

Laitance

Soft roe

Of all the soft roes used the most delicate is that of the carp. Next come herring and mackerel roes. Before being prepared, soft roes must be cleaned by soaking in cold water to whiten.

Laitance américaine

Soft roes American style

For 6 persons: *6 scollop shells; 300 gr. soft roe; 3 dl. sauce américaine; 1 dl. fish fumet; 5 cl. white wine; 30 gr. truffle; 30 gr. cooked lobster coral.* Cooking time: 8 to 10 minutes.

Poach the soft roes in the fish fumet and white wine; drain; cut up into thick scollops. Arrange in the shells. Reduce well the cooking liquor and mix with the sauce américaine. Mask the soft roes with the sauce; sprinkle with chopped truffle and coral. *(France.)*

Laitance à l'écossaise

For 6 persons: *12 small boat-shapes in lining paste, lightly baked; 250 gr. soft roe; 4 eggs; 1 dl. fresh cream; 60 gr. butter; 1 lemon; 1 coffee-spoonful of chopped parsley.* Cooking time: 8 to 10 minutes.

Poach the soft roe almost until dry with the butter and lemon juice; scollop. Prepare scrambled eggs with the eggs, cream, salt and pepper. Fill the small hot cases with the scrambled eggs and arrange the scollops on this. Sprinkle lightly with melted butter and chopped parsley. *(France.)*

Laitance maréchale

For 6 persons: *18 soft roes; 150 gr. butter; fresh white breadcrumbs; 4 dl. sauce Perigueux.* Cooking time: 15 minutes.

Poach the soft roes and sponge them. Dip them in melted butter; breadcrumb them and press them with a palette knife. Colour in clarified butter, and arrange on a serviette. Serve the sauce separately. *(France.)*

Laitance meunière

For 6 persons: *18 soft roes; 150 gr. butter; 1 soup-spoonful of chopped parsley; 1 lemon; flour.* Cooking time: 8 to 10 minutes.

Season, flour and cook the soft roe in butter. Arrange on a dish, squeeze the juice of a lemon on it, sprinkle with chopped parsley and noisette butter. *(France.)*

Laitance Villeroi

For 6 persons: *18 soft roes; ½ litre frying batter; 4 dl. sauce Villeroi; 25 gr. minced truffle.* Cooking time: 20 minutes.

Poach the soft roes in court-bouillon and cool under pressure. Cover with sauce Villeroi to which the minced truffle has been added after the sauce is cooled. Shape the roes; dip in batter and fry in very hot fat.

Omelette à l'aneth et aux laitances de carpe

For 6 persons: *18 eggs; 900 gr. carp soft roes; 1 soup-spoonful of chopped dill; 5 cl. fresh cream; the juice of one lemon; Worcestershire sauce.* Poaching time for the soft roe: 4 to 5 minutes.

Clean the roes by soaking in cold water; scollop them, and poach in butter. Remove them. Deglaze with lemon juice and a drop of Worcestershire sauce. Add the cream, and bring to the boil. Season with salt and pepper; add the dill and the roe. Prepare 6 omelettes and stuff them with the roe. If only two omelettes are prepared (for 6 people), 7 or 8 eggs will be enough for each omelette. *(Israel.)*

Omelette de homard

Lobster omelette

For 4 persons: *8 eggs; 40 gr. butter; 100 gr. cooked lobster meat; 1 dl. lobster sauce; 1 small truffle.* Cooking time over a brisk flame: 3 to 4 minutes.

Stuff the omelette with the lobster meat bound with a little lobster sauce. Carefully extract the meat of the claws and keep separately. Arrange the omelette; decorate with the slices of truffle and the meat from the claws. Run a border of the same sauce around the omelette. *(Germany.)*
(See illustration, page 214.)

Pizza Chioggia

For 6 persons: *650 gr. scampi; 80 gr. butter; 25 gr. flour; 4 eggs; 15 dl. milk; 1 cl. cognac; 1 soup-spoonful of chopped parsley; 10 gr. curry; bread-crumbs.* Cooking time in the oven: about 30 minutes.

Remove the scampi meat from their shells; dry it in a cloth, colour in the butter; flame with the cognac, and season. Prepare a very thick sauce with 30 gr. of butter, flour and milk. Remove from the fire, season with curry, salt and pepper. Add the parsley, the beaten eggs and then the scampi. Prepare 6 pizza with the pastry (see page 58), cover them with this preparation, sprinkle with breadcrumbs and melted butter. Cook in a moderate oven. Serve lukewarm. *(Italy.)*
(See illustration, page 212.)

Pizza du golfe

For 6 persons: *200 gr. provolone cheese; 5 aubergines; 3 large tomatoes, skinned, pipped and cut into slices; 24 anchovy fillets; 25 gr. stoned green olives; 25 stoned black olives; 12 small basil leaves; olive oil.* Cooking time in the oven: 30 minutes.

Cut the aubergines into slices, salt them, and allow them to soak in cold water for 3 to 4 minutes. Wipe and dry them; sauté in oil and allow to cool. Prepare 6 individual pizza, cover them over with half of the slices of aubergine; garnish with the cheese cut into small fine slices and the anchovies, and then cover over with the rest of the aubergines and the tomatoes. Sprinkle with basil leaves and a little oil. Cook in a moderate oven. *(Italy.)*

Pörkölt d'écrevisses

For 6 persons: *60 crayfish; 12 gr. caraway; 1 small bunch of parsley; 100 gr. butter; 10 gr. paprika; 15 gr. flour; 30 gr. crayfish butter; 15 cl. bouillon.* Cooking time for the crayfish: 10 minutes.

Cook the crayfish in boiling water, slightly salted, and seasoned with parsley and caraway. Shell the tails and remove the meat from the pincers; gut. Pound the shells and prepare a crayfish butter. Prepare a beurre manié worked up with 30 gr. of butter and the flour. Melt the rest of the butter and in it colour the tails and pincers. Sprinkle with paprika. Moisten with the bouillon, cook and bind with the beurre manié. Allow to cook for 2 or 3 minutes longer; adjust seasoning and consistency. Complete with the crayfish butter. Arrange in a timbale. Serve with a risotto mixed with chopped parsley. *(Hungary.)*

Quenelles de poisson à la sauce aux câpres

For 6 persons: *500 gr. cod or pike meat; 45 gr. flour; 3 egg whites; ¾ litre fresh cream; 100 gr. butter.* Sauce: *50 gr. butter; 40 gr. flour; 6 to 7 dl. fish fumet; 2 egg yolks; 75 gr. capers.* Poaching time for the quenelles: 12 to 15 minutes.

Pass the fish through the finest plate of a mincer, season with salt and pepper. Incorporate the whites of egg one by one, then the flour. Mix thoroughly and allow to cool. Work up with the cream, and incorporate the cooled melted butter. With a soup-spoon form quenelles and poach them in the hot fish fumet. Prepare a light golden-coloured roux with 50 gr. of butter and 40 gr. of flour; moisten with 6 dl. of fish fumet; allow to cook gently for 15 to 20 minutes. Bind the sauce with egg yolks and a little cream; pass through a tammy cloth; adjust seasoning and consistency, and add the capers. Arrange the quenelles on a hot dish and mask them liberally with caper sauce. *(Denmark.)*

Quiche de saumon

For 6 persons: *300 gr. salted salmon; 1 kg. 200 boiled potatoes; 6 dl. milk; 3 eggs; 1 soup-spoonful of chopped dill or slices of lemon; white milled pepper; a little milk with an equal quantity of water added; 120 gr. butter.* Cooking time: 30 to 40 minutes.

Soak the salmon for 12 hours in the milk with an equal quantity of water to remove the salt. Dry it and cut into equal slices. Butter a gratinating dish and line it with a layer of sliced potatoes. Add a layer of sliced salmon. Fill the dish with alternate layers of fish and potatoes, the last being a layer of potatoes. Sprinkle each layer with a little white pepper and chopped dill or a slice of lemon. Beat the eggs, together with the milk; fill the dish. Cook in a moderate oven. Serve sprinkled with melted butter. *(Finland.)*

Quiche de turbot à la façon des pères

For 6 persons: *600 gr. of fillets of turbot freed of skin; 350 gr. short pastry; 50 gr. hop shoots; 4 white of leek; about 6 dl. of Orval beer; 100 gr. butter; 2 chopped shallots; 1 coffee-spoonful of chopped chervil; 2 eggs; 2 egg yolks; ½ litre of fresh cream.* Cooking time: 20 to 25 minutes.

Line a flan ring with short pastry and raise the edge. Prick the bottom with a fork; cook until a pale colour. Mince the whites of leek; sweat in butter without colouring; moisten with the beer. Season and reduce to less than 1 dl. Drain carefully; reserve the cooking liquor. Butter the bottom of a fish tray, sprinkle it with chopped shallot and arrange on it the fillets of turbot. Season with salt and pepper and moisten with the cooking liquor reserved from the leeks; cover and poach gently. Garnish the bottom of the cooked flan with the chervil, leeks, hop shoots, and the drained turbot. Reduce the turbot cooking liquor by half; incorporate it with the beaten eggs and the cream; season and pour over the turbot. Sprinkle with flakes of butter and cook in a hot oven. *(Belgium.)*

Risotto aux fruits de mer

Seafood risotto

For 2 persons: *2 oysters; 4 raw halves of scampi; 100 gr. mussels; 40 gr. shrimps; 120 gr. fillets of sole; 3 thin slices of truffle; 2 dl. fish velouté; 5 dl. white wine; 5 dl. cream.*

Poach the fillets of sole, the oysters and the mussels in a fish fumet to which has been added the white wine and 2 chopped shallots. Arrange the fillets of sole in the middle of the separately cooked risotto. Reduce the cooking liquor of the fillets of sole; add to the well-seasoned fish velouté as well as the cream. Put the oysters back into their well-cleaned shells; mask them with sauce and garnish with a slice of truffle. Pass the scampi in batter and drop them into the frying fat. Then surround the fillets of sole with shrimps, scampi and mussels. Pass the whole rapidly under the salamander and serve immediately. *(Italy.)*
(See illustration, page 215.)

Rissoles

This name is given to a kind of croquette wrapped in a half-puff paste or a brioche paste without sugar. Rissoles are cooked by frying and are served on a serviette with fried parsley.

Rissoles indienne

For 6 persons: *200 gr. cooked lobster meat; 1 dl. sauce béchamel; 3 gr. curry powder; 6 poached and bearded oysters; 1 dl. sauce Villeroi; 200 gr. puff pastry trimmings; 1 egg yolk; breadcrumbs.* Cooking time: 7 to 8 minutes.

Prepare a salpicon with the lobster meat and the reduced béchamel, seasoned with the curry. Coat the oysters with hot sauce Villeroi; allow to cool. Roll out the pastry to 4 or 5 cm. thick; cut it with a round pastry cutter about 8 cm. in diameter. Place a little salpicon on each piece with an oyster on top and finish off with a little salpicon. Moisten the edges with water; fold the pastry into a turnover, coat with egg and breadcrumbs. Fry in hot deep fat. *(France.)*

Rissoles Joinville

For 6 persons: *150 gr. picked shrimp tails; 75 gr. mushrooms; 30 gr. truffle; 1 dl. sauce normande; 30 gr. shrimp butter; 200 gr. puff pastry trimmings.* Cooking time: 7 to 8 minutes.

Prepare a salpicon with the shrimp tails, mushrooms and truffle, bound with reduced sauce normande and finished with the shrimp butter. Garnish the thinly-rolled pieces of pastry with this salpicon; moisten the edges with water and fold into a turnover. Fry in deep hot fat. *(France.)*

Rissoles Nantua

For 6 persons: 6 rissoles: *200 gr. shelled crayfish tails; 60 gr. truffle; 1 dl. sauce béchamel; 30 gr. crayfish butter; 200 gr. puff pastry trimmings; 1 egg.* Cooking time: 7 to 8 minutes.

Prepare a salpicon with crayfish tails and truffle, bound with the béchamel, finished with the crayfish butter. Enclose the salpicon in thinly-rolled oval-shaped pieces of pastry. Moisten the edges with water and fold the pastry into a turnover. Fry in hot deep fat. *(France.)*

Rissoles normandes

For 6 persons: *150 gr. picked shrimp tails; 12 poached and bearded mussels; 1 dl. thickened sauce normande; 1 egg; 200 gr. puff pastry trimmings.* Cooking time: 7 to 8 minutes.

Prepare a salpicon with the shrimps, mussels and oysters, bound with sauce normande. Enclose the salpicon in thinly-rolled-out pieces of pastry of equal size. Moisten the edges with water and fold the pastry into turnovers. Fry in deep hot fat. *(France.)*

Rissoles Victoria

For 6 persons: *200 gr. lobster meat; 50 gr. truffle; 1 dl. reduced lobster sauce; 200 gr. puff pastry trimmings; 1 egg.* Cooking time: 7 to 8 minutes.

The same procedure as for the preparation of rissoles Nantua. *(France.)*

Sardines diable

For 6 persons: *12 sardines in oil with the heads, skin and bones removed; 12 rectangular croûtons; mustard; 2 eggs; fresh white breadcrumbs.* Cooking time: 3 to 4 minutes.

Spread the sardines with mustard seasoned with Cayenne pepper, egg and breadcrumbs. Fry them in hot deep fat, arrange them on the croûtons cut to the shape of the sardines and fried in butter. *(France.)*

Saucellis d'anchois

The same procedure as for the preparation dartois aux anchois. Saucellis is the Russian name for dartois. *(Russia.)*

Saucellis de filets de sole

See: dartois aux filets de sole. *(International cookery.)*

Saumon fumé Mannerheim

For 6 persons: *6 slices of fresh smoked salmon 80 to 100 gr. each; 2 dl. white wine; 2 dl. fish fumet; 1 dl. veal stock; 75 gr. mousse of foie gras; 75 gr. butter; 2 cl. cognac; the juice of half a lemon; 6 large and very white mushroom heads; 6 slices of truffle; dill.* Cooking time: 10 minutes.

Cut the salmon into rather thick scollops. Poach in the fish fumet and the wine; drain and keep hot. Mix the fish cooking liquor with the veal stock and allow to reduce to about a third. Incorporate the mousse of foie gras; add the butter and season with cognac and lemon juice. Arrange and mask with the sauce. Garnish with the slices of truffle and the dill. Serve with riz au beurre. This was the favourite dish of General Mannerheim at the Savoy Restaurant in Helsinki. *(Finland.)*

Soufflés de crustacés

For 6 persons: *150 gr. of cooked lobster, shrimp, crab, crayfish; 1 dl. sauce béchamel; 1 coffee-spoonful of fish glaze; 2 egg yolks; 2 egg whites; 30 gr. butter.* Cooking time: 12 minutes.

Pound the shellfish meat; pass it through a fine sieve. Mix this purée with the reduced béchamel; add the fish glaze and the egg yolks. Adjust seasoning and consistency. Incorporate the firmly-beaten whites of egg; pour into buttered cassolettes; cook in a moderate oven. *(France.)*

Soufflés de poisson (petits)

Small soufflés of fish

For 6 persons: *150 gr. raw fish flesh; 1 dl. sauce béchamel; 2 egg yolks; 3 egg whites; 50 gr. butter; 3 cl. fish fumet.* Cooking time: 10 to 12 minutes.

Stew the fish in butter; season and cut into dice. Pass through a fine sieve, mix with the reduced béchamel and add the reduced fish fumet. Add, away from the fire, the egg yolks, and incorporate the firmly-beaten egg whites. Pour this mixture into buttered cassolettes. Bake au bain-marie in a moderate oven.

Soufflés take their name from the fish which is used as the base: salmon, sole, whiting, smelt, etc. If smelt is used it is necessary to add two-thirds of other fish such as sole, whiting, etc., because of the special taste of the smelt. *(France.)*

Fish soufflé

Ingredients: *2 kg. 900 raw fish (to produce 700 gr. cooked fish, freed from skin and bone); 25 gr. chopped shallots; 275 cl. sauce béchamel; 6 egg yolks; 8 egg whites; 275 cl. dry white wine; 100 gr. butter; salt; Cayenne pepper.*

Suitable types of fish for this preparation include lemon sole, whiting, hake and fresh haddock. Wash, fillet and skin the fish. Place in a buttered pan previously sprinkled with the chopped shallots and salt. Moisten with the wine and cover with a heavily-buttered paper. Poach in the usual manner. Remove the fish, pound and sieve. Reduce the cooking liquor to a glaze and add to the purée. Re-heat with the boiling béchamel. Correct seasoning, adding a pinch of Cayenne. Allow to cool, and then incorporate the egg yolks. Now fold in the stiffly-beaten egg whites, taking care not to over-mix. Fill the buttered soufflé dish and level off. Cook in a moderate oven at 350° F. and serve immediately.

Spaghetti aux moules napolitaine

For 6 persons: *4 litres of mussels; 6 cl. olive oil; 30 gr. concentrated tomato purée; 800 gr. spaghetti; 1 chopped onion; 1 chopped clove of garlic; 1 soup-spoonful of chopped parsley.* Cooking time for the mussels: about 6 minutes.

Heat the mussels, previously brushed, washed and cleaned, in a saucepan. When they have opened, take them out, remove from the shells and drain them. Lightly cook the onion and garlic in oil; add the mussels, continue cooking until golden colour. Incorporate the concentrated tomato purée and the parsley; season with pepper and a little salt if necessary. Cook the spaghetti in the usual way. Drain and arrange and mask with the mussel mixture. *(Italy.)*
(See illustration, page 214.)

Tartelettes

Tartelettes for hot hors d'oeuvre or hot entrees can be lined with lining-paste and garnished uncooked, or cooked to a pale colour. In this case the tartlets are filled with the farce used for the preparation and passed for a moment through the oven until set.

Tartelettes Beatrix

For 6 persons: *6 tartlets cooked pale; 120 gr. thick mushroom purée; 120 gr. picked shrimp tails; 1½ dl. sauce normande; 6 oysters; 25 gr. butter.*

Fill the tartlets with mushroom purée; cover over with shrimp tails passed through hot butter. Mask lightly with sauce normande; place a poached and bearded oyster in the centre of each tartlet. *(Holland.)*

Timbales Dessoliers (petites)

For 6 persons: *150 gr. whiting farce; 30 gr. crayfish butter; 200 gr. shelled crayfish tails; 50 gr. cooked lobster meat; 1 dl. reduced sauce normande; 3 dl. fish velouté with crayfish butter; 30 gr. chopped truffle.* Cooking time: 12 to 15 minutes.

Butter small dariol moulds, sprinkle bottom and sides with chopped truffle; pass them for a few moments in the refrigerator to firm the butter. Coat them with whiting farce finished with the crayfish butter. Fill with a salpicon of crayfish tails and lobster meat bound with very thick lobster sauce. Cover over with farce; poach in the bain-marie and do not allow to boil. Allow to stand for two minutes before turning out of the moulds. Serve the sauce velouté separately. *(France.)*

Timbales Régine (petites)

For 6 persons: *180 gr. sole farce; 3 soup-spoonfuls of very thick mushroom purée; 200 gr. poached soft roe; 4 dl. fish velouté; 60 gr. crayfish butter; 20 gr. butter.* Cooking time: 15 minutes.

Butter small dariol moulds, and line them with sole farce mixed with mushroom purée. Fill the moulds with the scolloped soft roe bound with 1 dl. of thick velouté worked up with 20 gr. of crayfish butter. Cover with the remainder of the sole farce; poach in the bain-marie. Serve with the fish velouté finished with the crayfish butter.

Truite farcie Colorado

Stuffed Brook Trout Colorado

For 6 persons: *6 brook trout each of about 200 gr.; 300 gr. crab-meat; 1 dl. thick béchamel; 75 gr. butter; 2 dl. white wine; ¼ litre fresh cream; 200 gr. fresh minced mushrooms; 2 chopped shallots; 15 gr. flour.* Poaching time: 10 minutes.

Gut and wash the trout and remove the backbone. Cut up the crab meat into small dice; bind it with the béchamel, season and stuff the trout with it, and re-form them. Tie them up, or wrap them in buttered paper. Lay them in a sauteuse; moisten with the white wine, cover and poach in the oven. Lightly colour in butter both shallots and mushrooms. Sprinkle with flour and stew quickly. Moisten with the trout cooking liquor; reduce, bind with the cream; poach again for a moment, and adjust seasoning and consistency. Remove the paper. Arrange on a serving dish and mask with the sauce and serve very hot. *(United States.)*

Visnickis

For 6 persons: *250 gr. unsugared brioche paste, slightly firm; 300 gr. cooked fish flesh; 1½ dl. thick fish velouté; 1 coffee-spoonful of chopped fennel.* Cooking time: 6 to 7 minutes.

Flake the fish and bind it with the velouté; season with salt and pepper, and chopped fennel. Roll out the brioche paste to 3 or 4 mm. thickness; cut out 12 circles with a round pastry cutter, about 5 to 6 cm. in diameter. Arrange 6 on a baking sheet; moisten the edges, and garnish each piece with a ball of the fish mixture the size of a nut. Cover with the second 6 circles, press with the back of the pastry cutter. Leave for 20 to 25 minutes before frying in very hot deep fat. *(International cookery.)*

Vorschmack finlandais

For 6 persons: *6 small herrings or 12 small Swedish herrings; 600 gr. cold cooked potatoes; 300 gr. cooked ham; 4 eggs; 1 dl. sour cream; 100 gr. butter; breadcrumbs.* Cooking time: about 20 minutes.

Fillet the fish and cook in butter. Pass through the fine plate of a mincer with the potatoes and the ham. Add the sour cream and the egg yolks, salt and pepper. Beat the egg whites stiffly and incorporate them in the mixture. Butter six small ramequins and fill them with this preparation. Cover each one with a roundel of cooked potato. Sprinkle with breadcrumbs and melted butter. Cook in a moderate oven until the surface is a golden brown. *(Finland.)*

Buffets

Introduction

Guests will always enjoy a buffet carefully and tastefully arranged. This modern style in the art of reception allows an infinite variation in the presentation of dishes and can replace meals of any kind or any importance.
Fish and shellfish are the items of preference in the composition of a buffet.
Their preparation can vary greatly, from the canapé to the Miroir Traditions et Qualité.
Fish and shellfish dishes are an integral part of a buffet. Choice and presentation vary according to the occasion, the time and the importance of the reception. Dishes presented, hot or cold, simple or artistic, must be of unerring taste, delicate savour and impeccable presentation. A high point must be reached in aesthetics and the culinary art. (Illustrations, pages 225–230: 247–252.)
In this chapter we give a few suggestions. You will be able to compose quite easily your buffets when you have consulted the chapters: cold hors d'oeuvre, hot entrées, fish and shellfish dishes.

Recipes

Hot Buffets

Consult the chapters on hot entrées (page 197) and the fish and shellfish dishes served hot. Choose preparations to allow a quick service (presentation in portions).

Croustade de filets de sole

For 6 persons: *1 croustade; 3 soles of 400 gr.; 150 gr. mushrooms, blanched and cut into quarters; 300 gr. whiting flesh; 300 gr. picked shrimps; cut into dice; 1 truffle cut into slices; 1 litre shrimp sauce.* Cooking time for the fillets: 6 to 8 minutes.

Fillet the fish and clean by soaking in cold water; slightly flatten them, and spread the farce on the skin side (see Culinary Technique in pictures). Roll the fillets and place them in a buttered casserole, close to each other. Moisten with a fish fumet and white wine; cover with a buttered paper and poach in the oven. Allow to cool. Cut slices of paupiettes 1 cm. thick. Make up the garnishing of the croustade with the mushrooms, the shrimps and the slices of paupiettes by covering them with the hot sauce, kept au bain-marie. Fill the croustade with this mixture. The rest of the garnishing is served separately. Decorate the top with slices of truffle. *(Switzerland.)*
(See illustration, page 213.)

Darnes de cabillaud ou de saumon Condorcet

Darnes of fresh cod or salmon Condorcet

For 6 persons: *6 darnes of 2 cm. thick; 5 dl. white wine sauce (sauce vin blanc II); 6 tomatoes stuffed with cucumbers cut up in the shape of olives; 6 small timbales of rice pilaf; 3 cooked lobster tails cut up into medallions; potatoes dauphine; 6 picked shrimp tails; 2 peeled, pipped and chopped tomatoes; 6 slices truffle.* Cooking time: 15 minutes.

Poach the darnes in a court-bouillon, drain them and arrange on a dish. Place on top the medallions of lobster overlapping each other, and mask with sauce. Sprinkle truffle and parsley, and garnish with the chopped tomatoes. Arrange the other garnishings. *(Holland.)*
(See illustration, page 334.)

Filets de sole Caroline

For 6 persons: *12 fillets of sole; 12 fried croûtons triangular in shape; 120 gr. of fish farce; 600 gr. macédoine of vegetables; one whole truffle cut in strips; ½ litre white wine sauce (sauce vin blanc I); fresh white breadcrumbs; 2 whole eggs.*

Flatten the fillets; stuff them; fold and poach in a court-bouillon. Allow to cool. Give the fillets a triangular shape. Pass through the egg and breadcrumbs and deep fry. Arrange on the croûtons, and mask with the white wine sauce and glaze. Arrange in the shape of a crown, garnish the centre with the macédoine of vegetables bound with butter, and sprinkle with the strips of truffle. *(Holland.)*
(See illustration, page 368.)

Paupiettes de sole Beatrix

For 4 persons: *8 fillets of sole; 8 prawns with tails shelled; 8 fluted and cooked mushroom heads; 240 gr. picked shrimps; ½ litre white wine sauce with shrimp coulis; 8 slices of truffle.*

Form the sole into paupiettes and poach them. Arrange on a dish and mask with sauce. Place on each paupiette a mushroom head, and a prawn decorated with truffle embedded in it. Garnish the dish with the shrimps and the fluted mushrooms. *(See illustration, page 329.)*

Paupiettes de sole Boucanier

For 4 persons: *8 paupiettes of fillets of sole; 8 medallions made from maize flour; ½ litre of sauce cardinal; 4 scampi tails or picked shrimps; 120 gr. salpicon of shrimps bound with white wine sauce (sauce vin blanc II); 2 whole eggs; 8 slices of truffle; chopped parsley; fresh white breadcrumbs; pommes purée.*

Poach the paupiettes and arrange them on the medallions made of maize flour, coated with egg and breadcrumbs and shallow-fried and arranged to form a crown. Garnish the centre with the salpicon; place on it the shrimps or the scampi tails; sprinkle with chopped parsley. Place a paupiette on each; mask with sauce vin blanc and add a slice of truffle. Using a piping bag garnish with the potato purée. Decorate with picked parsley. *(Holland.)*
(See illustration, page 336.)

Turbot de la Manche Taj Mahal, p. 235 ▶ p. 225
Truite du lac Arthur Bolli, p. 235 ▶ p. 226
Galantine de homard Mary Crist Fleming, p. 232 ▶ p. 227
Miroir Traditions et Qualité, p. 232 ▶ p. 229
Truite Côte d'Azur, p. 234 ▶ p. 229

▲ Langouste en bellevue, IKA 1968, p. 454

Langouste en bellevue, présentation Palma

▲ Truite saumonée Intercontinental, p. 235

Pâté de turbot truffé W. Jungbluth, p. 233

Paupiettes de sole maître Adolfo Bader

For 4 persons: *8 fillets of sole; 8 portions of pommes duchesse; 32 asparagus tips; 4 fleurons of puff pastry; 120 gr. julienne of mushrooms and 1 truffle, cooked in butter; ½ litre white wine sauce (sauce vin blanc III); 8 prawns with the tails shelled; 8 fan-shaped slices of truffle; chopped fines herbes.*

Poach the paupiettes and arrange them in a crown; mask with white wine sauce and sprinkle with fine herbes. Place a slice of truffle on each paupiette. Embed with a prawn. Arrange in the middle of the dish the julienne of mushrooms and truffles; at the two ends the asparagus in small bunches and the golden pommes duchesse between the paupiettes. Garnish with the fleurons. *(Holland.)*
(See illustration, page 334.)

Cold Buffets

Brochet du lac farci à la mode de Kiev

Lake pike stuffed in the Kiev style

For about 20 people: *1 pike of about 3 kg.; pike farce; 2 kg. pike flesh; 1 kg. turbot flesh; 400 gr. panada; 8 dl. fresh cream; 100 gr. pistachio nuts; 150 gr. truffle; 100 gr. pimento; 1 litre white sauce chaud-froid; 24 large fluted cooked mushrooms; 12 small fluted cooked mushrooms; 250 gr. mousse of tunny; 2 litres of fish jelly; 4 crayfish cooked in court-bouillon; 6 hard-boiled eggs; stuffed olives; black olives; melon or water-melon pearls; pimento.* Cooking time: about 45 minutes.

Prepare a farce with the pike flesh, the turbot flesh, the panada and the cream. Season it well and incorporate the blanched skinned pistachios, the diced truffle and pimentoes. Scale the pike; open it along the belly; gut it; remove the bones, and wash and dry. Stuff the pike with the farce and wrap up in a serviette as if to form a galantine.
Another method: Scale the pike; open it along the belly; remove the 2 fillets which must remain whole; start with the abdominal fin and go up with the knife along the edge of the outside wall of the lateral fins; pass over the dorsal bone and go down on the other side. Place the prepared fish on a serviette, spread the farce and wrap up to form a galantine. Poach it in a fumet prepared with the bones; allow to cool in the stock.
Fill a buttered timbale with the mousse of tunny; poach au bain-marie; cool. Prepare 12 small quenelles in pike farce. Turn out the timbale; mask it with sauce chaud-froid; mask with fish jelly; decorate with stuffed olives and truffle slices, and the base with slices from 12 of the large mushrooms. Overlap the edge of this mousse with sliced stuffed pimento; dress as per illustration with remainder of mushrooms, pike quenelles, melon balls, hard-boiled egg and truffle slices. Finish decoration with crayfish. *(Switzerland, La Palma, Locarno.)*
(See illustration, page 252.)

Filets de sole Domino

For 12 persons: *700 gr. trimmed pike flesh; 200 gr. panada; 2 egg yolks; 2 dl. double cream; 400 gr. shelled scampi tails; 200 gr. picked shrimps; 12 fillets of sole each of 60 to 70 gr.; 12 cooked crayfish of medium size; 24 large mussels poached in the shell; 3 truffles; 1 red pepper; 1 piece of green pepper; 2 large tomatoes; 100 gr. Russian salad; 1 cooked carrot; 1½ litres white chaud-froid; 1 litre fish jelly; butter.* Poaching time for the terrine: 30 minutes.

Carefully remove the flesh of the crayfish tails from underneath so that the shells remain whole seen from above. Prepare a farce with the pike flesh, the panada and the egg yolks, working it on ice. Work up with the cream and season well. Cut the crayfish tails and truffles in a coarse large dice; incorporate with the farce, put into a round buttered terrine or mould, poach au bain-marie and allow to cool. Roll up in a serviette the remaining farce (the same procedure as for a small galantine) and poach. Allow to cool, and cut up this galantine into medallions.
Slightly flatten the fillets of sole, fold them, poach in the white wine and fish fumet and cool under slight pressure.
Coat the insides and bottom of a timbale mould with jelly, decorate the bottom with a star made from finely-cut red pimento placing a roundel of truffle in the centre. Fill with the carefully trimmed scampi and shrimp tails;

cover over with jelly and put to set. Turn out the pike terrine, mask with the sauce chaud-froid; decorate the upper edge with a mosaic of truffle and carrot and glaze all over with jelly. Arrange the terrine in the centre of the dish, decorate all around the base with the medallions of galantine slightly overlapping each other. Garnish each medallion with a roundel of stuffed olive and glaze with jelly.
Sponge well the folded fillets of sole; trim them up into rectangles of equal size; mask with the sauce chaud-froid. Make up some dominoes with small roundels of truffle; form the line of separation with the help of small fine slices of cooked green pepper. Stuff 12 large mussel shells with a salpicon of scampi and shrimp trimmings bound with jelly.
Turn out the timbale of scampi in the centre of the terrine masked with sauce chaud-froid. Arrange the dominoes all around and place in front of them the stuffed mussels, each on a base of jelly. Place at the top of the dish a sculpture in butter (optional). On the right and left arrange the crayfish, the tails being placed between the opened mussel shells. On each side a skinned tomato, opened on the underside, stuffed with Russian salad, glazed with jelly and presented in the form of a fancy fruit. *(Switzerland, La Palma, Locarno.)*
(See illustration, page 249.)

Galantine de homard Mary Crist Fleming

For 15 to 18 persons: *2 kg. of farce of pike and fillets of sole; 200 gr. smoked salmon in very thin slices; 1 kg. 800 cooked lobster (5 pieces); 8 scollop-shells; ½ litre sauce chaud-froid with lobster sauce; 2 litres well-seasoned fish jelly; asparagus tips; fresh figs; truffle; pimento; hard-boiled eggs; yolks of egg; balls of water-melon.* Cooking time: 40 to 45 minutes.

Lay the smoked salmon along a damp serviette forming a rectangle. Spread on top half of the farce, while leaving an edge of about ½ cm. Arrange in the middle, lengthwise, the meat from the lobster claws and the trimmings of smoked salmon. Cover over with the rest of the farce and roll up in the smoked salmon like a galantine. Wrap it up very tightly in the serviettes tying the two ends with string. Poach the galantine in a court-bouillon with white wine and allow to cool in the liquor. Unwrap the galantine; cut 6 slices from it of about 1½ cm. thick; mask these and the remainder of the galantine with sauce chaud-froid containing lobster butter. Garnish the galantine and the slices with medallions of lobster. Place on top a diamond of truffle and surround it with balls of water-melon. Glaze with jelly.
Garnishing: The empty lobster tails are stuffed with a salpicon of lobster trimmings, egg white, truffle and pimento, all bound with jelly. The scollop shells are filled with fish jelly, and topped with the poached scollops divided into two and stuffed with creamed yolks of hard-boiled egg. Form a ring with the balls of water-melon. Arrange the asparagus tips, the halves of hard-boiled egg, the quarters of fig and the lobster heads.
Serve a cocktail sauce or a mayonnaise sauce separately. *(Switzerland, La Palma, Locarno.)*
(See illustration, page 227.)

Miroir Traditions et Qualité

For 5 to 8 persons: *1 kg. 500 shelled picked scampi tails; 600 gr. cooked lobster or crawfish tails in medallions; 2 kg. smoked eel; 800 gr. prawns; 80 gr. truffle slices; 100 gr. stuffed olives; 1½ litres fish jelly.*

Coat three Savarin moulds with jelly, decorate them with medallions of lobster or crawfish and slices of truffle. Cut up the scampi into thick pieces; arrange them in the moulds; fill with jelly and allow to set in the refrigerator. Cut up one half of the eel into slices of about 1 cm.; decorate with a slice of stuffed olive and glaze with jelly. Cut up the other half similarly into slices of 1 cm. removing the skin by inserting the knife under the skin, starting on the belly side and continuing to remove it in this way almost to the top of the dorsel fin. Fold back the loosened skin outwards and in a curl-like fashion on either side.
Using a mirror as a base, arrange a sculptured decoration in butter (this is optional). Turn out the jellied mould inverted on to the mirror and garnish around the base with the prepared eel slices. Arrange a tasteful decoration of suitable garnishes as shown in the illustration. Accompany the decoration by the prawns, the tails of which should be shelled and arranged bunched together as shown in the illustration on page 229. *(Switzerland, La Palma, Locarno.)*

Palets d'esprots à la tallinoise

For 6 persons: *25 large Kiel sprats; 16 eggs; 5 gr. powdered gelatine; 20 gr. chopped shallots; 10 large poached mussels; 10 gr. chopped parsley; 50 gr. butter; oil.*

Skin the sprats and fillet carefully. Lightly oil a mould with a semi-circular bottom, about 15 cm. long, 10 cm. wide and 4·5 cm. deep; garnish it with the fillets of sprat. Beat the eggs well with the gelatine; season; pass through a conical strainer and sprinkle with chopped parsley.
Heat the butter in a deep pan; colour the shallots and add the mussels, bearded and cut into pieces. Add the previously beaten eggs. Prepare, preferably au bain-marie, from this mixture scrambled eggs left slightly under-done and pour them immediately, while still hot, into the mould garnished with fillets of sprat. Fold over the ends of the fillets on this mixture. Allow to cool a little before putting the mould into the refrigerator. After completely cooling, turn out, cut up into 6 slices of the same size, arrange on a long dish and garnish with picked parsley. *(Germany.)*

Parfait de homard

For 6 persons: *1½ kg. live lobsters, one of which should be a hen; 2 fine truffles; 2 bunches of dill; 1 bunch of herbs; 1 dl. Chablis; gelatine; ground caraway.* Cooking time: 30 minutes.

Quickly cut off the heads of the live lobsters and collect the liquid as it flows. Remove, with a silver fork, the eggs of the hen lobster and put them aside. Open the lobsters; remove the stomach sac and extract the creamy parts. Carefully disengage the meat from the claws, tails and arms. Detach the fine membranes from the tails in strips as wide as possible (proceed as for removing the skins of fillets of fish); the less skin remaining on the meat the whiter the parfait will be after cooking.
Divide the lobster meat into two parts. Slightly salt one part; pound it with a mortar to obtain a rather fine mass and incorporate little by little the liquid collected and the creamy parts. Chop rather coarsely the second half of the flesh, mix it with the first part. Season with salt, a little ground caraway, a small pinch of sugar and the pressed dill juice.
Line with foil a suitable mould, with a semi-circular or square bottom; 15 cm. long, 7 cm. wide and 6 cm. deep, and butter it. Pass through a hair sieve the lobster eggs and mix them with a little of the lobster mass to obtain a smooth mixture. Line the mould as far as possible with the lobster skins; it is of no importance if some places remain empty. Spread on top this smooth mixture. Pour half of the lobster mixture into the mould; garnish with a layer of truffle cut into pieces and fill to the edge with the rest of the mixture levelling it with a spatula. Cover over with buttered foil and seal well. Poach the parfait in a bain-marie in the oven with medium heat. Prepare a well-seasoned stock with the chopped carcasses and the bunch of herbs. With this stock prepare a jelly with soaked gelatine and heighten the flavour with Chablis.
After cooling, decorate the parfait tastefully; place it in a mould of appropriate size, previously coated with the jelly. For the service turn out the parfait, cut it up into slices and arrange on a dish. *(Germany.)*

Pâté de turbot truffé W. Jungbluth

For 12 perons: *1 kg. of turbot flesh, free from skin and bones; 200 gr. fresh white breadcrumbs; ½ litre cream; 2 to 3 truffles; 150 gr. dried lobster coral; 2 litres white wine jelly; 12 artichoke bases; 300 gr. smoked salmon trimmings; 100 gr. butter; 2 lemons; Worcestershire sauce.* Poaching time: 90 minutes.

Pass through the mincer, several times, the turbot flesh and the fresh white breadcrumbs, then finally through a fine hair sieve. Place this farce in a sautoir and arrange on ice. Chill, season with salt, white pepper and lemon juice. Incorporate the cream with the help of a wooden spatula—if frozen fish is used incorporate 3 egg whites in addition.
Coat a mould with buttered greaseproof paper and carefully fill it half full with the mixture. Build up this mixture carefully to avoid the formation of air bubbles. Arrange the peeled truffles on top; fill the mould with the rest of the mixture. Cover over with a buttered paper. Poach au bain-marie in moderate heat and allow to cool in the mould. Drain well and turn out on to a wire-mesh tray.
Pass the coral through a fine sieve, mix with 1 litre of very clear jelly. Mask the pâté three or four times with this jelly. Cool. Cut into slices and present on a mirror. Garnish with small cubes of jelly, the picked shrimps and the artichoke bases filled with salmon cream.
Artichoke bases: Pass the smoked salmon trimmings through a hair sieve; season with lemon juice and Worcestershire sauce and incorporate 75 gr. of butter. Work up to obtain a creamy consistency. Trim the artichoke bases and fill dome-shape with the salmon cream; decorate with a truffle motif and glaze with jelly. *(Germany.)* *(See illustration, page 230.)*

Saumon festival de Salzbourg

For 1 person: *150 gr. salmon; 1 picked shrimp; 1 stuffed hard-boiled egg; 1 roundel of cucumber.*

Cut the salmon into darnes, wrap them up in greaseproof paper and poach them gently in a small quantity of court-bouillon and white wine of first quality. Allow to cool in the cooking liquor; drain them, take them out of the paper, remove the skin, and divide into two pieces.

Arrange the fillets on a dish or on a mirror in an overlapping pattern. Place on each slice a roundel of fines herbes butter.

Coat a mould with jelly, garnish with truffle motifs, and fill with a very fine and seasoned fish farce. Turn out on the dish. Place around the picked shrimps attaching them to the dish with jelly. Arrange the egg garnished with a roundel of stuffed olive, and roundels of cucumber decorated with small medallions of farce. *(Austria.)* *(See illustration, page 247.)*

Savarins de truite Aga Khan

For 6 persons: *6 trout each of 200 gr.; 1 bunch of herbs; 20 gr. butter; 1 dl. fish fumet; 5 cl. white wine; 120 gr. chopped tips of fillet of beef (tartare); 60 gr. caviar.* Cooking time: 12 to 15 minutes. Smoking: 6 hours.

Remove the heads of the fish, fillet and skin. Prepare a thickened fumet with the heads, bones and skins, the bunch of herbs and ½ litre of water. Pass through a conical strainer; reduce to 1 dl. and allow to cool on ice.

Prepare a fine farce pounded in a mortar with half the fillets; season and work up with the cold fumet. Cut up the rest of the fillets into small dice; incorporate them carefully in the farce and divide this into small buttered savarin moulds, 8·5 cm. in diameter. Poach these savarins in the fish fumet and white wine and allow to cool completely. Turn out on a grill and smoke in moderate heat in a smoke cabinet for 6 hours. For the service arrange the savarins on a dish; fill the centre of each with 20 gr. of beef tartare topped with 10 gr. of caviar. *(Germany.)*

Terrine de poisson à la roumaine

For 8 to 10 persons: *500 gr. eels; 500 gr. sturgeon; 600 gr. pike flesh (skinned and boned); 30 small gutted crayfish tails; 150 gr. fresh and very white mushrooms; 150 gr. cooked lean ham (no fat); 2 dl. fresh cream; 4 finely-cut medium-sized shallots; 150 gr. fat bacon; 25 gr. butter; 2 soup-spoonfuls of oil; 1 bunch of dill; 1 bayleaf; 1 small sprig of thyme; fine lettuce leaves; about 200 gr. lemon butter.* Cooking time: 60 minutes.

Remove the skin and bones of the eel and sturgeon. Cut up the flesh into pieces the size of a haricot bean; mix it with the crayfish tails; marinate with salt, pepper, shallots and oil and put in the cool until the moment of using. Clean the mushrooms. Pound in a mortar with the pike flesh; pass through a hair sieve, and work up the mixture, on ice, into a fine farce with the cream. Incorporate in the farce the small pieces of eel and sturgeon flesh, the crayfish tails and the ham cut into dice. Adjust the seasoning. Line with thin slices of bacon an appropriate earthenware dish. Brush the bacon over with melted butter and sprinkle copiously with very finely-cut dill. Fill with the farce, heaping up well. Fold the ends of the sliced bacon over the farce and place in the centre the bayleaf and the sprig of thyme. Carefully close the earthenware dish and poach au bain-marie in the oven. Allow to cool well. After completely cooling, with the help of a flat slicing spoon, scoop the farce in the shape of shells and arrange on the lettuce. Serve separately a lemon butter of smooth and creamy consistency. *(Germany.)*

Truite Côte d'Azur

For 8 persons: *8 trout each of 160 gr.; 400 gr. fresh figs; 600 gr. asparagus tips; 10 small tomatoes; 300 gr. Russian salad; 9 radishes; 1 small truffle; 8 balls of Cavaillon melon; 1 grapefruit; 1 orange; 1 lemon; purée made from yolks of 4 hard-boiled eggs and 100 gr. butter; 10 stuffed green olives; 10 slices of black olives; 1 litre fish jelly; picked parsley; 2 green leaves.*

Five hours before use, kill the trout; gut and wash them; tie the heads and tails together with string and put to cool in the refrigerator. Poach in the usual way and allow to cool in the cooking liquor. Drain well. Remove the skin except from the heads; remove the string; garnish the backs of the trout with small stars of egg purée and place on top a very small slice of truffle. Fix a melon ball on the head with the help of a toothpick, glaze the trout with jelly. With the small tomatoes make some roses, formed with a very sharp knife; cut away the skin leaving a little of the tomato and form a spiral. Then give a shape to the rose by rolling the spiral over itself. Cut the large tomatoes in

two; empty them and season; drain them and fill with Russian salad; decorate with a slice of black olive and glaze with jelly. Form the radishes into rosettes. Place at the top of the dish a sculpture in butter (optional), and put on its right and left two green leaves. Arrange in the centre of the dish a bunch of parsley with a rosette of radishes on top; form a crown of tomato roses around and then arrange the trout, the head towards the centre of the dish. Place a small bunch of asparagus between each trout and complete the decoration with the figs cut into four, the stuffed tomatoes and the rosettes of radishes.
At the top of the dish, on the green leaves, place at each side a fluted half grapefruit, on top a fluted half orange and a fluted half lemon; between the orange and the lemon place a slice of egg-plant. Garnish each half lemon with a little parsley and two quarters of figs; place in the flutings of the grapefruit half a stuffed green olive, the cut side towards the outside. Fix all together with a silver skewer. *(Switzerland, La Palma, Locarno.)*
(See illustration, page 229.)

Truite du lac Arthur Bolli

For 18 persons: *2 fillets of lake trout, free from skin and bone, each of 1 kg. 100; 1 kg. 200 trout flesh; 300 gr. panada; ½ litre fresh cream; 50 gr. lobster butter; 1 kg. Russian salad; 1 litre white sauce chaud-froid; 2 litres fish jelly; 6 to 8 crayfish cooked in court-bouillon; 2 heads and one tail of lake trout; Argenteuil asparagus tips; pearls of water-melon or melon; 1 truffle; 1 cooked carrot; tomatoes; curly parsley; butter.* Cooking time for the cutlets: 8 minutes.

Prepare a farce with the trout flesh, the panada and the fresh cream and season it. Poach the farce in a buttered oval earthenware dish; allow to cool. With the rest of the farce fill 5 small timbale moulds; poach; cool.
Cut up each fillet into 8 cutlets. Poach the cutlets in the oven, after having placed them on a buttered fish tray, in a little court-bouillon. Cook the heads and tails very carefully in the court-bouillon without over cooking; allow to cool in the court-bouillon. Turn out the farce, mask it with sauce chaud-froid; decorate the edge with a mosaic of truffle and carrot; glaze with jelly. Place this mousse in the middle of the dish, garnish it with the jellied Russian salad and arrange on top three timbales, masked with sauce chaud-froid, decorated with truffle and glazed with jelly. Wipe the cutlets, mask them with sauce chaud-froid. Decorate each cutlet with two asparagus tips and a water-melon ball, a mosaic decoration of truffle and carrot; glaze with jelly.
Arrange the cutlets around the centre-piece, the two trout heads on each side of the sculpture in butter. Complete the garnishing with the crayfish, the tail of the trout, two timbales of mousse decorated with truffle, the stuffed tomatoes, and small bunches of curly parsley. Light mayonnaise sauce or green sauce served separately. *(Switzerland, La Palma, Locarno.)*
(See illustration, page 226.)

Truite saumonée Intercontinental

Prepare a trout and gut by the gills (size according to the number of guests). Lay it on the grill of the fish-kettle, attaching it with the help of cotton. Pass the cotton through the holes of the grill and fix it on the back of the trout making a knot, without tightening it too much, holding the trout by the belly. Repeat this manipulation until the trout is well fixed. Poach in a seasoned court-bouillon and allow to cool in the cooking liquor.
Take out the trout; remove the cotton; skin it and place it on a mirror. Surround it with fish jelly cut up into small cubes.
Garnish the back of the trout with shelled crayfish tails, place dill leaves between each one. Put on top roundels of hard-boiled egg white, overlapping them with roundels of truffle.
Cut green peppers into very wide strips; with the help of a suitable cutter, cut out lozenges. Cut out lozenges of smaller dimensions either in red pepper or tomato. Stick the red lozenges on the green ones with jelly. With the help of mayonnaise or softened butter lay the lozenges on the surface of the trout.
Garnishing: per person—1 stuffed hard-boiled egg and a boat-shaped pastry case of macédoine of vegetables bound with mayonnaise and garnished with half of a picked shrimp tail (cut lengthwise), with an asparagus tip and with truffle decorations. *(Germany.)*
(See illustration, page 230.)

Turbot de la Manche Taj Mahal

For 16 to 18 persons: *1 turbot of 2 kg. 500; 800 gr. farce of truffled turbot; 2 kg. Russian salad; 50 mussels cooked in white wine; 40 fluted mushrooms, cooked white; 16 halves of hard-boiled eggs stuffed with shrimp mousse; 3 trussed crayfish, cooked in court-bouillon; 1 litre white sauce chaud-froid; shelled Dublin Bay prawn tails; 2 litres fish jelly; stuffed olives; truffles; pimentoes; fish fumet with white wine; lemon.* Cooking time: 40 to 45 minutes.

Clean the turbot. Rub the white side well with lemon juice. Remove the two fillets from the black side; skin them and make incisions lengthwise. Flatten them lightly, stuff them with the farce and wrap them up in a serviette as for a galantine. Poach in the fish fumet and allow to cool in the cooking liquor. Remove the bones from the turbot; place the fish on the grill of a well-buttered turbot kettle; season; moisten with the fish fumet and white wine. Poach until just cooked and allow to cool in the cooking liquor. Drain and sponge the turbot, and place it in the middle of a mirror. Cover over with Russian salad the side from which the fillets have been removed. Cut up the galantine of turbot into slices of about 1 cm. thick, garnish them with a mushroom head and a roundel of truffle. Glaze the slices of turbot with jelly; arrange them on the Russian salad. Place the crayfish at the head of the turbot. Decorate it from the head to the tail and on the sides with medallions of Dublin Bay prawn tails; place a small roundel of truffle on each medallion. Remove one shell from each mussel; mask them with sauce chaud-froid; decorate with a roundel of stuffed olive; glaze with jelly. Place the mussels round the turbot and garnish with small bunches of curly parsley. Decorate the mirror with the hard-boiled eggs and the medallions left over, bunches of curly parsley and radish. Serve mayonnaise and tartare sauce separately. (See Culinary technique in pictures, page 81.) *(Switzerland, La Palma, Locarno.)*

(See illustration, page 225.)

Salt-Water Fish

Hot Dishes

Aiglefin au beurre fondu

Haddock

For 6 persons: *1 kg. 200 haddock; 1 kg. potatoes; 150 gr. butter; 2 lemons; parsley.* Cooking time: 20 minutes.

Clean and trim the fish, lay it on the grid of a fish-kettle, and cover it with salted water. Bring quickly to the boil, skim off, and keep the fish-kettle on the side of the stove, to complete the cooking process by poaching. Drain the fish, and arrange it on a folded napkin. Garnish with lemon quarters and parsley, and serve separately steamed potatoes and melted butter. *(France.)*

Aiglefin écossaise

For 6 persons: *12 medallions of haddock (60 gr. to 75 gr. each); 60 gr. butter; 60 gr. chopped shallot; 2 dl. fish fumet (containing white wine); 20 gr. celeriac; 30 gr. carrot; 30 gr. leek; 20 gr. onion; 30 gr. french beans; 3 dl. sauce hollandaise; 24 fish potatoes; 1 table-spoonful of white wine; 75 gr. butter; parsley.* Cooking time: 15 minutes.

Cut up the vegetables into a brunoise, and stew them in butter. Sprinkle the base of a buttered gratinating dish with shallot, place the medallions on top, and poach them in the fish fumet. As soon as the fish is cooked, remove it, and arrange it on a serving dish. Reduce the cooking liquor by three-quarters, and add the reduced sauce hollandaise and the brunoise. Use this sauce to coat the fish, sprinkle with chopped parsley, and surround with the potatoes.

(See illustration on page 266. N.B. Slightly different presentation.)

Filets d'aiglefin

Haddock fillets

Prepare and garnish as for filets de sole.

Aiglefin aux fines herbes

For 6 persons: *6 slices of haddock (250 gr. each); 150 gr. chopped mushrooms; 50 gr. chopped onion; 1 tablespoonful of chopped parsley; 2 dl. white wine; 75 gr. butter; 50 gr. breadcrumbs.* Cooking time: 15 minutes.

Sprinkle the base of a thickly-buttered gratinating dish with the onion, mushrooms and parsley. Place the slices of haddock on top, moisten with the white wine, and sprinkle with the breadcrumbs. Cover with shavings of butter, cook and brown in the oven.

Aiglefin flamande

Haddock Flemish-style

For 6 persons: *1 haddock, weighing 1 kg. 200; 1 table-spoonful of chopped mixed fines herbes; 2 chopped shallots; 12 roundels of peeled and pipped lemon; 2 dl. white wine; 3 or 4 rusks; 30 gr. butter.* Cooking time: 17 minutes.

Cut the fish into slices 2½ cm. thick. Season them with salt and pepper; arrange them in a thickly-buttered sauteuse, and moisten just to cover with the white wine. Add the chopped shallots and parsley, and arrange the roundels of lemon on top. Poach in the oven for 12 minutes. Arrange the slices on a serving dish, thicken the liquor with the crushed rusks, allow to boil for 5 minutes, and pour this sauce over the fish.

Aiglefin frit française

Fried haddock French-style

For 6 persons: *1 kg. 200 haddock; 2 lemons; parsley; flour; ½ litre milk.* Cooking time: 7 to 8 minutes.

Fillet the fish. Skin the fillets, and cut them into escalopes weighing 100 gr. to 110 gr. each. Dip them in salted milk, pass through flour, and fry in deep, hot fat. Arrange the fish on a napkin, and garnish with the fried parsley and lemon quarters. This dish is served without a sauce.

Aiglefin maître d'hôtel

For 6 persons: *6 slices of haddock (250 gr. each); 1 dl. oil; 30 gr. butter; 2 lemons; parsley; 150 gr. maître d'hôtel butter; 24 steamed potatoes; flour.* Cooking time: 15 minutes.

Season the slices with salt and pepper, flour them, and sauté in oil and butter. Arrange them on a serving dish, and coat them with half-melted maître d'hôtel butter (or serve it separately). Garnish with the parsley and lemon quarters. Serve the steamed potatoes separately.

Aiglefin du métayer

Crofter's style haddock fillets

For 6 persons: *6 fillets of haddock (170 gr. each); 100 gr. butter; 100 gr. crushed corn flakes; 3 (sieved) hard-boiled eggs; 6 tomato-halves; 1 tablespoonful of chopped parsley; flour.* Cooking time: 12 minutes.

Season the fillets with salt and pepper, pass them through melted butter and coat with the corn flakes. Grill gently, basting from time to time with melted butter. Arrange the fish on a serving dish, and sprinkle with the hard-boiled eggs and the chopped parsley. Garnish with the grilled tomato-halves. *(Great Britain.)*
(See illustration on page 262. N.B. Different presentation.)

Aiglefin Mistral

For 6 persons: *1 kg. 200 haddock; 300 gr. chopped tomatoes; 200 gr. thinly-sliced mushrooms; 1 clove of garlic; salt; pepper; 1 dl. white wine; 15 cl. oil; breadcrumbs; 1 tablespoonful of chopped parsley; 50 gr. butter.* Cooking time: 15 minutes.

Cut up the haddock into slices 2½ cm. thick, and sauté them in oil on both sides. Sauté the mushrooms in butter. Arrange the slices on a gratinating dish, and cover them with the chopped tomatoes, mushrooms, crushed garlic and chopped parsley. Pour the white wine on top, sprinkle with oil, and brown in the oven.

Aiglefin provençale

For 6 persons: *6 slices of haddock (250 gr. each); 60 gr. chopped onion; 2 dl. olive oil; 500 gr. chopped tomatoes; 2 crushed cloves of garlic; 2 tablespoonfuls of chopped parsley; 2 tablespoonfuls of capers; 18 (stoned) black olives; 50 gr. butter.* Cooking time: 12 to 15 minutes.

Colour the onion in oil, and add the chopped tomatoes, crushed garlic, capers, and half the parsley. Cook until the tomatoes have softened. Arrange the slices on a buttered gratinating dish, add the garnish and the olives, and pour the white wine on top. Cover the dish with a sheet of buttered paper, and cook in the oven. Before serving, sprinkle with chopped parsley.

Aiglefin sauté anglaise

For 6 persons: *12 escalopes of haddock (60 gr. each); 2 eggs; breadcrumbs; 120 gr. butter; 120 gr. maître d'hôtel butter; flour.* Cooking time: 8 to 10 minutes.

Season the escalopes with salt and pepper, flour them, and cover with egg and breadcrumbs. Cook in clarified butter until golden brown; arrange on a serving dish and cover with the maître d'hôtel butter.

Brochettes d'anguille

Unagi no kabayaki

For 6 persons: *900 gr. to 1 kg. of eel (skinned, gutted and cleaned); 5 cl.* sake *(Japanese rice alcohol); 2 tablespoonfuls of* shoju *(Japanese soya sauce); 2 tablespoonfuls of sugar; 300 gr. rice.* Cooking time: approximately 10 minutes.

Fillet the fish, cut up the fillets into small pieces about 3 cm. thick, and impale them on skewers. Mix the *sake* with the *shoju* and sugar, and dip the skewers into this liquor. Grill the eel over charcoal, basting with the liquor until the fish is just cooked and well glazed. Cook the rice in lightly-salted water, drain and dry it. Arrange it in a Japanese serving bowl, and garnish with the skewers of fish. *(Japan.)*
(See Culinary Technique, page 91.)

Anguille étuvée aux tomates

Eel

Al i gryta med tomat och kryddgront

For 6 persons: *1 kg. 800 of eel (skinned, and cut up into thick slices weighing 75 gr. each); 300 gr. chopped tomatoes; 3 dl. dry white wine; 3 cl. cognac; a sprig of parsley stalks and white of leek; a sachet (containing thyme, basil, tarragon and chervil); 3 chopped shallots; the juice of 1 lemon; 2 tablespoonfuls of oil; 50 gr. butter; 1 tablespoonful of beurre manié; chopped parsley; chopped chervil.* Cooking time: approximately 20 minutes.

Marinate the slices of eel with salt, pepper and lemon juice. Colour the chopped shallots in oil, add the fish, allow to sweat for a moment, flame with the cognac, and swill out with the white wine. Add the tomatoes, the sprig of parsley and leek, and the sachet, and cook, covered with a lid. Arrange the slices on a serving dish. After removing the sprig and the sachet, thicken the cooking liquor with the beurre manié, and monter au beurre. Check seasoning and consistency. Coat the fish with the unpassed sauce, and sprinkle with chopped parsley and chervil. Serve separately either buttered rice or plain boiled potatoes. *(Sweden.)*
(See Culinary Technique, page 91.)

Anguille frite aux pommes de terre à la crème

Stegt Al med stuvede kartofler

For 6 persons: *1 eel, weighing 1 kg. 500; 100 gr. butter; 2 eggs; 2 lemons; 1 kg. potatoes; ½ litre fresh cream; flour; breadcrumbs; parsley; nutmeg.* Cooking time for the eel: 10 to 12 minutes.

Skin, gut and wash the eel, cut it up into thick slices approximately 6 cm. long; flour, pass through beaten and seasoned egg, and coat with breadcrumbs. Pass the eel through deep fat, and finish the cooking in butter. Arrange on a serving dish with fried parsley and lemon quarters, and serve separately the creamed potatoes.

Pommes de terre à la crème: Steam the peeled potatoes or boil in salted water until they are just done. Cut them up into large dice, heat them in the cream, and season them with salt, pepper and a pinch of nutmeg. *(Denmark.)*

Anguille aux pousses de bambou japonaise

Japanischer Bambusaal

For 6 persons: *500 gr. eel (net weight); 120 gr. young bamboo shoots; 120 gr. mushrooms; 120 gr. green peppers; 12 leaves of* nori *(dried Japanese seaweed); 6 eggs; 15 cl.* sake *(Japanese rice liquor); 3 teaspoonfuls of soya sauce; 10 gr.* aji no moto *(a Japanese preparation); 1 pinch of sage; picked parsley.* Poaching time: 15 minutes.

Prepare 15 cl. cooking liquor with the bones and trimmings of eel, and pass through a conical strainer (chinois). Cut up the eel into fine escalopes. Thinly slice the mushrooms, bamboo shoots and pepper. Distribute all these ingredients, with the parsley and the *nori*, in six Japanese cooking bowls. Prepare a royale with the beaten eggs, the eel cooking liquor, the fresh cream, the *sake* and the soya sauce, the whole seasoned with salt, freshly-milled pepper, sage and *aji no moto*. Seal the bowls with their lids, and poach in a bain-marie in the oven. The royale must remain soft. *(Germany.)*
(See illustration, page 365.)

Anguille rotie Finlandia

Uunissa paistettu ankerias Finlandia

For 6 persons: *2 eels (weighing a total of 1 kg. 500); 50 gr. butter; 1 tablespoonful of chopped dill.* Cooking time: approximately 35 minutes.

Gut the eels, wash them carefully, and dry them without skinning. Remove the dorsal and ventral fins. Sprinkle the eels with salt and white pepper. Butter a grid, place the eels on it, and cook in the oven. Using a brush, baste with butter from time to time. When the cooking is finished, remove the skin, and cut up the fish into thin slices. Arrange on a serving dish and sprinkle with the dill. Serve with the accompaniment of a strong-flavoured sauce (mustard or piquante), and plain boiled or purée potatoes. *(Finland.)*

Anguilles de Bilbao

Angulas a la bilbaina

For 6 persons: *600 gr. of elvers; 3 dl. oil; 3 chopped cloves of garlic; 2 small chopped red peppers.* Cooking time: 2 to 3 minutes.

Wash the fish and dry them on a cloth. Pour the oil into six small fire-proof cocottes or ramequins, add the garlic and the peppers, and heat. When the oil is boiling, add the elvers, stir, cover, and then serve immediately with wooden forks. *(Spain.)*

Quenelles d'anguilles Caroline

For 6 persons: *1 kg. of skinned eels; 30 cl. beer (from the Abbaye de Maredsous); 350 gr. butter; 400 gr. flour; 10 eggs; 10 peeled tomatoes; 50 gr. chopped onion; 1 clove of garlic; 1 lemon; 1 tablespoonful of olive oil; 1 tablespoonful of beurre manié (made from 10 gr. flour and 15 gr. butter); 1 dl. fresh cream.* Cooking time: approximately 30 minutes.

Gut and clean the eels, fillet them, and cut the fillets into slices 1 cm. thick. Marinate them for 30 minutes in the beer, with a bayleaf, a sprig of thyme, and a pinch each of rosemary, pepper, salt and celery salt. Prepare a pâté à choux with ½ litre of water, 200 gr. butter, 400 gr. flour and a pinch of salt. Add the eggs one by one, the well-drained fillets of eel, and 100 gr. of melted butter. Mix thoroughly to obtain a smooth consistency. Shape the quenelles with a tablespoon and poach them in lightly-salted simmering water for 12 to 15 minutes. Colour the chopped onion in olive oil, and add the fish-bones, the tomatoes (cut into quarters), the thinly-sliced lemon, the crushed garlic, and the beer from the marination. Cook gently for 20 minutes. Pass through a conical strainer (chinois), thicken with the beurre manié, blend in the cream, and correct seasoning and consistency. Drain the quenelles and arrange them in a buttered gratinating dish. Coat with the sauce. Allow to swell for 15 minutes in a medium oven. *(Belgium.)*

Bar

Sea-perch

See Loup de mer, page 273.

Bar rayé New England

Striped bass New England style

For 6 persons: *1 striped bass, weighing 1 kg. 500; 50 gr. thinly-sliced onion; 75 gr. julienne (of carrots and celery); 200 gr. chopped tomatoes; 100 gr. butter; 1 lemon; thyme.* Cooking time: 25 to 30 minutes.

Scale, gut, clean and wash the fish. Season the inside and outside of it with salt, pepper and thyme. Place it on a sheet of aluminium foil, and cover with the julienne, tomatoes and onions. Pour melted butter on top. Wrap the fish in the aluminium foil, so that it is hermetically sealed, but leaving a little space inside. Cook in a medium oven. Unwrap the papillote (foil case) only at table. Serve parsley potatoes separately. *(United States.)*

Barbue

Brill

The flesh of the brill is a little softer than that of the turbot. All styles of preparation for turbot are applicable to the brill, except for fillets, which follow the designations for fillets of sole.

Barbue amiral

For 6 persons: *1 brill, weighing 1 kg. 500; 50 gr. red butter; ½ litre court-bouillon (containing white wine); 200 gr. shelled crayfish; 12 large poached and bearded mussels; 12 poached and bearded oysters; 12 mushroom heads; 12 bouchées mignonnes; ½ litre sauce Villeroi; ½ litre sauce normande; 30 gr. butter; 30 gr. crayfish butter; 2 eggs; breadcrumbs; 12 thin slices of truffle.* Cooking time: approximately 40 minutes.

Place the brill on the buttered grid of a turbot-kettle (turbotière), moisten with the court-bouillon, cover with a sheet of buttered paper, and cook covered with a lid in a medium oven. After cooking, drain the fish, and arrange it on a serving dish. Brush the surface of the fish with the red butter. Coat the mussels and oysters with the sauce Villeroi, egg and breadcrumbs, and fry them. Use the shelled crayfish to make a salpicon, bind it with the sauce normande, and use it to fill the bouchées mignonnes. Surround the brill with the mussels, oysters, bouchées mignonnes, mushrooms, and slices of truffle. Serve separately the sauce normande (containing a little reduced braising-stock finished with the crayfish butter), and plain boiled potatoes. *(France.)*

Barbue Bonnefoy

For 6 persons: *12 escalopes of fillets of brill (60 gr. each); 1 kg. potatoes; 100 gr. butter; flour; ½ litre sauce Bonnefoy.* Cooking time: 7 to 8 minutes.

Season the escalopes with salt and pepper, flour them, and sauté in butter. Arrange the fish on a serving dish and coat with the sauce Bonnefoy. Serve plain boiled potatoes separately. *(France.)*

Barbue Chauchat

For 6 persons: *6 pieces of fillet of brill (125 gr. each); 700 gr. potatoes; 75 gr. butter; 1 lemon; ½ litre sauce Mornay.* Cooking time: 15 to 18 minutes.

Season the fish with salt and pepper, and poach in the oven with butter and lemon juice (covered with a sheet of buttered paper). Mask a gratinating dish with sauce Mornay, arrange the pieces of fish on it, and surround them with thick roundels of freshly-boiled potatoes. Coat the fish and the garnish with sauce Mornay, and glaze either in a hot oven or under the salamander. *(France.)*

Barbue Denise

For 6 persons: *1 brill, weighing 1 kg. 500; 200 gr. thick mushroom purée; 400 gr. fish forcemeat; 2 dl. fresh cream; ½ litre white wine; 2 chopped shallots; 1 coffee-spoonful of paprika; 1 tablespoonful of chopped parsley; 2 dl. fish velouté; 1 dl. sauce béchamel; 40 gr. butter.* Cooking time: 35 to 40 minutes.

Score the brill (on the dark side) to right and left of the backbone, from just behind the head and as far as the tail. Loosen the fillets, and remove the backbone. Stuff the brill with two-thirds of the fish forcemeat (worked up with cream, and containing the mushroom purée and chopped parsley). Seal in the forcemeat by pressing the fillets together. Lay the fish, black side downwards, on the grid of a turbot-kettle (which has been buttered, and then sprinkled with chopped shallot), season with salt and pepper, moisten with the white wine, cover with a sheet of buttered paper, and poach, covered with a lid, in the oven. Drain, arrange on a serving dish, and coat with the velouté (which has been mixed with the sauce béchamel and with the reduced cooking stock). Garnish with quenelles (shaped with small spoons) made from the rest of the forcemeat. *(France.)*

Barbue Dieudonné

For 6 persons: *1 brill, weighing 1 kg. 500; 3 dl. white wine; 3 dl. fish fumet; ½ litre fresh cream; 250 gr. chopped tomatoes; 200 gr. button mushrooms; 1 tablespoonful of fines herbes; 75 gr. butter; 40 gr. beurre manié.* Cooking time: 30 minutes.

Stew together in butter the chopped tomatoes and the thinly-sliced mushrooms. Poach the brill in the white wine and fish fumet, drain it, and arrange it on a serving dish. Reduce the cooking liquor by half, add the cream, thicken with the beurre manié, allow to cook for a few minutes, correct seasoning and consistency, and pass. Add the mushrooms, tomatoes and fines herbes. Coat the fish with a little of this sauce. Serve the rest of the sauce separately. *(France.)*

Barbue Donier

For 6 persons: *12 escalopes of fillet of brill (60 gr. each); 300 gr. rice; 9 dl. fish fumet; 40 gr. chopped onion; 60 gr. butter; 70 gr. grated Parmesan cheese; 4 dl. sauce Mornay; 1 dl. sauce Nantua.* Cooking time: 15 to 18 minutes.

Poach the escalopes in the fish fumet. Prepare a basic risotto, but with fish fumet, and add, away from heat, 30 gr. grated Parmesan cheese and a nut of butter. Arrange the escalopes on the rice in a gratinating dish, coat with the sauce Mornay, sprinkle with cheese, and brown. Before serving, surround the dish with a thread of sauce Nantua.

Barbue Dugléré

For 6 persons: *6 slices of fillet of brill (110 gr. each); 350 gr. chopped tomatoes; 1 coffee-spoonful of chopped parsley; 30 gr. chopped onion; 60 gr. butter; 1 dl. white wine; 15 cl. fish velouté; ½ lemon.* Cooking time: 15 minutes.

Arrange the fish in a buttered gratinating dish. Add the chopped onion, the roughly-chopped tomatoes and the chopped parsley. Season with salt and pepper. Moisten with the white wine, cover with a sheet of buttered paper, and poach in the oven. Arrange the fish on a serving dish, reduce the cooking liquor, and add the velouté. Finish off with 40 gr. butter and a few drops of lemon juice, and use this sauce to cover the slices. *(France.)*

Barbue Edouard VII

For 6 persons: *1 brill, weighing 1 kg. 500; 2 chopped shallots; 12 poached and bearded mussels; 12 poached and bearded oysters; 12 mushroom heads; 12 thin slices of truffle; 12 very small potato croquettes; 3 shelled crayfish; 4 dl. sauce béchamel; 3 dl. fish fumet; ½ bottle dry champagne; 50 gr. crayfish butter; ½ coffee-spoonful of curry powder; 2 eggs; breadcrumbs.* Cooking time: 30 to 35 minutes.

Poach the brill, with the chopped shallots and the mushroom trimmings, in the fish fumet and champagne. As soon as it is cooked, drain the fish and arrange it on a serving dish. Reduce the cooking liquor by two-thirds, add the sauce béchamel, season with the curry powder, pass, and incorporate the crayfish (which have been cut into dice). Coat the fish with part of the sauce, and decorate it lengthwise with the slices of truffle and mushroom heads. Garnish with the mussels and oysters (coated with egg and breadcrumbs and fried) and with the croquette potatoes. Serve the rest of the sauce separately. *(France.)*

Barbue hôtelière

For 6 persons: *12 escalopes of fillet of brill (60 gr. each); 100 gr. butter; 2 tablespoonfuls of dry duxelles; 120 gr. maître d'hôtel butter; flour.* Cooking time: 10 to 12 minutes.

Season the escalopes with salt and pepper, flour them, and cook the meunière. Arrange them on a hot serving dish (on top of the maître d'hôtel butter containing the duxelles). Garnish with quarters of lemon, or border the dish with thin slices of lemon. *(France.)*

Barbue Laguipière

For 6 persons: *900 gr. skinned fillets of brill; 1 dl. white wine; 1 dl. fish fumet; 4 dl. white wine sauce; 50 gr. truffle.* Cooking time: 20 minutes.

Season the fillets with salt and pepper, and poach them in the white wine and fish fumet. Drain, and arrange on a serving dish. Reduce the cooking liquor by three-quarters, and add it to the white wine sauce. Coat the fillets with the sauce, and sprinkle with the truffle (cut into a brunoise). *(France.)*

Barbue riche

For 6 persons: *6 pieces of fillet of brill (110 gr. to 120 gr. each); 4 dl. sauce Nantua; 12 thin slices of truffle; 12 shelled crayfish; 2 dl. fish fumet.* Cooking time: 15 minutes.

Poach the fillets in the fumet. Drain them and arrange on a serving dish. Garnish with the crayfish and slices of truffle. Coat with the sauce Nantua. *(France.)*

Coulibiac de saumon, p. 403

Saumon Festival de Salzbourg, p. 234 ▼

▲ Homard en bellevue, p. 453

Homard au champagne, p. 453 ▼

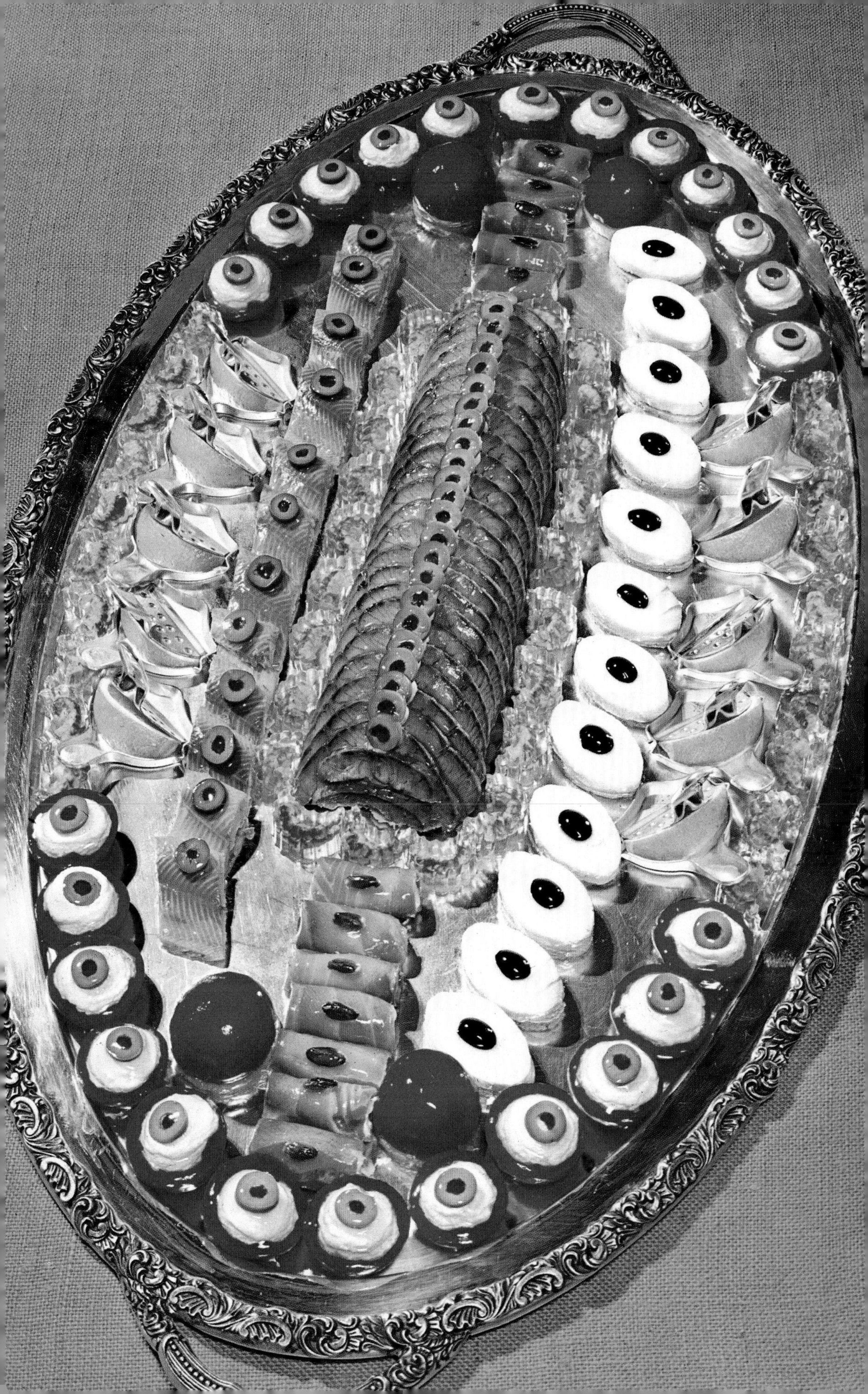

Barbue rôtie

For 6 persons: *1 brill, weighing 1 kg. 800; 150 gr. butter; parsley; 2 lemons; ½ litre sauce Saint-Malo.* Cooking time: 35 to 40 minutes.

Score the brill, season it with salt and pepper, and cook it in the oven on a thickly-buttered fish tray, basting frequently with the butter. Drain, arrange on a serving dish, and garnish with the parsley and the quartered lemons. Serve with the sauce Saint-Malo, or melted butter, or even a white wine sauce containing anchovy butter. *(France.)*

Barbue Saint-Germain

For 6 persons: *12 escalopes of brill (60 gr. each); 250 gr. breadcrumbs; 150 gr. butter; 3 dl. sauce béarnaise; 800 gr. noisette potatoes.* Cooking time: 10 to 12 minutes.

Season the escalopes with salt and pepper, and dip them in melted butter. Roll them in fine breadcrumbs (pressing them down with a palette knife). Sprinkle with melted butter, and grill gently. Arrange on a serving dish and garnish with the noisette potatoes. Serve the sauce béarnaise separately. *(France.)*

Barbue Sarah

For 6 persons: *6 fillets of brill (150 gr. each); 100 gr. truffle; 100 gr. carrots; 110 gr. celeriac; 4 dl. sauce Vénitienne; 2 dl. fish fumet; 50 gr. butter.* Cooking time: 15 minutes.

Cut up the carrots and celeriac into a fine julienne, and stew in butter. Cut up the truffle into a fine julienne. Poach the fillets in the fish fumet, drain it, and arrange on a serving dish. Coat with the sauce Vénitienne, and sprinkle with the julienne of carrot, celeriac and truffle.

Barbue soufflée Victoria

For 6 persons: *1 brill, weighing 1 kg. 200; 400 gr. fish forcemeat; 180 gr. raw salmon (skinned and boned); 1 egg white; 2 dl. cream; 6 large medallions of lobster tail; 6 large thin slices of truffle; ½ litre white wine; 4 dl. sauce Victoria; 50 gr. butter.* Cooking time: 35 to 40 minutes.

Prepare the brill as for Barbue Denise, but fill it with the fish forcemeat (containing a salmon forcemeat, and the egg white worked up with the cream). Poach the fish, in the white wine, in the oven. Drain it, and arrange it on a serving dish. Reduce the cooking stock by three-quarters, and add it to the sauce Victoria. Place the medallions of lobster, lengthwise, along the brill, alternating them with slices of truffle. Coat lightly with the sauce. Serve the rest of the sauce separately.

Barbue tyrolienne

For 6 persons: *12 escalopes of brill (60 gr. each); 500 gr. chopped tomatoes; 100 gr. butter; 24 roundels of onion; 2 chopped shallots; flour.* Cooking time: 12 to 16 minutes.

Pass the shallots through butter, add the chopped tomatoes, season with salt and pepper, and cook until the tomatoes are soft. Flour the escalopes and sauté them in butter. Arrange the tomatoes on a serving dish, place the escalopes on top, and garnish with deep-fried roundels of onion.

Barbue Wellington

For 6 persons: *6 fillets of brill (120 gr. each); ½ litre purée Soubise; 2 dl. fish fumet; 4 dl. sauce normande; 60 gr. grated Parmesan cheese; 50 gr. butter.* Cooking time: 20 minutes.

Poach the fillets in the fish fumet, and drain them. Cover the base of a gratinating dish with half the purée Soubise, and arrange the fillets on top. Cover with the rest of the purée Soubise, sprinkle with the grated Parmesan cheese, dot the surface with pieces of butter, and brown in a hot oven. Serve the sauce normande separately.

Baudroie

Angler

Because of the hideous appearance of its head, this fish—which the French also know as diable de mer (sea devil) or crapaud de mer (sea toad)—is sold only without its head and tail, and skinned. The flesh is white and delicate, but rather close-textured. It is used in bouillabaisse and bourride. It can also be prepared as for hake and fresh cod.

p. 249 ◄ Filets de sole Domino, p. 231
p. 250 ◄ Pie de queues d'écrevisses, p. 452
p. 251 ◄ Sélection de poissons fumés
p. 252 ◄ Brochet du lac farci à la mode de Kiev, p. 231

Bonite et boniton

Bonito and young bonito

This fish can be prepared in all styles applicable to tunny. *(See page 344.)*

Cabillaud ou morue fraîche

Fresh cod

Fresh cod is cooked in salted water. All sauces suitable for turbot are applicable to it. *(See Culinary Technique, page 66.)*

Cabillaud anglaise

Fresh cod English style

For 6 persons: *1 kg. 200 of fresh cod; 150 gr. butter; 1 kg. potatoes; 2 lemons; parsley.* Cooking time: 25 minutes.

Cook the cod in a court-bouillon (or simply in salted water containing vinegar). Drain the fish, and arrange it on a serving dish which has been covered with a napkin. Garnish with lemon quarters and parsley. Serve plain boiled potatoes and melted butter separately.

Cabillaud bâloise

Kabeljau auf basler Art

For 6 persons: *6 middle-cut slices of fresh cod (180 gr. each); 1 dl. oil; 80 gr. butter; 200 gr. onions; 5 cl. jus lié; 1 lemon; 1 tablespoonful of chopped parsley; flour.* Cooking time: 10 to 12 minutes.

Season the slices with salt and pepper, flour them, and colour them gently until golden in hot oil. Colour the onions (cut into roundels) in butter. Arrange the fish on a serving dish, cover it with the onions, sprinkle with lemon juice, and then with chopped parsley. Use the jus lié to make a border around the fish. *(Switzerland.)*

Cabillaud boulangère

For 6 persons: *3 middle-cut slices of fresh cod (400 gr. each); 200 gr. butter; 24 potatoes (olive shaped); 50 gr. breadcrumbs; 1 crushed clove of garlic; 1 tablespoonful of chopped parsley.* Cooking time: 25 minutes.

Place the slices in a large, thickly-buttered, gratinating dish, surround them with the potatoes, season with salt and pepper, and moisten liberally with melted butter. Bake in the oven, basting frequently. A few minutes before the end of the cooking time, sprinkle with the breadcrumbs (mixed with the garlic and parsley). *(See illustration, page 265.)*

Cabillaud Dimitri

For 6 persons: *6 slices of fresh cod (250 gr. each); 4 dl. white wine sauce; 150 gr. anchovy butter; 25 gr. fillets of anchovy; 24 pommes à l'anglaise.* Cooking time: 15 minutes.

Poach the slices in a court-bouillon, drain them, and arrange them on a serving dish. Work up the white wine sauce with the anchovy butter, and add it to the anchovy fillets (which have been cut into dice). Coat the slices with the sauce, and garnish with the pommes à l'anglaise.
(See illustration, page 268. N.B. Different presentation.)

Cabillaud flamande

Proceed as for the preparation of Aiglefin flamande. *(See page 242.)*

Cabillaud frit

Fried fresh cod

For 6 persons: *1 kg. 200 fresh cod; 2 lemons; 4 dl. sauce tartare (or sauce tomate); 2 eggs; breadcrumbs; flour.* Cooking time: 12 minutes.

Cut up the fish into slices 2 cm. to 3 cm. thick, and season them with salt and pepper. Flour the slices, coat with egg and breadcrumbs, and deep fry. Drain, and arrange on a serving dish, with lemon quarters and fried parsley. Serve the sauce separately.

Cabillaud grillé

Grilled fresh cod

For 6 persons: *1 kg. 200 of fresh cod; 150 gr. maître d'hôtel butter (or anchovy butter); 75 gr. butter (or 7 cl. oil); 2 lemons; parsley; flour.* Cooking time: 12 to 15 minutes.

Cut up the cod into slices 2 cm. to 3 cm. thick; season them with salt and pepper, and flour them. Sprinkle them with oil (or with melted butter), and grill them gently. Arrange them on a serving dish, with lemon quarters and parsley. Serve the maître d'hôtel butter or anchovy butter separately.

Cabillaud Kämp

Kampin turska

For 6 persons: *1 kg. of fillets of cod; 90 kg. butter; 15 cl. double cream; 3 dl. white wine.* Poaching time: 10 to 12 minutes.

Cut up the fillets into escalopes, salt them, arrange in a buttered sauteuse, sprinkle with the white wine, sprinkle with pieces of butter, and poach. Add the double cream, and cover the sauteuse with a sheet of buttered paper. Finish the poaching in the oven. Drain the fish, arrange it on a serving dish, and coat with the sauce. Serve with steamed potatoes, and a green salad. *(Finland.)*

Cabillaud Minerve

For 6 persons: *2 fillets of fresh cod (450 gr. each); 50 gr. chopped onion; 3 chopped shallots; 300 gr. chopped tomatoes; 100 gr. butter; 18 anchovy fillets; 500 gr. potatoes; ½ litre fish fumet.* Cooking time: 18 minutes.

Line a buttered gratinating dish with the chopped onion and shallot, arrange the fillets in it, and cover them with the chopped tomatoes. Moisten with the fish fumet, and cook in the oven. When the cooking is finished, drain the fish, and arrange it on a serving dish. Reduce the cooking liquor by two-thirds, and monter au beurre. Garnish the fish with freshly boiled potatoes (cut into roundels) and the anchovy fillets. Coat with the sauce.

Cabillaud Mistral

For 6 persons: *1 kg. 200 of fresh cod; 300 gr. chopped tomatoes; 200 gr. thinly-sliced mushrooms; 1 crushed clove of garlic; 15 cl. white wine; 15 cl. olive oil; 50 gr. breadcrumbs.* Cooking time: 20 minutes.

Cut up the cod into slices 25 mm. thick, season with salt and pepper; flour the slices and seal them in hot oil for two minutes on each side. Sauté the mushrooms, add the chopped tomatoes and the garlic, and soften them. Arrange the slices in a gratinating dish, add the tomatoes and mushrooms, moisten with the white wine, and sprinkle with the breadcrumbs. Sprinkle with the oil, and finish off the cooking by browning.
(See illustration, page 266.)

Cabillaud orientale

Bakala misrachi

For 6 persons: *6 thick slices of fresh cod (250 gr. each); 100 gr. butter; 200 gr. celery; 200 gr. carrots; 250 gr. onions; 1 parsley stalk; 200 gr. chopped tomatoes; 1 lemon; Worcestershire sauce; curry powder; sweet marjoram; paprika; saffron; flour.* Cooking time: 12 minutes.

Marinate the fish in lemon juice, Worcestershire sauce, salt and pepper, and a large pinch each of paprika, saffron, curry powder and marjoram. Cut up the celery, onion and carrots into small dice, and chop the parsley finely. Stew until cooking is almost complete, and add the tomatoes. Drain and dry the fish, season with salt and pepper, and gently colour both sides of the fish in butter. Place the vegetables in a sauteuse, arrange the fish on top, cover with a sheet of buttered paper, and finish off the cooking in the oven. *(Israel.)*

Cabillaud et pommes de terre à la sauce moutarde

Plukfisk af Torsk

For 6 persons: *1 fresh cod weighing 2 kg.; 1 kg. potatoes; ½ litre milk; 75 gr. butter; 35 gr. flour; finely-milled mustard grains.* Cooking time: 10 minutes.

Cut up the cod into slices 2 cm. thick, and poach them in boiling, salted water. Remove skin and bones, and flake the fish. Cook the potatoes (plain boiled) until they are just done, and cut them into dice 15 mm. thick. Prepare a roux with 40 gr. butter and 35 gr. flour, bring to the boil, season with the mustard flour, and cook for a few more minutes. Thicken the fish and the potatoes with the sauce (which must remain fairly clear). Arrange in a timbale, and sprinkle with small shavings of butter. *(Denmark.)*

Cabillaud portugaise

For 6 persons: *6 slices of fresh cod (250 gr. each); 50 gr. chopped onion; 1 crushed clove of garlic; 500 gr. chopped tomatoes; 2 dl. white wine; 50 gr. butter; 1 tablespoonful of chopped parsley.* Cooking time: 15 minutes.

Sprinkle a buttered sauteuse with the chopped onion, and arrange the slices in it. Season with salt and pepper, and add the peeled, de-seeded and chopped tomatoes, the garlic and the chopped parsley. Pour on the white wine, and poach (covered with a lid) in the oven. When the cooking is finished, arrange the slices on a serving dish, reduce the cooking liquor, and pour it (without passing) over the fish.

Cabillaud provençale

For 6 persons: *6 pieces of fresh cod fillet (120 gr. each); 400 gr. peeled, de-seeded and chopped tomatoes; 100 gr. chopped raw mushrooms; 1 chopped shallot; 2 crushed cloves of garlic; 1 tablespoonful of chopped parsley; 7 cl. olive oil; 1 dl. white wine; 1½ dl. fish fumet.* Cooking time: 15 minutes.

Pass the shallots through oil, and add the peeled, de-seeded and chopped tomatoes, mushrooms, garlic and parsley. Soften. Poach the fillets in the white wine and fish fumet, drain them, and arrange on a serving dish. Reduce the cooking liquor, blend it with the tomato fondue, bring to the boil, and pour this sauce over the fish.

Cabillaud reine

For 6 persons: *2 fillets of fresh cod (450 gr. each); 24 spoon-moulded quenelles of pike forcemeat; 12 thin slices of truffle; 4 dl. cream sauce; 2 dl. fish fumet.* Cooking time: 20 minutes.

Poach the fillets, and arrange them on a serving dish. Reduce the cooking liquor, and add it to the cream sauce. Place the slices of truffle on the fillets, garnish the fish with the quenelles, and coat all over with the sauce.

Cabillaud sauce persil, Steak de

Poached cod steaks with parsley sauce

For 6 persons: *6 fresh cod steaks (200 gr. each); 600 gr. pommes poisson; 4 dl. thick sauce béchamel; 1 dl. fresh cream; 40 gr. butter; 2 tablespoonfuls of chopped parsley; ½ litre milk; 50 gr. thinly-sliced onions; ½ bayleaf; 3 parsley stalks; 5 white pepper-corns; ½ lemon; 25 gr. salt.* Cooking time: 10 to 12 minutes.

Prepare a court-bouillon with 2 litres of water, and the milk, bayleaf, parsley-stalks, onion, pepper, lemon juice and salt. Plunge the cod steaks into the boiling court-bouillon, and poach gently. Drain them, and arrange them on a serving dish. Prepare a cream sauce with the sauce béchamel, cream and butter. Add the chopped parsley, and correct seasoning and consistency. Coat the fish with this sauce, and garnish with pommes poisson. *(Great Britain.)*

Cabillaud vierge

For 6 persons: *6 pieces of fresh cod fillet (120 gr. each); 2 dl. fish fumet; 2 dl. fish velouté; 2 dl. fresh cream; 1 coffee-spoonful of (mixed) chopped tarragon and chopped chervil; 50 gr. butter; 12 small puff-pastry fleurons.* Cooking time: 15 to 18 minutes.

Poach the fillets in the butter and fish fumet, and arrange them on a serving dish. Add the cooking liquor to the velouté, and reduce by half over a brisk flame. Add the cream, allow to simmer for a few minutes, and correct seasoning and consistency. Coat the fish with the sauce, sprinkle with the chopped tarragon and chervil, and garnish with the fleurons.

Carrelet ou plie franche

Plaice

This fish is rarely used in restaurant cookery. It can be prepared as for certain methods used for young turbot, but it is usually served fried, grilled or meunière.

Carrelet au beurre fondu, au persil et aux pommes nature

Kogt rodspaette med smeltet smör, hakket persille og hvide kartofler

For 6 persons: *3 plaice, weighing 700 gr. each; 1 kg. 500 potatoes; 300 gr. butter; 6 tablespoonfuls of chopped parsley.* Cooking time: 10 minutes.

Clean the plaice, place them in cold salted water, bring to the boil, and poach gently. Drain the fish, and arrange them on a napkin. Serve melted butter, chopped parsley, and pommes l'anglaise separately. *(Denmark.)*

Carrelet frits sauce rémoulade, Filets de

Stegte rödspaetterfileter, sauce remoulade

For 6 persons: *3 plaice, weighing 700 gr. each; 2 eggs; 250 gr. breadcrumbs; 2 lemons; 4 dl. sauce rémoulade; 100 gr. flour.* Cooking time: 4 to 5 minutes.

Fillet the plaice, flour the fillets, pass them through beaten egg, season with salt and pepper, and cover with breadcrumbs. Plunge them into very hot fat. Drain the fillets, and arrange them on a serving dish with quarters of lemon. Serve the sauce rémoulade separately. *(Denmark.)*

Carrelet à la petite sirène, Filets de

Fiskegryde Den lille Havfrue

For 6 persons: *18 fillets of plaice (50 gr. each); 50 gr. onion; 600 gr. fresh mushrooms; 3 large tomatoes; 7 cl. oil; 75 gr. capers; 150 gr. butter; 250 gr. shelled prawns; 2 lemons; 6 large potatoes; flour.* Cooking time for the fillets: 3 to 4 minutes.

Cut up the fillets into small batons 1 cm. thick, season them with salt and pepper, flour them, fry them in boiling oil, and remove them. Using the same oil, rissolé the chopped onion, drain and keep hot, with the fillets, in a gratinating dish. Thinly slice the mushrooms, sauté them in butter, and add the peeled, de-seeded and chopped tomatoes, the segments of peeled and pipped lemons, and the capers. Stew all these together, and pour over the fillets. Sauté the prawns lightly in butter, and distribute them over the fillets. Bake the potatoes in their jackets in the oven, and score them so as to be able to slip in a small piece of butter. Serve together the fillets and the baked potatoes. *(Denmark.)*

Carrelets de Friedrichshafen, sauce persil

Fridrickshavnpetter i persiljesås

For 6 persons: *2 plaice, weighing 1 kg. 500 each; 4 chopped shallots; 3 dl. white wine; 2 dl. fresh cream; 200 gr. butter; parsley-stalks; 3 dl. fish stock; 1 tablespoonful of flour; 2 egg yolks; chopped parsley.* Cooking time: 8 to 10 minutes.

Remove the heads and fins of the fish, and place these trimmings aside. Gut and clean the fish, and cut up each into three pieces. Prepare a fumet with the heads and trimmings. Line a buttered dish with the chopped shallots, and place in it the pieces of fish, season with salt, pepper and lemon juice, and cover with the parsley-stalks. Moisten, just to cover, with the white wine and the fish fumet, cover with a lid, and poach gently until just cooked. Pass the cooking stock, reserve a few tablespoonfuls of it, reduce the rest, bind it with beurre manié, and cook for a few more moments. Bind it with the cream and egg-yolks, monter au beurre (using fresh butter), and add the chopped parsley. Arrange on a hot serving dish, and sprinkle with the reserved stock. Serve the sauce separately, and also some plain boiled potatoes. *(Sweden.)*

Chinchard

Horse-mackerel; scad

This fish is similar to the mackerel, but has a coarser flesh. All methods of preparation appropriate to the mackerel are applicable to the horse-mackerel.

Chinchard à la créole, Filets de

Bluefish fillets Creole style

For 6 persons: *3 horse-mackerel (bluefish), weighing 500 gr. to 600 gr. each; 3 chopped shallots; the flesh of 2 unskinned green peppers; 60 gr. onion; 150 gr. fresh mushrooms; 150 gr. peeled, de-seeded and chopped tomatoes; 75 gr. butter; 1 dl. white wine; 1 lemon.* Poaching time: 10 to 15 minutes.

Fillet the fish, and arrange the fillets in a buttered gratinating dish (which has been lined with the shallots). Cut up the peppers and the mushrooms into a julienne. Cover the fish with this julienne, and also with the thinly-sliced onion and the peeled, de-seeded and chopped tomatoes. Season with salt and pepper, sprinkle with lemon juice, moisten with the white wine, and cover with a sheet of buttered paper. Poach the fillets in a moderate oven. Serve parsley potatoes separately, or rice (prepared créole). *(United States.)*

Colin

Hake

All styles of preparation for fresh cod and haddock are applicable to hake. It is served in small restaurants and in the home.

Colin basquaise

Merluza a la vasca

For 6 persons: *6 slices of hake (200 gr. each); 6 cockles; 6 shelled prawns; ½ litre fish fumet; 1 crushed clove of garlic; 1 onion; 1 tablespoonful of chopped parsley; 5 cl. oil; 3 hard-boiled eggs.* Cooking time: approximately 30 minutes.

Colour the chopped onion, and half the parsley, in oil. Swill out with the fish fumet, and cook gently for 15 minutes. Arrange the slices of hake in a gratinating dish, add the shelled cockles and the prawns, moisten with the fish fumet, season with salt and pepper, and poach gently for 12 minutes. Garnish with quarters of hard-boiled egg, and sprinkle with chopped parsley. *(Spain.)*

Colin Bercy

For 6 persons: *1 kg. 250 of hake; 3 dl. white wine; 3 chopped shallots; 1 tablespoonful of chopped parsley; 30 gr. flour; 75 gr. butter; 1 lemon; 40 gr. bread-crumbs.* Cooking time: 15 minutes.

Fillet the fish, and cut up each fillet into three pieces. Prepare a fumet with the bones and trimmings, pass it, and poach the fillets in it. Drain them, and arrange them on a buttered gratinating dish. Pass ¼ litre of the cooking liquor, season it with salt and pepper, and add the lemon juice and chopped parsley. Pass the chopped shallots through butter, moisten with the white wine, and reduce by half. Add the fish fumet, bring to the boil, and thicken (away from heat) with beurre manié (made from

25 gr. butter and 30 gr. flour). Allow to simmer for a few minutes, and butter lightly. Coat the fillets with this sauce, sprinkle with the breadcrumbs, dot with pieces of butter, and brown in a hot oven.

Colin bretonne

Proceed as for Colin Bercy, adding to the sauce a julienne of 75 gr. carrot, 75 gr. turnip and 75 gr. white of leek (stewed together in butter).

Colin florentine

For 6 persons: *1 kg. 200 of hake; 1 kg. leaf spinach; ½ litre sauce Mornay; 1 dl. white wine; 1 dl. fish fumet; 50 gr. grated Parmesan cheese; 50 gr. butter.* Cooking time: 15 minutes.

Fillet the fish, and poach the fillets in the white wine and fish fumet. Sauté the blanched spinach in butter, season with salt, pepper and a pinch of nutmeg, and arrange it in a gratinating dish masked with sauce Mornay. Arrange the fillets on the spinach, and coat them with thick sauce Mornay (containing the fish fumet reduced almost to a glaze). Sprinkle with the grated cheese, and brown in a hot oven.

Colin grillé

Grilled hake

For 6 persons: *6 fillets of hake (120 gr. each); 7 cl. oil; 2 lemons; parsley; 150 gr. maître d'hôtel butter; flour.* Cooking time: 15 minutes.

Season the fillets with salt and pepper, flour them, sprinkle them with oil, and grill gently. Arrange them on a serving dish with lemon quarters and the parsley. Serve the maître d'hôtel butter separately.

Colin Mornay

For 6 persons: *1 kg. 200 of hake; ½ litre sauce Mornay; 1 dl. white wine; 1 dl. fish fumet; 50 gr. grated Parmesan cheese; 30 gr. butter.* Cooking time: 15 to 18 minutes.

Fillet the fish, and cut each fillet into three parts. Poach them in the white wine and fish fumet. Mask the base of a gratinating dish with a little sauce Mornay, and arrange the fillets on top. Coat with the sauce Mornay (containing the cooking liquor, which has been reduced almost to a glaze), sprinkle with the grated cheese, then with melted butter, and brown in a hot oven (or under a salamander).

Colin en timbale

For 6 persons: *12 escalopes of fillets of hake (60 gr. each); 24 large poached and bearded mussels; 24 fish quenelles; 2 dl. fish fumet; ½ lemon; ½ litre sauce normande.* Cooking time: 12 minutes.

Poach the escalopes in the fish fumet and lemon juice. Drain them, arrange them in a timbale, and lay the quenelles and mussels on top. Coat with half of the sauce. Serve the other half separately.

Congre ou anguille de mer

Conger eel

The flesh of the conger is similar to that of the eel, but less delicate. Conger eel is used mostly for bouillabaisse and fish soups, but nearly all methods of preparing eel are appropriate to it.

Daurade

Gilt-poll

Daurade farcie

Stuffed gilt-poll

For 6 persons: *1 gilt-poll, weighing 1 kg. 200; 400 gr. creamed fish forcemeat; 1 tablespoonful of chopped fines herbes; 100 gr. butter; 1 bouquet garni; ¼ litre white wine.* Cooking time: 35 to 40 minutes.

Split the gilt-poll on the dorsal side, from head to tail, and remove the backbone, without spoiling the shape of the fish. Season the flesh of the inside with salt and pepper, stuff the fish with the forcemeat (containing the fines herbes), and press the fish together again. Lay the fish on a thickly-buttered cooking dish, moisten with equal parts of white wine and water, add the bouquet garni, cover with a sheet of buttered paper, and cook in the oven. Arrange the fish on a serving dish, reduce the cooking liquor, monter au beurre, and use this sauce to coat the fish.

Daurade au four

Besugo al horno

For 6 persons: *1 gilt-poll, weighing between 1 kg. 500 and 2 kg.; 500 gr. peeled potatoes; 75 gr. onion; 1 dl. oil; 1 coffee-spoonful of paprika; 2 tablespoonfuls of chopped parsley.* Cooking time: 35 to 50 minutes.

Oil a fish tray, line it with the potatoes and roundels of onion, and season with salt and pepper. Score the fish on both sides, at intervals of 2 cm., and decorate with half-slices of lemon. Place it on the potatoes, season with salt and paprika, sprinkle with oil and with chopped parsley, and cook in a medium oven, basting frequently. *(Spain.)*

Daurade au gratin

For 6 persons: *1 gilt-poll, weighing 1 kg. 200; ½ litre sauce gratin; 2 chopped shallots; 1 coffee-spoonful of chopped parsley; 1 coffee-spoonful of roughly-chopped parsley; 250 gr. raw mushrooms; 50 gr. butter; ½ lemon; breadcrumbs.* Cooking time: 30 to 35 minutes.

Mask a gratinating dish with a little sauce gratin, and add the shallots and chopped parsley. Arrange the fish on the dish, surround it with the mushrooms (cut into thick slices), and cover with sauce gratin. Sprinkle with the breadcrumbs, and then with melted butter, and cook until browned in the oven. Arrange on a serving dish, sprinkle with a little lemon juice, and finish with the chopped parsley.

Daurade en papillote

Orata in cartoccio

For 6 persons: *1 gilt-poll, weighing 1 kg. 500; 6 slices of cooked ham; 1 kg. 200 fruits de mer (shrimps, mussels, etc.); 50 gr. chopped onion; 2 cl. cognac; 1 dl. olive oil; 60 gr. butter; 1 large sheet of aluminium foil.* Overall cooking time: 40 minutes.

Clean, wash and dry the fish. Score it lightly. Cook it in the oven, in hot oil, until it is almost done. Meanwhile, heat the mussels, and shell them. Heat the chopped onion (without colouring it), add the shrimps and mussels, colour lightly, and flame with the cognac. Lightly colour the slices of ham in butter. Cut up the foil into a stylised heart-shape, and brush it with oil. Arrange on the foil: 3 slices of ham, then the fish, then 3 more slices of ham; and a layer composed of the fruits de mer. Sprinkle with chopped parsley, and hermetically seal the papillote by sticking the edges together with a little paste. (Leave some air in the papillote before sealing it, so that it will swell.) Place on an oiled fish-tray, and put into the oven. When the foil has turned brown, arrange on a serving dish, and open the papillote only at table. *(Italy.)*

Daurade à la mode des pirates

Orata alla pirata

For 6 persons: *1 gilt-poll, weighing between 1 kg. 500 and 1 kg. 800; 600 gr. mussels; 6 large scampi; 300 gr. 'sea dates' (a variety of small mussels); 6 cl. olive oil; 6 cl. fresh cream; 60 gr. butter; the juice of 2 lemons; 1 tablespoonful of chopped parsley.* Cooking time: approximately 30 minutes.

Scrub the mussels and the 'sea dates', wash them, and cook (the mussels separately from the 'sea dates') until they open. Pour off the cooking liquor, pass it through a cloth strainer, and keep it in reserve. Cook the scampi, and shell and gut them. Gut and clean the gilt-head, arrange it in an oiled and heated gratinating dish, colour it gently golden on both sides, season it with salt and pepper, sprinkle it with melted butter, and finish off the cooking in a medium oven. Remove the fish from the oven, drain it, and arrange it on a serving dish. Swill out the stock with a little mussel fumet, add the cream, and allow to simmer for a few moments. Season with lemon juice and Worcestershire sauce, add a little chopped parsley and pour this sauce over the fish. Garnish with clusters made from the mussels, 'sea dates' and scampi. *(Italy.)*

Daurade Portofino

Orata Portofino

For 6 persons: *1 gilt-poll, weighing 1 kg. 500; 150 gr. butter; 1 dl. white wine; 1 dl. fish fumet; 700 gr. fresh tomatoes (peeled, pipped and sieved); 20 gr. pine kernels; 100 gr. stoned green olives; 30 gr. chopped onion; 1 bouquet garni; a few leaves of basil; chopped parsley; triangular bread croûtons.* Poaching time: 20 minutes.

Season the gilt-poll with salt and pepper and, using 50 gr. hot butter, colour the fish gently golden on both sides. Moisten with the white wine and the fish fumet, add the bouquet garni, bring to the boil, and poach (covered with a lid) over gentle heat for 20 minutes. Melt the rest of the butter in a saucepan, use it to colour the onion, add the purée of tomatoes, and cook for 15 minutes. Add the olives, pine kernels and basil leaves, together with the passed and reduced cooking liquor. Allow to cook for 2 to 3 minutes. Arrange the fish on an oval gratinating dish, and coat it with the sauce. Pass it through a hot oven for 1 to 2 minutes, sprinkle with the chopped parsley, and garnish with the croûtons. *(Italy.)*

Daurade rôtie

Roast gilt-poll

For 6 persons: *1 gilt-poll, weighing 1 kg. 200; 50 gr. anchovy fillets; 75 gr. fat bacon; 5 cl. oil; 2 dl. white wine; 100 gr. butter; ½ lemon.* Cooking time: 30 to 35 minutes.

Stud the gilt-poll with fine lardons alternated with anchovy fillets. Wrap it in a sheet of greased or buttered paper, or in aluminium foil, and bake in the oven. Swill out the cooking dish with the white wine, reduce, and monter au beurre.

Dorade

Sea-bream

Small sea-bream can be grilled, fried, or prepared meunière. Larger sea-bream are prepared as for gilt-poll.

Dorade Bercy

For 6 persons: *1 sea-bream, weighing 1 kg. 200; 3 chopped shallots; 1 coffee-spoonful of roughly-chopped parsley; ¼ litre white wine; 150 gr. butter.* Cooking time: 25 to 30 minutes.

Score the fish, season it with salt and pepper, and lay it on a gratinating dish which has been buttered and then sprinkled with the chopped shallots and parsley. Moisten with the white wine, sprinkle with 25 gr. melted butter, and cook in the oven, basting frequently with the cooking liquor. Arrange the fish on a serving dish, reduce the cooking liquor almost to a glaze, and monter au beurre. Use this sauce to coat the fish. Glaze quickly in a hot oven (or under the salamander).

Éperlan

Smelt

Small smelt are especially suitable for deep frying, and also for cooking skewered or en buisson. Large smelt can be prepared as for whiting, taking the difference in size into account when calculating the cooking time.

Éperlans anglaise

For 6 persons: *36 smelt; 120 gr. maître d'hôtel butter; 2 eggs; breadcrumbs; 125 gr. butter.* Cooking time: 7 to 8 minutes.

Split open the smelt on the dorsal side, and remove the backbones. Coat with egg and breadcrumbs, and press down with a palette knife. Cook the smelt in clarified butter, arrange on a serving dish, and sprinkle with the half-melted maître d'hôtel butter.

Éperlans Bercy

Proceed as for Merlan Bercy, taking into account the difference in size.
(See page 276.)

Éperlans Boistelle

For 6 persons: *36 smelt (of medium size); 2 chopped shallots; 2 dl. white wine; 2 dl. fish fumet; 100 gr. thinly-sliced mushrooms; 75 gr. butter; ½ lemon; 1 coffee-spoonful of chopped parsley.* Cooking time: 8 to 12 minutes.

Arrange the smelt on a gratinating dish which has been buttered, and then sprinkled with the shallots and mushrooms. Moisten with the white wine and fish fumet, add the butter, and cook in the oven, basting frequently. The almost complete reduction of the cooking liquor must coincide with the cooking time of the fish. Glaze at the last minute, squeeze a few drops of lemon juice over the fish, and sprinkle with the chopped parsley.

Éperlans, Brochettes d'

For 6 persons: *36 smelt; flour; ½ litre milk; parsley; 2 lemons.* Cooking time: 7 to 8 minutes.

Dip the smelt into the milk, drain and flour them, and skewer them through their heads. Deep fry the fish, and arrange them on a napkin with fried parsley and with lemon quarters.

Éperlans en buisson

For 6 persons: *36 smelt; parsley; 2 lemons; flour; 2 eggs; breadcrumbs.* Cooking time: 7 to 8 minutes.

Coat with egg and breadcrumbs, and deep fry the smelt in hot fat. Arrange in a cluster on a napkin, with the fried parsley and with lemon quarters.

Éperlans Colbert

Proceed as for Éperlans anglaise, but serve them with sauce Colbert (instead of maître d'hôtel butter). *(See above.)*

Hareng Marie, p. 264

▲ Aiglefin Métayer, p. 242

Filets de morue milanaise, p. 282 ▼

▲ Merlan niçoise, p. 279

Haddock aux oeufs pochés, p. 270 ▼

▲ Filets de maquereau Cavendish, p. 274

Filets de merlan Doria, p. 277 ▼

▲ Maquereau aux fines herbes, p. 275

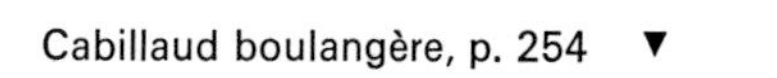

Cabillaud boulangère, p. 254 ▼

▲ Aiglefin écossaise, p. 242

Cabillaud Mistral, p. 255 ▼

▲ Sole Miramar I, p. 315

Sole Bartenbach, p. 298 ▼

▲ Harengs diable, p. 272

Cabillaud Dimitri, p. 254 ▼

Éperlans frits

Fried smelt

For 6 persons: *36 smelt; ½ litre milk; 120 gr. maître d'hôtel butter; parsley; lemons.* Cooking time: 7 to 8 minutes.

Steep the smelt for 1 hour in the salted milk. Drain and flour them, and deep fry them in smoking fat. Arrange on a serving dish with lemon quarters and the fried parsley. Serve the maître d'hôtel butter separately.

Éperlans au gratin

Proceed as for the preparation of Daurade au gratin, taking into account the difference in size when calculating the cooking time. *(See page 259.)*

Éperlans meunière

For 6 persons: *36 smelt; 1 lemon; 150 gr. butter; 1 tablespoonful of chopped parsley; flour.* Cooking time: 7 to 8 minutes.

Season the smelt with salt and pepper, flour them, and shallow fry them in butter in a frying-pan. Arrange the fish on a serving dish, squeeze the lemon juice on top, sprinkle them with the chopped parsley, and finish by sprinkling with noisette butter.

Éperlans Orly

For 6 persons: *36 smelt; ½ litre fish batter; parsley; 2 lemons; ½ litre sauce tomate.* Cooking time: 8 to 10 minutes.

Dip the smelt in fish batter, and deep fry them in hot fat. Arrange them on a napkin with fried parsley and lemon quarters. Serve the sauce tomate separately.

Éperlans sur le plat

Proceed as for the preparation of Sole sur le plat, taking into account the difference in size when calculating the cooking time. *(See page 322.)*

Éperlans polonaise

For 6 persons: *24 large smelt; 240 gr. fish forcemeat; 2 dl. white wine; 150 gr. butter; 1 hard-boiled egg; 1 tablespoonful of chopped parsley; 2 heaped tablespoonfuls of breadcrumbs.* Cooking time: 12 to 15 minutes.

Split open the smelt on the dorsal side, remove the backbones, and stuff the fish with the forcemeat. Poach them in the white wine with 30 gr. butter. Drain them, arrange them on a serving dish, and sprinkle them with chopped hard-boiled egg and chopped parsley. Finish by sprinkling with noisette butter (in which the breadcrumbs have been fried).

Éperlans Richelieu

Proceed as for the preparation of Éperlans anglaise, adding thin slices of truffle, and placing them on the maître d'hôtel butter. *(See page 260.)*

Éperlans au vin blanc

For 6 persons: *30 large smelt; 4 dl. white wine sauce; 1 dl. white wine; 1 dl. fish fumet; 2 chopped shallots; 30 gr. butter.* Cooking time: 12 minutes.

Arrange the smelt on a fish dish which has been buttered and then sprinkled with the chopped shallots. Moisten with the white wine and fish fumet, cover with a sheet of buttered paper, and poach in the oven. Drain the fish, and arrange it on a serving dish. Reduce the cooking liquor almost to a glaze, and add it to the white wine sauce. Use this sauce to coat the smelt, and glaze them briskly. (This preparation can also be served without glazing.)

Espadon messinoise

Chiotta di pesce spada alla messinese
Sword fish

For 6 persons: *6 slices of swordfish (200 gr. each); 50 gr. chopped onion; 50 gr. chopped celery; 1 dl. olive oil; 1 dl. white wine; 1 tablespoonful of shredded pine kernels; 2 peppers (pipped, and cut into a julienne); 3 potatoes; 50 gr. capers; 100 gr. blanched and stoned green olives; 6 large tomatoes.* Cooking time: 12 to 15 minutes.

Lightly colour the celery and onion in olive oil, and moisten with the white wine. Add the peeled, de-seeded and chopped tomatoes, the shredded pine kernels, the julienne of peppers and of blanched potatoes, and cook for 25 minutes over a moderate heat, stirring from time to time. Season the fish with salt and pepper, flour the slices, and cook them in oil. Arrange the fish on a serving dish, sprinkle with olives and capers, and coat with the sauce which has been reduced to the consistency of a purée. *(Italy.)*

Flétan

Halibut

All the methods of preparation for brill are applicable to halibut (*page 245*). Cooking requires particular care, as the flesh is delicate. Halibut is most often served in slices cooked in salted water or in a court-bouillon, and is then garnished with plain boiled potatoes. It is also accompanied with sauce hollandaise, sauce mousseline, sauce crevette, caper sauce or beurre fondu.
The fillets can be cut into escalopes, which are then grilled, fried, or prepared meunière.

Flétan maison, Tranches de

Helgeflundra Maison

For 6 persons: *6 slices of halibut (150 gr. each); 6 quartered hearts of globe artichokes; 6 thin slices of bacon (cut into thin strips); 2 apples (peeled, cored and cut into slices 5 mm. thick); 1 dl. sauce tomate; 100 gr. butter; 6 cold medallions of horse-radish butter; flour.* Cooking time: 10 to 12 minutes.

Colour the bacon brown in butter, add the apples, sauté, add the globe artichokes, and sauté all these together. Cook the slices of halibut meunière, and arrange them on a long serving dish, which has been covered with a thin layer of sauce tomate. Garnish one side of the dish with a mixture of the apples and globe artichokes, and the other side with the medallions of horse-radish butter. Serve separately a mixed salad and plain boiled potatoes. In the Scandinavian countries, a mixed salad usually comprises tomatoes, cucumber, cooked celeriac, lettuce-hearts and endive (or a combination of some of these ingredients). *(Sweden.)*

Germon

Albacore or white tunny

All methods of preparation appropriate to tunny are applicable to albacore.

Grelin

Rock salmon

This fish is of inferior quality and is usually prepared in the same way as salted cod. The flesh is dark and is sold as frozen fillets. It is not a fish for haute cuisine but preparation appropriate to cod is applicable.

Grondin

Gurnard or gurnet

This fish, which has a very large and cartilaginous head, is often—and incorrectly—sold under the description of red mullet. It is best used in the making of fish stew known as bouillabaisse.

Haddock, smoked

Smoked haddock is also known, especially in Scotland and England, as Finnan haddock or Finnan haddie. Immediately after catching, the fish is cut open, lightly rubbed with salt, and hung up to be smoked for 24 hours. In Scotland and England, it is often served as a breakfast delicacy, but it can also be served (as a proper fish course) at lunch.

Haddock grillé

For 6 persons: *1 kg. 200 of smoked haddock; 750 gr. potatoes; 150 gr. butter.* Cooking time: 15 to 18 minutes.

Remove the tail and the fins, and cut up the fish into two, lengthwise. Cut up each half into three pieces. Brush with melted butter or oil, and cook over gentle heat. Serve with pommes a l'anglaise and melted butter. *(International cookery.)*

Haddock Mr. Higgens

For 6 persons: *2 kg. of smoked haddock; 1 litre milk; 1 onion (studded with 1 bayleaf and 2 cloves); 1 kg. potatoes; 500 gr. onion; 250 gr. butter; 2 tablespoonfuls of chopped parsley.* Cooking time: 15 to 20 minutes.

Poach the smoked haddock in the milk with the studded onion. Cut up the potatoes into 1 cm. dice, blanch them, drain them well, and colour them golden in butter. Season with salt and pepper, and arrange them in the centre of an oval serving dish. Skin and bone the fish, and arrange it on top of the potatoes. Sauté the thinly-sliced onions in the rest of the butter, and pour them immediately over the fish. *(Germany.)*

Haddock aux oeufs pochés

Finnan haddock with poached eggs

For 6 persons: *6 pieces of smoked haddock (170 gr. each); 6 eggs; ¾ litre milk; 70 gr. butter.* Cooking time: 10 to 12 minutes.

Butter a fish tray, and place the pieces of haddock in it in such a way that they are not touching each other. Season with white pepper (but not with salt), moisten with the milk, and cover with shavings of butter. Cover with a sheet of buttered paper, and allow to simmer gently. Poach the eggs. As soon as they are cooked, remove the haddock from the heat, drain it, fillet it, and arrange it on a serving dish. Place a poached and trimmed egg on each piece of fish, and pour the cooking liquor around the fish. (N.B. The cooking liquor can be slightly thickened with arrowroot, or with beurre manié, or white roux, and then creamed.) *(Great Britain.)*

Haddock poché

Poached smoked haddock

For 6 persons: *1 kg. 200 of smoked haddock; ½ litre milk; 120 gr. butter.* Cooking time: 15 to 18 minutes.

Cut up the fish into two, lengthwise. Cut up each half into three pieces. Place the pieces of fish into boiling water containing milk, and finish off the cooking, covered, on the side of the stove. Arrange the fish on a napkin. Serve either melted or fresh butter separately. *(International cookery.)*

Hareng

Herring

Herring can be eaten fresh, but are also preserved in a large variety of forms. These are:

Hareng saur

Red herring

Dried and smoked herring

Hareng bouffi

Bloater

The bloater is lightly salted and smoked, but not barrelled.

Hareng Pec

Newly salted herring

Hareng au beurre de moutarde

Herring with mustard butter

For 6 persons: *6 herrings; 1 dl. oil; 125 gr. mustard butter; flour; parsley; 2 lemons.* Cooking time: 10 to 12 minutes.

Score the herrings, season them with salt and pepper, oil them, and grill them gently. Arrange on a serving dish, with the parsley and lemon quarters. Serve the mustard butter separately. *(France.)*

Hareng bouilli nordique

Keitetty silli phjoismaalaiseen tapaan

For 6 persons: *1 kg. 500 fresh herrings; 1 onion; 2 bayleaves; 12 peppercorns; 3 tablespoonfuls of cooking salt; 1½ tablespoonfuls of sugar.* Cooking time: 8 minutes.

Gut and clean the herrings, and then smear them with a mixture of salt and sugar. Leave them in the refrigerator for 24 hours. Rinse them off, and arrange them in a sauteuse. Cover with lukewarm water, add the onion (cut into roundels), the peppercorns and bayleaves, and bring to the boil. Skim off, and cook gently. Drain thoroughly. Arrange on a serving dish, and serve with plain boiled potatoes and parsley butter. *(Finland.)*

Hareng calaisienne

For 6 persons: *6 fresh herrings (225 gr. each); 100 gr. soft roe; 2 chopped shallots; 1 tablespoonful of chopped parsley; 50 gr. chopped mushrooms; 150 gr. maître d'hôtel butter; 5 cl. oil.* Cooking time: 12 to 15 minutes.

Open the herrings, on the dorsal side, to remove the backbones. Pass the soft roe through a sieve, and incorporate into the roe the maître d'hôtel butter, the shallots, mushrooms and parsley. Stuff the herrings with this mixture, seal them in an oiled papillote, and bake in the oven. *(France.)*

Hareng carélienne

Karjalainen silli

For 6 persons: *900 gr. of fillets of salted herring; 120 gr. butter; 150 gr. onions; 2 dl. fresh cream; 75 gr. crushed rusks.* Cooking time: 8 to 10 minutes.

Skin the fillets, and soak and rinse them. Dry them and roll them in the crushed rusks. Using half the butter, colour the fillets golden and, using the other half, lightly colour the onions (which have been cut into thin roundels). Arrange the fillets on a serving dish, and cover them with the onions. Swill out the sauteuse with the cream, reduce slightly, and pour this sauce over the herrings. Serve with a garnish of plain boiled potatoes or sautées potatoes. *(Finland.)*

Hareng en cocotte Antéro, Filets de

Anteron sillipata

For 6 persons: *900 gr. fillets of fresh herrings; 3 lemons; 15 to 18 button onions; 12 large tomatoes; 75 gr. butter; 1 tablespoonful of coarsely-chopped parsley; 1 tablespoonful of coarsely-chopped dill.* Cooking time: 20 minutes.

Colour the peeled onions for 5 minutes in butter, and then add a little salt. Roll up the fillets, keep them rolled with cocktail sticks, and place them in a thick-bottomed cocotte. Season lightly with salt and pepper. Moisten with the lemon juice mixed with ½ litre water. Add the onions, and the tomatoes (peeled, pipped and quartered). Sprinkle with the parsley and dill. Add the rest of the butter, cover the cocotte with a lid, and cook in a low oven. *(Finland.)*

Hareng diable

For 6 persons: *6 herrings (225 gr. each); 4 dl. sauce ravigote; mixed mustard; breadcrumbs; 5 cl. olive oil.* Cooking time: 12 minutes.

Score the herrings, smear them with the mixed mustard, sprinkle with the breadcrumbs, then with the olive oil, and grill. Serve the sauce ravigote separately. *(France.)*
(See illustration, page 268.)

Hareng grillé

Grilled herring

Method A
Clean, scale and wash the herrings, dry, score on both sides, season with salt and pass through flour. Place on a wire fish grill, brush with oil or melted clarified butter, and grill on both sides over a gentle heat until golden brown. Serve garnished with picked parsley and a twist of lemon. Serve mustard sauce separately.

Method B
Clean, scale the fish and remove the backbone. Wash, dry and pass through flour. Season with salt. Cook and serve as for Method A.

Herrings, Scotch

Clean the herrings and remove the backbone. Coat with fine seasoned oatmeal and shallow-fry in hot clarified butter on both sides, cut side downwards first, until brown; approximately 6 to 8 minutes.

Hareng grille maître d'hôtel

For 6 persons: *6 herrings (225 gr. each); 150 gr. maître d'hôtel butter; parsley; 5 cl. oil.* Cooking time: 10 to 12 minutes.

Season the herrings lightly with salt, sprinkle them with oil, and grill gently. Garnish with parsley. Serve the maître d'hôtel butter separately. *(France.)*

Hareng Marie

For 6 persons: *6 herrings (approximately 200 gr. each); 6 tomatoes; 2 chopped shallots; 1 heaped tablespoonful of freshly-chopped mixed herbs (hyssop, sage, basil, savory, lavender, dill and parsley); 2 dl. fish fumet; 2 dl. jus lié; 50 gr. beurre manié; 20 gr. mixed Dijon mustard; 50 gr. double cream; flour.* Cooking time: 10 minutes.

Gut, clean and wash the herrings. Season them with salt and pepper, flour them, and cook them meunière. Fillet the fish, and place the fillets side by side in a buttered gratinating dish. Place on top the peeled and sliced tomatoes, and keep them hot. Lightly sauté the herbs and the chopped shallots in butter, moisten with the fish fumet and jus lié and bring to the boil. Thicken with the beurre manié, cook for a few moments, and correct the seasoning with pepper and lemon juice. Pass the gratinating dish under the salamander to soften the tomatoes. Brush with the Dijon mustard and double cream, and coat with the sauce. Serve with a garnish of gratinated purée potatoes. *(Germany.)*
(See illustration, page 261.)

Hareng meunière

Proceed as for the preparation of any other fish designated meunière. *(See page 64.)* *(France.)*

Hareng nantaise

For 6 persons: *6 herrings (225 gr. to 250 gr. each); 120 gr. soft roes; 2 eggs; breadcrumbs; 200 gr. butter; 1 coffee-spoonful of mixed mustard; flour.* Cooking time: 10 to 12 minutes.

Score and flour the herrings, coat with egg and breadcrumbs, and cook them in butter. Poach the soft roes, and pass them through a fine sieve. Season this purée with salt and pepper, add the mustard, and monter au beurre (using 125 gr. butter). Arrange the herrings on a serving dish. Serve the purée separately. *(France.)*

Hareng Paramé

For 6 persons: *6 herrings (225 gr. each); 125 gr. butter; 6 tablespoonfuls of concentrated duxelles; the juice of 1 lemon; oil.* Cooking time: 15 minutes.

Score the herrings and seal them in butter. Wrap each in an oiled papillote, with a tablespoonful of duxelles, a few drops of lemon juice and a nut of butter. Fold the papillotes so as to seal them, and finish off the cooking in the oven. *(France.)*

Hareng portière

For 6 persons: *6 herrings (225 gr. each); 200 gr. butter; 50 gr. mixed mustard; 1 tablespoonful of chopped parsley; vinegar.* Cooking time: 12 minutes.

Prepare and cook the herrings as for the designation meunière. Drain them, smear them lightly with the mixed mustard, arrange them on a serving dish, and sprinkle them with the chopped parsley. Cover with noisette butter, and sprinkle them with a dash of vinegar (which has been heated in a pan). *(France.)*

Hareng tartare

For 6 persons: *12 fillets of herring; 2 eggs; breadcrumbs; parsley; 2 lemons; 1 dl. oil; 4 dl. sauce tartare; flour.* Cooking time: 10 minutes.

Season the fillets with salt and pepper, and coat with egg and breadcrumbs. Oil them, and grill them gently. Arrange them on a serving dish with the parsley and lemon quarters. Serve the sauce tartare separately. *(France.)*

Lieu jaune

Pollack

This fish belongs to the cod family, and is of first-class quality. The flesh is tasty and fairly firm. It is prepared as for fresh haddock and fresh cod.

Limande

Dab

The flesh of the dab is white, rather soft, but highly digestible. This fish is seldom used in restaurants. It can be grilled, fried, or prepared meunière.

Limande sole

Lemon sole

The lemon sole is a less expensive fish than the true sole. All methods of preparation appropriate to the sole are applicable to it.

Lingue

Ling

This fish, which belongs to the cod family, has fairly fine flesh. It is prepared as for fresh cod.

Lingue bleue

Blue ling

The blue ling belongs to the cod family. Its flesh, when salted like cod, has a very good flavour. When filleted, it is usually prepared as for whiting and fresh cod.

Loup de mer

Sea-perch

Nearly all methods of preparation appropriate to the salmon are applicable to the sea-perch. The smallest ones are usually grilled, fried, or prepared meunière.

Loup de mer bouilli, sauce crevette

For 6 persons: *1 sea-perch, weighing 1 kg. 500; parsley; 5 dl. sauce crevette.* Cooking time: 25 to 30 minutes.

Cook the fish in a court-bouillon, and arrange it on a napkin. Garnish with the parsley. Serve the sauce crevette separately, together with plain boiled potatoes. *(France.)*

Loup de mer rôti Jean-Bart

For 6 persons: *1 sea-perch, weighing 1 kg. 500; 6 large onions; 100 gr. butter; 4 dl. sauce Bercy; 1 coffee-spoonful of mixed mustard.* Cooking time: approximately 30 minutes.

Score the fish, season it with salt and pepper, and roast it in the oven, basting with butter. Cut up the onions into roundels, flour them, and fry them in oil, taking care to keep them very crisp. Arrange the fish on a serving dish, and surround it with the fried onions. Serve the sauce Bercy (to which a little mustard has been added) separately. *(France.)*

Maquereau anglaise

Mackerel English style

For 6 persons: *3 mackerel (250 gr. each); 100 gr. fennel; 200 gr. gooseberry purée.* Cooking time: 8 minutes.

Cut up the mackerel into thick slices and poach them in a court-bouillon (which has been seasoned with fennel). Arrange on a serving dish, and serve a slightly clear purée of gooseberries separately. *(France.)*

Maquereau bâtelière, Filets de

For 6 persons: *6 mackerel (250 gr. each); 1 dl. oil; 4 dl. sauce verte; flour.* Cooking time: 7 to 8 minutes.

Fillet the fish, and season the fillets with salt and pepper. Flour and oil them, and grill them gently. Arrange the fillets on a serving dish. Serve the sauce verte separately.

Maquereau Bonnefoy, Filets de

For 6 persons: *12 fillets of mackelel (approximately 70 gr. each); flour; 500 gr. pommes à l'anglaise; 4 dl. sauce Bonnefoy; 100 gr. butter.* Cooking time: 7 to 8 minutes.

Season the fillets with salt and pepper, flour them and cook them meunière. Arrange them on a serving dish, garnish with the pommes à l'anglaise, and coat overall with the sauce Bonnefoy (containing chopped tarragon). *(France.)*

Maquereau calaisienne

Proceed as for the preparation of Hareng calaisienne. *(See page 271.)*

Maquereau Cavendish, Filets de

Makrelenfilets Cavendish

For 6 persons: *12 fillets of mackerel (60 gr. each); 6 small bananas; 60 gr. shredded almonds; 7 cl. oil; 100 gr. butter; 1 lemon; flour; curry powder.* Cooking time: 4 to 5 minutes.

Lightly coat the fillets with the curry powder, season with a little salt, flour them, and cook in the oil (containing a nut of butter). Arrange the fillets on a serving dish. Skin the bananas, cut them in half lengthwise, flour them, and colour them golden in oil. Decorate each fillet with half a banana. In the frying pan, from which the oil has been poured off, and with the rest of the butter colour the almonds golden. Sprinkle the fish with lemon juice, pour on top the almonds and butter, and serve immediately. *(Germany.)*

(See illustration, page 264. N.B. Different presentation.)

Maquereau du chanoine, Filets de

For 6 persons: *12 fillets of mackerel; flour; 200 gr. shelled prawns; 200 gr. fish forcemeat; 1 dl. sauce béchamel; 20 gr. prawn butter; 4 dl. anchovy sauce.* Cooking time: 15 minutes.

Season the fillets with salt and pepper, flour them, and firm them in butter on the side from which the backbone was removed. Cool, under gentle downward pressure. Using a small star piping-tube, trace a figure eight (in fish forcemeat) on to each fillet. Arrange the fish on a buttered fish tray, and pass it through the oven to finish off the cooking of the fillets and forcemeat. After removing the fish from the oven, garnish each figure eight with a salpicon of prawns, bound with the sauce béchamel and finished with the prawn butter. Serve the anchovy sauce separately. *(France.)*

Maquereau à la crème, Filets de

Creamed fillets of mackerel

For 6 persons: *12 fillets of mackerel; 4 dl. cream sauce; 30 gr. chopped truffle; 2 dl. fish fumet.* Cooking time: 7 to 8 minutes.

Poach the fillets in the fish fumet. Drain them, and arrange them on a serving dish. Reduce the cooking liquor almost to a glaze, and add it to the cream sauce. Coat the fish with the sauce, and sprinkle with the chopped truffle.

Maquereau dieppoise

For 6 persons: *6 mackerel (225 gr. each); 1 dl. mushroom cooking liquor; 1 dl. dry white wine; 4 dl. white wine sauce; dieppoise garnish for 6 persons.* Cooking time: 10 minutes.

Open the mackerel on the dorsal side, and remove the backbones. Poach the fish in the white wine and mushroom liquor. Drain the mackerel, arrange them on a serving dish, and surround them with the dieppoise garnish. Coat the fish and the garnish with the white wine sauce, containing the passed and reduced cooking liquor. If desired, the whole dish can be glazed. *(France.)*

Maquereau aux fines herbes, Filets de

For 6 persons: *12 fillets of mackerel; 4 dl. sauce fines herbes; 1 dl. mushroom cooking liquor; 1 dl. white wine.* Cooking time: 7 to 8 minutes.

Poach the fillets in the white wine and mushroom liquor. Drain and skin the fillets, and arrange them on a serving dish. Coat with the sauce fines herbes, containing the reduced cooking liquor. *(France.)*
(See illustration, page 265.)

Maquereau Francillon, Filets de

Proceed as for the preparation of Rouget Francillon. *(See page 290.)*

Maquereau grillé I

Grilled mackerel

For 6 persons: *6 mackerel (225 gr. each); 80 gr. butter; 120 gr. maître d'hôtel butter; parsley; 2 lemons.* Cooking time: 12 minutes.

Remove the snouts of the mackerel, open the fish on the dorsal side, and remove the backbones, without splitting the fish in half. Season them with salt and pepper, sprinkle them with melted butter, and grill gently. Re-shape the fish, arrange them on a serving dish, and sprinkle them with half-softened maître d'hôtel butter. *(France.)*
(See Culinary Technique, page 83.)

Maquereau grillé II

Grilled mackerel

Mackerel can be grilled in the normal manner cutting 2 to 3 incisions in the thicker part on each side—or prepared as follows: Clean the mackerel without opening the belly, cut off the end of the mouth and open down the back but without dividing into two. Remove the backbone, season, brush with oil or clarified butter and grill gently, basting from time to time. When cooked, sprinkle with softened beurre maître d'hôtel and place the two halves together so as to re-form the fish. Serve garnished with lemon quarters and picked parsley. If desired, the fish may be served flat accompanied by beurre maître d'hôtel.

Maquereau indienne

For 6 persons: *6 mackerel (225 gr. each); 300 gr. rice; ½ litre curry sauce.*

Poach the mackerel in a court-bouillon, drain them, and skin them. Arrange them on a bed of plain boiled rice, and coat them with the curry sauce. *(International cookery.)*

Maquereau printanière, Filets de

For 6 persons: *12 fillets of mackerel; 4 dl. sauce bâtarde; 50 gr. printanier butter; 500 gr. new potatoes; 300 gr. peas; 50 gr. butter.* Cooking time: 7 to 8 minutes.

Poach the fillets in salted water, and skin them. Drain them, arrange them on a serving dish, and coat them with the sauce bâtarde, finished with the printanier butter. Garnish on one side with the plain boiled new potatoes, and on the other with the cooked peas bound in butter. *(France.)*

Maquereau Rosalie, Filets de

For 6 persons: *12 fillets of mackerel; 2 dl. nut oil; 100 gr. mushrooms; 50 gr. onion; 3 shallots; 1 clove of garlic; 1 tablespoonful of chopped parsley; flour; vinegar.* Cooking time: 10 minutes.

Season the fillets with salt and pepper, flour them, cook them in a frying-pan with the nut oil, and arrange them on a serving dish. Add to the oil in the pan the onion, mushrooms, chopped shallots and crushed garlic. Fry quickly and pour this mixture over the fillets. Heat in the very hot pan a few drops of vinegar, and pour over the fish. Sprinkle with chopped parsley. *(France.)*

Maquereau Saint-Jean, Filets de

For 6 persons: *12 fillets of mackerel; flour; 4 dl. sauce ravigote; parsley; 1 lemon; 80 gr. butter.* Cooking time: 7 to 8 minutes.

Season the fillets with salt and pepper, flour them, and cook them in butter. Arrange them on a serving dish with the parsley and lemon quarters. Serve the sauce ravigote separately. *(France.)*

Maquereau vénitienne, Filets de

For 6 persons: *12 fillets of mackerel; ½ litre sauce vénitienne; 24 pommes poisson.* Cooking time: 7 to 8 minutes.

Poach the fillets in salted water, skin them, and arrange them on a serving dish. Coat them with the sauce vénitienne, and garnish with the pommes poisson. *(France.)*
(See illustration, page 340. N.B. Different presentation.)

Merlan anglaise

Whiting English style

For 6 persons: *6 whiting (225 gr. to 250 gr. each); 2 eggs; breadcrumbs; flour; 80 gr. butter; 120 gr. maître d'hôtel butter.* Cooking time: 10 to 12 minutes.

Split open the fish on the dorsal side, and remove the backbones. Season the fish with pepper and salt, coat with egg and breadcrumbs, and cook them in clarified butter. Arrange on a serving dish, and cover with the half-softened maître d'hôtel butter. *(France.)*

Merlan Bercy

For 6 persons: *6 whiting; 3 chopped shallots; 75 gr. butter; 2 dl. white wine; 1 dl. fish fumet; ½ lemon; 1 tablespoonful of chopped parsley.* Cooking time: 10 to 12 minutes.

Split open the fish on the dorsal side, and remove the backbones. Place them on a thickly-buttered cooking dish (which has been sprinkled with chopped shallot). Moisten with the white wine and the fish fumet, add 50 gr. butter, and cook in the oven, basting frequently. The almost complete reduction of the moistening liquor must coincide with the completion of the cooking of the fish. Glaze at the last minute with the reduced cooking liquor. Arrange the fish on a serving dish, squeeze a few drops of lemon juice over them, and sprinkle with chopped parsley. *(France.)*

Merlan Boistelle

Proceed as for the preparation of Éperlans Boistelle, taking into account the difference in size when calculating the cooking time. *(France.)* *(See page 260.)*

Merlan bonne femme

For 6 persons: *12 fillets of whiting (approximately 70 gr. each); 125 gr. shelled prawns; 150 gr. butter; 50 gr. capers; 1 lemon; flour.* Cooking time: 8 to 10 minutes.

Season the fillets with salt and pepper, flour them, and cook them meunière. Arrange them on a serving dish, sprinkle them with the prawns and capers, squeeze the lemon juice on top, and sprinkle with noisette butter. *(France.)*

Merlan bretonne, Filets de

For 6 persons: *12 fillets of whiting (approximately 70 gr. each); 150 gr. butter; 125 gr. shelled prawns; 50 gr. capers; 1 lemon; flour.* Cooking time: 8 to 10 minutes.

Season the fillets with salt and pepper, flour them, and cook them meunière. Arrange them on a serving dish, garnish with the prawns and capers, squeeze the lemon juice over the fillets, and sprinkle with the noisette butter. *(France.)*

Merlan cancalaise

For 6 persons: *12 fillets of whiting; 12 oysters; 120 gr. shelled prawns; 4 dl. sauce normande; 2 dl. white wine.* Cooking time: 10 minutes.

Poach the fillets in the white wine. Arrange them on a serving dish, and garnish them with the prawns and the poached and bearded oysters. Coat with the sauce normande containing the reduced cooking liquor. *(France.)*
(See illustration, page 288. N.B. Different presentation.)

Merlan Cécilia, Filets de

For 6 persons: *12 fillets of whiting; 36 green asparagus-tips; 120 gr. butter; 50 gr. grated Parmesan cheese; flour.* Cooking time: 8 to 10 minutes.

Season the fillets with salt and pepper, flour them, and cook them in butter. Arrange them on a gratinating dish, and surround them with the asparagus-tips, which have been bound in butter. Sprinkle with the grated cheese, and glaze briskly. *(France.)*

Merlan Chauchat

Proceed as for the preparation of Barbue Chauchat. *(See page 245.)*

Merlan Colbert

For 6 persons: *6 whiting; 1 egg; breadcrumbs; 150 gr. maître d'hôtel butter.* Cooking time: 10 to 12 minutes.

Split open the fish on the dorsal side from head to tail, and remove the backbones. Coat with egg and breadcrumbs, and deep fry. Arrange on a long serving dish and fill in the cavities in the backs of the fish with the maître d'hôtel butter. *(France.)*

Merlan en colère

For 6 persons: *6 whiting; 3 eggs; breadcrumbs; parsley; 4 dl. sauce tomate.* Cooking time: 10 to 12 minutes.

Fix the tail of each whiting in its mouth, and coat with egg and breadcrumbs. Deep fry and drain. Arrange the fish on a napkin, with the fried parsley. Serve the sauce tomate separately. *(France.)*
(See Culinary Technique, page 68.)

Merlan aux crevettes

For 6 persons: *6 whiting; 125 gr. shelled prawns; 4 dl. sauce crevette; ¼ litre fish fumet.* Cooking time: 10 minutes.

Poach the whiting in the fish fumet, and arrange them on a serving dish. Surround them with the prawns, and coat with the sauce crevette, containing the reduced cooking liquor. *(France.)*

Merlan dieppoise

Proceed as for the preparation of Maquereau dieppoise. *(See page 274.)*

Merlan diplomate

For 6 persons: *6 whiting; 150 gr. mushrooms; 150 gr. peeled, pipped and chopped tomatoes; 2 shallots; 1 tablespoonful of chopped parsley; 6 chopped tarragon leaves; ¼ litre fish fumet; ½ litre sauce Mornay; 40 gr. butter; 50 gr. grated Parmesan cheese.* Cooking time: 12 to 15 minutes.

Split open the whiting, and remove the backbones (as for Merlan Colbert). Stuff with the mushrooms, which have been coarsely chopped, and reduced in butter, with the chopped shallots, parsley and tarragon, and the chopped tomatoes; all these ingredients bound with a little concentrated sauce Mornay. Re-shape the fish and poach them in the fish fumet. Drain the fish, arrange them on a gratinating dish, coat them with the rest of the sauce Mornay, sprinkle with the grated cheese, and brown. *(France.)*

Merlan Doria, Filets de

For 6 persons: *12 fillets of whiting; 150 gr. butter; 250 gr. cucumber (olive-shaped or shaped into small balls); 1 dl. fresh cream; 1 lemon; 1 tablespoonful of chopped parsley.* Cooking time: 8 to 10 minutes.

Stew the cucumber in butter, and bind it with the cream. Cook the fillets meunière, arrange them on a serving dish, and surround them with the cucumber garnish. Squeeze the lemon juice over them, sprinkle with the chopped parsley, and then with noisette butter. *(France.)* *(See illustration, page 264. N.B. Different presentation.)*

Merlan à la façon du chef, Filets de

Vitlingsfilé på chefens vis

For 6 persons: *6 fillets of whiting (150 gr. each); 500 gr. peeled, pipped and chopped tomatoes; 40 gr. chopped onion; 250 gr. chopped (fresh) mushrooms; 1 tablespoonful of chopped parsley; 2 dl. dry white wine; 200 gr. butter; 600 gr. spoon-cut, plain boiled potatoes; 1 lemon; breadcrumbs.* Cooking time: 10 to 12 minutes.

Marinate the fillets with salt, pepper and lemon juice. Colour the onion in butter, add the mushrooms, stew for a few minutes, moisten with the white wine, add the tomatoes, reduce to the consistency of a thick sauce, and season with salt, pepper and lemon juice. Season the fillets with salt and pepper, coat the upper side of each fillet with melted butter, sprinkle with breadcrumbs, and press down with a palette knife. Butter a gratinating dish, pour the sauce into it, and arrange the fillets on top (with the crumbed sides facing upwards). Sprinkle with melted butter, and cook in the oven until the fish is cooked and the breadcrumbs well-coloured. Garnish with the potatoes, and sprinkle with the chopped parsley. *(Sweden.)*

Merlan fécampoise

For 6 persons: *6 whiting; 125 gr. shelled prawns; 24 poached and bearded mussels; 4 dl. sauce crevette; ¼ litre fish fumet.* Cooking time: 10 to 12 minutes.

Poach the whiting in the fish fumet, and arrange them on a serving dish. Reduce the cooking liquor, and add it to the sauce crevette. Garnish the fish with the mussels and prawns, and coat with the sauce crevette. *(France.)*

Merlan française

For 6 persons: *12 fillets of whiting; 4 dl. sauce tomate; 1 lemon; parsley; flour; milk.* Cooking time: 8 to 10 minutes.

Pass the fillets through salted milk, flour, and deep fry them. Arrange them on a serving dish, with fried parsley and quarters of lemon. Serve the sauce tomate separately. *(France.)*

Merlan frit

Fried whiting

For 6 persons: *6 whiting; 2 eggs; breadcrumbs; parsley; 2 lemons.* Cooking time: 10 to 12 minutes.

Prepare the fish, coat with egg and breadcrumbs, and deep fry them. Arrange on a napkin with fried parsley and quarters of lemon. A sauce tartare or ravigote may be served separately. *(France.)*

Merlan au gratin

Proceed as for the preparation of Daurade au gratin, allowing for the difference in size when calculating the cooking time. *(See page 259.)*

Merlan grenobloise

For 6 persons: *6 whiting; 150 gr. butter; 1 lemon; 50 gr. capers; 1 tablespoonful of chopped parsley; flour.* Cooking time: 10 to 12 minutes.

Season the whiting with salt and pepper, flour them, and cook meunière. Arrange them on a serving dish, with a roundel of peeled lemon on each fish, sprinkle with capers and chopped parsley, and then with noisette butter. *(France.)*

Merlan hôtelière

Proceed as for the preparation of Barbue hôtelière. *(See page 246.)*

Merlan Jackson, Filets de

For 6 persons: *12 fillets of whiting; 200 gr. Soubise purée; 1 coffee-spoonful of chopped parsley; 8 chopped tarragon leaves; 24 button onions; 125 gr. butter; 1 dl. white wine; 2 dl. fish fumet.* Cooking time: 15 minutes.

Stew the onions in butter, without colouring them. Poach the fillets in the white wine and fish fumet. Mask a gratinating dish with the Soubise purée (containing the parsley and tarragon). Arrange the fillets on top, and surround them with the button onions. Reduce the cooking liquor, monter au beurre; use this sauce to coat the fillets, and glaze. *(France.)*

Merlan juive, Filets de

For 6 persons: *12 fillets of whiting; ½ litre batter; 4 dl. sauce tartare; parsley; 2 lemons.* Cooking time: 8 to 10 minutes.

Season the fillets with salt and pepper, coat with the batter, and deep fry them. Arrange the fish on a napkin, with fried parsley and quarters of lemon. Serve the sauce tartare separately. *(France.)*

Merlan en lorgnette

For 6 persons: *6 whiting; 2 eggs; breadcrumbs; parsley; 4 dl. sauce tomate.* Cooking time: 10 to 12 minutes.

Fillet the fish from tail to head, and remove the backbones by severing them just behind the head. Coat with egg and breadcrumbs, roll the fish into paupiettes, and keep each of them in this shape with a skewer. Deep fry. Remove the skewers, and arrange the fish on a serving dish, with fried parsley. Serve the sauce tomate separately. *(France.)*
(See Culinary Technique, page 68.)

Merlan marchand de vin

Proceed as for the preparation of Merlan Bercy, using red wine instead of white. *(France.)*
(See page 276.)

Merlan Médicis

Proceed as for the preparation of Merlan anglaise, and surround the whiting with six small grilled tomatoes, which have been hollowed out and filled with sauce béarnaise. *(France.)*
(See page 276.)

Merlan aux moules

Whiting with mussels

For 6 persons: *6 whiting; 4 dl. white wine sauce; 36 poached and bearded mussels; 2 dl. white wine; 5 cl. decanted mussel cooking liquor.* Cooking time: 10 to 12 minutes.

Poach the whiting in the white wine and mussel cooking liquor. Reduce all the cooking liquor, and add it to the white wine sauce. Arrange the whiting on a serving dish, surround them with the mussels, coat with the white wine sauce, and glaze. *(France.)*
(See illustration, page 285. N.B. Different presentation.)

Merlan niçoise

For 6 persons: *6 whiting; 400 gr. peeled, pipped and chopped tomatoes; 12 anchovy fillets; 18 stuffed olives; 1 dl. oil; flour; 1 clove of garlic.* Cooking time: 10 to 12 minutes.

Season the whiting with salt and pepper, flour and oil them, and grill. Arrange them on a serving dish, and cover with the chopped tomatoes which have been softened in oil, and seasoned with a touch of crushed garlic. Garnish with the anchovy fillets and the stuffed olives. *(France.)*
(See illustration, page 263. N.B. Different presentation.)

Merlan orientale

Proceed as for the preparation of Rouget orientale. *(See page 292.)*

Merlan Orly, Filets de

For 6 persons: *12 fillets of whiting; ½ litre batter; parsley; ½ litre sauce tomate.* Cooking time: 8 minutes.

Prepare the fillets as for Éperlans Orly. *(See page 269.)*

Merlan Rachel, Filets de

For 6 persons: *12 fillets of whiting; 250 gr. fish forcemeat; 1 dl. mushroom cooking liquor; 50 gr. butter; 4 dl. white wine sauce; 2 tablespoonfuls of green asparagus-tips; 40 gr. truffle.* Cooking time: 10 minutes.

Mask the fillets with the fish forcemeat. Fold them and poach (covered with a sheet of buttered paper) in the mushroom cooking liquor and butter. Arrange the fish on a serving dish. Reduce the cooking stock, and add it to the white wine sauce. Incorporate into the sauce the truffle (in small dice) and the asparagus-tips, and use this mixture to coat the fillets. *(France.)*
(See illustration, page 285. N.B. Different presentation.)

Merlan Réjane, Filets de

For 6 persons: *12 fillets of whiting; 400 gr. appareil à pommes duchesse; 4 dl. white wine sauce; 1 dl. fish fumet; 1 dl. white wine; 50 gr. watercress butter.* Cooking time: 10 minutes.

Poach the fillets in the white wine and fish fumet. Reduce the cooking liquor almost to a glaze, add it to the white wine sauce, and finish off with the watercress butter. Use this sauce to coat the fillets, and garnish them with rosettes made from the appareil à pommes duchesse (shaped with a star piping-tube, and coloured golden in the oven). *(France.)*

Merlan riche, Filets de

Proceed as for the preparation of Filets de barbue riche. *(See page 246.)*

Merlan russe

For 6 persons: *6 whiting; 3 small onions (cut up into roundels); 100 gr. carrot (cut up into thin roundels); 1 tablespoonful of picked parsley; 4 dl. white wine sauce; 50 gr. butter; 2 dl. white wine.* Cooking time: 15 minutes.

Pass the roundels of onion and carrot through butter, add the parsley and a little water, and cook. Place this appareil in a cooking dish, arrange the whiting on top, moisten with the white wine, and poach. Drain the fish, arrange on a serving dish, reduce the cooking stock almost to a glaze, add it (together with the vegetables) to the white wine sauce, and use this mixture to coat the fish. *(France.)*

Merlan Tabellion

For 6 persons: *6 whiting; 2 dl. fish fumet; 4 dl. white wine sauce; 12 slices of truffle.* Cooking time: 15 minutes.

Proceed as for the preparation of Merlan en lorgnette, but do not coat with egg and breadcrumbs. Poach the fish in the fish fumet, drain, and arrange them on a serving dish. Coat with the white wine sauce and garnish with the slices of truffle. *(France.)*
(See Culinary Technique, page 68.)

Merlan tyrolienne

For 6 persons: *6 whiting; 1 egg; breadcrumbs; parsley; 4 dl. sauce tyrolienne.* Cooking time: 10 to 12 minutes.

Prepare the whiting, and coat with egg and breadcrumbs as for Merlan en colère. Deep fry, drain, and arrange on a napkin, interspersed with the parsley. Serve the sauce tyrolienne separately. *(France.)*
(See Culinary Technique, page 68.)

Merlan Verdi, Filets de

For 6 persons: *12 fillets of whiting; 4 dl. sauce Choron; 30 gr. truffle, 1 dl. fish fumet; 1 dl. white wine.* Cooking time: 8 to 10 minutes.

Poach the fillets in the fish fumet and white wine. Reduce the cooking liquor, and add it to the sauce Choron. Drain the fillets, and arrange them on a serving dish. Coat the fillets with the sauce, and sprinkle them with the chopped truffle. *(France.)*

Merlan au vin blanc

Proceed as for the preparation of Sole au vin blanc. *(See page 343.)*

Morue

Salt cod

Salt cod must be freed of salt by soaking for at least 24 hours, with a change of water every 3 or 4 hours. The best salt cod is in the form of thick fillets having a white flesh.

Morue anglaise

Salt cod English style

For 6 persons: *900 gr. salt cod; 4 dl. sauce bâtarde; 2 hard-boiled eggs; 600 gr. parsnips; parsley.* Cooking time: 15 minutes.

Poach the fish in water, drain it, and free it of skin and bones. Arrange it on a napkin with the parsley. Serve at the same time the plain boiled potatoes and the sauce bâtarde (which has been mixed with the hard-boiled eggs cut into small dice). *(International cookery.)*

Morue Bamboche

For 6 persons: *900 gr. salt cod; 500 gr. macédoine of vegetables; 50 gr. butter; ¼ litre milk; flour.* Cooking time: 10 to 12 minutes.

Cut up the fish into long thin slices the size of fillets of sole. Dip them in the milk, flour them, and twist them into 'gimlets'. Deep fry them, and arrange in a timbale, on top of the macédoine (which has been bound in butter). *(France.)*

Morue bénédictine

For 6 persons: *700 gr. salt cod; 300 gr. potatoes; 1 dl. oil; 2 dl. milk; 50 gr. butter.* Cooking time: 20 minutes.

Poach the fish, skin and bone it, and pound it in a mortar with the potatoes (which have been cooked as for a purée, drained and dried), gradually absorbing the milk and the oil. Correct seasoning and consistency. Arrange this mixture in a buttered gratinating dish, smooth over the surface, sprinkle with melted butter, and colour in the oven. *(France.)*

Morue Benoîton

For 6 persons: *900 gr. cooked salt cod; 100 gr. thinly-sliced onion; 4 plain boiled potatoes; 1 dl. fish fumet; 4 dl. red wine; 5 cl. oil; 75 gr. butter; 1 clove of garlic; 30 gr. flour; breadcrumbs.* Cooking time: 20 minutes.

Colour the onion in oil and butter. Sprinkle it with flour, and allow it to cook for a few moments. Moisten with the fish fumet and red wine. Season with salt and pepper, simmer for 15 minutes, and add the plain boiled potatoes (cut into roundels), the flaked cod and the crushed clove of garlic. Pour this mixture into a buttered gratinating dish, sprinkle it with the breadcrumbs, and then with melted butter, and brown briskly. *(France.)*

Morue au beurre noir (ou au beurre noisette)

For 6 persons: *900 gr. salt cod; 150 gr. butter; 1 tablespoonful of chopped parsley; 1 lemon.* Cooking time: 15 to 18 minutes.

Poach the cod and drain, skin and flake it. Dry quickly, arrange on a serving dish, sprinkle with the chopped parsley, and then with lemon juice. Pour over the fish either beurre noir or noisette butter. *(France.)*

Morue biscaienne I

For 6 persons: *750 gr. salt cod; 700 gr. tomatoes; 300 gr. red peppers; 75 gr. chopped onion; 3 cloves of garlic; ¼ litre olive oil; 12 small heart-shaped croûtons.* Cooking time: 20 minutes.

Poach the cod, skin and bone it, and cut up the flesh into small pieces. Flour the fish, sauté in boiling oil, and remove. Colour the chopped onion in oil, add the tomatoes (peeled, pressed and cut into quarters), and cook until the tomatoes are softened. Cut the red peppers into long, thin strips (lanières), and stew them in oil. Arrange the pieces of fish in a timbale, interspersing them with the tomatoes and peppers. Surround with the croûtons (which have been fried in oil). *(France.)*

Morue biscaienne II

Bacalao a la vizcaina

For 6 persons: *1 kg. 500 salt cod (cut up into 12 square pieces); 12 thin slices of fresh bacon; 1 kg. peeled, pipped and chopped tomatoes; 75 gr. onion; 4 dried red peppers; oil.* Cooking time: 25 to 30 minutes.

Soak the fish in water for 10 to 12 hours, and bone it without removing the skin. Place the slices of bacon on an oiled fish tray, arrange the fish on top, and cook in the oven. Colour the chopped onions in oil, add the peppers (soaked in water, and diced) and the chopped tomatoes, season with salt and pepper, and cook for 15 minutes. Pass through a sieve, pour over the fish, and cook gently in a moderate oven for 12 to 15 minutes. *(Spain.)*

Morue, Brandade de

For 6 persons: *750 gr. salt cod; 4 dl. to 5 dl. olive oil; 2 dl. milk; 1 crushed clove of garlic; 50 gr. butter; 12 triangles of bread.* Cooking time: 20 minutes.

Cut up the fish into large squares, poach them for 8 minutes, and remove skin and bones. Heat 15 cl. oil in a sauteuse until the oil is smoking, and add the flaked cod and garlic. Using a spatula, work the mixture vigorously over heat until a fairly fine paste is obtained. Remove from heat and, on the corner of the stove, while continuing to work with the spatula, add gradually 2 dl. to 3 dl. oil. Break up the paste from time to time (adding 2 to 3 tablespoonfuls of boiled milk, and up to 2 dl. in all). The finished brandade should have the appearance of a white paste, and the consistency of purée potatoes. Correct seasoning and consistency. Arrange in a timbale, and garnish with the bread triangles, which have been fried in butter. *(France.)*

Morue à la crème

Creamed salt cod

For 6 persons: *900 gr. salt cod; ½ litre cream sauce.* Cooking time: 18 minutes.

Poach the cod, remove skin and bones, and flake. Simmer for a few minutes in a light cream sauce, and arrange in a timbale. *(France.)*

Morue créole

For 6 persons: *900 gr. salt cod; 100 gr. thinly-sliced onion; 6 tomatoes prepared provençale; 150 gr. butter; 3 sweet red peppers; ½ lemon.* Cooking time: 20 minutes.

Cook the sliced onion in butter, and spread the cooked onion over the base of a gratinating dish. Arrange the tomatoes on top, and place on top of them the cooked and flaked cod. Cover with the halved and grilled red peppers. Sprinkle with lemon juice and noisette butter, and pass through the oven for 2 to 3 minutes. *(France.)*

Morue aux épinards

Salt cod with spinach

For 6 persons: *900 gr. salt cod; 1 dl. oil; 700 gr. blanched spinach; 6 anchovy fillets; 1 dl. sauce béchamel; ½ crushed clove of garlic; 1 tablespoonful of chopped parsley; 20 gr. butter; breadcrumbs.* Cooking time: 20 minutes.

Poach the cod, remove the skin and bones, and flake the flesh. Heat the oil, add the coarsely-chopped spinach, and drain and dry it. Add the garlic, the cod, the diced anchovy fillets, the chopped parsley, and the sauce béchamel. Season with salt, pepper and a touch of nutmeg. Mix together thoroughly. Arrange in a buttered gratinating dish. Smooth into a dome-shape, sprinkle with the breadcrumbs, sprinkle with a little oil, and brown briskly. *(France.)*

Morue espagnole

Proceed as for the preparation of Morue biscaienne, adding 6 potatoes (plain boiled, and cut up into roundels), and covering the whole dish with sauce tomate.

Morue au gratin

For 6 persons: *900 gr. salt cod; ½ litre sauce Mornay; 60 gr. grated Parmesan cheese.* Cooking time: 18 minutes.

Poach the cod, remove the skin and bones, and flake the flesh. Mask a gratinating dish with 2 or 3 tablespoonfuls of sauce Mornay, and arrange the fish on top. Coat liberally with the rest of the sauce Mornay, sprinkle with the grated cheese, and glaze. *(France.)*

Morue hollandaise

For 6 persons: *900 gr. salt cod; 750 gr. potatoes; 150 gr. butter; parsley.* Cooking time: 15 minutes.

Poach the cod, remove the skin and bones, and arrange the fish on a napkin with the parsley. Serve the plain boiled potatoes at the same time, and either melted butter or a light sauce hollandaise. *(France.)*

Morue indienne

For 6 persons: *900 gr. salt cod; 300 gr. rice; ½ litre sauce indienne.* Cooking time: 15 minutes.

Poach the fish, flake it, and mix with the sauce indienne. Serve the plain boiled rice separately. *(International cookery.)*

Morue italienne

For 6 persons: *900 gr. salt cod; ½ litre sauce tomate; parsley; 2 lemons; flour.* Cooking time: 12 minutes.

Cut up the fish into dice, flour it, and sauté in oil. Arrange on a serving dish, with parsley and quarters of lemon. Serve the sauce tomate separately. *(France.)*

Morue milanaise

For 6 persons: *900 gr. salt cod; 2 eggs; 50 gr. grated Parmesan cheese; breadcrumbs; 1 lemon; 50 gr. butter; 5 cl. oil; 4 dl. sauce tomate; flour.* Cooking time: 15 minutes.

Cut up the fish into escalopes, season them with pepper, flour them, dip them in beaten egg, and roll them in a mixture of the cheese and breadcrumbs. Sauté the escalopes in butter and oil in a frying-pan. Arrange the fish on a serving dish, and sprinkle with lemon juice. Serve the sauce tomate separately. *(France.)*
(See illustration, page 262. N.B. Different presentation.)

Morue Parmentier

For 6 persons: *900 gr. salt cod; 500 gr. appareil à pommes duchesse; 4 dl. sauce Mornay; 50 gr. grated Parmesan cheese; 40 gr. butter.* Cooking time: 18 minutes.

Poach the cod, remove the skin and bones, and flake the flesh. Using a star piping-tube, border an oval (buttered) gratinating dish with the appareil. Arrange the fish in the centre. Coat with the sauce Mornay, sprinkle with the grated cheese and then with melted butter, and brown in a hot oven. *(France.)*

Morue provençale

For 6 persons: *900 gr. salt cod; 30 gr. chopped onion; 250 gr. peeled, pipped and chopped tomatoes; 100 gr. black olives; 1 dl. olive oil; 1 crushed clove of garlic; 50 gr. capers; 1 tablespoonful of coarsely-chopped parsley.* Cooking time: 25 minutes.

Sauté the chopped onion in oil. Add the chopped tomatoes, garlic, capers, black olives, parsley, and the cod (freshly cooked and flaked). Season with salt and pepper, and allow all the ingredients to simmer together for 10 minutes. Serve in a timbale. *(France.)*

Morue sautée lyonnaise

For 6 persons: *900 gr. salt cod; 500 gr. potatoes; 150 gr. butter; 75 gr. thinly-sliced onion; 1 tablespoonful of chopped parsley; 1 coffee-spoonful of vinegar.* Cooking time: 20 minutes.

Sauté the thinly-sliced onion in butter, and also the roundels of potatoes (after plain boiling). Add the fish (freshly cooked and flaked), season with salt and pepper, and sprinkle with the chopped parsley. Sauté all the ingredients together in a frying-pan for 3 to 4 minutes, and finish off with the vinegar. *(France.)*

Morue Valencia

For 6 persons: *750 gr. salt cod; 250 gr. rice; 100 gr. tomato purée; 200 gr. roundels of onion; 125 gr. butter; 3 hard-boiled eggs; 1 tablespoonful of breadcrumbs; fish fumet; oil; flour.* Cooking time: 20 minutes.

Poach the cod, remove the skin and bones, and flake the flesh. Cook the rice in the fish fumet. Arrange in a timbale, alternating the rice, fish, and tomato purée. Finish off with a layer of rice. Cover with roundels of onion (which have been floured and then fried in oil). Sprinkle with noisette butter (containing fine breadcrumbs). Garnish with quarters of hard-boiled egg. *(France.)*

Mulet, muge

Mullet

The most common varieties of this fish are the grey mullet and the striped mullet. The flesh is white, slightly fatty and quite delicate. Small mullet are either grilled or prepared meunière. The larger fish are prepared as for sea-perch.

Nonats, blanchaille

Nonats, whitebait

Nonats are the fry of an indeterminate species of small Mediterranean fish. As they begin to deteriorate soon after catching, they are not to be found except in the environs of the fishing-grounds.

Whitebait are, like nonats, rolled in flour and then deep fried in very hot oil. They must be kept very crisp. When they are taken out of the cooking oil, they are sprinkled with table salt (containing either black pepper or a touch of Cayenne pepper). They are arranged on a napkin, and garnished with fried parsley and with quarters of lemon.

Pagel

Gilt-head

This fish is of good quality, but not as fine as the gilt-poll. Preparations appropriate to the gilt-poll are applicable to the sea-bream and gilt-head.

Plie

Plaice

Plie farcie Folkestone

Baked stuffed plaice Folkestone style

For 6 persons: *3 plaice (650 gr. each); 175 gr. breadcrumbs; 60 gr. raw mushrooms; 2 eggs; 120 gr. butter; 2 lemons; 1 coffee-spoonful of chopped parsley; 1 coffee-spoonful of chopped chive; the zest of half a lemon; 1 pinch of sage and 1 pinch of thyme (both powdered); parsley.* Cooking time: approximately 35 minutes.

Remove the plaice heads, tails and fins. Loosen the fillets from the backbones (on the 'white skin' side) over a length of 10 cm., so as to make a cavity, and cut each backbone with scissors in various places so as to remove it. Mix the breadcrumbs with the parsley, chive, chopped mushrooms, chopped lemon-zest, and powdered sage and thyme, add the beaten eggs, and season with salt and pepper. Stuff the plaice with this mixture, and flour them. Arrange them on a buttered fish tray, sprinkle with melted butter and bake in a moderate oven. Arrange on a serving dish with lemon quarters and fried parsley. *(Great Britain.)*

Poisson aux amandes

Machchi Pellao

For 6 persons: *1 kg. 200 firm-fleshed fish; 1 dl. mustard-seed oil; 250 gr. onion; ½ coffee-spoonful of black peppercorns; ½ coffee-spoonful of cloves; 1 tablespoonful of coriander; ½ coffee-spoonful of cardamom; ¼ litre yoghurt; 120 gr. skinned and blanched almonds; a piece of cinnamon-stick (2 cm. long); 400 gr. Basmathi rice; 80 gr. melted butter; chenna flour (made from chick peas).* Cooking time: approximately 35 minutes.

Remove the fish-head(s) and use them to prepare a fish fumet (not more than 1 dl.). Coat the fish with chenna flour, and leave to rest for 10 minutes. Wash the fish carefully, drain it, cut up into thick slices, marinate it with the mustard-seed oil for 30 minutes, and wash it again. Prepare a paste with the onions, the peppercorns (freshly milled) and the yoghurt. Use this paste to coat the fish. Cook the rice gently in lightly-salted water for 12 minutes, drain, and reserve 1 dl. of the rice liquor. Arrange the fish, with the cloves, in a pan with hot butter, shake it, moisten with the rice liquor, and add the pounded almonds and the crushed coriander. Allow the fish to simmer until the liquor starts to thicken. Arrange half the rice in an earthenware cocotte (or in a gratinating dish), arrange the fish in the centre, cover it with the rest of the rice, and with the cardamom and cinnamon, sprinkle with the fish fumet and the rest of the melted butter, cover with a lid, and finish off the cooking in a moderate oven for 12 to 14 minutes. *(India.)*

Poisson de Méditerranée sfarde

Dag jam sfaradi

For 6 persons: *6 whole Mediterranean fish (or 6 darnes); 50 gr. pine kernels; 2 large cloves of garlic; the juice of 1 lemon; 4 cl. olive oil; 2 tablespoonfuls of chopped parsley.* Cooking time: 45 minutes.

Chop up the garlic and cook gently in the olive oil with the pine kernels until the garlic is coloured. Moisten with a little water and the lemon juice, season with salt, and bring to the boil. Arrange the fish in a sauteuse, and moisten half-way up with the unpassed stock. Cover with a lid, and cook over low heat. Just before serving, season with freshly-milled pepper, and sprinkle liberally with the chopped parsley. Hot: serve in the stock. Cold: allow to cool in the stock. *(Israel.)*

Poisson en papillote Georges Huhn

Cartoccio di pesce Giorgio Huhn

For 10 persons: *10 small slices of pike (40 gr. each); 10 small fillets of sole; 10 half slices of fresh salmon; 20 thin slices of scallop; 10 shelled scampi; 300 gr. shelled prawns; 10 medallions of red mullet (40 gr. each); 1 litre fish fumet; 3 dl. dry white wine; 3 dl. fresh cream; the juice of 1 lemon; 1 chopped shallot; 1 tablespoonful of chopped parsley; 100 gr. butter.*

Heat the chopped shallot (without colouring) with 40 gr. butter, and add all the fish (except the prawns). Pour on top half the white wine and ¼ litre fish fumet. Season with salt and pepper, cover with a lid, and cook in a low oven for about 10 minutes. Heat the prawns separately with 1 dl. fish fumet. Butter one side of a sheet of greaseproof paper, and oil the other side. Drain the fish and prawns thoroughly. Pass the cooking liquor through a conical strainer (chinois), completing it with the rest of the fish fumet and white wine. Reduce by half. Add the cream, cook gently, and work at the same time with a spatula until the sauce becomes thick and creamy. Finish off with the chopped parsley and the lemon juice, and work up the sauce with the rest of the butter. Correct seasoning and consistency. Coat the fish with a quarter of this sauce, and cook in a hot oven for 3 or 4 minutes. Serve the rest of the sauce separately. *(Switzerland.)*
(See illustration, page 340.)

Pompano Florida, Filets de

Fillets of pompano Florida style

For 6 persons: *3 pompanos (500 gr. each); 2 grapefruit; 2 large oranges; 1 lemon; 100 gr. butter; 5 cl. oil; 1 tablespoonful of chopped parsley; milk; flour.* Cooking time: 8 to 10 minutes.

Fillet the fish. Peel and pip the grapefruit and oranges, and skin the segments. Heat the segments in a little butter. Pass the fillets of fish through seasoned milk, flour them, colour them golden in hot oil, in a frying-pan with a little butter, drain them, and arrange on a serving dish. Garnish between each pair of fillets with the fruit segments, sprinkle with lemon juice, and then with chopped parsley. Pour over the whole dish some lightly-browned frothy butter. *(United States.)*

Raie

Skate

Skate is usually sold already gutted, and then cleaned. Only the wings are normally used, and the rest of the fish is not even brought ashore. However, it must, in any case, be carefully washed. It is poached in salted water, containing 12 gr. salt per litre of water. As soon as the cooking is finished, drain the fish, and skin it on both sides. If it is not to be served immediately, the pieces of fish can be kept hot in the passed cooking liquor.

Raie au beurre noir

Skate with black butter

Proceed as for the preparation of Morue au beurre noir.
(See page 280.)

Raie, Fritots de

Skate fritters

For 6 persons: *1 kg. 500 of skate; ½ litre batter; 150 gr. onion (cut into roundels); parsley; flour; 1 lemon; oil; thyme; bayleaf.* Cooking time: 15 minutes.

Choose the wings of very small skate, skin and bone them, and cut them up into pieces. Marinate them for 30 minutes with salt, pepper, lemon juice, oil, thyme and bayleaf. Wipe the pieces dry, dip them in the batter, and pass them through hot fat. Arrange them on a napkin, and garnish, on one side with fried parsley, and on the other with floured and fried roundels of onion. *(France.)*

Raie au gratin

Proceed as for the preparation of Daurade au gratin.
(See page 259.)

Raie Montrose

Skate Montrose

For 6 persons: *1 kg. 500 skate; 60 gr. thinly-sliced onion; 60 gr. thinly-sliced carrot; 6 white peppercorns; 2 cloves; 1 small bayleaf; 3 parsley-stalks; 1 dl. vinegar; 25 gr. salt; 60 gr. butter; 40 gr. capers; ½ lemon; 1 tablespoonful of chopped parsley.* Cooking time: 15 minutes.

Prepare a court-bouillon with 1½ litres of water, onion, carrot, bayleaf, parsley, vinegar and salt, and boil for 5 minutes. Cut up the wings of skate into 6 pieces, and place them in the boiling court-bouillon. Cook gently. As soon as the cooking is finished, drain the pieces of fish, skin them, and arrange them on a serving dish. Sprinkle with the lemon juice, then with the chopped parsley and the capers, and finish off with the noisette butter. *(Great Britain.)*

Raie normande

For 6 persons: *1 kg. 500 of skate; 50 gr. capers; 3 cl. vinegar; 4 dl. cream.* Cooking time: 15 minutes.

▲ Merlan aux moules, p. 278

Filets de merlan Rachel, p. 279 ▼

▲ Sardines basquaise, p. 294

Zephirs de sandre aux queues d'écrevisses, p. 398 ▼

▲ Paupiettes de sole Tsar Nicolas, p. 341

Filets de sole Dame Brune, p. 301 ▼

▲ Filets de merlan cancalaise, p. 276

Filets de sole Donizzetti, p. 301 ▼

Cut up the skate into thick slices and poach them in a court-bouillon. Arrange the fish on a serving dish, and coat them with thick cream, which has been heated and well-seasoned. Sprinkle with the capers, and then with the vinegar, which has been heated and reduced by half. *(France.)*

Raie provençale

For 6 persons: *1 kg. 500 skate; 500 gr. peeled, pipped and chopped tomatoes; 2 dl. fish fumet; 1 coffee-spoonful of anchovy essence; 1 lemon; 1 tablespoonful of chopped parsley; 25 gr. butter.* Cooking time: 20 minutes.

Cut up the skate into thick slices and arrange them in a buttered gratinating dish. Season with salt and pepper, and cover with the chopped tomatoes. Add the fish fumet, anchovy essence and lemon juice, and cook in the oven. Correct seasoning and consistency, and sprinkle with chopped parsley. *(France.)*

Rascasse du Nord berlinoise, Filets de

Rotbarschfilets auf berliner Art

Norway haddock

For 6 persons: *6 fillets of Norway haddock (125 gr. each); 300 gr. peeled potatoes; 250 gr. picked shrimps; 2 lemons; olive oil; 100 gr. butter; flour; 1 egg; meat-glaze; 1 tablespoonful of chopped parsley.* Cooking time: 10 minutes.

Marinate the fillets in oil with lemon juice, salt and pepper. Cut up the potatoes into small dice, blanch and refresh them, drain them, and colour golden in butter. Drain the fillets, flour them, pass through beaten egg, and sauté in equal quantities of oil and butter. Arrange them on a serving dish. Lightly colour the shrimps in the rest of the butter, add the potatoes, and mix all together. Sprinkle the fillets with lemon juice and meat-glaze, and cover with the mixture of shrimps and potatoes (in their butter). Sprinkle with chopped parsley. *(Germany.)*

Rascasse du Nord indienne

Indischer Dahlmouthfisch

For 6 persons: *1 kg. 500 fillets of Norway haddock; 500 gr. lentils; 1 litre bouillon du pot-au-feu; 10 gr. coriander; 5 gr. cardamom; 100 gr. onion; 250 gr. ghee (Indian clarified butter).*

Marinating liquor: *100 gr. yoghurt; 5 gr. curcuma; 10 gr. black caraway seeds; the juice of 1 lemon; 5 cl. mustard-seed oil.* Cooking time: 5 to 10 minutes.

Lightly colour the lentils with the onion, coriander, cardamom and a little oil. Moisten with the bouillon. Cook in the oven as for a risotto. Allow to cool, and mince finely, or pass through a cloth strainer (tamis). Lightly oil a fish tray, season the mixture lightly with salt, spread it over the tray (using a fork), and dry it off in a low oven. Marinate the fillets for 30 minutes in the yoghurt, curcuma and lemon juice. Roll them in the dried-off lentils (as if in breadcrumbs), and sauté them in the ghee. Sprinkle with the mustard-seed oil at the moment of serving. *(Germany.)*

Rouget, rouget-barbet

Red mullet

Provided that the gall-bladder and the gills are removed, the red mullet can be used without gutting or scaling. Red mullet are best when prepared sautés or grilled.

Rouget au basilic

Triglia di scoglio al basilico

For 6 persons: *6 red mullet (170 gr. each); 180 gr. raw mushrooms; 60 gr. chopped shallot (or onion); 300 gr. peeled, pipped and chopped tomatoes; 1 crushed clove of garlic; 50 gr. capers; 12 small basil leaves; 5 cl. white wine; 6 cl. meat stock; 25 gr. butter; the juice of ¾ lemon.* Poaching time: 10 to 12 minutes.

Wash and clean the red mullet, and score them lightly (without gutting them). Thickly butter a gratinating dish, line it with the shallot (or onion), arrange the fish in it, sprinkle with the white wine, season with salt and pepper, and add the mushrooms, cut up into small dice, the tomatoes and the capers. Cover with the garlic and the basil leaves, sprinkle with the lemon juice, add the meat stock, and poach in the oven. Serve with plain boiled potatoes. *(Italy.)*

Rouget bordelaise

For 6 persons: *6 red mullet (150 gr. each); 4 dl. sauce bordelaise (with white wine); 80 gr. butter.* Cooking time: 10 minutes.

Score the red mullet, season with salt and pepper, and cook them in butter. Arrange them on a serving dish. Serve the sauce bordelaise at the same time. *(France.)*

Rouget en caisse

For 6 persons: *6 red mullet (150 gr. each); 200 gr. peeled, pipped and chopped tomatoes; 150 gr. raw mushrooms; 3 dl. sauce italienne; 150 gr. butter; fresh breadcrumbs; 6 rectangular greased paper cases.* Cooking time: 15 minutes.

Season the red mullet with salt and pepper, and sauté them in butter. Mask the inside of each case with a tablespoonful of sauce italienne, place a fish on top, surround with the chopped tomatoes (softened in butter), and the thinly-sliced mushrooms (sautéd in butter). Coat with sauce italienne, sprinkle with the breadcrumbs, and then with melted butter, finish off the cooking and brown in the oven. *(France.)*

Rouget Cheltonia, Filets de

For 10 persons: *5 red mullet of 200 gr. each; 2 medium-sized lobsters; 400 gr. mushrooms; 250 gr. butter; 2 lemons; salt and peppercorns; 1 kg. 200 potatoes; 10 small peeled tomatoes.*

Cook the lobsters in a court-bouillon, remove the meat from the tail and cut into medallions. Leave the claws whole. Fillet the red mullet and cook them meunière. Chop the liver from the mullets and mix with the creamy parts (coral) from the lobster and pass through a hair sieve, dilute with a little mushroom cooking liquor and lobster cooking stock and reduce over the fire to a sauce consistency. Add butter, Cayenne and lemon juice, and mask the cooked fillets. Garnish with mushroom heads and lobster medallions. Accompany the dish with small tomatoes stewed in butter and spoon-cut potato balls sautéd au beurre.
Above recipe created by Mr. Henry Duthaler, Junior, Chef de Cuisine, Queens Hotel, Cheltenham.

Rouget Danicheff

For 6 persons: *6 red mullet; 2 dl. fish fumet; 3 chopped shallots; 40 gr. truffle; 120 gr. butter.* Cooking time: 10 minutes.

Lay the red mullet in a buttered gratinating dish sprinkled with the chopped onion. Season them with salt and pepper, moisten with the fish fumet, and add the truffle (cut into a julienne). Poach in the oven, reduce the cooking liquor and monter au beurre. Coat the fish with this sauce, and glaze briskly. *(France.)*

Rouget égyptienne

For 6 persons: *6 red mullet; 500 gr. tomatoes (peeled, pipped and quartered); 1 crushed clove of garlic; 2 dl. oil; breadcrumbs; flour; 1 tablespoonful of chopped parsley.* Cooking time: 12 to 15 minutes.

Soften the tomatoes in oil, season with salt and pepper, and add the garlic and parsley. Flour the red mullet, and sauté in oil. Sprinkle half the tomatoes on to a gratinating dish, arrange the red mullet on top, and cover with the rest of the tomatoes. Sprinkle with the breadcrumbs, and then with a trickle of oil, and brown in a hot oven. *(France.)*

Rouget épicurienne

For 6 persons: *6 red mullet; 500 gr. peeled, pipped and chopped tomatoes; 120 gr. butter; 3 chopped shallots; 1 dl. jus lié; flour.* Cooking time: 10 minutes.

Pass the shallots through butter, add the tomatoes, cook until the water has completely evaporated and incorporate the jus lié. Score and flour the red mullet, and cook in butter. Arrange them on a serving dish, mask them with the softened tomatoes, and sprinkle with a little noisette butter. *(France.)*

Rouget au fenouil

Red mullet with fennel

For 6 persons: *6 red mullet; 3 gr. chopped fennel; 1 dl. oil; 1 lemon; 150 gr. chopped fat bacon; 1 tablespoonful of chopped parsley.* Cooking time: 15 minutes.

Score the red mullet, and marinate for 3 hours with salt, pepper, lemon juice, oil and chopped fennel. Add the fat bacon and the parsley to the marinating liquor. Wrap each red mullet, with a little of the chopped herbs, in a greased paper papillote. Grill gently. Serve just as it is.

Rouget Francillon

For 6 persons: *6 red mullet; 300 gr. straw potatoes; 120 gr. butter; 100 gr. anchovy butter; 2 dl. sauce tomate; 15 cl. oil; 1 lemon; parsley; 6 bread croûtons.* Cooking time: 10 minutes.

Score the red mullet, marinate them for 25 minutes with the lemon juice and oil, and grill them. Arrange each red mullet on a croûton of the same shape, which has been fried in butter and spread with anchovy butter.

Arrange on a serving dish with the straw potatoes and fried parsley. Serve the sauce tomate separately (worked up with 60 gr. butter and 25 gr. anchovy butter). *(France.)*
(See illustration, page 306. N.B. Different presentation.)

Rouget au gratin

Proceed as for the preparation of Daurade au gratin, taking into account the difference in size when calculating the cooking time. *(See page 259.)*

Rouget grenobloise

Proceed as for the preparation of Merlan grenobloise. *(See page 278.)*

Rouget grillé

Grilled red mullet

For 6 persons: *6 red mullet; 120 gr. maître d'hôtel butter; 1 lemon; picked parsley; flour; oil.* Cooking time: 10 minutes.

Score the red mullet, season them with salt and pepper, flour them, and grill gently. Arrange them on a serving dish. Garnish with the parsley and lemon quarters. Serve the maître d'hôtel butter separately (or anchovy butter). *(France.)*
(See illustration, page 306. N.B. Different presentation.)

Rouget italienne

For 6 persons: *6 red mullet; 4 dl. sauce italienne; 1 dl. fish fumet; 1 dl. white wine.* Cooking time: 8 to 10 minutes.

Poach the red mullet in the fish fumet and white wine. Reduce the cooking liquor, blend it with the sauce italienne, and use this mixture to coat the fish. *(France.)*

Rouget juive

For 6 persons: *6 red mullet; 3 dl. oil; 4 dl. sauce tartare; picked parsley; 1 lemon; flour.* Cooking time: 8 to 10 minutes.

Score the red mullet, season with salt and pepper, flour them, and fry them in oil. Drain, and arrange them on a serving dish, with parsley and lemon quarters. Serve the sauce tartare separately. *(France.)*

Rouget livournaise I

For 6 persons: *6 red mullet; 2 dl. fish fumet; 2 chopped shallots; 250 gr. peeled, pipped and chopped tomatoes; 120 gr. butter; 40 gr. truffle.* Cooking time: 8 to 10 minutes.

Pass the chopped shallot through butter, add the chopped tomatoes, and soften them. Poach the red mullet in the fish fumet. Reduce the cooking liquor almost to a glaze, and monter au beurre. Incorporate the chopped tomatoes, and also the truffle (cut into a julienne). Use this mixture to coat the fish, and glaze briskly. *(France.)*

Rouget livournaise II

Triflie di scoglio alla livornese

For 6 persons: *6 red mullet (170 gr. each); 60 gr. chopped onion; 2 finely-chopped cloves of garlic; 6 cl. olive oil; 300 gr. chopped tomatoes; 4 finely-chopped anchovy fillets; 6 cl. dry white wine; 1 tablespoonful of chopped parsley; 12 plain boiled potatoes; 12 fried heart-shaped croûtons.* Poaching time: 10 minutes.

Wash and clean the red mullet, dry them, flour them, and colour golden on both sides in hot oil. Meanwhile, lightly colour the onion and garlic in oil, moisten with a little water, and reduce completely. Add the anchovy, chopped tomatoes, and parsley, season with salt and pepper, and cook gently for 10 minutes. Arrange the red mullet in an oval gratinating dish, coat with the mixture containing the chopped tomatoes, cook for 5 minutes on top of the stove, sprinkle with the white wine, and finish off the poaching in the oven. Arrange on a serving dish, and garnish round the edge with the potatoes and the croûtons. *(Italy.)*

Rouget meréchale, Filets de

For 6 persons: *6 red mullet (180 gr. each); 150 gr. melted butter; 180 gr. chopped truffle.* Cooking time: 8 minutes.

Fillet the fish, season the fillets with salt and pepper, and dip them in the melted butter. Roll them in the finely-chopped truffle, and press them down with the blade of a knife. Cook them gently in clarified butter. *(France.)*

Rouget meunière

Proceed as for the preparation of all other fish designated meunière. *(See page 64.)*

Rouget Monte-Carlo

For 6 persons: *6 red mullet; 90 gr. anchovy butter; 300 gr. straw potatoes; 100 gr. maître d'hôtel butter; oil; flour; 6 bread croûtons (shaped so that the fish will cover them exactly)*. Cooking time: 10 minutes.

Score the red mullet, season with salt and pepper, flour and oil them, and grill gently. Drain them, and arrange them on the croûtons (which have been fried and then spread with the anchovy butter). Sprinkle with the half-softened maître d'hôtel butter. Garnish round the edge of the serving dish with the straw potatoes. *(France.)*

Rouget Montesquieu, Filets de

For 6 persons: *6 red mullet (180 gr. each); 100 gr. chopped onion; 2 tablespoonfuls of chopped parsley; 180 gr. butter; 1 lemon.* Cooking time: 8 to 10 minutes.

Fillet the red mullet. Season the fillets with salt and pepper, dip them in melted butter, and roll them in the finely-chopped onion and chopped parsley, pressing them down with the blade of a knife. Cook the fillets gently in clarified butter. Arrange them on a serving dish, and sprinkle them with the cooking butter and with lemon juice. *(France.)*

Rouget nantaise

For 6 persons: *6 red mullet; the liver from the red mullet; 2 chopped shallots; 1 dl. white wine; 2 dl. half-glaze sauce; 1 coffee-spoonful of meat-glaze; 100 gr. butter; 6 channelled roundels of lemon; oil.* Cooking time: 8 to 10 minutes.

Score the red mullet, season with salt and pepper, and oil and grill them. Reduce the white wine with the chopped shallots, add the half-glaze sauce, and the cooked and crushed mullet livers, and finish off with the meat-glaze. Work up the sauce with butter, pour it on to the serving dish, and arrange the fish on top. Place on each fish a roundel of lemon. *(France.)*

Rouget niçoise

Proceed as for the preparation of Merlan niçoise. *(See page 279.)*

Rouget orientale

For 6 persons: *6 red mullet; 500 gr. chopped tomatoes; 2 chopped shallots; 1 dl. white wine; 15 cl. olive oil; 1 crushed clove of garlic; 1 pinch of saffron; 1 bayleaf; 1 tablespoonful of chopped parsley; flour.*

Score the red mullet, season with salt and pepper, flour them, and colour them in oil in a frying-pan. Arrange them in a gratinating dish. Colour the chopped shallots in oil, add the chopped tomatoes, and simmer for a few minutes. Moisten with the white wine, add the garlic, the saffron, the parsley and the bayleaf, season and boil again. Pour this mixture over the fish, and cook in the oven for 10 minutes. Serve the fish either hot or very cold. *(France.)*

Rouget sur le plat

For 6 persons: *6 red mullet; 2 dl. fish fumet; 100 gr. butter; 1 lemon.* Cooking time: 12 to 15 minutes.

Gently loosen the fillets from the backbone of each fish, and slip a nut of butter under each fillet. Arrange the fish on a thickly-buttered gratinating dish, season with salt and pepper, moisten with the fish fumet, and add the juice of half a lemon, and 60 gr. butter (in small pieces). Cook in the oven, basting frequently with the cooking liquor until this acquires a syrupy consistency. Arrange the fish on a serving dish, coat with the cooking liquor, and serve. *(France.)*

Rouget polonaise

For 6 persons: *6 red mullet; ¼ litre fish fumet; 2 dl. fresh cream; 2 egg yolks; 120 gr. butter; 1 tablespoonful of fresh breadcrumbs; flour.* Cooking time: 10 minutes.

Season the red mullet with salt and pepper, flour them, and cook in butter. Reduce the fish fumet by three-quarters, and thicken it (away from the heat) with the egg yolks and cream. Correct seasoning and consistency. Arrange the red mullet on a serving dish, coat with the sauce, and sprinkle the surface with fine breadcrumbs fried in butter.

Rouget au Porto

Place in a buttered fire-proof dish finely-chopped shallots, and 500 gr. skinned, pipped and diced tomatoes. Place on top 2 to 3 red mullet, season with salt and pepper, and add a

glass of white port. Cover with buttered greaseproof paper and poach in the oven. When the fish is cooked, strain off the cooking liquor and mix with an equal quantity of good fish velouté; add a squeeze of lemon juice and 2 dl. of fresh cream and 50 gr. of butter. Mask the fish with this sauce and sprinkle with chopped parsley.
Created by the former Chef de Cuisine of the Grand Hotel, Birmingham, Mr. J. F. Beer.

Rouget Porto Venere

Triglie di scoglio alla Porto Venere

For 6 persons: *6 red mullet (170 gr. each); 15 cl. olive oil; 1 chopped onion; the juice of 1 lemon; 1 small coffee-spoonful of chopped parsley; 1 coffee-spoonful of chopped fennel leaves; 150 gr. anchovy butter; 6 sheets of greaseproof paper (in the shape of stylised hearts).* Cooking time in the oven: 15 to 18 minutes.

Wash and clean the red mullet, dry them, and score them lightly. Marinate them for 1 hour with olive oil, lemon juice, onion, parsley and fennel. Drain and dry the fish, and colour them gently golden on both sides in oil. Brush each papillote with oil, smear it with anchovy butter, place a fish on it, sprinkle with a little of the marinating liquor, and seal the papillote by folding it in half and crimping the edges. Oil an oven-proof fish tray, arrange the papillotes in it, and cook in an already hot oven for 15 minutes, or until the paper browns and the papillotes start to swell. Arrange the papillotes on a serving dish, and open them only at table. Sprinkle each red mullet with the liquor contained in its papillote, and serve immediately. *(Italy.)*
(See illustration, page 307. N.B. Different presentation.)

Rouget portugaise

For 6 persons: *6 red mullet; 2 dl. fish fumet; 4 dl. sauce portugaise.* Cooking time: 8 to 10 minutes.

Poach the red mullet in the fish fumet. Reduce the poaching stock, and add it to the sauce portugaise. Arrange the red mullet on a serving dish, and coat them with the sauce. They may also be garnished with puff pastry fleurons. *(France.)*

Rouget provençale

Proceed as for the preparation of Aiglefin provençale. *(See page 243.)*

Rouget Théodore

For 6 persons: *6 red mullet; 100 gr. fish forcemeat; 120 gr. raw mushrooms; 2 dl. white wine; 4 dl. white wine sauce; 25 gr. butter.* Cooking time: 12 minutes.

Split open the red mullet on the dorsal side, and remove the backbones. Fill the fish with the chopped mushrooms, which have been mixed with the fish forcemeat. Re-shape the fish, arrange them on a buttered fish tray, poach them in the white wine, and arrange on a serving dish. Reduce the cooking liquor, add it to the white wine sauce, and use to coat the fish. *(France.)*

Rouget trouvillaise

For 6 persons: *6 red mullet; 240 gr. fish forcemeat; 1 dl. white wine; 50 gr. butter; 4 dl. sauce Colbert; 6 roundels of channelled lemon.* Cooking time: 12 to 15 minutes.

Prepare the red mullet as for Rouget Théodore, and fill them with the forcemeat. Re-shape the fish, and poach in the white wine and butter. Arrange them on a serving dish, and decorate each with a roundel of lemon. Serve the sauce Colbert separately.

Rouget vénitienne, Filets de

For 6 persons: *12 fillets of red mullet; 50 gr. butter; 5 cl. oil; 18 small mushroom-heads; 18 stuffed olives; 4 dl. sauce vénitienne; flour.* Cooking time: 8 minutes.

Season the fillets with salt and pepper, flour them, and cook in oil and butter. Arrange the fish on a serving dish, and garnish with the mushroom-heads and stuffed olives. Coat with the sauce vénitienne. *(France.)*

Rouget Villeroi, Filets de

For 6 persons: *12 fillets of red mullet; ½ litre sauce Villeroi; 2 eggs; fresh breadcrumbs; parsley; 2 lemons; olive oil.* Cooking time: 10 minutes.

Trim the fillets, and marinate them for 30 minutes with lemon juice, oil, salt and pepper. Drain and dry the fish, dip in the sauce Villeroi, and allow to cool. Coat with egg and breadcrumbs, and deep fry in oil. Arrange the fillets on a serving dish with the fried parsley and the lemon quarters. *(France.)*

Saint-pierre

John Dory

This fish has a very delicate flesh. It can be poached or grilled whole, or prepared in fillets as for brill or turbot. The John Dory is also an ingredient in the making of bouillabaisse.

Sardines

Sardines

Sardines antiboise

For 6 persons: *900 gr. sardines; 500 gr. chopped tomatoes; 2 eggs; 1 small crushed clove of garlic; 30 gr. butter; fresh breadcrumbs; oil.* Cooking time: 8 minutes.

Remove the heads, and open and bone the sardines. Coat with egg and breadcrumbs, and deep fry the fish in oil. Prepare a fondue with the chopped tomatoes, and season it with the garlic. Arrange the sardines round the edge of a serving dish, and garnish the centre with the fondue. *(France.)*

(See Culinary Technique, page 85.)

Sardines basquaise

For 6 persons: *900 gr. sardines; 4 dl. sauce béarnaise; 50 gr. small capers; 2 eggs; fresh breadcrumbs; oil.* Cooking time: 8 minutes.

Prepare the fish as for Sardines antiboise. Arrange the cooked sardines around the edge of a serving dish, and garnish the centre of the dish with the sauce béarnaise, to which the capers have been added. *(France.)*

(See illustration, page 286. N.B. Different presentation.)

Sardines bonne femme

For 6 persons: *900 gr. sardines; 100 gr. thinly-sliced small onions; 250 gr. tomatoes; 15 cl. olive oil; ½ coffee-spoonful of powdered fennel seeds; 50 gr. fresh breadcrumbs; 2 dl. white wine.* Cooking time: 15 minutes.

Lightly colour the onion in oil, add the white wine, and reduce the liquor by two-thirds. Add the tomatoes, which have been peeled, pressed, quartered, and sauté in oil, season with salt and pepper, and cook all these ingredients together. Pour the mixture into a gratinating dish, arrange the sardines on top, sprinkle with the breadcrumbs mixed with the fennel seeds, and then with the olive oil, and finish off by browning in the oven. *(France.)*

Sardines courtisane

For 6 persons: *12 large sardines; 75 gr. duxelles; 75 gr. fish forcemeat; 100 gr. purée of spinach; 2 dl. white wine; 3 dl. white wine sauce; 18 potato croquettes; 12 bread croûtons.* Cooking time: 12 to 15 minutes.

Remove the heads, open the sardines on the dorsal side, bone the fish, and mask the fillets with the fish forcemeat, to which the duxelles have been added. Re-shape the sardines, and poach them in the white wine. Drain the fish, arrange them on top of the croûtons (the same shape as the sardines) in a gratinating dish, and coat them with the white wine sauce mixed with the fine purée of spinach. Glaze the dish briskly in the oven, and then surround the fish with the small potato croquettes. *(France.)*

(See illustration, page 307. N.B. Different presentation.)

Sardines farcies génoise

Sardine fritte e farcite alla genovese

For 6 persons: *18 large sardines; 120 gr. fresh breadcrumbs dipped in milk; 4 eggs; 60 gr. grated Parmesan cheese; 15 gr. chopped parsley; 1 tablespoonful of chopped basil; 6 gr. chopped wild marjoram; 180 gr. breadcrumbs; 90 gr. flour; frying-oil.* Frying time: 6 to 7 minutes.

Gut and bone the sardines, and remove the heads. Wash the fish and fillet them. Using a fork, crush the soaked and pressed breadcrumbs. Add 3 beaten eggs and the basil, wild marjoram and parsley. Season with salt and pepper, and knead well together. Coat each fillet with a layer of forcemeat, and make 'sandwiches' by pressing the fillets together in pairs. Pass through flour and then through the beaten egg, and roll in the breadcrumbs mixed with the grated Parmesan cheese. Press down the 'sandwiches' lightly, and deep fry them in very hot oil. Remove and drain them. Arrange the fish on a paper napkin. Garnish with lemon quarters. *(Italy.)*

Sardines farcies palermitaine

Sardine ripiene alla palermitana

For 6 persons: *24 large sardines; 12 anchovy fillets (freed of salt by soaking); 90 gr. pine kernels; 90 gr. raisins; 120 gr. breadcrumbs; 1 tablespoonful of chopped parsley; 3 roughly-chopped bayleaves; 1 dl. olive oil; 12 gr. sugar; the juice of 1½ lemons.* Cooking time in the oven: 30 minutes.

Gut and bone the sardines, and remove the heads. Wash them and lay them on a cloth to allow them to drain. Heat 5 cl. oil, add half the breadcrumbs, and fry very gently. Pour into a terrine. Add the raisins, pine kernels, anchovy fillets, sugar and chopped parsley. Season with salt, pepper and a pinch of nutmeg, moisten with oil, and knead until a fairly soft paste has been obtained. Fill the sardines with this forcemeat, arrange them side by side on an oiled fish tray, and place between each pair a piece of bayleaf. Sprinkle with the remaining breadcrumbs, and then with the rest of the oil, and cook in a hot oven until the fish are well-coloured (30 minutes). Arrange the sardines on a serving dish, and sprinkle with the lemon juice. *(Italy.)*

Sardines frites italienne

For 6 persons: *18 sardines; ½ litre batter; 4 dl. sauce tomate; parsley.* Cooking time: 8 minutes.

Remove the heads, dip the sardines in the batter, and deep fry them. Arrange the fish on a napkin, and garnish with the fried parsley. Serve the sauce tomate separately. *(France.)*

Sardines havraise

For 6 persons: *12 large sardines; 150 gr. fish forcemeat; 24 poached and bearded mussels; 1 egg; fresh breadcrumbs; 4 dl. white wine sauce; 1 coffee-spoonful of meat-glaze; 1 dl. white wine; 1 dl. fish fumet.* Cooking time: 18 minutes.

Prepare the sardines as for the designation courtisane (*see page 294*), but omit the duxelles. Poach the fish in the white wine and fish fumet. Drain them, and arrange on a serving dish. Coat with the white wine sauce, and trace a thread of meat-glaze over the sauce. Surround the sardines with the poached and bearded mussels, which have been coated with egg and breadcrumbs and then fried. *(France.)*

Sardines hyéroise

For 6 persons: *12 large sardines; 150 gr. fish forcemeat; 150 gr. white of leek; 1 dl. white wine; 1 dl. mushroom cooking liquor; 125 gr. butter; 1 coffee-spoonful of chopped parsley; 2 egg yolks; 12 croûtons.* Cooking time: 18 minutes.

Pass the finely-chopped white of leek through butter, and moisten with the white wine and the mushroom cooking liquor. When the white of leek is cooked, poach the sardines (stuffed as for the designation havraise, *see above*) in this liquor. Arrange the sardines, on croûtons of similar shape (fried in butter), on a serving dish. Reduce the cooking liquor, thicken it with the egg yolks, monter au beurre, correct seasoning and consistency, finish off with the chopped parsley, and use this sauce to coat the fish. *(France.)*

Sardines ménagère

For 6 persons: *12 large sardines; 150 gr. fish forcemeat; 3 chopped shallots; 100 gr. butter; 200 gr. raw mushrooms; 2 dl. white wine; 1 lemon; 1 coffee-spoonful of mixed chopped parsley, chervil and tarragon.* Cooking time: 18 minutes.

Stuff the sardines as for the designation havraise, and arrange them in a buttered gratinating dish sprinkled with chopped shallot. Surround them with the thinly-sliced mushrooms, moisten with the white wine, sprinkle with melted butter, and poach in the oven. At the moment of serving, add the lemon juice and the chopped mixed herbs. *(France.)*

Sardines meunière

Proceed as for the preparation of any other fish designated meunière. *(See page 64.)*

Sardines niçoise

For 6 persons: *12 large sardines; 150 gr. concentrated duxelles; 24 flowers of vegetable marrow; 100 gr. butter; 1 litre 250 fish fumet; 1 coffee-spoonful of anchovy purée; 25 gr. flour.* Cooking time: 12 minutes.

Fillet the sardines, and season the fillets with salt and pepper. Coat each fillet on the backbone side with a thin layer of duxelles. Roll the fillets into paupiettes, and wrap them in the marrow flowers. Arrange the paupiettes in a buttered sauteuse, moisten them with the fish fumet, and poach them in the oven. Arrange the fish on a serving dish. Thicken the cooking liquor with 40 gr. beurre manié, add the anchovy purée to it, and use this sauce to coat the paupiettes. *(France.)*

Sardines pisane

For 6 persons: *24 fillets of sardine; 150 gr. fish forcemeat; 250 gr. blanched leaf spinach; 1 crushed clove of garlic; 120 gr. peeled, pipped and chopped tomatoes; 1 dl. white wine; 1 dl. mushroom cooking liquor; 25 cl. sauce béchamel; 3 hard-boiled eggs; 75 gr. butter; 1 coffee-spoonful of anchovy purée; 40 gr. grated Parmesan cheese; 1 tablespoonful of breadcrumbs.* Cooking time: 15 minutes.

Mask the fillets with the fish forcemeat, roll

them into paupiettes, arrange them in a buttered sauteuse, moisten with the white wine and the mushroom cooking liquor, and poach the fillets in the oven. Colour the chopped leaf spinach in butter, add the crushed garlic and the anchovy purée, and arrange them round the edge of a gratinating dish, with the paupiettes in the centre. Garnish round the edge of the dish with quarters of hard-boiled egg. Reduce the poaching liquor, add to it the sauce béchamel and the chopped tomatoes which have been glazed in butter, and cover overall with the sauce. Sprinkle with the grated cheese and the breadcrumbs, and brown briskly. *(France.)*

Sardines provençale

For 6 persons: *900 gr. sardines; 100 gr. butter; 1 crushed clove of garlic; thyme; 1 small bayleaf; 1 tablespoonful of chopped parsley; oil; flour; vinegar.* Cooking time: 8 minutes.

Season the sardines with salt and pepper, flour them, and cook meunière in oil, with the crushed garlic, the thyme and bayleaf. Arrange the sardines on a serving dish, sprinkle with the chopped parsley, add a trickle of vinegar, and sprinkle with noisette butter. *(France.)*

Sardines Savoia Beeler

Sardine Savoia Beeler

For 6 persons: *12 large sardines; 150 gr. creamed whiting forcemeat; 5 dl. white wine sauce; 2 dl. fish fumet; 3 dl. white wine; 6 roundels of hard-boiled egg; 12 bread croûtons (coloured golden); 6 small ball-shapes made from leaf spinach.* Cooking time: 12 to 15 minutes.

Open up the sardines on the dorsal side, and bone and gut the fish. Wash the fish, dry on a cloth, stuff them with the forcemeat, and poach them in the fish fumet and white wine. Drain the fish, and arrange them in a deep serving dish. Coat with the white wine sauce. Garnish the cooked croûtons with the roundels of hard-boiled egg, alternated with the ball-shapes of leaf spinach. Arrange the croûtons among the fish, as shown in the illustration. *(Italy.)*
(See illustration, page 305. N.B. Different presentation.)

Sardines sicilienne

For 6 persons: *18 sardines; 2 eggs; fresh breadcrumbs; 120 gr. butter; 50 gr. capers; 6 anchovy fillets; 1 hard-boiled egg; 18 slices of lemon; cooking oil.* Cooking time: 8 to 10 minutes.

Prepare the sardines as for the designation Colbert, and deep fry them in the oil. Arrange them on top of the slices of lemon, on a serving dish, and surround them with noisette butter, containing the capers, the chopped hard-boiled egg and the diced anchovy fillets. *(France.)*

Sardines toulonnaise

For 6 persons: *12 large sardines; 150 gr. creamed whiting forcemeat; 4 dl. white wine sauce; 2 dl. fish fumet; 36 poached and bearded mussels.* Cooking time: 12 to 15 minutes.

Remove the heads, bone the sardines, and stuff them with the forcemeat. Re-shape them, and poach in the fish fumet. Drain the fish, and arrange around the edge of a serving dish. Place the mussels in the centre of the serving dish, and coat overall with the white wine sauce. *(France.)*

Sardines vivandière

For 6 persons: *24 fillets of sardine; 24 roundels of cucumber; 150 gr. concentrated duxelles; 2 dl. mushroom cooking liquor; 40 gr. butter; 4 dl. sauce tomate; 1 coffee-spoonful of mixed chopped chervil and tarragon.* Cooking time: 15 to 18 minutes.

Mask the fillets with the duxelles, and roll them into paupiettes. Place each paupiette in a blanched roundel of cucumber which has been scooped out to accommodate the fish. Arrange the roundels in a buttered sauteuse, moisten with the mushroom cooking liquor, and poach in the oven, basting frequently. Arrange the fish on a serving dish. Reduce the cooking liquor, and add it to the sauce tomate. Coat the dish with this sauce, and finish off by sprinkling with the chopped chervil and tarragon. *(France.)*

Sole and fillets of sole

To serve soles whole, they should be trimmed down to the fillets before cooking. For two persons, a sole of 400 gr. is large enough, especially if it is served in a sauce and with a garnish. In the case of ungarnished soles, a fish of 450 gr. will serve two.
For soles which are fried, grilled or prepared meunière, the individual portion is a whole fish weighing about 200 gr.
Sole fillets are served two per portion, and weigh about 75 gr. each, or a little less if they are stuffed.

Sole ambassade I

For 6 persons: *3 soles (400 gr. each); 1 dl. fish fumet; 1 dl. white wine; 4 dl. white wine sauce; 1 dl. sauce américaine; 6 medallions of lobster-tail; 6 good slices of truffle.* Cooking time: 12 to 15 minutes.

Poach the soles in fish fumet and white wine. Arrange them on a serving dish. Garnish each sole with two lobster medallions and two slices of truffle. Reduce the poaching stock almost to a glaze, and add it to the white wine sauce. Use to coat the soles, glaze them quickly, and surround with a ring of sauce américaine. *(France.)*

Sole ambassade II

For 6 persons: *3 soles (400 gr. each); 1 dl. white wine; 1 dl. fish fumet; 3 dl. fresh cream; 50 gr. lobster butter; 6 medallions of lobster-tail; 6 good slices of truffle.* Cooking time: 12 to 15 minutes.

Poach the soles in fish fumet and white wine. Drain them, and arrange on a serving dish. Garnish each sole with two lobster medallions and two slices of truffle. Reduce the cooking liquor considerably, add the cream, allow to cook for a moment longer, work up with the lobster butter, and correct seasoning and consistency. Coat the soles with this sauce, and glaze quickly. *(France.)*
(See illustration, page 339.)

Sole ambassadrice, Filets de

For 6 persons: *3 soles (400 gr. each); ¼ litre fish fumet; 12 shelled crayfish; 6 crayfish shells filled with fish forcemeat; 4 dl. sauce normande.* Cooking time: 8 to 10 minutes.

Remove the fillets, fold them, and poach in fish fumet. Arrange them on a serving dish, and place a crayfish on each. Coat with sauce normande, and surround with the stuffed shells which have been lightly passed through the oven. *(France.)*

Sole amiral

Proceed as for the preparation of Barbue amiral, taking into account the difference the size will make to the cooking time. *(France.)*
(See page 245.)

Sole anglaise, Filets de

Fillets of sole English style

For 6 persons: *12 fillets of sole; 2 eggs; fresh white breadcrumbs; 120 gr. butter; 120 gr. beurre maître d'hôtel.* Cooking time: 8 to 10 minutes.

Leave the fillets flat, coat with egg and breadcrumbs, and cook gently in clarified butter. Arrange on a serving dish, and cover with softened beurre maître d'hôtel. *(France.)*

Sole Anthony, Fillet of

For 6 persons: *3 filleted Dover soles (580 gr. each); ¼ litre sauce vin blanc; 75 gr. julienne of white mushrooms cooked in butter; 12 thin slices of pineapple (fresh or tinned); 142 gr. butter; 250 gr. fresh white breadcrumbs; picked parsley.* Cooking time: approximately 20 minutes.

Season the fillets of sole, pass them through flour, melted butter and breadcrumbs. Place on a buttered tray and lightly colour under the grill (salamander). Finish cooking in the oven. Dry and brush the pineapple with melted butter, sprinkle with a little sugar and lightly caramelise under the grill. Combine the mushrooms and the white wine sauce and coat the bottom of the serving dish. Arrange the sole fillets on top, fan shape. Place 1 slice of pineapple on each fillet. Pass under the grill to glaze the sauce. Serve very hot, garnished with a bouquet of picked parsley.

Sole archiduc

For 6 persons: *3 soles (400 gr. each); 2 dl. fish fumet; 2 cl. whisky; 3 cl. port; 4 dl. fresh cream; 100 gr. brunoise of vegetables; 20 gr. finely-diced truffle; 75 gr. butter; 12 very small puff-pastry fleurons.* Cooking time: 12 to 15 minutes.

Stew the brunoise in butter. Poach the soles in fish fumet, whisky and port. Drain, and arrange on a serving dish. Reduce the cooking liquor considerably, add the cream, brunoise and truffle, and cook for a few moments. Add a little butter to the sauce, coat the soles, and surround the fleurons. *(France.)*

Sole Argenteuil

For 6 persons: *3 soles (400 gr. each); 4 dl. white wine sauce; 300 gr. cooked white asparagus-tips; 1 dl. white wine; 1 dl. fish fumet; 50 gr. butter.* Cooking time: 12 to 15 minutes.

Arrange the soles on a buttered dish, and poach them in white wine and fish fumet. Re-heat the asparagus quickly in butter, and season slightly. Arrange the soles on a serving dish, garnish with the asparagus, and coat with white wine sauce containing the reduced cooking liquor. *(France.)*

Sole Bartenbach, Filets de

For 6 persons: *12 fillets of sole; 240 gr. pilaff rice; 100 gr. raisins; 3 slices of pineapple; 1 red pepper; 30 gr. ground coconut; 3 bananas; 1 dl. ketchup; 125 gr. butter; 30 gr. shredded almonds; 1 coffee-spoonful chopped parsley; 4 dl. curry sauce; flour.* Cooking time: 20 minutes.

Soak the raisins in lukewarm water, seed, drain, and dry on a cloth. Dice half the pineapple and bananas, and sauté in butter. Stew the diced red pepper. Add all these, as well as the raisins and coconut, to the rice. Season the fillets, flour, and cook in butter. Shape the rice into a mound on a serving dish, and place the fillets on top. Dice the rest of the pineapple and bananas, sauté in butter, and garnish the fillets. Sprinkle with ketchup, chopped parsley and grilled almonds. Serve the curry sauce separately. *(International cookery.)*
(See illustration, page 267.)

Sole bella Marina, Suprême de

Sovrana di sogliole bella Marina

For 6 persons: *6 soles (200 gr. each); 300 gr. prawns; 80 gr. butter; 6 cl. fresh cream; 1 egg white; 3 dl. sauce hollandaise; 60 gr. truffles (julienne); 600 gr. mussels; 300 gr. rice; 1 dl. champagne (or very good white wine); 1 lemon; 1 tablespoonful chopped parsley; Worcestershire sauce.* Poaching time for the fillets: 8 to 10 minutes.

Shell the uncooked prawns, putting the shells aside, and make a purée of the flesh, gradually adding the egg white and cream. Fillet the soles, flatten the fillets, cover them with a layer of the prepared forcemeat, and stick them together in pairs to make 'sandwiches'. Prepare the prawn butter with the pounded prawn-shells mixed with 50 gr. butter. Mask a gratinating dish with the rest of the butter, arrange the fillets on it, season, moisten with the wine, cover with greased paper, and poach in the oven. Meanwhile, heat the mussels (previously scrubbed and washed) until they open. When the fillets are just cooked, reduce the poaching liquor, mix with a very thick sauce hollandaise, and finish with the prawn butter. Arrange the fillets on a serving dish, coat with the sauce, and sprinkle with the truffles. Decorate the dish round the edge with the mussels (in half-shells which have been sprinkled with lemon juice, a few drops of Worcestershire sauce and parsley). Serve with pilaf rice. *(Italy.)*

Sole Bercy

Prepare as for Merlan Bercy. *(See page 276.)*

Sole bordelaise

For 6 persons: *3 soles (450 gr. each); 3 chopped shallots; ¼ litre red wine; 30 gr. butter; 4 dl. sauce bordelaise.* Cooking time: 12 to 15 minutes.

Arrange the soles on a buttered dish sprinkled with chopped shallots. Moisten with red wine, poach and drain. Reduce the cooking liquor, add it to the sauce bordelaise, and coat the soles. *(France.)*

Sole Breteuil

For 6 persons: *3 soles (400 gr. each); 6 small barquettes (cooked pale); 150 gr. soft roes; 150 gr. butter; 1 coffee-spoonful chopped parsley; 300 gr. potatoes.* Cooking time: 15 minutes.

Poach the soles in short cooking liquor (court-bouillon). Slice the cooked roes on the slant (escalopes), stew them in butter, fill the barquettes, and sprinkle with chopped parsley. Drain the soles, arrange them on a serving dish and garnish with the barquettes and the boiled potatoes. Serve a sauce-boat of melted butter separately. *(France.)*

Sole bretonne

For 6 persons: *3 soles (400 gr. each); 2 dl. fish fumet; 4 dl. sauce bretonne; 18 cooked, turned mushroom heads; 12 small fleurons.* Cooking time: 12 to 15 minutes.

Poach the soles in the fumet. Drain, and arrange on a serving dish. Place on each sole 6 mushroom heads. Coat with sauce bretonne, and surround with fleurons. *(France.)*

Sole Cancalaise, Filets de

For 6 persons: *12 fillets of sole; 150 gr. shelled prawns; 18 cooked oysters; 50 gr. butter; 4 dl. sauce normande.* Cooking time: 8 to 10 minutes.

Fold the fillets and poach them in butter and oyster liquor. Arrange them in a circle-shape on a serving dish, and place in the centre the cooked prawns and the poached and bearded oysters. Coat completely with sauce normande containing the reduced poaching liquor. *(France.)*

Sole cardinal, Filets de

For 6 persons: *12 fillets of sole; 180 gr. whiting forcemeat, containing crayfish butter; 12 thin escalopes lobster-tails; 2 dl. fish fumet; 30 gr. lobster coral.* Cooking time: 10 to 12 minutes.

Mask the fillets with the forcemeat, fold them, and poach in the fish fumet. Arrange them in a circle on a serving dish, inserting an escalope of lobster between each pair of fillets. Coat with sauce cardinal. Sprinkle with chopped coral. *(France.)*
(See illustration, page 332.)

Sole Carême

For 6 persons: *3 soles (400 gr. each); 6 escalopes cooked lobster-tail; 6 soft roes; 6 oysters; 12 thin slices of truffle; 2 dl. fish fumet; 50 gr. butter; ½ lemon; 4 dl. white wine sauce; 50 gr. celery purée.* Cooking time: 12 to 15 minutes.

Poach the soles in the fish fumet, drain them, and arrange on a serving dish. Garnish with lobster escalopes. Add poached and bearded oysters, and soft roes (stewed in butter and lemon juice). Coat with the white wine sauce containing celery purée, and place 4 slices of truffle on each sole. *(France.)*

Sole "Carmelite", Fillets of

For 10 persons: *5 soles (350 gr. each); 24 crayfish; 500 gr. fillet of pike; 3 medium-sized cucumbers; 400 gr. butter; 8 dl. cream; ½ dl. cognac; 5 dl. white wine; 20 cooked mushrooms; 20 slices truffle.*

Fillet the sole, trim and flatten lightly, fold in two. With the bones and trimmings make ½ litre of good fish stock. Wash the crayfish, season and sauté in butter with a mirepoix bordelaise until they turn red, flame with cognac, add half the white wine and half the cream, cook for ten minutes. Shell and reserve the crayfish meat. Wash and place on one side 20 of the shells, pound the remainder of the shells in the mortar with 150 gr. butter. Pass through a hair sieve. Pound the pike flesh and mix with 2 dl. of cold thick béchamel, 3 dl. cream, 1 whole egg and 2 yolks. Season with salt and pepper. Pass through a hair sieve, sauté over a quick fire and with the aid of a piping-bag and suitable tube, fill the 20 empty shells with this mixture. Cut the cucumbers into large olive shapes, blanch and stew in butter and add to them the shelled crayfish tails. Poach the sole fillets in the remainder of the white wine and keep warm. Add the sole cooking liquor to the crayfish cooking liquor and the remainder of the cream; bring to the boil and thicken with beurre manié and crayfish butter. Dress the fillets of sole in a crown with the points to the centre on a large round dish. Top each fillet with a mushroom head, mask with the sauce and glaze under the salamander. At the moment of service, pile the cucumber, truffle and crayfish garnish in the centre of the dish and surround the dish with the stuffed crayfish shells and fleurons.
This dish was created by Marcel Haentzler, formerly Chef de Cuisine of the restaurant 'La Cigogne' in London.

Sole Castiglione, Filets de

For 6 persons: *12 fillets of sole; 12 escalopes cooked lobster-tail; 12 cooked mushroom heads; 300 gr. potatoes; 2 dl. fish fumet; 3 dl. white wine sauce; 1 dl. cream sauce.* Cooking time: 8 to 10 minutes.

Fold the fillets, and poach them in the fish fumet. Arrange them on a round serving dish, with the tips pointing towards the centre, and place on each fillet an escalope of lobster and a mushroom-head. Surround with thick roundels of plain boiled potatoes. Coat with white wine sauce mixed with the cream sauce, to which has been added the reduced cooking liquor. Glaze. *(France.)*
(See illustration, page 309.)

Sole au champagne

For 6 persons: *3 soles (400 gr. each); 150 gr. fillets of sole cut into goujons; 3 dl. dry champagne; 3 dl. fish velouté; 150 gr. butter; flour.* Cooking time: 12 to 15 minutes.

Season the soles, and poach them in the champagne. Drain. Reduce the wine by two-thirds, thicken it with the velouté, and work it up with 75 gr. butter. Arrange the soles on an oval serving dish, coat them with the sauce, and glaze. Place at each end of the dish the goujons, which have been floured, sautéd in butter, and kept crisp. *(France.)*

Sole aux champignons, Filets de

For 6 persons: *12 fillets of sole; 250 gr. raw mushrooms; 1 dl. white wine; 40 gr. butter; ½ lemon; 4 dl. white wine sauce; small puff-pastry fleurons.* Cooking time: 10 minutes.

Thinly-slice the mushrooms, cook in the butter without colouring them, with lemon juice and a little water. Drain. Fold the fillets, and poach them in the white wine and the mushroom cooking liquor. Arrange them in a circle on a serving dish, garnish the centre with the mushrooms, and coat the whole with the white wine sauce containing the cooking liquor. Surround with fleurons. *(France.)*

Sole Chauchat, Filets de

Prepare as for Barbue Chauchat. *(See page 245.)*

Sole Choisy, Filets de

For 6 persons: *12 fillets of sole; 12 very small braised lettuce-halves; 125 gr. raw mushrooms; 50 gr. butter; ½ lemon; 1 dl. white wine.* Cooking time: 10 to 12 minutes.

Cut the mushrooms into a julienne, and cook them in butter with lemon juice, a little water and a pinch of salt. Fold the fillets, and poach them in white wine and the mushroom cooking liquor. Arrange them on the trimmed lettuce-halves in a serving dish, and coat them with sauce Mornay to which is added the reduced cooking liquor and the mushrooms. Glaze. *(France.)*

Sole Cléopâtre

For 6 persons: *3 soles (400 gr. each); 180 gr. whiting forcemeat containing cream; 80 gr. truffle; 1 dl. white wine; 1 dl. mushroom cooking liquor; 40 gr. butter; 4 dl. white wine sauce.* Cooking time: 15 to 18 minutes.

Bone the soles, and fill them with the whiting forcemeat containing 30 gr. chopped truffles. Re-shape them, and poach in white wine, mushroom cooking liquor and butter. Drain, arrange on a serving dish and coat with the white wine sauce mixed with the reduced poaching liquor and 50 gr. truffles cut into a fine julienne. Glaze. *(France.)*

Sole Colbert

For 6 persons: *3 soles (450 gr. each) or 6 soles (200 gr. each); 2 eggs; fresh breadcrumbs; 150 to 180 gr. beurre maître d'hôtel; milk; flour.* Cooking time: 12 to 15 minutes.

Lift the fillets on the dark skin side, loosen them from the bone, and break the bone in two or three places so that it can be removed after cooking. Dip the soles in cold pre-boiled milk and in flour. Roll the fillets gently so as to free from the bone, and coat with egg and breadcrumbs. Fry the soles in hot, deep fat, until crisp and golden brown. Arrange the soles on a serving dish, and fill the cavities with beurre maître d'hôtel. *(France.)*
(See Culinary Technique, page 75.)

Sole Colinette, Filets de

For 6 persons: *12 fillets of sole; 150 gr. pike forcemeat; 30 gr. chopped fines herbes; 2 eggs; fresh breadcrumbs; flour; 4 dl. tomato sauce.* Cooking time: 15 minutes.

Slightly flatten the fillets, mask them with pike forcemeat containing fines herbes, fold, pass through flour and coat with egg and breadcrumbs. Fry, and arrange on a serving dish. Serve a light tomato sauce separately. *(France.)*

Sole Condé, Filets de

For 6 persons: *12 fillets of sole; 4 dl. white wine sauce; 1 dl. mushroom cooking liquor; 100 gr. butter; 100 gr. tomato purée.* Cooking time: 10 minutes.

Poach the fillets in the butter and mushroom liquor. Arrange them on a serving dish, and coat with white wine sauce containing the reduced poaching liquor. Mix the tomato purée with the melted butter, and make a border of the purée around the dish and a cross-shape over the sauce. Glaze. *(France.)*

Sole aux crevettes, Filets de

For 6 persons: *12 fillets of sole; 240 gr. picked shrimps; 4 dl. shrimp sauce; 1 dl. white wine; 1 dl. fish fumet.* Cooking time: 8 to 10 minutes.

Fold the fillets, and poach them in the white wine and fish fumet. Arrange in a circle, and garnish the centre with shrimps. Coat the fillets and the garnish with the shrimp sauce containing the reduced cooking liquor. *(France.)*

Sole Cubat, Filets de

For 6 persons: *12 fillets of sole; 240 gr. mushroom purée; 12 slices of truffle; 1 dl. mushroom cooking liquor; 40 gr. butter; 4 dl. sauce Mornay.*

Poach the fillets lengthwise in the mushroom liquor and butter. Mask the bottom of a gratinating dish with the mushroom purée. Arrange the fillets on top, place a slice of truffle on each fillet, and coat with sauce Mornay containing the reduced poaching liquor. Glaze.

Sole "Cyprien", Tonnelets de

Take 8 medium-sized fillets of Dover sole, spread with a whiting forcemeat, and roll into paupiettes. Arrange in a suitable pan previously buttered and sprinkled with chopped shallots. Moisten with fish stock and a glass of dry white wine, lemon juice and mushroom cooking liquor. Garnish the bottom of eight previously baked tartlet cases with a purée of mushrooms. Arrange the paupiettes on top and garnish each one with a scollop of cooked lobster meat topped with a truffle blade. Mask with a sauce Bercy and glaze in a hot oven or under the salamander. Arrange in a crown on a round serving dish and fill the centre with spoon-cut balls of potato cooked golden in butter.
The above recipe was created by the late Mr. A. C. Juriens, formerly Chef de Cuisine of the Caledonian Club, London, S.W.1.

Sole dame brune, Filets de

Filetti di sogliola dama bruna

For 6 persons: *12 fillets of sole; 300 gr. picked shrimps; 250 gr. small noodles; 150 gr. butter; 150 gr. mushrooms; 2 eggs; 60 gr. flour; 2 dl. red wine; 15 cl. jus lié; 50 gr. grated Parmesan cheese; 2 dl. tomato coulis; chopped parsley.* Cooking time for the fillets: about 5 minutes.

Slightly flatten the fillets, flour, coat with egg and breadcrumbs, colour golden, and keep hot. Sauté the quartered mushrooms in the butter used to cook the fillets, moisten with the red wine, add the jus lié, reduce gently, add the shrimps, and keep hot. Drain and season the noodles, which have been previously cooked 'al dente', and add the Parmesan cheese and a knob of butter. Shape the noodles to form a base on an oval serving dish, garnish with the fillets, coat with the sauce containing the shrimps and mushrooms, and sprinkle with chopped parsley. Surround with a border of tomato coulis. *(Italy.)*
(See illustration, page 287.)

Sole Déjazet, Filets de

For 6 persons: *12 fillets of sole; 100 gr. butter; 2 eggs; breadcrumbs; flour; 125 gr. tarragon butter; 24 blanched tarragon leaves.* Cooking time: 8 to 10 minutes.

Slightly flatten the fillets, flour and coat with egg and breadcrumbs, sprinkle with butter and grill gently. Arrange on the partially softened tarragon butter, and garnish each fillet with two tarragon leaves. *(France.)*

Sole Deland, Filets de

For 6 persons: *12 fillets of sole; 100 gr. raw mushrooms; 3 chopped shallots; 1 dl. fish fumet; 1 dl. white wine; 1 coffee-spoonful paprika; 200 gr. cooked noodles; 40 gr. raw noodles; 4 dl. fresh cream; 100 gr. butter.* Cooking time: 8 to 10 minutes.

Lay the fillets lengthwise on a dish which has been buttered, and then sprinkled with chopped shallots and thinly-sliced mushrooms. Moisten with the fish fumet and white wine, and poach. Drain, and arrange on the buttered cooked noodles. Reduce the cooking liquor (without straining it), and add cream and paprika. Allow to cook for a moment, add a little butter to the sauce, adjust seasoning and consistency, coat the fillets with the sauce, and glaze. Surround the fillets with a garnish of the raw noodles coloured in butter.

Sole dieppoise

Prepare as for Maquereau dieppoise. *(See page 274.)*

Sole Donizzetti

Sogliole Donizzetti

For 6 persons: *3 soles (400 gr. each); 1 dl. sauce Nantua; 2 dl. sauce crevettes; 4 dl. sauce vin blanc I; 6 zéphirs of crustaceans (prepared with 300 gr. crustacean forcemeat); 12 mussels; 30 stoned olives; 3 cooked mushroom heads; 9 thin slices of truffle; a few capers.* Cooking time: 12 to 15 minutes.

Poach the soles in the fish fumet, drain, arrange on a serving dish, and coat with the white wine sauce. Garnish with the mussels, poached in white wine and coated with sauce Nantua, and with the zéphirs (coated with sauce crevettes). Garnish the zéphirs and the soles with the slices of truffle. Decorate the fish with the mushrooms, olives and capers. *(Italy.)*
(See illustration, page 288.)

Sole Dugléré

Prepare as for Barbue Dugléré. *(See page 246.)* *(See illustration, page 329.)*

Sole écossaise

Scottish sea brunch

For 6 persons: *6 fillets of sole (75 gr. each); 6 bearded oysters; 6 escalopes cooked lobster; 12 shelled prawns; 2 eggs; 2 lemons; ½ litre batter; 300 gr. straw potatoes; 4 dl. sauce tartare; fine breadcrumbs; flour; parsley.* Cooking time: 6 to 8 minutes.

Cut the fillets into strips 5 cm. long and 12 mm. wide. Season and flour the soles and oysters, and coat with egg and breadcrumbs. Dip the lobster and prawns in the batter, and deep fry all these ingredients. Arrange on a bed of straw potatoes, and garnish with fried parsley and quarters of lemon. Serve the sauce tartare separately. *(Great Britain.)*

Sole à l'étouffée

For 6 persons: *3 soles (450 to 500 gr. each); 1 lemon; 60 gr. butter; 1 tablespoonful chopped parsley;* Cooking time: 12 to 15 minutes.

Remove the head, and cut each sole into three pieces. Season, then half steam the fish in butter in a deep dish. Add lemon juice, a few drops of water and chopped parsley. Finish the cooking in a closed container. *(France.)*

Sole Europe-Unie

Seezunge Vereinigtes Europa

(This dish was created to celebrate Europe Day)

For 6 persons: *6 soles (300 gr. each); 1 tablespoonful chopped shallots; ¼ litre dry white wine; ¼ litre fish stock; 1 dl. mushroom stock; 600 gr. leaf spinach; 100 gr. butter; 1 dl. sauce hollandaise; 60 gr. picked shrimps; 2 lemons; 1 tablespoonful beurre manié; peaches; 6 stoned red cherries.* Cooking time: 20 minutes.

Skin the soles, prepare Colbert, and marinate in lemon juice with salt and pepper. Arrange them upside down in a buttered fish-kettle. Moisten with boiling fish stock and mushroom stock. Add the white wine, cover with a sheet of buttered paper, and poach in the oven. Drain the soles carefully, arrange them, and keep them hot. Colour the shallots, add the blanched spinach, season, and cook quickly. Stuff the soles with this mixture, and garnish them on top with the shrimps which have been heated in butter. Reduce the fish stock by one-third, thicken with the beurre manié, complete with the sauce hollandaise, and correct seasoning and consistency. Coat the soles with the sauce, and glaze under the salamander. Decorate with the cherries, and also with the sliced peaches (arranged in fan-shapes). *(Switzerland.)*

Sole fécampoise, Filets de

For 6 persons: *12 fillets of sole; 24 large mussels; 12 picked shrimps; 4 dl. sauce crevette; 2 dl. fish fumet.* Cooking time: 8 to 10 minutes.

Poach the fillets in the fish fumet, drain, and arrange on a serving dish, surrounded by the mussels (poached and trimmed) and the shrimps. Coat with the sauce crevette. *(France.)*

Sole aux fines herbes

For 6 persons: *3 soles (450 gr. each); 4 dl. white wine sauce; 2 tablespoonfuls fines herbes; 2 dl. fish fumet.* Cooking time: 12 to 15 minutes.

Poach the soles in the fish fumet, drain, and arrange on a serving dish. Coat with white wine sauce containing fines herbes. *(France.)*

Sole florentine

For 6 persons: *3 soles (400 gr. each); 500 gr. blanched leaf spinach; 4 dl. sauce Mornay; 2 dl. fish fumet; 60 gr. butter; 50 gr. grated cheese.* Cooking time: 15 minutes.

Poach the soles in the fish fumet. When the spinach has been well squeezed, stew it in butter, and season it with salt, pepper and a pinch of nutmeg. Spread out the spinach on a gratinating dish, and arrange the soles on top. Coat with sauce Mornay to which the reduced poaching stock has been added, and sprinkle with grated cheese and melted butter. Brown in the oven or under the salamander. This method can also be used for fillets. *(France.)*

Sole froide Edwina, Filets de

Fillet a large Dover sole of about 550 to 600 gr. Trim and soak in cold water. Poach the fillets in the usual manner. Make a fish fumet from the bones and trimmings, with white wine, fish stock, a bouquet garni, strain and allow to cool. Stew together in olive oil 2 chopped shallots and 2 skinned, pipped and diced tomatoes. Moisten with the fish fumet and add 2 or 3 tarragon stalks, season with salt and pepper and allow to reduce by half. When

cold, add 2 spoonfuls of mayonnaise, a liqueur glass of sherry, 2 spoonfuls of olive oil, 1 dl. fresh cream and a few chopped tarragon leaves. Mask the sole fillets with this sauce and with a good scollop of cooked lobster on each fillet.
The above recipe was created by Mr. F. Girotti, formerly Chef de Cuisine at the Junior United Services Club, Charles II Street, London.

Sole "Futuriste", Filets de

Flatten lightly fillets of Dover sole, fold and poach in a good fish stock with white wine; arrange the fillets in a crown on a bed of square-cut raviolis. Arrange in the centre of the crown a salpicon of diced cooked lobster and diced cooked mushrooms bound with a sauce américaine and flavoured with cognac. Mask the fillets with a Mornay sauce, sprinkle with grated Parmesan cheese and brown in a hot oven or under the salamander.
Recipe created by Mr. C. B. Degiuli, Chef de Cuisine of the Stafford Hotel, London.

Sole Georgette, Paupiettes de

For 6 persons: *6 fillets of sole; 6 large potatoes of uniform size and shape; 150 gr. picked shrimps; 7 cl. white wine sauce; 3 dl. sauce Mornay; 2 dl. fish fumet; 40 gr. grated cheese; 25 gr. butter.* Cooking time: 15 minutes.

Bake the potatoes and scoop them out. Roll the fillets into paupiettes and poach them in the fish fumet. Garnish the inside of each potato with the shrimps which have been heated and bound with the white wine sauce. Drain the paupiettes thoroughly, place each inside a potato, coat with sauce Mornay, sprinkle with grated cheese, lightly sprinkle with melted butter, and brown in a hot oven. *(France.)*
(See illustration, page 311. N.B. Different presentation.)

Sole en goujons

For 6 persons: *12 fillets of sole; 2 lemons; parsley; flour; milk.* Cooking time: 6 to 7 minutes.

Cut the fillets lengthwise into short strips 2 cm. wide. Pass them through salted milk, flour them, and fry in smoking, deep fat. Arrange on a napkin, garnished with fried parsley and quarters of lemon. *(France.)*

Sole au gratin

Prepare as for Daurade au gratin. *(See page 259.)*

Sole grillée

Grilled sole

For 6 persons: *6 soles (200 gr. each); milk; flour; 2 lemons; parsley; oil.* Cooking time: 10 to 12 minutes.

Pass the soles through salted milk. Flour and oil them, and grill at a moderate temperature. Arrange on a serving dish, garnished with parsley and quarters of lemon. *(International cookery.)*
(See illustration, page 310.)

Sole Grimaldi, Paupiettes de

For 6 persons: *12 fillets of sole; 180 gr. cooked spaghetti; ½ litre sauce Nantua; 2 dl. fish fumet; 12 thin slices of truffle; 50 gr. butter.* Cooking time: 8 to 10 minutes.

Flatten the fillets, roll them into paupiettes, and poach them in the fish fumet. Bind the spaghetti in butter and arrange in a timbale. Place the paupiettes on top, coat them with the sauce, and garnish each with a slice of truffle. *(France.)*

Sole havraise

For 6 persons: *3 soles (400 gr. each); 24 large mussels (poached and trimmed); 2 dl. fish fumet; ½ litre sauce Bercy; 2 eggs; breadcrumbs.* Cooking time: 12 to 15 minutes.

Poach the soles in the fish fumet, drain, and arrange them. Coat with the sauce Bercy, and garnish with the mussels which have been coated with egg and breadcrumbs and deep fried. *(France.)*

Sole Héloïse

Prepare as for Merlan Bercy, replacing the shallots with 100 gr. chopped raw mushrooms. *(France.)* *(See page 276.)*

Sole hongroise

For 6 persons: *3 soles (450 gr. each); 75 gr. chopped onions; 200 gr. peeled, pipped and chopped tomatoes; 1 dl. fish fumet; 1 dl. white wine; 1 dl. fresh cream; 3 dl. fish velouté; 5 gr. paprika; 40 gr. butter.* Cooking time: 15 minutes.

Lay the soles in an oval metal dish which has been thickly buttered and sprinkled with chopped onions. Season, cover with the tomatoes, moisten with the white wine and the fumet, cover with greaseproof paper, and poach in the oven. When the fish is cooked, remove the cooking liquor (without the tomatoes), add it to the velouté, add the cream and the paprika, which has been dissolved in a little water, reduce the sauce to the required consistency, and correct seasoning. Pass the sauce, and use it to coat the soles and tomatoes. *(France.)*

Sole aux huîtres

For 6 persons: *3 soles (450 gr. each); 4 dl. white wine sauce; 18 oysters; 1 dl. white wine; 40 gr. butter.* Cooking time: 12 to 15 minutes.

Poach the oysters in their liquor, trim them, and keep the liquor. Poach the soles in the white wine, butter and oyster liquor. Arrange them on a serving dish, and garnish with the oysters. Coat the soles with the white wine sauce to which has been added the reduced cooking liquor. *(France.)*

Sole impériale

For 6 persons: *3 soles (400 gr. each); 4 dl. white wine sauce; 12 shelled crayfish; 40 gr. truffle; 12 large soft roes; 2 dl. fish fumet; 50 gr. butter; ½ lemon; 12 small fleurons.* Cooking time: 12 to 15 minutes.

Poach the soles in the fish fumet, and add the soft roes (cooked in butter and lemon juice). Blend the reduced cooking liquor with the white wine sauce. Arrange the soles on a serving dish, and garnish with the roes, and also with the crayfish which have been heated in butter. Coat with the white wine sauce. Sprinkle with a julienne of truffle, and surround with fleurons. *(France.)*

Sole infante, Filets de

For 6 persons: *12 fillets of sole; 4 dl. sauce Mornay; 180 gr. mushroom purée; 2 dl. fish fumet; 50 gr. grated cheese.* Cooking time: 8 to 10 minutes.

Poach the fillets in the fumet. Reduce the cooking liquor, and add it to the sauce Mornay. Place the mushrooms in a gratinating dish, and arrange the fillets on top. Coat with sauce Mornay, sprinkle with grated cheese, and glaze either in the oven or under the salamander. *(France.)*

Sole Isadore

For 6 persons: *6 Dover soles (of 200 gr. each); ¼ litre of white wine sauce; 120 gr. purée of cooked crabmeat; 1 dl. sauce américaine; 6 turned and cooked mushroom heads; 6 shelled prawns; fish stock; 6 slices of truffle; fleurons; butter.* Cooking time: 25 minutes.

Shallow poach the prepared soles in fish stock, drain well, and trim the side bones, keep warm covered with buttered paper. Heat the purée of crab in a little butter and bind with sauce américaine. Place the prepared crab on the bottom of the serving dish and arrange the soles on top. Mask with the hot white wine sauce. Arrange on each sole a turned mushroom head and prawn previously warmed in butter. Pass under the grill (salamander). Garnish with a slice of truffle on each sole and surround with fleurons.

Sole Jean-Bart, Filets de

For 6 persons: *12 fillets of sole; 2 dl. fish fumet; 18 small mussels; 100 gr. picked shrimps; 100 gr. small cooked mushroom heads; 4 dl. sauce normande; 1 dl. sauce béchamel; 1 dl. sauce Mornay; 12 large mussels.* Cooking time: 10 to 12 minutes.

Fold the fillets, and poach them in the fish fumet. Prepare a salpicon with the picked shrimps, mushrooms, and small mussels (poached and trimmed). Bind it with the sauce béchamel containing a little of the reduced cooking liquor. Cook the large mussels; shell and trim them, put them back into the half-shells; coat them with sauce Mornay and glaze. Arrange the fillets in a ring on a round flat serving dish, with the salpicon in the centre. Coat the fillets with sauce normande, and surround them with the glazed mussels. *(France.)*

Sole Jeannette, Paupiettes de

For 6 persons: *12 fillets of sole; 180 gr. fish forcemeat; 60 gr. purée de foie gras; 2 dl. fish fumet; 1 dl. fresh cream; 4 dl. white wine sauce; 12 thin slices of truffle; 50 gr. butter.* Cooking time: 10 to 12 minutes.

Flatten the fillets, mask them with fish forcemeat containing purée de foie gras, and roll them into paupiettes. Arrange in a buttered sauteuse, moisten with fish fumet, cover with buttered paper, and poach in the oven. Drain the paupiettes, and arrange them

▲ Sardines Savoia Beeler, p. 296

Sole Yvette, p. 344 ▼

▲ Rougets Francillon, p. 290

Rougets grillés, p. 291 ▼

▲ Rougets Porto Venere, p. 293

Sardines courtisane, p. 294 ▼

▲ Filets de sole Orlanda, p. 319

Paupiettes de sole mexicaine, p. 315 ▼

▲ Filets de sole Castiglione, p. 299

Filets de sole St. Valéry, p. 326 ▼

▲ Sole grillée, p. 303

Sole Savoy, p. 340 ▼

▲ Sole printanière, p. 322

Paupiettes de sole Georgette, p. 303 ▼

▲ Sole sultane, p. 326

Quenelles de brochet aux crevettes, p. 377 ▼

on a round serving dish. Reduce the poaching liquor (with the cream), and incorporate it in the white wine sauce. Coat the paupiettes and place a slice of truffle on each. This dish can be served cold, glazed with fish jelly. *(France.)*

Sole Joinville, Filets de

For 6 persons: *12 fillets of sole; 300 gr. Joinville garnish; 4 dl. sauce Joinville; 2 dl. fish fumet; 12 thin slices of truffle.* Cooking time: 8 to 10 minutes.

Fold the fillets, and poach them in fish fumet. Arrange them in a circle on a round serving dish, with the Joinville garnish in the centre. Coat the fillets and the garnish with sauce Joinville, and place a slice of truffle on each fillet.

Sole Léopold, Filets de

For 6 persons: *12 fillets of sole; 180 gr. picked shrimps; 2 dl. sauce crevette; 2 dl. sauce genevoise; 7 cl. white wine sauce; 2 dl. fish fumet; 20 gr. chopped truffle; 20 gr. chopped lobster coral.* Cooking time: 8 to 10 minutes.

Fold the fillets, and poach them in the fish fumet. Arrange them on a round serving dish, with the tips pointing towards the centre. Coat every other fillet with sauce crevette, and the rest with sauce genevoise. Sprinkle the 'pink' fillets with chopped truffle, and the 'brown' fillets with chopped coral. Garnish the centre with the shrimps bound with the white wine sauce. *(France.)*
(See illustration, page 339. N.B. Different presentation.)

Sole Liepaja, Filets de

Seezungenfilets Liepaja

For 6 persons: *6 large fillets of sole; 500 gr. boned and skinned fresh salmon; 6 large mushroom heads; 2 dl. fish fumet; 1 dl. fresh cream; 1 dl. sauce hollandaise; 30 gr. beurre manié; 50 gr. butter.* Poaching time: 10 to 15 minutes.

Flatten and lightly score the fillets. Press each fillet into a buttered cylindrical mould 8 cm. (approx. 3 in.) wide so that it is touching the inner surfaces, but with each end of the fillet protruding. Place the moulds on a buttered fish dish; fill them with the slightly salted and finely chopped salmon, and pile up this garnish to make a dome. Fold the ends of the fillets over on the salmon, and press them down to make them stick. Pour on a little fish fumet; cover with greased paper, and poach in the oven. Demould, and garnish each piece with a mushroom head. Reduce the fish fumet (to which has been added a little poaching stock), thicken with the beurre manié; add the cream, correct seasoning and consistency, and mix with the sauce hollandaise. Coat the fillets with this sauce, and glaze under the salamander. *(Germany.)*

Sole Louis XV

For 6 persons: *3 soles (450 gr. each); 4 dl. white wine sauce; 1 dl. fish fumet; 1 dl. white wine; 12 thin slices of truffle; 40 gr. chopped coral.* Cooking time: 12 to 15 minutes.

Poach the soles in the fish fumet and the white wine. Reduce the poaching liquor, and add it to the white wine sauce. Arrange the soles on a serving dish; coat them with the sauce; sprinkle with the coral, and place 4 slices of truffle on each. *(France.)*

Délices de sole "Mademoiselle Vingt-et-un"

Take some fresh Scotch salmon free of skin and bone, and an equal quantity of fresh cream and prepare a very light salmon mousse, sufficient to fill one ring mould. Poach gently au bain-marie. When cooked turn out on to a round serving dish; fill the centre with a salpicon of picked prawns, poached and bearded oysters bound with well-buttered sauce vin blanc. Surround the salmon mousse with previously prepared small paupiettes of sole poached in white wine and oyster poaching liquor, each paupiette masked with a creamed fish velouté. Garnish with truffle blades and very white, cooked turned mushrooms. Serve separately cooked cucumber cases filled with buttered asparagus tips.
The above recipe was created by the late Mr. Arthur Hope, formerly Chef de Cuisine of the Tregenna Castle Hotel, St. Ives, Cornwall, and of international repute.

Sole Manolo, Paupiettes de

For 6 persons: *12 small paupiettes of fillets of sole; 12 cooked globe artichoke-bases; 6 tablespoonfuls mushroom purée; 4 dl. sauce hollandaise; 2 dl. fish fumet; 50 gr. butter.* Cooking time for the paupiettes: 7 to 8 minutes.

Season the paupiettes, and poach in the fish fumet. Pass the artichoke-bases through butter, and arrange them in a buttered gratinating dish. Fill them with a little mushroom purée, and arrange on top the paupiettes (which have been well drained beforehand). Reduce the cooking liquor almost to a glaze, and blend it with the sauce hollandaise. Coat the paupiettes with sauce, and glaze quickly under the salamander. *(Spain.)*

Sole Marguéry, Filets de

For 6 persons: *12 fillets of sole; 24 poached and bearded mussels; 120 gr. picked shrimps; 2 dl. fish fumet; 4 dl. white wine sauce.* Cooking time: 8 to 10 minutes.

Leave the fillets flat, and poach them in the fish fumet. Arrange them on a serving dish, and surround them with the shrimps and mussels. Coat the fillets and the garnish with white wine sauce. Glaze quickly. *(France.)*

Sole marinière

For 6 persons: *3 soles (400 gr. each); 12 oysters; 18 small mussels; 120 gr. picked shrimps; 2 dl. fish fumet; 4 dl. sauce marinière.* Cooking time: 12 to 15 minutes.

Poach the soles in the fish fumet and the mussel liquor. Arrange the soles on a serving dish; place 4 poached and bearded oysters on each; surround with the shrimps and mussels, and coat with sauce marinière. *(France.)*

Sole mascotte, Paupiettes de

For 6 persons: *12 fillets of sole; 120 gr. fish forcemeat; 300 gr. purée duchesse; 150 gr. cooked lobster meat; 50 gr. truffle; 2 dl. fish fumet; 1 dl. fish velouté; 4 cl. fresh cream; 4 dl. sauce Mornay; 50 gr. butter.* Cooking time: 12 minutes.

Flatten the fillets, mask with fish forcemeat, and roll into paupiettes. Arrange these on a buttered fish dish; moisten with the fish fumet; cover with buttered paper and poach in the oven. Border a round gratinating dish with purée duchesse, using a star piping-tube. Prepare a salpicon with lobster and truffle, and bind with the lightly-creamed fish velouté. Arrange the paupiettes in a ring, place the salpicon in the centre, coat with sauce Mornay, and glaze. *(France.)*
(See illustration, page 335.)

Sole Mathilde

For 6 persons: *3 soles (400 gr. each); 100 gr. purée Soubise; 300 gr. cucumber, olive-shaped; 2 dl. fish fumet; 4 dl. white wine sauce; 60 gr. butter.* Cooking time: 12 to 15 minutes.

Stew the cucumber in butter, and season. Poach the soles in the fish fumet. Reduce the poaching liquor, add it to the white wine sauce, and incorporate the purée Soubise. Coat the soles, and arrange the garnish of cucumber at each end of the serving dish. *(France.)*

Sole Maurice

Proceed as for the preparation of Filets de sole fécampoise but leaving the soles whole. *(France.)* *(See page 302.)*

Sole ménagère

For 6 persons: *3 soles (450 gr. each); 120 gr. butter; ½ litre red wine; 25 gr. flour; 3 chopped shallots; bouquet garni.* Cooking time: 12 to 15 minutes.

Butter a fish dish, and sprinkle it with chopped shallots. Lay the soles on the dish, season, moisten with the red wine, add the bouquet garni, cover and poach. Drain the soles, and arrange them on a serving dish. Pass the cooking liquor, reduce it and bind it with beurre manié made from 40 gr. butter and 25 gr. flour. Monter au beurre, correct seasoning and consistency, and use to coat the soles. *(France.)*

Sole mère Récamier

For 6 persons: *6 soles (300 gr. each); 100 gr. button mushrooms; 100 gr. cooked lobster meat; 100 gr. picked shrimps; 50 gr. butter; 2 tablespoonfuls fish velouté; 2 dl. fresh cream; 1 tablespoonful sauce hollandaise; 6 thin slices of truffle; 2 eggs; fresh white breadcrumbs.* Cooking time: about 20 minutes.

Prepare the soles as for Colbert, coat with egg and breadcrumbs, and fry them in hot, deep fat. Lightly colour in butter the shrimps and the diced mushrooms and lobster. Blend with the fish velouté and fresh cream; allow to cook for a few minutes to ensure even mixing, and finish the sauce with the hollandaise. Correct seasoning and consistency. Remove the backbones from the cooked soles, and fill the cavities with the prepared garnish. Brown in a hot oven. Garnish each sole with a slice of truffle placed in the centre. *(Switzerland.)*
(See illustration, page 338.)

Sole Matternich, Filets de

For 6 persons: *12 fillets of sole; 4 dl. white wine sauce; 5 gr. paprika; 1 dl. fish fumet; 1 dl. white wine; 40 gr. butter.* Cooking time: 8 to 10 minutes.

Lay the fillets on a buttered dish, moisten with the white wine and fish fumet, and poach. Cook the paprika quickly in butter, add the poaching liquor, reduce and pass it, and blend it with the white wine sauce. Use the sauce to coat the fillets, and place a slice of truffle on each. *(France.)*

Sole meunière

For 6 persons: *3 soles (450 to 500 gr. each); 200 gr. butter; 1 lemon; flour; 1 tablespoonful chopped parsley; milk.* Cooking time: 15 minutes.

Dip the soles in milk, season and flour them, and shallow fry them in hot, clarified butter. Arrange them on a serving dish, squeeze the lemon juice over them, and sprinkle with the chopped parsley and beurre noisette. *(France.)*

Sole mexicaine, Paupiettes de

For 6 persons: *12 fillets of sole; 180 gr. fish forcemeat; 12 large mushroom heads; 120 gr. peeled, pipped and chopped tomatoes; 30 gr. diced red pepper; 2 dl. fish fumet; 1 tablespoonful tomato purée; 4 dl. sauce béchamel; 75 gr. butter.* Cooking time: 10 to 12 minutes.

Flatten the fillets, mask them with the forcemeat, roll them into paupiettes, and poach in the fish fumet. Grill the mushroom heads, and arrange them inverted on a round serving dish. Fill each with ½ tablespoonful of the chopped tomatoes, and place a paupiette on each. Coat the paupiettes with sauce béchamel containing tomato purée and the diced red peppers (which have been stewed in butter). *(France.)*
(See illustration, page 308. N.B. Different presentation.)

Sole mignonnette, Filets de

For 6 persons: *12 fillets of sole; 240 gr. cooked noisette potatoes; 150 gr. butter; 24 thin slices of truffle; 40 gr. meat glaze; the juice of 1 lemon; flour.* Cooking time: 8 to 10 minutes.

Cut each fillet into two escalopes, season, and flour. Colour them golden in hot clarified butter. Arrange them in a timbale, and surround them with the noisette potatoes. Place on the fillets the slices of truffle which have been passed through the meat glaze. Work up the glaze with butter, add the lemon juice, and pour over the fillets and the garnish. *(France.)*

Sole minute, Filets de

For 6 persons: *12 fillets of sole; 120 gr. butter; flour.* Cooking time: 8 minutes.

Flatten the fillets, season and flour them, and cook them gently in hot, clarified butter. Arrange them on a serving dish, and sprinkle them with the butter from the cooking. Serve very hot. *(France.)*

Sole Mirabeau, Filets de

For 6 persons: *12 fillets of sole; 120 gr. anchovy butter; 24 thin strips of anchovy fillets; 24 blanched tarragon leaves.* Cooking time: 8 to 10 minutes.

Season and flour the fillets, and cook them in the anchovy butter. Arrange them on a serving dish, and place on each fillet 2 strips of anchovy fillet and 2 blanched tarragon leaves. Sprinkle with the cooking butter. *(France.)*

Sole Miramar I

For 6 persons: *12 fillets of sole; 180 gr. pilaf rice; 2 egg-plants; 150 gr. butter; flour.* Cooking time: 8 to 10 minutes.

Cut each fillet into 3 escalopes, season and flour them, and cook them in butter. Cut the egg-plants into 12 roundels, flour them, and sauté in butter until they are very crisp. Arrange the rice in a timbale, place the roundels of egg-plant in a ring, and lay the fillets in the centre. Sprinkle the whole dish with noisette butter. *(France.)*
(See illustration, page 267.)

Sole Miramar II

Proceed as for the preparation of Cabillaud portugaise, adding a fine julienne of lettuce stewed in butter. *(France.)* *(See page 255.)*

Sole Mireille

For 6 persons: *3 soles (450 gr. each); 2 eggs; fresh white breadcrumbs; flour; 250 gr. peeled, pipped and chopped tomatoes; 1 crushed clove of garlic; 1 coffee-spoonful chopped fines herbes; 3 dl. sauce béarnaise; 2 dl. olive oil.* Cooking time: about 15 minutes.

Soften the tomatoes in oil, season them, and add the garlic and the fines herbes. Prepare

the soles as for Colbert, and fry them in oil. Arrange them on a serving dish, and remove the backbones. Fill the cavities with sauce béarnaise, and surround the soles with the tomatoes. *(France.)*
(See illustration, page 338.)

Sole Miromesnil

For 6 persons: *3 soles (450 gr. each); 100 gr. peeled, pipped and chopped tomatoes; 60 gr. fine julienne of lettuce; 40 gr. julienne of truffle; 100 gr. butter; 2 dl. fish fumet; 2 dl. white wine.* Cooking time: 12 to 15 minutes.

Place the soles on a buttered fish dish, and cover them with the julienne of lettuce (previously stewed in butter), the chopped tomatoes, and the julienne of truffle. Moisten with the fish fumet and white wine, cover, and poach. When the soles are cooked, drain them, and arrange them on a serving dish. Reduce the poaching liquor by two-thirds, monter au beurre, correct seasoning and consistency, and pour over the soles. *(France.)*

Sole Mogador, Filets de

For 6 persons: *12 fillets of sole; 150 gr. mousseline forcemeat; 250 gr. whiting forcemeat (containing cream and chopped truffle); 12 thin slices of truffle; 12 crayfish shells; 100 gr. picked shrimps; 200 gr. Nantua garnish; 4 dl. sauce Nantua; 1 dl. white wine; 1 dl. fish fumet; 40 gr. butter.* Cooking time: 18 to 20 minutes.

Mask the fillets with the mousseline forcemeat, fold them, and poach in the white wine and fish fumet. Fill a buttered, shallow savarin mould with whiting forcemeat, and poach in a bain-marie. Prepare a salpicon with the picked shrimps bound with a little of the whiting forcemeat. Use the salpicon to fill the crayfish shells, and pass them briefly through a low oven to poach. Take the whiting forcemeat from the mould on to a round serving dish, arrange the fillets on top, and place a slice of truffle on each fillet. Pour the Nantua garnish into the centre, and surround the edge of the dish with the crayfish shells. Serve the sauce Nantua separately. *(France.)*

Sole Monaco, Filets de

For 6 persons: *12 fillets of sole; 4 dl. white wine sauce; 1 tablespoonful chopped fines herbes; 1 tablespoonful tomato purée; 12 oysters; 2 dl. white wine; 60 gr. butter; 12 heart-shaped bread croûtons.* Cooking time: 8 to 10 minutes.

Flatten and fold the fillets, and poach them in the white wine. Mix the white wine sauce with the reduced poaching liquor, and add the tomato purée and the chopped fines herbes. Arrange the fillets on a serving dish, place on each a poached and bearded oyster, and coat with the sauce. Garnish with the croûtons fried in clarified butter. *(France.)*

Sole Monte-Carlo, Filet de

For 6 persons: *12 fillets of sole; 150 gr. butter; 6 gr. capers; anchovy essence; flour.* Cooking time: 8 to 10 minutes.

Season and flour the fillets, and cook them in butter. Arrange on a serving dish, and sprinkle with the capers, a few drops of anchovy essence, and beurre noisette. *(France.)*

Sole Montespan, Filets de

For 6 persons: *12 fillets of sole; 100 gr. raw mushrooms; 1 tablespoonful fines herbes; 100 gr. butter; 1 dl. white wine; 2 dl. fish fumet.* Cooking time: 8 to 10 minutes.

Sprinkle the base of a buttered fish dish with thinly-sliced mushrooms. Arrange the fillets on top, sprinkle with fines herbes, moisten with the white wine and fish fumet, cover with buttered paper, and poach in the oven. Drain off the cooking liquor, reduce it, and monter au beurre. Arrange the fillets (covered with the mushrooms) on a serving dish, and coat with the stock. *(France.)*

Sole Mongolfier, Filets de

For 6 persons: *12 fillets of sole; 30 gr. carrot; 30 gr. raw mushrooms; 30 gr. truffle; 2 dl. fish fumet; 4 dl. white wine sauce; 50 gr. butter; 12 small puff-pastry fleurons.* Cooking time: 8 to 10 minutes.

Cut the carrot, mushrooms and truffle into a fine julienne, and stew in butter. Poach the fish fillets in the fish fumet, and drain them. Reduce the poaching liquor, and add it to the white wine sauce. Add the julienne to this sauce, and use it to coat the fillets. Surround with the fleurons. *(France.)*

Sole Montreuil

For 6 persons: *3 soles (400 gr. each); 3 dl. white wine sauce; 1 dl. sauce crevettes; 1 dl. white wine; 1 dl. fish fumet; 240 gr. balls of potato cut to the size of walnuts with a spoon-cutter.* Cooking time: 12 to 15 minutes.

Poach the soles in the white wine and fish fumet. Drain them, arrange on a serving dish, and surround with the potatoes (which have been plain boiled and kept whole). Coat the soles with the white wine sauce, and the potatoes with the sauce crevettes. *(France.)*

Sole Montreux, Filets de

For 6 persons: *12 fillets of sole; 12 roundels of cooked potatoes; 24 thin slices of truffle; 4 dl. sauce Mornay; 30 gr. grated cheese; 2 dl. fish fumet.* Cooking time: 10 to 12 minutes.

Fold the fillets in two, and poach them in the fish fumet. Arrange on a serving dish, and surround with the roundels of potato alternating with the slices of truffle. Coat all over with the sauce Mornay, sprinkle with grated cheese, and brown. *(France.)*

Sole Montrouge, Filets de

For 6 persons: *12 fillets of sole; 200 gr. thinly-sliced cooked mushrooms; ½ litre sauce béchamel; 5 cl. fresh cream; 75 gr. mushroom purée; 2 dl. mushroom cooking liquor.* Cooking time: 8 to 10 minutes.

Fold the fillets, and poach them in the mushroom liquor. Arrange them in a ring on a serving dish, and garnish the centre with the sliced mushrooms bound with lightly-creamed sauce béchamel. Coat the fillets with creamed sauce béchamel blended with the reduced poaching liquor and cooked mushroom purée. *(France.)*

Sole Mornay

For 6 persons: *3 soles (450 to 500 gr. each); 2 dl. white wine; 4 dl. sauce Mornay; 40 gr. grated cheese; 25 gr. butter.* Cooking time: 12 to 15 minutes.

Poach the soles in the white wine, drain them, and arrange on a serving dish. Reduce the poaching liquor, and add it to the sauce Mornay. Coat the soles with this sauce, sprinkle with grated cheese, and brown in a hot oven (or under the salamander). *(France.)*

Sole aux moules

Sole with mussels

Proceed as for the preparation of Merlan aux moules. *(See page 278.)*

Sole Mourier

For 6 persons: *3 soles (400 gr. each); 2 dl. hock; 1 dl. fish fumet; 30 gr. celery; 30 gr. truffle; 12 large mushroom heads; 24 green asparagus tips; 12 small croquettes of lobster; 120 gr. butter.* Cooking time: 12 to 15 minutes.

Poach the soles in the hock and fish fumet containing the celery and truffle cut into a fine brunoise. Drain the soles, and arrange them on a serving dish. Reduce the cooking liquor by two-thirds, monter au beurre, correct seasoning and consistency, and use to coat the soles. Garnish with the mushroom heads (cooked and filled with asparagus tips bound in butter) and the cooked croquettes of lobster, alternating the two garnishes around the dish. *(France.)*

Sole Murat, Goujons de

For 6 persons: *12 fillets of sole; 200 gr. raw potatoes; 6 globe artichoke-bases; 12 thick roundels of tomato; 150 gr. butter; 5 cl. olive oil; 1 lemon; 1 coffee-spoonful chopped parsley; flour.* Cooking time: 10 to 12 minutes.

Dice the potatoes and raw artichokes and sauté them separately in butter. Cut up the fillets into goujons, season and flour them, and sauté in butter. Mix together the fillets, potatoes and artichokes, and sauté them for 2 or 3 minutes. Arrange in a timbale, and add the roundels of tomato (which have been seasoned and sautéed in smoking oil). Squeeze the lemon juice on top, and sprinkle with chopped parsley and noisette butter. *(France.)*

Sole Nantua

For 6 persons: *3 soles (400 gr. each); 18 shelled crayfish; 12 thin slices of truffle; 4 dl. sauce Nantua; 2 dl. fish fumet; 5 cl. mushroom cooking liquor.* Cooking time: 12 to 15 minutes.

Poach the soles in the fish fumet and mushroom liquor. Drain, and arrange them on a serving dish. Surround them with the crayfish, and coat with the sauce Nantua. Arrange 4 slices of truffle in the centre of each sole. *(France.)*

Sole Nelson, Filets de

For 6 persons: *12 fillets of sole; 12 escalopes of soft roe; 240 gr. noisette potatoes; 1 dl. white wine; 1 dl. fish fumet; 4 dl. white wine sauce; 75 gr. butter; ½ lemon.* Cooking time: 8 to 10 minutes.

Fold the fillets, and poach them in the fish fumet and white wine. Arrange in a ring on a serving dish. Coat the fillets with the white wine sauce blended with the reduced and lightly buttered poaching stock, and glaze. Garnish the centre of the dish with the noisette potatoes, and surround the fillets with the escalopes of soft roe, which have been stewed in butter and lemon juice. *(France.)*

Sole Nemours, Filets de

For 6 persons: *12 fillets of sole; 180 gr. fish forcemeat; 100 gr. poached escalopes of soft roe; 12 fish quenelles; 12 small cooked mushroom heads; 4 dl. sauce crevettes; 1 dl. sauce normande; 12 small shrimp croquettes rolled in beaten egg and chopped truffle; 12 thin slices of truffle; 100 gr. butter; 2 dl. fish fumet.* Cooking time: 10 to 12 minutes.

Flatten the fillets, mask them with forcemeat, fold them in two, and poach them in the fish fumet. Drain, and arrange in a ring on a serving dish. Place a slice of truffle on each fillet, and coat with sauce crevettes. Garnish the centre of the dish with a salpicon of soft roe, quenelles and mushroom heads, bound with sauce normande. Surround the fillets with the shrimp croquettes (fried in clarified butter). *(France.)*

Sole Newburg, Filets de

For 6 persons: *12 fillets of sole; 12 thin escalopes of cooked lobster-tails; 12 thin slices of truffle; 4 dl. fish fumet; 4 dl. sauce Newburg.* Cooking time: 8 to 10 minutes.

Fold the fillets, and poach them in the fish fumet. Arrange in a ring on a serving dish, and garnish each fillet with an escalope of lobster and a slice of truffle. Coat with sauce Newburg. *(France.)*
(See illustration, page 336.)

Sole niçoise

For 6 persons: *3 soles (400 gr. each); 250 gr. peeled, pipped and chopped tomatoes; 1 clove of garlic; 6 slices of peeled and pipped lemon; 12 black olives; 12 anchovy fillets; 100 gr. anchovy butter; 1 dl. oil; ½ coffee-spoonful chopped tarragon; flour.* Cooking time: 12 to 15 minutes.

Season, flour and oil the soles, and grill them lightly. Melt the chopped tomatoes in oil with a crushed clove of garlic and the chopped tarragon. Arrange the soles on a serving dish, and garnish them with the slices of lemon, the anchovy fillets and black olives. Surround with the chopped tomatoes, and pour on top the half-melted anchovy butter. *(France.)*

Sole Noilly

For 6 persons: *3 soles (400 gr. each); 1 dl. fish fumet; 1 dl. Noilly-Prat Vermouth; 150 gr. thinly-sliced raw mushrooms; 1 lemon; 60 gr. butter; 4 dl. white wine sauce.* Cooking time: 12 to 15 minutes.

Arrange the soles on a buttered fish dish which has then been sprinkled with the thinly-sliced mushrooms. Moisten with the fish fumet, vermouth and lemon juice. Season, cover with buttered paper, and poach in the oven. Arrange the soles on a serving dish with the mushrooms. Reduce the cooking liquor, blend with the sauce, and use to coat the soles. *(France.)*

Sole normande

For 6 persons: *3 soles (400 gr. each); 2 dl. fish fumet; 300 gr. normande garnish; 4 dl. sauce normande.* Cooking time: 12 to 15 minutes.

Poach the soles in the fish fumet, drain them, and arrange them on a serving dish. Surround with normande garnish, and coat with sauce normande. *(France.)*

Sole d'Offémont, Filets de

For 6 persons: *12 fillets of sole; 2 dl. fish fumet; 3 chopped shallots; 3 dl. white wine sauce; 2 dl. fresh cream; 150 gr. morels; 12 small truffles olive-shaped; 50 gr. butter.* Cooking time: 8 to 10 minutes.

Fold the fillets, arrange them on a buttered dish which has been sprinkled with chopped shallots, and poach in fish fumet. Reduce the fumet with 1 dl. cream, and add it to the white wine sauce. Stew the morels in butter, and bind them with the cream. Arrange the fillets in a ring on a serving dish, coat them with the sauce, and fill the centre of the dish with the morels and truffles. *(France.)*

Sole Olga, Paupiettes de

Proceed as for the preparation of Paupiettes de sole Georgette, but coat with white wine sauce, and glaze. *(See page 303.)*

Sole opéra

For 6 persons: *3 soles (400 gr. each); 2 dl. fish fumet; 4 dl. white wine sauce; 100 gr. truffle turned into small balls with a spoon-cutter; 150 gr. green asparagus tips; 50 gr. butter.* Cooking time: 12 to 15 minutes.

Poach the soles in the fish fumet, drain, and arrange them on a serving dish. Coat with the white wine sauce. Garnish with the truffle and also with the asparagus tips which have been bound in butter. *(France.)*

Sole orientale, Filets de

For 6 persons: *12 fillets of sole; 2 dl. fish fumet; 180 gr. rice; 4 dl. sauce Newburg; 3 gr. curry powder.* Cooking time: 8 to 10 minutes.

Fold the fillets, and poach them in the fish fumet. Drain and arrange them in a ring on a serving dish. Coat with sauce Newburg flavoured with curry. Arrange the plain boiled rice in the centre of the dish. *(France.)*

Sole Orlanda, Filets de

For 6 persons: *12 fillets of sole; 12 oval vol-au-vent cases; 120 gr. cooked mushrooms; 150 gr. clams (poached and shelled); 2 dl. fish fumet; 4 gr. curry powder; ½ litre sauce américaine.* Cooking time: 8 to 10 minutes.

Fold the fillets, poach them in the fish fumet, and drain them. Prepare a salpicon with the mushrooms and clams, and bind it with a few tablespoonfuls of sauce américaine. Use this salpicon to fill the vol-au-vent cases, place them on a serving dish, and arrange the fillets on top. Coat with sauce américaine flavoured with curry. The vol-au-vent cases can be replaced by boat-shaped puff-pastry cases lightly baked. *(France.)*
(See illustration, page 308.)

Sole Orléans, Paupiettes de

For 6 persons: *12 fillets of sole; 12 small puff-pastry cases; 180 gr. truffled whiting forcemeat; 60 gr. picked shrimps; 60 gr. cooked mushrooms; 20 gr. truffle; 12 slices of truffle; 12 prawns; 2 dl. fish fumet; 1 dl. white wine sauce; 4 dl. sauce crevettes.* Cooking time: 10 to 12 minutes.

Flatten the fillets, mask them with the forcemeat, roll them into paupiettes, and poach them in the fish fumet. Prepare a salpicon with the shrimps, mushrooms and truffle, and bind it with the white wine sauce. Fill the puff-pastry cases to two-thirds with this salpicon, and place a paupiette on each. Coat with sauce crevettes, place a slice of truffle on each paupiette, and skewer it with a cooked prawn, the tail of which has been shelled. *(France.)*

Sole Orly, Filets de

For 6 persons: *12 fillets of sole; ½ litre batter; 4 dl. sauce tomates; parsley.* Cooking time: 8 minutes.

Season the fillets, dip them in the batter, and fry immediately before serving. Arrange on a napkin, and decorate with fried parsley. Serve the sauce tomates separately. *(France.)*

Sole ostendaise, Filets de

For 6 persons: *12 fillets of sole; 120 gr. fish forcemeat; 24 oysters; 12 small diamond-shaped sole croquettes; 12 thin slices of truffle; 4 dl. sauce normande; 40 gr. butter.* Cooking time: 10 to 12 minutes.

Flatten the fillets, mask them with the fish forcemeat, fold them in two, and poach in the butter and oyster liquor. Arrange the fillets in a ring on a serving dish, with the poached and bearded oysters in the centre. Coat with the sauce normande containing the reduced poaching liquor. Place a slice of truffle on each fillet. Surround the fillets with the croquettes. *(France.)*

Sole Otéro, Paupiettes de

Proceed as for the preparation of Paupiettes de sole Olga. *(See page 318.)*

Sole Othello

For 6 persons: *3 soles (450 gr. each); 120 gr. raw mushrooms; 12 thin slices of truffle; 3 chopped shallots; 2 dl. fish fumet; 1 dl. white wine; 120 gr. butter.* Cooking time: 15 minutes.

Loosen the fillets from the backbones, and slip a nut of butter under each fillet. Place the soles on a buttered fish dish sprinkled with the chopped shallots and mushrooms. Moisten with the fish fumet and white wine, and poach in the oven. Remove the soles, and arrange them on a serving dish. Reduce the cooking liquor almost to a glaze, monter au beurre, use to coat the fillets, and glaze quickly. Place 4 slices of truffle on each sole. *(France.)*

Sole Pagani, Filets de

For 6 persons: *12 fillets of sole; 1 dl. white wine; 1 dl. mushroom cooking liquor; 12 large mussels; 12 oysters; 12 cooked mushroom heads; 4 dl. white wine sauce; 40 gr. grated cheese.* Cooking time: 8 to 10 minutes.

Poach the fillets in the white wine and mushroom liquor. Reduce the poaching liquor, and add it to the white wine sauce. Arrange the fillets on a serving dish, and garnish them with the mushroom heads and the poached and bearded oysters and mussels. Coat with the sauce, sprinkle with the grated cheese, and glaze. *(France.)*

Sole Paillard

For 6 persons: *3 soles (400 gr. each); 3 chopped shallots; 150 gr. morels; 100 gr. butter; 1 coffee-spoonful chopped parsley; 1 dl. fish fumet; 2 dl. white wine; ½ lemon; 6 shelled crayfish; 12 small heart-shaped croûtons.* Cooking time: 12 to 15 minutes.

Lay the soles on a heavily-buttered fish dish (sprinkled with chopped shallots). Moisten with the white wine and fish fumet, add 60 gr. butter, and cook in the oven, basting frequently. The near completion of the reduction must coincide with the completion of the cooking of the soles. Place the soles on a serving dish, glaze with the reduced cooking liquor, squeeze on top a few drops of lemon juice, and sprinkle with chopped parsley. Garnish with the morels (sautéed in butter), the fried croûtons, and the crayfish (cooked in a court-bouillon). *(France.)*

Sole Palace

For 6 persons: *3 soles (400 gr. each); 24 thick slices of raw mushrooms; 12 thick slices of skinned tomato; 3 chopped shallots; 10 tarragon leaves; 3 cl. cognac; 2 dl. white wine; 100 gr. butter.* Cooking time: 12 to 15 minutes.

Lay the soles on a fireproof gratinating dish which has been buttered and sprinkled with chopped shallots and chopped tarragon. Season, cover with the mushrooms and tomatoes, moisten with the cognac and white wine, and poach in the oven. Reduce the poaching liquor, monter au beurre, use to coat the soles, and glaze quickly. *(France.)*

Sole pannoise, Filets de

For 6 persons: *3 soles (350 gr. each); 200 gr. picked shrimps; 2 chopped shallots; 4 peeled, pipped and chopped tomatoes; 3 dl. fresh cream; 200 gr. butter; 1 dl. fish fumet; 5 cl. Noilly-Prat; 1 bouquet garni; 1 lemon; ½ coffee-spoonful chopped tarragon; 6 fleurons.* Cooking time: 7 to 8 minutes.

Fillet the soles, and prepare the fumet with the backbones. Line a buttered fish dish with the chopped shallots, and arrange on it the flattened fillets which have been folded in two. Moisten with the fish fumet and Noilly-Prat, season, add the chopped tomatoes and bouquet garni, cover with buttered paper, and poach in the oven. When the fillets are cooked, drain them, arrange on a buttered serving dish with the chopped tomatoes and cover. Strain the cooking liquor, reduce it by half, add the cream, reduce again, monter au beurre, incorporate the shrimps and lemon juice, and correct seasoning and consistency. Coat the fillets with the sauce, sprinkle with the chopped tarragon, and garnish with the fleurons. *(Belgium.)*

Sole parisienne I

For 6 persons: *3 soles (450 gr. each); 2 dl. white wine; 5 cl. mushroom cooking liquor; 12 thin slices of truffle; 12 thin slices of white mushrooms; 6 shelled crayfish; 40 gr. butter; 4 dl. white wine sauce.* Cooking time: 12 to 15 minutes.

Poach the soles in the white wine, mushroom liquor and butter. Reduce the cooking liquor almost to a glaze, and add it to the white wine sauce. Arrange the soles on a serving dish, and coat them with the sauce. Place on each of them 4 slices of truffle and 4 slices of cooked mushroom. Arrange the crayfish (cooked in a court-bouillon) at each end of the dish. *(France.)*

Sole parisienne II

For 6 persons: *3 soles (450 gr. each); 2 dl. fish fumet; 2 dl. white wine sauce; 2 dl. sauce crevettes; 18 small cooked mushroom heads.* Cooking time: 12 to 15 minutes.

Poach the soles in the fish fumet, drain them, and arrange on a serving dish. Coat each sole lengthwise, along one side with the white wine sauce, and along the other with sauce crevettes. Arrange 6 mushrooms along each sole to overlap both sauces. *(France.)*

Sole paysanne, Filets de

For 6 persons: *12 fillets of sole; 2 very small carrots; 2 button onions; 1 small stick of celery; 1 white of leek; 1 tablespoonful garden peas; 1 tablespoon french beans; 120 gr. butter.* Cooking time: 10 to 12 minutes.

Cut into small thin slices the carrots, onions, celery and leek. Season, stew slowly in butter, moisten with water, and add the peas together with the french beans cut into diamond shapes. Finish cooking by reducing the cooking liquor. Lay the fillets on a buttered gratinating dish, cover with the vegetables and the vegetable liquor, and poach in the oven. After poaching, remove most of the cooking liquor from the dish, reduce it to 1 dl. in a sauteuse, monter au beurre, correct seasoning and consistency, and use to coat the fillets. *(France.)*

Sole persane, Filets de

Proceed as for the preparation of Filets de sole Newburg, but season the sauce with paprika, and add diced cooked red peppers. Serve saffroned pilaf rice separately. *(France.)* *(See page 318.)*

Sole petit-duc

For 6 persons: *3 soles (400 gr. each); 120 gr. thinly-sliced raw mushrooms; 2 dl. fish fumet; 24 asparagus tips; 12 thin slices of truffle; 40 gr. butter; 4 dl. white wine sauce.* Cooking time: 12 to 15 minutes.

Sprinkle a buttered fish dish with the mushrooms, arrange the soles on top, and poach them in the fish fumet. Reduce the poaching stock, and add it to the white wine sauce. Arrange the soles on top of the mushrooms in a serving dish, garnish with the asparagus tips, place 4 slices of truffle on each sole, coat the fillets and garnish with the sauce, and glaze quickly. *(France.)*
(See illustration, page 333.)

Sole picarde, Filets de

Proceed as for the preparation of Filets de sole Marguéry, adding 12 poached and bearded oysters and 12 thin slices of truffle, but without glazing. *(France.)* *(See page 314.)*

Sole Piccadilly I

For 6 persons: *3 soles (400 gr. each); 20 gr. chopped onion; 2 chopped shallots; 10 chopped tarragon leaves; 2 dl. fish fumet; 2 cl. whisky; 2 cl. cognac; Worcestershire sauce; 100 gr. butter.* Cooking time (in the kitchen): 12 minutes. N.B. This preparation is finished at table.

Lay the soles on a buttered fish dish sprinkled with the onion, shallots and tarragon, moisten with the fish fumet, and poach in the oven. At table: the maître d'hôtel removes the fillets and keeps them hot between two plates. In a small saucepan on the flare-lamp, he reduces the cooking stock, flames it with the cognac and whisky, adds a few drops of Worcestershire sauce, monte au beurre, and uses this to coat the fillets (which have been plated in pairs). *(International cookery.)*

Sole Piccadilly II

Remove the black skin and scale the white skin of a Dover sole of between 280 to 300 gr. On the skinned side carefully incise from head to tail on the backbone lifting the fillets by sliding a sharp flexible knife against the bone towards the outside without detaching the fillets entirely, to form a pocket. Toss in hot butter 2 chopped shallots and 150 gr. of very white firm mushrooms finely chopped; add cooked and shelled lobster tail cut into dice and bind the whole with 2 dl. of fresh cream, finishing, off the fire, with the yolk of one egg. Stuff the cavity of the sole with this mixture and put in a buttered oval fireproof dish, moistened with a good glassful of dry white wine and a little fish stock. When the sole is cooked, reduce the cooking liquor, add 1 dl. of cream and a good nut of butter and pass under the salamander to glaze. Garnish with puff pastry crescents (fleurons).
The above recipe was created by Mr. L. Howe, Chef de Cuisine at the Public Schools Club, 100 Piccadilly, London.

Sole Pierre-le-Grand, Filets de

For 6 persons: *12 fillets of sole; 2 dl. fish fumet; 4 dl. white wine sauce; 40 gr. chopped cooked ham; 40 gr. chopped truffle.* Cooking time: 8 to 10 minutes.

Fold the fillets, and poach them in the fish fumet. Arrange on a round serving dish, with the tips pointing towards the centre. Coat the fillets with the white wine sauce, and sprinkle one half of each with ham and the other half with truffle. *(France.)*

Sole sur le plat

For 6 persons: *3 soles (450 to 500 gr. each); ¼ litre fish fumet; 100 gr. butter; 3 chopped shallots; ½ lemon.* Cooking time: 12 to 15 minutes.

Loosen the fillets from the backbones, and slip a nut of butter under each fillet. Lay the soles on a fish dish which has been heavily buttered and sprinkled with chopped shallots. Season, and moisten with the fish fumet and lemon juice. Cook in the oven, basting frequently until the cooking liquor is reduced almost to a glaze. Coat the soles with the liquor, and glaze lightly. *(France.)*

Sole Polignac

For 6 persons: *3 soles (400 gr. each); 50 gr. truffle; 75 gr. cooked mushrooms; 2 dl. fish fumet; 1 dl. fresh cream; 3 dl. white wine sauce; 12 small puff pastry fleurons.* Cooking time: 12 to 15 minutes.

Poach the soles in the fish fumet. Reduce the poaching liquor with the cream, add it to the white wine sauce, and incorporate the mushrooms and truffle both cut into a julienne. Arrange the soles on a serving dish, coat with this sauce, and surround with fleurons. *(France.)*

Sole Pompadour

For 6 persons: *3 soles (400 gr. each); 200 gr. peeled, pipped and chopped tomatoes; 4 dl. white wine sauce; 2 dl. fish fumet; 40 gr. truffle; 40 gr. butter.* Cooking time: 12 to 15 minutes.

Poach the soles in the fish fumet. Reduce the poaching liquor, and add it to the white wine sauce. Soften the tomatoes in butter. Arrange the soles on a serving dish, place on each a line of chopped tomatoes, coat with the white wine sauce, and sprinkle with a short julienne of truffle. *(France.)*

Sole Pompadour, Filets de

For 6 persons: *12 fillets of sole; 100 gr. butter; fresh white breadcrumbs; 4 dl. sauce béarnaise containing tomato (Choron); 12 thin slices of truffle; 240 gr. noisette potatoes.* Cooking time: 8 to 10 minutes.

Season the fillets, dip them in melted butter, roll in fresh breadcrumbs, press them down with the blade of a knife, sprinkle with melted butter, and grill gently. Arrange on a serving dish, place a slice of truffle on each fillet, and garnish the spaces between the fillets with a trickle of sauce Choron. Surround with the noisette potatoes. *(France.)*

Sole portugaise

Proceed as for the preparation of Cabillaud portugaise. *(See page 255.)*

Sole princesse

For 6 persons: *3 soles (400 gr. each); 4 dl. white wine sauce; 60 gr. purée of green asparagus; 24 green asparagus tips; 6 thin slices of truffle; 300 gr. purée duchesse; 1 egg; 2 dl. fish fumet; 60 gr. butter.* Cooking time: 12 to 15 minutes.

Poach the soles in the fish fumet. Prepare 6 round croustades made from the purée duchesse; gild them with beaten egg, and colour in the oven. Arrange the soles on a serving dish, and coat them with the white wine sauce containing the cooked asparagus purée. Garnish with the croustades filled with the asparagus tips (bound with melted butter), and place on each a slice of truffle passed through butter. *(France.)*

Sole princière, Filets de

For 6 persons: *12 fillets of sole; 4 dl. sauce Nantua; 20 gr. truffle; 2 dl. fish fumet; 12 thin slices of truffle.* Cooking time: 8 to 10 minutes.

Fold the fillets, poach them in the fish fumet, and arrange them on a serving dish. Coat them with sauce Nantua containing truffle (cut into small dice) and glaze. Place a slice of truffle on each fillet. *(France.)*

Sole printanière, Filets de

For 6 persons: *12 fillets of sole; 2 dl. fish fumet; 4 dl. sauce béchamel; 60 gr. beurre printanier; 200 fr. small spoon-cut potato-balls; 100 gr. carrots and 100 gr. turnips (spoon-cut parisienne); 5 cl. fresh cream; 50 gr. butter.* Cooking time: 15 to 18 minutes.

Fold the fillets, and poach them in the fish fumet. Cook the potatoes, keeping them whole. Cook the carrots and turnips in consommé and butter, reducing to a glaze. Arrange the fillets on a serving dish, and coat them with the creamed sauce béchamel finished with beurre printanier. Surround them with the potatoes, carrots and turnips. *(France.)*

(See illustration, page 311. N.B. Different presentation.)

Sole provençale

For 6 persons: *3 soles (400 gr. each); 2 dl. fish fumet; 4 dl. sauce provençale; 12 very small tomatoes prepared provençale; 4 cl. olive oil; ½ clove of garlic; 1 coffee-spoonful chopped parsley.* Cooking time: 12 to 15 minutes.

Poach the soles in the fish fumet, olive oil and crushed garlic. Reduce the poaching stock, and add it to the sauce provençale. Arrange the soles on a serving dish, surround them with the tomatoes, coat them with the sauce provençale, and sprinkle lightly with chopped parsley. *(France.)*

Sole Quo Vadis

For 6 persons: *3 soles (450 gr. each); 4 dl. white wine sauce; 50 gr. tarragon butter; 2 dl. fish fumet; 12 thin slices of truffle; 6 shelled crayfish.* Cooking time: 12 to 15 minutes.

Poach the soles in the fish fumet. Arrange them on a serving dish and coat them with the white wine sauce finished with the tarragon butter. Place 4 slices of truffle on each sole, and arrange the crayfish at each end of the dish. *(France.)*

Sole Rabelais

Proceed as for the preparation of Sole normande, but sprinkle the whole dish with chopped lobster coral. *(France.)* *(See page 318.)*

Sole Rachel I, Filets de

For 6 persons: *12 fillets of sole; 12 thin slices of truffle; 2 dl. fish fumet; 4 dl. sauce crevettes; 30 gr. truffle; 30 gr. butter.* Cooking time: 8 to 10 minutes.

Flatten the fillets, place on each of them a slice of truffle, fold them, arrange them on a buttered fish dish, and poach in the fish fumet. Reduce the poaching stock, add it to the sauce crevettes, and incorporate with it the truffle (cut into small dice). Arrange the fillets on a serving dish, coat them with the sauce, and glaze. *(France.)*

Sole Rachel II, Filets de

Proceed as for the preparation of Filets de sole Rachel I, but coat the fillets with white wine sauce containing truffle and cooked green asparagus tips (both cut into small dice). *(France.)*

Sole ravigote, Filets de

For 6 persons: *12 fillets of sole; 2 dl. fish fumet; 4 dl. hot sauce ravigote; 20 gr. butter.* Cooking time: 8 to 10 minutes.

Flatten the fillets, and poach them in the fish fumet. Drain them, arrange on a serving dish, and coat with the sauce ravigote. *(France.)*

Sole Régence

For 6 persons: *3 soles (400 gr. each); 300 gr. Régence garnish; 4 dl. sauce Régence; 2 dl. fish fumet.* Cooking time: 12 to 15 minutes.

Poach the soles in the fish fumet. Arrange them on a serving dish, surround them with the Régence garnish, and coat them with sauce Régence. *(France.)*

Sole reine Fiamette, Paupiettes de

For 6 persons: *12 fillets of sole; 2 dl. fish fumet; 180 gr. Joinville garnish; 2 dl. sauce Nantua; 2 dl. white wine sauce; 12 small puff-pastry croustadines; 50 gr. cooked lobster (cut into small dice); 30 gr. lobster coral (cooked and chopped).* Cooking time: 8 to 10 minutes.

Flatten the fillets, roll them into paupiettes, and poach them in the fish fumet. Fill the croustadines with Joinville garnish, arrange them on a serving dish, and place a paupiette on each. Coat 6 of the paupiettes with sauce Nantua sprinkled with the diced lobster, and the other 6 with white wine sauce sprinkled with the chopped coral. *(France.)*

Sole Réjane, Filets de

For 6 persons: *12 fillets of sole; 50 gr. watercress butter; 4 dl. white wine sauce; 240 gr. purée duchesse; 2 dl. fish fumet; 20 gr. butter; 1 egg.* Cooking time: 8 to 10 minutes.

Leave the fillets flat, and poach them in the fish fumet. Arrange them on a serving dish, and coat them with the white wine sauce containing the watercress butter. Surround with pommes duchesse, shaped with a star piping-tube, gilded with egg, and coloured in the oven. *(France.)*

Sole Rhodésia, Paupiettes de

For 6 persons: *12 fillets of sole; 180 gr. fish forcemeat; 12 escalopes cooked lobster-tail; 2 dl. fish fumet; 4 dl. sauce américaine; 5 cl. fresh cream.* Cooking time: 10 to 12 minutes.

Flatten the fillets, mask them with the forcemeat, roll them into paupiettes, and poach them in the fish fumet. Arrange each paupiette on a lobster escalope (prepared américaine), and place them in a ring on a round serving dish. Coat with sauce américaine worked up with cream. *(France.)*

Sole riche, Filets de

Proceed as for the preparation of Filets de barbue riche. *(See page 246.)*

Sole Richebourg, Filets de

For 6 persons: *12 fillets of sole; 100 gr. butter; 4 dl. sauce américaine; 12 oysters prepared Villeroi; 12 thin slices of truffle.* Cooking time: 8 minutes.

Season the fillets, and shallow fry them in butter (without too much coloration). Arrange them on a serving dish, and coat with sauce américaine. Place a slice of truffle on each fillet. Surround with oysters Villeroi. *(France.)*

Sole Richelieu

Proceed as for the preparation of Sole Colbert. Place large slices of truffle on the beurre maître d'hôtel. *(France.)*
(See Culinary Technique, page 75.)

Sole Richepin, Paupiettes de

For 6 persons: *12 fillets of sole; 120 gr. fish forcemeat; 60 gr. duxelles; 24 very small ravioli stuffed with spinach; 12 shelled crayfish; 12 thin slices of truffle; 2 dl. fish fumet; 4 dl. sauce Nantua; 5 cl. fresh cream.* Cooking time: 10 to 12 minutes.

Flatten the fillets, mask them with the fish forcemeat (containing the duxelles), roll them into paupiettes, and poach in the fish fumet. Arrange them in a ring on a round serving dish, and surround them with the crayfish. Coat the paupiettes and the garnish with the creamed sauce Nantua, and place a slice of truffle on each. Fill the centre with the ravioli. *(France.)*

Sole Riviéra, Goujons de

For 6 persons: *12 fillets of sole; 100 gr. mushrooms; 6 cooked artichoke-bases; 150 gr. peeled, pipped and chopped tomatoes; 150 gr. butter; ½ lemon; 1 coffee-spoonful chopped parsley; flour.* Cooking time: 10 to 12 minutes.

Cut the fillets into goujons, season and flour them, and sauté in butter. Add the mushrooms and artichoke-bases (which have been thinly-sliced or cut into a coarse julienne), and sauté in butter. Sauté all the ingredients together for 1 or 2 minutes, to ensure an even mixture. Arrange in a timbale, add the chopped tomatoes (stewed in butter), coat with beurre noisette, and finish with lemon juice and chopped parsley. *(France.)*

Sole rochelaise I

For 6 persons: *3 soles (450 gr. each); 3 dl. sauce crevette; 2 dl. sauce béarnaise; 2 dl. fish fumet.* Cooking time: 12 to 15 minutes.

Poach the soles in the fish fumet, and arrange them on a serving dish. Coat them with the sauce crevette, and surround them with a trickle of sauce béarnaise. *(France.)*

Sole rochelaise II

For 6 persons: *3 soles (400 gr. each); 24 mussels; 12 oysters; 12 good escalopes of soft roe; 40 gr. chopped onion; 100 gr. butter; ¼ litre red wine; 1 dl. fish fumet; 1 dl. sauce demi-glace.* Cooking time: 12 to 15 minutes.

Lay the soles in a fish dish (buttered, and sprinkled with onion which has been finely chopped and cooked in butter). Season the soles, moisten with the fish fumet and red wine, add 25 gr. butter, and poach gently. Drain the soles, arrange them on a serving dish, and garnish with the poached and bearded mussels and oysters, and also with the escalopes of soft roe (stewed in butter). Reduce the poaching stock, pass it through a tammy cloth, add the lightly buttered demi-glace and use it to coat the soles and the garnish. *(France.)*

Sole Rossini, Paupiettes de

For 6 persons: *12 fillets of sole; 200 gr. fish forcemeat; 50 gr. purée of foie gras; 6 small tartlet-cases; 6 thin slices of truffle; 30 gr. chopped truffle; 2 dl. white wine; 4 dl. white wine sauce; 25 gr. meat glaze.* Cooking time: 12 minutes.

Flatten the fillets, mask them with fish forcemeat mixed with the foie gras, roll into paupiettes, and poach in white wine. Fill the tartlet-cases with the mixture, and poach just inside the oven. Arrange the paupiettes on a serving dish, coat them with the white wine sauce containing the reduced poaching stock, and sprinkle them with the chopped truffle. Garnish with the tartlets, and with a slice of truffle (passed through meat glaze) on each tartlet. *(France.)*

Sole rouennaise

For 6 persons: *3 soles (400 gr. each); 3 dl. red wine; 3 chopped shallots; 100 gr. butter; 60 gr. picked shrimps; 12 mussels; 12 oysters; 12 small mushroom heads; 6 trussed crayfish; 6 headless smelts; 6 heart-shaped croûtons; 1 tablespoonful meat glaze; ½ lemon; flour.* Cooking time: 12 to 15 minutes.

Lay the soles on a buttered fish dish sprinkled with chopped shallots. Season, moisten with red wine, and poach in the oven. Drain the soles, arrange them on a serving dish, and garnish with the poached and bearded mussels and oysters. Then garnish with the cooked shrimps and mushrooms. Reduce the cooking liquor, add the meat glaze and a few drops of lemon juice, monter au beurre, correct seasoning and consistency, and use this sauce to coat the soles. Surround them with the smelts (floured, and cooked meunière), fried croûtons and crayfish (cooked in court-bouillon). *(France.)*

Sole Rougemont

For 6 persons: *3 soles (450 to 500 gr. each); 2 dl. fish fumet; 4 dl. white wine sauce; 30 gr. tomato purée.* Cooking time: 12 to 15 minutes.

Poach the soles in the fish fumet, and arrange them on a serving dish. Coat with the white wine sauce containing tomato. *(France.)*

Sole royale

For 6 persons: *3 soles (400 gr. each); 12 small cooked mushrooms; 12 small quenelles of fish forcemeat; 12 shelled crayfish; 12 thin slices of truffle; 240 gr. small spoon-cut potato-balls; 2 dl. fish fumet; 4 dl. sauce normande; 50 gr. butter.* Cooking time: 12 to 15 minutes.

Poach the soles in the fish fumet and butter. Reduce the poaching stock, and add it to the sauce normande. Arrange the soles on a serving dish, and place on them the mushrooms, crayfish, quenelles and slices of truffle. Surround with the plain-boiled potatoes, and use the sauce to coat the soles and the garnish. *(France.)*

Sole russe

For 6 persons: *3 soles (450 gr. each); 24 very thin roundels of serrated carrot; 3 small onions cut into very thin round slices; 1 tablespoonful picked parsley; 3 dl. water; 120 gr. butter; ½ lemon.* Cooking time: 20 to 25 minutes.

Pass the slices of carrot and onion through hot butter without coloration, add the parsley, water and 75 gr. butter, and cook for 10 minutes. Pour this preparation into a gratinating dish, lay on it the soles (previously scored on the upper side), and poach on the stove, basting frequently. When the soles are cooked, the cooking liquor must have reduced by half. Add the rest of the butter and the lemon juice, correct seasoning and consistency, and serve as it is. *(France.)*

Sole Saint-Arnould, Filets de

For 6 persons: *2 soles (500 gr. each); 3 dl. pale ale; 100 gr. hop shoots; 150 gr. butter; 3 chopped shallots; 1 tablespoonful beurre manié; 3 egg yolks; 1 dl. fresh cream; 125 gr. bread.* Poaching time: 8 to 10 minutes.

Remove the fillets, trim and flatten them, and fold them in two. Brown the shallots in 50 gr. butter, and use them to cover the bottom of a gratinating dish. Arrange the fillets in the dish, moisten with the beer, and marinate for 30 minutes. Season with mignonette pepper (with very little salt), cover with buttered paper, and poach without boiling. Stew the hop shoots in butter. Remove the fillets, arrange them on a serving dish, sprinkle them with the hop shoots, cover, and keep hot. Reduce the cooking liquor by half, and thicken lightly with beurre manié. Finish with a liaison of the egg yolks and fresh cream, work up with 50 gr. butter, whisking to make the mixture frothy, and correct seasoning and consistency. Coat the fillets with the sauce, and, at the last moment, sprinkle with small bread croûtons (dried in the oven and tossed in clarified butter). *(Belgium.)*

Sole Saint-Germain, Filets de

Proceed as for the preparation of Escalopes de barbue Saint-Germain. *(France.)* *(See page 253.)*

Sole Saint-Henry

For 6 persons: *3 soles (450 to 500 gr. each); 12 sea-urchins; 1 dl. fresh cream; 40 gr. butter; 1 lemon; parsley; flour; 1 dl. oil.* Cooking time: 12 to 15 minutes.

Season, flour and oil the soles, and grill them slowly. Arrange them on a serving dish with parsley and quarters of lemon. Serve separately a purée of urchin-coral montée au beurre and with cream (or sauce béchamel). *(France.)*

Sole Saint-Valéry

For 6 persons: *3 soles (400 gr. each); 120 gr. picked shrimps; 120 gr. cooked mushrooms; 2 dl. fish fumet; 4 dl. white wine sauce.* Cooking time: 12 to 15 minutes.

Poach the soles in the fish fumet, drain them, and arrange on a serving dish. Coat them with the white wine sauce containing the shrimps and the finely-diced mushrooms, and glaze. *(France.)*
(See illustration, page 309. N.B. Different presentation.)

Sole Salisbury, Filets de

For 6 persons: *12 fillets of sole; 120 gr. fish forcemeat; 180 gr. pilaf rice; 1 dl. white wine sauce; 4 dl. lobster sauce; 12 thin slices of truffle; 2 dl. fish fumet.* Cooking time: 10 to 12 minutes.

Flatten the fillets, mask them with the forcemeat, fold them in two, poach in the fish fumet, and arrange in a ring on a serving dish. Place a slice of truffle on each fillet, and coat with lobster sauce. Fill the centre of the dish with the pilaf rice bound with the white wine sauce. *(France.)*
(See illustration, page 333.)

Sole Salvator, Filets de

For 6 persons: *12 fillets of sole; 10 gr. paprika; 100 gr. thinly-sliced raw mushrooms; 12 shelled crayfish; 12 slices of peeled tomato; 12 roundels of lemon (peeled and pipped); 15 gr. chopped parsley; 3 dl. white wine sauce; 1 dl. fresh cream; 2 dl. fish fumet; 40 gr. butter.* Cooking time: 10 to 12 minutes.

Sprinkle the fillets with paprika, and lay them in a buttered gratinating dish which has been sprinkled with the mushrooms and parsley. Place a slice of tomato on each fillet, moisten with the fish fumet, cover with buttered paper, and poach in the oven. Reduce the poaching liquor with the cream, and add it to the white wine sauce. Place a roundel of lemon on each fillet, coat them with the sauce, and glaze. *(France.)*

Sole Sapho

For 6 persons: *3 soles (400 gr. each); 1 dl. white wine; 1 dl. fish fumet; 5 cl. truffle cooking liquor; 6 small puff-pastry croustades; 30 gr. truffle (julienne); 60 gr. cooked mushrooms (julienne); 12 very small lobster croquettes; 100 gr. Joinville garnish; 6 shelled crayfish (cooked in court-bouillon); 100 gr. butter.* Cooking time: 12 to 15 minutes.

Poach the soles in the white wine, fish fumet and truffle cooking liquor. Drain them, and arrange on a serving dish. Reduce well the poaching liquor, monter au beurre, add the julienne of truffle and mushrooms, and use to coat the soles. Garnish with the croustades (filled with the Joinville garnish), the lobster croquettes and the shelled crayfish. *(France.)*

Sole Sarah Bernhardt

For 6 persons: *3 soles (450 gr. each); 2 dl. fish fumet; 4 dl. sauce vénitienne; 50 gr. cooked julienne of carrot; 30 gr. julienne of truffle; 30 gr. butter.* Cooking time: 12 to 15 minutes.

Lay the soles in a buttered gratinating dish, and poach them in the fish fumet. Drain them, arrange them on a serving dish and coat them with the sauce vénitienne to which has been added the carrot and truffle. *(France.)*

Sole Savigny, Paupiettes de

For 6 persons: *12 fillets of sole; 150 gr. whiting forcemeat; 6 3 cm. lengths of blanched cucumber; 12 prawns (deep fried in batter); 12 thin slices of truffle; 2 tomatoes; 6 peeled, split and blanched almonds; 5 dl. sauce aurore.* Cooking time: 12 minutes.

Flatten the fillets, mask them with the whiting forcemeat, and roll them into paupiettes. Arrange the paupiettes on a buttered fish dish, moisten with the fish fumet, cover with buttered paper, and poach in the oven. Drain the paupiettes, arrange them in a ring on a serving dish, place the cucumber pieces (previously heated in the oven) in the centre, with a slice of tomato on each, and garnish each paupiette with a slice of truffle and half an almond, and finish with the prawns. Use the sauce aurore to coat the paupiettes and the garnish. *(Switzerland.)*
(See illustration, page 332. N. B. Different presentation.)

Sole Savoy

For 6 persons: *3 soles (400 gr. each); 1 dl. fish fumet; 1 dl. mushroom liquor; 1 dl. white wine; 5 cl. truffle liquor; 12 large slices of cooked mushroom; 12 thin slices of truffle; 150 gr. peeled, pipped and chopped tomatoes; 24 green asparagus tips; 125 gr. butter.* Cooking time: 12 to 15 minutes.

Poach the soles in the white wine, fish fumet, mushroom liquor and truffle liquor. Drain the soles, arrange them on a serving dish, garnish with the asparagus tips (heated in butter), and the chopped tomatoes (softened in butter). Place on each sole 4 slices of mushroom and 4 slices of truffle. Reduce well the poaching liquor, monter au beurre, use to coat the soles, and glaze briskly. *(France.)*

Sole Schneider

Proceed as for the preparation of Merlan Bercy, but garnish with 24 mussels (poached and bearded), and sprinkle the soles with breadcrumbs fried in butter. *(France.)* *(See page 276.)*

Sole "Scotts", Fillet of

For 6 persons: *12 fillets of sole (folded); 12 bearded oysters; 12 prawns; 12 cooked mussels; 12 small scollops of cooked lobster; 12 turned and cooked mushroom heads; chopped parsley; ½ litre sauce vin blanc glacée.* Cooking time: 20 minutes.

Heat the oysters, prawns, mussels and lobster in butter. Poach the fillets in fish stock and white wine; drain and keep warm. Reduce the fish cooking liquor and add it to the sauce vin blanc. Flame the shellfish with cognac and place in the centre of a round serving dish. Surround with the fillets of sole. Mask with sauce vin blanc and glaze under the salamander. Place a turned mushroom on each fillet and top with a pinch of chopped parsley. Serve very hot.

Sole sportive, Filets de

For 6 persons: *12 fillets of sole; 50 gr. thinly-sliced raw mushrooms; 3 chopped shallots; 50 gr. mirepoix bordelaise; 18 shelled crayfish; 1 dl. fish fumet; 1 dl. champagne; 1 dl. fresh cream; 100 gr. butter; 1 coffee-spoonful meat glaze; ½ lemon.* Cooking time: 10 to 12 minutes.

Fold the fillets, and lay them in a buttered fish dish which has been sprinkled with the chopped shallots, thinly-sliced mushrooms and mirepoix bordelaise. Moisten with the fish fumet and champagne, and poach in the oven. Drain the fillets, strain the poaching liquor, reduce it well with the cream, add the meat glaze, correct seasoning and consistency, and finish with a few drops of lemon juice. Arrange the fillets in a ring on a serving dish, with the crayfish in the centre, and coat all over with the sauce containing the cooked garnish. *(France.)*

Sole Suchet

For 6 persons: *12 fillets of sole; julienne of—30 gr. carrot, 30 gr. white of leek, and 30 gr. celery; 30 gr. truffle; 1 dl. fish fumet; 1 dl. white wine; 50 gr. butter; 4 dl. white wine sauce.* Cooking time: 10 to 12 minutes.

Stew the julienne of vegetables in butter with a few drops of water. Poach the fillets in the white wine and fish fumet, and drain them. Reduce the poaching liquor almost completely; add it to the white wine sauce; incorporate the vegetables and the truffle (cut julienne); arrange the fillets in a serving dish, and coat with the sauce. *(France.)*

Sole Sullivan, Filets de

For 6 persons: *12 fillets of sole; 24 asparagus tips; 12 thin slices of truffle; 2 dl. fish fumet; 4 dl. sauce Mornay; 40 gr. butter.* Cooking time: 8 to 10 minutes.

Fold the fillets, and poach them in the fish fumet. Arrange them on a buttered gratinating dish; garnish with the asparagus tips, coat with the sauce Mornay, and glaze. Place on each fillet a slice of truffle which has been passed through butter. *(France.)*

Sole Sully, Filets de

For 6 persons: *12 fillets of sole; 2 eggs; fresh breadcrumbs; 3 dl. sauce béarnaise; 100 gr. anchovy butter; 1 lemon; flour; picked parsley.* Cooking time: 10 minutes.

Slightly flatten the fillets, coat with egg and breadcrumbs and deep fry. Arrange on a napkin with quarters of lemon and fried parsley. Serve the sauce béarnaise and anchovy butter separately. *(France.)*

Sole sultane

For 6 persons: *3 soles (400 gr. each); 4 dl. white wine sauce; 50 gr. pistachio butter; 6 small puff-pastry cases; 100 gr. picked shrimps; 7 cl. sauce crevettes; 12 thin slices of truffle; 2 dl. fish fumet.* Cooking time: 12 to 15 minutes.

Poach the soles in the fish fumet. Arrange them on a serving dish, and coat with the white wine sauce finished with the pistachio butter. Place 4 slices of truffle on each sole. Garnish with the puff-pastry cases filled with a salpicon of shrimps bound with sauce crevettes. *(France.)* *(See illustration, page 312. N.B. Different presentation.)*

Sole Suzanne

Proceed as for the presentation of Sole Polignac, but add to the garnish 12 picked shrimps and 12 escalopes of soft roe (stewed in butter). *(France.)* *(See page 322)*

Sole Sylvette, Filets de

For 6 persons: *12 fillets of sole; 2 dl. fish fumet; 1 dl. sherry; 12 very small tomatoes; 120 gr. purée of cooked sole; 100 gr. brunoise of vegetables; 50 gr. raw mushrooms; 20 gr. truffle; 75 gr. butter; 40 gr. grated cheese.* Cooking time: 8 to 10 minutes.

Cut the mushrooms into a brunoise and the truffle into very small dice; add to the brunoise of vegetables, and stew in butter. Fold the fillets, and poach them in the fish fumet and sherry with the brunoise. Drain the fillets, arrange them on a serving dish with the brunoise, reduce the poaching liquor, incorporate the cream; cook for a few more moments, butter lightly, and correct seasoning and consistency. Coat the fillets with the sauce, sprinkle with the grated cheese, and brown. Garnish with the tomatoes which have been filled with the purée of cooked sole. *(France.)*

Sole Sylvia, Paupiettes de

For 6 persons: *12 fillets of sole; 90 gr. fish forcemeat; 30 gr. purée of globe artichokes; 12 globe artichoke bases; 2 dl. fish fumet; 4 dl. white wine sauce; 12 thin slices of truffle; 30 gr. butter.* Cooking time: 10 to 12 minutes.

Flatten the fillets, mask them with the fish forcemeat containing the cooked artichoke purée, roll them into paupiettes and poach in the fish fumet. Arrange each paupiette on an artichoke base (which has been heated in butter), lay them on a serving dish, coat with the white wine sauce, and place on top of each paupiette a slice of truffle. *(France.)*

Sole Talleyrand, Filets de

For 6 persons: *12 fillets of sole; 200 gr. cooked spaghetti; 50 gr. truffle; 1 dl. fresh cream; 60 gr. butter; 5 dl. white wine sauce.* Cooking time: 12 to 15 minutes.

Bind the spaghetti with the butter and cream, and the truffle (cut into julienne). Spread all these on the base of a buttered gratinating dish, and arrange on top the flat, raw fillets. Coat with thin white wine sauce, and cook in the oven. *(France.)*

Sole Théodora I

For 6 persons: *12 fillets of sole; 2 dl. fish fumet; 2 dl. white wine sauce; 2 dl. sauce vénitienne; 30 gr. chopped truffle.* Cooking time: 8 to 10 minutes.

Fold the fillets, and poach them in the fish fumet. Drain them. Arrange on a serving dish; coat alternately with white wine sauce and vénitienne, and sprinkle with the chopped truffle. *(France.)*

Sole Théodora II

Proceed as for the preparation of Merlan Bercy, but with a garnish of 12 oysters (poached and bearded), 12 thin slices of truffle, and 12 very small puff-pastry fleurons. *(France.)* *(See page 276.)*

Sole Thérèse, Paupiettes de

For 6 persons: *12 fillets of sole; 30 gr. cooked lobster coral; 4 dl. white wine sauce; 2 dl. fish fumet; 30 gr. butter.* Cooking time: 8 to 10 minutes.

Flatten the fillets, roll them into paupiettes, and poach them in the fish fumet. Arrange on a serving dish, and coat them with the white wine sauce containing the reduced poaching liquor. Sprinkle with the chopped lobster coral. *(France.)*

Sole thermidor

For 6 persons: *3 soles (450 gr. each); 1 dl. white wine; 1 dl. fish fumet; 4 dl. sauce Bercy; 1 coffeespoonful dry mustard; 1 tablespoonful meat glaze; 2 chopped shallots; 50 gr. butter.* Cooking time: 12 to 15 minutes.

Lay the soles on a buttered fish dish sprinkled with the chopped shallots. Moisten with the white wine and fish fumet, cover with buttered paper, and poach in the oven. Drain the soles, arrange them on a serving dish, and coat with the sauce Bercy lightly flavoured with the mixed mustard. Surround with a border of meat glaze. *(France.)*

▲ Sole Dugléré, p. 302

Paupiettes de sole Beatrix, p. 224 ▼

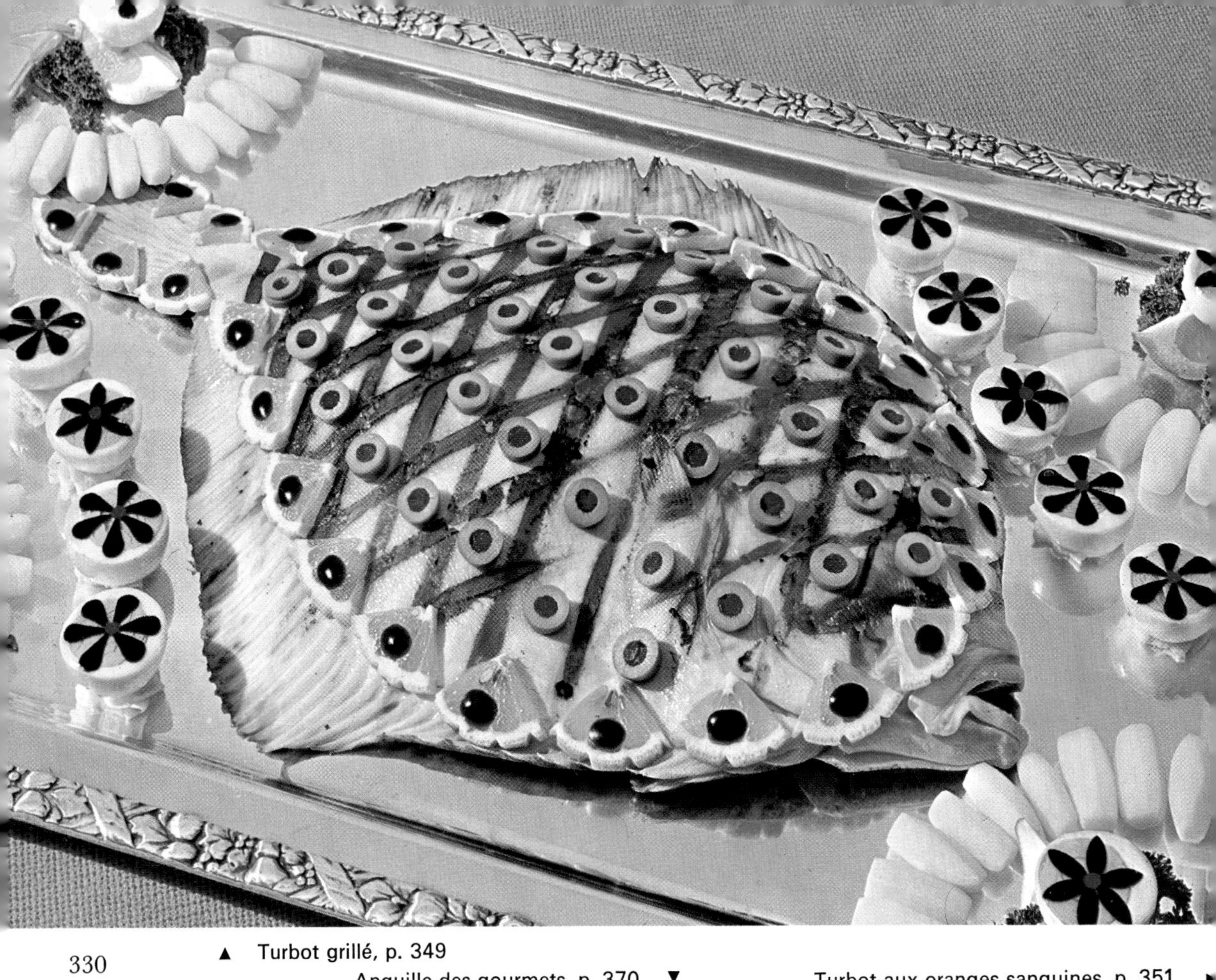

▲ Turbot grillé, p. 349

Anguille des gourmets, p. 370 ▼

Turbot aux oranges sanguines, p. 351 ►

▲ Filets de sole cardinal, p. 299

Paupiettes de filets de sole Savigny, p. 326 ▼

▲ Filets de sole Salisbury, p. 326

Filets de sole petit-duc, p. 321 ▼

▲ Paupiettes de sole maître Adolfo Bader, p. 231

Darnes de cabillaud ou de saumon Condorcet, p. 224 ▼

▲ Paupiettes de sole mascotte, p. 314

Homard Xavier Winthertur, p. 445 ▼

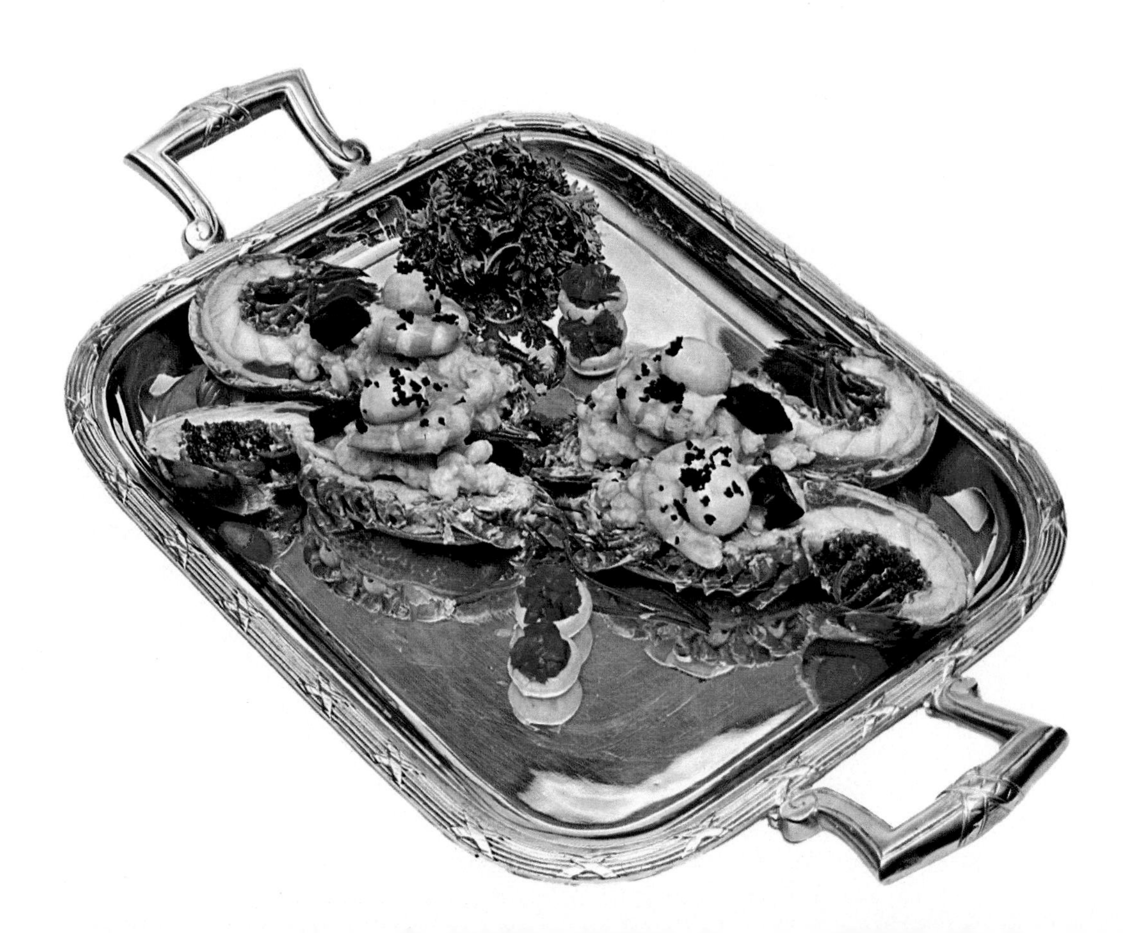

▲ Paupiettes de sole Boucanier, p. 224

Paupiettes de filets de sole Newburg, p. 318 ▼

▲ Turbot Floralies, p. 359

Turbot française, p. 349 ▼

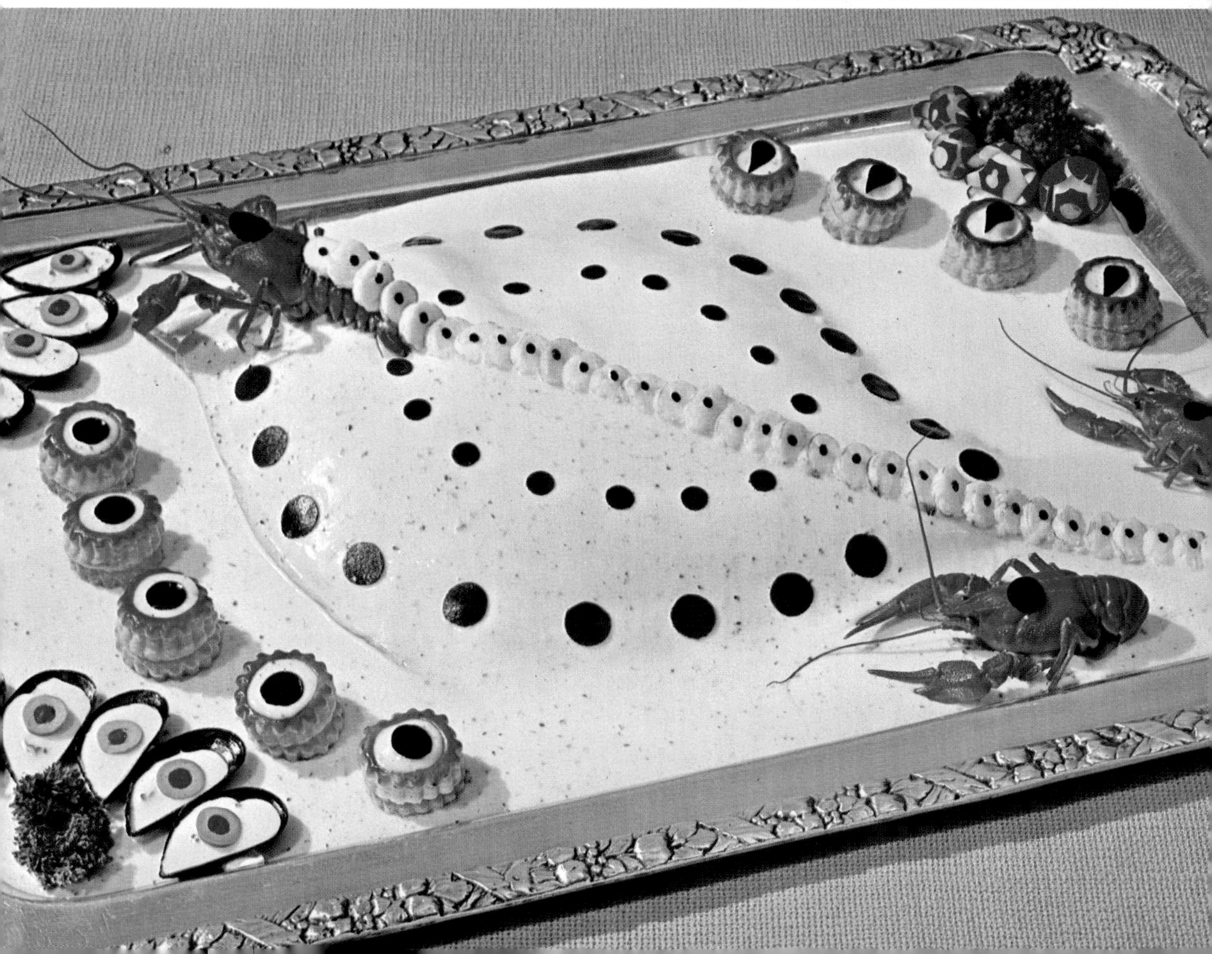

▲ Sole mère Récamier, p. 314

Sole Mireille, p. 315 ▼

▲ Sole ambassade II, p. 297

Filets de sole Léopold, p. 313 ▼

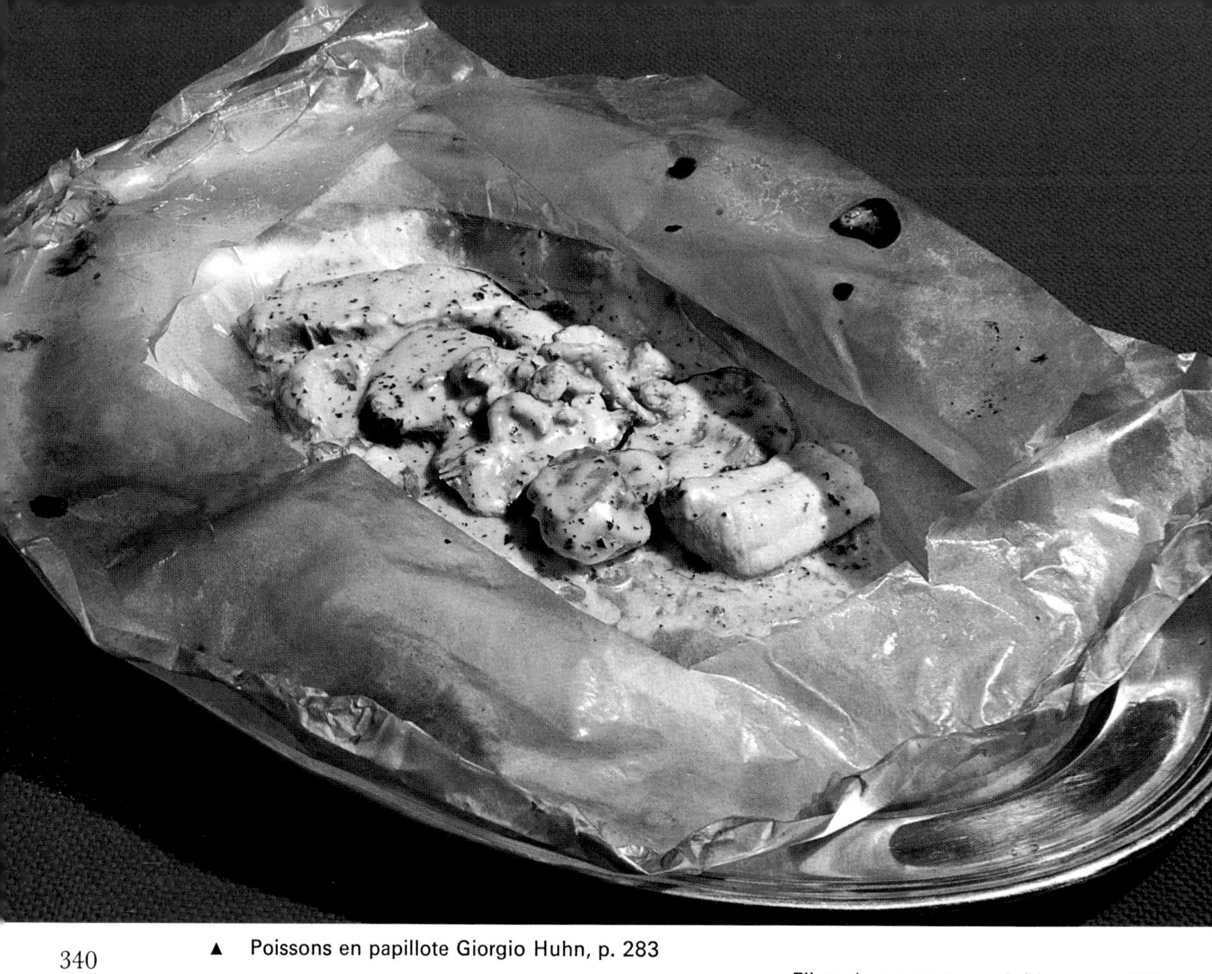

▲ Poissons en papillote Giorgio Huhn, p. 283

Filets de maquereau vénitienne, p. 275 ▼

Sole Tivoli, Filets de

For 6 persons: *12 fillets of sole; 12 oysters; 12 small cooked mushroom heads; 12 escalopes of soft roe; 4 dl. sauce genevoise; 100 gr. raw noodles; 2 dl. fish fumet.* Cooking time: 8 to 10 minutes.

Fold the fillets, and poach them in the fish fumet. Drain them and arrange in a ring on a serving dish. Arrange in the centre a garnish of escalopes of soft roe (stewed in butter), oysters (poached and bearded) and mushrooms. Coat all over with the sauce genevoise. Surround with the noodles which have been sauté in butter. *(France.)*

Sole Traviata

Proceed as for the preparation of Merlan Bercy, but surround the soles with 12 very small tomatoes cooked in the oven and filled with a salpicon Nantua. *(France.)* *(See page 276.)*

Sole Tsarine

For 6 persons: *3 soles (400 gr. each); 300 gr. cucumber formed into olive-shapes; 2 dl. fish fumet; 4 dl. sauce Mornay; 1 coffee-spoonful paprika; 50 gr. butter.* Cooking time: 15 minutes.

Stew the cucumber in butter, and season. Poach the soles in the fish fumet. Drain them, arrange on a serving dish, and coat with the sauce Mornay flavoured with paprika. Serve, glazed or unglazed, surrounded with the cucumber. *(France.)*

Sole Tsar Nicolas, Paupiettes de

For 6 persons: *6 fillets of sole (100 gr. each); 3 dl. fish fumet; 1 dl. fresh cream; 50 gr. beurre manié; 6 bearded oysters; 100 gr. mushrooms; 18 shelled crayfish; 1 dl. lobster sauce; 60 gr. caviar; 180 gr. puff-pastry; 1 egg yolk.* Poaching time for the fillets: 5 to 6 minutes.

Flatten the fillets, and trim them. Roll each fillet round a cork shape of suitable size made from a blanched potato. Wrap each paupiette in buttered tinfoil, and poach them in the fish fumet. Stiffen the oysters in their liquor, prepare a salpicon with the mushrooms and crayfish, and bind it with the lobster sauce. When the cooking is finished, remove the tinfoil and carefully take out each potato. Arrange the paupiettes in a buttered gratinating dish; fill the cavity of each with the salpicon, and place an oyster on top. Prepare a creamy sauce with fish fumet, cream and beurre manié, and use to coat the paupiettes. Garnish each with a little caviar, cover the gratinating dish with the puff pastry, gild with the egg yolk, and bake in a hot oven. *(Germany.)*
(See illustration, page 287. N.B. Different presentation.)

Sole d'Urville, Filets de

For 6 persons: *12 fillets of sole; 120 gr. fish forcemeat; 60 gr. truffle; 5 dl. sauce américaine; 12 small boat-shaped puff-pastry cases; 18 shelled crayfish; 2 dl. fish fumet.* Cooking time: 10 to 12 minutes.

Flatten the fillets, mask them with the forcemeat; fold them and stud each of them with a piece of truffle. Poach them in the fish fumet. Drain, arrange on a serving dish, and coat them with the sauce américaine. Garnish with the puff-pastry cases filled with a salpicon of crayfish bound with the same sauce. *(France.)*

Sole "Valentine", Filets de

For 10 persons: *20 fillets of Dover sole of 400 gr. each, trimmed and lightly pressed.* For the mousseline farce: *500 gr. fish flesh; the coral from 3 lobsters; 2 egg whites; 6 dl. fresh cream; a liqueur glass of sherry.*

Pound the fish flesh with the coral, salt, pepper and spices. When well pounded, add the egg whites and pass through a hair sieve. Place in an earthenware bowl on ice and work thoroughly with a wooden spatula adding the cream and the sherry a little at a time. Spread a layer of this mousseline upon each fillet of sole, fold in two and arrange in a well-buttered fish tray, season with salt and milled pepper and moisten with a good fish stock and a glass of champagne. Add thin roundels of new carrots, truffle blades and sliced white mushrooms. Poach for 10 minutes in the oven. Thicken the cooking liquor with beurre manié, egg yolk and cream, season and mask over the fillets. Garnish with fleurons, buttered asparagus tips and conserved sweet red pimentoes.
Created by Eugen Käufeler, Maître de Cuisine, Dorchester Hotel, London.

Sole Valentino, Filets de

For 6 persons: *12 fillets of sole; 250 gr. purée duchesse; 120 gr. rice; 20 gr. chopped onion; 40 gr. white truffle; 3 dl. white stock; 2 dl. fish fumet; 1 egg; 40 gr. butter; 4 dl. sauce Mornay.* Cooking time: 18 minutes.

Prepare a risotto piémontaise with rice, butter, chopped onion, white stock, white truffle (diced) and 6 boat-shaped cases made from the purée duchesse. Gild the cases with beaten egg, and colour them in the oven. Fold the fillets, and poach them in the fish fumet. Drain them, and arrange them on a serving dish. Coat with the sauce Mornay and glaze. Garnish with the cases filled with the risotto piémontaise. *(France.)*

Sole Valois

For 6 persons: *3 soles (450 to 500 gr. each); 2 dl. fish fumet; 4 dl. white wine sauce; 3 cl. tarragon vinegar; 2 cl. white wine; 1 chopped shallot; 10 tarragon leaves; 5 gr. chervil; 6 gr. crushed white peppercorns.* Cooking time: 12 to 15 minutes.

Prepare a reduction (as for sauce béarnaise) with vinegar, white wine, shallot, tarragon, chervil and peppercorns. Pass it through a tammy cloth, and add it to the white wine sauce. Poach the soles in the fish fumet, drain, arrange on a serving dish, and coat them with the sauce. *(France.)*

Sole van den Berg

For 6 persons: *3 soles (400 gr. each); 2 dl. fish fumet; 120 gr. peeled, pipped and chopped tomatoes; 100 gr. cooked diced mushrooms; 40 gr. butter; 4 dl. white wine sauce.* Cooking time: 12 to 15 minutes.

Poach the soles in the fish fumet, and drain them. Arrange them on a serving dish, and coat them with the white wine sauce containing the mushrooms and the chopped tomatoes (softened in butter). *(France.)*

Sole vasovienne

For 6 persons: *3 soles (450 gr. each); julienne of— 60 gr. carrot, 60 gr. celery, 3 button onions, and 1 tablespoonful roughly-chopped parsley; 100 gr. butter; 3 dl. fish fumet.* Cooking time: 12 to 15 minutes.

Poach the soles in the fish fumet with the julienne (which has been previously stewed in butter). Drain the soles and the julienne, and arrange them on a serving dish. Reduce the poaching liquor, monter au beurre. Use to coat the soles, and glaze. *(France.)*

Sole Vatel, Filets de

For 6 persons: *12 fillets of sole; 2 dl. fish fumet; 6 roundels of cucumber 2 cm. thick (scooped out and blanched); 4 dl. sauce Chambord; 3 fillets of sole (goujons); 90 gr. fish forcemeat; 50 gr. butter; flour.* Cooking time: 15 to 18 minutes.

Fill the roundels of cucumber with the fish forcemeat, arrange them on a buttered dish, and cook them, covered, in the oven. Fold the fillets, and poach them in the fish fumet. Season the goujons, and flour and fry them. Arrange the fillets on a serving dish; coat them with the sauce Chambord, and garnish with the cucumber and goujons. *(France.)*

Sole Vendôme, Paupiettes de

Proceed as for the preparation of Paupiettes de sole Grimaldi, but glaze. *(France.)* *(See page 303.)*

Sole vénitienne

For 6 persons: *3 soles (450 gr. each); 2 dl. white wine; 4 dl. sauce vénitienne.* Cooking time: 12 to 15 minutes.

Poach the soles in the white wine. Drain them, arrange on a serving dish, and coat them with the sauce vénitienne containing the poaching liquor. *(France.)*

Sole Verdi, Filets de

For 6 persons: *12 fillets of sole; 2 dl. fish fumet; 180 gr. cooked macaroni; 80 gr. cooked lobster meat; 40 gr. truffle; 1 dl. sauce béchamel; 4 dl. sauce Mornay; 30 gr. butter.* Cooking time: 10 to 12 minutes.

Poach the fillets in the fish fumet. Arrange them in a buttered gratinating dish on top of the macaroni (to which has been added the lobster meat and the diced truffle bound with a light sauce béchamel). Coat with the sauce Mornay and glaze. *(France.)*

Sole Véron, Filets de

For 6 persons: *12 fillets of sole; fresh white breadcrumbs; 150 gr. butter; 4 dl. sauce Véron.* Cooking time: 8 to 10 minutes.

Flatten the fillets, pass them through melted butter, and the breadcrumbs, and press down with the blade of a knife. Cook them in clarified butter. Arrange on a serving dish on top of the sauce Véron (or serve the sauce separately). *(France.)*

Sole Véronique, Filets de

For 6 persons: *12 fillets of sole; 1 dl. white wine; 1 dl. fish fumet; 5 cl. curaçao; 200 gr. peeled and seeded muscat grapes; 75 gr. butter.* Cooking time: 8 to 10 minutes.

Fold the fillets, and poach them in the white wine, fish fumet and curaçao. Arrange the fillets in a ring on a serving dish. Reduce the poaching liquor to the consistency of syrup; monter au beurre. Use this sauce to coat the fillets, and glaze briskly. Fill the centre of the dish with the chilled grapes. *(France.)*

Sole Victoria

For 6 persons: *3 soles (400 gr. each); 100 gr. cooked lobster meat (or crawfish meat); 50 gr. truffle; 2 dl. fish fumet; 4 dl. sauce Victoria.* Cooking time: 12 to 15 minutes.

Poach the soles in the fish fumet, and drain. Arrange them on a serving dish, surround with the lobster and truffle (both in small dice), and coat all over with the sauce Victoria. Glaze. *(France.)*

Sole farcie viennoise

For 6 persons: *3 soles (300 gr. each); 4 chopped shallots; 125 gr. diced fresh mushrooms; 150 gr. diced cooked lobster meat; 3 egg yolks; ¼ litre fresh cream; 1 dl. fish fumet; 1 dl. white wine; 125 gr. butter; 12 small fleurons.* Poaching time: 12 minutes.

Prepare and open the soles as for Sole Colbert. Brown the chopped shallots in 30 gr. butter; add the mushrooms and lobster meat; stew gently. Season and bind with the 3 egg yolks and 6 cl. cream. Stuff the soles with this mixture. Arrange them in a buttered gratinating dish; season with salt and white pepper; moisten with the white wine and fish fumet; cover with buttered paper and poach in the oven. When the cooking is finished, remove all the poaching liquor. Add to it the rest of the cream, reduce, add (away from the heat) the rest of the butter, and correct seasoning and consistency. Coat the soles with this sauce, and glaze quickly under the salamander. Serve decorated with a border of fleurons. *(Austria.)*

Sole Villeroi, Filets de

For 6 persons: *12 fillets of sole; 120 gr. fish forcemeat; 2 dl. fish fumet; ½ litre sauce Villeroi; 2 eggs; breadcrumbs; 4 dl. sauce tomate; parsley.* Cooking time: 10 to 12 minutes.

Flatten the fillets, mask them with the forcemeat, fold them and poach in the fish fumet. Drain them well, dip in the sauce Villeroi, and allow to cool. Coat with egg and breadcrumbs, and fry in hot, deep fat. Arrange the fillets on a napkin, garnish with the fried parsley, and serve the sauce tomate separately. *(France.)*

Sole au vin blanc

For 6 persons: *3 soles (450 to 500 gr. each); 1 dl. fish fumet; 1 dl. white wine; 30 gr. butter; 4 dl. white wine sauce.* Cooking time: 12 to 15 minutes.

Lay the soles, or flat fillets, on a buttered fish dish; moisten with the white wine and fish fumet, and poach. Drain, arrange on a serving dish, and coat with the white wine sauce containing the reduced poaching liquor. Glaze briskly, or serve unglazed. *(France.)*

Sole Walewska, Filets de

For 6 persons: *12 fillets of sole; 12 escalopes of cooked lobster tail (or 6 picked tails of langoustines); 12 thin slices of truffle; 2 dl. fish fumet; 25 gr. butter; 4 dl. sauce Mornay.* Cooking time: 10 minutes.

Poach the fillets flat in the fish fumet. Arrange them on a buttered gratinating dish. Place on each an escalope of lobster and a slice of truffle (or else decorate with a slice of truffle, and surround with the tails of langoustines which have been cut in two lengthwise). Coat with the sauce Mornay, and glaze. *(France.)*

Sole Walkyrie, Filets de

For 6 persons: *12 fillets of sole; 12 escalopes of cooked lobster tail; 12 thin slices of truffle; 2 dl. fish fumet; 3 dl. white wine sauce; 2 dl. sauce américaine.* Cooking time: 8 to 10 minutes.

Fold the fillets, and poach them in the fish fumet. Drain them, arrange on a serving dish, and place on each of them an escalope of lobster and a slice of truffle. Coat lightly with the white wine sauce. Serve the sauce américaine separately. *(France.)*

Sole Washington, Filets de

For 6 persons: *12 fillets of sole; 12 escalopes of lobster tail; 30 gr. truffle; 4 dl. sauce américaine; 80 gr. butter; flour.* Cooking time: 8 to 10 minutes.

Season and flour the fillets, and cook them gently in butter (without too much coloration). Arrange them on a serving dish, place on each an escalope of lobster, coat them with sauce américaine, and sprinkle them with a fine julienne of truffle. *(France.)*

Sole Wilhelmine, Paupiettes de

For 6 persons: *6 fillets of sole; 6 large oval potatoes; 6 oysters; 200 gr. diced cucumber; 2 dl. fish fumet; 1 dl. fresh cream; 50 gr. butter; 3 dl. sauce Mornay.* Cooking time: 15 to 20 minutes.

Bake the potatoes, and scoop them out (as for Paupiettes de sole Georgette. *See page 303*). Fold the fillets, and poach them in the fish fumet. Garnish the inside of each potato with a tablespoonful of cucumber stewed in butter and bound with cream. Place a fillet on each potato and, on top of that, a large oyster (poached and bearded). Coat with the sauce Mornay, glaze briskly, and arrange on a napkin. (N.B. Use fairly large fillets.) *(France.)*

Sole Yvette

Proceed as for the preparation of Sole aux fines herbes, but garnish with very small tomatoes (scooped out, and then filled with fish forcemeat, and cooked in a slow oven). *(France.)* *(See illustration, page 305. N.B. Different presentation.)*

Sole Yvette, Filets de

Proceed as for the preparation of Filets de sole aux crevettes, but place a thin slice of truffle on each fillet, and glaze. *(France.)* *(See page 300.)*

Tentation de Monsieur Janson

For 6 persons: *200 gr. anchovies in brine; 1 kg. 500 potatoes; 500 gr. onions; 4 dl. fresh cream; 150 gr. butter; breadcrumbs; dill leaves.* Cooking time: 20 minutes.

Soak the salt out of the anchovies, and bone and skin them. Dry them and cut each, lengthwise, into fillets. Peel the potatoes, and cut them into a julienne. Slice the onions thinly. Butter a large gratinating dish, and line it with a layer of potatoes. Garnish this layer with the anchovy fillets, cover with the onions, and finish off with a layer of potatoes. Spread the rest of the butter over the potatoes, sprinkle with the cream (which must not cover the border of the dish), and sprinkle with the breadcrumbs. Allow 20 minutes for cooking, in a medium oven, from the time when the cream starts boiling. Garnish with quarters of lemon and dill leaves. *(Sweden.)*

Thon

Tunny

A darne of fresh tunny is usually called a rouelle. For braising, the fish must be cut into pieces 4½ cm. to 5 cm. thick.

Thon bonne femme

For 6 persons: *1 roundel (rouelle) of tunny, weighing 900 gr.; 75 gr. chopped onion; 350 gr. peeled, pipped and chopped tomatoes; 100 gr. gherkins; 7 cl. oil; ½ litre white wine; 4 cl. vinegar; 40 gr. flour; 1 bouquet garni; 1 tablespoonful of chopped parsley.* Cooking time: 1 hour 20 minutes.

Blanch the tunny for 7 or 8 minutes. Drain and dry it, colour it in oil on both sides, and remove. In the same oil, lightly colour the onions, sprinkle them with flour, allow to cook for 2 or 3 minutes, and moisten with equal quantities of white wine, water and vinegar. Stir well. Season with salt and pepper, add the chopped tomatoes and the bouquet garni, and bring to the boil. Place the tunny in this liquor, and cook gently (covered) in the oven for 1 hour. Remove the bouquet garni, and add to the sauce the gherkins (cut into very thin slices) and the chopped parsley. *(France.)*

Thon braisé

Braised tunny

For 6 persons: *1 roundel (rouelle) of tunny, weighing 900 gr. to 1 kg.; 2 carrots; 2 onions; 1 bouquet garni; 7 cl. oil; 1 dl. white wine; bouillon.* Cooking time: 1 hour 30 minutes.

Place the tunny in an earthenware dish (which has been liberally oiled, and then lined with thick roundels of carrot and onion). Cover, and allow to sweat in the oven for 15 minutes. Moisten with the white wine, and reduce almost completely. Pour on enough bouillon just to cover the rouelle; season with salt and pepper; add the bouquet garni and cook gently (covered) for 1 hour 15 minutes. Arrange the tunny on a serving dish. Reduce the braising stock, pass and skin it, and correct seasoning and consistency. Coat the tunny with a little of the stock. Serve the rest of the stock separately, and a purée of spinach, sorrel, celeriac or even of potatoes. *(International cookery.)*

Thon grillé

Grilled tunny

For 6 persons: *6 roundels (rouelles) of tunny (150 gr. each, and 2 cm. to 2½ cm. thick); 1 small thinly-sliced onion; ½ bayleaf; 1 sprig of thyme; 6 stalks of parsley; 5 cl. white wine; 1 lemon; 15 cl. oil; 4 dl. sauce rémoulade (or tartare); browned breadcrumbs.* Cooking time: approximately 20 minutes.

Season the rouelles, and marinate them, for at least 1 hour, with the onion, parsley, thyme, bayleaf, white wine, lemon juice and oil. Drain and dry them, oil them, and grill gently. After cooking, sprinkle them on both sides with the breadcrumbs. Arrange them on a serving dish. Serve the sauce separately. *(International cookery.)*

Thon indienne

For 6 persons: *1 roundel (rouelle) of tunny, weighing 900 gr. to 1 kg.; 15 anchovy fillets; 2 carrots; 2 onions; ½ bayleaf; 1 sprig of thyme; 6 stalks of parsley; 5 cl. white wine; 1 lemon; 5 cl. oil; 2 dl. fish fumet; 300 gr. rice; 4 dl. curry sauce.* Cooking time: 1 hour 30 minutes.

Stud the rouelle with anchovy fillets, and marinate it for 1 hour with the carrot and onion (cut into roundels), the parsley, bayleaf, thyme, salt, pepper, white wine and lemon juice. Drain and dry the fish. Liberally oil a casserole; place in it the herbs from the marinating liquor, and lay the rouelle on top. Allow to sweat in the oven for 15 minutes. Moisten with the white wine from the marination and with the fish fumet, and cook gently (covered) in the oven for 1 hour 15 minutes. Arrange the rouelle on a serving dish. Pass and skim the cooking liquor, reduce it, and add it to the curry sauce. Coat the fish with a little of this sauce. Serve separately the rest of the sauce and the rice (cooked indienne). *(France.)*

Thon ménagère

For 4 persons: *500 gr. tunny; 50 gr. butter; 50 gr. onion; 10 gr. flour; 1 dl. white wine; 3 tablespoonfuls of tomato purée; 1 lemon; 150 gr. mushrooms.* Cooking time: 45 minutes to 1 hour.

Place a thick slice of tunny in a saucepan containing water, and blanch it for 6 to 8 minutes to remove the oil from the flesh. Drain the fish, and rissoler it on both sides in butter. Place it on a hot plate. In the butter which is left over, fry 1 chopped onion, sprinkle with 10 gr. flour, allow to cook for a moment, and moisten, first with equal quantities of white wine and of water, and then with the juice of 1 lemon and 3 spoonfuls of concentrated tomato purée. When this sauce comes to the boil, place the tunny in it, cover, and cook very slowly in the oven for approximately 1 hour. When the tunny is well braised, add, according to season, either the mushrooms, or fresh tomatoes (sautéd in butter). *(France.)*

Thon aux oignons et aux concombres sales, Darnes de

For 6 persons: *1 kg. fresh tunny; 1 kg. 500 potatoes; 250 gr. onions; 150 gr. butter; 12 small salted cucumbers; flour.* Cooking time: 12 to 15 minutes.

Cut up the tunny into 6 thick darnes (like steaks), season them with salt and pepper, flour and cook gently in butter on both sides. Arrange the darnes on a serving dish. Lightly colour the thinly-sliced onions in butter. Pour the onions and the butter over the tunny. Serve separately the plain boiled potatoes and the salted cucumbers. N.B. Thickness of the darnes: 1½ cm. to 2 cm. *(Denmark.)*

Thon Orly

For 6 persons: *750 gr. tunny; ½ litre batter; 4 dl. sauce tomate; parsley; flour.* Cooking time: 10 to 12 minutes.

Cut up the tunny into small aiguillettes. Season them with salt and pepper, flour them, dip in the batter and cook quickly in very hot, deep fat. Drain the fish, and arrange, with the fried parsley, on a napkin. Serve the sauce tomate separately. *(France.)*

Thon provençale

For 6 persons: *1 kg. tunny; 15 anchovy fillets; 300 gr. peeled, pipped and chopped tomatoes; 3 cloves of garlic; 50 gr. chopped onion; 3 dl. white wine; 7 cl. bouillon; 2 dl. sauce demi-glace; 30 gr. capers; 1 tablespoonful of chopped parsley; 1 lemon; 1 carrot; 1 onion; ½ bayleaf; 1 sprig of thyme; pinch of basil; 1 bouquet garni; 12 cl. oil.* Cooking time: 1 hour 30 minutes.

Stud the rouelle with the anchovy fillets, and marinate it with the carrot and the onion (cut into roundels), the thyme, bayleaf, salt, pepper, lemon juice and oil. Drain and dry the fish, and colour it well in the rest of the oil. Add the chopped onion, the crushed garlic, the chopped tomatoes, the bouquet garni, and pinch of basil. Stew for 20 minutes. Moisten with the white wine and the bouillon, and braise (covered) in the oven for between 1 hour 10 minutes and 1 hour 20 minutes. Remove and drain the fish, and arrange it on a serving dish. Pass and skim the cooking liquor, reduce it, and thicken it with the demi-glace. Complete the sauce with the capers and chopped parsley. Pour a little of it over the rouelle. Serve the rest of the sauce separately. *(France.)*

Turbot, turbotin

Turbot, young turbot

The flesh of the turbot and of the young turbot is firm, white and very tasty. Large turbot can be served whole as a relevé, but in restaurants they are also served cut up into slices or fillets. In this case, the turbot is cut up lengthwise along the backbone, and each half is cut into slices weighing approximately 250 gr. each. In the case of fillets, these are skinned, and served, depending on size, either whole or cut up into smaller pieces. Nearly all preparations of fillets of sole are applicable to fillets of turbot. For the cooking of a whole large turbot, a turbot kettle complete with grid is absolutely essential. If the turbot is to be poached, boiled or braised, a deep incision should be made on the dorsal side (dark side) along the length of the backbone to prevent the fish from losing its shape during cooking. To make sure that large turbot are still hot when served, the garnish should not be arranged around the serving dish. It is preferable to serve the garnish, and the sauce, separately. In this way, the fish is served more quickly. and remains very hot. *(See Culinary Technique, page 76.)*

Turbot Aïda, Filets de

For 6 persons: *6 fillets of young turbot (150 gr. each); 600 gr. leaf spinach (blanched); 4 dl. sauce Mornay; 25 gr. grated Parmesan cheese; 20 gr. browned breadcrumbs; 5 gr. paprika; 2 dl. fish fumet; 75 gr. butter.* Cooking time: 12 minutes.

Stew the spinach in butter, and season with salt and paprika. Poach the fillets in the fish fumet, and drain them. Arrange the spinach in a buttered gratinating dish, and place the fillets on top. Coat with the sauce Mornay, sprinkle with the grated cheese and browned breadcrumbs, and dot the whole surface with small pieces of butter. Brown in a hot oven. *(France.)*

Turbot ambassade, Filets de

Proceed as for the preparation of Sole ambassade. *(France.)* *(See page 297.)*

Turbot américaine, Filets de

For 6 persons: *6 fillets of turbot (150 gr. each); 12 escalopes of lobster tail; 2 dl. fish fumet; 4 dl. sauce américaine.* Cooking time: 12 minutes.

Season the fillets with salt and pepper, and poach them in the fish fumet. Drain them, and arrange them on a serving dish. Garnish each fillet with 2 escalopes of lobster tail (prepared américaine). Coat with sauce américaine. *(France.)*

Turbot andalouse

For 6 persons: *1 young turbot, weighing 1 kg. 500 to 1 kg. 800; 120 gr. butter; 3 thinly-sliced onions; 150 gr. tomatoes (peeled, pressed and thinly sliced); 120 gr. thinly-sliced raw mushrooms; 2 dl. white wine; 1 dl. fish fumet; 120 gr. red peppers (cut into thin strips); breadcrumbs.* Cooking time: 30 to 40 minutes.

Lightly colour the thinly-sliced onions in butter, and sprinkle on a thickly buttered gratinating dish. Lay the fish on the onions, season with salt and pepper, and place on top of the fish the mushrooms, tomatoes and red peppers. Moisten with the white wine and the fish fumet, sprinkle lightly with the breadcrumbs, and dot the surface with small pieces of butter. Cook in a low oven.

N.B. The gelatinous consistency of the fish makes thickening possible by the simple reduction of the moistening liquor. *(France.)*

Turbot arlésienne

For 6 persons: *1 young turbot weighing 1 kg. 500; 12 tomato halves; 150 gr. button onions (cut into roundels); 3 chopped shallots; 50 gr. butter; 2 dl. white wine; 1 dl. fish fumet; 4 dl. sauce Bercy.* Cooking time: 30 to 35 minutes.

Sprinkle the chopped shallots into a buttered turbot-kettle, place the turbot on the buttered grid, season the fish with salt and pepper, and moisten with the white wine and fish fumet. Braise in a moderate oven, basting frequently. Drain the fish, and arrange it on a serving dish. Strain the cooking liquor, reduce it, and add it to the sauce Bercy. Coat the fish with sauce, and glaze. Garnish with the tomato halves (which have been scooped out, cooked in the oven, and filled with the fried roundels of onion). *(France.)*

Turbot berlinoise, Fricassée de

For 6 persons: *2 kg. (approx.) of turbot; 12 medium-sized crayfish; 250 gr. pike forcemeat; 250 gr. small raw mushroom heads; 18 button onions; 2 egg flolks; 2 shallots; 1 button onion; 125 gr. butter; 2 dl. white Moselle; 1 dl. fresh cream; 6 parsley stalks; 5 peppercorns; the juice of ½ lemon; 30 gr. flour; 6 fleurons.* Poaching time for the turbot: 10 to 12 minutes.

Fillet the turbot, skin the fillets, and cut them up into square pieces weighing approximately 30 gr. each. Prepare ¾ litre of fish fumet with the chopped backbones, the single button onion (thinly sliced), and the parsley, peppercorns, white wine and some water. Poach the mushroom heads in a nut of butter, with the lemon juice and a pinch of salt. Gently cook the button onions in a little butter without colouring them. Cook the crayfish, shell and gut them, and prepare a crayfish butter with the pounded shells and 40 gr. butter. Using the pike forcemeat, prepare quenelles (of the size of a small coffee-spoon), and poach them in salted water. Prepare a white roux with 40 gr. butter and 30 gr. flour, pour the passed fish fumet into it, and stir until a velouté is obtained. Stew the shallots in a nut of butter, add the squares of turbot, colour quickly, and moisten with 2 or 3 tablespoonfuls of fish fumet which have been kept in reserve for this purpose. Season lightly, and poach gently (covered). Drain the turbot well, the mushrooms and the button onions, and add the cooking stock to the velouté. Reduce the sauce slightly, bind it with the cream and egg yolks, flavour with the lemon juice, and correct seasoning and consistency. Mix the pike quenelles and the crayfish tails with the squares of turbot, the mushrooms and onions, bind with the sauce, and heat without cooking. Arrange in a timbale, sprinkle with crayfish butter, and garnish round the dish with fleurons. *(Germany.)*

Turbot Boistelle, Filets de

For 6 persons: *6 fillets of turbot (150 gr. each); 120 gr. butter; 3 chopped shallots; 150 gr. thinly-sliced raw mushrooms; ½ lemon; 2 dl. fish fumet.* Cooking time: 12 to 15 minutes.

Arrange the fillets in a sauteuse (which has been buttered, and then sprinkled with chopped shallot). Add the thinly-sliced mushrooms, season with salt and pepper, and moisten with the fish fumet and lemon juice. Cover with a sheet of buttered paper, and poach in the oven. Drain the fillets and the mushrooms, and arrange them on a serving dish. Reduce the cooking stock, monter au beurre, correct seasoning and consistency, and pour this sauce over the fillets. *(France.)*

Turbot bonne femme, Filets de

Proceed as for the preparation of Filets de sole Boistelle, but surround the serving dish with thick slices of plain boiled potatoes. *(France.)*

Turbot bouilli

Boiled turbot

For 6 to 8 persons: *1 turbot, gross weight between 1 kg. 500 and 1 kg. 800; 750 gr. potatoes; 5 to 6 dl. sauce hollandaise (or sauce mousseline or crevette, or lobster or caper sauce, or beurre fondu); 20 gr. butter; parsley.* Cooking time: 35 to 40 minutes.

Lay the fish on the grid of a turbot-kettle, and moisten with salted cold water (15 gr. salt per litre of water). Add to each litre 1 dl. milk and a thin slice of peeled and pipped lemon. Bring slowly to the boil, then poach gently, counting the cooking time from the moment when boiling point is reached. Drain the fish, and arrange very carefully on a napkin on a serving dish. Pass a piece of butter over the whole surface of the fish, to give it a sheen, and garnish with parsley. Serve the plain boiled potatoes and the sauce (or beurre fondu) separately. *(International cookery.)*

Turbot, Cadgery de

Kedgeree of turbot

For 6 persons: *600 gr. turbot (cooked, skinned and boned); 50 gr. butter; 6 hard-boiled eggs; 300 gr. pilaf rice; 6 dl. sauce béchamel, 1 coffee-spoonful curry powder.*

Flake the turbot, and heat it in butter. Season the fairly clear sauce béchamel with the curry powder. Thicken the well-cooked pilaf rice with a third of the sauce. Arrange, in a timbale, the turbot flesh, the rice, and the hard-boiled eggs (cut into large dice), alternating these ingredients. Coat with the sauce. *(International cookery.)*

Turbot au Chambertin, Filets de

For 6 persons: *6 fillets of young turbot (150 gr. each); ½ litre Chambertin; 150 gr. butter; 150 gr. fillets of sole; ½ lemon; flour.* Cooking time: 12 to 15 minutes.

Lay the fillets of turbot on a butter fish tray, season with salt and pepper, moisten with the Chambertin, and poach in the oven (covered with a sheet of buttered paper). Drain the fillets, and arrange them on a serving dish. Reduce by half the wine from the cooking, add a little freshly-milled pepper and a few drops of lemon juice, and thicken with beurre manié (made with 75 gr. butter and 20 gr. flour). Coat the fish with this sauce, and glaze quickly. Garnish with the fillets of sole, cut into a julienne, floured, sautéd in clarified butter, and kept very crisp. *(France.)*

Turbot au champagne, Filets de

Proceed as for the preparation of Sole au champagne. *(France.)* *(See page 299.)*

Turbot Chauchat, Filets de

Proceed as for the preparation of Filets de sole Chauchat. *(France.)* *(See page 300.)*

Turbot au cidre, Délice de

For 6 persons: *900 gr. fillets of skinned turbot; 2 pippin apples; 2 lemons; 75 gr. butter; 2 dl. cider; 2 egg yolks; 6 black olives; 1 bayleaf; 3 cloves; 3 coriander seeds; 6 round croûtons; flour.* Cooking time: approximately 15 minutes.

Cut up the fillets into 6 thick medallions, and colour them for 1 or 2 minutes with the juice of one lemon and a pinch of salt. Peel the apples, cut each into 3 thick slices, core them and cook them in butter. Drain and dry the medallions, flour them, and sauté in butter. Using the sauteuse in which the medallions have been coloured, swill out with the juice of the second lemon and the cider, add the bay-leaf, cloves and coriander, season with salt and pepper, and bring to the boil. Mix the egg yolks with ½ coffee-spoonful of flour. Use to thicken the cooking liquor; bring to the boil again, and correct seasoning and consistency. Arrange the medallions on top of the croûtons in a serving dish, and coat with the sauce which has been passed through a sieve. Garnish each medallion with a slice of apple and a black olive. *(Israel.)*

Turbot commodore

For 6 persons: *1 young turbot, weighing between 1 kg. 500 and 1 kg. 800; 18 large noisette potatoes; 12 fish quenelles (moulded with coffee-spoons); 6 oysters (prepared Villeroi); 6 small lobster croquettes; 6 trussed crayfish; 4 dl. sauce normande; 30 gr. anchovy butter; 20 gr. butter.* Cooking time: 35 to 40 minutes.

Poach the turbot in salted water. Drain the fish, and arrange it on a serving dish. Rub the surface of the fish with butter, and surround with an alternating garnish of the noisette potatoes, oysters Villeroi and lobster croquettes. Serve the sauce normande separately (finished with the anchovy butter). *(France.)*

Turbot à la crème au gratin

For 6 persons: *900 gr. (net weight) of cooked turbot; 4 dl. sauce Mornay; 450 gr. purée duchesse; 40 gr. grated Parmesan cheese; 20 gr. butter; 1 egg yolk.* Cooking time: 6 to 8 minutes.

Using a star piping-tube, border a buttered gratinating dish with the purée duchesse. Coat the dish with part of the sauce Mornay. Fill two-thirds of the dish with the hot cooked turbot (which has been cut into escalopes). Cover with the rest of the sauce Mornay, and sprinkle with the grated cheese, and then with melted butter. Brush with beaten egg. Place in a low oven to brown. *(France.)*

Turbot dieppoise, Filets de

Proceed as for the preparation of Merlan dieppoise. *(France.)* *(See page 277.)*

Turbot Dugléré

Proceed as for the preparation of Barbue Dugléré. *(France.)* *(See page 246.)*

Turbot braisé Elisabeth

For 6 to 8 persons: *1 turbot (weighing 2 kg. to 2 kg. 500); 500 gr. fresh white bread (without crusts); ¾ litre milk; 12 poached and bearded oysters; 12 large shelled prawns; 150 gr. brunoise of celeriac (lightly cooked; 5 egg yolks; 3 dl. fish fumet; ½ litre fresh cream; 150 gr. butter; 1 dl. champagne; fleurons; aromatic herbs.* Cooking time: approximately 40 to 50 minutes.

Clean and trim the turbot. Make an incision on the 'black skin' side, and loosen the fillets so as to facilitate the removal of the backbone. Steep the bread in the milk, press it gently, pound it well with the egg yolks, season strongly, add the brunoise, the oysters, and the prawns (cut into tronçons), and mix well together.

Stuff the turbot with this mixture. Line a turbot-kettle with the onions, carrots and celery (all thinly sliced), picked parsley, 1 bayleaf, 1 sprig of thyme, 1 clove, a few white peppercorns, and the pounded crayfish shells. Place the turbot on the grid of the buttered turbot-kettle, with the 'black skin' side down, moisten with the champagne (or any other dry white wine of good quality), cover and braise in the oven, basting frequently. Drain the turbot, arrange it on a serving dish, and keep it hot, covered with a sheet of buttered paper. Pass the cooking liquor, reduce it by half, blend in the cream, reduce until the sauce clings to a spatula, and monter au beurre. Skin the turbot, coat it with part of the sauce, and garnish with the fleurons. Serve the rest of the sauce separately. *(International cookery.)*

Turbot Empire, Filets de

For 6 persons: *6 fillets of turbot (150 gr. each); 6 thin slices of truffle; 6 large oysters; 6 medallions of lobster tail; 6 large turned mushroom-heads; 4 dl. sauce Nantua; 2 dl. fish fumet; 12 small puff-pastry fleurons.* Cooking time: 12 to 15 minutes.

Poach the fillets in the fish fumet. Drain them, arrange them on a serving dish, and garnish with the medallions of lobster tail, the poached and bearded oysters, the slices of truffle, and the mushrooms. Coat with the sauce Nantua, and surround with the fleurons. *(France.)*

Turbot fermière, Filets de

For 6 persons: *2 fillets of turbot (450 gr. each); 1 dl. white wine; 1 dl. fish fumet; 1 carrot; 2 young onions; the white of 1 leek; 1 stick of celery; 2 shallots; 100 gr. butter; 2 dl. fresh cream.* Cooking time: 18 to 20 minutes.

Cut up the vegetables into very thin slices, and stew them in butter. Sprinkle a buttered fish tray with chopped shallots, arrange the thinly-sliced vegetables in a layer on top, and then the fillets. Season with salt and pepper, moisten with the white wine and fish fumet, cover with a sheet of buttered paper, and poach gently in the oven. Drain the fillets well, arrange them on a serving dish, and cover them with the vegetables. Pass the cooking stock, add the cream, reduce by one-third, butter, and correct seasoning and consistency. Coat the fillets with this sauce. Serve very hot. *(France.)*

Turbot française

For 6 persons: *1 turbot (weighing from 1 kg. 500 to 1 kg. 800); ½ litre white wine sauce; 30 gr. tarragon butter; 12 bouchées mignonnes; 12 poached and bearded mussels; 8 crayfish (cooked and shelled); 40 gr. truffle; 7 cl. sauce poulette; 1 dl. white wine; 1 dl. fish fumet; 25 gr. butter.* Cooking time: 35 to 40 minutes.

Lay the turbot on the buttered grid of a turbot kettle, season with salt and pepper, moisten with the white wine and fish fumet, and braise in the oven. Prepare a salpicon with the mussels, crayfish and truffle, bind it with the sauce poulette, and use it to fill the bouchées. Drain the turbot, and arrange it on a serving dish. Coat one half of the fish (lengthwise) with half of the white wine sauce, and the other half with the rest of the white wine sauce (finished with the tarragon butter). Surround it with the bouchées. *(France.)*
(See illustration, page 337. N.B. Different presentation.)

Turbot François Ier, Filets de

Proceed as for the preparation of Filets de barbue Dugléré, adding 150 gr. mushrooms, thinly sliced and stewed in butter. *(See page 246.)*

Turbot grillé

Grilled turbot

Sprinkle the turbot with oil, and then grill it, in accordance with the cooking method described on page *64*.
(See illustration, page 330.)

Turbot Hasselbacken, Filets de

For 6 persons: *6 skinned fillets of young turbot; 1 tablespoonful of chopped shallot; 1 tablespoonful of chopped parsley; 250 gr. chopped fresh mushrooms; 3 dl. white wine; 1 dl. fish fumet; 200 gr. butter; 1 coffee-spoonful of meat-glaze (glace de viande); the juice of half a lemon; 40 gr. grated Parmesan cheese; 6 fleurons.* Cooking time: 10 to 12 minutes.

Marinate the fillets with salt, pepper and the lemon juice. Arrange them in a buttered gratinating dish, season with salt and pepper, moisten with the fish fumet, cover with a sheet of buttered paper, and poach in the oven. Colour the shallots in melted butter, add the chopped mushrooms, and cook until all the water has evaporated. Moisten with the fish cooking liquor and the white wine, and reduce by two-thirds. Add the meat-glaze and the chopped parsley. Work up, away from the heat, with 125 gr. butter, and correct seasoning and consistency. Coat the fillets with this sauce, sprinkle with the grated cheese, and brown briskly under the salamander. Garnish with the fleurons. Serve pilaf rice separately. *(Sweden.)*

Turbot hollandaise

For 6 persons: *1 young turbot (weighing 1 kg. 500 to 1 kg. 800); 4 dl. sauce hollandaise; 750 gr. potatoes; parsley.* Cooking time: 35 to 40 minutes.

Poach the fish in salted water. Drain, arrange on a serving dish, and garnish with the parsley. Serve separately the sauce hollandaise and the plain boiled potatoes.
N.B. The sauce hollandaise can be replaced by plain beurre fondu. *(France.)*

Turbot hongroise, Filets de

For 6 persons: *6 fillets of turbot (150 gr. each); 2 dl. fish fumet; 4 dl. white wine sauce; 1 coffee-spoonful of paprika; 750 gr. potatoes.* Cooking time: 12 to 15 minutes.

Poach the fillets in the fish fumet. Drain them, and arrange them on a serving dish. Coat with the white wine sauce seasoned with the paprika, and garnish with the plain boiled potatoes. *(France.)*

Turbot aux huîtres

Proceed as for the preparation of Sole aux huîtres, allowing for the difference in size when calculating the cooking time. *(France.)* *(See page 304.)*

Turbot impériale, Filets de

For 6 persons: *2 whole fillets of turbot (450 gr. each); 6 empty crayfish-shells; 120 gr. salpicon Nantua; 6 oysters and 6 large mussels (all these prepared Villeroi); 250 gr. potatoes (shaped with a large spoon cutter); 150 gr. whitebait; 2 dl. sauce Victoria; 2 dl. fish fumet; flour.* Cooking time: 18 to 20 minutes.

Poach the fillets in the fish fumet. Drain them and arrange them on a serving dish. Garnish with the crayfish shells stuffed with the salpicon Nantua, the oysters and mussels, the plain boiled potatoes, and the whitebait (these last floured and fried).
N.B. The sauce Victoria can be replaced by sauce genevoise or sauce hollandaise. *(France.)*

Turbot Kléber

For 6 persons: *1 young turbot (weighing 1 kg. 500 to 1 kg. 800); 50 gr. butter; 2 dl. fish fumet; 75 gr. cooked mushrooms; 75 gr. shelled prawns; 40 gr. truffle; 4 dl. sauce Bercy; 1 tablespoonful of meat-glaze (glace de viande).* Cooking time: 35 to 40 minutes.

Braise the turbot (covered) with the fish fumet. Drain it, and arrange it on a serving dish. Reduce the cooking liquor considerably, and add it to the sauce Bercy (which has been finished off with the meat-glaze). Incorporate into the sauce the mushrooms, truffle and prawns (all these cut into small dice), and use this mixture to coat the fish. *(France.)*

Turbot Laguipière

For 6 persons: *1 young turbot (weighing 1 kg. 500); 12 very small potato croquettes; 12 deep half-shells of oysters (filled with salpicon Joinville); 4 dl. sauce normande; 40 gr. truffle.* Cooking time: approximately 35 minutes.

Poach the turbot in a court-bouillon containing white wine. Drain the fish, and arrange it on a serving dish. Coat with the sauce normande, and sprinkle with the truffle, cut into small dice. Surround with the half-shells (filled with the salpicon Joinville), and with the potato croquettes (kept very crisp). *(France.)*

Turbot ligurienne

For 6 persons: *1 turbot (weighing 1 kg. 500); 1 dl. olive oil; the juice of two lemons; 6 small basil leaves; 2 bayleaves; 100 gr. butter; 100 gr. blanched walnuts; 20 gr. blanched pistachio nuts; 4 anchovy fillets; 1 kg. potatoes (olive-shaped).* Cooking time: approximately 35 minutes.

Prepare the turbot, score it, and marinate it for 30 minutes with olive oil, lemon juice, bayleaves and freshly-milled pepper. Drain and dry the fish, and cook it on a charcoal grill, basting frequently with the marinating liquor. Pound in a mortar, or pass through a mixing machine: the walnuts, pistachios, anchovy fillets, basil and parsley, and blend these with the butter. Melt this mixture in a saucepan, add to it the juice of ½ lemon, and pour over the fish which has been arranged in a serving dish. Garnish around the border of the dish with the plain boiled potatoes. *(Italy.)*

Turbot marquise, Escalopes de

For 6 persons: *12 escalopes of fillet of turbot (75 gr. each); 400 gr. duchesse potatoes; 2 tablespoonfuls of tomato concentrate; 2 dl. fish fumet; ½ dl. sauce crevette; 12 small quenelles (made from salmon forcemeat); 12 small pieces of truffle (olive-shaped); 125 gr. shelled prawns; 1 egg yolk.* Cooking time: 12 to 15 minutes.

Poach the escalopes in the fish fumet. Using a star piping-tube, border a round gratinating dish with the duchesse potatoes (mixed with the tomato concentrate), brush with the egg yolk and colour in the oven. Drain the escalopes, and arrange them round the dish. Fill the centre with the quenelles, truffles and prawns. Without touching the border of the dish, coat the fish and the garnish with the sauce crevette. *(France.)*

Turbot meunière

For cooking in the style designated meunière, the turbot is cut up into escalopes or fillets. However, small young turbot, weighing not more than 1 kg., can be cooked meunière, allowing for the difference in size when calculating the cooking time. The fish should be scored before cooking. *(France.)*

Turbot meunière aux amandes, Filets de

For 6 persons: *6 skinned fillets of turbot (150 gr. each); 200 gr. butter; 75 gr. flaked almonds; 4 lemons; 1 tablespoonful of chopped parsley.* Cooking time: approximately 10 minutes.

Wash the fillets, and dry them on a cloth. Season with salt and pepper, and flour (moderately, but patting the flour down carefully). Place the fillets in a hot fish frying-pan with lightly-coloured butter. As soon as one side of the fillets is coloured, carefully turn the fish over. (It must be coloured just golden; the butter must never turn black). Garnish the serving dish with half slice twists of lemon. Arrange the fillets on the serving dish. Lightly colour the almonds in butter, and sprinkle over the fillets. Decorate each fillet with a thin slice of peeled raw lemon. Sprinkle with the chopped parsley. *(Belgium.)*

Turbot Mirabeau

For 6 persons: *1 young turbot (1 kg. 500); 2 dl. sauce genevoise; 2 dl. white wine sauce; 12 anchovy fillets; 12 thin slices of truffle; 12 blanched leaves of tarragon.* Cooking time: approximately 35 minutes.

Poach the turbot in a court-bouillon containing white wine. Drain the fish, and arrange it on a serving dish. Coat one half of the fish (lengthwise) with the sauce genevoise, and the other half with the white wine sauce. Arrange the slices of truffle on the white wine sauce, the leaves of the tarragon on the sauce genevoise, and the anchovy fillets between the two sauces. *(France.)*

Turbot Nelson, Filets de

Proceed as for the preparation of Filets de barbue Dugléré, but garnish the fillets with very small potato croquettes shaped like marbles. *(France.)* *(See page 246.)*

Turbot aux oranges sanguines, Filets de

For 6 persons: *the 2 upper fillets of a turbot weighing together 1 kg. 500; 10 blood oranges; 5 egg yolks; 500 gr. butter; 30 gr. beurre manié; 1 dl. whipped cream; 1 lemon.* Poaching time: approximately 35 minutes.

Poach the fillets in deep water (containing the lemon juice, a little salt, and all the zest of 1 orange). Prepare a sauce with 1 dl. cooking liquor, the juice of 4 blood oranges and the beurre manié. Prepare a sauce hollandaise with the egg yolks, the butter, and the juice of 1 blood orange. Blend the two sauces together, and incorporate the whipped cream. Skin the rest of the oranges, and sauté the segments gently in butter. Drain and skin the fillets, and arrange on a serving dish. Cover with the orange segments, and coat lightly with the sauce. Serve the rest of the sauce separately. *(Germany.)*
(See illustration, page 331.)

Turbot ostendaise, Filets de

Fillet the turbot, and proceed as for the preparation of Filets de sole ostendaise. *(France.)* *(See page 319.)*

Turbot prince de Galles

For 6 persons: *1 young turbot (weighing 1 kg. 500); 4 dl. white wine sauce; 5 cl. crayfish coulis; 1 coffee-spoonful of curry powder; 12 oysters and 12 mussels (all prepared Villeroi); 12 very small croquette potatoes; 2 dl. fish fumet; 50 gr. butter.* Cooking time: approximately 35 minutes.

Braise the fish in the fish fumet and butter. Drain the fish, and arrange it on a serving dish. Reduce the braising stock, and add it to the white wine sauce (which has been seasoned with the curry powder, and finished with the crayfish coulis). Use this sauce to coat the fish. Garnish with the mussels and oysters (prepared Villeroi), and with the croquette potatoes. *(France.)*

Turbot Rachel, Filets de

Proceed as for the preparation of Filets de sole Rachel. *(See page 323.)*

Turbot Régence

For 6 persons: *1 turbot (weighing 1 kg. 500 to 1 kg. 800); 1 dl. mushroom cooking liquor; 1 dl. white wine; 50 gr. butter; 12 small fish quenelles (containing crayfish butter); 6 large turned mushroom heads; 6 pieces of truffle (olive-shaped); 6 large oysters (poached and bearded); 6 escalopes of soft roe; 4 dl. sauce normande (containing truffle essence).* Cooking time: 35 to 40 minutes.

Braise the turbot in the white wine, mushroom liquor and butter. Drain the fish, and arrange it on a serving dish. Reduce well the cooking liquor, and add it to the sauce normande. Surround the fish with the quenelles, mushroom heads, soft roes (stewed in butter), oysters and truffles. Serve the sauce separately. *(France.)*

Turbot royale

Proceed as for the preparation of Carpe royale. *(See page 382.)*

Turbot suédoise

Proceed as for the preparation of Turbot Mirabeau. *(See page 351.)*

Turbot Thuillier, Médaillons de

For 6 persons: *12 medallions of turbot (75 gr. each); 2 dl. Noilly-Prat; 2 dl. fish fumet; 3 dl. fish velouté; 2 tablespoonfuls of sauce hollandaise; 125 gr. shelled prawns; 1 small red pepper (cut into a julienne); 180 gr. fine noodles; 40 gr. butter; 50 gr. grated Parmesan cheese.* Cooking time: 12 to 15 minutes.

Poach the medallions in the Noilly-Prat and the fish fumet. Reduce the cooking liquor considerably, blend it with the velouté, simmer gently, remove to the side of the stove, and add the sauce hollandaise. Cook the noodles in salted water, drain them completely, season with salt and pepper, butter lightly, and incorporate the shelled prawns, and the julienne of red pepper (stewed in butter). Arrange the noodles in 6 gratinating dishes, and place 2 medallions of turbot in each. Coat with the sauce, sprinkle with the grated cheese, and glaze. *(International cookery.)*

Turbot Valentino, Filets de

Proceed as for the preparation of Filets de sole Valentino. *(See page 341.)*

Turbotin amiral

For a turbot weighing from 1 kg. 500 to 1 kg. 800, proceed exactly as for the preparation of Barbue amiral. *(France.)* *(See page 245.)*

Turbotin Gavarni

For 6 persons: *1 young turbot, weighing from 1 kg. 500 to 1 kg. 800; 4 dl. sauce hollandaise; 40 gr. truffle; parsley.* Cooking time: 35 to 40 minutes.

Poach the turbot in salted water. Drain it, arrange it on a napkin, and garnish with the parsley. Serve separately the sauce hollandaise, which has been mixed with the truffle cut into very small dice. *(France.)*

Turbotin Mercator, Filets de

For 6 persons: *6 fillets of young turbot (150 gr. each); 1 litre of mussels; 250 gr. fresh mushrooms; ¼ litre fresh cream; 2 egg yolks; 150 gr. butter; 1 lemon; 1 onion; 1 stick of celery; parsley stalks; 4 dl. batter; flour.* Cooking time: 10 minutes.

Skin the fillets, season them with salt and pepper, flour them, and cook in hot butter. When the fillets are cooked golden, arrange them on a serving dish, and keep hot. Cook the mussels with the onion, the thinly-sliced celery, and the parsley. Shell and beard them. Slice the mushrooms thinly, rissoler in butter, moisten with the cream, cook for a few minutes, and blend with the egg yolks and the lemon juice. Away from the flame, add a nut of butter, and correct seasoning and consistency. Pass the mussels through the batter, and plunge them into deep fat. Coat the fillets with the cream (containing the mushrooms), sprinkle with chopped parsley, and garnish with the fried mussels. *(Belgium.)*

Turbot parisienne

For 6 persons: *1 young turbot weighing approximately 1 kg. 500; 1 dl. mushroom cooking liquor; 50 gr. butter; 15 large thin slices of truffle; 15 large escalopes of cooked mushrooms; 6 trussed crayfish (cooked in a court-bouillon); 4 dl. white wine sauce.* Cooking time: approximately 35 minutes.

Poach the turbot in the white wine, mushroom liquor and butter. Drain it, and arrange it on a serving dish. Reduce the cooking liquor well, and add it to the white wine sauce. Surround the fish with a border of alternating slices of truffle and mushrooms. Coat the fish and the garnish with the white wine sauce, and arrange the crayfish at the tail end of the fish. *(France.)*

Turbotin Polignac

Proceed as for the preparation of Sole Polignac, allowing for the difference in size when calculating the cooking time. *(See page 322).*

Turbotin soufflé Reynière

For 6 to 8 persons: *1 young turbot, weighing 1 kg. 500; 300 gr. whiting forcemeat (containing cream); 12 turned mushrooms (cooked white); 12 cooked soft roes; 12 anchovy fillets; 1 dl. fish fumet; 1 dl. mushroom cooking liquor; 60 gr. butter; 3 dl. white wine sauce; 100 gr. purée Soubise.* Cooking time: approximately 40 minutes.

Score the back of the turbot on each side of the backbone, from behind the head and as far as the tail. Loosen the fillets, break off the backbone at each end, and remove it (by loosening the ventral fillets). Season the inside of the fish with salt and pepper, fill it with the forcemeat, and close it again by pressing the dorsal fillets together. Turn the fish upside down, lay it on the buttered grid of a turbot-kettle (turbotière), and poach it gently in the fish fumet and mushroom liquor. Drain the fish, and place it carefully on the serving dish. Arrange down the middle of the fish a line of mushrooms, and, on each side, the soft roes (alternating with the anchovy fillets). Serve separately the white wine sauce containing the reduced poaching stock and the purée Soubise. *(France.)*

Turbotin Rostand

For 6 persons: *1 young turbot weighing 1 kg. 500; 30 gr. julienne of truffle; 100 gr. thinly-sliced cèpes; 2 dl. fish fumet; 5 cl. truffle cooking liquor; 6 bouchées mignonnes (filled with a lobster salpicon prepared américaine); 6 boat-shaped pastry cases filled with asparagus tips bound in butter; 150 gr. whitebait; flour; 100 gr. butter.* Cooking time: 35 minutes.

Poach the turbot in the fish fumet, truffle liquor and the mushroom liquor, with the cèpes and truffle. Drain the fish and arrange it on a serving dish. Pass the cooking liquor, put aside the cèpes and the julienne of truffle; reduce the cooking liquor to a syrupy consistency, monter au beurre, correct seasoning and consistency, add the cèpes and truffle. Use this sauce to coat the fish and glaze briskly. Garnish with the bouchées mignonnes, the pastry cases and the floured and fried whitebait. *(France.)*

Turbotin Saint-Malo

For 4 persons: *1 young turbot (weighing from 1 kg. to 1 kg. 200); 1 dl. olive oil; 500 gr. noisette potatoes; 4 dl. sauce Saint-Malo.* Cooking time: approximately 25 minutes.

Score the fillets on both sides, season with salt and pepper, sprinkle with the olive oil, and grill gently. Arrange the fish on a serving dish, and surround with the noisette potatoes. Serve the sauce separately. *(France.)*

Harengs russe

For 6 persons: *12 fillets of smoked herring; 500 gr. potatoes (cooked in their jackets, and then peeled); 2 chopped shallots; 1 tablespoonful of a mixture of chervil, fennel, and tarragon (all chopped); 1 dl. olive oil; 4 cl. vinegar.*

Skin the fillets, and cut them up into thin escalopes. Arrange them on a dish, alternating them with slices of potato. Season with oil and vinegar, and sprinkle with the chopped shallot and mixed herbs. Allow to marinate for at least 2 hours before serving.

Macquereaux marinés

Preparation as for Harengs marinés. *(See page 356.)*

Maquereaux au yogourt

For 6 persons: *6 mackerel (225 to 250 gr. each); 150 gr. yoghurt; 1 pippin; 10 gr. chopped gherkins; ½ coffee-spoonful chopped chive; 50 gr. butter; 4 cl. oil; flour.* Cooking time: 5 to 6 minutes.

Fillet the fish, season with salt and pepper, flour and colour golden on both sides in butter and oil. Arrange on a serving dish, allow to cool. Peel and pip the apple, cut into fine dice, mix with the yoghurt, gherkins and chive. Pour mixture over the fillets. Serve very cold. *(Great Britain.)*

Rougets en daube

For 6 persons: *2 kg. of small red mullet; 1 litre Pilsener beer; 1 kg. large onions; 1 bouquet garni; 15 leaves of gelatine; 2 egg whites; 12 gherkins; 2 lemons.* Cooking time: approx. 5 minutes.

Remove the heads and tails from the mullet, wash the fish and cut up into pieces weighing approximately 25 gr. each. Slice the onions thinly. Heat the beer with the onion and the bouquet garni. When the liquor simmers (without boiling) add the mullet, and poach for 5 minutes over low heat. Remove the saucepan from the heat. Remove the fish and onion when almost cold, and arrange in a deep serving dish made of earthenware or glass. Prepare the jelly with the cooking beer, the beaten egg whites, and the gelatine (which has previously been softened in cold water). Correct seasoning and consistency. Pass through a damp cloth. Pour the almost cold jelly over the mullet. Decorate with channelled slices of lemon, and slices of gherkin (arranged in a fan-shape). Keep in a cool place for 24 hours before serving. *(Belgium.)*

Rougets en escabèche

Proceed as for the preparation of Éperlans en escabèche, allowing for the difference in size when calculating the cooking time. *(See page 356.)*

Sardines en escabèche

Preparation as for Eperlans en escabèche, using only large sardines. *(See page 356.)*

Sole Bramana, Filets de

For 6 persons: *12 fillets of sole (60 gr. each); 6 apples; 120 gr. cooked rice; 6 slices of pineapple; 6 small boat-shaped puff-pastry cases (filled with mango chutney); ½ litre fish jelly; 100 gr. mayonnaise; 5 cl. whipped cream; 6 thin slices of truffle; 12 round thin slices of preserved ginger; 1 lemon; curry powder; 50 gr. butter; 1 dl. white wine; 4 dl. white sauce chaud-froid.* Cooking time: 7 to 8 minutes.

Flatten the fillets, fold them in two, and poach them in the butter and white wine. Allow them to cool (while being lightly pressed down). Coat with the sauce chaud-froid (seasoned with curry powder); decorate each fillet with a roundel of ginger, and glaze with jelly. Remove a cap from stalk side of each apple, core and peel them, sprinkle them with lemon juice, place them in water containing lemon juice, blanch for 2 or 3 minutes, and allow to cool. Drain and fill each apple with rice bound with mayonnaise (seasoned with curry powder and mixed with the whipped cream). Decorate each apple with a slice of truffle, and coat all over with jelly. Arrange the fillets on a round serving dish, with the tips pointing towards the centre. Surround with the apples (each placed on a round slice of pineapple) alternating with the pastry cases. *(Netherlands.)*

Sole farcis Colette, Filets de

For 6 persons: *12 fillets of sole (60 gr. each); 12 thin slices of raw salmon (of the same shape and size as a half-fillet of sole); 4 dl. white sauce chaud-froid; 75 gr. prawn butter; 24 balls of cooked carrot (shaped with a spoon cutter); 24 'pearls' of truffle; 6 boat-shaped puff-pastry cases, each filled with salmon mousse, a poached and bearded oyster, and a thin slice of truffle; 6 small tomatoes (scooped out, and filled with a fine macédoine of vegetables bound with mayonnaise); 6 cornets of smoked salmon (filled with creamed hard-boiled egg yolks, and decorated with a touch of caviar on top); 1 dl. white wine; 1 dl. light fish fumet; 1 egg white.* Cooking time: 8 to 10 minutes.

Flatten the fillets, and brush them over with egg white. Arrange a slice of salmon on one half, fold each fillet in two, press down lightly, and poach the fillets in the white wine and fish fumet. Allow to cool in the cooking liquor (under slight downward pressure). Dry and trim the fillets, and coat them with the sauce chaud-froid containing the prawn butter. Decorate each fillet with 2 'pearls' of truffle and 2 balls of carrot, and glaze over with the jelly. Use the jelly to glaze the pastry cases, tomatoes and cornets. Arrange the fillets on a serving dish, and garnish them with an alternation of pastry cases, tomatoes and cornets. Surround with jelly cut into small dice. *(Netherlands.)*

Sole Austria, Filets de

For 6 persons: *3 soles (300 gr. each); 6 large tomatoes; 3 chopped shallots; 12 medallions of cooked lobster tail; 1 dl. white wine; 1 bouquet garni; 5 cl. oil; 4 cl. dry sherry; 3 dl. stiff mayonnaise; 5 cl. double cream; ½ coffee-spoonful of chopped tarragon.* Poaching time for the fillets: 7 to 8 minutes.

Fillet the soles. Prepare a stock, with the backbones and the bouquet garni, in 1 dl. to 2 dl. of water. Flatten the fillets, fold them in two and trim them; season with salt and pepper, and poach them in the stock (to which the white wine has been added). Allow to cool. Chop finely the peeled and pipped tomatoes, and cook them in the oil with the chopped shallots. Season with salt and pepper, and add the tarragon and 1 dl. of stock. Cook for 10 minutes, and allow to cool. Add the mayonnaise to this mixture, and incorporate the sherry and the double cream. Drain the fillets well, and arrange them, with the tips pointing to the centre, on a glass serving dish, or on a ravier. Coat with the sauce, and garnish each fillet with a medallion of lobster. *(Austria.)*

Sole moscovite, Filets de

For 6 persons: *12 fillets of sole; 12 round cases (made from channelled, scooped and blanched pieces of cucumber); 60 gr. caviar; ½ litre of jelly; 4 dl. sauce russe; 2 dl. fish fumet; 1 lemon; oil; vinegar.* Cooking time: 8 to 10 minutes.

Marinate the blanched cucumber cases with the salt, pepper, oil and vinegar. Flatten the fillets, roll them into paupiettes, and poach them in the light fish fumet (with the lemon juice, to keep them white). Allow to cool. Drain and sponge the paupiettes, arrange them in the cucumber cases, and decorate them with a touch of caviar in the centre. Glaze with the half-set jelly. Arrange the cases in a ring on a round serving dish, and garnish the centre with chopped jelly. Serve the sauce separately. *(France.)*

Sole sur mousse d'écrevisses, Filets de

For 6 persons: *12 small fillets of sole; 300 gr. crayfish mousse; 12 small shelled crayfish; picked chervil; 1 dl. white wine; 1 dl. white fish fumet; 3 dl. jelly containing white wine.* Cooking time: 8 to 10 minutes.

Flatten the fillets, and fold them in two. Season with salt and pepper, and poach gently in the fish fumet and white wine (covered with a sheet of buttered paper). Allow to cool in the cooking liquor, under slight downward pressure. Drain and dry the fillets. Decorate each of them with chervil and a crayfish (trimmed and split lengthwise). Arrange the fillets on the mousse in a deep serving dish. Cover it all over with a fine and clear jelly containing white wine. *(France.)*

Timbale de filets de sole riche

For 6 persons: *9 fillets of sole (75 gr. each); 180 gr. truffled whiting forcemeat; 300 gr. crayfish mousse; ¾ litre of fish jelly containing white wine; 5 cl. white wine; 1 dl. light fish fumet; 1 lemon; 1 small truffle.* Cooking time: 10 to 12 minutes,

Flatten the fillets, mask them with forcemeat, roll them into paupiettes, arrange side by side in a sauteuse, moisten with the white wine, fish fumet and lemon juice, season with salt and pepper, cover with a sheet of buttered paper, and poach gently in the oven. Allow to cool in the cooking liquor. Drain and sponge the paupiettes, and trim them. Cut each of them into 3 slices (1 cm. thick), and decorate with a round slice of truffle dipped in the half-set jelly. Line a dome-mould or a timbale with jelly. Arrange the slices in superimposed layers, against the inside of the mould, with the decorated sides facing outwards, after dipping them in the half-set jelly to stick them against the outer surfaces. Garnish the centre of the mould with the cold crayfish mousse. Allow to set in a cool place, and seal the mould when the jelly is half set. Keep cold until the moment of serving. Turn out of the mould on to a round serving dish. Garnish with triangles of jelly. Serve a sauce Chantilly (optional) separately. *(International cookery.)*

Sole à la sauce raifort, Filets de

For 6 persons: *6 fillets of sole (75 gr. each); 180 gr. fine macédoine of mixed vegetables; 200 gr. mayonnaise; 5 cl. whipped cream; 30 gr. grated horse-radish; 180 gr. shelled prawns; a julienne of 20 gr. each of carrot and leek (cooked and well-drained); 20 gr. julienne of truffle; 4 dl. jelly containing white wine; 1 dl. light fish fumet; the juice of 1 lemon.* Cooking time: 7 to 8 minutes.

Flatten and fold the fillets, and poach them in the fish fumet and lemon juice. Allow them to cool, under slight downward pressure. Mix 100 gr. mayonnaise with the grated horse-radish and the whipped cream, correct seasoning and consistency, and firm gently with the jelly. Coat the fillets with this sauce, and sprinkle them with the julienne of carrot, leek and truffle. Garnish six silver scallop shells with the macédoine blended with the mayonnaise. Arrange a fillet in each, with the tip pointing towards the 'hinge' of the shell. Surround with the prawns, and coat all over with the jelly. Arrange the shells on a napkin. Decorate with picked parsley. *(Netherlands.)*

Thon Saint-Georges, Roulade de

Tunny Saint-Georges

For 6 persons: *700 gr. fresh tunny; 200 gr. bone-marrow; 6 egg yolks; 3 hard-boiled eggs (shelled); 200 gr. poached mushrooms; 2 small black truffles; gherkins; red peppers in vinegar; ¾ litre of fish jelly.* Poaching time: 1½ hours.

Cut 300 gr. of tunny into long, broad and very thin slices, and cut the rest of the fish into dice. Steep the bone-marrow in milk for 1 hour, and drain well. Mince the diced tunny and the bone-marrow, season with salt and pepper, and use to prepare a forcemeat (blending in the egg yolks). Incorporate into this forcemeat the chopped mushrooms, the chopped hard-boiled eggs, and the finely-diced truffles. Arrange the slices of tunny side by side, cover them with a layer of forcemeat, roll them in a serviette (as for a galantine), tie with string, and poach in a highly-seasoned court-bouillon. Allow to cool in the cooking liquor, and then remove. Decorate with gherkins and peppers, and glaze with fish jelly. Allow to rest in a cool place. Arrange on an oval serving dish, and garnish with dice of fish jelly. *(Italy.)*

Turbot Floralies

For 10 persons: *1 turbot, weighing approximately 1 kg. 600; 400 gr. prawn forcemeat; 20 hard-boiled eggs; 10 thin slices of truffle; 1 dl. mayonnaise blended with 1 litre sauce tartare; 20 turned mushroom heads; 1 yellow pepper; 1 green pepper; 2 spoon-cut balls of water-melon; parsley.* Cooking time: 40 to 50 minutes.

Proceed as for the preparation of Turbot Helgoland. After draining the fish, dry it, and arrange it on a serving dish. Fill the halved eggs with a purée made from the hard-boiled yolks and the mayonnaise. Coat the fish carefully with a thick sauce tartare, and decorate it with the turned mushrooms, the halves of hard-boiled eggs, peppers, spoon-cut water-melon and truffles (as shown in the illustration). *(Switzerland.)*
(See illustration, page 337.)

Turbot Helgoland

For 10 persons: *1 turbot weighing 1 kg. 800; 400 gr. zéphyr forcemeat; 1 cooked lobster, weighing 700 gr.; 10 to 12 thin slices of truffle; 75 gr. mushrooms (cooked white); 2 dl. white fish fumet; 2 dl. white wine; 2 lemons; 1 litre of fish jelly containing white wine; 50 gr. butter; 1 litre sauce Chantilly.* Cooking time: 40 to 50 minutes.

Gut and clean the fish. Rub the white side thoroughly with lemon juice. Score on both halves of the dorsal side, from just behind the head to the tail. Loosen the fillets from the backbone, and remove the bone, after carefully loosening the ventral fillets. Stuff the turbot with the zéphyr forcemeat (containing the flesh from the lobster claws, and the mushrooms, all cut into small dice). Seal in the forcemeat by pressing the fillets together. Turn the fish over, lay it on the buttered grid of a turbot-kettle (turbotière), season with salt and pepper, and moisten with the white wine, fish fumet and lemon juice. Cover with a sheet of buttered paper, and poach in a medium oven, basting from time to time. Allow to cool in the cooking liquor. Drain and dry the fish. Arrange it on a large serving dish which has been glazed with set jelly. Decorate lengthwise, i.e. from head to tail, with escalopes of lobster, alternating with slices of truffle. Glaze with jelly, and surround with diced jelly. Serve the sauce separately. *(Germany.)*

Fresh Water Fish

Hot Dishes

Alose anglaise

Shad English style

For 6 persons: *1 shad (1 kg. 200); 150 gr. butter; 750 gr. potatoes; picked parsley; 1 lemon; 3 cl. oil; thyme; ½ bayleaf; parsley stalks.* Cooking time: approximately 30 minutes.

Score the shad, and marinate it for 1 hour with oil, lemon juice, thyme, bayleaf, parsley, salt and pepper. Drain, smear with butter and grill gently, basting frequently. Arrange on a serving dish with the parsley. Serve beurre fondu and fish potatoes separately. *(France.)*

Alose Bercy

For 6 persons: *1 shad (1 kg. 200); 5 cl. oil; 4 dl. sauce Bercy.* Cooking time: 30 to 35 minutes.

Score the shad, season it, and wrap in greased paper. Bake. Open the paper at table. Serve the sauce Bercy separately. *(France.)*

Alose farcie

Stuffed shad

For 6 persons: *1 shad (1 kg.); 300 gr. pike forcemeat; 3 chopped shallots; 1 tablespoonful fines herbes; 75 gr. butter; 600 gr. fish potatoes; 1 tablespoonful chopped parsley; 4 dl. sauce Bercy.* Cooking time: 35 to 40 minutes.

Empty the shad through the gills. Open the back, and remove the bone. Mix the forcemeat with the chopped shallots (which have been passed through butter) and the fines herbes, and use to stuff the fish. Wrap it in buttered paper (or aluminium foil) and bake. Remove the fish from the paper or foil, arrange it on a serving dish, and garnish with parsley potatoes. Serve the sauce Bercy separately. *(France.)*

Alose au gratin

Proceed as for the preparation of Daurade au gratin, modifying the cooking time to allow for any difference in size. *(France.)* *(See page 259.)*

Alose grillée

Grilled shad

Proceed as for the preparation of Alose anglaise. *(International cookery.)* *(See above.)*

Alose grillée à l'oseille

Grilled shad with sorrel

Proceed as for the preparation of Alose grillée, but serve with it 600 gr. purée of sorrel and 150 gr. beurre fondu. *(France.)*

Alose hollandaise

For 6 persons: *2 shad, 600 to 650 gr. each; 1 dl. vinegar; 10 white peppercorns; 750 gr. fish potatoes; 4 dl. sauce hollandaise; picked parsley; parsley stalks.* Cooking time: approximately 25 minutes.

Cook the fish in salted water with the parsley stalks, peppercorns and vinegar. Drain them, arrange on a napkin, and garnish with the picked parsley. Serve the sauce hollandaise and the plain boiled fish potatoes separately. *(France.)*

Alose maître d'hôtel

For 6 persons: *1 shad (1 kg. 200); 1 lemon; 1 sprig of thyme; ½ bayleaf; parsley stalks; 1 dl. oil; picked parsley; 150 gr. maître d'hôtel butter.* Cooking time: approximately 30 minutes.

Marinate the shad for 1 hour with lemon juice, parsley stalks, bayleaf, thyme, salt, pepper and oil. Dry, flour, oil and grill gently. Arrange on a serving dish, and garnish with the picked parsley. Serve the maître d'hôtel butter separately. *(France.)*

Alose provençale

For 6 persons: *1 shad (1 kg.); 300 gr. fish forcemeat; 1 clove of garlic; 1 dl. olive oil; 300 gr. peeled, pipped and chopped tomatoes; 1 tablespoonfu roughly-chopped parsley; 50 gr. anchovy butter; 15 cl. white wine.* Cooking time: 35 to 40 minutes.

Empty the fish through the gills. Open the back, remove the bone, wash the fish, dry, and season the inside. Stuff the fish with the forcemeat (slightly flavoured with crushed garlic), lay it on an oiled dish, season with salt and pepper, add the chopped tomatoes, white wine, and 3 tablespoonfuls of olive oil. Braise in the oven. Arrange the cooked fish on a serving dish with the chopped tomatoes, and pour on top the reduced poaching liquor (to which has been added 2 tablespoonfuls of olive oil) worked up with the anchovy butter. Sprinkle with the chopped parsley. *(France.)*

Anguilles aux pousses de bambou japonaise, p. 244 ▶

SUPER-SEASONING
AJI-NO-MOTO
AJI·NO·MOTO
A VEGETABLE PROTEIN
DERIVATIVE

▲ Féra au bleu.

Filets de perche du gourmet, p. 394 ▼

▲ Esturgeon en cocotte, p. 383

Filets de perche Murat, p. 394 ▼

▲ Anguille Sainte Ménéhould, p. 372

Filets de sole Caroline, p. 224 ▼

Pâté d'anguille anglaise

Eel pie

For 6 persons: *1 kg. of eel; 6 hard-boiled eggs; 2 dl. white wine; 300 gr. puff pastry; 2 dl. demi-glace containing fish essence; 1 tablespoonful chopped parsley; 30 gr. butter; 1 egg.* Cooking time: approximately 1½ hours.

Bone the eel, cut the fillets into escalopes, blanch them in salted water, drain, season with salt and pepper, and add a pinch of grated nutmeg. Arrange the escalopes in a long, shallow pie-dish, alternating them with thick slices of hard-boiled egg. Moisten to cover with the white wine, sprinkle with the chopped parsley and with a little beurre fondu. Cover with a layer of puff pastry. Score, and decorate as required. Brush with beaten egg and make an opening in the centre to allow steam to escape. Bake in a medium oven. At the moment of serving, pour the demi-glace into the pie through the opening. *(International cookery.)*

Anguille Beaucaire

For 6 persons: *1 eel (900 gr.); 250 gr. whiting forcemeat; 100 gr. duxelles; 3 chopped shallots; 15 cl. white wine; 5 cl. cognac; 150 gr. butter; 150 gr. small raw mushrooms; 150 gr. peeled button onions.* Cooking time: 20 to 25 minutes.

Bone the eel, and fill it with the forcemeat containing the duxelles. Re-shape the eel, sew it up, shape it into an oval ring; stiffen it in butter, and season. Butter an oven-proof terrine; sprinkle it with the shallots, and place the eel on top. Moisten with the white wine and cognac; add the small mushrooms and button onions (both previously coloured in butter) and 75 gr. butter. Cover the terrine with a lid, and braise the eel in the oven. Serve in the same container. *(France.)*

Anguille Benoîton

For 6 persons: *1 kg. 200 of eel; 4 chopped shallots; 6 parsley stalks; 3 dl. red wine; 100 gr. butter; picked parsley; flour.* Cooking time: 12 minutes.

Bone the eel, cut the fillets into thin strips 10 cm. long, and twist them into 'ringlet'-shapes. Season, flour and fry. Arrange the fish on a napkin with the fried picked parsley. Reduce the red wine by two-thirds with the eel trimmings, parsley stalks and chopped shallots. Pass through a conical strainer (chinois), monter au beurre, and correct the seasoning and consistency. Serve this sauce separately. *(France.)*

Anguille bouillie anglaise

Eel and parsley sauce

For 6 persons: *1 kg. of eel; 4 dl. parsley sauce; 750 gr. potatoes.* Cooking time: 10 to 12 minutes.

Cut the eel into tronçons 6 to 7 cm. long, and poach them in salted water. Drain, arrange them on a serving dish, and coat them with the parsley sauce. Serve the plain boiled potatoes separately. *(Great Britain.)*

Anguille bourguignonne

For 6 persons: *1 kg. of eel; 150 gr. button onions; 150 gr. small mushrooms; 2 chopped shallots; 6 white peppercorns; 6 parsley stalks; 1 small crushed clove of garlic; 4 dl. red wine; 75 gr. butter; 40 gr. beurre manié; ½ lemon.* Cooking time: 25 minutes.

Cut the eel into tronçons 6 to 7 cm. long. Prepare a stock with the red wine, peppercorns, shallots, garlic and parsley stalks. Cook gently for 12 minutes. Pass through a conical strainer (chinois), pour on to the tronçons, and cook gently. Sauté the mushrooms and glaze the onions in butter. When the eel is cooked, thicken the cooking liquor with the beurre manié, add a few drops of lemon juice, and correct seasoning and consistency. Place the eel, mushrooms and onions together in a timbale, and coat with the sauce. *(France.)*

Anguille à la broche

For 6 persons: *1 kg. 200 of eel; 5 cl. oil; 1 lemon; picked parsley; 4 dl. fish velouté (or 150 gr. maître d'hôtel butter).* Cooking time: 12 to 15 minutes.

Cut the eel into tronçons 5 cm. long, skewer them, season and oil them, and grill gently. Arrange them on a serving dish, and garnish with the parsley and quarters of lemon. Serve the velouté (or maître d'hôtel butter) separately. *(France.)*

Anguille, coulibiac

For 6 persons: *1 kg. of eel; 500 gr. savoury brioche paste; 100 gr. semolina (or 100 gr. rice); 2 eggs; 100 gr. thinly-sliced mushrooms; 50 gr. chopped onion; 150 gr. butter; breadcrumbs.* Cooking time: approximately 40 minutes.

Fillet the skinned eel, cut the fillets into small escalopes, and stiffen them in butter. Roll out the brioche paste into a thin rectangle measuring approximately 28 cm. by 18 cm. Garnish the centre with superimposed layers of semolina kasha (or rice cooked in consommé and cooled), escalopes of eel, thinly-sliced mushrooms, chopped onion and chopped hard-boiled egg. Finish with a layer of kasha. Lightly moisten the edges of the paste, fold in the sides and ends towards the centre, and seal. Place the coulibiac, sealed side downwards, on a buttered tray, decorate with a few pieces of paste, and allow to rest for 25 minutes. Brush the coulibiac with beurre fondu, sprinkle with fine breadcrumbs, and make an opening in the centre to allow steam to escape. Bake in a medium oven. Before serving, pour some beurre fondu into the opening. *(International cookery.)*

Anguille Durand

For 6 persons: *1 kg. of eel; 300 gr. pike forcemeat; 100 gr. mirepoix bordelaise; 2 dl. dry white Burgundy; 75 gr. butter.* Cooking time: 20 minutes.

Cut up the eel into tronçons 6 cm. long, bone them, fill with the forcemeat, and reshape them. Wrap each tronçon in a small piece of muslin, and tie up with string. Stew the mirepoix in butter, moisten with the white wine and 1 dl. water, cook for 10 minutes, and pour over the fish. Season and poach slowly. When cooked, unwrap the tronçons, and arrange them on a gratinating dish. Strain and reduce the cooking liquor, pour it over the fish, and glaze in the oven. *(France.)*

Anguille frite

Fried eel

For 6 persons: *1 kg. 200 of eel; 4 dl. sauce tartare (or ravigote); picked parsley; flour.* Cooking time: 12 minutes.

Cut the eel into tronçons 6 to 7 cm. long, season, flour and fry. Arrange on a napkin with fried parsley. Serve the sauce separately. *(France.)*

Anguille frite anglaise

Fried eel English style

For 6 persons: *1 kg. of eel; 1 lemon; oil; 1 egg; breadcrumbs; 4 dl. sauce bâtarde (or 150 gr. maître d'hôtel butter or anchovy butter); flour.* Cooking time: 10 to 12 minutes.

Cut the eel into tronçons, season with salt and pepper, and marinate for 1 hour with lemon juice and oil. Dry and flour the tronçons, coat with egg and breadcrumbs, and deep fry. Arrange on a napkin with fried parsley. Serve the sauce (or butter) separately. *(France.)*

Anguille des gourmets

For 6 persons: *1 kg. of eel; 2 dl. Chablis; 3 dl. sauce béchamel; 1 dl. fresh cream; 12 shelled crayfish; 50 gr. crayfish butter.* Cooking time: 15 minutes.

Cut the eel into tronçons, season them, and poach in the Chablis. Drain them, arrange on a serving dish, and garnish with the crayfish (which have been gently heated in the crayfish butter). Reduce the poaching stock, add it to the sauce béchamel, incorporate the cream, simmer gently for a few minutes, finish with the crayfish butter, and correct seasoning and consistency. Coat the eel with this sauce. *(France.)* *(See illustration, page 330.)*

Anguille mâconnaise

For 6 persons: *1 kg. of eel; 18 button onions; 18 small mushroom heads; 12 shelled crayfish; 12 heart-shaped bread croûtons; 3 chopped shallots; 40 gr. beurre manié; 4 dl. red wine; 100 gr. butter.* Cooking time: 15 to 18 minutes.

Cut the eel into tronçons, and poach in the red wine and chopped shallots. Drain. Reduce the cooking liquor by one-third, strain, thicken with the beurre manié, butter moderately, and correct seasoning and consistency. Sauté the mushrooms in butter. Colour the onions, and glaze them. Arrange the tronçons in a timbale, add the mushrooms, onions and crayfish, and coat with the sauce. Surround with the fried croûtons. *(France.)*

Anguille, matelote d'

For 6 persons: *1 kg. of eel; 18 button onions; 18 small mushroom heads; 50 gr. thinly-sliced onion; 30 gr. mushroom trimmings; 1 clove of garlic; 1 bouquet garni; 6 white peppercorns; 2 dl. red wine; 5 cl. cognac; 2 dl. sauce demi-glace maigre; 30 gr. beurre manié; 50 gr. butter; 6 trussed crayfish.* Cooking time: 15 minutes.

Cut the eel into tronçons, and brown them in butter with the sliced onion. Flame the cognac, swill out with the red wine, and add mushroom trimmings, crushed garlic, bouquet garni and white peppercorns. Season, and cook briskly. Drain the tronçons, and arrange them on a serving dish. Add the cooked mushrooms and the button onions (blanched), strain the cooking liquor, thicken it slightly with the beurre manié, boil, add the sauce demi-glace, and pour on to the matelote. Surround with the crayfish cooked in court-bouillon. *(France.)*

Anguille ménagère

For 6 persons: *1 kg. 200 of eel; 6 gherkins; picked parsley; oil; 1 coffee-spoonful mustard; 150 gr. maître d'hôtel butter.* Cooking time: 12 to 15 minutes.

Cut the eel into tronçons, and season them with salt and pepper. Oil them, and grill gently. Arrange on a serving dish, and garnish with the gherkins (arranged in fan-shapes or thin slices) and parsley. Serve the maître d'hôtel butter, flavoured with mustard, separately. *(France.)*

Anguille normande

Proceed as for the preparation of Matelote d'anguille, but moisten with cider (not white wine), and replace the crayfish with poached and bearded oysters. *(France.)*

Anguille Orly

For 6 persons: *1 kg. of eel; ½ litre batter; 4 dl. sauce tomate; picked parsley.* Cooking time: 8 to 10 minutes.

Fillet the fish, and cut the fillets into aiguillettes. Season them, dip in batter, and then into hot, deep fat. Arrange on a napkin with the fried parsley. Serve the sauce tomate separately. *(France.)*

Anguille, pàté d'

Eel pie

For 6 persons: *1 kg. of eel; 500 gr. lining-paste (or pie paste); 300 gr. fish forcemeat; 1 tablespoonful chopped truffle; 5 cl. white wine; 3 cl. cognac; 2 cl. oil; 3 chopped shallots; 1 coffee-spoonful chopped parsley; 75 gr. butter; 1 egg; 4 dl. sauce demi-glace maigre.* Cooking time: 1½ hours to 1 hour 50 minutes.

Fillet the eel, cut into escalopes, and marinate for 2 hours with salt, pepper, white wine, cognac and oil. Stiffen the escalopes in butter with shallot and parsley, and allow to cool. Line a pie-mould with two-thirds of the paste, and smear the sides of the mould with a layer of forcemeat mixed with chopped truffle. Fill the mould with an alternation of layers of eel and forcemeat, sprinkling the last layer (forcemeat) with 2 tablespoonfuls of beurre fondu. Cover with the rest of the paste, decorate with leaf-shapes made from paste, make an opening in the centre to allow steam to escape, and brush with beaten egg. Bake in a medium oven. Serve the sauce demi-glace separately. *(France.)*

Anguille Pompadour

For 6 persons: *900 gr. of eel; ½ litre sauce Villeroi; 4 dl. tomato-flavoured sauce béarnaise; 300 gr. very small potatoes (prepared dauphine); 1 egg; fresh white breadcrumbs; picked parsley.* Cooking time: 15 to 18 minutes.

Score the eel, and cut into tronçons 5 cm. long. Poach in a court-bouillon with white wine. Drain and dry thoroughly. Mask the tronçons with boiling sauce Villeroi, and allow to cool. Coat the tronçons with egg and breadcrumbs and dip (to colour them) in very hot fat. Arrange the tronçons on a napkin with fried parsley. Garnish with the potatoes. Serve the sauce béarnaise separately. *(France.)*

Anguille poulette

For 6 persons: *1 kg. of eel; 1 bouquet garni; 50 gr. chopped onion; 250 gr. small mushroom heads; 2 egg yolks; 15 cl. fresh cream; 75 gr. butter; 25 gr. flour; ½ lemon; 1 coffee-spoonful chopped parsley.* Cooking time: 12 to 15 minutes.

Cut the eel into tronçons. Sweat the onion in butter (without colouring), add the tronçons, stiffen them, sprinkle with flour and moisten with water. Season, add the bouquet garni, and cook gently. Drain and arrange in a timbale with the mushrooms (cooked with a nut of butter, the lemon juice and a pinch of salt). Strain the cooking liquor, thicken it with the egg yolks and cream, correct seasoning and consistency, and pour over the tronçons. Sprinkle with the parsley. *(France.)*

Anguille provençale

For 6 persons: *1 kg. of eel; 300 gr. peeled, de-seeded and chopped tomatoes; 3 chopped shallots; 1 crushed clove of garlic; 75 gr. chopped onion; 5 cl. oil; 2 dl. white wine; 1 tablespoonful fines herbes (parsley, chervil, tarragon) minced.* Cooking time: 15 minutes.

Cut the eel into tronçons. Colour the shallots and onion in oil. Add the tronçons, the chopped tomatoes, garlic and fines herbes. Season, moisten with the white wine, and cook gently. Correct seasoning and consistency. Arrange in a timbale. *(France.)*

Anguille romaine

For 6 persons: *1 kg. of eel; 300 gr. freshly-shelled peas; 1 lettuce; 75 gr. butter; 3 dl. white wine; 30 gr. beurre manié.* Cooking time: 15 to 18 minutes.

Cut the eel into tronçons 5 to 6 cm. long, season and stiffen them in butter. Add the lettuce (chiffonnade), the peas, 50 gr. butter and the white wine. Stew slowly together. Bind with beurre manié, and correct seasoning and consistency. Arrange in a timbale. *(France.)*

Anguille rouennaise

For 6 persons: *1 kg. of eel; ¼ litre red wine; 2 dl. sauce espagnole; 200 gr. small (cooked) mushroom heads; 200 gr. escalopes of poached soft roe; 12 poached and bearded oysters; 200 gr. headless smelts; 100 gr. mirepoix; 60 gr. butter; flour.* Cooking time: 15 minutes.

Cut the eel into tronçons, season them, poach in the red wine with the mirepoix, and glaze. Arrange on a serving dish, and garnish with the mushrooms, soft roe and oysters. Reduce the cooking liquor, strain, blend with the sauce espagnole, and use to coat the garnish. Surround with the very small smelts (floured and cooked meunière). *(France.)*

Anguille Saint-Martin, tourte d'

For 6 persons: *900 gr. of eel; 300 gr. fish forcemeat (containing fines herbes); 350 gr. lining-paste; 3 chopped shallots; 150 gr. raw mushrooms; 100 gr. butter.* Cooking time: 35 to 40 minutes.

Fillet the eel, cut the fillets into small escalopes, and stiffen them in butter with the chopped shallots (previously stewed in butter). Allow to cool. Prepare a circular layer of paste (18 cm. wide and 5 mm. thick). Arrange on top a layer of forcemeat (leaving a narrow border of paste uncovered). Fill with the escalopes of eel and thinly-sliced mushrooms, and cover with the forcemeat. Moisten the edges of the paste, cover with a second layer of paste, and seal by folding over the edges. Score, make an opening in the centre to allow steam to escape, and brush with egg. Bake in a medium oven. At the moment of serving, pour a little beurre fondu into the opening. *(France.)*

Anguille Sainte-Ménéhould

For 6 persons: *1 kg. of eel; 200 gr. fresh white breadcrumbs; 50 gr. chopped raw mushrooms; 100 gr. butter; 6 gherkins; 4 dl. sauce hachée; 10 anchovy fillets.* Cooking time: 15 to 18 minutes.

Cut the eel into tronçons, poach them in a court-bouillon containing white wine, drain them, dip in beurre fondu, and coat with the breadcrumbs (containing chopped mushrooms). Sprinkle with beurre fondu, and grill gently. Arrange on a serving dish, and garnish with the gherkins arranged in fan-shapes or thin slices. Serve separately the sauce hachée (containing the finely-diced anchovy fillets). *(France.)*
(See illustration, page 368. N.B. Different presentation.)

Anguille au soleil

For 6 persons: *1 kg. 200 of small eels; 2 eggs; fresh white breadcrumbs; picked parsley; 75 gr. butter; 4 dl. sauce tomate.* Cooking time: 10 to 15 minutes.

Skin the eels, roll them into spirals, and coat with egg and breadcrumbs. Sprinkle with clarified butter, and grill gently. Arrange on a serving dish with fried parsley. Serve the sauce tomate separately. *(France.)*

Anguille Suffren

For 6 persons: *6 tronçons of eel (150 gr. each); 18 anchovy fillets; 2 dl. white wine; 50 gr. tomato purée; 75 gr. butter; ½ coffee-spoonful of anchovy essence.* Cooking time: 12 to 15 minutes.

Stud the tronçons with the anchovy fillets, and poach in the white wine. Drain. Strain the cooking liquor, reduce, and blend with the tomato purée. Work up lightly with butter, and season with anchovy essence and a touch of Cayenne pepper. Arrange the tronçons on a serving dish, and pour the sauce over them. *(France.)*

Anguille tartare

For 6 persons: *1 kg. 200 of eel; 6 gherkins; 1 egg; fresh white breadcrumbs; picked parsley; 4 dl. sauce tartare.* Cooking time: 15 to 18 minutes.

Cut the eel into tronçons, and poach in a court-bouillon. Drain the tronçons, sponge, coat with egg and breadcrumbs, and deep fry. Arrange them on a serving dish bordered with thin slices of gherkin and garnished with fried parsley. Serve the sauce tartare separately. *(France.)*

Anguille vénitienne

For 6 persons: *1 kg. of eel; 250 gr. soft roe; 200 gr. small (cooked) mushroom heads; 3 dl. sauce vénitienne; 15 cl. white wine; 50 gr. butter.* Cooking time: 12 to 15 minutes.

Cut the eel into tronçons, and poach them in the white wine with butter. Reduce the cooking stock almost to a syrupy consistency, and glaze in the oven. Arrange the tronçons on a serving dish, garnish with the soft roe (stewed in butter and cut into large dice) and the cooked mushrooms (re-heated in butter). Coat the garnish with the sauce vénitienne. *(France.)*

Anguille Villeroi

For 6 persons: *1 kg. of eel; ½ litre sauce Villeroi; 2 eggs; fresh white breadcrumbs; parsley; 4 dl. sauce tomate.* Cooking time: 15 minutes.

Fillet the eel, and cut the fillets into tronçons 5 cm. long. Season, and coat with the boiling sauce Villeroi. Cool, coat with egg and breadcrumbs, and deep fry. Arrange on a napkin with fried parsley. Serve the sauce tomate separately. *(France.)*

Anguille au vert anversoise

For 6 persons: *2 kg. of eels (each the size of a finger); 3 chopped shallots; 30 gr. chopped onion; ½ litre white wine; 3 dl. fish fumet; 1 dl. fresh cream; 3 egg yolks; 30 gr. coarsely-chopped sorrel; 10 gr. parsley; 10 gr. artemisia; 5 gr. chopped mint leaves; 1 lemon; 1 coffee-spoonful fecula; 1 bouquet garni; 50 gr. butter.* Cooking time: approximately 10 minutes.

Clean the skinned eels, cut them into tronçons 8 cm. long, wash and drain them. Brown the shallots and onion in butter, add the eels, and sweat for 4 minutes. Season with pepper and salt, moisten with the white wine and fish fumet, add the sorrel, parsley, artemisia and mint leaves, and cook for 4 minutes. Drain. Reduce the cooking liquor by one-third, add the lemon juice, thicken with the fecula (mixed with a little water), boil up once, add the tronçons, and cook for 1 minute. Thicken with the egg yolks and cream, and correct seasoning and consistency. Serve (hot or cold) with lemon. *(Belgium.)*

Barbeau, barbillon

Barbel

As the flesh of the barbel is rather tasteless, lacks firmness, and is full of bones, it is most frequently used in matelotes with other types of fish. It can, however, also be prepared meunière, Bercy, or grilled. It is then accompanied with a butter (mustard, shallot or anchovy). The young barbel (barbillon) weighs from 400 to 600 gr.

Barbeau bourguignonne

For 6 persons: *2 barbels (750 to 800 gr. each); 40 gr. mushroom trimmings; 60 gr. butter; ½ litre red wine; 1 bouquet garni; 40 gr. beurre manié.* Cooking time: 30 minutes.

Place the barbels on the well-buttered grid of a fish-kettle. Season, add the mushroom trimmings, 40 gr. butter and the bouquet garni, moisten with the red wine, and braise in the oven. Drain, and arrange on a serving dish. Strain the cooking liquor, reduce slightly, thicken with the beurre manié, correct seasoning and consistency, and pour over the fish. *(France.)*

Barbeau rôti

Roast barbel

For 6 persons: *2 barbels (750 to 800 gr. each); 18 anchovy fillets; 150 gr. anchovy butter; picked parsley; 7 cl. oil.* Cooking time: approximately 25 minutes.

Skin the barbels, and stud them finely with the anchovy fillets. Season, sprinkle with oil, and roast in the oven on a buttered roasting tray. Arrange on a serving dish with the picked parsley. Serve the anchovy butter separately. *(France.)*

Barbeau aux sauces diverses

Barbel with various sauces

For 6 persons: *1 barbel (1 kg. 500 to 1 kg. 800); 4 dl. sauce hollandaise (or sauce Bercy or caper sauce); picked parsley; 750 gr. fish potatoes.* Cooking time: 30 to 35 minutes.

Poach the barbel in a court-bouillon containing vinegar. Drain, and arrange on a serving dish with the parsley. Serve the sauce and the plain boiled fish potatoes separately. *(International cookery.)*

Barbillon grillé

Grilled barbel

For 6 persons: *3 small barbels (500 to 600 gr. each); 180 gr. maître d'hôtel butter; 50 gr. chopped shallot; picked parsley.* Cooking time: 20 minutes.

Score the barbels, season with salt and pepper, oil them, and grill gently. Arrange on a serving dish, and garnish with the parsley. Serve the maître d'hôtel butter (containing the blanched and pressed shallots) separately. *(France.)*

Bhiriani de poisson

Bhiriani Machchi

For 6 persons: *1 kg. 200 of fish (pike, haddock, etc.); 5 cl. mustard oil; ½ litre yoghurt; 2 onions cut into roundels; ¾ tablespoonful curcuma; 125 gr. beurre fondu; 2 tablespoonfuls coriander; 4 cardamom seeds; 6 cloves; 2 tablespoonfuls aniseed; 2 large tomatoes; 1 large sweet red pepper; 400 gr. rice; chenna flour (Indian flour made from chick peas)*. Cooking time: approximately 40 minutes.

Cut the fish into large pieces, wash it several times, dry carefully, and rub lightly with mustard oil. Leave for 15 minutes, wash again, and rub with chenna flour and pounded aniseed. (This operation is intended to remove the 'fishy' smell and to impart a delicate aroma to the fish.) Wash it once more, and marinate it in a marinade prepared as follows: gently colour the onions in mustard oil, and add the pounded cloves and cardamom, and half the yoghurt. Place all in a lidded casserole. At the same time, blanch the rice for 10 minutes, drain, wash in cold water, and drain thoroughly. Sprinkle the fish with half the curcuma and half the coriander, season with salt, and sprinkle with half the butter. Add the rice, the rest of the coriander, curcuma, aniseed, yoghurt and butter, the sliced tomatoes and the sweet pepper (pipped and thinly sliced), and moisten with 2 dl. water. Cover the casserole, shake slightly, start the cooking on the stove for 3 or 4 minutes, and finish by cooking in the oven for about 30 minutes. *(India.)*

Blanchaille

Whitebait

These are very small fish (of the herring family, Clupeidae) which originate at the mouth of the River Thames, and are in season from February to September, being at their best from February to May. They are now available all the year round in frozen form. They deteriorate quickly and should be cooked as soon as possible after they are caught. Whitebait are always fried. After being rolled in flour, they are fried in deep, hot oil, while being kept very crisp. They are sprinkled with table salt containing a touch of Cayenne pepper, and arranged on a napkin with fried parsley and quarters of lemon.

Whitebait with lemon

Dip the washed whitebait into seasoned milk, drain and dredge in flour, place on a sieve and shake off the surplus flour. Plunge immediately into a clean friture of very hot oil and cook for about 1 minute until crisp and golden brown. Drain well and season with a mixture of salt and pepper and serve on a dish on paper with fried parsley and lemon. Serve brown bread and butter separately.

Bondelles neuchâteloise

For 6 persons: *1 kg. 500 of bondelles (small white fish of the Coregonus family); 80 gr. butter; 250 gr. brunoise (of carrot, leek, celery, fennel and shallot); 3 dl. white wine; 1 dl. cream; the juice of ½ lemon; 1 coffee-spoonful chopped parsley; flour.*

Brown the brunoise in butter in a sauteuse. Add the cleaned and seasoned bondelles, moisten with the white wine, cover, and poach gently. Remove the fish, and arrange them on a serving dish. Reduce the cooking stock, thicken with the cream, monter au beurre, and add, if necessary, a little beurre manié. Flavour with the lemon juice, and correct the seasoning and consistency. Coat the bondelles with the sauce, and sprinkle with the chopped parsley. (N.B. Bondelles weigh from 80 to 150 gr.) *(Switzerland.)*

Brochet angevine

Pike

For 6 persons: *1 kg. 200 of pike; 100 gr. butter; ¼ litre white Anjou wine; 3 chopped shallots; 2 gr. English mustard; 5 cl. fresh cream; 30 gr. beurre manié; ½ lemon; 12 small heart-shaped croûtons.* Cooking time: 12 to 15 minutes.

Cut the pike into tronçons about 3 cm. long, and stiffen them in butter. Season, moisten with the white wine, and add the chopped shallots and a pinch of grated nutmeg. Cook and also reduce. Drain the fish, and arrange it in a timbale. Thicken the cooking liquor with the beurre manié mixed with dry mustard, and allow to simmer. Finish it with the cream, the finely-pounded pike liver, the lemon juice and a little butter. Correct seasoning and consistency. Pour over the fish and surround with the fried croûtons. *(France.)*

(See illustration, page 388. N.B. Different presentation.)

Brochets anglaise, Filets de

Fillets of pike English style

Proceed as for the preparation of Filets de sole anglaise. *(See page 297.)*

Brochet Benoîton, Filets de

Proceed as for the preparation of Filets d'anguille Benoîton. *(See page 369.)*

Brochet au beurre blanc

For 6 persons: *1 pike (1 kg. 500); 200 gr. unsalted butter.* Cooking time: 35 to 40 minutes.

Cook the pike in an ordinary court-bouillon. Drain and skin it, and arrange on a serving dish. Coat liberally with unsalted butter. *(International cookery.)*

Brochet, Blanquette de

For 6 persons: *1 kg. 500 of pike; 100 gr. butter; 200 gr. small mushroom heads; 200 gr. button onions; 3 dl. white wine; 1 dl. fresh cream; 2 egg yolks; 1 bouquet garni; ½ lemon; 25 gr. flour.* Cooking time: 20 minutes.

Fillet the pike, remove skin and bones, cut into 75 gr. escalopes, stiffen them in butter, sprinkle with flour, moisten with the white wine and a little water, season, and cook gently for 10 minutes. Add the raw mushroom heads and the button onions (previously cooked in butter) and finish the cooking. At the last moment, bind with the egg yolks and cream, correct the seasoning and consistency, add a few drops of lemon juice, and arrange in a timbale. *(International cookery.)*

Brochet au bleu

For 6 persons: *1 pike (1 kg. 500 to 1 kg. 800); 180 to 200 gr. butter; 750 gr. fish potatoes; picked parsley; 1 lemon.* Cooking time: 35 to 45 minutes.

The fish must still be alive when preparation starts; it must be gutted as gently as possible and without being scaled. Place the fish on the grid of a fish-kettle. Pour on top the fairly-hot court-bouillon, bring it to the boil, and keep it simmering during the cooking. Arrange the pike on a napkin, and surround it with the parsley. Serve beurre fondu, and plain-boiled fish potatoes separately. *(International cookery.)*

Brochet bordelaise

For 6 persons: *1 kg. 500 of pike; 100 gr. mirepoix bordelaise; 2 chopped shallots; ½ litre red wine; 40 gr. beurre manié; 50 gr. butter.* Cooking time: 15 minutes.

Cut the pike into tronçons about 3 cm. long. Season and poach in the red wine with the mirepoix and chopped shallots. When the cooking is finished, remove the tronçons, drain them, and arrange in a timbale. Strain the cooking liquor, thicken it with the beurre manié, butter lightly, correct seasoning and consistency, and pour over the fish. *(France.)* *(See illustration, page 388. N.B. Different presentation.)*

Brochet château de Gruyère

For 6 persons: *1 pike (2 kg.); 100 gr. lardons; 100 gr. shallots; 4 dl. white wine; 3 dl. cream; 100 gr. butter; 1 dl. brown veal stock; 1 lemon; flour.* Cooking time: approximately 25 minutes.

Skin the pike, stud it with lardons, season, and flour. Butter the base of a fish-kettle, garnish it with chopped shallots, and place the fish on top. Moisten with white wine, cream and veal stock. Braise in the oven, and baste frequently with the stock until the fish is brown and well glazed. Arrange on a serving dish. Strain the cooking stock, reduce, monter au beurre, flavour with lemon juice, correct seasoning and consistency, and use this sauce to coat the fish. *(Switzerland.)*

Brochet, Côtelettes de

Pike cutlets

For 6 persons: *750 gr. pike forcemeat; 150 gr. cooked mushrooms; 50 gr. truffle; 1 dl. sauce allemande; 150 gr. butter; fresh white breadcrumbs; 4 dl. sauce Soubise.* Cooking time: 20 minutes.

Prepare a salpicon of mushroom and truffle, bind it with reduced sauce allemande, and allow to cool. Smear 12 small buttered cutlet-moulds with forcemeat, fill the centre with the salpicon, cover with the forcemeat, and poach in salted water. De-mould the cutlets, dry them completely, dip in beurre fondu, and coat with fine breadcrumbs. Colour in clarified butter, and arrange in a ring. Serve the sauce Soubise separately. *(France.)*

Brochet à la crème aigre

For 6 persons: *1 pike (1 kg. 500); 120 gr. butter; ¾ litre sour cream.* Cooking time: 30 to 35 minutes.

Place the pike on the buttered grid of a fish-kettle, sprinkle liberally with beurre fondu, season, and colour golden in the oven, basting frequently with butter. Add the sour cream, and cook the fish to a turn (basting from time to time). Arrange on a serving dish. Slightly reduce the cream (if necessary), pass through a tammy cloth, and use to coat the fish. *(Russia.)*

Brochet lyonnaise, Quenelles de

For 6 persons: *600 gr. raw, filleted, pike meat; 250 gr. beef suet; 4 eggs; 50 gr. butter; ¼ litre milk; 4 dl. sauce.* Cooking time: 15 minutes.

Prepare a panada of the consistency of pâte à choux with: 2 eggs, the flour, the cold milk, the butter and a pinch of salt. Allow to cool. Pass the suet and pike meat through the finest mincer-plate. Incorporate the panada, mix all the ingredients well together, add 2 eggs, and correct the seasoning and consistency. Pass through a hair sieve, and work over once more with a spatula. Test a little of this mixture in boiling water to ensure a firm consistency, adding a little more egg if necessary. Form into quenelles with the aid of tablespoons. Poach these in a covered sauteuse, with a small quantity of fish fumet, for 10 minutes. Remove the quenelles, using a perforated spoon, and coat with lobster, crayfish or shrimp sauce. *(France.)*

Brochet meunière

Proceed as for the preparation of all other fish designated meunière.
(See illustration, page 387.)

Brochet Montebello

For 6 persons: *1 pike (1 kg. 200); 300 gr. fish forcemeat; 6 fillets of sole; 200 gr. rice; 6 trussed crayfish; 6 thin slices of truffle; 6 small croquettes of shelled prawns; 6 small boat-shapes (made from poached escalopes of soft roe); 12 small oysters (poached and bearded); 3 dl. white wine; 4 dl. fish velouté; 30 gr. anchovy butter; 1 carrot; 1 onion; parsley stalks.* Cooking time: 40 to 45 minutes.

Fill the pike with forcemeat. Remove the skin from two-thirds of one side, and mask the exposed part with forcemeat. Garnish this part with the flattened fillets of sole of suitable size, and decorate with truffle. Braise the pike in white wine, on a bed of aromatics, in a covered container. Drain and arrange on a serving dish on a socle of cooked rice. Garnish with the croquettes of shrimp, barquettes of soft roe, and trussed crayfish (cooked in a court-bouillon). Serve the fish velouté (finished with the anchovy butter) and the oysters separately. *(France.)*

Brochet Nantua, Quenelles de

For 6 persons: *600 gr. raw pike meat; 250 gr. beef suet; 4 eggs; 50 gr. butter; ¼ litre milk; 12 thin slices of truffle; 18 shelled crayfish; 4 dl. sauce Nantua; 2 dl. fish fumet.* Cooking time: 15 minutes.

Proceed at first as for the basic preparation of Quenelles de brochet lyonnaise (12 quenelles). Poach them in the fish fumet. Drain them, and arrange in a round serving dish. Garnish each quenelle with a slice of truffle, and arrange the crayfish in the centre. Coat the quenelles and the garnish with sauce Nantua. (The quenelles can also be prepared with a mousselin of pike forcemeat.) *(France.)*

Brochet normande

For 6 persons: *1 kg. 200 of pike; 300 gr. fish forcemeat; 300 gr. normande garnish; 4 dl. white wine; 1 carrot; 1 onion; parsley stalks; 4 dl. sauce normande.* Cooking time: 40 minutes.

Stuff the pike, and braise it in white wine on a bed of aromatics. When the cooking is finished, drain the fish, skin it, and arrange on a serving dish. Surround with the normande garnish, and coat with the sauce normande containing the reduced cooking liquor. *(France.)*

Brochet Orly

Proceed as for the preparation of all other fish designated Orly.
(See illustration, page 407.)

Brochet à l'oseille, Grenadins de

For 6 persons: *12 medallions of pike fillet (60 gr. each); 2 gherkins; 1 blanched carrot; 60 gr. butter; 2 dl. fish fumet; 2 dl. fish velouté; 300 gr. purée of sorrel.* Cooking time: 15 minutes.

Stud the medallions with small pieces of gherkin and carrot, season, stiffen in butter, moisten with the fish fumet, and finish off the cooking. Drain the medallions, arrange them in a ring, and coat very lightly with the fish velouté containing the reduced cooking stock. Serve the cooked purée of sorrel separately. *(France.)*

Brochet, Pain de

Pike loaf

For 6 persons: *750 gr. creamed pike forcemeat; 12 large mushroom heads (cannelées); 12 thin slices of truffle; 4 dl. sauce bâtarde; 25 gr. butter.* Cooking time: 20 to 25 minutes.

Butter a hinged, cylindrical mould, fill it with the forcemeat, and poach in a bain-marie. Leave in the mould for a few minutes, and de-mould into a serving dish. Garnish with the truffle and mushrooms. Serve the sauce separately. *(France.)*

Brochet au persil

Pike with parsley

For 6 persons: *1 kg. 500 of pike; 6 quarters of lemon; 150 gr. butter; 2 tablespoonfuls picked parsley.* Cooking time: 15 minutes.

Cut the pike into darnes, and poach them in a court-bouillon. Drain them, and arrange on a serving dish with the quarters of lemon. Serve noisette butter, containing the picked parsley, separately. *(France.)*

Brochet sauce au beurre blanc

For 6 persons: *1 pike (1 kg. 600); 750 gr. fish potatoes; 1 dl. wine vinegar; ½ litre dry white wine; 3 litres water; 2 shallots; 1 clove of garlic; 1 small carrot; 1 bayleaf; 1 sprig of thyme; 8 peppercorns.*

Sauce: *1 dl. wine vinegar; 1 tablespoonful chopped shallots; 1 dl. fresh cream; 200 gr. unsalted butter; 50 gr. beurre manié; 3 dl. cognac.* Cooking time: approximately 20 minutes.

Prepare a court-bouillon with water, wine vinegar, white wine, shallots and carrots cut into roundels, crushed garlic, bayleaf, thyme, pepper and salt. Simmer for 15 minutes. Add the pike, and cook gently for 20 minutes. To make the sauce, almost completely reduce the vinegar with the chopped shallots, add the unsalted butter, and stir with a spatula until the butter is melted. When a white froth forms on the butter, incorporate the beurre manié and 1 dl. court-bouillon. Simmer for a few minutes, add the cream, and heighten the flavour with the cognac. Arrange the fish (sprinkled with chopped parsley) on a serving dish, and serve accompanied by the sauce and fish potatoes. *(Austria.)*

Brochet poché, sauce câpres

Poached pike with caper sauce

For 6 persons: *1 kg. 500 to 1 kg. 800 of pike; 4 dl. caper sauce; picked parsley; 750 gr. potatoes; 25 gr. butter.* Cooking time: 35 to 40 minutes.

Poach the pike in a court-bouillon. Drain, skin, arrange on a serving dish, and glaze with butter. Garnish with the parsley. Serve the sauce and the plain boiled potatoes separately. (N.B. The caper sauce can be replaced by a sauce hollandaise, vénitienne or ravigote (hot).) *(France.)*

Brochet poché, sauce persil

Poached pike with parsley sauce

For 6 persons: *1 kg. 500 to 1 kg. 800 of pike; 1 sprig of parsley; 4 dl. parsley sauce; 750 gr. potatoes; picked parsley.* Cooking time: 35 to 40 minutes.

Cook the pike in a court-bouillon containing a large sprig of parsley. Drain, arrange on a napkin, and surround with the picked parsley. Serve the parsley sauce and plain boiled potatoes separately. *(International cookery.)*

Brochet, Quenelles de

For 6 persons: *750 gr. mousseline of pike forcemeat; 4 dl. sauce homard (or sauce Nantua or shrimp sauce); 10 gr. butter.* Cooking time: 10 to 12 minutes.

Mould the quenelles with a tablespoon (or else pipe the forcemeat through a piping-bag, as for a meringue, into a buttered sauteuse). Cover them with salted, boiling water, and poach slowly. (The quenelles are cooked when the forcemeat is firm to the touch.) Drain them on a cloth, arrange on a serving dish, and coat with an appropriate sauce. *(France.)*
(See illustration, page 312. N.B. Different presentation.)

Brochet Régence, Filets de

For 6 persons: *12 oval medallions of pike fillets (60 gr. each); 300 gr. Régence garnish; 6 trussed crayfish; 50 gr. butter; 1 dl. white wine; 15 cl. fish fumet; 4 dl. sauce Régence.* Cooking time: 15 minutes.

Arrange the medallions in a thickly-buttered sauteuse, season them, and poach in the white wine and fish fumet. Drain. Reduce the cooking liquor almost to a syrupy consistency, coat the medallions and glaze them. Arrange them in a ring on a serving dish, with the garnish in the centre, and surround with the trussed crayfish (cooked in a court-bouillon). Serve the sauce Régence separately. *(France.)*

Brochet Taillevent, Terrine de

For 10 persons: *frangipane panada (made from 125 gr. flour, 4 egg yolks, 100 gr. butter, ¼ litre milk, salt, white pepper); 200 gr. fresh morels (or, if these are out of season, button mushrooms); 600 gr. cleaned and filleted pike meat; 3 egg whites; 125 gr butter; 50 gr. unsalted butter; ½ litre fresh cream; 250 gr. pike fillets; 5 shallots; 10 gr. chopped parsley; white wine.* Cooking time: 1¼ hours.

Marinate the pike fillets in the white wine for 1 hour. Pound the pike meat, and incorporate gradually: the panada, butter and egg whites. When the forcemeat is smooth, pass it through a fine sieve, turn it out into a terrine, work it (on ice) with a spatula, and work up with cream. Keep in a cool place. Gently sweat the morels (cut into thin slices) in a plat à sauter, and drain them. Stiffen the pike fillets in the same butter, and add the thinly-sliced shallots and chopped parsley. Remove the fillets, pour the marinade into the plat à sauter, reduce, and pour the essence thus obtained over the fillets. Fill a terrine with successive layers of forcemeat, fillets and morels, finishing with forcemeat. Cover the terrine with a lid, and finish the cooking in a bain-marie. Serve hot in the terrine, with a sauce-boat of unsalted butter. *(France.)*

Brochet valaisane, Filets de

For 6 persons: *1 kg. pike fillets; 3 dl. white wine; 75 gr. butter; 2 chopped shallots; 300 gr. to 400 gr. duchesse potatoes; 250 gr. asparagus tips.* Cooking time: approximately 15 minutes.

Arrange the fillets in a fish tray which has been buttered and sprinkled with chopped shallots. Season, moisten with the white wine, cover with a sheet of buttered paper, and poach in the oven. Remove the fish, pass the cooking stock, reduce, monter au beurre, and correct seasoning and consistency. Border the rim of a gratinating dish with the duchesse potatoes, arrange the fish on it, garnish with the asparagus tips, coat with the sauce, and glaze quickly under the salamander. *(Switzerland.)*

(See illustration, page 407. N.B. Different presentation.)

Brochet zurichoise

For 6 persons: *1 pike (1 kg. 800); 3 dl. white Zurich wine; 15 cl. fresh cream; 150 gr. small mushroom heads; 24 button onions; 80 gr. butter; 1 tablespoonful mixed herbs (parsley, dill and sage).* Cooking time: approximately 25 minutes.

Gut the pike, and sew it up. Place it in a fish-kettle, add the mushrooms and onions, season, moisten with the white wine, cover with a lid, and poach. Remove the fish and the garnish from the stock, and arrange on a serving dish. Reduce the cooking stock, bind it with the cream, monter au beurre, add the chopped herbs, and correct the seasoning and consistency. (As white Zurich wine is fairly acid, there is no need to use lemon juice.) Coat the pike with the sauce. *(Switzerland.)*

(See illustration, page 405. N.B. Different presentation.)

Brocheton grillé

Grilled small pike

For 6 persons: *3 young pike (500 gr. to 600 gr. each); 1 lemon; 2 chopped shallots; olive oil; 4 dl. mayonnaise; 50 gr. finely chopped, skinned walnuts; flour; picked parsley.* Cooking time: approximately 20 minutes.

Marinate the pike for at least 1 hour with lemon juice, chopped shallot and a trickle of olive oil. Dry the fish, score it, flour, oil, and grill gently. Arrange on a serving dish with the parsley. Serve separately the mayonnaise containing the chopped walnut. *(France.)*

Brocheton martinière

For 6 persons: *3 young pike (500 gr. to 600 gr. each); 2 chopped shallots; 1 lemon; olive oil; 4 dl. mayonnaise; 50 gr. finely-chopped, skinned hazel-nuts; flour; picked parsley.* Cooking time: 20 minutes.

Proceed as for the preparation of Brocheton grillé, but serve instead a mayonnaise finished with the hazel-nuts. *(France.)*

Carassin à la crème aigre

For 6 persons: *1 kg. 800 of crucian carp; 120 gr. butter; 70 gr. flour; 4 dl. sour cream; 40 gr. fresh white breadcrumbs.* Cooking time: 18 to 20 minutes.

Season the carp, flour it, brush with butter, and keep in a hot place. Prepare a white roux with 40 gr. butter and 30 gr. flour. Add the sour cream, cook for a few minutes, correct seasoning and consistency, and pass through a conical strainer. Coat the fish with the sauce, sprinkle with breadcrumbs, then with beurre fondu, and brown quickly in a hot oven. (N.B. The crucian carp has no barbels.) *(Russia.)*

Carpe à l'aigre-doux

Sweet and sour carp

For 6 persons: *1 carp (1 kg. 500); 7 cl. saké; 75 gr. onion cut into roundels; 6 cl. peanut-oil; 50 gr. stem ginger; 250 gr. sweet-and-sour cucumber; 1 tablespoonful honey; 1 tablespoonful soy sauce; 2 tablespoonfuls vinegar; 1 tablespoonful sugar; green stems of spring onions, or red peppers.* Cooking time: approximately 30 minutes.

Skin and gut the carp, remove the head, wash the fish, and cut it in two lengthwise. Cut each half into 3 pieces and marinate them for 1 hour with salt, pepper and saké. Dry the pieces, flour them, and sauté in peanut-oil, on each side, until they are done to a turn. Keep them hot. Brown the roundels of onion in peanut-oil, add the ginger and cucumber (both cut into thin slices), and moisten with the marinade and a little water. Add the honey, soy sauce, vinegar and sugar. Cook gently for 15 minutes. Thicken slightly with a little fecula diluted in water, and correct seasoning with salt and pepper. Arrange the fish on a serving dish, coat with the sauce, and sprinkle with a julienne of the onions or red peppers. *(China.)*
(See Culinary Technique, page 96.)

Carpe alsacienne

Carp Alsatian style

For 6 persons: *1 carp (1 kg. 500); 300 gr. fish forcemeat; 2 dl. white wine; 2 dl. fish fumet; 750 gr. sauerkraut; 600 gr. fish potatoes; 40 gr. beurre manié; 50 gr. butter.* Cooking time: 30 to 35 minutes.

Fill the carp with the forcemeat, and poach it slowly in the white wine and fish fumet. Drain it, and arrange on a serving dish. Garnish with the sauerkraut (previously cooked and kept white) and the plain boiled potatoes. Strain the poaching stock, reduce it, thicken it with the beurre manié, butter lightly, and correct seasoning and consistency. Serve this sauce separately. *(France.)*

Carpe à l'ancienne mode juive

Carp in the traditional Jewish style

For 6 persons: *6 pieces of carp (300 gr. each); 200 gr. onions; 200 gr. carrots; 150 gr. sultanas; 100 gr. skinned almonds; 100 gr. crumbed gingerbread; 1 tablespoonful of honey; 1 lemon; 1 bayleaf; 3 cloves; 6 coriander seeds.* Cooking time: 1½ hours.

Cut the onions and carrots into roundels, moisten with 1 litre of water, and add honey, bayleaf, cloves, lemon (peeled, pipped and sliced), coriander and a little salt, and cook gently for 40 minutes. Add the pieces of carp and, if necessary, enough water to cover the fish. Bring to the boil. Add the raisins, gingerbread and grated almonds and cook with gentle heat for about 50 minutes, so that the fish is done to a turn and the sauce creamy. Correct the seasoning and consistency. Serve hot or cold. *(Israel.)*

Carpe à la bière

Carp with beer

For 6 persons: *1 carp (1 kg. 500); 250 gr. soft roe; 100 gr. thinly-sliced onion; 50 gr. thinly-sliced celery; 1 bouquet garni; 50 gr. gingerbread; 1 litre brown ale; 3 cl. vinegar; 100 gr. butter.* Cooking time: approximately 30 minutes.

Line a fish kettle with the onion and celery (both stewed in butter). Arrange the carp on top, moisten (to cover) with the beer, add the finely-diced gingerbread and the bouquet garni. Braise (covered) in the oven. Drain the fish, and arrange it on a serving dish. Strain the cooking liquor (thickened with the gingerbread) through a tammy cloth. Heat it, add the vinegar, butter lightly, and pour over the fish. Garnish with the soft roe (cut into escalopes and stewed in butter). *(International cookery.)*

Carpe au bleu

Proceed as for the preparation of all fish designated au bleu. *(See page 64.)*
(For serving, see page 121.)

Carpe canotière

For 6 persons: *1 carp (1 kg. 200); 300 gr. fish forcemeat; 250 gr. raw button mushrooms; 4 chopped shallots; 125 gr. butter; 3 dl. white wine; 6 trussed crayfish; 12 very small gudgeons; fine breadcrumbs; fresh breadcrumbs.* Cooking time: approximately 30 minutes.

Fill the carp with the forcemeat. Season. Lay the fish on a thickly-buttered gratinating dish which has been sprinkled with the chopped shallots. Surround with the raw mushrooms, moisten with the white wine, add 75 gr. butter, and bake in the oven, basting frequently.

5 to 6 minutes before cooking is finished, sprinkle with fine breadcrumbs and then with beurre fondu, and brown lightly. Surround with the gudgeons (coated with egg and breadcrumbs and fried), cooked mushrooms and trussed crayfish (the last cooked in a court-bouillon). *(France.)*

Carpe Chambord

For 8 persons: *1 mirror carp (2 kg.); 1 kg. fish forcemeat (suitable for quenelles); 100 gr. carrot; 100 gr. onion; 100 gr. celery; 10 parsley stalks; ½ bottle claret; 4 dl. fish fumet; 8 soft roes of carp; 1 dl. white wine; 16 oysters; 4 dl. sauce Villeroi; 16 turned mushroom heads; 16 small gudgeons; 4 large quenelles shaped with a spoon and decorated with truffle; 16 small round quenelles containing truffle; 2 truffles; 8 trussed crayfish; 2 eggs; fresh white breadcrumbs; 100 gr. butter; ½ litre sauce genevoise.* Cooking time: 50 to 60 minutes.

Empty the carp through the gills, and remove the skin from the centre of one side. Fill the inside with forcemeat, and sew up. Mask the exposed surface with forcemeat, and decorate it with half-moon shapes of truffle (pressed down, and arranged in a pattern of fish-scales). Season and cover with buttered paper. Spread over the base of a fish-kettle a layer of vegetables (cut into roundels) and the parsley stalks. Lay the carp on the buttered grid of the fish-kettle, moisten with the red wine and fish fumet, and braise in the oven, basting frequently. Drain the fish, and arrange it on a serving dish. Garnish with the large and small poached quenelles, the soft roes (cooked in white wine, cut in escalopes, egg and breadcrumbed and fried), the oysters (poached and bearded, dipped in the boiling sauce Villeroi, egg and breadcrumbed and fried), the gudgeons (breadcrumbed and fried), the turned mushrooms (cooked), and the trussed crayfish (cooked in a court-bouillon). Strain the cooking liquor, reduce it well, and add it to the sauce genevoise. Serve this sauce separately. *(France.)*

Carpe aux champignons

Carp with mushrooms

For 6 persons: *1 kg. 200 of fillets of carp; 15 cl. white wine; 15 cl. fresh cream; 100 gr. butter; 150 gr. finely-diced mushrooms; 30 gr. chopped onion; 1 tablespoonful chopped parsley; 25 gr. flour.* Poaching time: 20 minutes.

Cut the fillets into large pieces, and arrange them in a buttered cocotte. Salt, sprinkle with white wine, cover with a sheet of buttered paper, and poach in a low oven. Tomber au beurre the onion in a sauteuse, add the mushrooms, and sauté gently. Correct the seasoning, add the parsley, sprinkle with flour, cook for a few minutes, and moisten with the poaching stock. Add the cream, blend well, and cook for 3 or 4 minutes. Correct the seasoning and consistency, monter au beurre (with the rest of the butter), arrange the fish on a serving dish, and pour the sauce on top. Serve accompanied with pommes sautées persillées. *(Hungary.)*

Carpe à la crème de raifort

For 6 persons: *1 carp (1 kg. 500 to 1 kg. 800); 2 lemons; picked parsley; 2 dl. fresh cream; 40 gr. grated horse-radish; 750 gr. potatoes.* Cooking time: 30 to 35 minutes.

Poach the carp in a court-bouillon. Drain and arrange on a napkin with the parsley and the quartered lemons. Serve the plain boiled potatoes separately, and also the whipped cream blended with the horse-radish and seasoned with a pinch of sugar and a touch of Cayenne. *(International cookery.)*

Carpe farcie I

Stuffed carp I

For 6 persons: *1 carp (2 kg.); 1 small chopped onion; finely-chopped parsley; chives; 50 gr. butter; 100 gr. soaked white breadcrumbs; 3 eggs; 100 gr. butter; 300 gr. mushrooms; ½ litre red wine.* Cooking time: approximately 50 minutes.

Open the carp through the back to remove the backbone, reserve the soft roe and the liver, and clean and dry the fish. Quickly colour the soft roe and the liver in butter (into which has been blended the finely-chopped and cooked onion, parsley and chives). Allow to cool. Thicken with the squeezed breadcrumbs and the beaten eggs. Season with salt and nutmeg. Add enough forcemeat to fill the cavity in the carp, and sew it up. Arrange it in a sauteuse, and brush it with noisette butter on both sides. Moisten with the red wine and simmer. Add, after 15 minutes of cooking, the mushrooms (previously quartered and then rissolés in butter). Finish the cooking in the oven, in a covered container. Arrange on a long serving dish. Pour the mushrooms and the cooking liquor over the fish. *(Austria.)*

Carpe farcie II

Stuffed carp II

For 6 persons: *2 small carp (750 to 900 kg. each); 4 thinly-sliced onions; 100 gr. butter; 3 hard-boiled eggs; 4 raw eggs; 30 gr. sugar.* Court-bouillon: *6 carrots (cut into roundels); 8 button onions; 30 gr. salt; 15 gr. freshly-milled pepper; 60 gr. sugar.* Cooking time: 1 hour.

Prepare a court-bouillon with the roundels of carrot, sliced onions, salt, pepper, sugar and approximately 3½ litres of water. Scale the carp without damaging the skin, gut and bone them, and keep the skins whole. Stew the sliced onions in butter, and allow them to cool. Using a bowl chopper, chop the filleted fish flesh, the hard-boiled eggs and the onions, incorporate the raw eggs, and season with salt and freshly-milled pepper. Use this mixture to stuff the skins of the carp, sew them up, and poach them lightly in the prepared court-bouillon. Allow to cool gently. Arrange on a serving dish. Immediately before serving, sprinkle with the stock. *(Israel.)*

Carpe hongroise

Carp Hungarian style

For 6 persons: *2 kg. of carp; 100 gr. chopped onion; 35 gr. lard; 75 gr. green peppers cut into small dice; 75 gr. peeled, de-seeded and chopped tomatoes; 6 gr. paprika.* Poaching time: 20 minutes.

Fillet the fish (already gutted and cleaned) and skin. Cut the fillets into large pieces, and salt. Prepare a stock from the heads, bones and trimmings. Colour the onion in the lard, sprinkle with paprika, and moisten with the stock. Cook gently for 30 to 35 minutes. Moisten the fish with the stock, add the peppers and the chopped tomatoes, and poach gently for 20 minutes. Serve with an accompaniment of galuska, which is a Hungarian farinaceous paste looking like fine pearl barley. *(Hungary.)*

Carpe juive

Carp Jewish style

For 6 persons: *1 kg. 800 of carp; 150 gr. thinly-sliced onions; 6 small carrots; 30 gr. salt; 60 gr. sugar; 15 gr. white peppercorns.* Cooking time: 40 minutes.

Prepare a court-bouillon with the onion, whole carrots, salt, peppercorns, sugar and approximately 3½ litres of water. Cut up the fish, and place the pieces in the hot court-bouillon. Cook gently in the oven for 40 minutes. When the cooking is finished, remove the fish, and drain it. Arrange on a serving dish, and garnish with the carrots cut into roundels. *(Israel.)*

Carpe au letcho

For 6 persons: *1 kg. 200 of fillets of carp; 60 gr. lard; 60 gr. onion; 250 gr. green peppers (emptied out and cut into rings); 150 gr. skinned tomatoes (cut into roundels); 12 gr. paprika.* Cooking time: 40 minutes.

Lightly score the fillets, cut them into pieces, season with salt, sprinkle with half the paprika, and arrange in a sauteuse smeared with lard. Colour the onion in lard, sprinkle with the rest of the paprika, add the peppers and tomatoes, and a few drops of water, season with salt, and cook (covered) for 20 minutes. Pour the letcho on the fish, cover, and stew gently for another 20 minutes. Arrange on a serving dish, and serve with an accompaniment of parsley potatoes. (N.B. Letcho is a mixture of peppers, tomatoes and onions.) *(Hungary.)*

Carpe nivernaise

For 6 persons: *1 carp (1 kg. 500); 100 gr. butter; 200 gr. thinly-sliced onions; 2 cloves of garlic; 150 gr. thinly-sliced raw mushrooms; 200 gr. button onions; 4 dl. red wine; 1 dl. clear sauce tomate; ½ bayleaf; 1 sprig of thyme; 40 gr. beurre manié; 2 cl. cognac; 1 tablespoonful of chopped parsley.* Cooking time: 30 to 35 minutes.

Lightly colour the onion in butter, and spread it over the base of a buttered fish tray. Add chopped parsley, thyme, bayleaf and crushed garlic. Lay the carp on top, and season. Moisten with the sauce tomate and red wine, cover with buttered paper, and cook in the oven. Strain the cooking liquor, bind it with the beurre manié, add the cognac, and correct the seasoning and consistency. Coat the fish with this sauce. Garnish with the slices of mushroom (cooked in butter) and the button onions (cooked in red wine). *(France.)*

Carpe au paprika

For 6 persons: *2 carp (1 kg. 500 each); 1 kg. potatoes; 60 gr. pieces of bacon; 120 gr. lard; 35 cl. dry white wine; 1 red pepper cut into roundels; 2 onions; 60 gr. paprika; 80 gr. paprika butter; 2 dl. sour cream; 100 gr. flour; salt; Cayenne pepper; 2 litres of water.* Preparation time: 50 to 60 minutes.

Scale, clean and fillet the fish. Carefully remove the remaining bones, take out the gills, and wash the fillets and heads. Peel the potatoes, and cut them into roundels 3 mm. thick. Blanch them in salted water, and arrange them in a gratinating dish greased with 20 gr. lard. Cut the fillets into portions, season, and colour in paprika butter. Arrange them on top of the potatoes in the gratinating dish. Cut the pieces of bacon and one of the onions into thin strips of equal width, colour them in a sauteuse, and spread them evenly over the fish. Cut up the bones and heads into small pieces, colour them with chopped onion in 100 gr. lard, sprinkle with paprika and flour, and add the white wine and 2 litres of water. Cook for 25 minutes, strain through a tammy cloth. Use this sauce to coat the potatoes and fish, and cook for another 20 minutes in the oven. At the last minute, place dabs of paprika butter on the dish, coat with cream, and cover with roundels of peppers. *(Hungary.)*

Carpe au poivre

For 6 persons: *6 pieces of carp (300 gr. each); 1 tablespoonful crushed peppercorns; 1 bayleaf; 1 sprig of thyme; 3 cloves of garlic; 1 dl. tarragon vinegar; the juice of 1 small lemon; 1 litre water; ¼ litre red wine; picked parsley; 150 gr. carrots; 150 gr. celery; 300 gr. onions.* Poaching time; 15 minutes.

Prepare a court-bouillon with the water, peppercorns, bayleaf, thyme, garlic and tarragon vinegar. Cook over a low flame for 30 minutes, and strain through a chinois. Prepare a coarse brunoise, and cook it in the stock for 12 minutes. Add any hard roe from the carp, whisk, blend in the red wine, and cook for a few minutes. Place the pieces of carp in the stock, salt slightly, add the lemon juice, and poach. Arrange on a serving dish, and coat with the reduced stock and the brunoise. Sprinkle with the parsley. *(Austria.)*

Carpe polonaise

Carp Polish style

For 6 persons: *1 kg. 500 of carp; 100 gr. butter; 3 dl. brown ale; 1 dl. red wine; 2 thinly-sliced onions; 6 parsley stalks; ½ bayleaf; 1 sprig of thyme; 2 cloves; 6 white peppercorns; 5 cl. vinegar; 50 gr. sultanas; 50 gr. shredded almonds; 50 gr. gingerbread; 50 gr. sugar.* Cooking time: 20 minutes.

Line a buttered sauteuse with onion, parsley stalks, bayleaf, thyme, cloves and peppercorns. Cut up the carp into slices 3 cm. thick, arrange them on the base of aromatics; season; moisten with the ale and red wine, add the gingerbread (cut into small dice), and cook gently, covered with a lid, When the cooking is finished, remove the fish, arrange it on a dish, and keep it hot. Dissolve the sugar (cooked to a pale caramel stage) with the vinegar, add the cooking liquor (passed through a hair sieve), and reduce if necessary. Place the carp in the sauce, add the sultanas (previously swollen in lukewarm water) and the almonds. Correct the seasoning and consistency, and allow to simmer for 3 or 4 minutes. Arrange in a timbale. *(International cookery.)*

Carpe, Quenelles de

Proceed as for the preparation of Quenelles de brochet, replacing the pike forcemeat with a mousseline forcemeat of carp. *(See page 377.)*

Carpe Ratz

For 6 persons: *1 kg. 200 of carp fillets; 120 gr. thinly-sliced onion; 60 gr. lard; 12 gr. paprika; 15 gr. flour; 180 gr. thinly-sliced green peppers; 150 gr. peeled tomatoes (cut into roundels); 600 gr. cooked potatoes (peeled, and cut into roundels); 60 gr. smoked bacon; 3 dl. sour cream.* Cooking time: 20 minutes.

Cut up the fillets into pieces, and lard each piece with a thin slice of bacon. Season lightly with salt, and sprinkle with paprika. Arrange the potatoes in a gratinating dish, and place the fish on top. Cover with the onion, peppers and tomatoes. Sprinkle with melted lard (or beurre fondu), and cook, covered, in the oven. After 10 minutes of cooking, add the sour cream (which has been well blended with the flour). Finish the cooking in the oven. *(Hungary.)*

Carpe royale

For 6 persons: *1 carp (1 kg. 800); 2 dl. Chablis; 1 dl. fish fumet; 2 chopped shallots; 12 thin slices of truffle; 12 escalopes of soft roe of carp; 12 small turned mushroom heads; 12 small pieces of truffle turned olive-shaped; 4 dl. sauce normande; 50 gr. butter.* Cooking time: 15 minutes.

Fillet the carp, clean it, and cut each fillet into 6 escalopes. Season, and poach in the Chablis and fish fumet. Drain, and arrange in a ring. Fill the centre with the escalopes of soft roe (cooked in butter), the mushrooms and the olives of truffle. Coat the fish and the garnish with the sauce normande (containing the reduced cooking liquor), and place a slice of truffle on each escalope. *(France.)*

Carpe grillée turque

Grilled carp Turkish style

For 6 persons: *3 kg. of carp; 2 onions; 7 dl. local red wine; the juice of 1 lemon; 12 tomatoes; 150 gr. carrots; 150 gr. celeriac; 100 gr. leek; 50 gr. concentrated tomato purée; 2 dl. olive oil; 1 clove of garlic; rosemary, wild marjoram, thyme, bayleaf and sage; lemon-peel; salt and pepper.*

Scale and clean the fish, and fillet (beginning at the dorsal edge). Cut the fillets into pieces, and season with salt and pepper. Prepare a marinade with lemon juice, a very-finely-chopped onion, crushed garlic, rosemary, thyme, wild marjoram, sage, lemon-peel and bayleaf. Marinate the fish for 1 hour.
Prepare a fine julienne with 1 onion, the leeks, celeriac and carrots. Lightly colour these vegetables, one after another, in the olive oil. Season with salt and freshly-milled pepper; add the concentrated tomato purée, and moisten slowly with the wine. Reduce the wine until it has almost evaporated. At the last moment, add the tomatoes, peeled, pipped and cut into a julienne. Stew. Keep warm. Cut the marinated fillets into small squares, pass them through olive oil, and grill them over very hot charcoal. Serve, separately, the julienne (in red wine) and white bread. *(Turkey.)*

Carpe tzigane

For 6 persons: *6 pieces of carp (300 gr. each); 1 kg. potatoes (cooked in their jackets and then peeled); 250 gr. onions; 250 gr. thin slices of smoked bacon; 60 gr. butter; 1 litre sour cream; very sweet paprika; chopped parsley.* Cooking time: approximately 30 minutes.

Pour a little beurre fondu into a gratinating dish. Arrange, layer by layer, roundels of potato, the thinly-sliced onions and the slices of bacon. Place on top the pieces of carp, sprinkle with half of the cream, and simmer in the oven for about 25 minutes. Pour on the rest of the cream, replace in the oven, and cook for another 5 or 6 minutes. Serve in the cooking dish. Sprinkle with paprika, and then with chopped parsley. Add, when available, a fine julienne of green peppers. *(Austria.)*

Chevesne, chevaine

Chub

This fish, with fine white flesh, can be prepared meunière, grilled (with a sauce maître d'hôtel), or fried (with a sauce tartare or rémoulade).

Esturgeon bourgeoise

Sturgeon

For 6 persons: *2 darnes of sturgeon (600 gr. each); 1 carrot; 1 onion; 50 gr. celery; 8 parsley stalks; 1 dl. white wine; 2 dl. fish fumet; 1 dl. fresh cream; 40 gr. beurre manié; 750 gr. potatoes (turned into large olive-shapes).* Cooking time: approximately 25 minutes.

Line a buttered sauteuse with roundels of carrot and onion, thinly-sliced celery, and parsley stalks. Place the darnes on the aromatics, season, moisten with the white wine and fish fumet, and braise in the oven. Remove the darnes, drain and skin them, and arrange them on a serving dish. Strain the cooking liquor, reduce it by a quarter, thicken with the beurre manié, incorporate the cream, and correct the seasoning and consistency. Coat the darnes with this sauce, and surround them with the potatoes (cooked in salted water and kept olive-shaped). *(France.)*

Esturgeon en cocotte

For 6 persons: *2 darnes of sturgeon (600 gr. each); 150 gr. fat bacon; 150 gr. small cooked mushrooms; 150 gr. button onions; 100 gr. small carrots; 200 gr. noisette potatoes; 3 dl. white wine; 2 tablespoonfuls tomato purée; 150 gr. butter.* Cooking time: 25 to 30 minutes.

Skin the darnes, stud them with bacon, arrange them in a buttered sauteuse, season, moisten with the white wine, and braise (covered) in the oven. Stew the carrots in butter, glaze the onions, and gild the noisette potatoes. Pour the garnish into the sauteuse, and simmer all for 4 or 5 minutes. Pour the cooking liquor into a saucepan, add the tomato purée, monter au beurre lightly, and correct seasoning and consistency. Arrange the darnes, with their garnish, in a cocotte, and coat with the sauce. *(France.)*
(See illustration, page 367. N.B. Different presentation.)

Côtelettes d'esturgeon

Proceed as for the preparation of Côtelettes de brochet (cutlets of pike), but with a mousseline forcemeat of sturgeon. *(See page 375.)*

Esturgeon livonienne

For 6 persons: *1 piece of fillet of sturgeon (1 kg.); 150 gr. fat bacon; 3 dl. white wine; 1 bouquet garni; 30 gr. butter; 3 dl. white wine sauce; 1 dl. sour cream.* Cooking time: 25 minutes.

Skin the fillet, stud it with small pieces of bacon, and lay it on a thickly-buttered fish tray. Moisten with the white wine, add the bouquet garni, season, and cook (covered) in the oven. Remove the fillet, drain it, and arrange on a serving dish. Reduce the cooking liquor almost to a glaze, add it to the white wine sauce, blend in the cream, simmer gently, correct the seasoning and consistency, strain, and pour on to the fish. *(International cookery.)*

Matelote d'esturgeon

Proceed as for Eel Matelote, but with fillets of sturgeon, skinned and cut up into large dice. *(See page 370.)*

Esturgeon normande

Cut up the skinned fillet of sturgeon into escalopes, and then proceed as for the preparation of Sole normande. *(See page 318.)*

Esturgeon russe

Cut up the sturgeon into darnes. Proceed as for the preparation of Sole russe, taking into account the difference in size when calculating the cooking time. *(See page 325.)*

Esturgeon en tortue

For 6 persons: *2 darnes of sturgeon (600 gr. each); 20 anchovy fillets; 1 onion; 1 carrot; 50 gr. celery; 6 parsley stalks; 1 sprig of thyme; ½ bayleaf; 3 dl. white wine; 300 gr. turtle garnish; 4 dl. turtle sauce; 25 gr. butter.* Cooking time: 25 to 30 minutes.

Skin the darnes, and stud them with the anchovy fillets. Cut the onion and carrot into roundels, and place them in a sauteuse with the thinly-sliced celery, parsley stalks, thyme and bayleaf. Arrange the darnes on the aromatics, season, moisten with the white wine, and braise (covered) in the oven. When the cooking is finished, remove the darnes, drain them, and arrange on a serving dish. Strain the cooking liquor, reduce it considerably, and add it to the turtle sauce. Surround the darnes with the garnish, and coat them and the garnish with the sauce.

Turtle sauce: This is a Madeira sauce boiled up with a little tomato purée and seasoned with an infusion of turtle herbs (which can be bought or can be made with a pinch each of marjoram, rosemary, basil, very little sage, pouring a little hot stock on top, covering and allowing to simmer but not boil). Strain through a tammy cloth. *(France.)*

Féra

Whitefish

The féra is a highly delicate fish, and is the equal of the best freshwater trout. All methods of preparing trout are applicable to the féra.
(See illustration, page 366.)

Féra tessinoise, Filets de

For 6 persons: *1 kg. fillets of whitefish; 50 gr. butter; 2 chopped shallots; 200 gr. red and green peppers; 50 gr. cèpes; 1 lemon; 5 cl. oil; 4 cl. brown veal stock; 100 gr. onion; flour.* Cooking time: 6 to 7 minutes.

Sweat the chopped shallots in butter, add to them the peppers and cèpes (all these ingredients diced); season and stew. Season the fillets, flour them, and colour golden in oil. Arrange them on top of the ragoût, sprinkle with the lemon juice, cover with roundels of fried onion, and pour the veal stock around the fish. *(Switzerland.)*
(See illustration, page 387.)

Féra trois nations, Filets de

For 6 persons: *12 fillets of whitefish (60 gr. each); 300 gr. creamed pike-perch forcemeat; 250 gr. peeled, de-seeded and chopped tomatoes; 150 gr. raw mushrooms; 3 dl. cream; 1 dl. white wine; 1 dl. fish fumet; 2 chopped shallots; 100 gr. butter; 1 lemon; 30 gr. beurre manié.* Cooking time: 10 to 12 minutes.

Mask the fillets with the forcemeat, fold them in two, season them and lay them on a buttered fish tray sprinkled with the chopped shallots; moisten with the white wine and fish fumet. Cover with buttered paper, and cook in the oven. Cut up the mushrooms into thick slices, and cook them with a nut of butter, the juice of half a lemon, and a pinch of salt. Season the

▲ Carpe à la japonaise Shasimi, p. 421

Darnes de saumon grillées, p. 404 ▼

▲ Truite Antoine Clessé, p. 412

Filets de perche bernoise, p. 393 ▼

▲ Brochet meunière, p. 376

Filets de féra tessinoise, p. 384 ▼

▲ Brochet angevine, p. 374

Brochet bordelaise, p. 375 ▼

tomatoes with salt and pepper, and melt them in butter. Arrange them in a gratinating dish, and cover them with the cooked sliced mushrooms. Drain the fillets, and arrange them on top of the mushrooms. Reduce the cooking liquor with the mushroom liquor, bind lightly with the beurre manié, blend in the cream, and simmer gently. Finish this sauce with 50 gr. of butter and a few drops of lemon juice; correct the seasoning and consistency; pour the sauce over the fillets, and glaze. *(Switzerland.)*
(See illustration, page 405. N.B. Different presentation.)

Féra au vin de Moselle

For 6 persons: *6 whitefish (200 to 225 gr. each); ½ bottle medium-dry Moselle; 4 dl. sauce mousseline; 600 gr. potatoes.* Cooking time: 12 minutes.

For this method, the whitefish must be chosen live, and killed only 10 minutes before use. Gut and clean them quickly. Place them in a court-bouillon (containing the Moselle wine) which is just deep enough to cover them, and poach, preferably in a small silver fish-kettle suitable for service. Serve the sauce mousseline separately, and the plain boiled potatoes. *(International cookery.)*

Fogasch (ou Sandre) Bakony

Pike-perch

For 6 persons: *1 pike-perch weighing 1 kg. 500; 60 gr. thinly-sliced onion; 100 gr. lard; 15 gr. paprika; 200 gr. diced raw mushrooms; 35 gr. butter; 20 gr. flour; 2 dl. fresh cream; 75 gr. diced green peppers; 75 gr. roundels of green peppers; chopped parsley.* Poaching time for the fillets: approximately 12 minutes.

Remove the head and gut, clean, wash and fillet the fish. Skin the fillets, cut them into pieces, season with salt, and arrange in a buttered sauteuse. Prepare a stock with a little water and the roughly-chopped head and backbone. Colour the sliced onion in lard, and add the mushrooms. Sauté. Sprinkle with paprika, and add the peppers. Moisten with the stock (which has been passed through a sieve), and cook for 4 to 5 minutes. Bind with the flour mixed with the cream, stir well and cook gently for 10 minutes. Pour the sauce over the fish, and poach in the oven. Arrange the fish on a serving dish, coat it with the unpassed sauce, garnish with the thinly-sliced roundels of peppers, and sprinkle with chopped parsley. Serve with plain-boiled fish potatoes. *(Hungary.)*

Fogasch au paprika

For 6 persons: *1 pike-perch weighing 1 kg. 500; 75 gr. onion (cut into roundels); 60 gr. lard; 15 gr. paprika; 15 gr. flour; 15 cl. fresh cream; 100 gr. seeded green peppers; 30 gr. butter.* Poaching time for the fillets: 15 minutes.

Remove the head and gut, clean, wash and fillet the fish. Skin the fillets, season with salt, and arrange in a buttered cocotte. Colour the roundels of onion in the lard, sprinkle with paprika, add the trimmings and the backbone, cover with water, salt lightly, and cook for 30 to 40 minutes. Pass the fish stock, and add to it the flour (which has been previously mixed with the cream), and allow to cook for 2 to 3 minutes. Pour the sauce over the fish, and bake in the oven for 15 minutes. Arrange the fish on a serving dish, coat with the sauce, and garnish with rings of green peppers. Serve with an accompaniment of galuska or of potatoes (the latter finished with parsley butter). *(Hungary.)*

Fogasch (ou Sandre) poêlé

For 6 persons: *1 pike-perch weighing 1 kg. 500; 80 gr. brown breadcrumbs; 120 gr. lard.* Cooking time: 10 to 12 minutes.

Remove the head, and gut, clean, wash and fillet the fish. Skin the fillets, and season them with salt. Roll them (with pressure) in the breadcrumbs. Sauté them in lard in a frying-pan, and colour them on both sides. Drain them on a cloth, and arrange them on a serving dish. Serve with a garnish of quarters of lemon, and accompanied, separately, with parsley potatoes and sauce tartare. *(Hungary.)*

Fogasch poêlé hongroise

For 6 persons: *1 pike-perch weighing 1 kg. 500; 40 gr. flour; 120 gr. lard.* Cooking time: 12 minutes.

Remove the head and gut, clean, wash and fillet the fish. Skin the fillets, cut them into pieces, and season with salt. Incorporate the paprika with the flour, and use the mixture to coat the fish. Gild the fillets on both sides in very hot lard. Drain them on a cloth. Arrange on a serving dish, and garnish with quarters of lemon. Serve parsley potatoes and sauce tartare separately. *(Hungary.)*

Goujons

Gudgeon

These small fish are usually fried. Larger specimens can, however, be prepared meunière. Gudgeon are used in first-class cookery as a garnish for certain other, and much larger fish. For this purpose, gudgeon are egg and bread-crumbed and fried.

Huch, huchon

Hucho

This fish, belonging to the salmon family, has white and tasty flesh. All the methods of preparation for salmon are applicable to it.

Huch goulasch

For 6 persons: *1 kg. 600 of filleted flesh; 500 gr. onions; 200 gr. lard; 30 gr. mild paprika; 10 gr. caraway; 100 gr. concentrated tomato purée; 500 gr. potatoes; 1 lemon.* Complete cooking time: 45 minutes.

Cut up the fish into pieces weighing about 40 gr. each, sprinkle them with lemon juice, and marinate for 30 minutes. Colour the thinly-sliced onions in very hot lard, sprinkle with the paprika, and cook for a few minutes. Add the tomato concentrate, the caraway, and the finely-diced raw potatoes. Moisten with water, salt lightly, and allow to simmer until the potatoes are cooked. Add the fish, bring all to the boil, and poach, covered, for 10 to 15 minutes. *(Austria.)*

Lavaret Gmunden

For 6 persons: *6 lavarets (200 gr. each); 6 dl. oil; 2 dl. milk; 150 gr. butter; 3 anchovies; 30 gr. capers; 3 lemons; chopped parsley; 3 dl. sour cream.* Cooking time: approximately 30 minutes.

Season the lavarets with salt and pepper, dip them in the milk, and roll them in the flour. Seize them in very hot fat, and arrange on a thickly-buttered gratinating dish. Place on each fish some roundels of peeled and pipped lemon. Chop the capers, the lemon-zest and the de-salted anchovies, toss them in noisette butter, and pour the mixture over the fish. Sprinkle liberally with chopped parsley, and cook in a low oven. During the cooking, coat with the cream, and sprinkle with small pieces of butter. *(Austria.)*

Lotte au four

Burbot, baked

For 6 persons: *1 kg. 200 of burbot (without head); 150 gr. unsalted fat bacon; 2 dl. white wine; 100 gr. butter; 1 carrot; 1 onion; ½ bayleaf; 1 sprig of thyme; 8 parsley stalks.* Cooking time: 30 to 35 minutes.

Skin the burbot, and stud it on one side with fine lardons. Season, and wrap it in thickly-buttered paper. Arrange it on a base of aromatics in a baking tray, moisten with white wine, and bake in the oven. After 25 minutes, remove the paper, and finish off the cooking, while basting frequently. Drain, and arrange on a serving dish. Pass the cooking stock, reduce it by half, add a little butter, and serve separately. *(France.)*

Lotte ménagère

For 6 persons: *1 burbot (weighing 1 kg. 500); 100 gr. chopped onion; 2 dl. clear veal stock; 1 dl. white wine; 50 gr. chopped ham; 2 egg yolks; 1 tablespoonful chopped parsley; 1 tablespoonful grated horse-radish; 75 gr. butter.* Cooking time: 30 to 35 minutes.

Skin the burbot, and lay it on a fish tray which has been buttered, and then sprinkled with the chopped onion and ham. Moisten with the veal stock, add 50 gr. of butter, and braise in the oven until the fish is cooked and well coloured. Cut the liver of the burbot into escalopes, and sauté in butter until it is well done. Arrange the fish on a serving dish, and garnish with the escalopes of liver. Reduce the cooking liquor by a quarter, pass it, and blend with the white wine mixed with the egg yolks. Add the chopped and grated horse-radish. Serve the sauce separately. *(France.)*

Lotte, Quenelles de

Prepare a forcemeat with the burbot flesh (as indicated in the method for the preparation of Quenelles de brochet). Mould and poach the quenelles in the same way. Serve them with the same sauces. *(France.)* *(See page 377.)*

Lotte de rivière suédoise

For 6 persons: *2 kg. 500 of burbot; 200 gr. carrots; 50 gr. celery; 600 gr. potatoes; the white of 2 leeks and one medium-sized onion (all these ingredients thinly-sliced); 1 sprig of parsley; 1 bay-*

leaf; mace; 4 dl. white wine; 2 dl. fresh cream; 2 egg yolks; 100 gr. butter; 2 lemons; chopped parsley; heart-shaped croûtons. Cooking time: 20 minutes.

Skin and gut the fish, wash it, and cut into 6 tronçons. Reserve, whole, the hard roes and liver from the fish. Line a buttered fish tray with the thinly-sliced vegetables, and place the fish on top. Season with salt and pepper, add a bouquet of parsley and bayleaf, the mace and a little lemon-zest, moisten with the white wine and a little water, cover with a sheet of buttered paper, and cook gently. Remove the fish as soon as it is cooked. Poach the eggs and the burbot liver in a little stock. Pass the rest of the stock, reduce it slightly, bind it with beurre manié, and with the cream which has been blended with the egg yolks. Correct the seasoning and consistency, flavour with lemon juice, and incorporate some small pieces of fresh butter. Arrange the burbot on a hot serving dish, garnish with the sliced liver and roes which have been poached, coat with the sauce, and sprinkle with chopped parsley. Surround with croûtons fried in butter. Serve plain-boiled fish potatoes separately. *(Sweden.)*

Marène

This fish, which is of the family Coregonus, is very rare and has white and fine flesh. All methods of preparation appropriate to river trout and small salmon-trout apply to it.

Matelote canotière

For 6 persons: *600 gr. carp; 600 gr. eel; 200 gr. mushrooms; 200 gr. button onions; 12 small goujons; 6 trussed crayfish; 100 gr. butter; 3 cl. cognac; 4 dl. white wine; 40 gr. beurre manié; 1 bouquet garni; 1 egg; breadcrumbs.* Cooking time: 20 minutes.

Cut the carp and eel into tronçons, flame with cognac, moisten with white wine, season, add the bouquet garni, and cook, covered, in the oven. Remove the bouquet garni, pour off the cooking liquor, bind it with the beurre manié and finish the sauce with 50 gr. butter. Put together in a saucepan the fish, the mushrooms (cooked white), the button onions (glazed white in butter), and the sauce. Simmer on the side of the stove for a few minutes, and arrange in a timbale. Garnish with the crayfish (cooked in a court-bouillon) and the goujons (egg and breadcrumbed and fried).

Matelote Lovran

For 6 persons: *1 small carp; 1 small pike; 1 small eel; 1 small tench (total weight of the four fish being approximately 2 kg.); 150 gr. unsalted fat bacon; 15 button onions; 3 cloves of garlic; ½ litre dry white wine; 15 cl. red Burgundy; chopped parsley; 1 dl. fresh cream; 70 gr. beurre manié.* Cooking time: 25 minutes.

Cut the fish into equal-sized pieces, and season with salt and pepper. Cut the bacon into dice, and cook without colouring. Add the onions (previously blanched) and cook together until golden. Add the fish and the crushed garlic, moisten with the white wine, and bring to the boil. Add the red wine, and cook gently for 20 minutes. Arrange in a timbale, and keep hot. Bind the cooking stock with the beurre manié, cook for a few minutes, and add the cream. Correct the seasoning of the sauce, and pour the sauce over the fish. Sprinkle with chopped parsley. *(Austria.)*

Matelote marinière

For 6 persons: *1 kg. 200 of various fish (carp, pike, eel and tench); 4 dl. fish velouté; 3 dl. white wine; 3 cl. cognac; 200 gr. button mushrooms; 200 gr. button onions; 6 trussed crayfish; 12 small heart-shaped croûtons; 1 bouquet garni; 100 gr. butter.* Cooking time: 15 to 20 minutes.

Cut the fish into tronçons, flame with the cognac, moisten with the white wine, season, add the bouquet garni, and cook, covered, in the oven. When the cooking is finished, place the tronçons in another saucepan, and add the cooked mushrooms and the onions (which have been glazed without colouring). Pass the cooking liquor, reduce by two-thirds, add it to the velouté, simmer, correct the seasoning and consistency, and pour over the fish. Allow to simmer for a few more minutes, arrange in a timbale, garnish with the crayfish (cooked in a court-bouillon) and the croûtons (fried in clarified butter). *(France.)*

Matelote meunière

For 6 persons: *1 kg. 200 of various fish; 3 cl. cognac; 4 dl. red wine; 40 gr. beurre manié; 100 gr. butter; 6 trussed crayfish; 12 heart-shaped croûtons; 1 bouquet garni.* Cooking time: 20 minutes.

Proceed as for the preparation of Matelote canotière, but moisten with red wine. Bind the cooking liquor with beurre manié, butter lightly, correct seasoning and consistency, and pour over the fish. Garnish with the trussed crayfish and the croûtons (fried in clarified butter). *(France.)*

Matelote meurette

For 6 persons: *1 kg. 200 of various fish; ½ litre red wine; 4 cl. brandy; 2 cloves of garlic; 100 gr. butter; 40 gr. beurre manié; 12 square bread croûtons; 1 bouquet garni.* Cooking time: 20 minutes.

Proceed as for the preparation of Matelote canotière, but moisten with red wine, after flaming with brandy. Cook in beurre manié, butter lightly, and pour over the fish. Garnish with the square buttered croûtons dried out in the oven, and rubbed with garlic. *(France.)* *(See page 391.)*

Matelote normande

For 6 persons: *1 kg. 200 of fish (sole, gurnard, small conger); 200 gr. mushrooms; 12 poached and bearded oysters; 12 shelled crayfish; 12 heart-shaped croûtons; 3 cl. Calvados; 4 dl. cider; 3 dl. fish velouté; 1 dl. fresh cream; 50 gr. butter; 1 bouquet garni; 12 poached and bearded mussels.* Cooking time: 20 minutes.

Cut the fish into tronçons, season, flame with the Calvados, moisten with the cider, add the bouquet garni, and cook, covered, in the oven. When the tronçons are just cooked, transfer them to another saucepan, and add the oysters, mussels, cooked mushrooms, and cooked shelled crayfish. Pass the cooking liquor, reduce it well, bind it with the velouté, adjust with the cream, and correct the seasoning and consistency. Pour this mixture over the fish, and simmer for a few minutes. Arrange in a timbale, and surround with the croûtons (fried in clarified butter). *(France.)*

Matelote pochouse

For 6 persons: *1 kg. of fish (eel, carp, pike and tench); 3 cl. brandy; 4 dl. red wine; 150 gr. streaky bacon; 150 gr. button mushrooms; 150 gr. button onions; 100 gr. butter; 40 gr. beurre manié; 12 small square croûtons (as for Matelote meurette).* Cooking time: 20 minutes.

Proceed as for the preparation of Matelote meurette, but flame with brandy, and then moisten with red wine. Add the bacon (previously diced and blanched), and the raw mushrooms and, at the last minute, the onions (glazed in butter). Bind with the beurre manié, butter lightly, and arrange in a timbale. Surround with the croûtons. *(France.)*

Omble chevalier

Sea-Char

The char is a fish of very fine quality, and is highly esteemed by gastronomes. Small char are prepared like trout, and the larger specimens as for salmon-trout.

Omble chevalier bourgetine

For 6 persons: *3 char (400 gr. each); 300 gr. raw pike flesh; 2 chopped shallots; 2 dl. fish fumet; 2 dl. fish velouté; 3 dl. fresh cream; 150 gr. butter; 12 shelled crayfish; 12 small fleurons; 50 gr. crayfish purée; the white of 1 egg; the juice of 1 lemon.* Cooking time: 10 minutes.

Prepare a forcemeat with the pike flesh, the egg-white, the crayfish purée and the cream, and season liberally. Fillet the char, and remove skin and small bones. Mask the fillets with the forcemeat, and sandwich them together on a buttered fish-tray which has been sprinkled with chopped shallot. Moisten with the white wine and the fish fumet, add a few drops of lemon juice, season, cover, and poach in the oven. Arrange the fillets on a gratinating dish. Pass the cooking stock, reduce it by three-quarters, add the velouté and cream, and cook for a few more moments. Remove from the heat, butter, and correct the seasoning and consistency. Garnish the char with the shelled crayfish, coat with the sauce, and glaze quickly under the salamander. Serve the rest of the sauce separately. *(International cookery.)*

Omble chevalier genevoise

For 6 persons: *1 char weighing between 1 kg. 200 and 1 kg. 500; 3 dl. white wine; 1 bouquet garni; 15 cl. fresh cream; 50 gr. butter; 2 egg yolks.* Cooking time: 20 to 25 minutes.

Season the fish, and poach it, with the bouquet garni, in the white wine. Remove the fish, pass the cooking stock, bind with the egg yolks and cream, and monter au beurre. Correct the seasoning and consistency. Season the sauce with a pinch of Cayenne, and use this sauce to coat the fish (which has been arranged in a serving dish). *(Switzerland.)*

Omble chevalier du lac de Thoune Saint-Béat

For 6 persons: *1 char weighing 1 kg.; 200 gr. fresh mushrooms; 2 chopped shallots; 2 dl. white wine; 3 dl. to 4 dl. sauce hollandaise.* Cooking time: approximately 12 minutes.

Split the fish open to remove the backbone, salt and flour it, and place it open side down in a buttered gratinating dish. Colour golden in the oven, basting frequently with butter. Add the chopped shallots, moisten with the white wine and reduce. Thinly-slice the mushrooms, season with pepper and salt, sauté them in butter, and use them to stuff the fish. Coat with the sauce hollandaise containing the reduced cooking stock. Glaze quickly under the salamander. *(Switzerland.)*

Omble chevalier au vin blanc

Char cooked in white wine

For 6 persons: *6 char (200 gr. to 225 gr. each); 3 dl. dry white wine; 2 chopped shallots; 100 gr. butter; 600 gr. potatoes (spoon-cut into large ball-shapes).* Cooking time: 12 to 15 minutes.

Lay the fish on a tray which has been buttered and sprinkled with chopped shallot. Season moderately with salt and pepper, moisten with the white wine, add 75 gr. butter, and cook in the oven, basting frequently. Drain the fish, and arrange them on a serving dish. Pass the cooking liquor, reduce it by half, correct the seasoning and consistency, and pour this over the fish. Garnish with the potatoes (cooked in salt water). (N.B. The white wine used for this preparation must be of first quality). *(Switzerland.)*

Ombre écailles

Grayling

The grayling can be favourably compared with the trout, and can be prepared like the char.

Ombre écailles genevoise

For 6 persons: *3 grayling (400 gr. each); 250 gr. small mushroom heads; 100 gr. mirepoix bordelaise; 3 dl. red wine; 40 gr. beurre manié; 100 gr. butter; ½ lemon.* Cooking time: 18 to 20 minutes.

Season the fish, and poach them gently in the red wine and with the mirepoix. Drain them, arrange them on a serving dish, and garnish with mushrooms (sautéd in butter). Pass the cooking liquor, reduce it by a quarter, bind with the beurre manié, butter lightly, add a few drops of lemon juice, correct the seasoning and consistency, and pour over the fish. *(Switzerland.)*

Ombre écailles lausannoise

For 6 persons: *4 grayling (300 gr. to 325 gr. each); 3 chopped shallots; 200 gr. raw mushrooms; 3 dl. white wine; 2 dl. sauce demi-glace maigre; 75 gr. butter; ½ lemon.* Cooking time: 15 to 20 minutes.

Lay the fish on a buttered gratinating dish which has been sprinkled with the chopped shallots. Add the thinly-sliced mushrooms, season with salt and pepper, moisten with the white wine, cover with a sheet of buttered paper, and poach in the oven. When the fish is cooked, pour the cooking stock into a small saucepan, reduce it by two-thirds, and add it to the sauce demi-glace. Add a few drops of lemon juice and correct the seasoning and consistency. Pour the sauce over the fish. *(Switzerland.)*

Perche aux amandes, Filets de

Perch fillets with almonds

For 6 persons: *900 gr. of fillets of perch; 2 eggs; 150 gr. shredded almonds; 200 gr. butter; 1 lemon.* Cooking time: 6 to 10 minutes.

Season the fillets with salt and pepper, and pass them through beaten egg. Colour them golden in butter, and arrange on a serving dish. Colour the almonds slightly in the cooking butter, and sprinkle them over the fillets. Garnish with roundels of lemon which have been cut into half-moon shapes. *(Switzerland.)*

(See illustration, page 406. N.B. Slightly different presentation.)

Perche bernoise, Filets de

For 6 persons: *900 gr. fillets of perch; 150 gr. butter; 500 gr. potatoes, steamed in their jackets, and peeled; 4 dl. sauce Mornay; ½ lemon; flour; 40 gr. grated Parmesan cheese.* Cooking time: 7 to 10 minutes.

Season the fillets with salt, pepper and lemon juice. Flour, and colour golden in butter. With the potatoes, prepare the rösti (see page *476*). Coat each fillet separately with sauce Mornay, arrange the fillets on a serving dish which has been garnished with the rösti, sprinkled with the grated Parmesan cheese, then with the beurre fondu, and brown. *(Switzerland.)*

(See illustration, page 386.)

Perche en cocotte Orso

For 6 persons: *6 large (or 12 small) perch; 2 dl. white wine; 75 gr. butter; 2 chopped shallots; 1 lemon; 1 tablespoonful chopped parsley; 600 gr. fish potatoes.* Cooking time: 18 minutes.

Scale the fish, gut, wash and dry them, and sprinkle with salt. Butter liberally an oval gratinating dish, and sprinkle it with the chopped shallots and chopped parsley. Arrange the perch on top, with the dorsal side uppermost, and sprinkle with more shallots and parsley. Moisten with the lemon juice and the white wine, and begin the cooking, covered, on the stove. Then place in the oven, and poach (12 to 15 minutes, and 18 to 20 minutes for the large ones). Serve in the cooking dish, with the fish potatoes served separately. *(Finland.)*

Perche aux figues, Filets de

For 6 persons: *6 fillets of perch (200 gr. each); 6 fresh figs; 200 gr. butter; 2 lemons; 1 orange; flour.* Cooking time: 6 to 10 minutes.

Marinate the fillets for 30 minutes with the juice of both lemons, and season with salt and pepper. Dry and flour the fillets, and cook them meunière. Arrange them on an oval cooking dish, and cover with the figs (cut into thin slices). Grate the rinds of 1 lemon and 1 orange. Add the rest of the butter to the cooking butter, and allow to colour and froth. Moisten with the juices of the lemon and the orange, and add the grated rinds. Immediately sprinkle the fish and the figs with this flavoured butter. Serve a saffroned risotto separately. *(Germany.)*

Perche du gourmet, Filets de

For 6 persons: *6 fillets of perch (120 gr. each); 2 eggs; 100 gr. butter; 1 lemon; 3 dl. sauce béarnaise; 2 tomatoes; 600 gr. potatoes; 2 tablespoonfuls olive oil; picked parsley.* Cooking time: 8 to 10 minutes.

Marinate the fillets for 30 minutes with the lemon juice, most of the oil, and salt and pepper. Sponge and flour, pass them through beaten eggs (containing a little olive oil), and colour them golden in butter. Arrange them on a serving dish, and garnish with the plain boiled potatoes and the parsley. Serve the sauce béarnaise (containing peeled, pipped and chopped tomatoes) separately. *(France.)* *(See illustration, page 366. N.B. Different presentation.)*

Perche hollandaise

For 6 persons: *6 perch (300 gr. each); 150 gr. butter; 1 tablespoonful chopped parsley; ½ lemon; 600 gr. potatoes; picked parsley.* Cooking time: 18 to 20 minutes.

Plunge the fish into a boiling court-bouillon (containing 1 tablespoonful of vinegar per litre, and also 1 bouquet garni). Cover and poach on the top of the stove. When the cooking is finished, drain the fish, skin them, and place them back in the court-bouillon. Drain them again, arrange on a napkin, and garnish with the picked parsley and with the fish potatoes. Serve beurre fondu (containing lemon juice and chopped parsley) separately. *(France.)*

Perche Murat, Filets de

Proceed as for the preparation of Filets de sole Murat. *(France.)* *(See page 317.)*
(See illustration, page 367.)

Perche Riehen, Filets de

For 6 persons: *900 gr. fillets of perch; 120 gr. butter; 600 gr. potatoes; 1 lemon.* For the sauce: *75 gr. onion; 3 dl. white wine; 4 dl. fish fumet; 120 gr. fresh breadcrumbs; 15 cl. cream; 6 cl. cognac; 1 clove; 1 small bayleaf.* Cooking time: 30 minutes.

Mix together the fish fumet and the white wine, and add the chopped onion and the bayleaf and clove. Cook for 10 minutes. Incorporate the breadcrumbs, return to the heat for 10 minutes, and pass all through a fine sieve. Thicken with the cream, work up with 50 gr. butter, add the cognac, and correct the seasoning and consistency. Season and flour the fillets, cook them (without colouring) in butter, and arrange on a serving dish. Coat with the very hot sauce. Serve with a garnish of plain boiled potatoes. *(Switzerland.)*

Perche de Tibériade au tschina

For 6 persons: *6 perch (300 gr. each); 3 seeded green peppers; 75 gr. chopped onion; 300 gr. peeled, pipped and chopped tomatoes; 600 gr. peeled potatoes; 300 gr. tschina; 1 crushed clove of garlic; 1 tablespoonful chopped parsley; 3 egg yolks; the juice of ½ lemon; 100 gr. butter.* Preparing time: approximately 30 minutes.

Clean, salt and flour the perch, and colour them golden on both sides in either butter or olive oil. Sweat the chopped onion, add the peppers and tomatoes, and colour. Cut the potatoes into fairly thin slices, season them, and stew in butter with a few drops of water. Arrange the fish on a layer of roundels of potato in a gratinating dish. Season the tomatoes and peppers with lemon juice and a pinch of cayenne, pour the mixture over the fish and braise in the oven. Blend the tschina with the egg yolks, add the garlic, and flavour with lemon juice. Use this mixture to coat the fish, and glaze under the salamander. *(Israel.)* (N.B. Tschina is the oily residue obtained from the production of sesame seeds, and is sold in Europe in preserved form.)

Poisson en brochette Pallastunturi

For 6 persons: *3 perch of 500 gr. to 600 gr. each; 150 gr. butter; 6 cl. white wine; 1 tablespoonful of mixed chopped chervil and chopped tarragon (or 1 tablespoonful chopped dill); ½ lemon; freshly-milled black pepper; fennel; sage; bayleaves; rosemary.* Cooking time: 20 to 25 minutes.

Scale the fish, gut, wash and dry them. Stuff each fish with the fines herbes. Fix them on a skewer, season with salt and pepper, and brush with melted butter. Blend the rest of the melted butter with the white wine. Pass under a hot grill, basting frequently with the mixture of butter and white wine. The fish is sufficiently cooked when the fins can be detached without difficulty, or fall off of their own accord. Arrange the fish on a serving dish, accompanied by melted butter containing the chopped dill and the lemon juice. This speciality dish is often served with a garnish of purée potatoes. *(Finland.)*

Poisson grillé libanaise

For 6 persons: *1 kg. 200 of fish (pike, gilt-poll, or scad etc.); 1 lemon; sumac; Sauce Taratour a la tachine: ¼ litre tachine; 1 lemon; 1 clove of garlic; 1 coffee-spoonful chopped parsley.* Cooking time for the fish: approximately 20 minutes.

Scale the fish and open it just enough to gut it. Wash and dry it, and rub it thoroughly with lemon juice, salt, pepper and sumac. Stick the fish on a spit, and grill it over charcoal. Arrange on a serving dish, and serve with the fish a sauce Taratour, together with thickly-sliced fresh cucumber covered with chilled yoghurt which has been seasoned with crushed garlic and a little salt, and then sprinkle with mint-leaves (either freshly chopped or dried and pounded).

Sauce Taratour: Mix the tachine with a little water and the lemon juice, and add the crushed garlic with a little salt as well as the chopped parsley.

N.B. Tachine is the oily residue obtained from the production of sesame seeds, and is sold in Europe in preserved form.

N.B. Sumac is the sharp-flavoured powdered spice obtained from the seeds of the plant called sumac. *(Lebanon.)*

Sandre anglaise, Filets de

Pike-perch English style, Fillets of

Proceed as for the preparation of Filets de sole anglaise. *(See page 297.)*

Sandre bouillie

Boiled pike-perch

For 6 persons: *1 pike-perch (1 kg. 200); 180 gr. butter; 1 lemon; picked parsley; 750 gr. potatoes.* Cooking time: approximately 25 minutes.

Lay the pike-perch on the grid of a fish-kettle, cover with cold water, and add 8 gr. salt and 1 coffee-spoonful of vinegar per litre of water. Bring rapidly to the boil. Remove from the heat, and poach, covered, on top of the stove. Drain, arrange on a napkin, and garnish with parsley and quarters of lemon. Serve beurre fondu and plain boiled potatoes separately. The beurre fondu may be replaced by various sauces, such as hollandaise, mousseline, Nantua, shrimp or lobster. *(International cookery.)*

Sandre Butterfly, Filets de

For 6 persons: *6 fillets of pike-perch (150 gr. each); 3 thick slices of pineapple (cut into quarters); 200 gr. butter; 2 dl. sauce tomate; 1 coffee-spoonful curry powder; 2 eggs; flour; fresh breadcrumbs.* Cooking time: 8 to 10 minutes.

Take the fillets and egg and breadcrumb them, adding a little curry powder to the bread-crumbs. Arrange the fillets on a buttered fish tray, sprinkle with beurre fondu, start the cooking on the stove, and finish it off either in the oven or under the salamander. Arrange the fillets on a serving dish, and coat with a thin layer of sauce tomate. Sauté the pineapple in curry butter, and arrange it on top of the fillets. Serve saffroned risotto or fish potatoes separately, and the rest of the sauce tomate. *(Sweden.)*

Sandre aux champignons, Filets de

Pike-perch with mushrooms, Fillets of

For 6 persons: *6 fillets of pike-perch (120 gr. to 150 gr. each); 2 dl. fish fumet; 180 gr. raw mushrooms; 3 chopped shallots; 3 dl. fish velouté; 75 gr. butter.* Cooking time: 12 to 15 minutes.

Lay the fillets on a gratinating dish which has been buttered, and then sprinkled with the chopped shallots. Season with salt and pepper, cover with the sliced mushrooms, moisten with the fish fumet, cover with a sheet of buttered paper, and poach in the oven. When the cooking is finished, reduce the poaching stock, and add it to the velouté. Butter lightly, correct the seasoning and consistency; use this sauce to coat the fillets, and glaze them briskly. *(France.)*

Sandre chancelier, Filets de

For 6 persons: *6 fillets of pike-perch (120 gr. to 150 gr. each); 1 dl. fish fumet; 1 dl. white wine; 2 chopped shallots; 1 dl. fish velouté; 3 dl. sauce hollandaise; 300 gr. potatoes; 200 gr. button onions; 75 gr. butter; 30 gr. caviar; ½ lemon.* Cooking time: 12 to 15 minutes.

Lay the fillets on a fish tray which has been buttered and then sprinkled with chopped shallot. Moisten with the white wine and the fish fumet, season with salt and pepper, cover with a sheet of buttered paper, and poach in the oven. Arrange on a serving dish, and garnish with the potatoes (cut with a round spoon-cutter, plain boiled, and passed through butter) and with the button onions (glazed white in butter). Reduce the cooking liquor, blend it with the velouté, and incorporate the sauce hollandaise. Add a few drops of lemon juice, and the caviar. Use this sauce to coat the fillets and serve immediately. *(France.)*

Sandre châtelaine, Filets de

For 6 persons: *6 fillets of pike-perch (120 gr. each); 1 dl. white wine; 2 dl. fish fumet; 2 egg yolks; 1 dl. fresh cream; 60 gr. butter; 12 poached and bearded oysters; 12 shelled crayfish; 12 small dauphine potatoes; ½ lemon.* Cooking time: 12 to 15 minutes.

Poach the fillets in the white wine and the fish fumet. Drain them, and arrange them on a serving dish. Pass the poaching stock, reduce it by one-third, bind it with the egg yolks and cream, butter lightly, add a few drops of lemon juice, and correct the seasoning and consistency. Garnish with the oysters and the crayfish, and coat the fillets and the garnish with this sauce. Surround with the dauphine potatoes. *(France.)*

Sandre Concordia, Filets de

For 6 persons: *6 fillets of pike-perch (200 gr. each); 10 jasmine flowers; 4 dl. fish fumet; 3 dl. brown veal stock; 100 gr. celery; 150 gr. cucumber; 50 gr. smoked bacon; 40 gr. butter; 60 gr. beurre manié; 1 clove of garlic; 3 tablespoonfuls sauce hollandaise; 4 tablespoonfuls ketchup.* Poaching time for the fillets: 10 minutes.

Poach the fillets in the fish fumet with the jasmine flowers. Drain them, and arrange them on a serving dish. Make a coarse julienne with the bacon, celery and cucumber. Sauté au beurre, and season with salt, pepper and crushed garlic. Pass the fish fumet over the julienne, add the veal stock, and reduce by three-quarters. Thicken with the beurre manié, and incorporate the sauce hollandaise with a pinch of cayenne. Coat the fillets with this sauce, and decorate with threads of ketchup. *(Germany.)*

Sandre à la crème au gratin

Proceed as for the preparation of Turbot à la crème au gratin. *(See page 348.)*

Sandre du Danube au paprika

For 6 persons: *6 portions of pike-perch (250 gr. each); 350 gr. onions; 1 clove of garlic; 100 gr. butter; 30 gr. mild paprika; 1 litre water; 50 gr. flour; ¼ litre white wine; ½ litre fresh cream.* Poaching time: 15 minutes.

Colour the finely-chopped onions in butter, sprinkle them with paprika, add the water, and season with salt and crushed garlic. Cook, covered, for 30 minutes. Place the portions of pike-perch in the resultant stock, and simmer on the side of the stove for 15 minutes. Remove the fish from the heat, trim, arrange on a serving dish, and keep hot. Make a bay with the flour, blend in the white wine and the cooking stock, and cook to a creamy consistency. Pass this sauce, blend it with the cream, and pour it (hot) over the fish. *(Austria.)*

Sandre du Danube Vieux-Vienne

For 6 persons: *1 pike-perch weighing 2 kg.; 20 gr. butter; 1½ dl. white wine; 60 gr. grated Parmesan cheese.* Stuffing: *250 gr. cleaned and filleted flesh of pike-perch; 30 gr. onion; 30 gr. butter; 1 table-spoonful chopped parsley; 100 gr. fresh mushrooms.* Risotto: *50 gr. butter; 20 gr. chopped onion; 300 gr. rice.* Sauce: *2 dl. fish fumet; 1 egg; 3 egg yolks; 50 gr. butter; 5 gr. flour; lemon juice.* Poaching time: 15 minutes.

Lightly colour the chopped onion in butter, add the chopped mushrooms and the parsley, colour them, season with salt and pepper, and allow to cool. Pound the pike-perch flesh, pass it through a sieve and incorporate it into the cooled mixture. Cut up the whole fish into thick slices, arrange them in a buttered sauteuse, and fill the centre of each with forcemeat. Sprinkle with white wine, cover, and poach in the oven. Prepare the risotto with water. Prepare the sauce with all the ingredients, as for a sauce hollandaise. Spread the rice on a gratinating dish, arrange the fish on top, coat with the sauce, sprinkle with grated Parmesan cheese, and brown in a hot oven. *(Austria.)*

Sandre duchesse, Filets de

For 6 persons: *6 fillets of pike-perch (120 gr. each); 300 gr. pommes duchesse mixture; 12 shelled crayfish; 18 white asparagus tips; 2 dl. fish fumet; 3 dl. fish velouté; 40 gr. grated Parmesan cheese; 50 gr. butter; 1 egg yolk.* Cooking time: 15 to 18 minutes.

Poach the fillets in the fish fumet. Using a star piping-tube, border a gratinating dish with the pommes duchesse mixture, and brush over with the egg yolk. Drain the fillets. Reduce the poaching stock, add it to the velouté, and butter lightly. Mask the dish with a table-spoonful of this sauce, arrange the fillets on top, and place on each 2 shelled crayfish and 3 asparagus tips. Coat with the sauce (avoiding the edge of the dish), sprinkle with the grated Parmesan cheese, and brown. *(France.)*

Sandre au four

Pike-perch, Baked

For 6 persons: *2 skinned fillets of pike-perch (375 gr. to 400 gr. each); 150 gr. poached and bearded mussels; 150 gr. cooked and quartered mushrooms; 100 gr. small fish quenelles; 1 dl. white wine; 2 dl. fish fumet; 1 dl. fresh cream; 4 dl. fish velouté; 50 gr. butter; 40 gr. grated Parmesan cheese.* Cooking time: 20 minutes.

Season the fillets, lay them in a buttered gratinating dish, and moisten with the white wine, containing 1 dl. fish fumet. Cover with a sheet of buttered paper, and cook for not more than 10 minutes. Drain the stock, and set it aside. Heat quickly the mussels, mushrooms and quenelles in the fish fumet, and drain. Blend this stock with the cooking liquor, reduce quickly, add the velouté, simmer, thicken with the cream, and correct the seasoning and consistency. Bind the ragoût with a little sauce, and spread it over the fillets. Coat all over with the sauce, sprinkle with the grated cheese and then with butter. Pass through the oven to complete the cooking, and brown. *(France.)*

Sandre Hämeensilta

For 6 persons: *1 pike-perch weighing about 1 kg. 500; 125 gr. mushroom heads; 2 dl. white wine; 30 gr. crayfish butter (beurre d'écrevisse); 4 dl. sauce écrevisse; 20 shelled crayfish; 6 thin slices of truffle; 10 gr. caraway seeds; 1 sprig of parsley; the juice of ½ lemon.* Poaching time for the fillets: 12 to 15 minutes.

Fillet the fish. Prepare a very concentrated stock with the head, the bones, the caraway seeds and the sprig of parsley. Arrange the fillets in a buttered fish tray, season with salt and pepper, and sprinkle with the white wine and an equal quantity of fish stock. Cover with a sheet of buttered paper, and poach in the oven. Poach the mushrooms with a nut of butter, the lemon juice and a pinch of salt. Re-heat the crayfish in a little crayfish butter. Once the cooking is finished, pour the cooking stock on top, blend it with the mushroom liquor, and reduce almost completely. Pass through a conical strainer and mix with the crayfish sauce (which has been kept thick). Arrange the fillets on a long serving dish, garnish with the mushrooms and the crayfish, and coat with the crayfish sauce. Garnish with thin slices of truffle, and sprinkle with melted crayfish butter. Serve with fish potatoes. *(Finland.)*

Sandre hôtel de ville Enköping, Filets de

For 6 persons: *3 pike-perch (800 gr. each); 50 gr. chopped dill; 1 lemon; 250 gr. butter; oil.* Cooking time: approximately 10 minutes.

Fillet, bone and skin the fish, and marinate with lemon juice, salt and pepper. Mix 200 gr. butter with the chopped dill. Smear the fillets with this butter, and sandwich them together in pairs. Butter three pieces of suitably-sized aluminium foil, and use them to wrap up and seal the three double fillets. Heat some oil in a plat à sauter, arrange the papillotes, and moisten them several times with hot oil. Allow to swell, then cook in a hot oven. Remove the papillotes, arrange them on a serving dish, and open them up only at table. Serve at the same time the following sauce: mix mayonnaise sauce with a little whipped cream, and then mix with a little grated horse-radish and tomatoes, peeled, pipped and diced. Serve plain-boiled fish potatoes separately. *(Sweden.)*

Sandre Metternich

For 6 persons: *1 pike-perch weighing 2 kg.; 60 gr. butter; 1 dl. fish fumet; the juice of 1 lemon; ¾ litre sauce béchamel, ¼ litre fresh cream; 20 gr. paprika; 12 thin slices of truffle.* Poaching time: approximately 30 minutes.

Poach the fish, covered, in the fish fumet with the butter and lemon juice. Add to the sauce béchamel the fumet (which has been passed through a conical strainer and then reduced). Bind with the cream, and colour with the paprika. Arrange the pike-perch on a long serving dish, coat with part of the sauce, and decorate with the slices of truffle. Serve plain-boiled fish potatoes and the rest of the sauce separately. *(Austria.)*

Sandre meunière

Proceed as for the preparation of any other fish designated meunière, taking care to choose only small fish or, better still, fillets. *(See page 64.)*

Sandre milanaise, Filets de

For 6 persons: *12 escalopes of pike-perch (weighing 60 gr. each); 2 eggs; 100 gr. fine breadcrumbs; 60 gr. grated cheese; 120 gr. butter; 300 gr. macaroni prepared milanaise; flour.* Cooking time: 12 minutes.

Season and flour the fillets, pass them through beaten egg, and then coat them with bread-crumbs mixed with grated cheese. Cook in clarified butter, and then arrange in a ring on a round serving dish. Fill the centre of the dish with the macaroni milanaise. *(France.)*

Sandre polonaise

Pike-perch Polish style

For 6 persons: *1 pike-perch weighing 1 kg. 500; 2 hard-boiled eggs; 1 tablespoonful of chopped parsley; 40 gr. fresh breadcrumbs; 150 gr. butter.* Cooking time: approximately 15 minutes.

Cut up the pike-perch into slices 5 cm. thick, cook them in a court-bouillon, drain them completely, and arrange them on a heated serving dish. Sprinkle with the chopped hard-boiled egg and with the parsley. At the moment of serving sprinkle with noisette butter (in which the very-finely-chopped breadcrumbs have been fried). *(France.)*

Sandre aux queues d'écrevisses, Zéphirs de

For 6 persons: *750 gr. forcemeat zéphirs of pike-perch; 24 shelled crayfish; 4 dl. white wine sauce; 3 tablespoonfuls sauce hollandaise; 30 gr. butter; 20 gr. crayfish butter (or any other red butter).* Cooking time: 10 to 12 minutes.

Butter some small dariole moulds, and fill them with the forcemeat, or carefully lay it in a buttered sauteuse, using a star piping-tube (as for small meringues). Moisten with salt-water, and poach. Dry the zéphirs on a cloth, and arrange them around the edge of a serving dish. Fill the centre of the dish with the shelled crayfish (which have been passed through butter). Coat the zéphirs and the crayfish with the white wine sauce (to which has been added the sauce hollandaise), and sprinkle the zéphirs with a few drops of melted crayfish butter. *(France.)* *(See illustration page 286.)*

Sandre royale, Filets de

For 6 persons: *6 fillets of pike-perch (120 gr. each); 100 gr. cooked lobster tail; 100 gr. cooked mushrooms; 100 gr. cooked calf's sweetbreads; 300 gr. pommes duchesse mixture; 2 dl. white wine; 4 dl. lobster sauce; 40 gr. grated Parmesan cheese; 50 gr. butter; 1 egg yolk.* Cooking time: 15 minutes.

Season the fillets, poach them in the white wine, and drain. Reduce the poaching stock, and add it to the lobster sauce. Decorate the rim of a gratinating dish with the pommes duchesse mixture, and brush over with the egg yolk. Lightly butter the bottom of the dish, and arrange the fillets on top. Prepare a coarse salpicon (made from the lobster, mushrooms and sweetbreads), bind it with a little lobster sauce, and arrange it over the fillets. Coat with lobster sauce, avoiding the edge of the dish, sprinkle with the grated Parmesan cheese, and then with beurre fondu, and brown. *(France.)*

Sandre Rust, Filets de

For 6 persons: *1 pike-perch weighing 2 kg.; 120 gr. unsalted fat bacon; 50 gr. onion; 100 gr. mushroom trimmings; ½ litre white Burgundy; 4 egg yolks; 3 dl. fresh cream; 1 small bayleaf; 1 sprig of thyme; mild paprika; 50 gr. butter.* Poaching time: 12 minutes.

Remove the two fillets, skin them, stud them with bacon, sprinkle with paprika, and season them with salt. Butter a fish tray, line it with the mushroom trimmings, chopped onion, bayleaf and thyme. Arrange the fillets on top. Moisten with the white wine, cover with a sheet of buttered paper, and poach in the oven. Arrange in a buttered gratinating dish. Pass the cooking stock through a conical strainer, and reduce it by half. Meanwhile, work up the egg yolks, with cream, in a bain-marie, to a light consistency. Add the reduced cooking liquor, and flavour with a few drops of lemon juice. Coat the fish with the sauce, and glaze quickly under the salamander. *(Austria.)*

Sandre vénitienne, Filets de

Pike-perch Venetian style, Fillets of

For 6 persons: *6 fillets of pike-perch (150 gr. each); 1 dl. white wine; 1 dl. fish fumet; 4 dl. sauce vénitienne; 600 gr. potatoes; 30 gr. butter.* Cooking time: 12 minutes.

Poach the fillets in the white wine and fish fumet. Drain. Reduce the poaching stock, and add it to the sauce vénitienne. Arrange the fillets on a long serving dish, coat them with the sauce, and garnish with the potatoes (which have been cut with a round spoon-cutter, plain boiled, kept whole, and passed through butter). *(France.)*

Sandre Tempéré

For 6 persons: *1 pike-perch weighing 1 kg. 500; 100 gr. diced onions; 1 tablespoonful tomato purée; 60 gr. butter; 25 gr. flour; 2 dl. sour cream.* Poaching time: 12 minutes.

Fillet the fish, and trim the fillets. Prepare a stock with the head and the bones. Cut the fillets into coarse squares, and season with salt. Sprinkle with lemon juice, and place aside. Colour the onion golden in butter, sprinkle with a little flour, colour brown for a few minutes, mix with the cooking stock (which has been passed through a conical strainer), and season with pepper. Reduce the sauce to a thick consistency, and add the tomato purée. Pour the sauce over the fish, and poach until the cooking is complete. Arrange the fish on a serving dish with the sauce. Sprinkle at the last moment with the sour cream. Serve with plain boiled fish potatoes, or with buttered rice. *(Finland.)*

Sandre Villeroi, Filets de

Proceed as for the preparation of Filets de sole Villeroi. *(See page 343.)*

Saumon

Salmon

Salmon is generally prepared as follows:

whole, poached or braised;
in slices approximately 1½ cm. thick, and weighing 200 gr. to 250 gr.;
in darnes 3 cm. to 4 cm. thick;
in tronçons, of variable size;
in escalopes, weighing approximately 120 gr. and cut from the skinned fillet. *(See Culinary Technique, page 87.)*

Saumon Alexandra, Médaillons de

For 6 persons: *1 kg. 800 of salmon; 500 gr. raw pike flesh; 6 dl. fresh cream; 35 cl. white wine sauce; 2 dl. sauce hollandaise; 500 gr. green asparagus tips; 12 small thin slices of truffle; 12 small fleurons; 3 chopped shallots; 1 dl. fish fumet; 1 dl. white wine; 50 gr. butter; 1 egg yolk.* Cooking time: 8 to 10 minutes.

Fillet the salmon, skin and bone the fillets, and cut them into 12 medallions 2 cm. thick. Prepare a light forcemeat with salmon trimmings, the pike, the egg yolk and 3 dl. cream, and season well. Place the medallions in a buttered plat à sauter sprinkled with chopped shallots, garnish each with forcemeat (piped through a star piping-tube) and decorate each with a slice of truffle. Moisten with the white wine and fish fumet, cover with a sheet of buttered paper, and poach in the oven. Pass the asparagus tips through butter, and season lightly. Drain the medallions and arrange them along the edge of a round serving dish. Reduce the cooking liquor almost completely, add the white wine and the cream, cook for a few minutes, pass through a cloth strainer, work up with the sauce hollandaise, add a few drops of lemon juice, and correct the seasoning and consistency. Coat the medallions with a little of this sauce, arrange the asparagus tips in the centre of the dish, and surround the medallions with the fleurons. Serve the rest of the sauce separately. *(France.)*

Saumon Alexandra, Mousseline de

For 6 persons: *500 gr. raw salmon flesh; 2 egg whites; 7 dl. fresh cream; ½ litre sauce Mornay; 12 thin slices of truffle; 250 gr. green asparagus tips (or 300 gr. very small petits pois); 60 gr. butter.* Cooking time: 15 minutes.

Prepare a forcemeat as for Mousse de saumon (but without the final addition of egg whites en neige). *(See page 423.)* Mould quenelles with a tablespoon (or else pipe them through a piping-bag into a buttered sauteuse, giving them the shape and size of meringues). Cover with boiling salted water, and poach slowly. Dry on a cloth, and arrange round the edge of a buttered gratinating dish. Place a slice of truffle on each quenelle, coat with sauce Mornay, and glaze in the oven. Remove the dish from the oven, and garnish the centre with the asparagus tips (or the peas bound in butter). *(France.)*

Saumon américaine, Escalopes de

Proceed as for the preparation of Filets de turbot américaine. *(See page 346.)*

Saumon amiral

Proceed as for the preparation of Barbue amiral. *(See page 245.)*

Saumon amiral Courbet

For 6 persons: *3 darnes of salmon (400 gr. each); 300 gr. fish forcemeat; 1 truffle; 12 crescent-shaped fish quenelles; 12 turned mushroom heads; 12 fried smelt; 6 poached trussed crayfish; 4 dl. sauce normande; ½ bottle dry champagne; 30 gr. butter; 1 egg white.* Cooking time: approximately 25 minutes.

Skin the darnes, and mask them with the forcemeat. Smooth the surfaces, moisten with the egg white, and decorate with thin slices of truffle (cut into half-moon shapes). Lay the darnes in a thickly-buttered sauteuse, season with salt and pepper, moisten with the champagne, and poach gently (covered). Drain the darnes, and arrange them on a serving dish. Reduce the cooking liquor considerably, and add it to the sauce normande. Use this sauce to coat the darnes. Garnish with the quenelles, the mushrooms, the fried smelt and the crayfish. *(France.)*

Saumon anglaise, Escalopes de

Proceed as for the preparation of Filets de sole anglaise. *(See page 297.)*

Saumon d'Artois

For 6 persons: *2 darnes of salmon (600 gr. each); 250 gr. whiting forcemeat; 1 truffle; 12 small quenelles made from whiting forcemeat; 6 small tartlet-cases made from lining paste; 200 gr. shelled prawns; 6 thin slices of truffle; 6 small turned mushroom heads; 75 gr. butter; 3 dl. white wine; ½ litre shrimp sauce.* Cooking time: 30 minutes.

Skin the darnes, mask them on one side with the forcemeat, and decorate with the truffle. Lay them in a buttered sauteuse, season with pepper and salt, moisten with the white wine, add 50 gr. butter, cover with a buttered paper, and poach (covered) in the oven. When the cooking is finished, drain off the poaching stock, reduce it, add it to the shrimp sauce and garnish with the whiting quenelles and with the tartlet-cases (filled with a salpicon of prawns bound with shrimp sauce and each decorated with a slice of truffle and a mushroom head.) *(France.)*

Saumon d'Artois, Côtelettes de

For 6 persons: *6 cutlets of salmon III; 150 gr. fish forcemeat; 6 thin slices of truffle; 1 egg white; 75 gr. butter; 4 dl. oyster sauce.* Cooking time: 15 minutes.

Mask the cutlets with the forcemeat, moisten the surface with the egg white, and decorate each cutlet with a slice of truffle. Arrange them in a sauteuse containing hot clarified butter, and cook in the oven (covered with a sheet of buttered paper). Arrange on a serving dish. Serve the sauce separately. N.B. Trimmings may be used for the preparation of the fish forcemeat. *(France.)*

Saumon bâloise

Salmon Basle style

For 6 persons: *6 slices of salmon (200 gr. each); 1 dl. olive oil; 80 gr. butter; 200 gr. thinly-sliced onions; 1 lemon; 1 tablespoonful chopped parsley; 5 cl. brown veal gravy; flour.* Cooking time: 12 to 15 minutes.

Season the slices with salt and pepper, flour them and cook them in oil. Stew and colour the sliced onion in butter. Arrange the slices on a serving dish, cover them with the onion, sprinkle with lemon juice, and then with the chopped parsley. Pour the veal gravy around the dish to form a cordon. *(Switzerland.)*

Saumon au beurre d'anchois

Salmon with anchovy butter

For 6 persons: *6 slices of salmon (200 gr. to 250 gr. each); 150 gr. anchovy butter; 600 gr. plain-boiled fish potatoes; 6 quarters of lemon; parsley; oil.* Cooking time: 12 to 15 minutes.

Season the slices with salt and pepper, oil them, and grill them gently. Arrange the slices on a serving dish with the parsley and the quarters of lemon. Serve the fish potatoes and the anchovy butter separately. *(France.)*

Saumon bouilli

Boiled salmon

For 6 persons: *6 slices of salmon (200 gr. to 250 gr. each); 750 gr. potatoes; 4 dl. sauce (see method); court-bouillon; parsley.* Cooking time: 10 to 12 minutes.

Poach the slices in the court-bouillon, drain them, and arrange on a napkin with the parsley. Serve at the same time the plain boiled potatoes, and the sauce, which can be hollandaise, mousseline, lobster, shrimp, Nantua, genevoise or vénitienne. This dish can also be prepared with darnes or whole fish. *(International cookery.)*

Saumon braisés aurore, Filets de

For 6 persons: *1 fillet of salmon weighing 1 kg. (or 6 slices weighing 150 gr. each); 1 tablespoonful of chopped shallots; 3 dl. tomato juice; 3 dl. white wine; 3 dl. fresh cream; 200 gr. butter; 2 tablespoonfuls of sauce hollandaise; 2 tablespoonsfuls of chopped chive; rice; beurre manié; 12 white asparagus tips; 6 small fleurons.* Cooking time: fillet—10 to 12 minutes; slices—8 minutes.

Butter a fish tray, sprinkle with shallot, and place in it the fillet of salmon, skin side upwards. Season with salt and pepper, moisten with the white wine and tomato juice, cover with a sheet of buttered paper, and braise in a medium oven. When the cooking is finished, arrange the fish on a gratinating dish, and remove the skin. Pass the cooking stock, and reduce it by half. Thicken it lightly with beurre manié, add the cream, and reduce a little more. Work up this sauce with butter and with the sauce hollandaise and add the chopped chive. Coat the fish with this sauce (which should be pale pink in colour), and glaze quickly under the salamander. Garnish with the asparagus tips (heated in butter) and the fleurons. Serve rice, cooked white, separately. *(Sweden.)*

Saumon Brillat-Savarin

For 6 persons: *3 darnes of salmon (400 gr. each); 1 onion; 1 carrot; 50 gr. celery; 1 sprig of thyme; ½ bayleaf; 8 parsley stalks; 3 dl. white wine; 2 dl. fresh cream; 75 gr. butter; 12 turned mushroom heads; 12 pieces of truffle (turned olive-shaped); 12 crayfish shells (filled with whiting forcemeat).* Cooking time: approximately 25 minutes.

Lay the darnes in a buttered sauteuse (on a base of aromatics). Season with salt and pepper, moisten with white wine, and braise (covered) in the oven. Drain, and arrange on a serving dish. Pass the cooking liquor, reduce, blend it with the cream, add butter and correct the seasoning and consistency. Coat the skinned darnes with this sauce. Garnish with the mushrooms, truffles and cooked crayfish shells. *(France.)*

Saumon, Cadgery de

Salmon kedgeree

Proceed as for the preparation of Cadgery de turbot. *(See page 347.)*

Saumon cancalaise, Escalopes de

Proceed as for the preparation of Filets de sole cancalaise. *(See page 298.)*

Saumon Chambord

Prepare the salmon (in large darnes, in tronçons, or whole) according to the method for the preparation of Carpe Chambord. For a small salmon, weighing 3 kg., allow 50 minutes for the braising. *(See page 380.)*

Saumon Champerrée

For 6 persons: *6 slices of salmon (200 gr. to 250 gr. each); 200 gr. rice; 250 gr. button onions; 100 gr. butter; 4 dl. white wine; 4 dl. sauce normande; parsley.* Cooking time: 10 to 12 minutes.

Season the slices with salt and pepper, and poach them with butter in the white wine. Drain them, and arrange them on a serving dish. Reduce the poaching stock, and add it to the sauce normande. Arrange the slices on a socle of pilaf rice, coat with the sauce, and garnish with the onions (cooked white in butter) and the fried parsley. *(France.)*

Saumon Clarence, Côtelettes de

For 6 persons: *100 gr. raw salmon-flesh; 400 gr. salmon forcemeat; 100 gr. lobster forcemeat; 12 cooked turned mushroom heads; 12 small shelled prawns; 4 dl. sauce Newburg.* Cooking time: 12 minutes.

Line 12 small buttered cutlet-moulds with a very thin layer of salmon. Fill with the salmon forcemeat mixed with the lobster forcemeat. Poach in a bain-marie. De-mould and drain the cutlets, dry them, arrange them on a serving dish, and coat them lightly with sauce Newburg. Garnish each cutlet with a mushroom-head which has been studded with a prawn. Serve the rest of the sauce Newburg separately. *(France.)*

Saumon, Côtelettes de I

For 6 persons: *300 gr. raw salmon-flesh; 200 gr. cooked mushrooms; 100 gr. shelled prawns; 50 gr. truffle; 2 dl. sauce béchamel; 2 egg yolks; 2 eggs; fresh breadcrumbs; flour; parsley.* Cooking time: 7 to 8 minutes.

Prepare a salpicon with the salmon, mushrooms, prawns and truffle. Thicken it with the reduced sauce béchamel and the egg yolks, spread it on a tray and allow to cool. Divide it into portions weighing approximately 70 gr. each. Shape into cutlets on a floured surface, inserting a piece of macaroni to represent a cutlet-bone, coat in egg and breadcrumbs, and deep fry. Arrange on a serving dish with fried parsley and cutlet-frills. Serve a garnish of vegetables or any chosen sauce separately. *(France.)*

Saumon, Côtelettes de II

For 6 persons: *600 gr. of forcemeat made from mousseline of salmon; 150 gr. cooked mushrooms; 50 gr. truffle; 7 cl. reduced sauce allemande; fresh breadcrumbs; 150 gr. butter; 4 dl. of any chosen sauce.* Total cooking time: 18 to 20 minutes.

Prepare a fine salpicon with the mushrooms and truffle (bound with the sauce allemande), and allow to cool. Line 12 small buttered cutlet-moulds with forcemeat, garnish the centre of each with a little salpicon, cover with forcemeat, smooth over the surface, and poach in salted water. De-mould the cutlets, dry them completely, dip them in beurre fondu, coat with fine breadcrumbs, cook them in clarified butter, and arrange them in a ring on a serving dish. Serve the chosen sauce separately. *(France.)*

Saumon, Côtelettes de III

For 6 persons: *3 darnes of salmon, weighing approximately 300 gr. each; 2 dl. white wine (or 1 dl. white wine and 1 dl. fish fumet); 4 dl. of any chosen sauce; garnish as required.* Cooking time: approximately 10 minutes.

Skin the darnes, remove the backbone and the small bones, and cut each darne into two pieces lengthwise. Trim them, and shape each half into a cutlet. Season with salt and pepper, and poach in the white wine. Drain off the poaching stock, pass it, reduce, and add it to the chosen sauce. Arrange the cutlets on a serving dish, coat them with the sauce, and garnish as required. The cutlets can also be cooked in clarified butter, or else egg and breadcrumbed and fried. *(France.)*

Saumon, Coulibiac de

For 6 to 8 persons: *750 gr. savoury brioche paste (without sugar and kept a little firm); 600 gr. skinned fillet of salmon; 50 gr. chopped onion; 75 gr. chopped raw mushrooms; 150 gr. semolina kasha (or 150 gr. rice cooked in white stock); 300 gr. coarsely-chopped spinal sturgeon-marrow (vésiga); 2 chopped hard-boiled eggs; 150 gr. butter; breadcrumbs.* Cooking time: approximately 45 minutes.

Cut the salmon into small escalopes, and seize them in butter. Pass the chopped onion and mushrooms through butter, and allow to cool. Roll out the paste into a rectangle measuring 32 cm. by 18 cm. Garnish the centre with superimposed layers of kasha, salmon, vésiga,

mushrooms, eggs and onion, finishing with a layer of kasha. Moisten the edges, fold in the paste towards the centre from both sides and both ends, to cover the garnish, and seal. Place the coulibiac upside down on a buttered fish tray. Allow the paste to ferment for 20 to 25 minutes. Make an opening in the centre to allow steam to escape, smear with beurre fondu, and sprinkle with the breadcrumbs. Cook in a moderately hot oven. After removing the coulibiac from the oven, pour a few spoonfuls of beurre fondu through the opening. N.B. the brioche paste can be replaced by puff paste.
Vésiga: The soaking time, in cold water, for normal swelling, is 5 hours. 10 gr. of dry vésiga, when swollen, become 50 gr. Cooking time: approximately 4 to 4½ hours. *(International cookery.)*
(See illustration, page 247.)

Saumon danoise

For 6 persons: *3 darnes of salmon (400 gr. each); 4 dl. sauce bâtarde; 50 gr. anchovy butter; 750 gr. potatoes; parsley.* Cooking time: 20 minutes.

Poach the darnes in salt water, drain them, and arrange them on a napkin with the parsley. Serve separately the sauce bâtarde (finished with the anchovy butter) and the plain-boiled fish potatoes. *(France.)*

Saumon Daumont

For 6 persons: *2 darnes of salmon (600 gr. each); 12 round fish quenelles decorated with truffle; 4 dl. white wine; 12 large cooked mushroom heads; 12 small shelled crayfish; 12 escalopes of soft roe (panées); ½ litre sauce Nantua; 50 gr. butter.* Cooking time: approximately 25 minutes.

Poach the darnes in a court-bouillon containing white wine. Drain them, arrange on a serving dish, coat them with sauce Nantua, and surround them with the mushrooms (stuffed with a salpicon of crayfish bound with sauce Nantua), the quenelles, and the escalopes of soft roe (fried in clarified butter). *(France.)*

Saumon dieppoise

Prepare the salmon in slices or escalopes, and proceed as for the preparation of Maquereau dieppoise. *(See page 274.)*

Saumon écossaise

For 6 persons: *3 darnes of salmon (400 gr. each); 4 dl. sauce hollandaise; 4 dl. white wine; 100 gr. brunoise of vegetables; 50 gr. butter; picked parsley.* Cooking time: 20 minutes.

Poach the darnes in a court-bouillon containing white wine. Arrange them on a napkin, and surround with the parsley. Stew the brunoise in the butter, allow it to cool slightly, and add it to the light sauce hollandaise. Serve this sauce separately. *(France.)*

Saumon Edward VII, Coquilles de

For 6 persons: *6 scallop-shells; 750 gr. salmon (cooked, skinned, boned and flaked); 4 dl. white wine sauce; 5 cl. fresh cream; 6 thin slices of truffle; 4 gr. curry powder; 60 gr. butter.* Cooking time: 6 to 8 minutes.

Heat the salmon in butter. Use the curry to season the white wine sauce, thicken it with the cream, and butter lightly. Mask the shells with a tablespoonful of sauce and arrange the flaked salmon on top. Place a slice of truffle in the centre of each shell, coat with sauce, and glaze briskly. *(France.)*

Saumon fumé naïde, Filets de

For 6 persons: *1 fillet of slightly smoked salmon, weighing 1 kg. 500; 100 gr. carrots; the white of 2 leeks and 1 onion (thinly sliced); 4 tablespoonfuls of mixed herbs (parsley, dill, chervil and chive); 4 dl. white wine; ½ litre sauce hollandaise; 1 lemon; 600 gr. potatoes; 1 kg. 500 leaf spinach; 1 dl. fish fumet; 1 tablespoonful flour; 300 gr. butter.* Cooking time: 15 to 18 minutes.

Stew the sliced leeks and onion, and spread them over a fish tray. Bone the salmon, and arrange the flesh on the vegetables. Moisten with the fish fumet, cover with a sheet of buttered paper, and braise in a moderate oven. Blanch the spinach, refresh, squeeze, sauté in noisette butter, and season with salt and pepper. Place the spinach in the centre of a large oval gratinating dish, and arrange the skinned fillet on top. Strain the braising stock, reduce it slightly, and thicken it with beurre manié. Allow to cool slightly, work up with the sauce hollandaise, flavour with the lemon juice, and incorporate half of the mixed herbs. Coat the salmon with this sauce, and glaze briskly under the salamander. Roll the pommes poisson in beurre fondu and the rest of the mixed herbs, and arrange around the fish, or serve them separately. *(Sweden.)*

Saumon grillé

Grilled salmon

For 6 persons: *6 slices of salmon (200 gr. to 250 gr. each); 75 gr. butter; 4 dl. sauce béarnaise; parsley; flour.* Cooking time: 12 to 15 minutes.

Season the darnes with salt and pepper, flour them, brush them with clarified butter, and grill them gently, basting frequently with butter. Arrange with the parsley on a serving dish. Serve the sauce béarnaise (or maître d'hôtel butter) separately. *(France.)*

Saumon italienne, Côtelettes de

For 6 persons: *6 salmon cutlets (110 gr. each); 150 gr. concentrated mushroom purée; 2 egg yolks; 2 eggs; fresh breadcrumbs; grated Parmesan cheese; 4 dl. anchovy sauce; parsley.* Cooking time: 10 to 12 minutes.

Thicken the mushroom purée with the egg yolks. Dip the cutlets in the purée, allow to cool, and paner twice, in a mixture of two parts of breadcrumbs to one part of grated cheese. Deep fry the cutlets, and arrange them, with the parsley, on a serving dish. Serve the sauce separately. *(France.)*

Saumon Lucullus

For 6 persons: *2 darnes of salmon (600 gr. each); 2 truffles; 6 small tartlet cases made from lining paste (pâte à foncer); 6 bouchées mignonnes; 6 soft roes; 6 large shelled crayfish; 6 mousseline of oysters (poached in dariole moulds); ½ bottle dry champagne; 100 gr. butter; 50 gr. crayfish butter; 1 onion; 1 carrot; 50 gr. celery; 1 small bayleaf; 1 sprig of thyme.* Cooking time: 30 minutes.

Skin each of the darnes on one side, stud the skinned sides with truffle, season the darnes with salt and pepper, and braise them, on a bed of aromatics, in champagne (covered and in the oven). Drain them, and arrange them on a serving dish. Pass the cooking liquor, reduce it to a syrupy consistency, and work it up with equal proportions of butter and crayfish butter. Garnish the darnes with the tartlet cases (filled with escalopes of soft roe sautées in butter), the bouchées mignonnes (filled with a salpicon of crayfish bound with a little sauce), and the mousseline of oysters. Serve the sauce separately. *(France.)*

Saumon Marcel Prévost

For 6 persons: *2 darnes of salmon (600 gr. each); 24 poached and bearded mussels; 500 gr. blanched leaf spinach; 3 dl. white wine; 4 dl. sauce marinière; 50 gr. butter; aromatic herbs.* Cooking time: 30 minutes.

Braise the darnes in the white wine on a base of aromatic herbs. Drain them, and arrange them (on a bed of spinach previously stewed in butter) on a serving dish. Reduce the cooking liquor, strain it, and add it to the sauce marinière. Surround the fish with the mussels, and use the sauce to coat both the fish and the garnish.

Saumon maréchale, Côtelettes de I

For 6 persons: *6 cutlets of salmon III; 120 gr. fish forcemeat; 6 thin slices of truffle; 12 turned mushroom heads; 12 shelled crayfish; 6 trussed crayfish; 6 fleurons; 80 gr. butter; 4 dl. sauce Nantua; 6 cutlet-shaped croûtons; 1 egg white.* Cooking time: 15 minutes.

Mask the cutlets with the forcemeat. Moisten the surface of each cutlet with egg white, and decorate each with a slice of truffle. Arrange them in a sauteuse (containing hot clarified butter), and bake in the oven. Arrange the cutlets, in a serving dish, on top of the fried croûtons. Garnish with the mushrooms, and the crayfish and trussed crayfish (cooked in a court-bouillon). Coat lightly with sauce. Serve the rest of the sauce separately. *(France.)*

Saumon maréchale, Côtelettes de II

For 6 persons: *6 cutlets of salmon II; 175 gr. butter; 150 gr. fine fresh breadcrumbs; 40 gr. chopped truffle; 6 thin slices of truffle; 300 gr. green asparagus tips.* Cooking time: 10 to 12 minutes.

Season the cutlets, dip them in beurre fondu, and coat with the breadcrumbs mixed with chopped truffle. Cook gently in clarified butter. Arrange on a serving dish. Place a slice of truffle on each cutlet, and garnish with the asparagus tips (passed through butter). *(France.)*

Saumon Médicis, Médaillons de

For 6 persons: *6 medallions of salmon (120 gr. each); 12 very small tomatoes; ¼ litre sauce béarnaise; 1 egg; fresh breadcrumbs; oil.* Cooking time: 10 to 12 minutes.

▲ Brochet zurichoise, p. 378

Filets de féra trois nations, p. 384 ▼

▲ Truite farcie maître Fonçon, p. 413

Filets de perche aux amandes, p. 393 ▼

▲ Brochet Orly, p. 376

Brochet valaisane, p. 378 ▼

▲ Homard Fra Diavolo, p. 437

Scampi frits, beurre maître d'hôtel ▼

Take the medallions, egg, breadcrumb and oil them, and grill over low heat. Arrange on a serving dish. Garnish with the tomatoes (scooped out and baked in the oven) filled with the sauce béarnaise. *(France.)*

Saumon Mornay, Coquilles de

For 6 persons: *6 scollop-shells; 600 gr. salmon (cooked, skinned, boned and flaked); 4 dl. sauce Mornay; 300 gr. pommes duchesse mixture; 50 gr. grated cheese; 30 gr. butter.* Cooking time: 6 to 8 minutes.

Using a star piping-tube, border the shells with the pommes duchesse mixture. Mask each shell with a tablespoonful of sauce Mornay, and arrange the flaked salmon on top. Coat with sauce Mornay, sprinkle with grated cheese, sprinkle lightly with beurre fondu, and brown. *(France.)*

Saumon Nesselrode

For 6 persons: *1 large darne of salmon (900 gr.); 200 gr. lobster forcemeat; 100 gr. pike forcemeat; 500 gr. to 600 gr. pie-paste; 200 gr. unsalted fat bacon; ½ litre sauce américaine; 12 small oysters (poached and bearded); 30 gr. butter.* Cooking time: 1 hour to 1½ hours.

Skin the darne, remove the backbone and the other bones, and fill the inside with the lobster forcemeat mixed with the pike forcemeat. Line a round pie mould with rolled out paste (kept firm), and line the inside with thin slices of bacon. Season the salmon, and place it upright in the mould. Cover with thin slices of bacon, seal with rolled out paste, make an opening in the top to allow steam to escape, and cook in a medium oven. After removing the pie from the oven, turn it upside down to drain the bacon and the liquid inside (without de-moulding). Slide the pie on to the serving dish, and remove the mould. Serve separately the sauce américaine to which the oysters have been added. *(France.)*

Saumon Pojarski, Côtelettes de

For 6 persons: *450 gr. raw salmon flesh; 150 gr. white bread (steeped in milk); 175 gr. butter; 1 egg; fresh breadcrumbs; flour.* Cooking time: 15 minutes.

Chop the salmon with the bread (soaked and pressed) and 75 gr. softened butter. Chop finely so as to obtain a smooth paste. Season with salt and pepper, shape (on a floured surface) 6 or 12 cutlets, egg and breadcrumb and cook them in clarified butter (turning them over carefully) and arrange them on a serving dish.

N.B. The designation Pojarski refers to the method of preparation, but not to the garnish. This latter can be a fine macédoine of creamed vegetables, or of peas, or of buttered asparagus tips. *(France.)*

Saumon Radziwill

For 6 persons: *2 darnes of salmon (600 gr. each); 250 gr. shelled prawns; 50 gr. truffle; 12 thin slices of truffle; 1 dl. sauce crevette; 400 gr. cucumber (spoon-cut olive-shaped); 4 dl. white wine sauce; 50 gr. butter.* Cooking time: approximately 30 minutes.

Poach the darnes in a court-bouillon, skin them, and arrange them on a serving dish. Fill the centre of the dish with a salpicon of crayfish and truffle (thickened with sauce crevette). Decorate the darnes with the slices of truffle, and coat them with white wine sauce. Surround with the cucumber (stewed in butter). *(France.)*

Saumon Régence

Proceed as for the preparation of Turbot Régence. *(See page 352.)*

Saumon, sauce homard, Mousse de

For 6 persons: *500 gr. raw salmon flesh; 5 dl. fresh cream; 4 egg whites; 25 gr. butter; 4 dl. lobster sauce (sauce homard).* Cooking time: 35 to 40 minutes.

Mince the salmon through the finest plate. Season with salt and pepper, add gradually 2 egg whites, and pass through a sieve. Place this forcemeat in a sauteuse, work it up with a spatula, and keep it on ice for 1 hour. Using the cream, relax the consistency with a spatula, and finally incorporate 2 small firmly-beaten egg whites. Using a plain piping-tube, fill a well-buttered mould with this forcemeat, and poach (covered with a sheet of buttered paper) in a bain-marie, in a moderate oven. Remove from the oven and leave for 5 to 6 minutes before de-moulding on to a serving dish. Serve the sauce separately. *(France.)*

Saumon Valois

For 6 persons: *3 darnes of salmon (400 gr. each); 250 gr. soft roe; 600 gr. potatoes; 4 dl. white wine; 6 trussed crayfish; 4 dl. sauce Valois; 75 gr. butter.* Cooking time: 20 to 25 minutes.

Poach the salmon in a court-bouillon containing the white wine. Drain and skin it and arrange on a serving dish. Garnish with the potatoes (cut with a round spoon cutter, cooked in salt water, kept whole, and passed through butter), the escalopes of soft roe (stewed in butter), and the crayfish (cooked in a court-bouillon). Serve the sauce separately. *(France.)*

Saumon Vernet

For 6 persons: *2 darnes of salmon (600 gr. each); 4 dl. white wine sauce; 4 dl. white wine; 50 gr. anchovy butter, and a julienne made from 30 gr. hard-boiled egg white, 30 gr. truffle, and 30 gr. cooked mushrooms.* Cooking time: approximately 30 minutes.

Poach the darnes in a court-bouillon containing the white wine. Drain and skin them and arrange on a serving dish. Coat them with the white wine sauce (finished with the anchovy butter and containing the julienne). *(France.)*

Saumon Victoria

For 6 persons: *2 darnes of salmon (600 gr. each); 1 dl. white wine; 1 dl. fish fumet; 4 dl. sauce Victoria; 12 escalopes of lobster tail; 12 thin slices of truffle; 12 very small puff paste fleurons; aromatic herbs.* Cooking time: 30 minutes.

Braise the darnes in the white wine and fish fumet on a bed of aromatics. Drain and skin them and arrange on a serving dish. Arrange on each darne 6 escalopes of lobster alternated with 6 slices of truffle, and coat with the sauce Victoria containing the passed and reduced braising stock. Surround with the fleurons. *(France.)*

Saumon Victoria, Coquilles de

For 6 persons: *6 scollop shells; 600 gr. salmon (cooked, skinned, boned and flaked); 6 cooked escalopes of lobster; 6 thin slices of truffle; 300 gr. pommes duchesse mixture; 4 dl. sauce Nantua.* Cooking time: 6 to 8 minutes.

Border the scollop shells with the pommes duchesse mixture. Mask the bottom of each shell with sauce Nantua, and arrange the flaked salmon on top. Place in the centre of each shell an escalope of lobster and a slice of truffle, coat with sauce Nantua, and glaze. *(France.)*

Silure â la choucroute

Sheat-fish

For 6 persons: *1 sheat-fish (weighing 1 kg. 500); 1 kg. 200 sauerkraut; 100 gr. thinly-sliced onion; 100 gr. finely-diced green peppers; 30 gr. smoked bacon; 30 gr. lard; 25 gr. flour; 2 dl. sour cream; 15 gr. paprika; 1 small sprig of fennel leaves (chopped).* Cooking time: 1½ hours.

Fillet the fish (after it has had the head removed, and been gutted, cleaned and washed). Skin the fillets, and cut them up into pieces. Prepare a court-bouillon with the trimmings and backbone. Pass the stock, and add the sauerkraut to it. Colour the bacon (which has been cut into slices), add the green peppers, and sweat gently. Mix the bacon and the peppers with the sauerkraut, cover, and stew for 1 hour. Add the fish, and continue the cooking for 20 minutes, over a low flame. Prepare a roux with the flour and lard. Add to it the onion, fennel and paprika. Carefully remove the fish from the sauerkraut, thicken it with the roux, add the sour cream, and bring to the boil. Replace the fish, and cook everything together for a few moments. For serving, arrange the fish on a serving dish, cover it with the sauerkraut, and sprinkle with the fennel. *(Hungary.)*

Silure du Danube aux amandes et aux noisettes

For 6 persons: *6 slices of Danubian sheat-fish (250 gr. each); 200 gr. butter; 100 gr. skinned and shredded almonds; 100 gr. skinned and shredded hazel-nuts; 1 coffee-spoonful of chopped sage and rosemary.* Cooking time: 10 minutes.

Cook the fish in a well-seasoned court-bouillon, and remove it. Drain carefully, and arrange on a serving dish. Gently froth the butter in a frying-pan, and slightly colour the almonds and hazel-nuts. Add the sage and rosemary. Pour immediately over the fish and serve. *(Germany.)*

Silure au fenouil, Filets de

For 6 persons: *1 sheat-fish, weighing 1 kg. 500; 1 small sprig of fennel leaves (chopped); 60 gr. thinly-sliced onion; 60 gr. lard; 15 gr. paprika; 20 gr. flour; 15 cl. fresh cream; 100 gr. green peppers (cut into fine roundels); 35 gr. butter.* Poaching time: 15 minutes.

After removing its head, gutting, cleaning and washing it, fillet the fish. Skin the fillets, cut them into pieces, season them with salt, and arrange them in a buttered cocotte. Colour the onion in the lard, sprinkle with the paprika, add the trimmings and bones and a few small pieces of green peppers; moisten to cover, salt slightly, and cook for 30 to 35 minutes. Pass the stock, thicken with the flour blended with the cream, allow to cook for a few minutes, pass, and mix with the fennel leaves. Pour the sauce over the fish, and cook, covered, in a medium oven. Correct the seasoning and consistency. Arrange on a serving dish, and coat with the sauce. Garnish with the green peppers. Serve with a garnish of galuska or of plain-boiled fish potatoes. *(Hungary.)*

Sterlet karpatique

For 6 persons: *6 slices of sterlet (250 gr. each); 15 small crayfish; 60 gr. butter; 20 gr. flour; 15 cl. fresh cream; 2 dl. white stock; 150 gr. thinly-sliced raw mushrooms; 30 gr. crayfish butter; 5 gr. caraway seeds; 1 small sprig of parsley; 1 small sprig of fennel leaves (chopped).* Braising time: approximately 20 minutes.

Bone the slices, blanch them briefly, skin them and place them in a buttered sauteuse. Cook the crayfish in salted water (containing the caraway seeds and the sprig of parsley). Remove the tails and claws from the crayfish. Using the shells (pounded), prepare a crayfish butter. Sauté the mushrooms in butter. Prepare a white roux with the flour and 30 gr. butter, moisten with the stock, stir, allow to cook for 3 to 4 minutes, blend in the cream, and allow to cook for a few more minutes. Season with salt, white pepper and fennel. Add the crayfish flesh and the mushrooms, and complete with the crayfish butter. Pour this sauce over the fish, and braise, covered, in the oven. When the cooking is complete, arrange the fish on a serving dish, and coat over with the sauce. Serve with a garnish of parsley (fish) potatoes. *(Hungary.)*

Sudak couvent

For 6 persons: *2 fillets of sudak (400 gr. to 450 gr. each); 600 gr. potatoes (cooked in their jackets and then peeled); 300 gr. peeled, salted cucumber; 2 dl. fish fumet; 15 gr. flour; 25 gr. fresh breadcrumbs; 25 gr. grated cheese; 50 gr. butter; chopped parsley.* Cooking time: 12 to 15 minutes.

Butter an oval gratinating dish, and coat the bottom of the dish with potatoes (cut into roundels) and with some roundels of cucumber. Arrange the fillets on top, season with salt and pepper, and cover alternately with potatoes and cucumber. Sprinkle lightly with flour, and moisten to cover with the fish fumet. Sprinkle generously with the breadcrumbs and the grated cheese, sprinkle with beurre fondu, cook and, at the same time, brown in a medium oven. Serve sprinkled with chopped parsley. N.B. Sudak: a type of pike-perch living in Russian waters. *(Russia.)*

Tanche farcie

Stuffed tench

For 6 persons: *6 tench (200 gr. each); 450 gr. pike forcemeat; 2 dl. white wine; 2 chopped shallots; 180 gr. thinly-sliced raw mushrooms; 1 coffee-spoonful chopped parsley; 4 dl. sauce allemande; 40 gr. butter; 1 lemon.* Cooking time: 20 minutes.

Fill the tench with the forcemeat, and arrange the fish on a fish tray (which has been buttered, and then sprinkled with the shallots, parsley and part of the mushrooms). Season with salt and pepper, moisten with the white wine and lemon juice, cover with a sheet of buttered paper, and cook in the oven. Drain and skin the fish, and arrange them, on a bed of cooked sliced mushrooms, in a serving dish. Reduce the cooking stock, add it to the sauce allemande, and use it to coat the fish. *(France.)*

Tanche lorraine

For 6 persons: *6 tench (225 gr. each); 40 gr. thinly-sliced onions; 2 chopped shallots; 6 stalks of parsley; ½ bayleaf; 1 sprig of thyme; ½ lemon; 2 egg yolks; 2 dl. fresh cream; 1 dl. white wine; 1 coffee-spoonful chopped parsley.* Cooking time: 20 minutes.

Lay the tench in a fish tray on a bed of onion, thyme, bayleaf, parsley stalks and 6 peppercorns. Season with salt, moisten with equal parts of white wine and water, cover with a sheet of buttered paper, and cook in the oven. Drain the fish, and place them in a buttered gratinating dish which has been sprinkled with chopped shallot. Reduce the cooking liquor by half, pass it, add three-quarters of the cream (previously heated), allow to cook for 2 minutes, and thicken with the egg yolks blended with the rest of the cream. Coat the fish with this sauce, and pass through the oven for 5 minutes. Before serving, sprinkle with chopped parsley, and then sprinkle also with a few drops of lemon juice. *(France.)*

Tanche à la sauce aneth

Tench with dill sauce

For 6 persons: *6 tench (225 gr. each); 4 dl. fish velouté; 3 tablespoonfuls of sauce hollandaise; 1 heaped tablespoonful of chopped fresh dill.* Cooking time: 12 to 15 minutes.

Poach the tench in salted water containing a little vinegar. Drain and skin them, arrange them on a serving dish, and coat them with the velouté (containing the chopped dill and finished with the sauce hollandaise). *(Germany.)*

Tanche à la sauge

For 6 persons: *6 tench (225 gr. to 250 gr. each); 8 to 10 leaves of fresh sage; 50 gr. butter; 4 dl. cream.* Cooking time: approximately 15 minutes.

Place the sage leaves on a thickly-buttered gratinating dish. Place the tench on top, season with salt and pepper, and moisten with cream (previously brought to the boil). Add 30 gr. butter, and cook in the oven (basting frequently with the cream). Serve. *(France.)*

Tanche tourangelle

For 6 persons: *6 tench (225 gr. each); 2 chopped shallots; 1 coffee-spoonful of mixed chopped chives and parsley; 150 gr. thinly-sliced raw mushrooms; 4 dl. fresh cream; 30 gr. butter; 1 tablespoonful of mixed parsley, chives and chervil (all finely chopped).* Cooking time: approximately 15 minutes.

Butter a gratinating dish and sprinkle it with chopped chives, chopped parsley and the thinly-sliced mushrooms. Place the tench on top. Season them with salt and pepper and moisten them with the cream (previously brought to the boil). Cook in the oven, basting from time to time. On removing from the oven, correct the seasoning and consistency. Serve sprinkled with the parsley, chives and chervil. *(France.)*

Truites aux amandes

Trout with almonds

For 6 persons: *6 trout (200 gr. each); 200 gr. butter; 150 gr. shredded almonds; milk; flour.* Cooking time: 8 to 10 minutes.

Pass the trout through salted milk, and then through flour, cook them in butter, and arrange them on a serving dish. Colour the almonds lightly in butter. Sprinkle the trout with noisette butter and the almonds. *(France.)*

Truite Antoine Clessée

For 6 persons: *6 live trout (225 gr. to 250 gr. each); approximately 6 dl. light ale; 3 small carrots; 6 button onions; 4 egg yolks; 225 gr. noisette butter; 2 chopped shallots; beurre manié (made from 10 gr. flour and 15 gr. butter); 1 tablespoonful of mixed chopped parsley and chervil.* Poaching time: 10 minutes.

Arrange the trout (previously killed, gutted and cleaned) in a buttered fish tray (which has been sprinkled with chopped shallots). Season with salt and pepper, moisten with the light ale, and poach gently in the oven. After cooking, skin the trout, arrange them on a serving dish, cover and keep hot. Thinly slice the carrots and onions, and cook them with a little water and a pinch each of salt and sugar. Pass the trout cooking liquor, pour three-quarters of it over the vegetables, and reduce to a glaze. Thicken the rest slightly with the beurre manié, and allow to cook for a moment. Work up the egg yolks with the noisette butter, incorporate the thickened trout cooking liquor, and then the vegetables, parsley and chervil. Correct the seasoning and consistency. Use this sauce to coat the trout. Serve very hot. *(Belgium.)*
(See illustration, page 386. N.B. Slightly different presentation.)

Truite au bleu

For 6 persons: *6 live trout (200 gr. each); 150 gr. beurre fondu (or 4 dl. sauce hollandaise); 600 gr. potatoes (optional); parsley; 6 quarters of lemon.* Cooking time: 10 minutes.

For cooking au bleu, it is absolutely necessary to have fresh and live fish. Have ready some boiling salted water. Ten minutes before cooking starts, kill the trout (with a sharp blow on the head), and gut and clean them quickly. Do not touch the trout too much, so as not to remove the outer mucosity which gives the fish its bluish tinge on cooking. Plunge the trout into boiling water in a fish-kettle and, when the water reaches boiling point again, remove the fish-kettle to the side of the stove, and finish off the cooking by poaching. Arrange the fish on a napkin, with the parsley and quarters of lemon. Serve the beurre fondu (or the sauce hollandaise) separately.

N.B. It is not absolutely necessary, when cooking trout au bleu, to include vinegar in the court-bouillon. Vinegar may, in fact, impair the flavour of the trout. *(International cookery.)*
(See illustration for Féra au bleu, page 366.)

Truite bretonne

For 6 persons: *6 trout (200 gr. each); 150 gr. thinly-sliced raw mushrooms; 150 gr. shelled crayfish; 150 gr. butter; 1 lemon; 1 tablespoonful of chopped parsley; flour.* Cooking time: 10 minutes.

Season the trout with salt and pepper, flour them, and cook them meunière. Sauté the mushrooms and crayfish in the cooking butter, and sprinkle them over the trout. Squeeze the lemon juice on top, sprinkle with the chopped parsley, and then sprinkle with the noisette butter. *(France.)*

Truite Caruso, Filets de

For 6 persons: *12 fillets of trout (approximately 60 gr. each); 180 gr. lobster forcemeat; 12 small shelled crayfish; 12 thin slices of truffle; 2 dl. white wine; 1 dl. fish fumet; 40 gr. beurre manié; 6 bouchées mignonnes; 60 gr. caviar.* Cooking time: 10 to 12 minutes.

Mask the fillets with the forcemeat, smooth them, and place a shelled crayfish in the centre of each. Moisten with the white wine and with the fish fumet, add 40 gr. butter, cover with a sheet of buttered paper and poach in the oven. When the cooking is finished, drain the fillets carefully, and arrange them on a serving dish. Reduce the poaching liquor and thicken it with the beurre manié. Use this sauce to coat the fillets, decorate them with the slices of truffle, and glaze. Surround with hot bouchées mignonnes (filled, at the last minute, with very cold caviar). Serve immediately. *(France.)*

Truite au chambertin

Proceed as for the preparation of Filets de turbot au chambertin. *(See page 347.)*

Truite au champagne

Proceed as for the preparation of Sole au champagne. *(See page 299.)*

Truite Cléopâtre

For 6 persons: *6 trout (200 gr. each); 150 gr. shelled crayfish; 150 gr. soft roe; 180 gr. butter; 30 gr. capers; 1 tablespoonful of chopped parsley.* Cooking time: approximately 10 minutes.

Prepare the trout meunière. Surround them with the crayfish (sautées in butter) and with escalopes of the soft roe (stewed in butter). Sprinkle with the capers and chopped parsley, and then with lemon juice and noisette butter. *(France.)*

Truite, Coulibiac de

Proceed as for the preparation of Coulibiac de saumon. *(See page 402.)*

Truite Doria

For 6 persons: *6 trout (200 gr. each); 120 gr. butter; 300 gr. cucumber (spoon-cut olive-shaped, and stewed in butter); 1 coffee-spoonful of chopped parsley; flour.* Cooking time: 10 minutes.

Season the trout with salt and pepper, and cook them in butter. Arrange them on a serving dish, sprinkle them lightly with the chopped parsley, and then sprinkle with noisette butter. Surround with the cucumber 'olives'. *(France.)*

Truite farcie

Stuffed trout

For 6 persons: *6 trout (200 gr. each); 300 gr. fish forcemeat; 4 dl. sauce marinière; 6 quarters of lemon; parsley; oil.* Cooking time: 15 minutes.

Cut open the trout at the back, remove the backbones, gut, wash and dry the fish, and fill them with the forcemeat. Season with salt and pepper. Wrap in greased paper, and grill gently. Arrange on a serving dish with the fried parsley and the quarters of lemon. Serve the sauce separately.

N.B. Unwrap the trout at the last moment, and then only at table. *(France.)*

Truite farcie maître Fonçon

For 6 persons: *6 trout (250 gr. each); 6 shelled scampi; 6 fillets of sole; 200 gr. raw pike flesh; 3 dl. white wine; 3 dl. fish fumet; 1 egg; 100 gr. butter; 15 gr. flour; 100 gr. finely-chopped chives; ½ lemon; 2 dl. cream.* Cooking time: approximately 20 minutes.

Open the trout at the back, remove the backbones, and gut, wash and dry the fish. Prepare a forcemeat, using the pike flesh, the fillets of sole, the scampi, 1 egg, 1 dl. cream, 30 gr. chives, salt and pepper. Stuff the trout with this forcemeat, place them in a plat à sauter, and butter them. Season them with salt and pepper, sprinkle with the white wine and fish fumet, cover with a sheet of buttered paper, and poach gently in the oven for approximately 15 minutes. After cooking, skin the trout very carefully. Keep them hot, covered with a sheet of buttered paper. Reduce the cooking stock by half, and prepare a sauce with this stock and a small roux (made with 25 gr. butter and 15 gr. flour).

Add 1 dl. cream, and allow to cook until the sauce becomes creamy. Add the rest of the chives, and work up the sauce with 50 gr. butter. Arrange the trout on a serving dish, coat them with the sauce, and serve very hot. *(Switzerland.)*
(See illustration, page 406. N.B. Different presentation.)

Truite farcie au vin blanc

Stuffed trout with white wine

For 6 persons: *6 trout (200 gr. each); 300 gr. pike forcemeat; 60 gr. chopped mushrooms; 2 chopped shallots; 60 gr. butter; 2 dl. cream; 2 dl. white wine.* Cooking time: 15 minutes.

Open the trout at the back, remove the backbones, gut, wash and dry the fish, fill them with the forcemeat (containing the chopped mushrooms), and arrange them in a buttered gratinating dish which has been sprinkled with chopped shallot. Moisten with the white wine, season with salt and pepper, add 50 gr. butter, and start off the cooking. Add the cream (which has been previously heated), and complete the cooking in the oven, basting from time to time. *(France.)*

Truite au four Kinross

Baked trout Kinross

For 6 persons: *6 trout (225 gr. each); 150 gr. fresh breadcrumbs; 70 gr. chopped onion; 1 coffee-spoonful of chopped parsley; 1 pinch of sweet marjoram; 1 pinch of sage; 6 large field mushrooms; 125 gr. cucumber; 1 egg; 1 egg yolk; 50 gr. butter; 2 lemons; flour.* Cooking time: approximately 15 minutes.

Mix the breadcrumbs with the onion, parsley, sweet majoram and sage. Add the whole egg and the egg yolk (both beaten). Season with salt and pepper. Stuff the trout with this mixture, flour them, arrange the fish on a buttered fish-tray, sprinkle them with beurre fondu, and cook in a medium oven. Arrange them on a serving dish, and garnish with the mushrooms (grilled), the cucumber (grooved but not peeled, thinly sliced, and cooked in butter) and quarters of lemon. Serve maître d'hôtel butter separately (optional). *(Great Britain.)*

Truite frite

Fried trout

For 6 persons: *12 very small trout (100 gr. each); 2 eggs; parsley; fresh breadcrumbs; 2 lemons; flour; 4 dl. sauce mayonnaise (or sauce tartare).* Cooking time: 10 minutes.

Season the trout with salt and pepper, flour them, egg and breadcrumb, fry in hot, deep fat, and drain them. Arrange them on a napkin with fried parsley and quarters of lemon. Serve the sauce separately. *(France.)*

Truite Gavarni

For 6 persons: *6 trout (200 gr. each); 150 gr. maître d'hôtel butter; 600 gr. potatoes; oil.* Cooking time: 15 minutes.

Wrap each trout, with 25 gr. maître d'hôtel butter (in greased paper, or in aluminium foil), and cook in the oven. Arrange on a serving dish, and unwrap at table. Serve plain boiled potatoes separately. *(France.)*

Truite George Sand, Filets de

For 6 persons: *12 fillets of trout (approximately 60 gr. each); 120 gr. shelled prawns; 12 thin slices of truffle; 24 small fish quenelles; 4 dl. sauce crevette; 2 dl. fish fumet.* Cooking time: 8 minutes.

Season the fillets with salt and pepper, and poach them in the fish fumet. Drain them, skin them very carefully, and arrange them on a serving dish. Place a slice of truffle on each fillet, and surround the dish with a garnish of prawns and quenelles. Coat the fillets and the garnish with the sauce crevette. *(France.)*

Truite grenobloise

Proceed as for the preparation of Merlan grenobloise (whiting grenobloise). *(See page 278.)*

Truite hollandaise

For 6 persons: *6 trout (200 gr. each); 4 dl. sauce hollandaise; parsley; 750 gr. potatoes.* Cooking time: 10 minutes.

Poach the trout in a court-bouillon. Drain them, and arrange them on a napkin, with the parsley. Serve the sauce hollandaise and plain boiled potatoes separately. *(France.)*

Truite hôtelière

For 6 persons: *6 trout (200 gr. each); 120 gr. maître d'hôtel butter; 1 tablespoonful of dry duxelles; 1 egg; fresh breadcrumbs; flour; 1 lemon.* Cooking time: 10 minutes.

Season the trout with salt and pepper, flour them, egg and breadcrumb, and fry. Arrange them on a serving dish (on top of the maître d'hôtel butter, which has been slightly softened and to which the duxelles has been added). Border the dish with thin half-slices of lemon (or garnish with quarters of lemon). *(France.)*

Truite hussarde

For 6 persons: *6 trout (200 gr. each); 150 gr. fish forcemeat; 40 gr. chopped onion; 2 dl. Chablis; 50 gr. butter; 80 gr. thinly-sliced onion; 3 dl. white wine sauce.* Cooking time: 15 minutes.

Fill the trout with the fish forcemeat (containing the chopped onion, which has been stewed in butter and then cooled). Season with salt and pepper, and arrange on a fish-tray (on a bed of thinly-sliced and blanched onion). Moisten with the Chablis, add 50 gr. butter, and poach in the oven (covered with a sheet of buttered paper). Drain and arrange the fish on a gratinating dish. Pass the cooking stock and the onion through a sieve, add to the white wine sauce, and correct the seasoning and consistency. Coat the trout with this sauce, and glaze briskly. *(France.)*

Truite juive

For 6 persons: *6 trout (200 gr. each); parsley; 4 dl. sauce tartare; flour; oil.* Cooking time: 10 minutes.

Season the trout with salt and pepper, flour them, and fry them in oil. Arrange on a napkin with the fried parsley. Serve the sauce tartare separately. *(France.)*

Truite Mantoue

For 6 persons: *6 trout (200 gr. each); 150 gr. fish forcemeat; 30 gr. chopped truffle; 4 dl. sauce italienne; 15 cl. white wine; 5 cl. mushroom cooking liquor; aromatics; 30 gr. butter.* Cooking time: 15 minutes.

Bone the fillets (without detaching them from the heads), cut away the backbones from just behind the heads, and remove. Mask the fillets with the forcemeat containing the chopped truffle, and re-shape the trout (using thread to hold them together). Arrange the fish on a buttered fish-tray containing a bed of aromatics, moisten with the white wine and the mushroom liquor, and cook in the oven. Remove the thread very carefully, arrange the trout on a serving dish, and coat them with the sauce italienne (containing the passed and reduced cooking liquor). *(France.)*

Truite Médicis, Médaillons de

Proceed as for the preparation of Médaillons de saumon Médicis. (Salmon.) *(See page 404.)*

Truite meunière

Proceed as for the preparation of any other fish designated meunière. *(See page 64.)*

Truite monseigneur

For 6 persons: *6 trout (175 gr. each); 6 small poached and trimmed eggs; 12 soft roes (escalopes stewed in butter); 12 small barquettes made from lining-paste; 2 dl. red wine; 12 thin slices of truffle; 12 small turned mushroom heads; 2 chopped shallots; 20 gr. butter; 7 cl. white wine sauce; 4 dl. red wine sauce.* Cooking time: 10 to 12 minutes.

Poach the trout in red wine on a buttered fish-tray which has been sprinkled with chopped shallot. Drain them, and arrange them on a serving dish. Pass and reduce the cooking stock, and add it to the red wine sauce. Place 2 mushroom heads on each trout and coat with the red wine sauce. Garnish with 6 barquettes (each containing a poached egg coated with red wine sauce and decorated with a slice of truffle) and the other 6 barquettes (each filled with escalopes of soft roe coated with white wine sauce and decorated with a slice of truffle). *(France.)*

Truite piémontaise

For 6 persons: *6 trout (200 gr. each); 4 dl. white wine sauce; 2 dl. fish fumet; 30 gr. butter; 30 gr. fine julienne of truffle; 240 gr. rice piémontaise.* Cooking time: 10 minutes.

Arrange the trout on a buttered fish-tray, season with salt and pepper, and poach them in the fish fumet. Drain and skin the trout, and arrange them on a base made from the rice, on a serving dish. Coat them with the white wine sauce, and sprinkle with the julienne of truffle. *(France.)*

Truite Suchet

For 6 persons: *6 trout (200 gr. each); 50 gr. red of carrot; 50 gr. celery; 50 gr. leek; 40 gr. truffle; 80 gr. butter; 2 dl. fish fumet; 4 dl. white wine sauce.* Cooking time: 12 minutes.

Cut into a fine julienne the carrot, celery and leek, and stew all these in butter. Add to these vegetables the truffle cut into a julienne. Fillet the trout, and lay the fillets in a buttered gratinating dish. Cover them with the julienne, season with salt and pepper, and moisten with the fish fumet. Cover with a sheet of buttered paper, and poach in the oven. Drain off the poaching stock, reduce it well, and add it to the white wine sauce. Arrange the fillets on a serving dish, and coat them with the sauce. *(France.)*

Truite vauclusienne

Proceed as for the preparation of any other fish designated meunière, replacing the butter with olive oil. *(France.)* *(See page 64.)*

Truite Wallis

For 6 persons: *6 trout (200 gr. each); 3 dl. white wine; 75 gr. butter; 40 gr. beurre manié; 200 gr. white grapes (peeled and pipped); 1 coffee-spoonful chopped fines herbes.* Cooking time: 12 minutes.

Season the trout with salt and pepper, and poach them in the white wine (containing 50 gr. butter). Drain them, arrange on a serving dish, and garnish with the grapes (heated in butter). Reduce the poaching stock by a quarter, thicken it slightly with the beurre manié, correct the seasoning and consistency, and use this sauce to coat the fish. Sprinkle with the fines herbes.

Truite Yvette

Proceed as for the preparation of Sole Yvette. *(See page 344.)*

Truite Zoug

For 6 persons: *6 trout (200 gr. each); 50 gr. chopped shallots; 100 gr. butter; 3 dl. white wine; 15 cl. cream; 1 tablespoonful of chopped mixed herbs (parsley, chervil, thyme, sage, sweet marjoram and tarragon); parsley.* Cooking time: approximately 10 minutes.

Line a buttered sauteuse with the chopped shallots, arrange the trout in it, season with salt and pepper, moisten with the white wine, cover with a sheet of buttered paper, and poach. Remove the fish from the cooking stock, and keep hot. Add the mixed herbs to the stock, reduce it slightly, thicken with the cream, and monter au beurre. Arrange the trout on a serving dish, coat them with the sauce, and sprinkle with the chopped parsley. *(Switzerland.)*

Truite de lac Schönbrunn

For 6 persons: *1 lake trout weighing 1 kg. 500; 250 gr. fresh mushrooms; 250 gr. tomatoes; 1 dl. white wine; 3 dl. fish fumet; 1 dl. fresh cream; 1 dl. sauce hollandaise; ½ teaspoonful chopped tarragon; ½ lemon; 125 gr. butter; 30 gr. flour.* Poaching time: 10 minutes.

Remove the fillets. Prepare a stock with the head and the bones. Cut up the fish into pieces, season with salt and pepper, and poach in the fish fumet and white wine. Make a brunoise of the mushrooms, and stew it in a little butter (containing lemon juice and salt). Also stew the tomatoes (peeled, pipped and chopped) to the point of almost complete reduction, and season with salt and pepper. Prepare a roux (with 50 gr. butter and 30 gr. flour), and moisten with the fish fumet and the mushroom cooking liquor, to obtain a velouté. Blend in the cream, bring to the boil, pass, correct the seasoning and consistency, and add the sauce hollandaise and the tarragon. Arrange the fillets in a gratinating dish, cover them with the mushrooms and tomatoes, coat with the sauce, and glaze quickly under the salamander. Garnish with noisette potatoes and with glazed cucumbers (which have been turned in the shape of large cloves of garlic). *(Austria.)*

Truite saumonée américaine, Escalopes de

Salmon-trout

For 6 persons: *6 escalopes of salmon-trout (125 gr. each); 2 dl. fish fumet; 4 dl. sauce américaine; 20 gr. butter; 6 escalopes of lobster tail.* Cooking time: 10 minutes.

Poach the escalopes in the fish fumet, in a buttered fish-tray. Drain them, arrange them on a serving dish, and place on each an escalope of lobster tail (prepared américaine). Coat with sauce américaine. *(France.)*

Truite saumonée Cambacérès

For 8 to 10 persons: *1 salmon-trout weighing 1 kg. 500; 500 gr. fish forcemeat; 40 gr. truffle; 60 gr. red of carrot; 4 dl. dry white wine; 60 gr. butter; ¾ litre white wine sauce; 12 escalopes of soft roe; 500 gr. morels; 30 stoned olives; 12 thin slices of truffle; 150 gr. fat bacon; aromatics; 1 dl. sauce hollandaise.* Cooking time: 35 to 40 minutes.

Gut and clean the trout, remove the gills, and skin on one side from 2 cm. behind the head to 5 cm. from the tail. Stud the skinned surface with truffle and red of carrot. Separate the two fillets very carefully, leaving the head attached to one and the tail to the other. Cut up the backbone, remove it, and then clean the inside of the fish very carefully. Season both fillets on the inside with salt and pepper, mask them on the inside with forcemeat, and press them together again to re-shape the trout. Cover with thin slices of bacon (which can be replaced with a sheet of buttered paper), tie with string, and place on a bed of aromatics, with the studded side facing upwards. Moisten with white wine, and braise (covered) in the oven, basting from time to time. Remove the trout, and arrange it on a long serving dish. Pass the cooking stock, reduce it well, and add it to the sauce hollandaise. Coat the fish lightly with this sauce, and decorate with the slices of truffle. Garnish with the escalopes of soft roe (stewed in butter), the morels (sautéd in butter) and the blanched olives. Serve the rest of the sauce separately. *(France.)*

Truite saumonée au coulis d'écrevisse

For 6 persons: *1 salmon-trout weighing 1 kg. 200; 100 gr. crayfish purée; 2 dl. fresh cream; 2 dl. fish velouté; 50 gr. butter.* Cooking time: 20 to 25 minutes.

Poach the trout in a court-bouillon containing white wine. Drain and skin the trout, and arrange it on a serving dish. Reduce the cream by half, add the velouté, allow to simmer, blend in the crayfish purée, finish with the butter, and correct the seasoning and consistency. Coat the trout lightly with this sauce. Serve the rest of the sauce separately. *(France.)*

Truite saumonée écossaise

Proceed as for the preparation of Saumon écossaise. (Salmon.) *(See page 403.)*

Truite saumonée Felix, Filets de

For 6 persons: *2 fillets of salmon-trout (400 gr. each); 120 gr. butter; 4 dl. sauce américaine.* Cooking time: 15 minutes.

Skin the fillets, season them with salt and pepper, flour them, and cook in clarified butter. Arrange on a serving dish, and coat with the sauce américaine. *(France.)*

Truite saumonée genevoise

For 6 persons: *1 salmon-trout weighing 1 kg. 200; 750 gr. potatoes; 4 dl. sauce genevoise; parsley.* Cooking time: 20 to 25 minutes.

Poach the trout in a court-bouillon containing white wine. Drain it, arrange on a napkin, and surround with the parsley. Serve the sauce genevoise and the plain boiled potatoes separately. *(France.)*

Truite saumonée impériale

For 6 persons: *1 salmon-trout weighing 1 kg. 200; 60 gr. truffle; ½ bottle dry champagne; 1 dl. fish fumet; 12 shelled prawns; 12 escalopes of soft herring roes; 30 gr. julienne of truffle; 75 gr. butter; 40 gr. beurre manié.* Cooking time: 20 to 25 minutes.

Skin the trout on one side (from 2 cm. behind the head to 5 cm. from the tail). Stud the skinned surface with truffle. Season the trout with salt and pepper, and poach it (covered in the oven), in the champagne and fish fumet. Drain the fish, and arrange it on a serving dish. Reduce the poaching stock by a quarter, thicken with the beurre manié, butter lightly, and correct the seasoning and consistency. Coat the trout with this sauce, and sprinkle it with the julienne of truffle. Garnish with the prawns and escalopes of soft roe (all these stewed in butter). *(France.)*

Truite saumonée Ivanhoe, Escalopes de

For 6 persons: *6 escalopes of salmon-trout (120 gr. each); 3 dl. white wine sauce; 50 gr. crayfish butter; 6 thin slices of lemon (peeled and pipped); 2 pippin apples; 3 large globe artichoke-bases; 100 gr. butter; flour.* Cooking time: 12 to 15 minutes.

Season the escalopes with salt and pepper, flour them, cook them in butter, and arrange them in a timbale. Peel and pip the apples, slice them thinly, and sauté in butter. Slice thinly the artichoke-bases, and sauté them in butter. Arrange the sliced apples and the artichoke-bases on the escalopes, and place the slices of lemon on top. At the last moment, coat all over with the white wine sauce (which has been finished off with the crayfish butter). *(France.)*

Truite saumonée Mont d'or, Suprême de

For 10 persons: *1 salmon-trout weighing 2 kg.; ¼ litre white wine; 250 gr. fresh mushrooms; 500 gr. peeled, pipped and chopped tomatoes; 2 dl. fresh cream; ½ tablespoonful chopped tarragon; 100 gr. butter; 40 gr. flour; lemon juice; 750 gr. plain boiled spoon-cut potatoes; 750 gr. cucumber (spoon-cut and glazed); ¼ litre sauce hollandaise.* Cooking time: 8 minutes.

Remove the head and tail of the trout, and fillet the fish. Skin the fillets, and cut them into 10 portions. Prepare ¾ litre of fish fumet with the head, bones, trimmings and the usual aromatics. Poach the suprêmes (fillets) in this stock (to which the white wine has been added). Cut the mushrooms into small dice, and cook them with 30 gr. butter, the juice of half a lemon, and a pinch of salt. Stew the chopped tomatoes in butter, to the point of complete evaporation, and season with pepper and salt. Prepare ¾ litre of velouté, composed of a roux (made with 50 gr. butter and the flour), together with the fish fumet and the mushroom cooking liquor. Pass it, work it up with the sauce hollandaise, and season with lemon juice and the chopped tarragon. Arrange the suprêmes in a buttered gratinating dish, cover them with the mushrooms and the chopped tomatoes, coat with the sauce, and glaze briskly under the salamander. Garnish one side of the dish with the potatoes, and the other side with the cucumber. *(International cookery.)*

Truite saumonée Montgolfier, Escalopes de

Proceed as for the preparation of Filets de sole Montgolfier. *(See page 316.)*

Truite saumonée Nantua

For 6 persons: *1 salmon-trout weighing 1 kg. 200; 4 dl. sauce Nantua; 18 shelled crayfish; 12 thin slices of truffle; 50 gr. butter; 1 dl. white wine; 1 dl. fish fumet.* Cooking time: 20 to 25 minutes.

Season the trout with salt and pepper, place it on a buttered fish-tray, moisten with the fish fumet and white wine, cover with a sheet of buttered paper, and poach in the oven. When the cooking is finished, remove the fish, skin it, and arrange it on a serving dish. Reduce the poaching stock, and add it to the sauce Nantua. Decorate the trout with the slices of truffle, surround it with the shelled crayfish, and coat the fish and the garnish with the sauce. *(France.)*

Truite saumonée Régence

Proceed as for the preparation of Turbot Régence. *(See page 352.)*

Truite saumonée Romanoff

For 6 persons: *the fillets from a salmon-trout weighing 2 kg.; 250 gr. soft roe of fresh carp; ¼ litre fish fumet; 3 shallots; 300 gr. button mushrooms; 1 dl. fresh cream; 40 gr. beurre manié; 200 gr. butter; 2 lemons; 5 cl. dry vermouth; 18 puff-paste bouchées mignonnes filled with caviar.* Poaching time: 10 minutes.

Pass the raw soft roes through a sieve and mix them with the fish fumet. Butter a fish-tray, sprinkle it with chopped shallots, cover with the thinly-sliced mushrooms, place the fillets on top, sprinkle with the fish fumet, cover with a sheet of buttered paper, and poach. When the poaching is finished, drain the fillets, arrange them on a serving dish, cover them with the mushrooms, and keep them hot. Reduce the stock by half, work it up with the cream, and thicken with the beurre manié. Work up the sauce with butter, and blend in the vermouth, lemon juice and a touch of Cayenne. Use this sauce to coat the fillets, and garnish with the bouchées of caviar. *(Germany.)*

Truite saumonée au vin blanc

Cut up the trout into slices (tranches) or darnes, and proceed as for the preparation of Sole au vin blanc. *(See page 343.)*

Truite saumonée au vin rouge

Prepare as for the preparation of Truite saumonée au vin blanc, using red wine instead of white.

Fresh-Water Fish:

Cold Dishes

Escabèche d'anguilles aux cèpes

Eel

For 6 persons: *900 gr. eel, gutted and skinned; 300 gr. cèpes; 1 small carrot; 50 gr. onion; 3 unpeeled cloves of garlic; 2 dl. sweet olive oil; 1 dl. wine vinegar; 1 lemon; 8 white peppercorns; 1 bunch of herbs; flour.* Cooking time for the eel: 8 to 10 minutes.

Carefully wash the eel, dry it, cut it into thick slices 5 cm. in length, season, flour, cook in a third of the oil. Take out the slices and put them into a fireproof earthenware dish. Cut the onions and the carrot in fine roundels and the cèpes into thick slices. Sauté the cloves of garlic in the rest of the oil, take them out when they are brown. In the same oil sauté rapidly the cèpes, carrot, onions. Add the vinegar, 1 litre of water, the peppercorns, the bunch of herbs and allow to cook gently for 15 minutes. Add at the last moment the lemon juice and pour this boiling marinade over the slices of eel almost to cover. Cover and allow to marinate for 24 to 36 hours. Serve very cold sprinkled with the marinade and chopped mixed herbs. *(Germany.)*

Anguille marinée au vin blanc

For 6 persons: *1 kg. 200 of skinned eel; 125 gr. finely-chopped onion; 50 gr. butter; 1 bunch of herbs; court-bouillon with white wine.* Cooking time: 20 minutes.

Stew the onion in the butter. Cut up the eel in thick slices of 4 to 5 cm. Arrange them on the onion in a shallow stew pan. Cover with court-bouillon, add the bunch of herbs, and cook slowly. Allow to cool in the cooking liquor. Take out the bunch of herbs. Arrange on an hors d'oeuvre dish, cover with the cooking liquor. *(France.)*

Anguille au vert

For 6 persons: *1 kg. 200 of skinned eel; 75 gr. sorrel leaves; 15 tender nettle leaves; 10 gr. parsley; 5 gr. burnet; 3 gr. green sage; 2 gr. savory; 2 gr. tarragon; 50 gr. butter; 4 dl. white wine; 3 egg yolks; ½ lemon.* Cooking time: 12 minutes.

Cut up small eels in slices of 5 to 6 cm. Melt the sorrel in the butter, add the other herbs (chopped) and stiffen the eel in the herbs. Moisten with the white wine; salt and pepper sparingly, allow to cook for 10 minutes. Bind with the egg yolks, complete with some drops of lemon; adjust seasoning and consistency. Allow to cool completely. Arrange in a timbale. *(Belgium.)*

Anguilles Charleroi

For 6 persons: *2 kg. of large eels; ½ litre dry white wine; ¼ litre of water; 1 large onion; 1 parsley root; 1 clove of garlic; 2 cloves; 1 bayleaf; 1 sprig of thyme; 18 gr. gelatine; 2 whites of egg; 1 lemon; 1 pinch of sweet marjoram; 12 pickled onions; 6 gherkins; 2 skinned tomatoes; tarragon leaves; 7 cl. oil; flour.* Cooking time: 10 minutes.

Skin and clean the eels. Cut them up into slices of about 6 cm. Wash them, dry on a cloth. Season, flour and cook the slices in the hot oil in the frying pan. After colouring, allow to cook gently and completely. Drain. Prepare a marinade with white wine, vinegar, water, thinly-sliced onion, bayleaf, thyme, marjoram, parsley, garlic and cloves and allow to cook gently for 20 minutes. Strain. Add the gelatine (previously soaked); clarify with the whipped egg whites. Adjust the seasoning. Strain the jelly through a cloth. Arrange the eels in a hollow dish, decorate with slices of fluted lemon, pickled onions, slices of tomato, fans of gherkin and tarragon leaves. Pour the half-set jelly over all. Keep cool for 24 hours before serving. *(Belgium.)*

Anguilles en gelée à la mode de Londres

Jellied eels London fashion

For 6 persons: *1 kg. 200 of eel (skinned and head removed); 1 bayleaf; 2 sprigs of thyme; 50 gr. finely-chopped carrot; 50 gr. finely-chopped onion; 50 gr. finely-chopped white of celery; 2 parsley leaves; ½ lemon; 8 gr. English pepper.* Cooking time: about 30 minutes.

Cut up the eel into slices of 3 cm. Moisten with cold water to cover; bring to the boil. Season, add the spices. When the eel is cooked remove the slices, arrange them in a porcelain or glass timbale. Strain the cooking liquor, reduced if necessary. The slices should be just covered. Keep cold in order to gell. *(Great Britain.)*

Carpe aigre-douce à la juive orientale

Carp

For 6 persons: *1 kg. 500 to 1 kg. 800 of small size carp; 2 carrots; 1 lemon; 2 finely-chopped onions; 1 bayleaf; 3 cloves; 150 gr. sultanas; 100 gr. gingerbread; 100 gr. sugar.* Cooking time: 45 minutes.

Cut the carp into pieces and salt them. The vinegar will have been cooked with ½ litre of water, onions, carrots, sliced and seeded lemon, bayleaf, cloves, sultanas and sugar. Pour over the pieces of carp. Allow to cook slowly for 30 minutes; add the crumbled gingerbread and continue the cooking for 15 minutes. Arrange the carp in a serving dish, sprinkle with the cooking liquor and garnish with sultanas. Serve cold. *(Israel.)*

Carpe farcie traditionnelle au raifort

For 6 persons: *1 kg. 500 of live carp; 400 gr. of onion; 150 gr. of carrots; 250 gr. breadcrumbs; 50 gr. chopped almonds; 4 eggs; 100 gr. celery; 50 gr. butter; 1 beetroot; 100 gr. horse-radish; 3 to 4 leaves of gelatine; vinegar.* Cooking time: about 90 minutes.

Kill the carp. Allow them to stay for a moment before scaling them. Remove the heads, gut and wash them; skin, leaving a little flesh on the skin. Hold these skins in reserve. Soak the breadcrumbs; lightly colour 250 gr. of finely-chopped onion in the butter, allow to cool. Pass together the fish flesh, onion and breadcrumbs through the fine plate of a mincer. Knead thoroughly with the eggs and add the chopped almonds; season with salt and pepper. Fill the carp skins with this preparation. Poach the fish in a court-bouillon prepared with the rest of the onions, the carrots, the celery, a few white peppercorns, water, salt and a little sugar. After cooking allow to cool in the court-bouillon. Remove the fish, strain the court-bouillon and dissolve in it the softened gelatine. Garnish the carp with roundels of cooked carrot and glaze with the jelly. Serve accompanied with finely-grated beetroot and horse-radish seasoned with vinegar, sugar and salt. *(Israel.)*

Carpe à la japonaise "Shasimi"

For 6 persons: *1 live carp of 2 kg.; 150 gr. cucumbers; 150 gr. bamboo shoots; 150 gr. carrots; 50 gr. radish; 50 gr. kopu (Japanese seaweed); 20 gr. Japanese poppy; vinegar; powdered green Japanese horse-radish; Japanese soy sauce.*

Kill, gut and wash the fish. Fillet and leave the fillets for 30 minutes in iced water. Dry and cut into very thin scollops. Prepare a fine julienne of cucumbers, bamboo shoots, radish, carrots and kopu; marinate with salt, pepper, vinegar and Japanese poppy. Arrange the small slices of carp on the vegetables, setting them out in rosettes. With the shasimi serve for each person a little bowl of soy sauce and a little bowl of horse-radish powder, slightly salted and moistened with water. All Japanese salads are prepared without oil. *(Germany.)*
(See illustration, page 385.)

Carpe à la juive

For 6 persons: *1 kg. 200 of carp; 120 gr. chopped onion; 3 chopped shallots; 50 gr. flour; 4 dl. oil; ¾ litre white wine; 1 bunch of herbs; 1 coffee-spoonful of chopped parsley; 2 crushed cloves of garlic.* Cooking time: 30 minutes.

Cut up the carp into slices of 1½ cm. Place them in a shallow stew pan with onion and shallot (previously stewed in oil). Sprinkle with flour, allow the latter to cook for a moment, moisten with white wine and an equal quantity of water. Season. Add 1 dl. of oil, the garlic, the bunch of herbs. Allow to cook gently for 25 minutes. Drain the slices, arrange them on a long dish in the shape of the fish. Reduce the cooking liquor by two-thirds, work it up (away from the fire) with ¼ litre of oil. Correct seasoning and consistency. Pour this sauce over the carp, allow to gell. At the moment of serving, sprinkle with chopped parsley. *(Israel.)*

Carpe marinée

For 6 persons: *1 kg. 800 to 2 kg. of carp; 250 gr. onion cut into rings; 600 gr. tomatoes, skinned, pipped and chopped; 1 soup-spoonful of tomato purée; 4 dl. dry white wine; 3 dl. sunflower oil; 4 lemons; 1 bayleaf; paprika; flour.* Cooking time: 10 to 25 minutes.

Remove the heads, cut up the fish into equal parts, season with salt and paprika, flour it, seize it in the oil, and arrange the pieces in a shallow stew pan. Cook the onion to a golden colour in the oil, add the chopped tomatoes and mask over the fish. Mix the tomato purée with the white wine and the juice of 2 lemons, and the rest of the oil; lightly season with salt and pepper; cover the fish with this preparation. Add the bayleaf, cover, complete the cooking in the oven. Allow the fish to cool in its own liquor. Arrange in a serving dish, cover over again with the base (not strained); garnish with slices of lemon and serve very cold. *(Rumania.)*

Carpe orientale

For 6 persons: *1 kg. 200 of carp; 120 gr. chopped onion; 3 chopped shallots; 50 gr. flour; ¾ litre white wine; 4 dl. oil; 1 bunch of herbs; 2 crushed cloves of garlic; 60 gr. chopped almonds; 1 gr. saffron; 1 coffee-spoonful of chopped parsley.* Cooking time: 30 minutes.

Proceed as for the preparation of Carpe à la juive, but add to the cooking liquor, when it is reduced and worked up with oil, the saffron and the chopped almonds. *(Israel.)*

Carpe Ploesti

For 6 persons: *2 carp, each 1 kg.; 2 eggs; 1 lemon; 2 cl. olive oil; flour; frying oil; a bunch of parsley;* Sauce: *3 soup-spoonfuls of red pimentoes; 8 skinned almonds; 1 small clove of garlic; 2 dl. olive oil; wine vinegar.* Cooking time: 10 minutes.

Fillet, cut into three, allow to marinate for 1 hour in the olive oil with salt and lemon juice. Dry, flour, pass through the beaten egg. Fry. Garnish with fried parsley and with quarters of lemon. Serve with a sauce prepared with the purée of peppers, a pinch of salt and sugar, grated nut and finely-crushed clove of garlic, incorporating the olive oil, stirring with a whisk, as for a mayonnaise. Adjust with vinegar. The sauce must not get too cold, to prevent separation. *(Germany.)*

Médaillons d'esturgeon en gelée

Sturgeon

For 6 persons: *6 medallions of sturgeon (150 gr. each); 600 gr. Russian salad; 6 dl. fish jelly; 600 gr. mayonnaise; 10 gr. grated horse-radish; 1 dl. white wine; ½ lemon; 25 gr. butter; olive oil; vinegar; chervil leaves.* Cooking time: 15 minutes.

Poach the medallions in white wine, butter and lemon juice. Allow to cool in the cooking liquor. Remove and sponge, trim, decorate with the chervil leaves; glaze with the jelly. Marinate in advance the salad with the vinegar and the oil. Bind lightly with the mayonnaise and a little jelly; glaze a round dish with the jelly. Arrange the medallions on it in the shape of a crown and set out the Russian salad in the shape of a dome in the centre. Serve separately the mayonnaise, to which has been added some grated horse-radish. *(International cookery.)*

Côtelettes de saumon Alaska

Salmon

For 6 persons: *6 salmon cutlets, each of 150 gr.; 600 gr. Russian salad; 3 dl. white sauce chaud-froid; 1 dl. white wine; ½ lemon; 25 gr. butter; 8 slices of truffle; 500 gr. mayonnaise; 4 dl. fish jelly.* Cooking time: 7 to 8 minutes.

Season the cutlets, moisten them with the white wine and the lemon juice; add the butter, cover with buttered paper, poach in the oven. Allow to cool in the cooking liquor under light pressure. Drain, remove the skin, trim, sponge, coat with sauce chaud-froid. Decorate with slices of truffle, or, according to taste, glaze with jelly. Arrange in the shape of a crown and in the centre a pyramid of Russian salad bound with mayonnaise. Serve a light mayonnaise separately. *(France.)*

Saumon en bellevue

For 10 persons: *1 cut of salmon (2 kg.); 1½ litres fish jelly; 1 truffle; hard-boiled white of egg; 10 small tartlets made from lining paste; 10 halves of hard-boiled eggs; 300 gr. macédoine of vegetables; 10 small turned mushroom heads; 10 small shelled crayfish tails; 150 gr. mayonnaise; ¾ litre sauce verte or Chantilly; tarragon leaves; chervil leaves; 40 gr. butter.* Cooking time: about 30 minutes.

Poach the salmon gently in a court-bouillon with white wine. Allow to cool in the cooking liquor. Take out, drain, skin, place upright on the belly. Decorate tastefully with truffle, white of hard-boiled egg, tarragon leaves, chervil leaves, dipping first each decoration in jelly, then glaze the salmon well with half-set jelly. Arrange the salmon on a dish glazed with a thin layer of jelly. Surround with tartlets (filled with a fine macédoine of vegetables bound with mayonnaise and each decorated with a crayfish tail and a mushroom head) and with stuffed hard-boiled egg, using the sieved yolks mixed with a little butter and mayonnaise and decorated with a star in truffle as well as with croûtons of jelly. Serve the sauce separately. There is no strict rule for the presentation of Saumon en bellevue. There are numerous variations in garnishings and decoration. *(France.)*

(See Culinary Technique, page 87.)

Saumon au beurre de Montpellier

For 6 persons: *2 thick slices of salmon, each 600 gr.; 150 gr. Montpellier butter; 2 truffles; ¾ litre fish jelly.* Cooking time: about 25 minutes.

Poach the thick slices of salmon in a court-bouillon with white wine. Allow to cool in the cooking liquor. Drain, sponge. Skin the slices, mask them on one side with Montpellier butter. Decorate with thin crescents of truffle, imitating the scales, glaze with the half-set jelly, masking several times. Decorate and border with croûtons of jelly. *(France.)*

Saumon au Chambertin

For 6 persons: *1 thick slice of salmon; 1 kg. 200; ½ litre Chambertin; 1 truffle; hard-boiled white of egg; tarragon leaves; chervil leaves; gelatine; 1 raw white of egg.* Cooking time: about 25 minutes.

Poach the salmon in the court-bouillon and the white wine in sufficient quantity to cover it. Allow to cool in the cooking liquor. Remove, sponge, skin, place in a deep glass bowl, keep cold. Strain the court-bouillon, reduce it, add enough soaked gelatine to prepare a light jelly, clarify with white of egg, adjust seasoning. Decorate the salmon according to taste; cover it entirely with half-set jelly. The jelly must be limpid, light and savoury. For service place on a serviette surrounded with crushed ice (optional). *(France.)*

Saumon froid mariné Tivoli

For 6 persons: *1 kg. of fresh salmon; 250 gr. picked shrimps; 2 carrots; ½ celeriac; 1 onion; 1 bayleaf; 1 coffee-spoonful of white peppercorns; 4 dl. white wine; 2 soup-spoonfuls tomato purée; 3 soup-spoonfuls of finely-chopped dill; 1 soup-spoonful of mustard; 1 dl. olive oil.* Poaching time: 10 minutes.

Split the salmon lengthwise, skin it and remove the bones. Cut up each half in slices 2 cm. thick. Make a julienne of the carrots and celery; thinly-slice the onion. Line a shallow stew pan with these vegetables. Arrange the slices of salmon on top, add the peppercorns and the bayleaf (wrapped in a muslin bag), cover with a sheet of oiled paper, poach, and allow to cool in its own liquor. Take out the slices of salmon, arrange them on a shallow glass dish, surround with the julienne, and decorate with the picked shrimps. Strain 2 dl. of the cooking liquor through a cloth-strainer, incorporate in it the tomato purée, the mustard, and the dill. Work up with oil. Rectify seasoning and consistency. Pour the marinade over the salmon and serve very cold. *(Denmark.)*

Mayonnaise de saumon

For 6 persons: *600 gr. of cooked salmon free from skin and bones; 2 small lettuce; 300 gr. mayonnaise; 6 to 8 anchovy fillets; 3 hard-boiled eggs; 12 stoned green olives; 30 gr. capers; 3 lettuce hearts.*

Garnish the bottom of a salad bowl with a coarse julienne of lettuce lightly seasoned. Arrange the flaked salmon on top. Mask with mayonnaise, smooth into a dome shape. Decorate with thin strips of anchovy fillets, olives, capers, quarters of hard-boiled eggs, and quarters of lettuce hearts. *(France.)*

Côtelettes de saumon Mécène

For 10 persons: *1 fillet of salmon (1 kg.) skinned and boned; 20 shelled crayfish tails; 600 to 700 gr. of cucumber balls (shaped with a spoon-cutter); 10 hard-boiled eggs; 1½ litres white wine jelly; 3 stuffed green olives; 75 gr. butter; 2 soup-spoonfuls of red pepper purée; 2 soup-spoonfuls of thick mayonnaise; 1 small truffle; vinegar; olive oil; ¾ litre Chantilly sauce.* Cooking time: 12 to 14 minutes.

Wrap the fillet in a buttered paper, poach it in a buttered fish tray, in a court-bouillon in the oven until just cooked. Blanch the cucumber balls, marinate them with vinegar, olive oil, and a little salt. Drain. Coat a dome-shaped mould or a timbale with jelly. Decorate the bottom with a good slice of truffle. Fill the timbale with cucumber balls, cover with half-set jelly, and keep cold. Cut up the fillet into ten equal slices, dry, decorate each cutlet with a thin slice of stuffed olive, mask with jelly. Remove one-third of the hard-boiled eggs, cut a small slice off the ends to make them stand upright, remove the yolks without damaging the whites and pass them through a fine sieve. Combine them with 50 gr. of softened butter, the mayonnaise, and the pepper purée. Adjust seasoning. Stuff the whites with this preparation using a piping-bag and star tube. Decorate with a small roundel of truffle and with a point of white of hard-boiled egg, and glaze with jelly. Turn out the timbale of cucumber into the centre of a large round dish (glazed with a thin layer of jelly). Trim the crayfish tails, arrange them (one next to the other) around the timbale. Glaze them with a brush with the half-set jelly. Arrange the salmon slices around the timbale, a stuffed egg between each. Surround with jelly in the shape of small dice. Serve the sauce separately. *(Germany.)*

Mousse de saumon

For 6 persons: *500 gr. of salmon (cooked, cold); 2 dl. velouté of fish; ¼ litre of white wine jelly; ¼ litre of whipped double cream; 12 slices of truffle.*

Skin the salmon, pass through a fine plate of the mincer. Incorporate half of the velouté, pass through a fine sieve. Place in an earthenware dish, add the rest of the velouté and 15 cl. of cold jelly. Season, and work with a wooden spatula. When the purée begins to thicken, incorporate the whipped cream, and adjust seasoning and consistency. Pour the composition into a timbale (or a glass coupe) up to 1 cm. from the top, and allow to set cold. Decorate with a crown of slices of truffle, and cover over with a thin layer of clear light jelly. *(France.)*

Saumon norvégienne

For 10 persons: *1 slice of salmon (2 kg.); 10 small cucumber cases, blanched, marinated and filled with purée of smoked salmon; 10 halves of hard-boiled eggs, the yolks removed, creamed and used to stuff the whites; 10 small cases of cooked beetroot filled with picked shrimps with mayonnaise; 10 small, skinned tomatoes, each compressed to a round shape, decorated with leaves of green butter; 1½ litres fish jelly; 10 large prawns with the tails shelled; ¾ litre of Russian sauce.* Cooking time: about 30 minutes.

Poach the salmon in a white wine court-bouillon. Allow to cool in the cooking liquor. Take out, drain, skin, glaze with jelly. Stick in the middle a row of prawns. Arrange on a dish glazed with a thin layer of jelly. Garnish with cucumber cases, halves of stuffed hard-boiled eggs, beetroot cases, tomatoes, and jelly croûtons. Serve the sauce separately. *(France.)*

Saumon parisienne

For 10 persons: *1 slice of salmon (2 kg.); 50 gr. Montpellier butter; 10 artichoke bases; 300 gr. macédoine of vegetables; 700 gr. mayonnaise; 1 litre of fish jelly; chopped white and yolk of egg; chopped lobster coral.* Cooking time: about 30 minutes.

Poach the salmon in a white wine court-bouillon. Allow to cool in the cooking liquor. Drain. Skin, but only on the back, a rectangle two-thirds of the total surface. Mask the bared part with a thin layer of lightly-gelled mayonnaise. Once set, border it with a thin ring of Montpellier butter using a piping bag and small star tube. Decorate the centre of the rectangle with chopped yolk and white of egg and lobster coral. Glaze the salmon completely with jelly, arrange it on a dish glazed with a thin layer of jelly. Garnish with small previously marinated cooked artichoke bases, garnish in the shape of a dome, with a fine macédoine of vegetables bound with the lightly-gelled mayonnaise. Serve a mayonnaise sauce separately. *(France.)*

Côtelettes de saumon Reval

For 6 persons: *6 salmon cutlets (each 150 gr.); 6 small shelled crayfish tails; 6 white asparagus heads; 6 hard-boiled eggs; 30 gr. caviar; ¾ litre fish jelly; 50 gr. mayonnaise; 75 gr. butter; 1 dl. white wine; ½ lemon; 4 dl. sauce verte; tarragon leaves.* Cooking time: 7 to 8 minutes.

For the cooking, proceed as for the preparation of Côtelettes de saumon Alaska. Cool under slight pressure, skin, and trim. Decorate each cutlet with a crayfish tail, with an asparagus head, with two leaves of blanched tarragon. Glaze with jelly. Cut the eggs in two by serrating with a small knife, remove the yolk, pass through a fine sieve. Combine with the mayonnaise and 50 gr. of slightly-softened butter, season, stuff the whites of egg using a piping-bag and plain tube. Place a little caviar in the centre, and glaze with jelly. Arrange the cutlets, garnish with the eggs. Serve the sauce verte separately. *(Germany.)*

Saumon Riga

For 10 persons: *1 slice of salmon (2 kg.); 500 gr. macédoine of vegetables; 10 cucumber cases (fluted, blanched, marinated); 10 small short paste tartlets; 10 empty crayfish shells; 100 gr. crayfish mousse; 10 halves of hard-boiled eggs; 75 gr. caviar; 1 litre fish jelly; 250 gr. mayonnaise.* Cooking time: about 30 minutes.

Poach the salmon in the court-bouillon. Allow to cool in the cooking liquor. Proceed as for the preparation Saumon parisienne. Glaze with jelly. Garnish with cucumber cases filled with a macédoine of vegetables bound with mayonnaise, with tartlets garnished with the same salad, each decorated with a crayfish shell stuffed with crayfish mousse and with halves of hard-boiled eggs, after removing the yolk with the point of a small knife and replacing it with caviar, and with croûtons of jelly. *(France.)*

Petits soufflés de saumon

Line small fireproof cassolettes with a band of greaseproof paper, rising 15 mm. above the edge of the mould. Run a thin layer of jelly in the bottom of each cassolette. Fill almost to the top with a salmon mousse preparation. Allow to set in the cold. Decorate with a slice of truffle, and cover with a thin layer of clear jelly. Keep cool until the moment of serving. Remove the paper carefully. Serve one cassolette per person. *(France.)*

Côtelettes de saumon suédoise

Proceed as for the preparation Côtelettes de saumon Alaska, without masking with sauce chaud-froid. *(France.)* *(See page 422.)*

Truite Carlton

For 6 persons: *6 trout (each 180 gr.); 200 gr. capers; 100 gr. peeled, de-seeded and chopped tomatoes; 3 dl. white wine; the juice of 1 lemon; 25 gr. butter; bayleaf; oil.* Poaching time: 10 minutes.

Remove through the dorsal side the bones of the previously cleaned trout; cut off the heads, open the fish flat. Mix the capers and the tomatoes, season with milled pepper. Distribute this mixture over the internal surface of the trout, season, roll and tie up each fish in a sheet of oiled paper. Butter well a shallow stew pan, arrange the rolled up fish in it side by side, sprinkle with white wine, add a bayleaf, cover, and poach in the oven. Once cooled take the trout carefully out of their paper, pass the cooking liquor, slightly reduce, season with lemon juice, and pour, when cold, over the trout. This dish can equally well be served hot, accompanied with rice pilaf. *(Italy.)*

Truite Célesta

For 6 persons: *6 trout, each 200 gr.; 3 tomatoes; 3 hard-boiled eggs; 12 anchovy fillets; 2 cucumbers; 2 red peppers; 4 dl. white wine jelly; 12 stuffed olives; 3 dl. tomatoed mayonnaise sauce.* Cooking time: 8 to 10 minutes.

Arrange the trout on a buttered fish tray, moisten with court-bouillon, cover with a buttered paper, and poach in the oven. Allow to cool in the cooking liquor. Remove the skin. Decorate with alternate roundels of skinned tomato and hard-boiled egg. Arrange anchovy fillets in thin strips on top, and mask with jelly. Peel the cucumbers, cut and remove the pips, as also the peppers, in a very fine and short julienne, bind them with a little half-set jelly, and arrange them on the base of a serving dish. Place the trout on this bed, and surround them with stuffed olives. Serve the tomatoed mayonnaise separately. *(Holland.)*

Truite au Chablis

For 6 persons: *6 trout, each 200 gr.; ½ litre of fish jelly; 26 blanched tarragon leaves; 4 dl. sauce tartare.* Cooking time: 8 to 10 minutes.

Poach the trout in a white wine court-bouillon. Let them cool in their cooking liquor. Take them out, skin them, decorate with tarragon leaves, glaze them with jelly. Arrange on a serving dish, garnish with dice-shaped jelly. Serve the sauce separately. *(International cookery.)*

Filets de truite à la mode de Chorin

For 6 persons: *6 trout, each 200 gr. to 225 gr.; 18 shelled crayfish tails; 18 large white asparagus heads; 12 small quarters of tomato, skinned and pipped; ¾ litre of fish jelly with white wine; fennel leaves; olive oil; vinegar.* Cooking time: 7 to 8 minutes.

Fillet the trout, poach them, scarcely covered in a court-bouillon with white wine. Allow to cool in the cooking liquor. Take them out, skin them, sponge carefully. Pour a little jelly into a large oval earthenware dish and, as soon as set, arrange the fillets on it slantwise. Garnish in the middle, lengthwise, with tomato quarters, and, on both sides, with alternate crayfish tails and asparagus tips, previously marinated with salt, pepper, oil and vinegar, and well drained. Decorate with very green fennel leaves. Cover all with light, clear and tasty half-set jelly. Serve a Chantilly sauce separately (optional). *(Germany.)*

Truite à la juive en gelée

For 6 persons: *6 trout, each 200 to 225 gr.; court-bouillon with Chablis; tarragon leaves; chervil leaves; white of egg; gelatine.* Cooking time: 8 to 10 minutes.

Poach the trout gently in the court-bouillon. Drain them, allow to cool. Make a jelly with the court-bouillon. Remove the skin of the trout carefully, decorate sparingly with, for example, tarragon leaves, white of egg, and chervil leaves. Arrange the trout in a hollow dish, mask completely with a very clear and very good jelly. *(France.)*

Truite saumonée en bellevue

Salmon-trout

Proceed as for the preparation of Saumon en bellevue, choosing for preference whole trout of 2 to 2 kg. 500. *(See page 422.)*
(See illustration, page 230, and Culinary Technique page 87.)

Truite saumonée farcie Nova Scotia

Stuffed salmon trout Nova Scotia

For 6 persons: *1 salmon-trout of 1 kg. 500; 125 gr. smoked salmon; 150 gr. of pike flesh; 2 whites of egg; 3 dl. fresh cream; 1 dl. white wine; fish stock; 1 bunch of dill; 16 gelatine leaves; stuffed olives; 4 dl. sauce verte.* Cooking time: 15 to 20 minutes.

Scale the salmon-trout, gut and wash it, cut off the head and the tip of the tail, remove all bones. Prepare a stuffing with the smoked salmon and the pike flesh, incorporating 1 white of egg, work up with the cream, and season. Stuff the trout with this mixture. Tie it up in a cloth as for a galantine, poach it gently in a fish stock; allow it to cool in it. Prepare some jelly with 1 litre of white stock clear of fat and the gelatine; clarify with the white of an egg; correct seasoning and consistency; pass through a cloth and add the white wine. Drain the trout well, remove the cloth from the fish, and cut the fish into slices of 2 cm. Decorate with dill leaves and stuffed olives; glaze with the jelly. Arrange the slices on a serving dish garnished with diced jelly. Serve the sauce verte separately. *(United States.)*

Mousse de truite saumonée

Proceed as for the preparation Mousse de saumon. *(See page 423.)*

Truite saumonée norvégienne

Proceed as for the preparation Saumon norvégienne. *(See page 424.)*

Truite saumonée, Ondines de

For 6 persons: *600 gr. salmon-trout mousse; 120 gr. picked shrimp tails; 24 large prawns; ¾ litre very good fish jelly with white wine; chervil leaves.*

Coat generously with trout mousse some hinged egg shape moulds. Garnish the centres with a few shrimp tails. Close the moulds, allow to cool. Turn out the ondines; arrange them in a deep silver dish on a bed of half-set jelly. Between each place two prawns with only the tails shelled, cover all, gradually, with layers of half-set jelly and chervil leaves between each layer. The ondines must be completely covered; the jelly must be light, clear and of very good quality. *(France.)*

Salmon Trout "Penatang"

Fillet four large Dover soles, trim them and spread with a fish farce. Roll into paupiettes and cook in fish stock and white wine. When cold, cut each paupiette into roundels of about 1 cm. thick and spread each with a little fish farce on either side. Egg and breadcrumb and fry in clarified butter. Cut ten egg-plants into roundels of 1½ cm. in thickness, pass through flour and pancake batter containing a little paprika pepper and sauté them in clarified butter. Remove the backbone of a salmon-trout weighing about 1 kg. 500 by incising along each side of the backbone and sliding the knife against the bone from head to tail, lifting the fillet at the same time towards the stomach of the salmon-trout. Break off the backbone carefully at the head and the tail and discard. Wash carefully and discard black tissue and blood and other intestinal matter. Season the fish with salt and milled pepper and pass through flour. Cook the fish meunière style and arrange on a large oval silver dish. Garnish the centre of the fish with overlapping roundels of the sole and egg-plant. Surround with spoon-cut balls of cucumber cooked in butter and lightly sprinkled with mixed spice. Sprinkle with lemon juice and chopped parsley and mask with foaming beurre noisette. The above recipe was created by Mr. John Bongers, ex-Chef de Cuisine and a Governor of the Academy of Chefs, in London.

Shellfish (Crustacés)

Hot Dishes

Bordure des pêcheurs

Fischbordure Trianon—Speciality of the Restaurant Trianon, Stockholm

For 6 persons: *lining-paste made of 150 gr. flour, 150 gr. butter, 5 cl. water, 1 pinch of salt; 1 small coarsely shredded lettuce; 125 gr. Emmentaler cheese, cut into dice; 200 gr. flaked cooked salmon; 200 gr. picked shrimp tails; 20 poached and bearded mussels; 20 cooked mushrooms, cut into four; 2 soup-spoonfuls of chopped dill; 1 soup-spoonful of chopped parsley; a royale of 4 eggs; 4 dl. cream or milk; salt; paprika; ½ litre sauce hollandaise; 1 small spoonful of chopped truffle; 75 gr. butter.* Cooking time: about 30 minutes.

Line evenly a savarin mould with a fine layer of paste; allow to stand in the cold for half an hour. Trim and level off. Sprinkle the lettuce on the bottom and garnish the mould with alternate layers of cheese, salmon, shrimps, mussels, mushrooms. Incorporate the dill with the royale; pour into the mould. Cook au bain-marie until the paste is coloured and the royale set. Allow to stand for a few minutes. Turn out on a round dish. Melt the butter, mix it with parsley and a few drops of hot water, and pour around the bordure. In the centre pour a few spoonfuls of sauce hollandaise and sprinkle with parsley. Serve the rest of the sauce, mixed with the truffle, separately. *(Sweden.)*

Crab and Dressed Crab

For cooking crab and the preparation of dressed crab, see page 449.

Crabe bretonne

For 6 persons: *2 crabs each about 1 kg.; 3 chopped shallots; 150 gr. chopped raw mushrooms; 1 dl. white wine; 4 dl. béchamel sauce; 50 gr. butter; 50 gr. grated cheese; bouquet garni.* Cooking time: 45 minutes.

Cook the crabs, extract the meat and flake it, retain the creamy parts. Prepare a reduction of white wine with mushrooms and the bouquet garni. Remove the bouquet garni, add 15 cl. of béchamel sauce, the crabmeat and the creamy parts. Allow to simmer for 5 to 6 minutes, season, and butter lightly. Garnish the shells with this mixture, mask with béchamel sauce, and sprinkle with grated cheese, and brown. *(France.)*

Curried crab with rice

Ingredients: *450 gr. crabmeat; 50 gr. shallots; 50 gr. onion; 100 gr. mushrooms; 450 gr. tomatoes, skinned and pipped; 225 gr. rice; 25 gr. curry powder; 100 gr. butter; ½ litre fish stock; bouquet garni.*

Sweat the finely chopped shallots and onion in the butter, add the curry powder and cook for 3 minutes. Add the picked rice, blend together, moisten with fish stock and add the bouquet garni and seasoning. Cover with a buttered paper and lid and simmer on the side of the stove for approximately 18 minutes. Remove the bouquet garni. Meanwhile, slice the peeled and washed mushrooms, and sweat in a little butter for 3 minutes. Add the diced tomato flesh and cook for 3 minutes. Fork into the prepared rice together with the re-heated, seasoned crabmeat. Correct seasoning. The crabmeat is re-heated in a buttered sauteuse covered with a buttered greaseproof paper, and passed through the oven. Serve in a timbale.

Crab diable I

Devilled crab

For 6 persons: *3 crabs each of 700 gr.; 100 gr. chopped onion; 3 dl. sauce béchamel; 1 coffee-spoonful of mustard; Worcestershire sauce; Chili sauce; Cayenne pepper; 75 gr. butter; brown bread-crumbs.* Cooking time: 25 minutes.

Cook the crabs, extract the meat. Colour the chopped onion in 50 gr. of butter, add the flaked crabmeat, allow to cook for a moment. Bind with béchamel, season strongly with mustard, a few drops of Worcestershire sauce, chili sauce, and a pinch of Cayenne pepper. Garnish the shells with this mixture, sprinkle with breadcrumbs and with melted butter, and brown. *(France.)*

Crab diable II

Ingredients: *4½ kg. crab in shell, or 900 gr. crab-meat; 100 gr. onions; 50 gr. shallots; 100 gr. butter; ¼ litre béchamel sauce; 50 gr. brandy; 50 gr. French mustard (or 12 gr. English mustard—pre-pared with salt and cayenne).*

Finely chop the shallots and onions and heat in the butter. Swill the pan with the brandy, de-glaze and add the mustard and béchamel sauce. Fold in the crabmeat lightly, mix and season well. Serve in the crab shells. This dish may be browned after sprinkling with white crumbs and melted butter. Individual portions may be served in fireproof eared dishes. Rice pilaf or brown bread and butter may be served as an accompaniment.

Crab guadeloupéene

For 6 persons: *600 gr. of cooked crabmeat; 6 crab-shells or 6 scollop shells; 220 gr. butter; 125 gr. fresh white breadcrumbs; 3 chopped cloves of garlic; 2 chopped shallots; 3 sieved yolks of hard-boiled eggs; 1 small spoonful of dry mustard; 20 gr. paprika; 3 small coffee-spoonfuls of chopped parsley; brown breadcrumbs; Worcestershire sauce.* Cooking time: about 15 minutes.

Flake the crabmeat, rejecting the cartilaginous parts. Heat 70 gr. butter, add garlic and shallot, allow to cook for 1 minute without colouration. Add the fresh white breadcrumbs, and the mustard, work well with a spatula, and allow to stand for 10 minutes. Incorporate the crabmeat, the hard-boiled eggs and parsley. Season with paprika, a pinch of salt, a pinch of Cayenne pepper, a few drops of Worcestershire sauce. Add 120 gr. butter, and work this mixture with a spatula until it is very smooth. Fill the crab-shells or scollop-shells with this mixture, smooth into a dome-shape, sprinkle with breadcrumbs and melted butter, and brown in a hot oven. Serve quarters of lemon separately. *(Guadeloupe.)*

Crab indienne

For 6 persons: *2 crabs each of 1 kg.; 4 dl. curry sauce; 200 gr. cooked rice; 1 dl. coconut milk; 50 gr. butter.* Cooking time: 45 minutes.

Cook the crabs, extract the meat and the creamy parts, and retain the shells. Flake the meat and moisten with the coconut milk and 2 dl. of curry sauce. Allow to simmer for 8 to 10 minutes. Pound the creamy parts and incorporate them in the butter, pass through a hair sieve, and add the rest of the curry sauce. Garnish the shells with the crabmeat, and mask with sauce. *(International cookery.)*

Crab à la King

Ingredients: *900 gr. crabmeat; 225 gr. sliced mushrooms; 4 green pimentoes; 2 red pimentoes; 50 gr. finely-chopped shallots; 6 egg yolks; ½ litre cream; 50 gr. butter; whisky (or sherry); Worcester-shire sauce.*

Skin the pimentoes if fresh, and remove the seeds; cut into a julienne. Melt the butter, sweat the shallot and when soft add the mush-rooms and pimentoes. Cook for a few minutes until tender, then add the prepared crabmeat, moisten with the whisky and allow to cook gently. Make a liaison with the yolks of egg and cream. When the whisky has been reduced sufficiently, pour the liaison over the crabmeat and toss over and over until the sauce thickens without boiling. Season well, adding a little Worcestershire sauce. Serve accompanied by a rice pilaf. A trellis of red pimento may be placed across the crabmeat before serving.

Crab Mornay

For 6 persons: *6 small crabs; 4 dl. Mornay sauce; 50 gr. grated cheese; 50 gr. butter; brown breadcrumbs.* Cooking time: 20 minutes.

Cook the crabs, extract the meat and the creamy parts and pound them with a little butter. Pass through a hair sieve. Mix the flaked meat with half the sauce and garnish the shells with it, mask with Mornay sauce to which the creamy parts have been added, sprinkle with grated cheese, and brown breadcrumbs and melted butter. Brown in a hot oven. *(France.)*

Coquille de crabe Mornay

For 6 persons: *600 gr. cooked crabmeat; 4 dl. Mornay sauce; 50 gr. grated cheese; 50 gr. butter; 300 gr. pommes duchesse mixture.* Cooking time: 5 to 6 minutes.

Heat the flaked crabmeat in the butter. Border 6 scollop-shells with pommes duchesse mixture, mask the bottom of each shell with a soup-spoonful of Mornay sauce. Garnish with the crabmeat, mask with Mornay sauce, sprinkle with grated cheese and melted butter. Brown in a hot oven. *(France.)*

Pilaf de crabe

For 6 persons: *600 gr. cooked crabmeat; 4 dl. shrimp sauce; 300 gr. rice pilaf; 50 gr. butter.* Preparation: 10 minutes.

Flake the meat, heat it in butter. Add the creamy parts passed through a hair sieve, bind with 15 cl. shrimp sauce. Line a savarin mould with alternate layers of rice and crab, finishing the top layer with rice. Turn out on a round dish and surround with a cordon of shrimp sauce. Serve the rest of the sauce separately. *(International cookery.)*

Crab portugaise

For 6 persons: *500 gr. cooked crabmeat; 50 gr. chopped onion; 150 gr. minced raw mushrooms; 150 gr. tomatoes, skinned, pipped and diced; 1 soup-spoonful of chopped parsley; 2 dl. tomato sauce; 75 gr. butter; brown breadcrumbs.* Cooking time: 20 minutes.

Stew the chopped onion in butter. Add the minced mushrooms and tomatoes, skinned, pipped and diced; allow to cook for 6 or 7 minutes. Incorporate the flaked crabmeat, bind with the boiling tomato sauce, and adjust the seasoning and consistency. Pour into a buttered gratinating dish. Sprinkle with breadcrumbs mixed with chopped parsley and melted butter, and brown in the oven.

Crabe géant Onondaga

Crabmeat Onondaga

For 6 persons: *750 to 900 gr. of crabmeat; 2 chopped shallots; 2 cl. whisky; 2 cl. cognac; 3 dl. fresh cream; 4 egg yolks; 750 gr. pommes duchesse mixture; 1 very small chopped truffle; 4 chopped cooked mushrooms; 75 gr. butter; 40 gr. grated cheese; lemon juice.* Cooking time: about 20 minutes.

Colour the chopped shallot in butter, add the flaked crabmeat and sauté lightly. Flame with the whisky and cognac, season with salt, pepper, paprika and lemon juice. Reduce almost completely the cooking liquor. Prepare a liaison with the yolks of egg and cream, mix it with the crabmeat. Re-heat gently and take care that the mixture does not come to the boil. Mix truffle and mushrooms with the pommes duchesse mixture and, with this, edge a buttered oval gratinating dish, using the piping-bag and star tube. Fill the dish with the crabmeat preparation, sprinkle with grated cheese and melted butter. Brown in a hot oven or under the salamander. *(United States.)*

Shrimps

Shrimps are often sold ready cooked. Live shrimps are cooked in well-salted boiling water to which pepper and a bouquet garni have been added. The cooking time is 8 to 10 minutes, according to the size of the shrimps. Drain but do not refresh. *(See Description of Crustacés p. 37.)*

Pilaf de crevettes américaine

Proceed as for the preparation Pilaf de crevettes au curry, replacing the curry sauce with a sauce américaine.

Feuilleté de crevettes cardinal

For 6 persons: *600 gr. picked shrimps; 2 dl. fresh cream; 1 dl. fish stock; 50 gr. crayfish butter; 3 soup-spoonfuls sauce hollandaise; 2 soup-spoonfuls of whipped cream; 2 dl. dry white wine; 5 dl. cognac; 25 gr. beurre manié; 6 small oval or fish-shaped vol-au-vent cases.* Cooking time: 15 minutes.

Toss the shrimps in the crayfish butter, flame in the cognac, de-glaze with the white wine. Allow to cook gently for 5 minutes, and remove the shrimps and keep hot. Add to the de-glazing the fish stock and the fresh cream, reduce by a quarter and bind with the beurre manié. Put the shrimps back in the sauce and add whipped cream and sauce hollandaise, stir to bind well, and adjust the seasoning and consistency. Fill the vol-au-vent cases with the shrimps. Serve very hot. *(Switzerland.)*
(See illustration, page 213.)

Coquilles de crevettes

For 6 persons: *600 gr. picked shrimps; 4 dl. white wine sauce; 8 slices of truffle; 300 gr. pommes duchesse mixture.* Cooking time: 7 to 8 minutes.

Border 6 scollop shells with the pommes duchesse mixture. Mask the bottom of each shell with a soup-spoonful of white wine sauce, garnish with shrimp tails lightly bound with the same sauce. Place a slice of truffle in the centre, mask with white wine sauce and glaze. *(France.)*

Pilaf de crevettes au curry

For 6 persons: *600 gr. picked shrimps; 300 gr. rice; ½ coffee-spoonful of curry powder; 3 dl. curry sauce; 30 gr. butter.* Cooking time: 10 minutes.

Heat the shrimp tails and bind them with about 1 dl. of curry sauce. Butter the bottom and sides of a timbale with rice pilaf, previously cooked and seasoned with curry. Fill the centre with shrimps and cover over with rice pilaf. Turn out on a round dish and surround with a cordon of curry sauce. *(International cookery.)*
(See illustration, page 442.)

Fried shrimps I

For 6 persons: *600 gr. picked shrimps; olive oil; 300 gr. cooked buttered rice (optional); parsley.* Cooking time: 4 to 6 minutes.

Sauté the shrimps in the oil. Drain them, sprinkle with salt mixed with a pinch of Cayenne pepper. Garnish with parsley. Serve the buttered rice separately.

Fried shrimps II

For 6 persons: *600 gr. picked shrimps; parsley; ½ litre batter.* Cooking time: 6 to 7 minutes.

Pass the shrimps in a light batter and fry them in very hot frying-fat. Arrange on a serviette with fried parsley. Serve a tomato sauce separately (optional). *(International cookery.)*

Coquilles de crevettes Gustave

For 6 persons: *400 gr. picked shrimps; 150 gr. green asparagus tips; 50 gr. truffle; 300 gr. pommes duchesse mixture; 4 dl. Mornay sauce; 50 gr. butter.* Cooking time: 10 minutes.

Edge silver or porcelain shells with pommes duchesse mixture. Heat the asparagus, cut into small dice, and the truffle en julienne in butter. Garnish the bottom of each shell with a soup-spoonful of this mixture. Place the shrimp tails, heated in butter, on them. Mask with Mornay sauce, and glaze. *(France.)*

Crevettes indienne

For 6 persons: *600 gr. picked shrimps; 50 gr. chopped onion; 50 gr. butter; 3 dl. fish velouté; 5 cl. fresh cream; ½ coffee-spoonful of curry powder; 300 gr. saffroned rice (riz à l'indienne).* Cooking time: 10 minutes.

Stew the chopped onion in butter. Add the curry powder and the shrimps, allow to simmer for a moment. Incorporate the skimmed velouté and allow to cook for 2 to 3 minutes; arrange in a timbale. Serve the saffroned rice separately. Variation: Arrange the shrimps on a bed of saffroned rice. *(International cookery.)*
(See illustration, page 210.)

Bordure de riz aux crevettes et aux morilles

For 6 persons: *250 gr. rice; 6 dl. white stock; 50 gr. grated Parmesan; 2 chopped shallots; 600 gr. fresh morels or 1½ tins of preserved morels; 4 dl. fresh cream; 400 gr. fresh picked shrimps or 200 gr. frozen shrimps; 12 very small whiting fillets; 150 gr. butter; 3 cl. sherry; 1 coffee-spoonful of curry; parsley; flour; 3 dl. tomato sauce.* Cooking time for the rice: 16 to 18 minutes.

Cook the rice in the white stock and bind it with butter and Parmesan. Press it into a buttered savarin or ring mould. Mince the morels coarsely and blanch them for 1 minute; drain and press them. Colour them in butter with the shallot. Moisten with the cream, season, allow to reduce a little, bind with a spoonful of beurre manié, and add the sherry. If frozen shrimps are used dip them in tepid water, drain, press, heat in butter but without allowing them to dry out, season with the curry. Roll the whiting fillets into paupiettes held with a cocktail stick, season and flour them, and cook in hot deep frying fat. Fry the parsley. Turn the rice ring on to a round dish, fill the centre with the morels. Arrange the shrimps on top, garnish around the ring with the paupiettes and the fried parsley. Serve the tomato sauce separately. *(Sweden.)*

Coquilles de crevettes Mornay

For 6 persons: *600 gr. picked shrimps; 4 dl. Mornay sauce; 300 gr. pommes duchesse mixture; 50 gr. butter; 50 gr. grated cheese.* Cooking time: 10 minutes.

Edge six scollop shells with pommes duchesse mixture. Mask the bottom of each shell with a soup-spoonful of Mornay sauce, add the shrimps previously heated in butter, and mask with Mornay sauce, sprinkle with grated cheese and glaze. *(France.)*

Pilaf de crevettes Nantua

Proceed as for the preparation Pilaf de crevettes au curry, replacing the curry sauce by a sauce Nantua.

Pilaf de crevettes orientale

For 6 persons: *600 gr. picked shrimps; 300 gr. rice; 3 dl. white wine sauce; 100 gr. skinned, pipped and diced tomatoes; a pinch of saffron; 50 gr. butter.* Cooking time: 10 minutes.

Stew the tomatoes in butter, mix them with the rice pilaf flavoured with saffron. Line a buttered timbale with rice, fill the centre with the shrimps bound with the white wine sauce. Cover over with rice, turn out on a dish. Surround with a cordon of white wine sauce. *(France.)*

Crevettes sautées New Orleans

Jumbo prawns New Orleans style

For 6 persons: *1 kg. 200 of picked raw jumbo prawns; 125 gr. minced onion; 500 gr. tomatoes, skinned, pipped and diced; ¼ litre white wine; ¾ litre fish stock; ¼ litre olive oil; 4 cl. whisky; the juice of one lemon; 30 gr. flour.* Cooking time: 15 to 20 minutes.

Sauté for 2 minutes the shelled prawns in very hot oil to colour them lightly. Retain the oil, flame the shrimps in the whisky, de-glaze with the white wine. Add half the fish stock and bring to the boil. Colour the minced onion in the oil which has been retained, sprinkle with flour; stir all, and cook for 2 minutes; add the diced tomatoes. Moisten with the remainder of the fish stock, bring to the boil and simmer for 2 minutes. Add the prawns, and season with salt, pepper, a pinch of Cayenne pepper and lemon juice. Allow to simmer until the prawns are cooked. Dress in a timbale. Serve a rice pilaf separately. *(United States.)*

Crayfish

Crayfish used in most of the following recipes are about 80 gr. in weight, and crayfish used for garnishing about 60 gr. Before every preparation the crayfish must be washed and gutted. The operation consists of taking out the intestine by seizing it with the point of a small knife through the opening to be found under the median phalanx and withdrawing it gently in order not to break it. To leave this appendix in would give the crayfish a bitter taste. In Germany and in several European countries it is forbidden to gut or sauté live crayfish. They must be thrown into boiling salt water for a moment to kill them before preparation.

Mousseline d'écrevisses Alexandra

For 6 persons: *700 gr. of crayfish mousseline; 12 small slices of truffle; 12 very small crayfish tails; 75 gr. butter; 4 dl. Mornay sauce; 250 gr. green asparagus tips, or 300 gr. extra fine peas.* Cooking time: about 15 minutes.

Butter 12 shallow dariole moulds, garnish the bottom with a roundel of truffle and two half-tails of crayfish. Fill the moulds to the top with mousseline, poach in the oven au bain-marie without boiling. Turn out in a crown on a round gratinating dish, mask the quenelles with Mornay sauce, and glaze. Garnish the centre of the dish with asparagus tips bound with butter or, if out of season, with buttered peas. *(France.)*

Queues d'écrevisses à l'aneth

For 6 persons: *36 large crayfish; ½ a bottle of white wine; 1 onion stuck with a small bayleaf and 2 cloves; 1 small bunch of dill; 60 gr. butter; 35 gr. flour; ¼ litre sauce hollandaise; 1 soup-spoonful of chopped dill.* Cooking time: 10 minutes.

Prepare a court-bouillon with two-thirds of water and one-third of white wine, the studded onion, the bunch of dill and very little salt.

Brush and wash the crayfish, put them in the boiling court-bouillon and just cook them. Allow them to cool before shelling them. Break the large claws and extract the meat. Pass the court-bouillon, reduce it by one-quarter, bind it with a white roux made with 50 gr. butter and flour, and allow this sauce to cook for 10 to 12 minutes. Pass through a tammy cloth, work up with the sauce hollandaise, add the chopped dill previously passed through butter. Bind the crayfish tails with the sauce, sprinkle with chopped dill. Serve a creole rice separately. *(Germany.)*

Ecrevisses bordelaise

For 6 persons: *36 crayfish; 100 gr. mirepoix bordelaise; 3 dl. white wine; 1 dl. fish stock; 1 dl. fish velouté; 1 coffee-spoonful of meat-glaze; 150 gr. butter; 5 cl. cognac; chopped parsley.* Cooking time: 15 minutes.

Sauté the crayfish and the mirepoix bordelaise in butter until the shells are very red. Flame in the cognac, moisten with the white wine, reduce by one-third. Adjust with the fish stock and the velouté, cook, covered, for 10 minutes; arrange the crayfish en timbale. Reduce the sauce, add the meat-glaze, work up with 100 gr. butter, finish with the chopped parsley, pour over the crayfish. *(France.)*

Coquilles d'écrevisses cardinal

For 6 persons: *36 shelled crayfish claws and tails; 3 dl. sauce cardinal; 300 gr. pommes duchesse mixture; 6 slices of truffle; 30 gr. butter; 1 egg yolk.* Cooking time: 6 to 7 minutes.

Edge some silver or porcelain scollop shells with a border of pommes duchesse mixture, using a piping-bag and star tube. Brush with beaten egg and glaze golden. Heat the claws and tails in butter. Garnish each scollop shell with 6 tails and 12 claws. Mask with sauce cardinal; place a slice of truffle in the centre. *(France.)*

Queues d'écrevisses à la crème au xérès

For 6 persons: *36 large crayfish; ½ litre béchamel; 1 dl. fresh cream; 5 dl. dry sherry; 2 soup-spoonfuls of mirepoix bordelaise; 150 gr. butter; 3 cl. cognac; 2 dl. dry white wine; white stock.* Cooking time: 12 minutes.

Put the crayfish in boiling water, take them out after 3 minutes, drain them, gut them. Colour lightly the mirepoix in butter, add the crayfish, flame in cognac, de-glaze with white wine, season, add the white stock just to cover. Cook for 6 minutes covered. Shell claws and tails. Pound one-third of the shells with 50 gr. butter to make crayfish butter. Pass the cooking liquor and reduce it to one-quarter. Incorporate the stock and the rest of the pounded shells with the béchamel and cook gently for 20 minutes to obtain a smooth thick sauce. Pass at first through a strainer and then a tammy cloth. Add the sherry to the sauce, bring to the boil, bind with cream, adjust the seasoning and consistency. Heat again the tails and claws in half the crayfish butter; add the sauce. Arrange en timbale and sprinkle with the crayfish butter. Serve with creole rice. *(Germany.)*

Ecrevisses danoise

For 6 persons: *4 to 5 dozen live crayfish; 50 gr. caraway; 4 bunches of dill.* Cooking time: 8 to 10 minutes.

Prepare a court-bouillon with lightly-salted water, caraway and dill; put in the crayfish, previously washed and drained. Cover and allow to cook for 8 to 10 minutes. Arrange en timbale with the cooking liquor. Serve with bread and butter. *(Denmark.)*

Soufflé d'écrevisses florentine

For 4 to 6 persons: *75 gr. flour; 3 dl. boiled milk; 50 gr. butter; 70 gr. grated cheese; 2 soup-spoonfuls of crayfish coulis; 24 small shelled crayfish tails; 12 slices of truffle; 4 eggs.* Cooking time: 20 to 25 minutes.

Melt the butter and incorporate the flour, adding immediately the hot milk. Work with a whisk until coming to the boil for the first time. Add, away from the fire, the coulis or a purée of crayfish, the grated cheese, 4 egg yolks; season and mix well. Incorporate the 4 firmly-beaten egg whites. Arrange in a buttered timbale. The filling should be made in alternate layers of crayfish tails and slices of truffle. Cook in a moderate oven. *(France.)*

Ecrevisses Georgette

For 6 persons: *6 large potatoes of even shape and size; 36 shelled crayfish tails; 4 dl. thick sauce Nantua; 50 gr. butter; 50 gr. grated cheese.* Cooking time: 10 minutes.

Bake the potatoes in the oven in advance. Remove one-third from the top of the cooked potato and scoop out most of the pulp leaving a strong shell. Pass the crayfish tails through butter for a moment and bind them with a little sauce Nantua and garnish the potato shells with the salpicon. Mask with sauce Nantua, sprinkle with grated cheese and melted butter, and brown. Arrange on a serviette. *(France.)*

Gratin d'écrevisses

For 6 persons: *36 crayfish; 250 gr. duxelles (dry); 3 dl. white wine; 3 dl. half-glaze; 50 gr. butter; 400 gr. pommes duchesse mixture; ½ a bayleaf; 1 sprig of thyme; 1 coffee-spoonful of chopped parsley; brown breadcrumbs.* Cooking time: 20 minutes.

Sauté the crayfish in butter until the shells are very red. Moisten with white wine, add thyme and bayleaf, salt sparingly and cook, covered, for 10 minutes. Remove the crayfish and shell them, keep them hot with a little stock. Reduce the cooking liquor by half, pass, incorporate the duxelles and the half-glaze. Allow to cook for another moment, add the chopped parsley, and adjust the seasoning and consistency. Edge a gratinating dish with pommes duchesse mixture, pour a little sauce on the bottom and place the crayfish tails on top. Mask with sauce, sprinkle with breadcrumbs and melted butter, and brown in a hot oven. *(France.)*

Ecrevisses liégeoise

Proceed as for the preparation Ecrevisses à la nage. Arrange en timbale. Pass the cooking liquor and reduce by three-quarters, work up with 75 to 100 gr. of butter, pour on the crayfish, and sprinkle with chopped parsley. *(France.)*

Ecrevisses Magenta

For 6 persons: *36 crayfish; 100 gr. mirepoix bordelaise; 3 dl. white wine; 5 cl. olive oil; 50 gr. butter; 1 coffee-spoonful of chopped parsley; 100 gr. tomatoes, skinned, pipped and diced; basil.* Cooking time: 15 minutes.

Sauté the crayfish in the oil until the shells turn red. Season, moisten with white wine, add the diced tomatoes and the chopped parsley, cook for 10 minutes, covered. Remove the crayfish and arrange them en timbale. Complete the cooking with 50 gr. of butter and a pinch of basil and pour over the crayfish. *(France.)*

Ecrevisses marinière

For 6 persons: *36 crayfish; 3 dl. white wine; 3 dl. fish velouté; 1 sprig of thyme; 1 small bayleaf; 50 gr. butter; 1 coffee-spoonful of chopped parsley.* Cooking time: 15 minutes.

Cook, covered, for 10 minutes, the crayfish in the white wine with thyme and bayleaf. Drain and arrange en timbale. Pass the cooking liquor, reduce by three-quarters; add the velouté and allow to cook for a moment. Work up with butter, pour over the crayfish and sprinkle with chopped parsley. *(France.)*

Ecrevisses à la nage

For 6 persons: *36 crayfish; a brunoise of: 50 gr. carrot; 50 gr. onion; 6 parsley stalks; chopped shallots; thyme; bayleaf; 3 dl. white wine; 2 dl. fish stock; 50 gr. butter.* Cooking time: 10 minutes.

Prepare in advance a court-bouillon with the brunoise of vegetables, shallots, a pinch of thyme and a pinch of powdered bayleaf, white wine, fish stock, and a very little salt. Put the crayfish into the boiling court-bouillon, cook, covered, for 10 minutes, stirring from time to time. Arrange the crayfish en timbale, add the butter and a pinch of Cayenne pepper to the cooking liquor and pour it over the crayfish. *(France.)*

Queues d'écrevisses Nantua

For 6 persons: *36 shelled crayfish tails; 200 gr. cooked mushrooms; 24 small quenelles of fish; 12 slices of truffle; 50 gr. butter; 3 dl. sauce Nantua.* Cooking time: 10 minutes.

Pass the crayfish tails through the butter. Heat the mushrooms (cut into quarters) and the quenelles. Bind all with a little sauce Nantua; arrange en timbale. Mask with the rest of the sauce and garnish with slices of truffle. *(France.)*

Queues d'écrevisses norvégienne

For 6 persons: *6 dozen crayfish; 120 gr. butter; 1 dl. sherry; 4 dl. fresh cream; 2 soup-spoonfuls of chopped dill; 12 slices of truffle (optional); 1 small bunch of dill.* Cooking time: 10 minutes.

Cook the crayfish in the court-bouillon with the bunch of dill. Shell the tails. Sauté the tails for a moment in the noisette butter; de-glaze with the sherry, and reduce by half. Add the cream and the dill, season and cook for a few minutes. Arrange en timbale or in small individual fireproof cocottes; garnish with slices of truffle. Serve a rice pilaf separately. *(International cookery.)*

Timbale de queues d'écrevisses parisienne

For 6 persons: *36 shelled crayfish tails; 300 gr. cooked macaroni; 250 gr. raw mushrooms; 12 slices of truffle; 3 dl. sauce Nantua; 1 dl. fresh cream; 50 gr. crayfish butter; 50 gr. butter.* Cooking time: 10 minutes.

Bind the freshly-cooked macaroni with the crayfish butter and the cream. Arrange en timbale. Place the crayfish tails, bound with the sauce Nantua, on top. Cover with thick slices of mushroom, sautéd in butter, and with slices of truffle. *(France.)*

Risotto d'écrevisses

For 6 persons: *300 gr. risotto; 36 shelled crayfish tails; 4 dl. sauce Nantua; 1 coffee-spoonful of chopped truffle; 20 gr. butter; 25 gr. crayfish butter.* Cooking time for the risotto: 15 to 18 minutes.

Fill a buttered savarin mould with risotto. Turn out on a round dish. Heat lightly the crayfish tails in the crayfish butter. Bind with sauce Nantua. Garnish the centre of the ring mould, surround with the crayfish tails and sprinkle with chopped truffle. Serve the rest of the sauce separately. *(France.)*

Soufflé d'écrevisses Rothschild

Proceed as for the preparation Soufflé florentine, and add 50 to 75 gr. cooked green asparagus tips placed between layers of the soufflé mixture. *(France.)* *(See page 433.)*

Lobster

Lobsters are in season throughout the year, and are at their best during the summer months. They vary in weight and size; the usual size for catering purposes is 560 to 700 gr. giving half a lobster per person. Larger lobsters can be used for garnishes, sauces, and portioning, i.e. salads, cocktails and bouchées. They must be purchased alive whenever possible. Many preparations demand live lobsters. If purchased cooked, the source of supply must be beyond reproach. The lobsters should feel heavy in proportion to size and should be lively.

The hen lobster is distinguished by its broad tail; the first two feelers nearest the head are soft and covered with fine hairs. The cock lobster has a narrower tail and the first two feelers near the head are of a brittle shell. The lobsters should be cooked as soon as they are landed. Live lobsters are cooked in a boiling court-bouillon allowing 15 minutes to 450 gr. They can also be cooked from cold in a court-bouillon, bringing to the boil, and allowing 10 minutes boiling, and then they are cooled in the cooking liquor. The hen lobster is better for the making of sauces.

Homard américaine

For 6 persons: *3 live lobsters each of 600 gr.; 4 cl. cognac; 3 dl. white wine; 4 dl. fish stock; 5 cl. oil; 4 chopped shallots; 100 gr. tomato, skinned, pipped and diced; 2 soup-spoonfuls of tomato purée; 100 gr. butter; 1 coffee-spoonful of meat-glaze; 1 small crushed clove of garlic; 1 coffee-spoonful of chopped parsley, chervil and tarragon.* Cooking time: 25 minutes.

Sever the head from the trunk and cut the tail into tronçons, crack the claws to facilitate the extraction of the meat after cooking, and split the head in two lengthwise. Remove from the head and reject the sac containing sand. Retain the creamy parts and the coral. Heat in a plat à sauter the oil to which has been added 40 gr. butter. Sauté the lobster tronçons in this until the shell has taken a bright red colour. Drain the oil by tilting the pan while keeping the lid on. Flame in the cognac, moisten with white wine and fish stock, and add the chopped shallot, the skinned, pipped and diced tomato, the tomato purée, the garlic, the meat-glaze and a pinch of Cayenne pepper. Allow to cool with the cover on for 15 to 20 minutes. Remove the tronçons and extract the meat from them and from the claws. Arrange in a timbale; place the two halves of head on top. Reduce the cooking liquor by half, bind it with the creamy parts and the coral mixed with a little butter and cook for a moment. Pass through a fine strainer, heat without boiling and incorporate the rest of the butter. Adjust the seasoning and consistency and pour over the lobster. Sprinkle with chopped parsley, chervil and tarragon. Serve a pilaf of saffroned rice separately (optional). *(France.)*
(See Culinary Technique, page 96–98.)

Homard Auld Reekie

For 6 persons: *3 cooked lobsters each of 650 gr.; 150 gr. raw mushrooms; 60 gr. grated Cheddar cheese; 12 cl. double cream; 7 cl. Scotch whisky; 6 gr. powdered English mustard; 3 small tomatoes; leaf parsley.* Cooking time: 12 to 15 minutes.

Detach claws and legs, split the lobster, and break the claws. Extract the meat from the claws and from the body; cut it up into dice. Clean and dry the half-shells. Cut up the mushrooms into dice, and stew them in butter for 5 minutes. Add the lobster meat, moisten with the cream, and reduce by half. Incorporate the whisky and the diluted mustard. Allow to cook for a moment until the sauce coats the spoon. Adjust the seasoning and consistency. Fill the shells with this mixture. Place on top a few slices of tomato, sprinkle with grated Cheddar cheese, and glaze under the salamander. Arrange on a serviette with leaf parsley. *(Great Britain.)*

Homard bordelaise

For 6 persons: *3 live lobsters each of 600 gr.; 4 chopped shallots; 3 cl. oil; 100 gr. butter; 100 gr. mirepoix bordelaise; 4 cl. cognac; 2 dl. white wine; 2 dl. fish stock; 100 gr. tomatoes, skinned, pipped and diced; 1 crushed clove of garlic; 1 coffee-spoonful of meat-glaze; ½ lemon; 1 coffee-spoonful of chopped parsley.* Cooking time: 20 to 25 minutes.

Detach the claws and legs. Crack the claws and split the lobster lengthwise, reject the sand-sac, retain the creamy parts and the coral. Toss and colour the lobster in very hot oil and butter; season, flame in cognac, moisten with the white wine and fish stock. Add the tomato, skinned, pipped and diced, garlic, and meat-glaze. Cook for 15 minutes, covered with a lid. Remove the lobster, extract the meat from the claws and the tail and scollop them. Add the mirepoix bordelaise, prepared in advance, to the cooking liquor and the pieces of lobster, and heat to boiling point. Simmer for 4 to 5 minutes. Arrange the lobster en timbale. Reduce the cooking liquor, incorporate the creamy parts and the coral pounded with a little butter. Pass through a fine strainer. Reheat without allowing to boil, work up with the rest of the butter, adjust the seasoning and consistency, complete with a few drops of lemon juice, and pour over the lobster. Sprinkle with chopped parsley. *(France.)*

Homard cardinal

For 6 persons: *3 live lobsters each of 600 gr.; 200 gr. cooked mushrooms; 18 slices of truffle; 4 dl. sauce cardinal; 50 gr. grated cheese; leaf parsley.* Cooking time: 20 minutes.

Cook the lobsters in the court-bouillon. Detach claws and legs, and split the lobster in two lengthwise. Extract the meat from the claws and the tails, cut that of the claws into dice and that of the tails into scollops. Place the half-shells on a dish. Mask the bottom of each one with a spoonful of sauce cardinal; garnish with diced meat of the claws and the diced mushrooms. Arrange the scollops on top in an overlapping pattern, separated by slices of truffle. Mask with sauce cardinal, sprinkle with grated cheese, and brown in a hot oven. Arrange on a serviette with leaf parsley. *(France.)*

Homard Chantecler

For 6 persons: *3 lobsters each of 600 gr.; 2 dl. curry sauce; 2 dl. sauce Nantua; 200 gr. cooked rice; 6 turned heads of mushrooms; 6 shelled prawn tails; 6 coxcombs; 1 small coffee-spoonful of curry powder; 100 gr. butter.* Cooking time: about 20 minutes.

Detach claws and legs, and split the lobster in two lengthwise. Break the claws, sprinkle the meat of the tails with curry powder. Place tails and claws in a shallow stew-pan containing hot butter, colour on both sides, cover, and cook in the oven. Take out the lobster, and extract the meat. Scollop the meat from the tails and dice that from the claws. Mix the diced claw-meat with the rice and fill the half-shells with it. Place the scollops on top in an overlapping pattern. Mask with curry sauce mixed with sauce Nantua, and glaze. Decorate each half-shell with a coxcomb, a shelled prawn and a cooked turned mushroom. *(France.)*
(See illustration, page 444.)

Homard Churchill

For 6 persons: *3 lobsters each of 600 gr.; 150 gr. mustard butter; leaf parsley.* Cooking time: 20 minutes.

Detach legs and claws; split the tail in two lengthwise. Smear the meat of the tails with mustard butter seasoned with a pinch of Cayenne pepper. Cook in a moderate oven. Arrange on a dish surrounded by leaf parsley. *(International cookery.)*

Homard Clarence I

For 6 persons: *3 lobsters each of 600 g.; 200 gr. cooked rice; 18 slices of truffle; 4 dl. Mornay sauce.* Cooking time: 20 minutes.

Cook the lobsters in the court-bouillon. Split the tails in two lengthwise. Extract the meat and cut it into scollops. Two-thirds fill the shells with cooked rice. Arrange the scollops on top in an overlapping pattern, separated by slices of truffle. Mask with Mornay sauce and glaze, and garnish with fleurons. *(France.)*
(See illustration, page 441.)

Homard Clarence II

Proceed as for the preparation Homard Clarence I but replace the Mornay sauce by a creamed béchamel to which the creamy parts of the lobster have been added and condimented with curry. Do not glaze. *(France.)*

Côtelettes de homard

Lobster cutlets

For 6 persons: *300 gr. of cooked lobster meat; 200 gr. cooked diced mushrooms; 50 gr. truffle; 3 dl. fish velouté; 2 egg yolks; 50 gr. lobster butter; 2 eggs; fresh white breadcrumbs; parsley.* Cooking time: 5 to 6 minutes.

Prepare a salpicon with the lobster meat, mushrooms and truffle. Bind it on full heat with the reduced velouté and the egg yolks; complete the liaison with the lobster butter, and allow to cool. Mould in the shape of cutlets of about 75 gr.; egg and breadcrumb and insert a small piece of blanched macaroni to represent the cutlet bone. Fry in hot deep fat. Add a cutlet-frill to each cutlet; arrange on a serviette with fried parsley. Serve a suitable sauce separately. *(France.)*

Homard à la crème

Creamed lobster

For 6 persons: *3 live lobsters each of 600 gr.; 4 cl. cognac; 4 dl. fresh cream; 2 small fresh or preserved peeled truffles; 60 gr. butter; 1 soup-spoonful of pale meat glaze; ½ a lemon.* Cooking time: 18 to 20 minutes.

Cut up the lobsters as for the preparation Homard américaine. Sauté in the butter until the shells turn bright red. Season, flame in the cognac, moisten with the cream, add the sliced truffle and allow to cook gently. Remove, extract the meat from the tronçons and claws, and arrange en timbale with the truffle slices. Reduce the cooking liquor by a quarter, add the meat-glaze and a few drops of lemon juice, and adjust the seasoning and consistency. Pass the sauce and pour it on to the lobster. *(France.)*

Homard au curry

Curried lobster

For 6 persons: *750 gr. cooked lobster meat; 4 dl. curry sauce; 300 gr. rice (cooked Indian way); 40 gr. butter.* Cooking time: 6 to 7 minutes.

Cut up the lobster meat into scollops and heat in the butter. Bind with curry sauce and arrange in a timbale. Serve the saffroned rice separately. *(International cookery.)*

Homard Dumas

For 6 persons: *3 lobsters each of 600 gr.; 1 dl. white wine; 3 dl. half-glaze; 1 soup-spoonful of tomato purée; 60 gr. butter; 12 small fleurons.* Cooking time: 20 to 25 minutes

Cook the lobsters in a court-bouillon. Remove them and extract the meat from the tails and claws. Cut it into scollops. Sauté the scollops in the butter, season with salt and a pinch of Cayenne pepper, moisten with the white wine, and reduce by three-quarters. Add the tomato purée and the half-glaze, bring to the boil two or three times, and arrange in a timbale. Surround with fleurons.

Homard Fra-Diavolo

For 6 persons: *600 gr. cooked lobster; 400 gr. tomatoes, skinned, pipped and diced; 30 gr. butter; 30 gr. chopped parsley; 1 large clove of garlic; 5 cl. olive oil; pepper; a little powdered sweet marjoram.* Cooking time: 25 minutes.

Cut the lobster in two lengthwise, leaving a half-shelled claw on each side. Arrange it on a gratinating dish. Heat lightly in the oven. Sauté the diced tomatoes and the garlic in the olive oil, adding the chopped parsley and the marjoram, then pour all over the lobster. Garnish with a bunch of parsley and quarters of lemon. Serve accompanied with rice pilaf. *(France.)*
(See illustration, page 408.)

Homard française

For 6 persons: *3 live lobsters each of 600 gr.; 100 gr. small carrots; 75 gr. small onions; 50 gr. chopped parsley; 1 dl. fish stock; 2 dl. fish velouté; 4 dl. cognac; 2 dl. white wine; 125 gr. butter.* Cooking time: 20 minutes.

Cut the tails into tronçons, and crack the claws. Sauté in clarified butter until the shells turn red. Season, flame in the cognac, moisten with the white wine, and add the carrots, minced onions (previously half-cooked in butter), chopped parsley and fish stock. Finish cooking with the lid on. Remove the pieces, extract the meat, arrange in a timbale. Reduce the cooking liquor, bind it with the velouté, butter lightly, adjust the seasoning and consistency, and pour over the lobster. *(France.)*

Grilled lobster I

For 6 persons: *3 live lobsters each of 600 gr.; 100 gr. butter; 3 dl. sauce diable; leaf parsley.* Cooking time: 20 minutes.

Detach the legs and claws and split the tail in two lengthwise. Season with salt mixed with a pinch of Cayenne pepper, sprinkle with melted butter, grill over moderate heat, sprinkling with butter from time to time. Break the claws to facilitate extraction of the meat. Arrange on a serviette and surround with leaf parsley. Serve the sauce diable or melted butter separately. Preferably, the lobsters should be three-quarters cooked in court-bouillon first and grilled afterwards. Treated in this way the lobster meat does not go hard as when it is grilled in a raw state. *(International cookery.)*

Grilled lobster II

Cut a live lobster in half lengthwise to provide two portions. Remove the pouch and season the flesh with salt and pepper after cracking the claws. Grill slowly on a moderate fire, brushing with melted butter from time to time. Serve on a dish paper garnished with picked parsley, and sauce diable served separately.

Grilled lobster III

Cook the lobster in a court-bouillon for 15 minutes, then cut in half and proceed as for II. This gives a less dry result.

Grilled lobster Glen Sannox

For 6 persons: *3 live lobsters each of 650 gr.; 75 gr. brown breadcrumbs; 75 gr. mustard butter; 5 cl. oil; 1 coffee-spoonful of chopped parsley; leaf parsley.* Cooking time: 25 minutes.

Cook the lobsters in salt water for 15 minutes. Drain them, and split them lengthwise while still hot. Smear the halves of the tails with mustard butter and sprinkle them with breadcrumbs mixed with chopped parsley. Sprinkle with a few drops of oil, pass through the oven for about 10 minutes at moderate heat. Arrange on a dish with leaf parsley. *(Great Britain.)*

Homard hollandaise

For 6 persons: *3 lobsters each of 600 gr.; 150 gr. melted butter or 3 dl. sauce hollandaise; 600 gr. fish potatoes; leaf parsley.* Cooking time: 15 to 18 minutes.

Cook the lobsters in a court-bouillon. Detach the claws and legs and split the lobsters in two lengthwise, to include one shelled claw on each half. Arrange on a serviette with leaf parsley and fish potatoes. Serve the melted butter or sauce hollandaise separately. *(France.)*

Homard hongroise

Proceed as for the preparation Homard Newburg, raw, without Marsala, but with the addition of 100 gr. chopped onion stewed in butter and a good coffee-spoonful of paprika. *(France.)* *(See page 439.)*

Pilaf de homard Hortense

For 6 persons: *3 live lobsters each of 600 gr.; 4 cl. whisky; ½ coffee-spoonful of chopped tarragon; 200 gr. cooked mushrooms; 2 dl. fish stock; 1 dl. white wine; 3 dl. sauce américaine; 1 dl. fresh cream; 300 gr. pilaf of rice; 50 gr. red peppers; 50 gr. very small green peas; 5 cl. oil; 5 gr. butter; 1 bunch mixed herbs; 1 gr. saffron.* Cooking time: 20 minutes.

Cut the lobsters into tronçons, sauté in oil with a nut of butter until the shells are red. Flame in the whisky, de-glaze with the white wine, season, moisten with the fish stock, add the bunch of mixed herbs; cook with the lid on. Extract the meat, cut it into large dice as well as the mushrooms. Keep hot, covered. Reduce the cooking liquor by three-quarters, add the cream, previously boiled, and allow to cook for a moment longer. Pass, add the sauce américaine, and incorporate the chopped tarragon. Cut the pepper into small dice and stew in butter. Cook the peas. Incorporate pepper and peas in the saffroned pilaf of rice. Fill the rice into a ring mould, level, and turn out on a round dish. Garnish the centre with the salpicon bound with the sauce. Serve the rest of the sauce separately. *(International cookery.)* *(See illustration, page 443; another presentation.)*

Homard Mornay

Proceed as for the preparation Homard cardinal, but replace the sauce cardinal by a Mornay sauce. *(France.)* *(See page 436.)*

Homard Newburg I, with raw lobster

For 6 persons: *1 kg. 800 of live lobsters; 100 gr. butter; 5 cl. oil; 3 cl. cognac; 2 dl. Marsala; 1 dl. fish stock; 4 dl. fresh cream.* Cooking time: 20 minutes.

Proceed as for the preparation Homard américaine. As soon as the shell is coloured, flame with the cognac, de-glaze with the Marsala. Reduce the wine by two-thirds, season, add the cream and the fish stock, and allow to cook for 15 minutes. Remove the tronçons and the claws, and extract the meat. Arrange in a timbale and keep hot. Bind the sauce with the creamy parts and the coral pounded with 50 gr. butter; allow to cook for a moment longer. Pass the sauce through a hair strainer, adjust the seasoning and consistency, heat without boiling, and pour over the lobster. Lobster Newburg, American in origin, is nearly always prepared with sherry and not Marsala in the United States. *(International cookery.)*

Homard Newburg II, with cooked lobster

For 6 persons: *1 kg. 800 of lobster; 50 gr. butter; 2 dl. Madeira; 4 dl. fresh cream; 4 egg yolks.* Cooking time: 20 minutes.

Cook the lobster in a court-bouillon. Extract the meat from the tail and cut it into even scollops. Arrange the scollops in a thickly-buttered shallow stew-pan and heat them on both sides, season sparingly with salt and a good pinch of paprika, moisten with the Madeira and reduce by three-quarters. At the moment of serving add a liaison of egg yolks and cream; heat without boiling until the cooking of the yolks is assured. Serve immediately in a double silver timbale, the base of which should contain very hot water.

Homard Palestine

For 6 persons: *1 kg. 800 of live lobster; 4 dl. fish stock; 200 gr. fine mirepoix; 5 cl. oil; 75 gr. butter; 3 cl. cognac; 4 dl. white wine; 3 dl. fish velouté; 300 gr. saffroned rice; 3 gr. curry powder.* Cooking time: 35 minutes.

Cut the lobster into tronçons and sauté in butter with 100 gr. mirepoix. Flame with the cognac, moisten with the white wine and fish stock, season, and allow to cook for 15 minutes. Shell, keep the meat hot in a covered stew-pan. Pound trunks and shells and toss in hot oil with the rest of the mirepoix, moisten with the lobster cooking liquor and cook for 15 minutes. Add the velouté, reduce, add the creamy parts and coral pounded with a little butter and the curry. Allow to cook for a moment longer. Pass through a fine conical strainer, heat without boiling, butter lightly, and adjust the seasoning and consistency. Arrange the lobster in the centre of a saffroned rice ring (using a ring mould), and mask with sauce. Serve the rest of the sauce separately. *(France.)*

Homard au Pernod

For 6 persons: *3 live lobsters each of 600 gr.; 120 gr. butter; 15 cl. olive oil; 30 gr. chopped onion; 3 chopped shallots; 1 small diced carrot; 1 small crushed clove of garlic; 1 bouquet garni; 50 gr. tomato purée; 2 tomatoes, skinned, pipped and diced; 2 dl. dry white wine; 3 cl. cognac; 6 dl. fish stock; 15 cl. fresh cream; the juice of half a lemon; 1 soupspoonful of Pernod.* Cooking time: 15 to 18 minutes.

Split the lobsters in two lengthwise, crack the claws, extract the coral and creamy parts from the head and retain them. Heat the oil in a shallow stew-pan, and place the lobsters in it; sauté until the shells turn red. Strain off the oil, put a little butter in the stew-pan with onion, shallot, carrot, and garlic; allow to colour for a moment. Flame with the cognac, de-glaze with the white wine and add the tomatoes, skinned, pipped and diced, the tomato purée, and the bouquet garni. Season, cover and cook. Remove the lobster, extract the meat from the claws and tails and cut it into large pieces. Retain the half-shells. Pass the stock through a hair sieve and reduce by two-thirds. Bind with coral and creamy parts mixed with 50 gr. of butter; pass through a fine strainer. Heat without boiling; work up with butter and cream, season with a few drops of lemon juice, a pinch of Cayenne pepper and the Pernod. Bind the pieces of lobster with the sauce, fill the half-shells, and glaze quickly under the salamander. Serve a creole rice separately. *(International cookery.)*

Homard phocéene

Proceed as for the preparation Homard américaine, but with a little more garlic. Condiment with saffron. Add to the sauce a julienne of 3 sweet peppers stewed in butter. Serve the lobster in a ring of saffroned rice using a ring mould. *(France.)* *(See page 435.)*

Homard Pompadour

Proceed as for the preparation Homard américaine but moisten with the fish stock and the cream. Reduce the cooking liquor, bind it with the creamy parts and coral pounded with a little butter, pass, and work up lightly with butter. *(France.)* *(See page 435.)*

Lobster for two

For 2 persons: *1 lobster of 500 gr.; 1 plaice of 600 gr.; 150 gr. fresh mushrooms; 50 gr. butter; 4 slices of truffle; 1 dl. white wine; 1 dl. fresh cream; ½ litre sauce hollandaise; ½ a lemon; fleurons.* Cooking time for the lobster: 10 to 12 minutes.

Cook the lobster in a court-bouillon and let it cool in the cooking liquor. Crack the claws, split the head in two lengthwise, and extract the meat from the claws and tail. Prepare 4 good medallions from the tail of the lobster and cut the rest, as well as the meat from the claws, into dice. Fillet the plaice, skin and bone, fold and trim. Butter a shallow stew-pan thickly and arrange the fillets in it, season them and add the mushrooms cut into quarters, sprinkle with white wine, and poach. Take care that the fillets are not over-cooked. Remove the fillets and place to keep hot with the medallions of lobster in a little melted butter. Pour the cream over the mushrooms; reduce, bind, away from the fire, with half the sauce hollandaise. Season and add the diced lobster. Fill the two halves of the shells with this mixture; place 2 fillets of plaice on each one, garnish with 2 medallions of lobster and 2 slices of truffle. Arrange on a hot dish; mask with the rest of the sauce hollandaise. Serve the fleurons separately. *(Denmark.)*

Lobster Soufflé

Ingredients: *2 kg. 750 raw lobster (to produce 350 gr. cooked purée of lobster); 75 gr. diced cooked lobster; 250 cl. sauce béchamel; 6 egg yolks; 8 egg whites; 75 gr. lobster coulis; salt; pepper; nutmeg.*

Dilute the béchamel with the coulis and reduce until the normal béchamel consistency is reached. Remove from the fire and add the lobster purée and the egg yolks. Mix well. Add seasoning. Carefully fold in the diced cooked lobster and the whipped egg whites. Then proceed as for fish soufflé.
Note: To improve the colour, any of the following can be incorporated:
12 gr. of paprika pepper, or
25 gr. of tomato purée, or
50 gr. of lobster butter.

Homard Suchet

For 6 persons: *3 lobsters each of 600 gr.; julienne of carrot (50 gr.), celery (50 gr.), parsley leaves (1 soup-spoonful); 30 gr. truffle; 1 dl. white wine; 1 dl. Mornay sauce; 3 dl. white wine sauce; 50 gr. butter.* Cooking time: 20 minutes.

Cook the lobsters in a court-bouillon, allow to cool in the cooking liquor. Detach legs and claws and split the tails in two lengthwise. Extract the meat from the claws and tails, cut the meat from the claws into dice and the meat from the tails into scollops. Heat in the white wine. Stew in butter the julienne (carrot, celery, parsley), add the truffle en julienne and the diced lobster, and bind with a little white wine sauce. Garnish the shells with this mixture, and arrange the scollops on top in an overlapping pattern. Mask with Mornay sauce mixed with the remainder of the white wine sauce; glaze quickly. *(France.)*

Homard suédoise

For 6 persons: *700 gr. of lobster farce mousseline; 12 scollops of cooked lobster; 50 gr. butter; 125 gr. anchovy butter.* Cooking time: 20 minutes.

Fill a buttered ring mould with the farce using a piping tube. Poach au bain-marie in a moderate oven. After cooking allow to stand 2 to 3 minutes before turning out. Surround with scollops of lobster heated in butter. Mask lightly with anchovy butter both mousse and scollops of lobster. Serve the rest of the anchovy butter separately. *(France.)*

▲ Langouste normande, p. 446

Homard Clarence I, p. 437 ▼

▲ Pilaf de crevettes au curry, p. 431

Pilaf de langouste et crevettes ▼

▲ Coquilles St. Jacques Mornay, p. 459

Pilaf de homard Hortense, p. 438 ▼

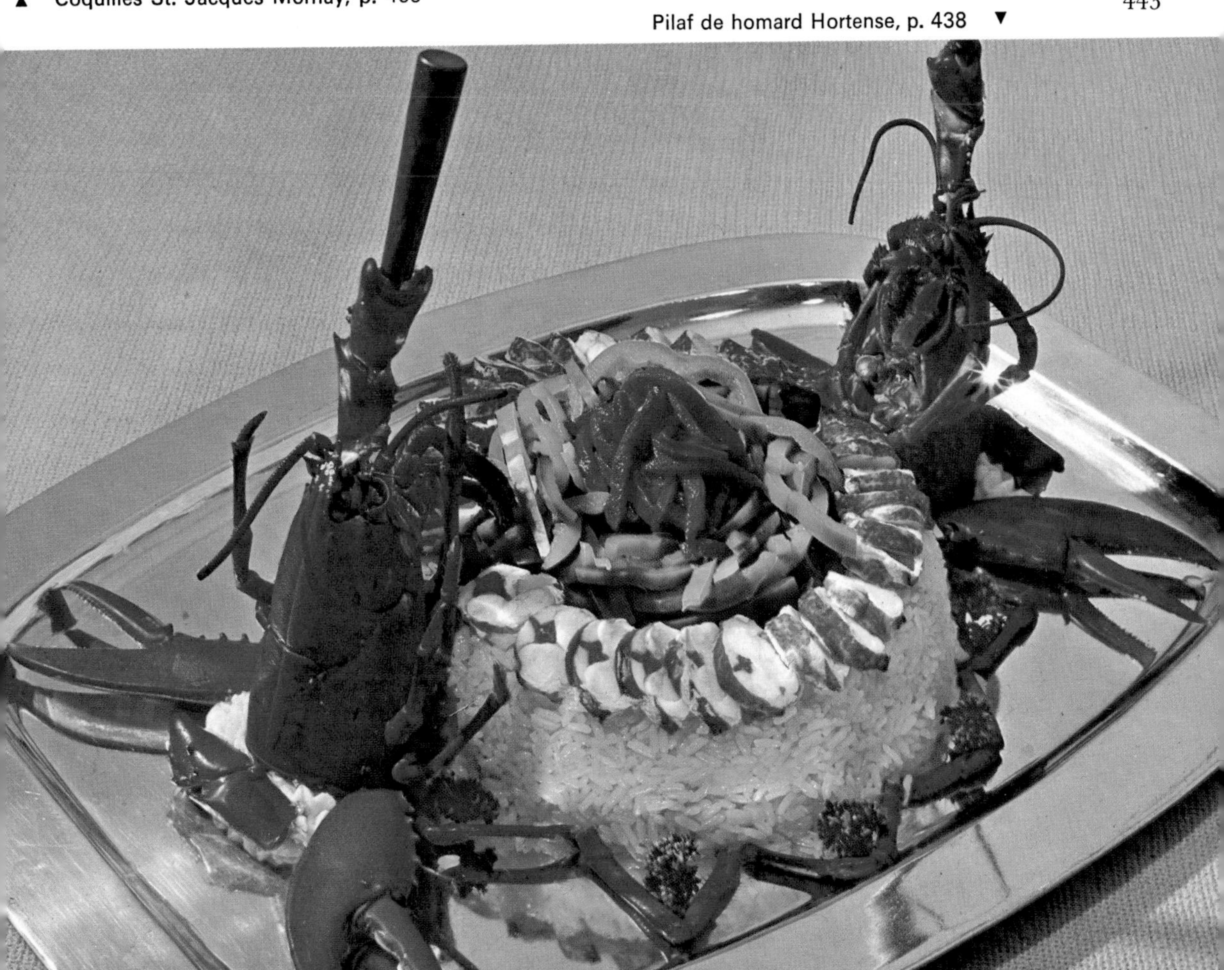

▲ Homard Chantecler, p. 436

Coquilles d'écrevisses cardinal, p. 433 ▼

Homard Thermidor

For 6 persons: *3 cooked lobsters each of 600 gr.; 1 dl. sauce béchamel; 3 dl. sauce Bercy; 3 to 4 gr. English mustard; 50 gr. grated Parmesan cheese.* Cooking time: 15 minutes.

Detach legs and claws, split the lobster in two lengthwise, and crack the claws. Extract the meat. Cut the meat from the claws into small dice and the meat from the tails into scollops. Mix the béchamel with the sauce Bercy and condiment with mustard. Bind the diced meat with a little of this sauce and garnish the shells with it. Arrange the scollops on top, mask with sauce, sprinkle with grated Parmesan cheese, and glaze in a hot oven. Arrange on a serviette. *(France.)*

Risotto de Homard Tourville

For 6 persons: *600 gr. cooked lobster meat; 200 gr. cooked mushrooms; 18 poached and bearded mussels; 12 poached and bearded oysters; 12 slices of truffle; 2 dl. sauce normande; 2 dl. Mornay sauce; 50 gr. butter; 30 gr. grated cheese; 300 gr. risotto.* Cooking time: 18 minutes for the risotto.

Cut the lobster meat and the mushrooms into large dice and add the mussels, oysters and slices of truffle; heat in butter. Press the risotto into a buttered ring mould, and turn out on a round gratinating dish. Bind the salpicon with sauce normande, arrange it in the centre of the ring, mask it with Mornay sauce without touching the risotto, sprinkle it with grated cheese, and glaze quickly under the salamander. *(France.)*

Homard Valencay

For 6 persons: *3 live lobsters each of 600 gr.; 100 gr. red peppers; 200 gr. tomatoes, skinned, pipped and diced; 3 chopped shallots; 30 gr. tomato purée; 1 soup-spoonful of chopped parsley; 1 coffee-spoonful of meat-glaze; 3 gr. English mustard; 2 dl. fish stock; 75 gr. butter; brown breadcrumbs.* Cooking time: 20 minutes.

Cook the lobsters in a court-bouillon, split them in two lengthwise, and crack the claws. Extract the meat from the tails and claws and cut it up into large dice. Colour the shallots in butter, add the small diced peppers and stew for 4 to 5 minutes. Incorporate the tomato and chopped parsley; season. Add the tomato purée, meat-glaze, mustard, and 50 gr. butter. Adjust the seasoning and consistency. Garnish the shells with the lobster salpicon heated in butter, mask with the sauce, and sprinkle with brown breadcrumbs. Brown lightly. *(France.)*

Homard Vanderbilt

For 6 persons: *3 live lobsters each of 600 gr.; 4 dl. sauce américaine; 1 dl. fresh cream; 12 shelled crayfish tails; 50 gr. truffle; 24 slices of truffle; 2 egg yolks.* Cooking time: 20 minutes.

Proceed as for the preparation Homard américaine, completing the sauce américaine with 7 cl. of cream. Extract the meat from the tails and scollop it. Prepare a salpicon with the crayfish tails and the truffle, bind it with a little sauce américaine. Garnish the bottom of the shells with this salpicon. Arrange the lobster scollops on top, separated by small slices of truffle. Bind the lobster sauce with egg yolks and the rest of the cream. Mask the scollops and glaze. *(France.)*

Homard Victoria

For 6 persons: *3 cooked lobsters each of 600 gr.; 200 gr. cooked mushrooms; 2 small peeled and cooked mushrooms; 4 dl. sauce Victoria; 30 gr. butter.* Cooking time: 10 minutes.

Detach legs and claws, split the lobster lengthwise and extract the meat. Prepare a coarse salpicon with the claw meat, mushrooms, and truffle. Scollop the tails. Heat the salpicon in butter and bind it with a little sauce Victoria. Garnish the half-shells with this salpicon and arrange the scollops on top. Mask with sauce Victoria and glaze. *(France.)*

Homard Washington

Another designation for the preparation Homard américaine. *(See page 435.)*

Homard Winthertur

Proceed as for the preparation Homard cardinal replacing the lobster salpicon with picked shrimps. Mask with sauce cardinal, and sprinkle with chopped truffle. *(France.)* *(See page 436.) (See illustration, page 335.)*

Crawfish

Langouste

All the preparations for hot lobster are applicable to crawfish.

Timbale de langouste épicurienne

For 6 persons: *1 kg. 500 crawfish; 24 small fish quenelles; 24 small cooked mushroom heads; 12 slices of truffle; 3 dl. sauce béchamel; 1 dl. fresh cream; 2 egg yolks; 100 gr. butter; ½ coffee-spoonful of paprika; ½ lemon.* Cooking time: 25 minutes.

Cook the crawfish in a court-bouillon, extract the meat, and scollop it. Pound the creamy parts with a little butter and add it to the béchamel; allow to cook for 3 to 4 minutes. Bind with cream and egg yolk, season with the paprika and a few drops of lemon juice, adjust the seasoning and consistency, and pass through a tammy cloth. Heat the scollops, mushrooms and quenelles in butter, bind with the sauce, and arrange in a timbale. Place the truffle slices on top. Serve the rest of the sauce separately. *(France.)*

Langouste grillée diable

Proceed as for the preparation Grilled Lobster. *(See page 438.)*

Langouste normande

For 6 persons: *3 small crawfish each of 600 gr.; 1 litre of cooked and bearded mussels; 200 gr. cooked mushrooms; 75 gr. truffle; 12 slices of truffle; ½ litre sauce normande.* Cooking time: 25 minutes.

Cook the crawfish in a court-bouillon; split them in two lengthwise. Extract the meat. Cut into large dice and the other half into scollops. Cut mushrooms and truffle into dice, adding mussels and crawfish dice and bind with a little sauce. Garnish with half-shells. Arrange the scollops on top; mask with sauce normande and glaze. Decorate each half crawfish with 2 slices of truffle, and surround with fried Gudgeon or goujons of fillet of sole.
(See illustration, page 441.)

Pilaf de langouste

Pilaf of crawfish

For 6 persons: *600 gr. cooked crawfish meat; 300 gr. pilaf of rice; 4 dl. sauce cardinal; 50 gr. butter.* Cooking time for the rice: 18 minutes.

Line the bottom and sides of a buttered timbale with a thick layer of rice. Fill the centre with a coarse salpicon of crawfish meat heated in butter and bound with sauce cardinal. Cover over with rice to the top of the timbale; press down evenly. Turn out on a round dish. Surround with a border of sauce. Serve the rest of the sauce separately. *(France.)*

Queues de Langouste Tortola

For 6 persons: *6 frozen or fresh crawfish tails, each of 200 gr.; 3 dl. tomato sauce; ½ a coffee-spoonful of Dijon mustard; 5 cl. Antilles rum; 2 dl. sauce hollandaise; 2 soup-spoonfuls of shredded coconut; 300 gr. rice.* Cooking time: 20 minutes.

Cook the crawfish tails in a court-bouillon (if frozen do not de-frost) for 10 minutes. Allow to cool slightly, split the tails in two lengthwise, extract the meat, and retain the half shells. Cut the meat into large dice, add tomato sauce and rum, allow to simmer for 5 to 6 minutes. Season with mustard and milled pepper. Garnish the half-shells with this salpicon. Mask lightly with sauce hollandaise, sprinkle with shredded coconut, and brown quickly in a hot oven. Serve creole rice separately. *(Antilles.)*

Dublin Bay prawns

Dublin Bay prawns (langoustines) are prepared as crayfish. It has become customary to call them scampi. The weight must be taken into account for cooking times.

Scampi barcelonaise

For 6 persons: *24 raw scampi, shelled and gutted; 50 gr. chopped onion; 250 gr. skinned, pipped and diced tomatoes; 3 cl. cognac; 2 dl. white wine; 1 soup-spoonful of chopped parsley; olive oil.* Cooking time: 12 minutes.

Sauté the scampi in oil, and add the chopped onion. Flame in the cognac, moisten with the white wine, season, and reduce by half. Add the diced tomatoes and finish cooking. Adjust the seasoning and consistency. Arrange in a timbale, and sprinkle with chopped parsley. Serve creole rice separately (optional). *(International cookery.)*

Scampi au blanc de Bordeaux

For 6 persons: *900 gr. shelled, cooked scampi; 120 gr. fine brunoise of vegetables; 120 gr. butter; 5 cl. cognac; 3 dl. dry white Bordeaux; 3 dl. fish stock; 150 gr. skinned, pipped and diced tomatoes; 1 coffee-spoonful of meat-glaze; 1 coffee-spoonful of chopped tarragon; 5 cl. oil.* Cooking time: 12 to 15 minutes.

Sauté the scampi in very hot oil, flame in the cognac, add the brunoise and half the butter, and colour for a few minutes. De-glaze with the white wine, add the tomatoes and the fish stock. Allow to simmer for 3 to 4 minutes more. Incorporate the meat-glaze, and season with tarragon, salt and a pinch of Cayenne pepper. Add the rest of the butter, and adjust the seasoning and consistency. Serve accompanied with creole rice. *(Switzerland.)*

Scampi en brochette

Skewered scampi

For 6 persons: *18 large raw scampi tails; 1 lemon; 120 gr. maître d'hôtel butter; oil; flour; parsley.* Cooking time: 12 minutes.

Clean and gut the tails. Season, flour, and skewer in threes. Oil and grill under gentle heat. Arrange and garnish with leaf parsley and quarters of lemon. Serve the maître d'hôtel butter separately. *(International cookery.)*

Scampi catalane

For 6 persons: *18 raw scampi; 300 gr. Patna rice; 2 red peppers; 350 gr. tomatoes; 100 gr. raw mushrooms; 50 gr. raw ham; 2 shallots; 1 dl. white wine; 50 gr. onion; 1 pinch of saffron; 1 pinch of basil; 1 pinch of thyme; 1 clove of garlic; 1 dl. olive oil; 1 litre white veal stock.* Cooking time for the scampi: 10 to 12 minutes. Cooking time for the rice: 18 minutes.

Colour the chopped onion and the peppers, diced small, in half the oil. Add the rice, colour lightly while stirring. Moisten with 1 litre of white veal stock. Season, add the saffron, and cook covered. In the rest of the oil, stew the chopped ham and shallots. Colour quickly the scampi tails, previously shelled and gutted, each cut into three. Add the minced mushrooms, moisten with the white wine and allow to reduce by half. Add the skinned, pipped and diced tomatoes, and season with salt, pepper, thyme, and basil. Simmer until cooked. Press the rice into an oiled ring mould, even off, turn out on a round dish, and fill the centre with scampi and sprinkle with parsley. *(Germany.)*

Brochettes de scampi Eden

For 6 persons: *72 large shelled scampi or 6 portions of scampi, each of 150 gr.; 300 gr. rice pilaf; 125 gr. butter; 2 sage leaves; 1 clove of garlic; 3 anchovies; 1 soup-spoonful of chopped parsley; 3 cl. cognac; 1 pinch of curry powder; the juice of a lemon; a few drops of tabasco; 6 cl. olive oil.* Cooking time: 15 to 18 minutes.

Prepare a rice pilaf, keep it hot. Skewer the scampi in sixes or twelves, season them and sprinkle with oil; grill them for 10 to 12 minutes, turning them to grill evenly. Soften the butter in a bowl with sage leaves, parsley, clove of garlic and anchovies, all finely chopped. Season with salt, pepper, curry, cognac and lemon juice until the mass is thick and creamy. Arrange a bed of rice pilaf on a gratinating dish; place the scampi in the centre, cover over with the prepared butter, and pass through a hot oven for a few minutes to brown. *(Switzerland.)*
(See illustration, page 211.)

Scampi Emerico Bianchi

For 6 persons: *750 gr. large scampi; 6 fillets of sole cut en goujons; 40 gr. lobster butter; 4 fresh hearts of artichoke; 2 dl. dry white wine; 50 gr. butter; 2 dl. fish velouté; 2 dl. fish stock; 2 dl. fresh cream; 1 chopped shallot; 3 leaves of basil; 1 egg; brown breadcrumbs.* Cooking time: 15 minutes.

Colour the chopped shallot and the scampi in hot butter, and season with salt, white pepper, a pinch of Cayenne pepper. Add the basil. De-glaze with the white wine, and allow to cook gently for 5 minutes. Remove the scampi and keep them hot. Reduce the white wine until almost dry, add the velouté, the fish stock and the cream; allow to cook until the sauce is rather thick. Work up, away from the fire, with the lobster butter, pass the sauce, re-heat it without allowing to boil. Mask the scampi with this sauce; garnish with the goujons of sole, egg and breadcrumbs, and deep fried, and the hearts of artichoke cut into quarters and passed through butter. *(Switzerland.)*
(See illustration, page 210.)

Scampi Ernesto

Cook in a court-bouillon with white wine, 10 good lively crayfish or large Dublin Bay prawns. When cool, shell and sauté the tails in butter, flame with cognac, add a good ladleful of coulis d'écrevisse made from the pounded shells, and a ladleful of fresh cream. Season with salt, cayenne and a squeeze of lemon juice; simmer for 1 minute. Remove from the heat and add a good ladleful of sauce hollandaise. Arrange in a gratinating dish and pass under the salamander to glaze.
Recipe created by Bartholomew Calderoni, former Chef de Cuisine of the Normandie Hotel, London.

Scampi frits cantonaise

For 6 persons: *600 gr. raw scampi; 400 gr. fresh pineapple; 1 lemon; 1 dl. soy sauce; 75 gr. rice flour; 2 eggs; powdered ginger; wine vinegar; 60 gr. butter.* Cooking time; 10 to 12 minutes.

Marinate the shelled and gutted scampi in lemon juice, salt, pepper, and a pinch of powdered ginger. Cut up into small dice half of the pineapple, squeeze out the juice from the other half, and pass it through a cloth. Dry the dice, pass them through rice flour and colour golden in butter. Dust copiously again with rice-flour. Colour quickly, moisten with the soy sauce and the pineapple juice, stir, add very little water, allow to cook for 20 minutes over a slow fire. Add a pinch of sugar and salt, a few drops of vinegar, and a pinch of ginger. Roll the scampi in the rice flour, pass them through the beaten egg and cook in deep fat. Arrange in a bunch and serve the hot sauce separately. *(Germany.)*

Grilled scampi

For 6 persons: *6 large or 12 small scampi; 100 gr. beurre maître d'hôtel, to which half a clove of crushed garlic has been added.* Cooking time: 12 minutes.

Put the scampi into boiling salt water, cook and allow to cool in the cooking liquor. Shell, gut and split in two, cover with hard beurre maître d'hôtel, and grill quickly under the salamander. Serve very hot, covered with softened beurre maître d'hôtel. *(Spain.)*
(See illustration, page 211.)

Scampi italienne

For 6 persons: *24 shelled scampi tails; 200 gr. skinned, pipped and diced tomatoes; 2 chopped shallots; 2 crushed cloves of garlic; 1 coffee-spoonful of fresh chopped rosemary leaves; 1 coffee-spoonful of chopped parsley; olive oil.* Cooking time: 10 minutes.

Colour the shallot in oil, and add the diced tomatoes, the garlic and rosemary. Season. Sauté the scampi tails in the oil, mix with the tomatoes, bring to the boil once or twice. Arrange in a timbale, and sprinkle with chopped parsley. *(International cookery.)*

Scampi Ravanusa

For 6 persons: *450 gr. shelled raw scampi tails; 6 aubergines; 2 eggs; 225 gr. brown breadcrumbs; 1 soup-spoonful of chopped wild marjoram; ¼ litre oil.* Cooking time: about 10 minutes.

Colour the scampi in oil, roll them in brown breadcrumbs. Cut the aubergines lengthwise, and then into thin slices, fry them in oil and place on a sheet of paper to drain surface fat. Roll 2 scampi in each slice of aubergine and skewer, pass several times through the beaten and seasoned eggs, and then through the breadcrumbs. Sprinkle with a little oil and wild marjoram, and cook on the grill. Serve very hot. *(Italy.)*

Scampi 'Scotts' style

For 6 persons: *48 raw scampi; 170 gr. julienne of red and green peppers; ½ litre sauce américaine; 170 gr. pilaf of rice; fresh cream; butter; cognac.* Cooking time: 20 minutes for the scampi.

Prepare and place to cook the pilaf of rice; sauté the scampi in butter until tender without colouring; add the peppers and stew together. Flame with cognac, add the well-creamed sauce américaine and combine together gently. Serve in a timbale with the rice pilaf separately. The above dish was introduced by Mr. H. Slack, the Sous Chef de Cuisine of 'Scotts' Restaurant, London.

Flake the crabmeat and bind it with the well-seasoned mayonnaise to which the whipped cream has been added. Arrange in a salad bowl or on a glass dish on heart of lettuce leaves. Garnish with asparagus tips, previously marinated with oil, lemon juice, salt and pepper. Sprinkle the salad with a fine short julienne of red peppers. *(United States.)*

Mayonnaised e crevettes à l'ancienne

Shrimp mayonnaise

For 6 persons: *360 gr. of picked shrimps; 1 good lettuce; 8 anchovy fillets; 3 hard-boiled eggs; 12 stoned green olives; 3 hearts of lettuce; 250 gr. mayonnaise.*

Set out the coarsely-shredded lettuce on the bottom of a salad bowl. Arrange the shrimps on top. Mask with mayonnaise and smooth into a dome shape. Garnish with anchovy fillets in a trellis work, quarters of hard-boiled egg, halves of lettuce hearts, and olives. *(France.)*

Aspic de crevettes

Shrimp aspic

For 6 persons: *400 gr. picked shrimps; 200 gr. mayonnaise; ¾ litre fish jelly with white wine; truffle; white of eggs; chervil leaves.*

Line a suitable mould with jelly. Decorate it with truffle, white of egg, chervil leaves, according to taste. Bind the shrimps with the mayonnaise combined with tepid fish jelly and fill the mould with it. Top with jelly and allow to set in the refrigerator. Turn out on a dish, and garnish with croûtons of jelly. *(France.)*

Mousse de crevettes

Proceed as for the preparation Mousse d'écrevisses. *(See page 452.)*

Aspic de crevettes roses

Prawn aspic

For 6 persons: *75 to 80 gr. of large picked prawn tails; 400 to 450 gr. prawn mousse; 1 litre fish jelly with white wine.*

Coat a dome mould with very clear jelly. Arrange the prawn tails on the sides in rows placed above one another and by dipping each prawn in the half-set jelly. Garnish the centre of the mould with a mixture of prawn mousse, cover over entirely with jelly, and allow to cool. Turn out on a round dish, and garnish with croûtons of jelly.

Prawn mousse: Pound the shells from the prawns. Add 5 cl. reduced fish velouté to 200 gr. of purée. Pass through a hair sieve, season, incorporate 1 dl. of cold fish jelly and, when it begins to set, add 15 cl. of whipped cream. It may be seasoned with paprika. *(France.)*
(See Culinary Technique, page 103.)

Suprême d'écrevisses au champagne

Crayfish

For 6 persons: *24 large live crayfish; 100 gr. mirepoix bordelaise; ¼ litre champagne; 100 gr. butter; 3 leaves of gelatine; 3 dl. fish velouté; ¼ litre whipped cream; 12 slices of truffle; 15 cl. jelly with white wine.* Cooking time: 15 minutes.

Sauté the crayfish in butter with the mirepoix until the shells are red. Moisten with the champagne and cook with the lid on. Shell the tails as soon as they are cooked, trim them, and keep them cold. Pound the shells with 75 gr. of butter, put them into a saucepan, add the crayfish cooking liquor (passed through a conical strainer), the velouté, the previously soaked gelatine, and allow to cook gently for 2 or 3 minutes. Pass through a hair sieve without pressure, then through a tammy cloth. Stir with the whisk, adjust the seasoning and consistency, and, when it begins to thicken, incorporate the whipped cream. Fill two-thirds full a silver or porcelain timbale, and allow to set firm in the refrigerator. When the mousse has set, decorate with crayfish tails and slices of truffle. Mask with a thin layer of half-set jelly. Keep in the cool. Serve on crushed ice or on an ice socle. *(France.)*

Timbale d'écrevisses en gelée

For 8 to 10 persons: *60 to 70 cooked crayfish; 200 gr. white asparagus tips; 250 gr. skinned, pipped and diced tomatoes; 200 gr. mayonnaise; 1 litre clear fish jelly with white wine; ¾ litre sauce Chantilly; 1 thin slice of truffle.*

Shell the tails and trim them. Crack the claws and extract the meat. Coat with jelly a dome mould, embedded in crushed ice. Place a slice of truffle on the bottom. Line the sides with the crayfish tails, the convex side towards the outside of the mould, after previously soaking in the half-set jelly to affix them on the side. Run jelly into the mould again leaving a free space. Fill this space with a salad of: asparagus tips cut into pieces, tomatoes, claw-meat and trimmings from the crayfish tails, all bound with the mayonnaise combined with fish jelly on setting point. Cover over entirely with half-set jelly. Keep cold until the moment of serving. Turn out on a round dish; garnish with triangles of jelly. Serve the sauce separately. *(International cookery.)*

Salade d'écrevisses Louis Ferdinand

For 6 persons: *36 crayfish cooked in a court-bouillon; 24 turned cooked small mushrooms; 18 slices of truffle cut out with a round column cutter; 200 gr. minced white celery; 2 pippin apples, peeled, cored, cut into quarters and diced; 2 small red peppers in a fine short julienne; 200 gr. mayonnaise; 1 small heart of lettuce; 1 coffee-spoonful of chopped dill; 2 soup-spoonfuls of ketchup; 3 dl. fish jelly with white wine.*

Shell the tails and trim them. Crack the claws and extract the meat. Prepare a salad with: white of celery, pippin apples, peppers, claws and remnants from the crayfish tails. Bind with the mayonnaise to which has been added the ketchup and chopped dill lightly bound with fish jelly on setting point. Arrange the salad in a round glass or crystal dish, leaving the edges free by about 4 cm. Smooth the surface. Surround the salad with crayfish tails arranged side by side with the underside towards the edge of the bowl. On the salad place the mushroom heads in a crown and the slices of truffle across the centre. Glaze all with jelly, including the crayfish tails. Surround the tails with a cordon of chopped jelly. Place the lettuce heart in the centre of the salad.
Optional: A sauce Chantilly may be served separately. *(Germany.)*

Mayonnaise d'écrevisses

Mayonnaise of crayfish

Proceed as for the preparation Shrimp mayonnaise, allowing tails and claws of six large crayfish per person. *(See page 451.)*

Mousse d'écrevisses

For 6 persons: *36 small crayfish; 100 gr. mirepoix bordelaise; 3 cl. cognac; 1 dl. white wine; 1 dl. fish velouté; 50 gr. crayfish butter; 3 dl. jelly with white wine; 2 dl. fresh cream; 6 slices of truffle; 30 gr. butter.* Cooking time: 12 minutes.

Sauté the crayfish in butter, with the mirepoix until they are red. Add: cognac, flame, and add white wine. Cook covered for 10 minutes. Remove the crayfish, shell the tails, crack the claws, and extract the meat. Retain 6 good tails and trim them. Pound or pass through a mincer the rest of the tails and the trimmings, adding the cooking liquor reduced by two-thirds. Incorporate the velouté; pass through a hair sieve. Add the softened crayfish butter, work on ice, add 15 cl. of jelly, and season. When the purée begins to set, mix the whipped cream with it. Pour the mousse into a silver timbale up to 1 cm. from the edge. Allow to set in the refrigerator. Decorate with the tails retained and the slices of truffle; cover over with a thin layer of jelly. *(France.)*

Petits soufflés d'écrevisses

Prepare a crayfish mousse as above. Run a thin layer of jelly in the bottom of small porcelain cassolettes or some small silver timbales. Surround them with a band of paper rising about 1½ cm. above the edges. Fill the cassolettes with mousse to the level of the top of the paper. When the mousse has solidified, decorate each cassolette with a slice of truffle, and a crayfish tail, split lengthwise. Cover over with a thin layer of jelly. Keep cold until the moment of serving. Remove the paper and arrange on a serviette. *(France.)*

Crayfish pie

For 10 persons: *10 fillets of sole; 6 dozen crayfish tails; 250 gr. fresh mushrooms; 100 gr. onion; parsley leaves; 1 small bunch of dill; 1 bayleaf; 250 gr. puff-paste; ½ litre jelly; Worcestershire sauce.* Cooking time: 30 minutes.

In a buttered pie-dish arrange the flattened fillets of sole in a fan shape. Sprinkle with onions cut into dice and picked parsley leaves, season with milled pepper, and cover with thick slices of mushrooms. Fill with the crayfish tails cut in small dice and clear jelly in small dice; add a little Worcestershire sauce. Sprinkle with a little more diced onion, parsley, and slices of mushroom to fill the pie-dish to the top. Place the bayleaf and the bunch of dill in the centre. Cover the pie-dish with puff-pastry decorated with puff-pastry leaves. Brush with beaten egg yolk. Cook in the oven. Allow to cool completely. Cut into portions while still in the dish. The jelly being incorporated with the ingredients during the cooking is flavoured and constitutes an agreeable liaison. *(Germany.)*
(See illustration, page 250.)

Aspic de homard

Lobster aspic

For 6 persons: *2 cooked lobsters each of 750 gr.; 18 slices of truffle; 1 dl. fish jelly with white wine.*

Detach the claws and crack them, and extract the meat. Shell the tails. Scollop the tail and claw meat. Fill a suitable mould with scollops of lobster alternating with slices of truffle and layers of jelly. Allow to set in the refrigerator. Turn out on a round dish; surround with triangles of jelly. Serve a sauce verte or Chantilly separately. *(France.)*

Homard en bellevue

Proceed as for the preparation Crawfish en bellevue, choosing large lobsters.
(See illustration, page 248.)

Homard Carnot

For 6 persons: *600 gr. lobster mousse; 12 scollops of lobster; 12 slices of truffle; ¾ litre fish jelly; 3 dl. Russian sauce.*

Coat a ring mould with jelly, fill it with lobster mousse, allow to set in the cold, and top with jelly. Decorate each lobster scollop with a slice of truffle; glaze the scollops with jelly. Turn out the mousse on a dish and arrange the scollops in a crown on top. Surround with croûtons of jelly. Serve the sauce separately. *(France.)*

Homard au champagne

Lobster with champagne

For 6 persons: *1 live lobster of 1 kg. 200; 2 good dessert apples; ¼ litre milk; 2 dl. fresh cream; 3 eggs; 3 leaves of gelatine; ½ bottle of champagne; 1 bunch of dill; 3 cl. cognac; 5 cl. white wine; the juice of ¼ of a lemon; caraway.* Preparation: 1 hour.

Cook the lobster in a court-bouillon and allow to cool in the cooking liquor. Crack the claws. Extract the meat of the claws and the tail; scollop it. Retain the coral. Peel the apples, cut into quarters and poach them in white wine and lemon juice. Drain them on a cloth. Pound in the mortar the coral and the shells and cook them for 15 minutes in the milk with a pinch of salt and caraway; reduce by a third. Pass through a conical strainer. Incorporate the cream and the cognac. Prepare a royale with this composition and the beaten eggs; poach it in a natural or artificial sausage-casing, of sufficient diameter, until cooked, to provide good slices after cooling. Arrange the lobster and the slices of royale in an overlapping pattern in a glass dish on crushed ice. Decorate with the quarters of apple. Sprinkle with dill. Allow to cool for 30 minutes. Melt the previously softened gelatine au bain-marie, add half a glass of champagne and heat to 30° C. Incorporate carefully the rest of the champagne (kept at cellar temperature) and put to cool. Once the jelly is half-set, pour it gently over the lobster and allow to set in the refrigerator. Serve with hot potato crisps. *(Germany.)*
(See illustration, page 248.)

Homard Chevreuse

For 6 persons: *3 cooked lobsters each of 600 gr.; 300 gr. asparagus tips; 2 small truffles; 4 dl. mayonnaise sauce; olive oil; vinegar; ¼ litre fish jelly.*

Detach the claws, crack them, and extract the meat. Split the tails lengthwise, remove the meat and cut it into scollops. Cut up into a salpicon the claw meat and the asparagus tips and marinate with vinegar, salt and pepper. Drain. Fill the half-shells with this salpcon. Arrange the scollops on top alternating with slices of truffle. Glaze with jelly. Arrange on a serving dish. Serve the mayonnaise separately. *(France.)*

Homard Grammont

For 6 persons: *3 cooked lobsters each of 600 gr.; 4 dl. fish jelly; 360 gr. lobster mousse; 10 gr. paprika; 18 oysters, poached and bearded; 18 slices of truffle; 3 hearts of lettuce; leaf parsley; 4 dl. sauce Chantilly.*

Detach the claws, crack them and extract the meat. Split the tails in two lengthwise and extract the meat. Extract the creamy parts from the trunks. Prepare a mousse with the claw-meat and the creamy parts, season it with paprika. Scollop the meat of the tails, and decorate each scollop with a fluted slice of truffle.Glaze with jelly. Mask the oysters with jelly. Fill the half-shells level with mousse and allow to set. Arrange the scollops on this mousse alternating them with oysters. Arrange the half-shells on a serviette with a lettuce heart in the middle and a bunch of parsley at each end of the dish. Serve the sauce Chantilly separately. *(France.)*

Homard parisienne

Proceed as for the preparation Crawfish parisienne, choosing large lobsters.
(See page 455.) (See Culinary Technique, page 102.)

Homard russe

Proceed as for the preparation Crawfish parisienne, but masking the medallions with a combined mayonnaise and fish jelly. *(France.)*

Soufflé de homard

For 6 persons: *4 dl. lobster purée; 15 cl. fish velouté; 15 cl. jelly; 2 dl. whipped cream.*

Prepare a lobster mousse (*see crayfish mousse, page 452*) and season it highly. Proceed for this soufflé as for small crayfish soufflés. *(France.)*

Homard Tivoli

For 6 persons: *3 cooked lobsters each of 600 gr.; 200 gr. of diced white asparagus; 200 gr. cooked minced mushrooms; 200 gr. tomatoes, skinned, pipped and diced; 250 gr. mayonnaise; 6 hard-boiled eggs; 40 gr. butter; 30 gr. caviar; 1 litre of fish jelly; oil; vinegar; 4 dl. sauce verte.*

Detach the claws and crack them. Split the lobster in two lengthwise. Extract the meat from tails and claws. Trim the tails, glaze them with jelly, on the red side. Mask the claw-meat lightly with jelly. Marinate the tomatoes, asparagus and mushrooms in oil, vinegar, a little salt, and pepper. Drain. Bind with 200 gr. of mayonnaise, combined with fish jelly. Fill a dome-shaped mould previously coated with jelly, with this salad, cover again with jelly and allow to set. Cut the eggs to two-thirds of their height and empty out the yolk. Pass the yolks through a sieve, incorporate with them the softened butter and a soup-spoonful of mayonnaise, season with salt and paprika, and fill the eggs with this mixture using a piping bag with a fluted tube. Place a point of caviar in the centre, and glaze with jelly. Glaze lightly a large round dish with jelly. Turn out the salad in the centre. Arrange around this, alternately, the half-tails and the claws. Garnish with the stuffed eggs and large dice of jelly. Serve the sauce separately. *(International cookery.)*

Médaillons de Homard Windsor

For 8 medallions: *1 cooked lobster of 700 to 800 gr.; 100 gr. white of hard-boiled egg; 100 gr. cooked celeriac; 100 gr. blanched green peppers; 150 gr. mayonnaise; ½ a coffee-spoonful of curry powder; 8 slices of truffle; ½ litre of fish jelly; oil; vinegar; 8 tartlets in lining-paste, cooked pale.*

Detach the claws and crack them. Shell the tail. Extract the meat of the claws and tail. Cut up the tail into 8 fine scollops. Decorate each of them with a slice of truffle; glaze with jelly. Cut up into dice: white of egg, pepper, celeriac, claw-meat, and trimmings from the tail. Marinate in oil, vinegar, salt and pepper. Drain, bind with the mayonnaise, seasoned with curry and to which the sieved creamy parts have been added. Fill the tartlets to the top with this salpicon. Place a scollop of lobster on each of them, surrounded by chopped jelly. *(France.)*

Médaillons de langouste Bagration

Crawfish

For 12 medallions: *12 good scollops of cooked crawfish tail; 12 tartlets in lining-paste cooked pale; 400 gr. mayonnaise; 4 dl. fish jelly; 1 coffee-spoonful of chopped fennel; 1 coffee-spoonful of chopped parsley; 400 gr. Russian salad.*

Mask lightly with jellied mayonnaise the scollops of crawfish. Sprinkle with chopped parsley and fennel; glaze with jelly. Bind the Russian salad with mayonnaise, and adjust the seasoning and consistency. Fill the tartlets level with this salad. Place a scollop of crawfish on each tartlet and surround it with a cordon of chopped jelly. *(France.)*

Langouste en bellevue

For 6 to 8 persons: *1 live crawfish of 1 kg. 500 to 1 kg. 800; 8 small tomatoes; 8 small artichoke-bases; 8 hard-boiled eggs; 200 gr. fine macédoine of vegetables; 1 litre of fish jelly; 2 lettuce; 6 small radish; 1 truffle; 250 gr. mayonnaise; chervil leaves; ½ litre mayonnaise sauce.* Cooking time: about 30 minutes.

Fix the crawfish, with tail well stretched out, on a small board. Cook it in a court-bouillon in a sufficiently large receptacle to prevent the breaking of the antennae. Allow to cool in the cooking liquor; drain. Along the whole length of the shell make two parallel incisions 4 cm. apart and without cutting into the meat. Extract the entire tail carefully. Extract from the head the rest of the meat and the creamy parts. Cut the tail up into 12 to 14 even scollops. Decorate each one with: 2 lozenges of truffle and a chervil leaf. Glaze with jelly. Glaze a large oval or rectangular dish with jelly. Fill the inside of the shell with coarsely-shredded lettuce and arrange the shell on the jelly. Arrange the scollops on the reconstituted shell, beginning with the head and in an overlapping pattern. Garnishing: tomatoes cut to two-thirds of their height, emptied and stuffed with crawfish meat cut up into dice, bound with mayonnaise, decorated with a small slice of truffle, and glazed with jelly; artichoke-bases marinated and filled in a dome shape with a vegetable salad bound with mayonnaise, decorated with a crown of slices of radish and glazed with jelly; hard-boiled eggs, emptied, stuffed with creamed egg yolks, and glazed with jelly. Decorate also with croûtons of jelly. Serve separately a light mayonnaise to which has been added the creamy parts of the crawfish passed through a hair sieve. There is no strict rule for the presentation of Langouste en bellevue. Numerous variations are acceptable in the garnishing and decoration. *(International cookery.)*

(See Culinary Technique, page 99, and illustration, page 228.)

Langouste parisienne

For 6 to 8 persons: *1 live crawfish of 1 kg. 500 to 1 kg. 800; ½ litre white sauce chaud-froid; 8 artichoke-bases; 8 hard-boiled eggs; 2 lettuce; 2 small truffles; 300 gr. Russian salad; 150 gr. mayonnaise; 1 litre jelly; 40 gr. butter.*

For the cooking and the extraction of the tail proceed as for the preparation Langouste en bellevue. Divide the tail into 13 or 14 scollops of equal size. Remove the meat from the trunk, cut it into dice, and add it to the Russian salad. Bind with about 100 gr. of mayonnaise to which the sieved creamy parts have been added. Arrange the salad in a dome shape on the artichoke-bases, decorate with a point of truffle; glaze with jelly. Fill the shell with coarsely-shredded lettuce. Arrange the scollops on this. Arrange the crawfish on a dish glazed with jelly. Garnish with the artichoke-bases and the hard-boiled eggs stuffed with creamed egg yolks—or simply filled with the same salad as the artichoke-bases, and surround with croûtons of jelly. *(France.)*

(See Culinary Technique, page 99.)

Scampi or Dublin Bay prawns

All the methods given for the preparation of crawfish are applicable to Dublin Bay prawns and scampi.

Langoustines à la mayonnaise

For 6 persons: *30 Dublin Bay prawns or scampi; 3 lemons; 3 to 4 dl. mayonnaise.* Cooking time: 5 to 6 minutes.

Put the Dublin Bay prawns into boiling salt water, cook gently, allow to cool in the cooking liquor. Drain, arrange on a dish, garnish with quarters of lemon, and serve the mayonnaise separately. *(Spain.)*

Coquilles Saint Jacques Mornay

For 6 persons: *6 large scollops; 300 gr. pommes duchesse mixture; 4 dl. Mornay sauce; 50 gr. grated cheese; 40 gr. butter.* Cooking time: 12 minutes.

Shell the scollops and cook them in a court-bouillon with white wine. Drain and cut into slices slantwise. Mask the bottom of each deep shell, edge with pommes duchesse mixture by using a piping bag with fluted tube, place a soup-spoonful of Mornay sauce on the bottom of the shell and the scollops on top. Mask with Mornay sauce, sprinkle with grated cheese and melted butter, and brown. *(France.)* *(See illustration, page 443.)*

Coquilles Saint Jacques nantaise I

For 6 persons: *12 scollops; 200 gr. cooked mushrooms; 4 dl. white wine sauce; 2 soup-spoonfuls of sauce hollandaise.* Cooking time: 12 minutes.

Poach the scollops in a court-bouillon with white wine, drain and cut into slices slantwise. Mask the bottom of a gratinating dish with white wine sauce. Arrange the scollops in the centre and surround with thick slices of mushrooms. Mask with white wine sauce to which sauce hollandaise has been added, and glaze. *(France.)*

Coquilles Saint Jacques nantaise II

For 6 persons: *6 large scollops; 12 poached and bearded oysters; 12 poached and bearded mussels; 4 dl. white wine sauce.* Cooking time: 12 minutes.

Shell the scollops, poach them in a court-bouillon with white wine, drain and cut into slices slantwise. Mask the bottom of each deep shell with a soup-spoonful of white wine sauce. Arrange the scollops on top, surround each one with two oysters and two mussels. Mask with white wine sauce, and glaze. *(France.)*

Coquilles Saint Jacques ostendaise

For 6 persons: *6 large scollops; 120 gr. picked shrimps; 100 gr. cooked mushrooms; 12 poached and bearded oysters; 6 slices of truffle; 4 dl. sauce Nantua. Cooking time: 10 minutes.*

Shell the scollops and poach them in a court-bouillon with white wine, drain and cut into slices slantwise. Mask the bottom of each deep shell with a soup-spoonful of sauce Nantua. Arrange the scollops on top, alternating with shrimp tails, oysters and slices of mushrooms. Mask with sauce Nantua. Place a slice of truffle on each shell. *(France.)*

Coquilles Saint Jacques parisienne

For 6 persons: *6 large scollops; 300 gr. pommes duchesse mixture; 4 dl. white wine sauce; 30 gr. chopped truffle.* Cooking time: 12 minutes.

Shell the scollops and poach them in a court-bouillon with white wine, drain them and cut into slices slantwise. Edge the deep shells with pommes duchesse mixture, using a piping bag with fluted tube. Mask the bottom of the shells with a soup-spoonful of white wine sauce. Arrange the scollops on top, mask them with white wine sauce to which chopped truffle has been added. Pass through a hot oven to glaze the sauce and colour the pommes duchesse. *(France.)*

Coquilles Saint Jacques au vin blanc

For 6 persons: *12 scollops; 2 dl. white wine; 40 gr. butter; 4 dl. white wine sauce; 2 soup-spoonfuls of sauce hollandaise.* Cooking time: 12 minutes.

Poach the scollops in white wine and butter. Drain, and cut into slices slantwise. Reduce the cooking liquor by three-quarters, and mix it with the white wine sauce; add the sauce hollandaise; adjust the seasoning and consistency. Arrange the prepared scollops on a dish, and mask with sauce. Glaze (optional). *(France.)*

Oysters

Real connoisseurs prefer to eat oysters raw. All the same, certain hot preparations are much appreciated. These preparations are usually presented in the well-cleaned deep oyster shells.

To poach oysters they are removed from the shell and heated to boiling point in their own liquor. One or two minutes are enough to poach them. If left longer they become toughened and shrivelled.

(See Culinary Technique, page 107.)

Huîtres américaine

For 6 persons: *36 oysters; 75 gr. butter; 2 lemons; fresh white breadcrumbs; leaf parsley.* Cooking time: 3 to 4 minutes.

Beard the raw oysters and put them back into the hollow shells; arrange them on a tray sprinkled with coarse salt. Sprinkle each oyster with a few drops of lemon juice and fresh white breadcrumbs mixed with a pinch of Cayenne pepper. Sprinkle with melted butter and brown in a hot oven. Arrange on a serviette with picked parsley. *(France.)*

Angels on horseback

For 6 persons: *36 oysters; 36 thin slices of bacon; 6 pieces of toast; white breadcrumbs.* Cooking time: 4 to 5 minutes.

Beard the raw oysters and wrap each one in a slice of bacon. Skewer them, six at a time, on metal skewers and grill them under a salamander. Arrange on rectangular pieces of toast, and sprinkle with a pinch of Cayenne.

Attereaux d'huîtres

For 6 persons: *24 large oysters; 24 thick slices of mushroom; ½ litre sauce Villeroi; 2 eggs; fresh white breadcrumbs; parsley.* Cooking time: 5 minutes.

Poach the oysters for 1 minute in their liquor. Drain and beard them. Skewer them, six on a skewer, alternating with mushrooms slices. Dip the skewers in boiling sauce Villeroi, and allow to cool. Coat with egg and breadcrumbs, fry in hot deep fat, and arrange on a serviette with fried parsley. *(France.)*

Oysters Baltimore

For 6 persons: *24 large oysters; 75 gr. butter; 50 gr. grated cheese; 50 gr. fresh white breadcrumbs; 1 soup-spoonful of chopped parsley.* Cooking time: 4 to 5 minutes.

Remove the oysters from the shells. Wash and dry the deep shells, butter them lightly. Place a bearded oyster in each one. Sprinkle with grated cheese, mixed with fresh white breadcrumbs and chopped parsley. Sprinkle with melted butter, cook and brown in a hot oven. *(United States.)*

Barquettes aux huîtres

For 6 persons: *6 small boat-shaped pastry cases made from puff pastry trimmings and cooked pale; 24 poached and bearded oysters; 3 dl. cream sauce; 30 gr. truffle.* Cooking of the oysters: 1 minute.

Garnish each hot pastry case with four oysters. Mask with cream sauce to which the reduced oyster cooking liquor has been added. Sprinkle with chopped truffle. *(France.)*

Huîtres Bercy

For 6 persons: *36 oysters; 4 dl. sauce Bercy; picked parsley.* Cooking time: 3 to 4 minutes.

Poach the oysters for 1 minute, and beard them. Place each one in a deep shell, mask with sauce Bercy, and glaze. Arrange on a serviette with picked parsley. *(France.)*

Huîtres bretonne

For 6 persons: *36 poached oysters; 3 dl. sauce Bercy; 75 gr. toasted white breadcrumbs; picked parsley.* Cooking time: 3 to 4 minutes.

Proceed as for the preparation Huîtres Bercy, but without glazing. Sprinkle them with toasted white breadcrumbs; arrange on a serviette with picked parsley. *(France.)*

Devilled Oysters

For 6 persons: *36 oysters; 100 gr. butter; fine white breadcrumbs; 4 dl. sauce diable; picked parsley.* Cooking time: 5 to 6 minutes.

Skewer the poached, bearded and drained oysters, six at a time, on small metal skewers. Dip them in melted butter, roll them in the fine white breadcrumbs, grill them under gentle heat. Season with salt to which a pinch of Cayenne pepper has been added; arrange on a serviette with picked parsley. Serve the sauce separately. *(France.)*

Huîtres favorite

For 6 persons: *36 poached and bearded oysters; 36 slices of truffle; 60 gr. grated cheese; 4 dl. Mornay sauce; 60 gr. butter.* Cooking time: 3 to 4 minutes.

Pour the equivalent of half a coffee-spoonful of Mornay sauce into each deep shell. Place the oysters in them with a slice of truffle on each one. Mask with Mornay sauce. Sprinkle with grated cheese, and brown. Arrange on a serviette with picked parsley. *(France.)*

Huîtres florentine

For 6 persons: *36 oysters; 300 gr. blanched leaf spinach; 3 dl. Mornay sauce; 60 gr. grated cheese; 75 gr. butter; parsley.* Cooking time: 3 to 4 minutes.

Chop the spinach coarsely and stew in butter. Season and put a small amount in the bottom of each shell. Arrange on top the poached and bearded oysters, mask with Mornay sauce, sprinkle with grated cheese and melted butter, and brown. Arrange on a serviette with picked parsley. *(France.)*

Baked oysters on half-shell

For 6 persons: *36 oysters; 150 gr. butter; 1 crushed clove of garlic; 1 soup-spoonful chopped parsley; 75 gr. finely crushed rusks; ½ a coffee-spoonful of paprika; 1 soup-spoonful of Worcestershire sauce; 2 cl. anisette liqueur; 2 cl. gin; 2 lemons.* Cooking time: 6 to 8 minutes.

Open the oysters, drain them, retain their liquor and leave them intact in the hollow shells without detaching them. Soften the butter with garlic, parsley, rusk, paprika, Worcestershire sauce, anisette, gin, the oyster liquor and very little salt. Mask each oyster with a coffee-spoonful of this mixture. Cook in a hot oven. Serve with quarters of lemon. *(United States.)*

Fried Oysters I

For 6 persons: *36 oysters; milk; flour; 2 lemons; parsley.* Cooking time: 2 to 3 minutes.

Poach and beard the oysters, dip them in milk, drain them, roll them in the flour and shake well to remove excess flour. Plunge in very hot deep frying fat, drain, season with fine salt. Arrange on a serviette with fried parsley and quarters of lemon. *(France.)*

Fried Oysters II

For 6 persons: *36 oysters; 2 eggs; fresh white breadcrumbs; 2 lemons; parsley.* Cooking time: 3 to 4 minutes.

Poach, beard, drain, and sponge the oysters. Coat with egg and breadcrumbs, and fry in hot deep frying fat. Arrange on a dish with fried parsley and quarters of lemon. *(France.)*

Fritots d'huîtres

For 6 persons: *24 large oysters; flour; ½ litre of batter; parsley.* Cooking time: 5 to 6 minutes.

Poach, beard, drain and lightly flour the oysters. Dip them in the batter and fry in hot deep frying fat. Arrange on a serviette with fried parsley. *(France.)*

Huîtres au gratin

For 6 persons: *24 large oysters; 100 gr. duxelles; 24 very small cooked mushroom heads; 3 dl. sauce italienne; 60 gr. butter; 1 lemon; 1 soup-spoonful of chopped parsley; brown breadcrumbs; fried parsley.* Cooking time: 6 to 7 minutes.

Poach the oysters in their liquor, drain them, and beard them. Put them back in the deep shells on a bed of very fine duxelles. Place a mushroom head on each one. Mask with sauce italienne to which reduced cooking liquor had been added. Sprinkle with brown breadcrumbs and melted butter, and brown. On taking out of the oven, sprinkle each shell with a few drops of lemon juice and chopped parsley. *(France.)*

Huîtres maréchale

For 6 persons: *24 oysters; ½ litre batter; 6 roundels of lemon; parsley.* Cooking time: 5 to 6 minutes.

Poach, drain and beard the oysters. Dip them in the light batter, and fry in hot frying fat. Arrange them in threes on a roundel of lemon. Garnish with picked parsley. *(France.)*

Huîtres Mornay

Proceed as for the preparation Huîtres favorite, but without slices of truffle. *(See page 460.)*

Huîtres polonaise

For 6 persons: *6 shells; 24 oysters; butter-fried fresh white breadcrumbs; 3 hard-boiled eggs; chopped parsley.* Cooking time: 4 minutes.

Put the bearded raw oysters back in the deep shells. Sprinkle with sieved egg yolk and a little chopped parsley. Heat in a hot oven. At the moment of serving, sprinkle each oyster with a small spoonful of butter-fried breadcrumbs. Finish with noisette butter. *(France.)*

Huîtres soufflées

For 6 persons: *24 oysters; 1 white of egg; 100 gr. pike farce; 2 dl. cream.* Cooking time: 6 to 8 minutes.

Pound 12 oysters incorporating little by little the white of egg. Pass through a hair sieve. Put this purée in an earthenware bowl on crushed ice, work, incorporating the pike farce and about 2 dl. of fresh cream. Season, put a half-spoonful of farce into each deep shell. Place a poached and bearded oyster on top, cover over with farce, and smooth into a dome shape. Cook in a moderate oven. Arrange on a serviette. *(France.)*

Huîtres Villeroi

For 6 persons: *24 large oysters; 3 dl. sauce Villeroi; 2 eggs; 2 lemons; fresh white breadcrumbs; parsley.* Cooking time: 5 to 6 minutes.

Poach, drain, sponge and beard the oysters. Lightly flour them, dip them in boiling sauce Villeroi, and allow to cool. Egg and bread-crumb, and fry in hot deep frying fat. Arrange on a serviette with fried parsley and quarters of lemon. *(France.)*

Huîtres Wladimir

For 6 persons: *36 poached and bearded oysters; 4 dl. sauce suprême; 50 gr. grated Gruyère cheese; brown breadcrumbs.* Cooking time: 3 to 4 minutes.

Arrange the oysters in the deep shells. Mask with thick sauce suprême, sprinkle with grated cheese and brown breadcrumbs, and brown. *(France.)*

Mussels

Mussels must first be very carefully cleaned, whatever their preparation. Scrape the shells and brush them. Wash them one by one. Mussels must be tightly closed, as an open mussel indicates unsafeness. Too heavy a mussel may contain sand or mud. Once cleaned, mussels must be washed again several times altogether in plenty of water.
To open mussels and to cook them is the same operation. Mussels are put in a saucepan adding a little white wine, minced onion and shallot and milled pepper. When the mussels are open and the cooking liquor is about to overflow, they are cooked. It is important to stir well during the cooking so that all the mussels are equally well cooked. Too well cooked a mussel becomes leathery and tough. Mussels must always be bearded unless served in half-shells. *(See Culinary Technique, page 112.)*

Moules américaine

For 6 persons: *36 mussels; 4 dl. sauce américaine.* Cooking time: 7 to 8 minutes.

Cook the mussels. Keep only one shell. Arrange in a timbale, mask with sauce américaine. *(France.)*

Moules Bangalore

For 6 persons: *4 litres of mussels; 1 litre white wine; 2 dl. fresh cream; ¼ litre fish velouté; 3 egg yolks; 100 gr. carrots; 50 gr. peppers; 50 gr. shallots; 100 gr. head of fennel; 50 gr. butter; 5 gr. curcuma; ½ a coffee-spoonful of ground cloves; 4 gr. curry; 1 gr. saffron.* Cooking time for the mussels: 5 to 6 minutes.

Prepare the mussels and cook in white wine until they open, remove from the shells, beard them and keep hot in a little cooking liquor. Strain off the stock, decant it, pass it and reduce it slightly with the velouté, bind it with the egg yolks and cream. Prepare a julienne of carrot, fennel, peppers and shallot. Colour in butter and season with curry, curcuma, ground clove, and saffron. Incorporate with the sauce. Arrange the mussels in a gratinating dish, mask them with the sauce, sprinkle with melted butter, and glaze under the salamander. *(Germany.)*

Moules bonne femme

For 6 persons: *3 litres mussels; 75 gr. raw mushrooms; 75 gr. white of celery; 3 chopped shallots; 40 gr. chopped onion; 2 dl. white wine; 40 gr. beurre manié; 5 cl. fresh cream.* Cooking time: 7 to 8 minutes.

Cook the mussels in white wine with chopped shallot and onion, a fine julienne of mushrooms and celery, and a little milled pepper (no salt). Drain. Keep only one shell. Arrange. Reduce the cooking liquor by half, bind it with the beurre manié, add the cream, and bring to the boil once or twice. Without passing it, pour the sauce over the mussels. *(France.)*

Moules catalane

For 6 persons: *3 litres of mussels; 6 parsley stalks; 2 chopped shallots; 50 gr. chopped onion; 2 dl. white wine; 2 egg yolks; ½ a lemon.* Cooking time: 7 to 8 minutes.

Cook the mussels in white wine with parsley stalks, chopped shallot and onion, and milled pepper. Drain, and keep only one shell. Arrange en timbale. Pass the cooking liquor; reduce by half. Bind with the egg yolk diluted in a little cooking liquor. Season this sauce with a little lemon juice; pour over the mussels. *(France.)*

Fried mussels

For 6 persons: *2 litres of large mussels, cooked, shelled and bearded; ¾ litre of batter; 1 lemon; 3 cl. olive oil; 1 coffee-spoonful of chopped parsley; parsley.* Cooking time: 4 to 5 minutes.

Marinate the mussels for 30 minutes in the lemon juice and oil with chopped parsley and milled pepper. Dip in the light batter; fry in hot deep frying fat. Arrange on a serviette with fried parsley. *(France.)*

Moules marinère I.

For 6 persons: *3 litres of mussels; 2 dl. white wine; 2 chopped shallots; 50 gr. chopped onion; 6 to 8 parsley stalks; 1 dl. fish velouté; 50 gr. butter; 1 soup-spoonful of chopped parsley.* Cooking time: 7 to 8 minutes.

Cook the mussels in white wine with parsley stalks, chopped shallot and onion, and a little milled pepper. Drain, and keep only one shell. Arrange en timbale. Pass and decant the cooking liquor, reduce it by two-thirds, add the velouté and the butter, and bring to the boil once or twice. Pour over the mussels, and sprinkle with chopped parsley. *(France.)*

Moules marinère II

For 6 persons: *3 litres of mussels; 75 gr. butter; parsley; 2 chopped shallots; 2 dl. white wine; 50 gr. onion; 1 soup-spoonful of chopped parsley.* Cooking time: 6 to 7 minutes.

Cook the mussels in white wine with butter, finely chopped shallot and onion, and a little milled pepper. Serve them as they are in their cooking liquor, sprinkled with chopped parsley. *(France.)*

Moules messinoise

For 6 persons: *4 litres of mussels; 50 gr. butter; 25 gr. flour; 15 cl. milk; 1 gr. saffron; 60 gr. sultanas; 30 gr. pine kernels; 300 gr. blanched julienne of red and yellow peppers; curry; 1 chopped onion; a small bunch of parsley, chopped.* Cooking time: 7 minutes.

Colour onion and parsley lightly in olive oil. Add the mussels, previously cleaned, and pepper lightly. Cook covered. When the mussels are open, remove from their shells. Pass the cooking liquor through a muslin cloth and retain it. Prepare a white roux with 30 gr. of butter and 25 gr. of flour, moisten with the milk and the decanted mussel liquor, and prepare a smooth and creamy sauce. Season with saffron, a pinch of curry and a pinch of grated nutmeg. Add the sultanas, pine kernels and the julienne of peppers. Butter a gratinating dish and pour the mussels in it, mask with sauce and brown in a moderate oven. *(Italy.)*

Paêlla of mussels

For 6 persons: *3 litres of mussels; 400 gr. rice; 40 gr. onion; 1 clove of garlic; ½ litre olive oil; 2 gr. saffron; 1 cooked pimento cut into strips.* Cooking time: about 20 to 25 minutes.

Clean the mussels and cook them on a quick fire in 1 litre of water. When the mussels are well open, about 5 to 8 minutes, drain them and retain the liquor. Remove half the mussels from their shells and keep the others hot in their half-shells with a little cooking liquor. Colour in the oil the chopped onion and garlic, add the rice, the saffron, and stew for 5 minutes stirring constantly. Moisten with the previously decanted cooking liquor, add the mussels which were removed from their shells, pour all into a large gratinating dish and, without stirring, cook in a moderately hot oven. Before serving, stick the mussels left in half-shells in a crown on the rice, the shell side in the rice, and garnish the centre with the strips of red pimento. *(Spain.)*

Pilaf of mussels

For 6 persons: *2½ litres of mussels; 3 dl. curry sauce; 250 gr. rice pilaf; 30 gr. butter.* Cooking time: 6 to 7 minutes.

Cook the mussels and remove from their shells; beard them. Butter thickly a timbale or a large bowl; line it with rice pilaf. Garnish the centre with the mussels bound with the curry sauce, cover over with rice, and turn out on a round dish. Surround with a cordon of curry sauce. *(France.)*

Moules pizzaiola

For 6 persons: *4 litres of mussels; 9 cl. olive oil; 1 dl. white wine; 600 gr. tomatoes, skinned, pipped and diced; 1 small de-pipped red pepper; 1 soup-spoonful chopped parsley; 2 crushed cloves of garlic; 6 chopped anchovy fillets; the juice of ¾ to 1 lemon.* Cooking time: 15 to 20 minutes.

Heat the mussels, previously brushed, washed and cleaned, just enough so that they open but their flesh remaining almost raw. Sweat the garlic in the hot oil, add the anchovies, mussels, chopped pepper; moisten with white wine, and allow to reduce almost completely. Add tomatoes and parsley, and allow to cook until complete reduction of the cooking liquor is achieved. Season with the lemon juice. Add salt only if it is required. *(Italy.)*

Moules rochelaise

For 6 persons: *3 litres of mussels; 50 gr. butter; 2 chopped shallots; 50 gr. chopped raw mushrooms; 50 gr. chopped white celery; 2 dl. white wine; 1 coffee-spoonful chopped chives; fine fresh white breadcrumbs.* Cooking time: 7 to 8 minutes.

Cook the mussels in the white wine with butter, chopped shallot, mushrooms, celery and chive, milled pepper and a pinch of nutmeg. Drain. Retain only one shell. Arrange the mussels in half-shells on a dish. Reduce the cooking liquor and bind it with a little fresh white breadcrumbs. Mask the mussels with this sauce, and brown at the last moment. *(France.)*

Moules à la sauce piquante

For 6 persons: *4 litres of mussels; 5 large cucumbers in vinegar; 30 gr. finely chopped onion; 1 soup-spoonful of chopped parsley; 1 soup-spoonful of chopped capers; 5 cl. ketchup; 1 dl. olive oil.* Cooking time for the mussels: 5 to 6 minutes.

Heat the previously brushed, washed and cleaned mussels in a saucepan until they open. Chop the cucumbers finely. Toss the onion in oil without colouration. Add the cucumbers, capers, parsley, then ketchup, and allow to cook on very gentle heat. Remove half a shell from each mussel; pour the hot sauce over them. This speciality can be served hot or cold. *(Italy.)*

Risotto de moules toulousaine

For 6 persons: *2½ litres of mussels; 250 gr. rice; 50 gr. butter; 50 gr. chopped onion; 7 dl. fish stock; 3 dl. white wine sauce.* Cooking time: 6 to 7 minutes.

Prepare a risotto with rice, butter, chopped onion, and fish stock. Cook the mussels, remove them from the shells, and beard them. Pass and decant 1 dl. of cooking liquor, reduce it by two-thirds, and add it to the white wine sauce. Press the risotto into a buttered ring mould; turn out on a round dish. Bind the mussels with the sauce and arrange them in the centre of the bordure. *(France.)*

Sea-urchins

The only edible part of the sea-urchin is a red substance which clings to the bottom of the shell and is commonly called the coral.
Before opening the sea-urchins, reject the spines. Then with scissors make a circular incision on the concave side, that is the side on which the mouth is, turn the shell inside out to empty it of water and to gut. Only the coral remains at the bottom and it is detached with a small spoon.
The coral may be eaten dipping in fingers of bread and butter, or it may be passed through butter as a filling for an omelette. Passed through a hair sieve, raw sea-urchin is excellent to complete fish sauces.

Small bivalve molluscs, cockles, venus, clams, etc.

Palourdes, praires

Usually these shellfish are eaten raw, but they may also be cooked as mussels.

Shellfish (Coquillages)

Cold Dishes

Sea Food (Fruits de Mer)

Under this name are usually included oysters, mussels and other small shellfish, molluscs etc. served cold, either raw or after cooking.

Andalusian Oysters

For 6 persons: *24 large poached and bearded oysters; 2 dl. fish jelly with white wine; 24 small slices of truffle; 250 gr. tomato mousse; 1 coffee-spoonful of pink paprika.*
Decorate each oyster with a small slice of truffle, fluted and dipped in the half-set jelly. Wash and dry 12 shells, selected from the best; fill them with a heaped soup-spoonful of tomato mousse, smoothing into a dome-shape, and allow to set. Garnish each shell with two oysters, glaze with jelly. Arrange on a round dish on crushed ice.
Tomato mousse: 200 gr. tomato flesh without skin or pips; 25 gr. butter; 1 soup-spoonful of velouté; 2 soaked leaves of gelatine; 7 cl. cream. Soften the tomatoes in butter until evaporation is complete. Add the velouté and the previously soaked gelatine. Season with: salt and paprika. Pass through a fine sieve, allow to cool. When the purée begins to set, incorporate the half-whipped cream. *(France.)*

Oyster tartlets with caviar

For 6 persons: *12 large bearded Limfjords oysters; 12 small tartlets in thinly rolled short pastry, lightly baked; 75 gr. caviar; 12 small truffle stars; 2 lemons; leaf parsley.*
Decorate each oyster with a truffle star. Glaze with jelly. At the moment of serving, garnish each tartlet with a very small spoonful of caviar and place an oyster on top. Arrange on lace paper, garnish with quarters of lemon and leaf parsley. *(International cookery.)*

Oyster tartare

For 6 persons: *36 poached and bearded oysters; 4 dl. sauce tartare; leaf parsley.*
Clean and dry the hollow shells. Replace an oyster in each shell. Lightly mask with sauce tartare. Arrange on crushed ice. *(France.)*

Mussels fécampoise

For 6 persons: *60 to 72 cooked and bearded mussels; 500 gr. raw celeriac; 400 gr. mayonnaise; 5 cl. decanted mussel cooking-liquor; 1 soup-spoonful of chopped mixed herbs; olive oil; vinegar.*
Cut the celeriac into a julienne and blanch for one minute, refresh, marinate with: salt, pepper, oil and vinegar. Arrange in a salad-

bowl or in a hors d'oeuvre dish with the mussels on top. Mask with mayonnaise to which the reduced and cooled mussel cooking-liquor has been added. Sprinkle with mixed herbs. *(France.)*

Mussels French style

For 6 persons: *72 large cooked and bearded mussels; 3 dl. mayonnaise; 1 coffee-spoonful of mustard; 1 coffee-spoonful of mixed herbs; oil; lemon juice.*
Marinate the mussels with: oil, lemon juice, milled pepper, (no salt). Bind with the mayonnaise condimented with mustard. Arrange in a hors d'oeuvre dish or in a suitable glass, sprinkle with mixed herbs. *(France.)*

Mussels Francillon

For 6 persons: *60 to 72 large poached and bearded mussels; 600 gr. potatoes cooked in their jackets; skinned and cut into roundels; 3 dl. mayonnaise lightly flavoured with mustard; 5 cl. mussel poaching-liquor; olive oil; vinegar; 1 coffee-spoonful of chopped parsley.*
Bind the mussels with the flavoured mayonnaise to which has been added the strongly reduced mussel poaching-liquor. Marinate the potatoes with: oil, vinegar, salt and pepper. Arrange the mussels in a hors d'oeuvre dish, surround with a crown of potato roundels, sprinkle with chopped parsley. *(France.)*

Mussels tartare

Proceed as for the preparation Oyster tartare. Arrange them in suitable glasses. (See page 465.)
(France.)

Molluscs

Fried squid

Calamaras fritas

For 6 persons: *600 gr. of cleaned squid; ½ litre of oil; 3 lemons; flour.* Cooking time: 5 to 6 minutes.

Cut the squid into small tronçons, flour them and fry them in very hot deep oil. Drain, salt, arrange on a serviette and garnish with quarters of lemon. *(Spain.)*

Stuffed cuttlefish

For 6 persons: *1 kg. 800 of cuttlefish, allowing one per portion; 600 gr. skinned, pipped and diced tomatoes; 3 eggs; 80 gr. grated Parmesan cheese; 3 de-salted anchovy fillets; 1 large crushed clove of garlic; 225 gr. fresh white breadcrumbs; 1 dl. white wine; 1 dl. fish stock; 2 dl. milk; 5 cl. olive oil; 1 soup-spoonful of chopped parsley.* Cooking time: 30 minutes.

Remove the skin and the ink sac from the cuttlefish; bone the head, wash and dry. Cut off the tentacles. Soak the fresh white breadcrumbs in milk and squeeze thoroughly. Add the tentacles passed through the mincer, the pounded anchovies, the beaten eggs, the parsley and garlic. Season, mix well and stuff the cuttlefish with this mixture; sew them up and place in an oiled sauteuse. Sprinkle with oil, colour quickly, deglaze with white wine, and allow to reduce almost completely. Add the tomatoes and fish stock, cover, and allow to cook on gentle heat for 30 minutes. When just cooked, remove them, arrange in a serving dish, sprinkle with the cooking liquor passed through a hair sieve. Serve accompanied with steamed fish potatoes and buttered peas. *(Italy.)*

Seiches pizzaiola

For 6 persons: *1 kg. 500 of squid; 120 gr, stoned green olives; 30 gr. capers; 30 gr. anchovy purée; 6 gr. wild marjoram; 1 small red pepper pipped and cut into a julienne; 900 gr. potatoes in small dice; 1 dl. olive oil; 2 crushed cloves of garlic; 50 gr. chopped onion; 200 gr. skinned, pipped and diced tomatoes; 1 dl. white wine; the juice of 1 lemon; chopped parsley.* Cooking time: 1 hour.

Remove the brown skin and the ink sac from the previously washed cuttlefish and cut the flesh into small pieces. Lightly colour the onion and garlic in olive oil, add the cuttlefish and the julienne of pepper; allow to colour for 2 to 3 minutes. Moisten with white wine; add the tomatoes, potatoes, olives, capers, anchovy purée, wild marjoram, and 2 dl. of water or stock. Season and cook for one hour on very gentle heat until just cooked, and the stock entirely reduced. Serve sprinkled with lemon juice and chopped parsley. *(Italy.)*

Accompanying Dishes and Garnishes

Vegetables

A great number of vegetables, cereals and also pasta serve as a garnish to accompany fish dishes. Great care has to be taken in cooking the vegetables. In several European countries it is the custom always to serve vegetables with fish. The vegetables, cereals and pasta presented here are limited to those most often served.

Artichoke bases

Cooking time: about 30 minutes

Trim the artichokes, of average size, rejecting the leaves and keeping only the base with the choke. Rub them with lemon and put them as soon as they are ready into cold acidulated water. Mix a little flour with cold water, add hot salted water, whisking well, and bring to the boil. Put the bases to cook in this 'blanc' until the choke is easily detached.

Artichoke bases stewed in butter

Proceed as above but remove the choke from the bases while still raw. Blanch for 10 minutes only. Drain and refresh. Place the bases in a buttered stew-pan, season, sprinkle with melted butter, and stew gently for 18 to 20 minutes.

Fonds d'artichauts Angenteuil

6 cooked artichoke bases; 30 cooked white asparagus tips each 4 cm. long; 30 gr. butter; 15 cl. sauce crème.

Pass the artichoke bases through butter. Heat the asparagus tips in boiling water, drain completely. Place 5 tips on each artichoke base, and mask lightly with sauce crème. They may also simply be sprinkled with melted butter.

Artichoke bases stuffed with mushroom purée

6 cooked artichoke bases; 250 to 300 gr. mushroom purée; 50 gr. butter; 40 gr. grated cheese. Cooking time: 5 to 6 minutes.

Arrange the artichoke bases on a buttered tray. Garnish them with a thick mushroom purée. Smooth the purée into a dome shape, sprinkle with grated cheese and melted butter, and brown in a hot oven.

Fonds d'artichauts florentine

6 cooked artichoke bases; 250 gr. blanched spinach; 2 soup-spoonfuls of thick sauce béchamel; 1 coffee-spoonful of anchovy purée; 15 cl. Mornay sauce; 40 gr. chopped onion; 60 gr. butter; 30 gr. grated cheese. Cooking time: 12 to 15 minutes.

Colour the chopped onion in butter. Add the chopped spinach. Stir over a hot fire to dry thoroughly. Add the anchovy purée and the béchamel; allow to cook gently for 10 minutes. Garnish the artichoke bases with spinach mixture and arrange on a buttered tray. Mask with Mornay sauce; glaze.

Artichoke bases as a garnish for cold dishes

Cook the artichoke bases in the usual way. Refresh and drain. Allow to marinate for 30 minutes at least with salt, a little pepper, olive oil, and vinegar or lemon juice.

White asparagus tips

As a garnish choose asparagus of medium size. After scraping and washing them, retain the tips about 6 cm. long. Put them into small bundles of 7 or 8 and cook in boiling salt water for 15 to 18 minutes. Keep them rather firm. Drain them.
To garnish hot fish they are passed through butter. For cold fish or shellfish they must be marinated for at least 30 minutes in oil, vinegar or lemon juice with a little salt and pepper.

Green asparagus tips

Break off level the tender upper part of the asparagus, the part called the tip. Put these tips into small bundles of 8 to 10 and tie them up. Cut off the lower part of these small bundles into pieces of 1 cm., retaining tips of about 5 cm. Cook in boiling salt water. Add the small bundles, after cooking for 4 minutes. Boil very fast for 6 to 8 minutes. Drain and refresh. The cut pieces are usually dried for a moment, then bound with butter or cream. Place on top the small bundles heated in salt water, dried and lightly sprinkled with butter.

Fried aubergines or egg-plants

Cut the aubergines into thin roundels. Season, flour, and fry them in very hot oil. Serve immediately while the aubergines are still crisp.

Glazed carrots

1 kg. of carrots; 50 gr. butter; 20 gr. sugar. Cooking time: 18 to 20 minutes.

Small new carrots are cooked whole; large ones are split in two or in four. If the carrots are old they are turned olive or barrel-shape and well blanched before cooking. Barely cover the carrots with water, add a little salt, butter and sugar. Cook uncovered until the moisture is almost evaporated to obtain a syrupy consistency and give the carrots a glossy appearance.

Fluted mushrooms

Choose fresh, very white mushrooms, all the same size. Reject the earthy part of the stalks. Wash them quickly in plenty of water, and drain them. Then cut the stems level with the heads. Flute the latter with a suitable knife incising them regularly. Put them in the boiling cooking liquor prepared thus: boil together 1 dl. of water, 40 gr. of butter, the juice of half a lemon and 5 gr. of salt. Allow the mushrooms to cook for 5 minutes. Place them together with cooking liquor in an earthenware dish covered over with buttered paper.

Mushroom purée

1 kg. fresh and very white mushrooms; 2 dl. sauce béchamel; 1 dl. fresh cream; 1 lemon; 50 gr. butter. Cooking time: 10 to 12 minutes.

Reduce the béchamel with the cream down to 2 dl. Reject the earthy parts of the stalks, wash and drain the mushrooms. Put them in a large earthenware dish, add the lemon juice and a large handful of salt. Quickly rub the mushrooms in the hands to remove the skin, and wash them again in plenty of water. Drain and dry on a cloth. Pass through a hair sieve. Put this purée of raw mushrooms in a shallow stew-pan, dry out on a quick fire, stirring with a spatula. Add the béchamel, and season with salt, pepper and a pinch of nutmeg; mix well, cook a few moments longer, and finish, away from the fire, with the butter.

Mushroom heads

Choose very small and even sized heads. Proceed as for the preparation of fluted mushrooms, but without incising them.
(See page 470.)

Buttered cucumbers

Proceed as for creamed cucumbers but stewing them completely in butter.

Creamed cucumbers

500 gr. cucumbers turned olive shape; 50 gr. butter; 15 cl. fresh cream; 5 cl. sauce béchamel. Cooking time: about 15 minutes.

Blanch the cucumbers (2 minutes), and drain them. Season moderately. Stew them in butter until three-parts cooked. Moisten with boiling cream. Add the béchamel to bind lightly. Adjust the seasoning and consistency.

Glazed cucumbers

Cooking time: about 15 minutes.

Peel the cucumbers and divide into four lengthwise, and remove the pips. Cut the cucumbers into pieces and fashion them into large olive shapes. Blanch them for a moment, drain them and treat as for glazed carrots.

Leaf spinach

1 kg. spinach; 60 gr. butter. Cooking time: 8 to 10 minutes.

Stalk the spinach, clean it and wash it with plenty of water. Cook in boiling salt water for about 6 to 7 minutes. Drain well without refreshing or pressing. Allow the butter to melt in a sauteuse, add the spinach and season with salt, pepper and a pinch of nutmeg. Dry out over the fire; fork well together.

Creamed spinach

1 kg. spinach; 50 gr. butter; 2 dl. fresh cream. Cooking time: 15 to 18 minutes.

Cook the spinach after stalking, cleaning and washing with plenty of water. Refresh, drain and press well to exude all moisture; chop well. Dry over the fire with butter. Season, add the cream, and allow to simmer over gentle heat for 10 minutes.

Spinach purée

1 kg. spinach; 50 gr. butter; 2 dl. thick sauce béchamel. Cooking time: 15 to 18 minutes.

Cook in salt water the spinach already stalked, cleaned and washed in plenty of water. Refresh and press to exude all moisture, and pass through a sieve. Dry out the spinach on the fire in butter. Season with salt, pepper and a pinch of nutmeg, and incorporate the béchamel. Allow to stew on gentle heat for 10 minutes.

Braised lettuce

5 lettuce; 1 carrot; 75 gr. onion; 150 gr. fat bacon; 2 dl. veal stock or dégraissis. Cooking time: 1 hour.

Clean the lettuce stumps without detaching the leaves. Wash them, and blanch them (15 minutes). Refresh, press well, divide them lengthwise and fold in two. Line the bottom of a sauteuse with thin slices of bacon, roundels of carrot and onion. Arrange the lettuce on top, shrink over the fire, season lightly, and moisten with the veal stock or the dégraissis. Cover over with a buttered paper, and braise, covered, in a moderate oven.

Creamed morels

1 kg. morels; 50 gr. butter; 3 dl. fresh cream. Cooking time: about 15 minutes.

Trim the morels, wash them several times, in fresh water each time, and very carefully remove the earth contained in the honeycomb cells. If the morels are large, divide them into two or four. Heat the butter in a sauteuse; add the morels, season with salt and pepper; stew. When they are cooked, add the boiling cream. Allow to cook until the cream is almost reduced.

Small glazed onions

To glaze brown: *750 gr. small onions; 50 gr. butter; 1 pinch of powdered sugar.* Cooking time: 15 to 18 minutes.

Peel, without cutting into them, the small onions of the same size. Cook then gently in the butter with the sugar until they are tender and well coloured.
To glaze white: *750 gr. small onions; 50 gr. butter; ½ litre white stock.* Cooking time: 15 to 18 minutes.
Proceed as for the preparation of glazed carrots. *(See page 470.)*

Sorrel purée

1 kg. of sorrel; 80 gr. butter; 30 gr. flour; ½ litre of white stock; 2 dl. thick sauce béchamel; 1 egg; 2 egg yolks; milk. Cooking time: 1 hour to 1½ hours.

Pick the sorrel and wash it several times, in fresh water each time; drain. Soften it with very little water; drain it again. Mix it with a white roux made with 50 gr. butter and 30 gr. flour. Season, and braise gently, covered, in a moderate oven. Pass through a sieve, heat up again in another receptacle, add the béchamel, and allow to simmer a few minutes longer. Bind with the egg yolks and the egg beaten in two soup-spoonfuls of milk; adjust the seasoning and consistency; complete with the rest of the butter.

Palm-tree hearts in butter

450 gr. preserved tinned palm stalks; 50 gr. butter. Cooking time: 6 to 7 minutes.

Split the stems in two lengthwise and cut up into thick slices of about 5 cm. Heat them in the preserving liquor. Drain completely, season, and allow to simmer in butter for a few minutes.

Buttered peas

1 litre shelled new peas; 60 gr. butter. Cooking time: 15 minutes.

Cook the peas quickly in boiling salted water, drain and dry off over the fire. Season with a pinch of sugar and bind with the butter off the fire.

Petits pois à la française

1 litre shelled peas; 1 lettuce; 12 small onions; 1 small bunch of parsley and chervil; 75 gr. butter; 15 gr. sugar; 7 gr. salt. Cooking time: about 20 minutes.

Shred the lettuce very coarsely. Mix with the peas, butter and other ingredients. Add 3 soup-spoonfuls of water, and cook gently, covered. Remove the bunch of herbs, and make a liaison, away from the fire, with a little beurre manié.

Stuffed sweet peppers

6 very small green or red peppers; 120 gr. half-cooked pilaf of rice; 75 gr. diced skinned tomatoes; 1 coffee-spoonful of chopped mixed herbs; 1 dl. olive oil. Cooking time: 25 to 30 minutes.

After removing the stalks, empty the peppers. Mix the rice pilaf with the tomatoes, mixed herbs and 2 soup-spoonfuls of olive oil. Fill the peppers three-quarters full with this mixture; arrange them in an oiled sauteuse. Sprinkle with the rest of the oil, and stew gently, covered, in a moderate oven.

Tomatoes piémontaise

6 tomatoes; 250 gr. risotto; 40 gr. grated Parmesan cheese; fresh white breadcrumbs; olive oil. Cooking time: 7 to 8 minutes.

Cut the tomatoes in two, empty them of their seeds and water; season. Fill them with the risotto to which the grated Parmesan has been added; arrange them on an oiled tray. Sprinkle with fresh white breadcrumbs and oil, cook and brown in the oven.

Tomatoes provençale

6 tomatoes; 100 gr. fresh white breadcrumbs; 1 soup-spoonful of chopped parsley; 1 crushed large clove of garlic; olive oil. Cooking time: 8 to 10 minutes.

Cut the tomatoes in two and press them lightly to remove seeds and water. Sprinkle with fresh white breadcrumbs mixed with the chopped parsley and the crushed garlic. Sprinkle with oil, and cook in the oven.

Truffles

Truffles are used particularly as a garnish and an element of decoration. They must be prepared very simply because of their strong aroma.

Truffles as garnish and decoration

250 gr. fresh truffle; 50 gr. mirepoix bordelaise; 2 dl. Madeira or Port, good quality white wine, or champagne. Cooking time: 20 minutes.

Brush and wash the truffles without peeling them. Season and cook gently, covered, in the chosen wine with the mirepoix bordelaise. Allow to cool in the cooking liquor, then peel the truffles and keep the peelings to flavour sauces. *(See Culinary Technique, page 87.)*

Creamed truffles

250 gr. raw truffle; 50 gr. butter; 15 cl. fresh cream; 5 cl. sauce béchamel; 1 cl. cognac. Cooking time: 20 minutes.

Brush, wash and peel the truffles. Cut them into thick slices. Season with salt and pepper, and stew gently in butter and cognac (flambe). As soon as the cooking is finished, reduce well the cream with the béchamel; add the truffle cooking liquor. Mix the truffles with this sauce.

Potatoes

Appareil à pommes duchesse

1 kg. peeled potatoes; 2 eggs; 4 egg yolks; 100 gr. butter. Cooking time: 20 minutes.

Cut the potatoes into quarters and cook until just tender. Drain, dry and pass through a sieve. Dry off over the fire with butter, season with salt, pepper and a pinch of nutmeg. Bind, away from the fire, with the eggs and egg yolks, mixing well.
(See Culinary Technique, page 114.)

Pommes allumettes

Large peeled potatoes. Cooking time: 6 to 7 minutes.

Trim the potatoes square and cut these into small matchstick shapes, wash them and dry them in a cloth. Fry them in small quantities in hot cooking fat until crisp and golden brown, and sprinkle lightly with fine salt.

Pommes anglaise

Cooking time: 18 minutes.

Peel the potatoes and shape them to the size of large olives. Cook them in salted water or by steaming.

Pommes Berny

750 gr. appareil à pommes croquettes; 75 gr. chopped truffle; 2 beaten eggs; shredded almonds. Cooking time: 5 to 6 minutes.

Add the chopped truffle to the appareil à pommes croquettes. Divide into small apricot shaped pieces of 60 gr. Pass through the beaten egg and roll in the shredded almonds. Fry in very hot, deep frying fat.

Pommes château

1 kg. 200 potatoes; 100 gr. butter; chopped parsley. Cooking time: 18 minutes.

Turn the potatoes barrel shape, blanch, strain, season and cook in clarified butter until soft and golden. Sprinkle with chopped parsley. If using new potatoes select them of an even size and scrape or peel before blanching.

Pommes croquettes

1 kg. peeled potatoes; 4 eggs; 4 egg yolks; 100 gr. butter; fresh white breadcrumbs or brown breadcrumbs. Cooking time: 5 to 6 minutes.

Prepare the mixture as for purée duchesse with 2 eggs and 4 egg yolks. Divide this mixture into pieces of 60 gr. or, if used for garnishing, into portions of 40 gr. Mould them into the shapes of corks or small pears or apricots. Egg and breadcrumb. Fry in very hot deep fat.

Pommes dauphine

500 gr. appareil à pommes croquettes; 150 gr. very firm choux paste without sugar; flour. Cooking time: 6 to 7 minutes.

Mix the appareil à pommes croquettes with the choux paste. Divide into small balls of 40 gr. and mould with flour into cigar shapes. Fry in hot deep fat.

Pommes duchesse

Mould the appareil duchesse to form small rolls, brioche or other shapes, and place onto a buttered tray, or, with the aid of a piping bag and tube, pipe onto a buttered tray. Brush with beaten egg and colour golden in the oven. *(See Culinary technique, page 114.)*

Pommes noisettes

1 kg. 200 large peeled potatoes; 100 gr. butter. Cooking time: 18 minutes.

With a round spoon-cutter form small ball shapes from the potatoes, and blanch them (2 minutes). Drain them, salt them and cook gently in butter until they are golden coloured and soft.

Pommes olives

1 kg. 200 large peeled potatoes; 100 gr. butter. Cooking time: 15 to 18 minutes.

With an oval spoon-cutter make small olive shapes from the potatoes. Salt and cook them gently in butter until they are golden in colour and soft.

Straw potatoes

1 kg. peeled potatoes. Cooking time: 6 to 7 minutes.

Cut up the potatoes into a fine julienne, wash them, drain them and dry in a cloth. Place in a frying basket and cook in hot deep frying fat until golden brown and crisp. Drain and season with salt.

Pommes parisienne

Prepare the potatoes as for pommes noisettes but a little smaller. When they are cooked, roll them in very reduced veal stock, or in meat glaze. Sprinkle with chopped parsley.

Parsley potatoes

Cook the potatoes as for pommes anglaise. Drain and dry them. Brush with melted butter and sprinkle with chopped parsley.

Pommes poisson

Cooking time: 18 minutes.

Cut up the potatoes in the shape of very large elongated olives. Cook them in salted water or by steaming. Drain and toss them in melted butter.

Rösti

Prepare potatoes by steaming in their jackets. Allow to cool and peel them. Using a mandolin, cut them into fine slices. Melt butter in a sauteuse. Add the potatoes, stirring with a fork, until the potatoes are impregnated with butter. Using a palette knife lightly press the potatoes against the bottom of the sauteuse to form a small round flat cake. Turn to a golden colour until the underneath forms a crust. Turn over on a serving dish and serve very hot. *(Switzerland.)*

Cereals and Pasta

Riz au blanc

500 gr. Carolina rice; 100 gr. butter. Cooking time: 30 minutes.

Wash the rice and put it in a thick bottomed saucepan. Moisten with cold water until just covered; salt, blanch (15 minutes). Drain and put it in a sauteuse, add the butter divided into very small pieces, mix with a fork and place the covered sauteuse in a very gentle oven for 15 minutes.

Creole rice I

1 kg. Patna rice. Cooking time: 1 hour.

Wash the rice several times in fresh water each time. Drain and put into a thick bottomed saucepan. Barely cover with water. Salt sparingly. Cook on a quick fire. When the rice is cooked place the covered saucepan on the corner of the stove or on very gentle heat to evaporate completely.

Creole rice II

500 gr. Carolina rice; 100 gr. butter.
Cooking time: 18 to 20 minutes.

Put the rice in a saucepan with 50 gr. of butter. Moisten with 1 litre of slightly salted water. Bring to the boil, cover and allow to cook gently without stirring. When the rice is cooked, add the rest of the butter divided into very small pieces; fork the rice well before use.

Curried rice

500 gr. rice; 50 gr. chopped onion; 1 coffee-spoonful of curry powder; 100 gr. butter; 1 litre white stock. Cooking time: 18 to 20 minutes.

Lightly colour the onion in half the butter. Add the rice and the curry, stir well and allow to impregnate for a moment. Moisten with the white stock, salt sparingly, cover and cook gently. Add the rest of the butter divided into very small pieces. Fork the rice before use.

Indian rice

Riz a l'indienne

500 gr. Basmathi rice. Cooking time: 15 minutes.

Blanche the rice (15 minutes) in salted water, stirring occasionally. Drain and refresh, and drain again. Put it in a serviette placed on a tray and fold the edges of the serviette over to enclose the rice. Dry out in the hot plate or in the mouth of a gentle oven for 15 minutes.

Pilaf of rice

500 gr. Patna or Carolina rice; 100 gr. butter; 50 gr. chopped onion; 1 litre white stock. Cooking time: 20 minutes.

Colour the onion in half of the butter. Add the rice and stir on the fire until the grains are well impregnated with butter. Moisten with the white stock, salt sparingly, cover and cook on gentle heat. When the rice is cooked mix with it the butter divided into very small pieces.

Risotto

500 gr. rice; 50 gr. chopped onion; 60 gr. butter; 60 gr. grated Parmesan; white stock. Cooking time: 20 minutes.

Toss the onion in hot butter without colouring. Add the rice and stir it over the fire until the grains are well impregnated with butter. Moisten the rice, twice as much as just to cover, with the white stock, adding this gradually five or six times until it is well absorbed by the rice. Finish cooling with the lid on. When the rice is cooked, change saucepans. Add the rest of the butter and the Parmesan, carefully, so as not to break the grains.

Risotto milanaise (Italian method)

500 gr. rice; 60 gr. butter; 30 gr. chopped onion; 3 gr. saffron; 5 cl. olive oil; 5 cl. white wine; 1 litre bouillon; 60 gr. grated Parmesan. Cooking time: 18 minutes.

Lightly colour the onions in the oil with a nut of butter. Moisten with the white wine, and reduce. Add rice and saffron, salt, and moisten with the bouillon adding it five or six times gradually as it is being absorbed by the rice. Finish cooking with the lid on. Mix in the rest of the butter and the Parmesan, away from the fire.

Risotto piémontaise

Prepare the risotto in the usual way. Add white truffles, cut in shavings, or ham cut into dice.

Fresh noodles

500 gr. flour; 2 eggs; 4 egg yolks; 10 gr. salt. Cooking time: 12 to 15 minutes.

Knead together into a firm paste the sifted flour, the eggs, the yolks and the salt. Wrap this paste in a cloth, and allow to stand in the cool for at least 3 to 4 hours. Roll out the paste into several strips as thin as possible, flour them and fold them over themselves, and cut into very fine strips. Dry them and cook them in salted water. After cooking drain the noodles and bind them with butter or cream. The noodles may be made with 4 or 5 whole eggs, but they are not so fine.

Green noodles

700 gr. flour; 4 eggs; 1 dl. olive oil; about 5 cl. of water; 500 gr. spinach, blanched, pressed and passed through a fine sieve; 12 gr. salt. Cooking time: 12 to 15 minutes.

Knead together into a firm paste the sifted flour, the eggs, the oil, the spinach, the water and the salt. Allow to stand for 1 hour; roll it as thin as possible. Flour, dry, and cut up into fine strips of about 2 cm. Cook them in salted water. After cooking, drain the noodles and bind them with butter.

Salads

Garnishes for fish and shellfish

Vegetable salad or macédoine

Cooked carrots, turnips, potatoes, French beans, peas, artichoke bases—150 gr. of each; 300 gr. clear mayonnaise.

Cut up into small dice the carrots, turnips, potatoes, artichoke bases and, into lozenges, the French beans. Mix all the vegetables and bind them well with well-seasoned mayonnaise.

Fresh vegetable salad

Carrots, turnips, potatoes, French beans, peas, asparagus tips, and cauliflower in equal parts; olive oil; vinegar; parsley; chopped chervil.

Cut up into small dice the carrots, turnips, potatoes, and asparagus and, into lozenges, the French beans. Cook all the vegetables separately. Allow to cool, but do not refresh. Mix and season with salt, pepper, oil and vinegar; add chopped parsley and chervil. The carrots, turnips and potatoes can equally well be shaped with an oval spoon-cutter.

Parmentier salad

1 kg. of raw potatoes, shaped with a small oval spoon-cutter; 300 gr. clear mayonnaise; 1 coffee-spoonful of chopped chervil. Cooking time: 12 to 15 minutes.

Cook the potatoes in salted water, carefully keeping them whole. Drain completely while they are still warm and season with the mayonnaise additionally flavoured with chopped chervil.

Russian salad

100 gr. each of cooked carrots, turnips, potatoes, mushrooms, French beans and peas; 100 gr. gherkins; 50 gr. capers; 50 gr. anchovy fillets; 275 gr. mayonnaise.

Cut into small dice the carrots. turnips, potatoes, mushrooms, peeled gherkins, anchovy fillets and, into lozenges, the French beans. Mix together with the peas and capers, and bind with mayonnaise. Russian salad, as a garnish for cold fish dishes, has no ham, sausage or lobster.

Waldorf salad

500 gr. celeriac; 500 gr. pippin apples; 150 gr. fresh walnuts; 300 to 350 gr. clear mayonnaise; 1 lemon.

Cut into small dice the celeriac, blanch it (1 minute) and drain it. Mix it with the apples, peeled and cored, and cut into dice. Allow to marinate for at least 1 hour with lemon juice and a pinch of salt. Bind with the mayonnaise, adjust the seasoning and consistency, and sprinkle with shredded fresh walnuts. The celeriac and the potatoes can equally well be cut into a julienne and mixed with shredded nuts.

Glossary

Abaisser: To extend pastry with a rolling pin. (Abaisse – a piece of pastry which has been rolled out).

Appareil: Various ingredients blended together for a certain preparation.

Aspic: A clear brilliant jelly made from stock used for glazing or decorating cold dishes of fish.

Bain-marie: A utensil for keeping food hot, and providing a gentle method of cooking. It usually consists of a fairly large shallow vessel containing hot water, into which are placed smaller pans containing food such as sauces, stews and soups. In the domestic kitchen a double saucepan could be used. Sometimes food which is to be cooked at a very low temperature may be placed in a baking tin half-filled with hot water in the oven. This will prevent the food from overheating and spoiling.

Bard (*barder*): To cover fish with thin slices of pork fat or unsmoked bacon while being braised.

Basting: Keeping fish etc. moist while cooking by pouring over it the juices or fat in the pan.

Blanchir (*blanch*): (a) to cook in boiling water for a few minutes, and then to plunge into cold water to retain colour; (b) to whiten or reduce the strong flavour of food by putting it in cold water, then bringing to the boil.

Beurrer: To butter or to incorporate butter.

Beurre fondu: Melted butter.

Beurre manié: Butter-paste. A mixture of four ounces of butter, kneaded with three ounces of flour. Used for thickening sauces, vegetables etc.

Beurre noir: Black butter, that is, butter heated beyond the noisette stage.

Bisque: Name given to a thick, rich, fish or shellfish soup.

Blondir: To shallow fry to a light colour, using butter, oil or fat.

Bondelles: Small *féras* (whitefish) of 80 to 150 gr.

Bouillon: A rich strong clear stock.

Bouquet: Simple: parsley only; garni: parsley, thyme and bayleaf; sometimes with tarragon, basil etc.

Braising: See *Cooking Methods*, page 63.

Brioche: A light yeast dough.

Brunoise: A mixture of vegetables cut into very small dice and cooked in butter or other fat; it is used in forcemeats, sauces etc.

Chapelure: Grated breadcrumbs.

Chenna: (Flour) chick pea.

Chiffonnade: Shredded lettuce, sorrel, spinach, etc. in butter.

Chinois: Wire sieve or strainer, conical in shape.

Ciseler: To slash lightly with a sharp knife, making incisions along the backs of such fish as trout, herring, etc. to facilitate their cooking. To shred into a fine *julienne* such vegetables as sorrel and lettuce.

Clarify: To clear stock with slightly beaten egg whites and minced raw fish or veal.

Clouter: To stud something with truffle, tongue or ham etc.

Colorer: The addition of something to colour; to pass over or through heat.

Concasser: To chop coarsely (especially tomatoes, after peeling and de-seeding).

Contiser: Incising pieces of fish with a sharp knife to allow slices of truffle or mushroom to be inserted.

Cordon: Thin line of sauce or thickened gravy surrounding a finished preparation.

Coucher: To arrange the main ingredient on a bed or layer of one of the garnishing elements such as spinach, noodles, etc.

Croûtons: Small cubes of bread fried in butter and used as a garnish for soups. Also various shapes of sliced bread fried in butter or oil, or toasted and used as a garnish for fish and entrées.

Cuire à blanc: To cook pastry crust for tartlets, timbales etc. without the normal filling, using instead rice, beans or nuts.

Cuire au gras: To cook with a fat element.

Cuire au maigre: To cook without a fat element.

Cuisson: The cooking process; liquor in which ingredients have been cooked.

Darioles: Small individual moulds.

Darne: Thick, middle cut of fish, such as salmon or cod.

Décanter: To decant, to obtain a liquid free from any deposit by pouring carefully from one vessel into another.

Déglacer: To deglaze, to moisten with wine, cooking liquor or any liquid.

Demi-glace: Brown sauce, semi-clear and glossy.

Dépouiller: To skin, to free fish from skin and bone.

Dessécher: To dry thoroughly.

Détendre: To clarify, to thin by adding liquid.

Dorer: To glaze, to colour golden, to brush beaten egg on an article preparatory to placing in the oven.

Dresser: To arrange correctly for serving.

Duxelles: Preparation containing chopped mushrooms and shallots cooked together in butter.

Ebarber: To cut the fins of fish; to remove the beards from oysters, mussels etc.

Effiler: To shred almonds.

Emincer: To slice thinly.

Emonder: To skin almonds, tomatoes, by blanching.

Escaloper: To cut or slice on the bias, slantwise.

Etuver: To stew; cook slowly; to cook with a given quantity of fat keeping covered and without moistening.

Farce: Stuffing, forcemeat.

Foncer: To line a mould, with paste.

Fondre: To dissolve, to melt, to cook certain vegetables (keeping covered), with little or no liquid.

Fraiser: To knead with a downward pressure of the hand.

Frapper: To chill, to put on ice.

Friture: The special pan used for deep frying; also the name given to certain foods cooked by the deep frying method.

Fumet: Light essence to strengthen the taste of sauces and stocks; concentrated stock of fish.

Galuska: Moulded fish forcemeat with a base of flour, milk, eggs, butter and sour cream (Hungarian cooking).

Glace: Stock reduced to a syrupy consistency.

Glacer: To ice, to refrigerate.

Glaze (*glacer*): To give a golden coloured skin to heavily buttered sauces under the grill or in a fierce oven. To brush preparations with heavily reduced stocks to give a brilliant, shiny appearance.

Goujons: Gudgeon: see also *goujons de sole, Illustrated Culinary Technique,* page 73.

Gratiner: To gratinate, to brown under the grill or quickly in the oven. Dishes cooked in this way are often sprinkled with breadcrumbs, butter and possibly grated cheese.

Hachis: Mince.

Julienne: Fine strips of vegetables, fish.

Jus lié: Thickened gravy.

Kaché (*Kasha*): Preparation with a base of buckwheat flour, butter and water, and cooked in the oven. (Russian cookery).

Laitance: Soft roe.

Lame: Thin slice.

Lanière: Strip.

Larder: To lard with strips of larding bacon; to introduce small or large pieces of fat bacon with a special needle to enrich an article.

Lardoire: Larding needle.

Lardons: Strips or small dice of larding bacon.

Letcho: Mixture of small peppers, tomatoes and onions.

Liaison: The binding or thickening agent used in soups and sauces. This may be egg yolks, beurre manié, roux or cream.

Losange: Lozenge or diamond shape.

Macédoine: A variety of different coloured vegetables cut into small even cubes and used for garnish or hors d'oeuvre.

Macerate: To soak in syrup, liquor, brandy, etc.

Marinate: To steep pieces of fish in a prepared liquid of wine, water and aromatics to both tenderise and flavour. Smaller pieces may be marinated in lemon juice, wine, spirits or oil with the addition of aromatics.

Marquer: To prepare an article before cooking.

Mask (*masquer*) : To cover with a layer of cream or sauce, etc.

Médaillon: A round slice of fish.

Meunière: See *Cooking Methods*, page 64.

Mie de pain: Crumbs of bread without crust; fresh white breadcrumbs.

Mijoter: To stew in sauce at a low temperature for a lengthy period.

Mirepoix: More or less large dice of vegetables, carrots, celery, ham or lean bacon, with melted butter.

Moisten (*mouiller*) : To cover with liquid (stock, wine, etc.) or to add a specific amount of liquid as directed in the recipe.

Monter: To aerate by whisking or beating egg whites, cream etc. Monter au beurre – to finish a sauce by beating whilst adding nuts of butter.

Moule: Mould. Moule à manqué – a tinned round mould with a lip 5 cm. high. There are many varieties of moulds such as moule à charnière – hinged mould. Mussel.

Mousse: A light aerated mixture of eggs, cream, fish jelly and fish.

Mousseline: A lighter mousse.

Napper: Synonymous with the word masquer – to mask. Also used to indicate the moment in cooking when a substance has thickened sufficiently to cover a spoon or spatula without flowing.

Neige: Battre en neige – to beat stiffly (egg white) to a frothy consistency.

Noisette butter: This is a butter which has been heated until it acquires a pale brown colour and nutty aroma. It is often called simply brown butter.

Paner: To coat with egg and breadcrumbs; to cover with breadcrumbs.

Papillote (*en*) : Paper or foil cases in which food is cooked or served.

Parer: To trim away what is useless or uneatable. Parures – trimmings.

Pignon: Also pignoli, pine-seed, pine-kernel.

Pincer: To shrink by cooking; to colour food in a pan by turning it over in very hot butter; to pinch – to use pastry tweezers to crimp pastry.

Piquer: To stud with small pieces of bacon or truffle using a larding needle.

Poach (*pocher*) : To simmer in a liquid between 90 and 95 degrees centigrade without allowing to boil.

Poche: Strong cloth or nylon bag of a conical shape to which various piping tubes are adapted.

Poêler: To braise lightly; method of cooking in a closed vessel; to pot roast.

Point: The point of a small knife inserted into a finely powdered condiment such as cayenne pepper, and removed, leaving only a minute quantity on the knife; about half a gramme.

Poissonière: Fish-kettle.

Ragoût: A stew.

Raidir: To stiffen without colouring.

Reduce (*réduire*) : To reduce stocks, sauces, to their required consistency and flavour, by boiling or simmering uncovered.

Refresh (*refraîchir*) : To place under cold running water fish and vegetables which have been previously blanched.

Revenir: To turn more or less brown as desired in fat.

Rissoler: To give a golden colour: to obtain a crisp or crusty surface, by turning the food over in a pan, usually in hot shallow butter or fat.

Roux: See *The Cooking of Fish: Basic Preparations,* page 56.

Ruban: A composition which falls in wide undulations like a ribbon.

Salamander: Grill for gratinating.

Salpicon: Various ingredients cut into small dice and bound with sauce. These are used to fill vol-au-vent cases, bouchées, canapés, and used to make croquettes, rissoles.

Sangler: To surround a receptacle with ice and salt to freeze the contents.

Sauter: To shallow fry lightly in hot fat, shaking the pan frequently; Sauteuse – a shallow sloping-sided saucepan of various sizes; Sautoir – a deep pan to sauter.

Seize (*saisir*) : To begin cooking with a fierce heat.

Socle: Base, e.g. of rice, on which to stand made-up preparations.

Soubise: A purée of onions enriched with cream.

Spatula: A flat wooden spoon.

Suprêmes: Term used for fillets of fish.

Sweat: To stew gently in butter without colouring, with added seasoning so that the ingredients cook in their own essences or juices.

Tabasco: Brand name of a hot, pungent, pepper sauce, originating in Louisiana.

Tammy: A sieve or tammy cloth; *tamis de crin* – a hair sieve; *tamis de fer* – a wire sieve.

Timbale: A drum-shaped mould; a drum-shaped silver serving dish.

Tomatoes concassées: Tomatoes skinned, de-seeded and coarsely chopped.

Tomatoes fondues: Tomatoes concassées, gently stewed in butter or oil, with a little chopped shallot, until the moisture has evaporated and the product becomes a firm pulp.

Tomber à glace: To evaporate a stock to a syrupy consistency, that is, to make a glaze.

Tourner: To turn; to give a round shape when peeling or paring.

Trancher: To slice or carve.

Travailler: To work or knead with the hands or an instrument.

Tronçons: Thick slices or steaks of fish, including the bones, from larger fish such as turbot, brill or halibut.

Truss: To tie together; to insert the claws of crayfish into their bodies for decorative purposes.

Turn (*tourer*) : The rolling and folding of puff pastry; to shape with a knife into barrel or olive shapes.

Vanner: To stir sauces occasionally to prevent the formation of a skin.

Velouté: A foundation white sauce made from fish, stock, etc.; white soup of similar foundations.

Vésiga: The spinal marrow of the sturgeon.

Zest: The outer coloured rind of citrus fruits, thinly pared off for flavouring and garnishing.

Zucchini (*courgette*) : Species of very small vegetable marrows.

Index

C

D

E

F

G

H

T

V

W

Z

Index of National and Regional Dishes

GERMANY

GREAT BRITAIN

GUADELOUPE

HOLLAND

HUNGARY

INDIA

ISRAEL

ITALY

JAPAN

LEBANON

RUMANIA

RUSSIA

SPAIN

SWEDEN

SWITZERLAND

TURKEY

UNITED STATES

WEST INDIES